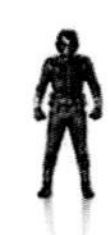

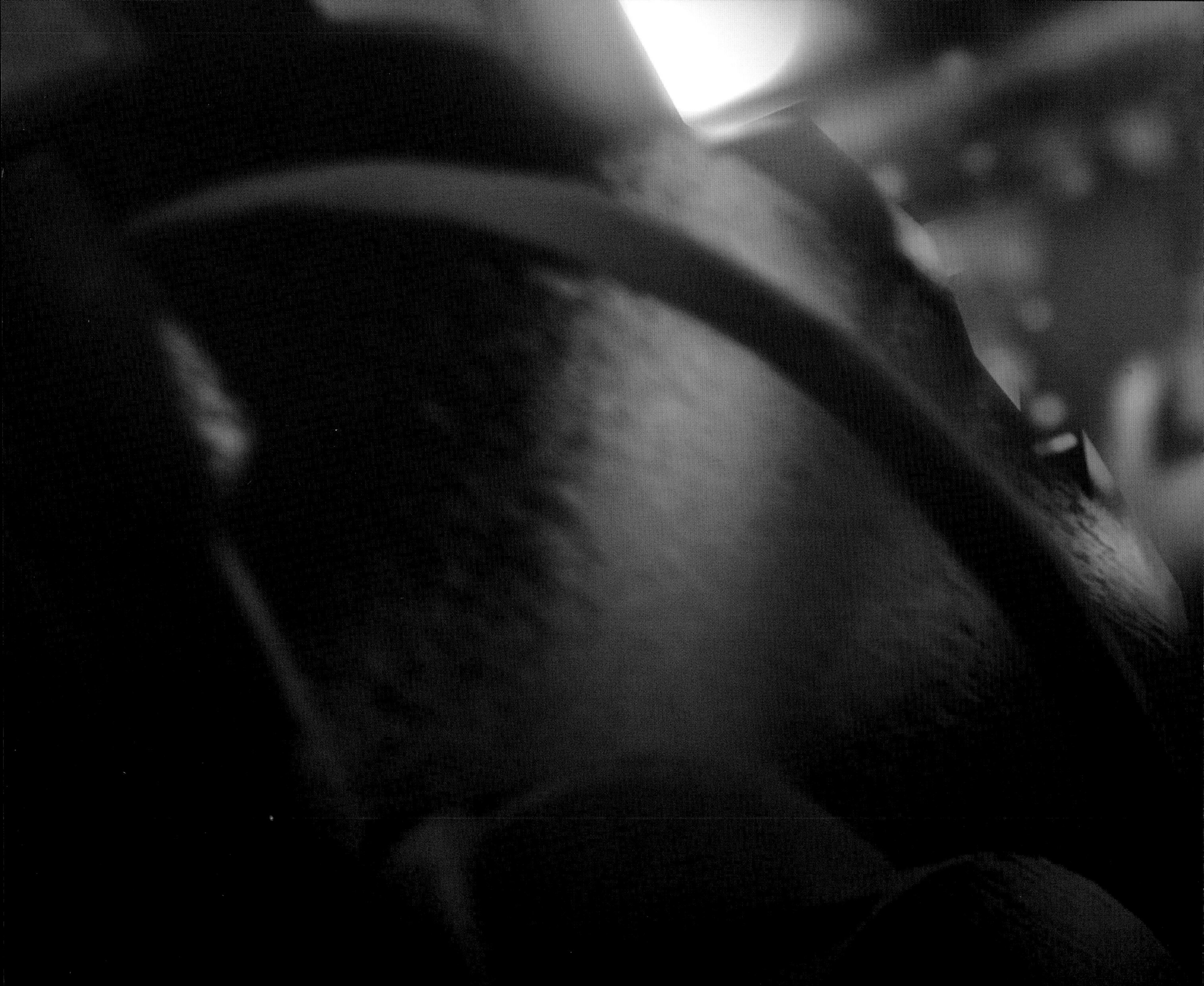

Jackson Sze keyframe.

MARVEL STUDIOS

THE INFINITY SAGA

THE ART OF MARVEL STUDIOS ANT-MAN

WRITTEN BY
JACOB JOHNSTON

FOREWORD BY
PEYTON REED

BOOK DESIGN BY
JEFF POWELL

DUSTJACKET ART BY
ANDY PARK

ANT-MAN CREATED BY
STAN LEE, LARRY LIEBER & JACK KIRBY

TITAN BOOKS

MARVEL STUDIOS: THE INFINITY SAGA - ANT-MAN: THE ART OF THE MOVIE

ISBN: 9781803367873

First edition: March 2025

10 9 8 7 6 5 4 3 2 1

Published by Titan Books
A division of Titan Publishing Group Ltd
144 Southwark St, London SE1 0UP

www.titanbooks.com

A CIP catalogue record for this title is available from the British Library.

Printed in China

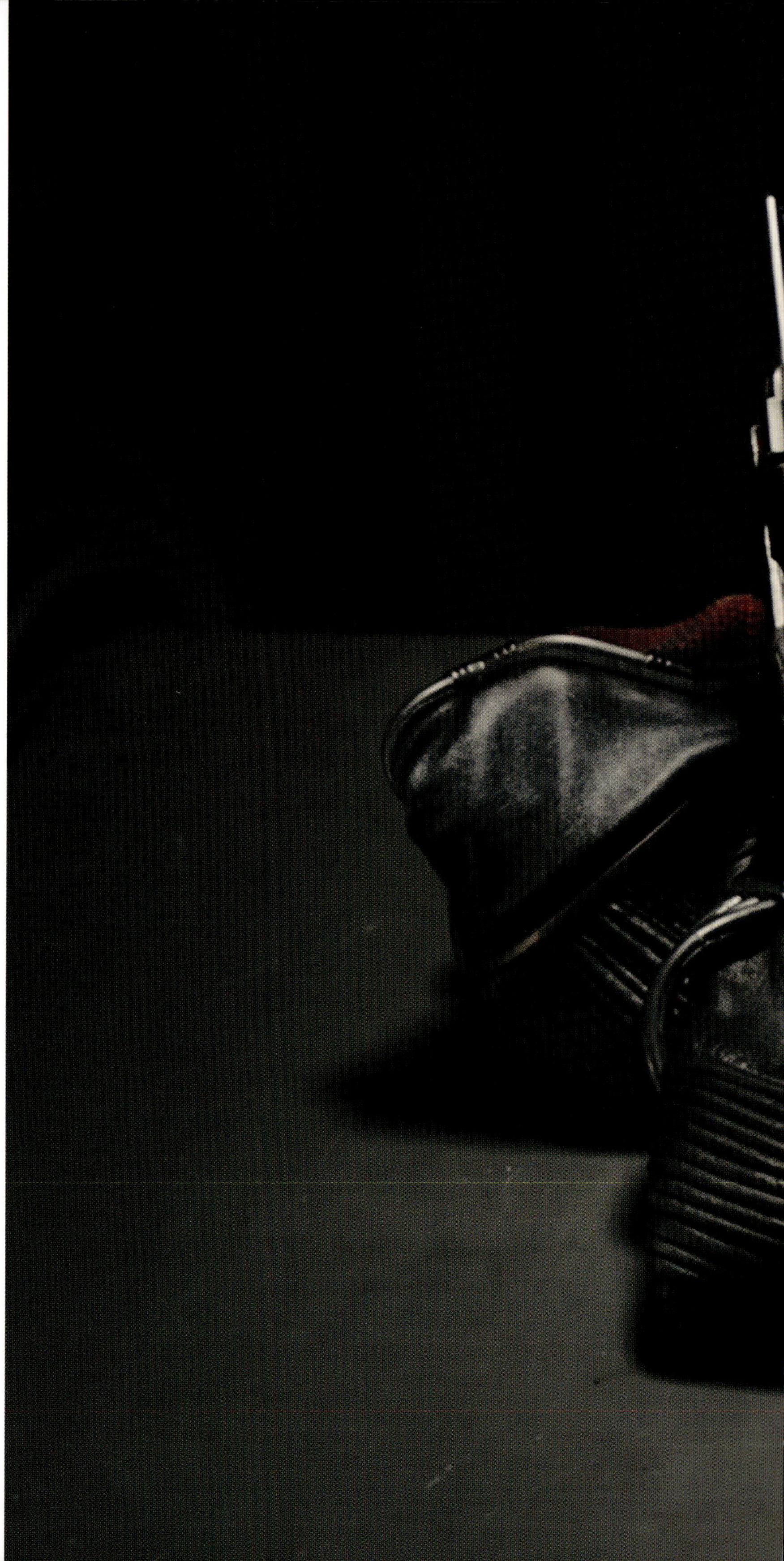

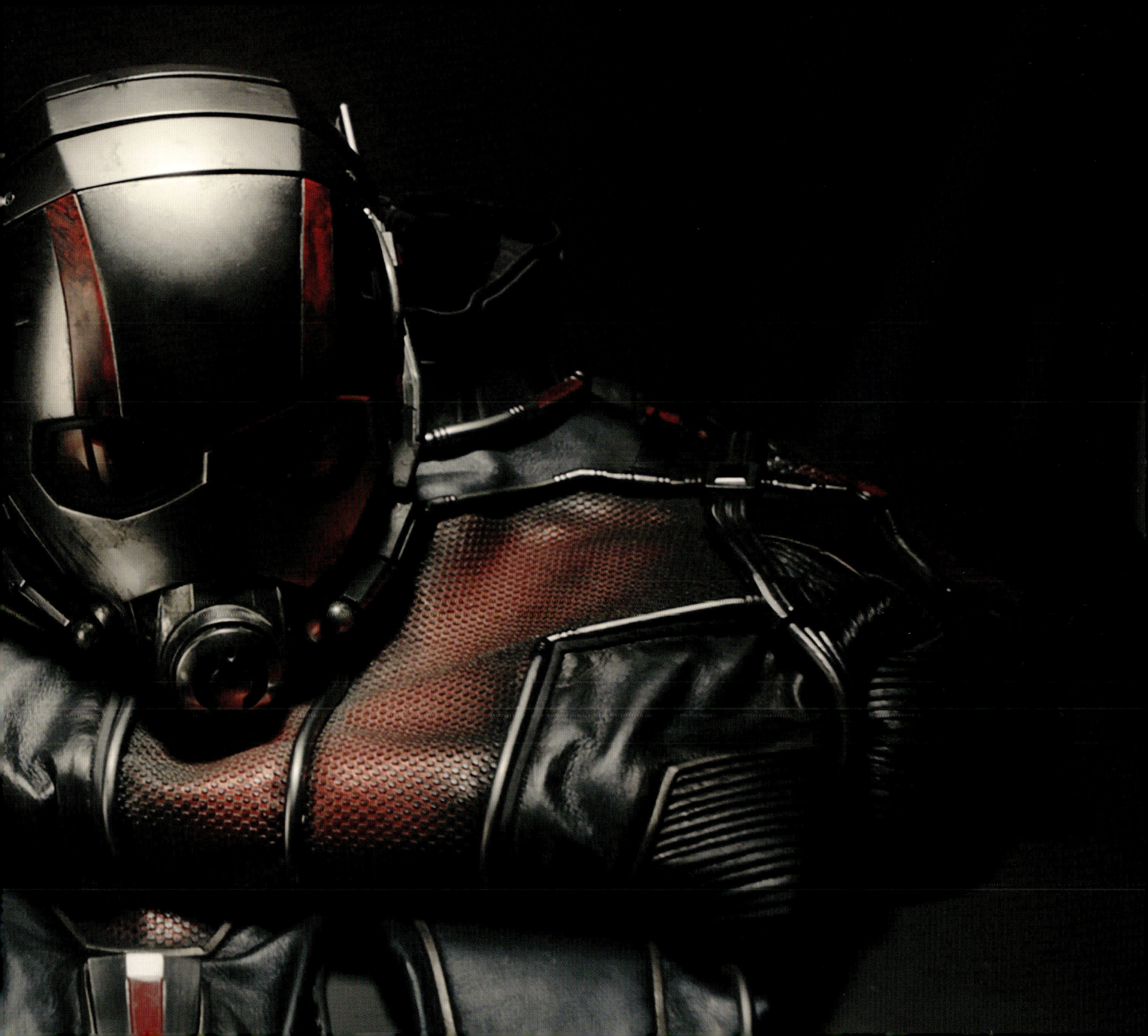

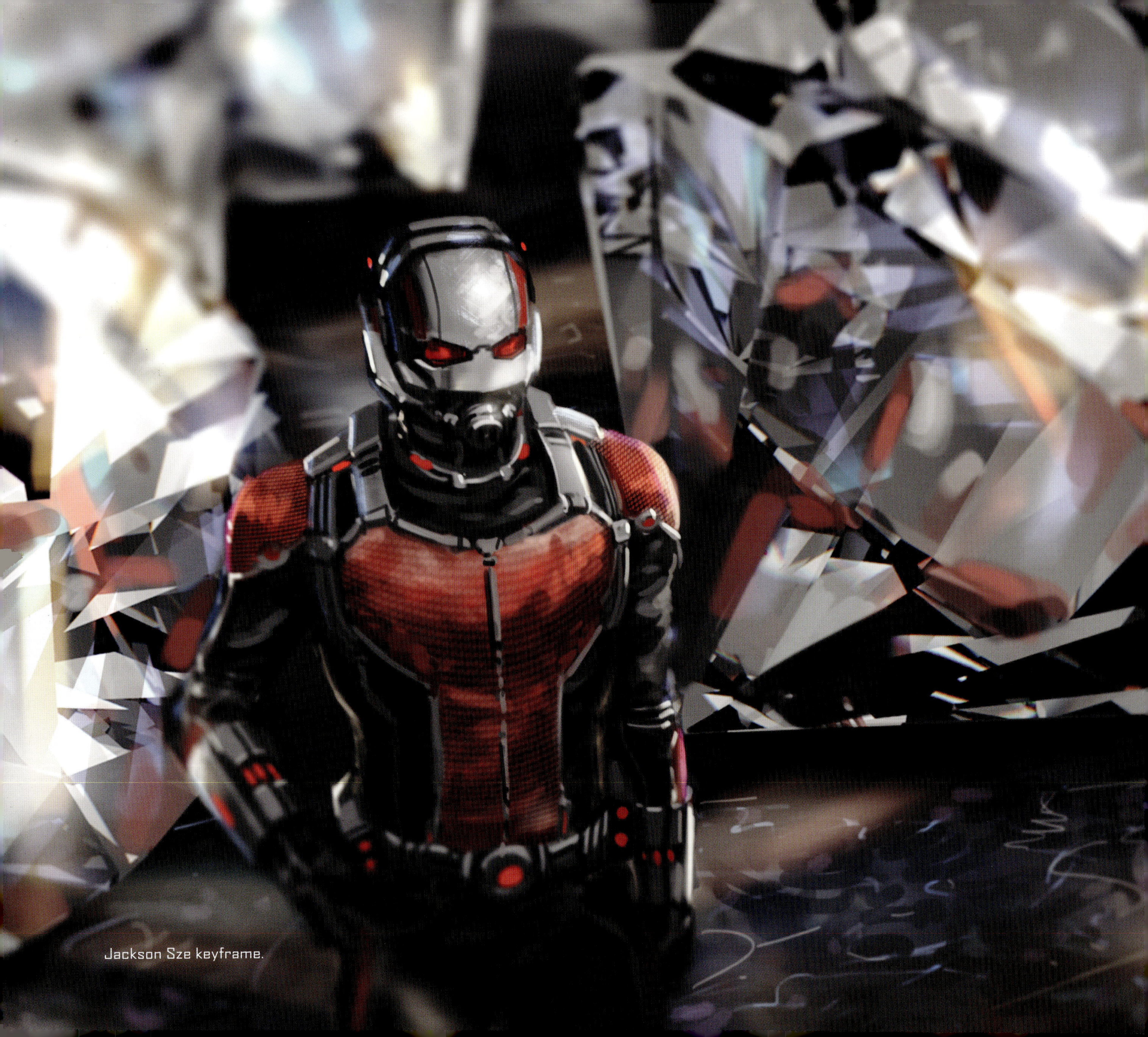

Jackson Sze keyframe.

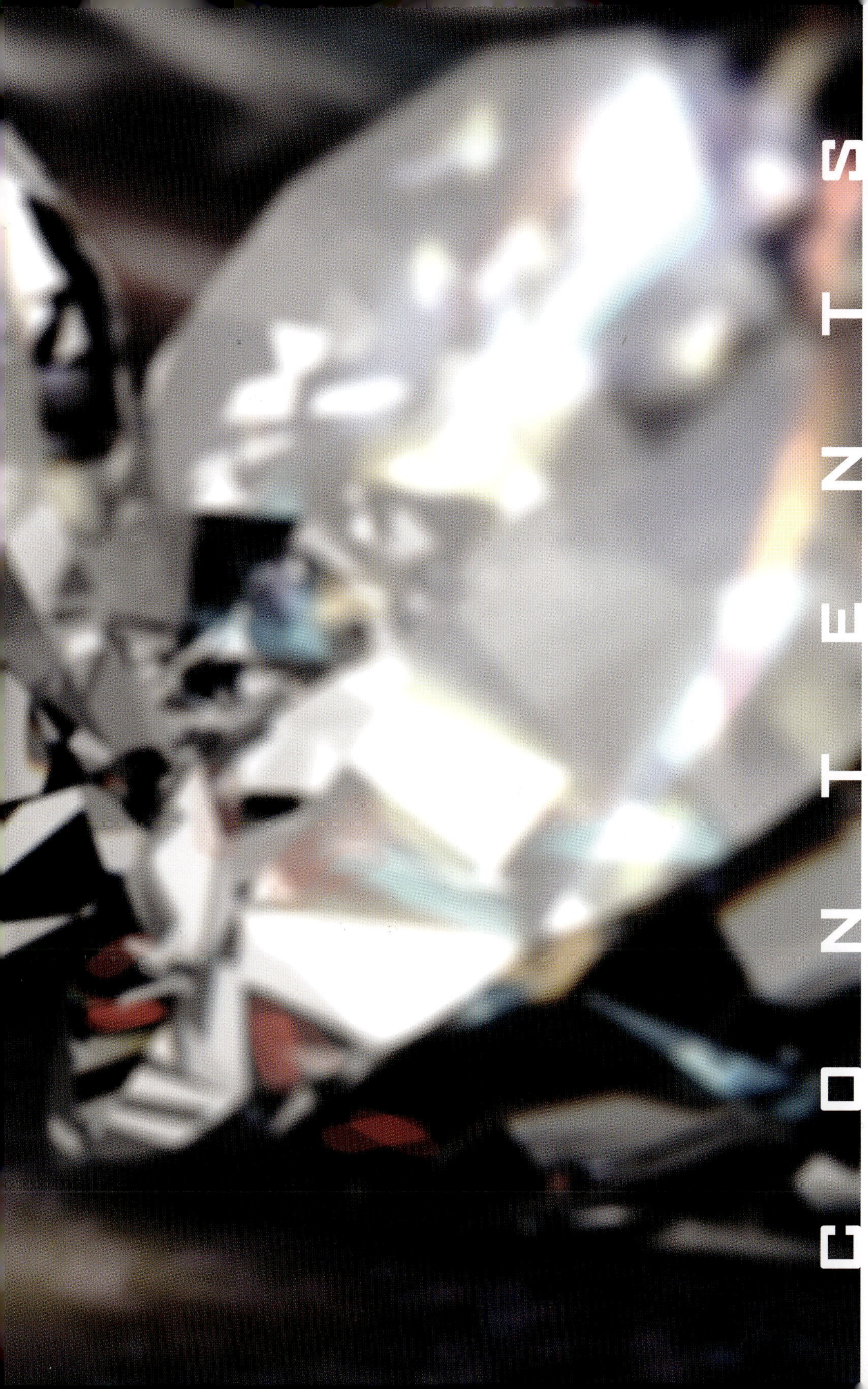

CONTENTS

9 **FOREWORD**
BY PEYTON REED

10 **INTRODUCTION**

16 **CHAPTER ONE**
"I'M NOT A SOLDIER, I'M A SCIENTIST"

40 **CHAPTER TWO**
"I BELIEVE THAT EVERYONE DESERVES A SHOT AT REDEMPTION."

94 **CHAPTER THREE**
"THE END OF WARFARE AS WE KNOW IT: THE YELLOWJACKET!"

132 **CHAPTER FOUR**
"YOU'VE YET TO LEARN ABOUT YOUR GREATEST ALLIES."

178 **CHAPTER FIVE**
"DID YOU THINK YOU COULD STOP THE FUTURE?"

204 **CHAPTER SIX**
"PICK ON SOMEONE YOUR OWN SIZE!"

244 **CHAPTER SEVEN**
NO HAMMER. NO SHIELD. NO PROBLEM!

250 **CONTRIBUTOR BIOS**

252 **ACKNOWLEDGMENTS**

255 **ARTIST CREDITS**

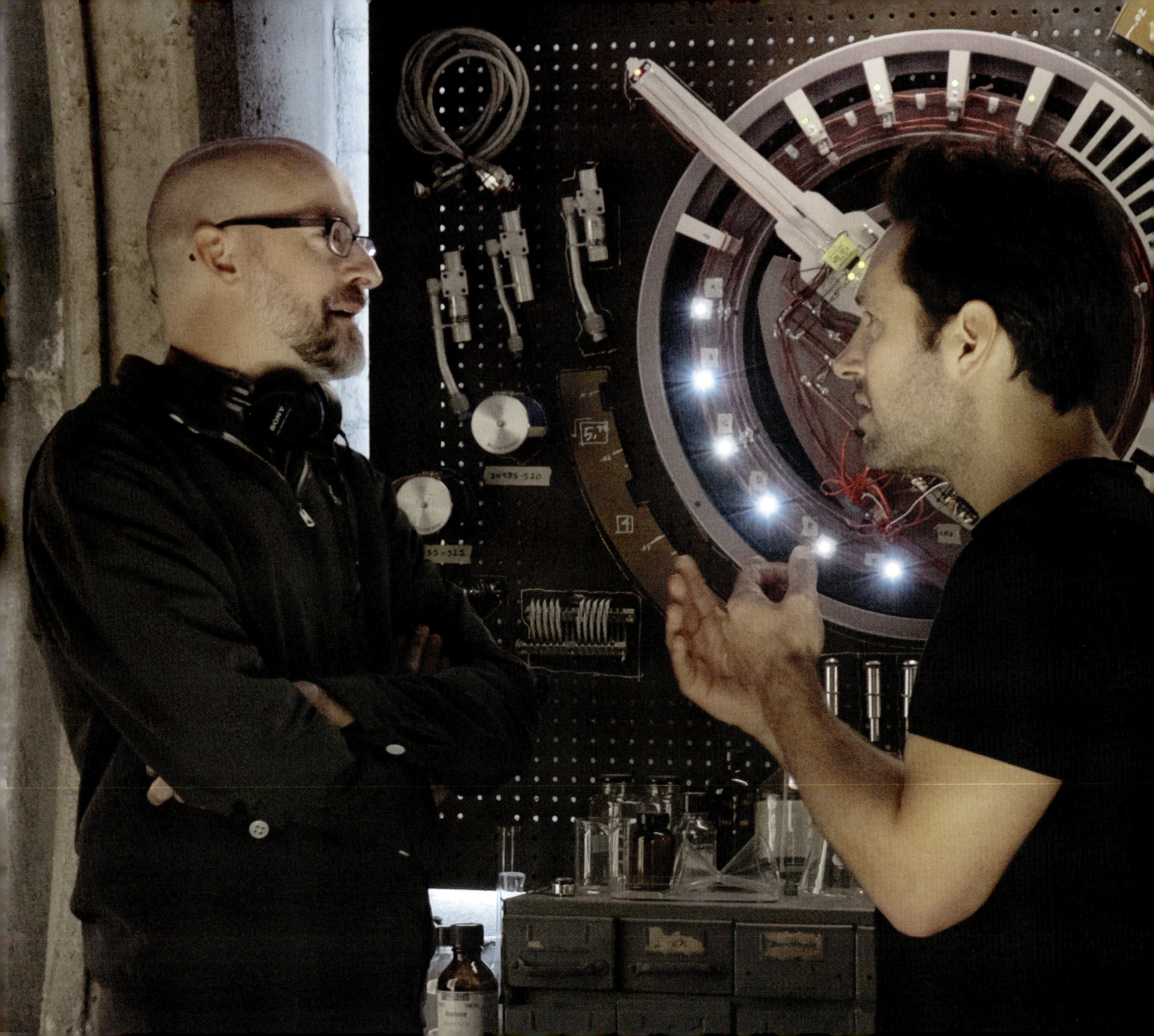

FOREWORD 2015

Let's face it: Ant-Man might just be the single most challenging hero in the history of Marvel. True, he was a founding member of the Avengers, but he never even had his own comic. (Until 2006, that is, but that was Eric O'Grady, the third Ant-Man.) Hell, he didn't even have a suit when he first appeared in *Tales to Astonish #27*. In that story, "The Man in the Ant Hill!," he was simply Henry Pym—a scientist who created a shrinking serum, had a harrowing encounter in an ant tunnel, and lived to tell the tale.

Pym finally got a suit in *Tales to Astonish #35*. But Ant-Man proved to be a constant challenge for Stan Lee and the Marvel writers, who changed him from Ant-Man to Giant-Man to Goliath to Yellowjacket to the Wasp (!) and back again.

He was also a challenge for the Marvel artists, and their collective sense of scale and perspective. Stan himself told me that he constantly hounded the likes of Jack Kirby, Don Heck, and Dick Ayers not to make him too large in the frame, to always place objects alongside him for scale, and to accentuate the low angles that represented Ant-Man's POV of the world.

Yes, Ant-Man was always a challenge.

So why should the Marvel Cinematic Universe's Ant-Man be any different?

Our movie has its origins in 1979's "To Steal an Ant-Man" from *Marvel Premiere #47*. In that story, Scott Lang—an ex-con coming straight off a prison stint—inherits (steals) the mantle of Ant-Man in an attempt to help save his daughter. The film takes elements of that issue, adds original Ant-Man Hank Pym, and creates an entirely new storyline.

It's a story of redemption between fathers and daughters wrapped up in a science-fiction concept with a heist-movie structure and a comedic rhythm that keeps it all beating. It takes place in our world—but it's experienced, in part, from a radically different perspective.

The movie would pose all the same challenges as the comics—and then some—and would require the imaginations of the best artists and visualists working in Hollywood today. Luckily, Marvel Studios is full of them: incredibly talented, creatively hungry people working at the peak of their powers to create an interlocking cinematic universe unlike anything that has existed before it.

A movie of this—or any—size is an extremely collaborative endeavor. I'd like to thank all those who poured their creative energies into *Ant-Man* and refused to shrink (sorry) before its many challenges:

To Producer Kevin Feige: Thanks for letting me fulfill a lifelong dream. Thanks also for your tirelessness, your sense of humor, and your deep, deep well of nerdiness (one that I relate to far too well).

To Executive Producer Louis D'Esposito: Thanks for your insight and energy, your experience and point-of-view, and those weird green juice drinks.

To Executive Producer Victoria Alonso: Thanks for your constant support and encouragement, your keen eye, and your beautiful accent.

To Co-Producer Brad Winderbaum: Thanks for being my comrade-in-arms every single day of this process. I don't think anyone fought harder for Ant-Man than you.

To Production Designer Shepherd Frankel, Cinematographer Russell Carpenter, Visual Effects Supervisor Jake Morrison, Visual Effects Producer Diana Giorgiutti, Editor Dan Lebental, Editor Colby Parker Jr., Costume Designer Sammy Sheldon Differ, Head Specialty Costume Creator Ivo Coveney, Executive Producer Michael Grillo, First A.D. Lars Winther, and the many, many others who helped bring Ant-Man to life—I am tremendously indebted to you.

I'd also like to thank all those responsible for the beautiful imagery that awaits you within these pages.

To Heads of Visual Development Charlie Wen and Ryan Meinerding: Thanks for your artistry. It is clear to me now what a crucial element you are to the MCU. You make the most difficult things seems easy. And they are not.

To Concept Artist Andy Park: Thanks for the final Ant-Man costume design. I think it's the best suit in the MCU. (Just because I'm biased doesn't mean I'm not right!) Thanks also for the final Wasp costume design. It is a thing of beauty.

To Concept Artist Jackson Sze: Thanks for the final, unbelievably great Yellowjacket costume design and all those amazing keyframes.

To Concept Artist Anthony Francisco: Thanks for all of your amazing ant designs and keyframes.

To Concept Artists Andrew Kim and Rodney Fuentebella: Thanks for your iconic keyframes.

Thanks also to our intrepid gang of storyboard artists: Bryan Andrews, Danelle Davenport, David Krentz, Jim Magdaleno, Steve Markowski, Jay Oliva, and Jim Rothwell (animatics).

Additional thanks to Michael Oliveri for the use of his amazing nano-micrographs, both in Hank Pym's Secure Room and as inspiration for the Quantum Realm.

And finally—thanks to you, Marvel fans. You already know what the rest of the world is about to learn:

Underestimate Ant-Man at your own risk.

THE MAN IN THE ANT HILL

The year was 1962. Splashed across the cover of *Tales to Astonish #27* was the horrified face of Hank Pym, desperately trying to escape the clutches of an army of ravenous ants. Much like the other issues in the series, "The Man in the Ant Hill!" was presented as a standalone monster story featuring an overzealous scientist who doesn't consider the consequences of his miracle invention: a shrinking formula. The comic ends with Hank dumping his potion down the drain so no one will be tempted to use it again. But creators Stan Lee, Larry Lieber, and Jack Kirby must have seen potential in the character and his invention.

A mere eight issues later, in *Tales to Astonish #35*, Hank Pym returns—in costume—in a story aptly titled "Return of the Ant-Man," transforming Tales to Astonish from a monster/sci-fi anthology into Marvel's newest super-hero series. Knowing that his invention could change the world, Hank had kept his recipe—just in case he ever felt daring enough to face the ants again. To better prepare himself for insect encounters, Hank develops a protective mesh suit and a helmet that allows him to communicate with ants. *Tales to Astonish* would continue to track Hank's adventures as Ant-Man—later Giant-Man—and his partner, the Wasp. Ant-Man and the Wasp would also appear as founding members of Earth's Mightiest Heroes in the pages of *Avengers*.

Flash forward to 1979's *Marvel Premiere #47-48*: The dynamic creative team of David Michelinie and John Byrne introduce the second Ant-Man, Scott Lang. The character had appeared a month earlier as an employee of Stark Industries in an issue of *Avengers*, but readers would witness his full origin in this two-part tale. Tragic hero Scott Lang breaks into Hank Pym's home and steals his Ant-Man equipment as a means of rescuing the only doctor who can save the life of his daughter, Cassie. Scott takes down violent kidnappers, saving the doctor's life—and Cassie's. In the end, Hank absolves Scott of his crimes—formally ushering in the next era of Ant-Man.

Backed by more than five decades of comic-book history, the screen adaptation needed to capture a flavor distinct from the other installments in the Marvel Cinematic Universe. "The tone of *Ant-Man* is very specific," Director Peyton Reed says. "I think if you don't know anything about Marvel comics or the Marvel Universe, and you go to the theater and you see a poster for Ant-Man, and maybe it's a guy flying around on an ant, you're gonna think, 'Oh, that looks really silly.' And then you're going to go and sit down in this movie theater, and for about two hours you're going be proven profoundly wrong. One of the

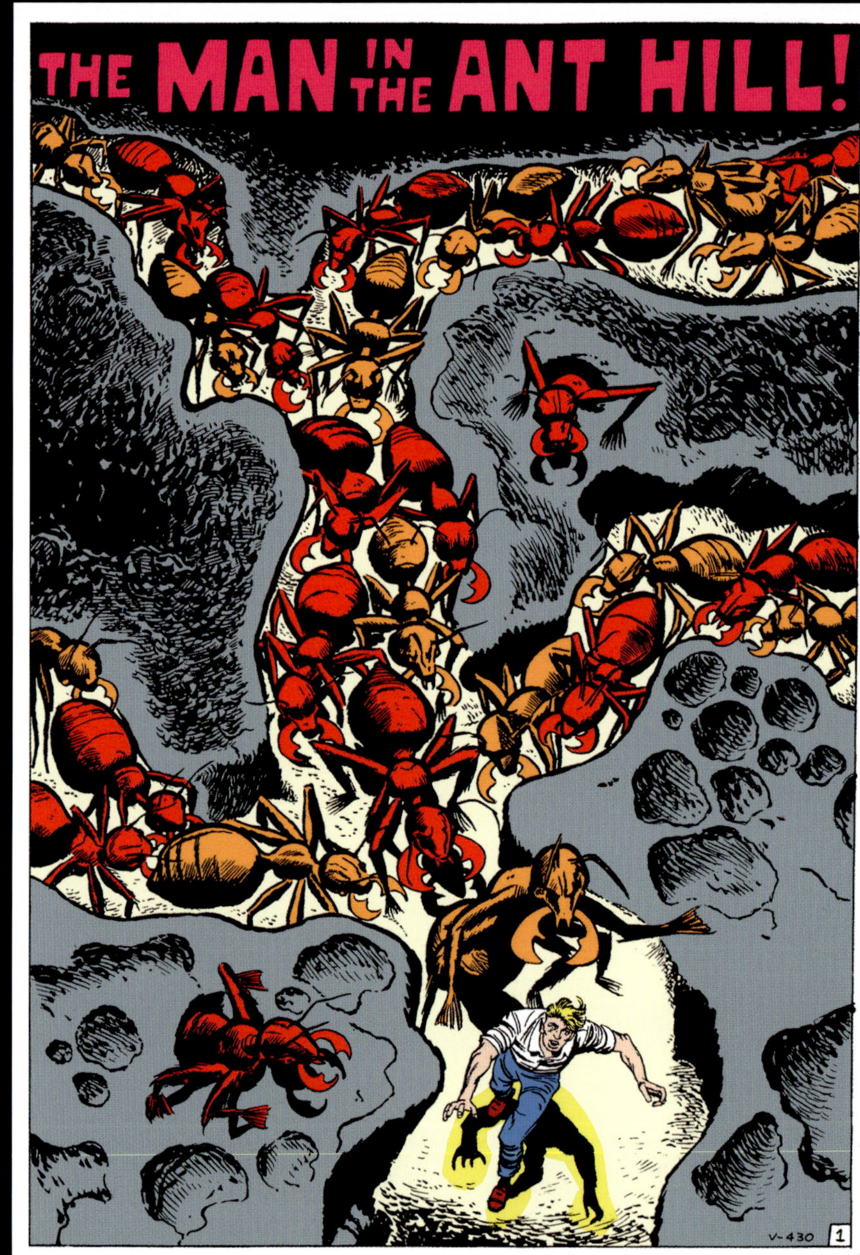

Hank Pym's first microscopic misadventure, from the cover of *Tales to Astonish (1959) #27*—written by Stan Lee and Larry Lieber, penciled by Jack Kirby, and inked by Dick Ayers.

fun things about this is it's going to twist people's expectations about Ant-Man. It is kind of a whimsical notion."

The film borrows a number of key elements from the early *Ant-Man* comics, focusing on the theme of redemption as a new hero rises under the mentorship of an old one. "It will be the first movie after Marvel's *Avengers: Age of Ultron* comes out, which is going to be a huge epic film where all the characters have to come together," Executive Producer Brad Winderbaum says. "But as we did with the first *Iron Man*, we're bringing down the scale to one single hero and his personal conflicts, and how the drama of his own life forces him to become a hero."

Scott certainly doesn't start out as a champion of morality—but as in the comics, his devotion to and love for his daughter transcend his dark past. As the film opens, Scott is fresh out of prison; he sets out to leave behind his life of thievery for a future he and his daughter both can be proud of. But his status as an ex con doesn't pave the way for a meaningful career—or even a part-time job. He eventually caves in and takes on one last heist to make enough money to get back on his feet.

"Obviously, all of these Marvel movies are big special-effects movies," Reed says. "But the great thing about the Marvel Cinematic Universe is at the center of these, the human story is really what counts. We've all seen a bunch of movies that are special-effects extravaganzas that you don't give a crap about, and this is something where what really draws you in is this guy who is a thief, an ex-con, and he's trying to figure out his life all over again. And suddenly, unbeknownst to him, he's drawn into the world of Henry Pym."

Further tying together the MCU, Hank's past is profoundly connected to the early days of S.H.I.E.L.D. in the 1960s, when his colleagues included Peggy Carter and Howard Stark. We've seen a little bit of the '60s in the way it relates to Stark Industries, to the Stark Expo, to some of what Howard was doing back in the '60s and '70s," Executive Producer Kevin Feige says. "And in this movie, we do put Hank Pym in that era as an active Ant-Man—as a part of S.H.I.E.L.D., working alongside those characters that people kno w—and showing how that sort of went awry. Hank was on to something before many people were, which is S.H.I.E.L.D. might not be the best place to work. And he steps out of that role, and he puts the Ant-Man suit in mothballs and focuses on his new company. And now as we open this film in the present day, things have changed. And there is a danger lurking that involves Pym's own technology being used in a way that he successfully avoided for 30 years after breaking with S.H.I.E.L.D."

Modern-day Hank Pym presents himself as a wealthy but frail old man—the perfect target for an expert thief like Scott, who makes

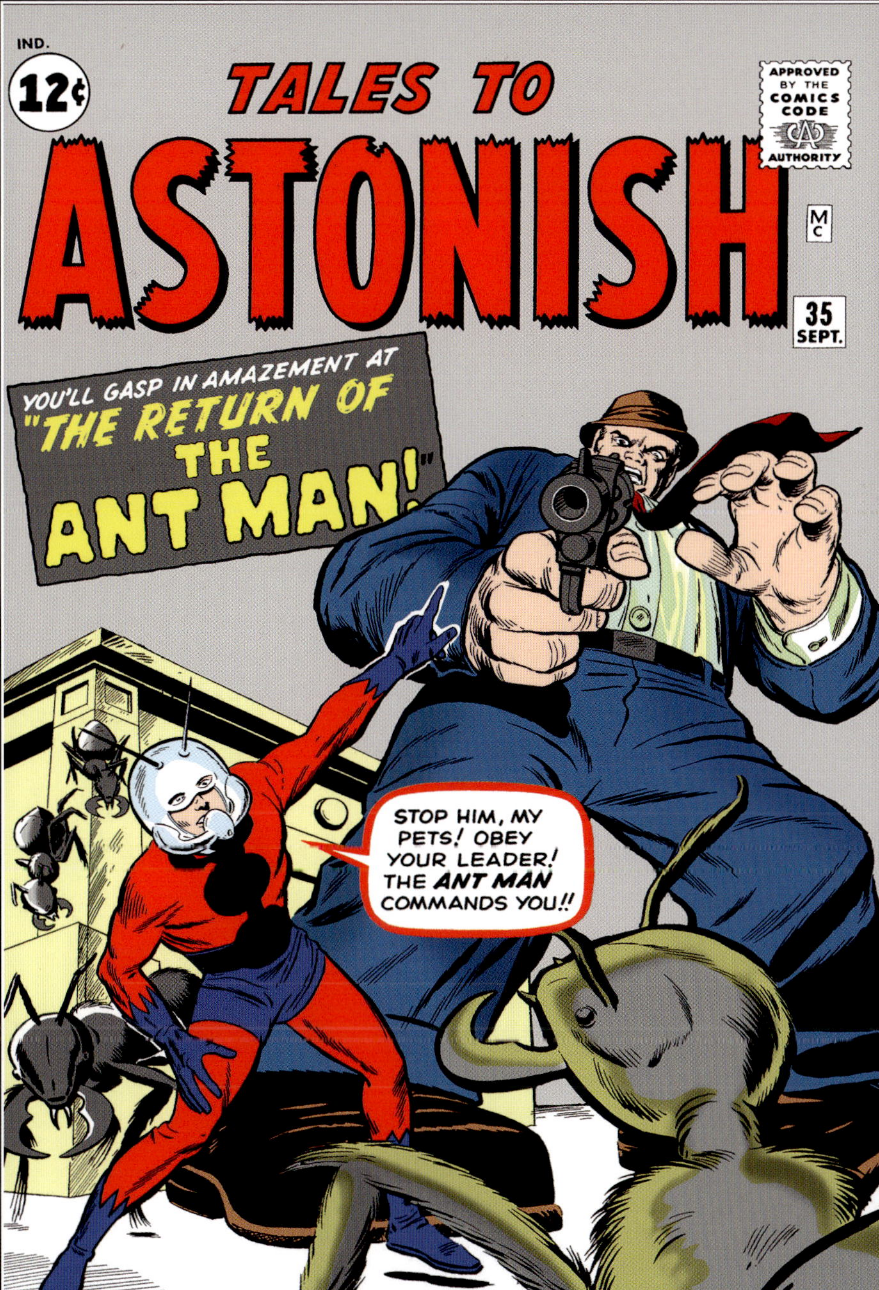

Cover to *Tales to Astonish (1959) #35*, penciled by Jack Kirby and inked by Dick Ayers.

his way through Pym's house with ease. But it isn't money, jewels, or antiques he finds in the highly secured basement vault. Instead, he discovers what appears to be a vintage motorcycle suit. The robbery is a bust, and Scott is devastated—and to top it all off, he gets arrested on the way out.

But appearances can be deceiving, especially for a former member of S.H.I.E.L.D. "It's all a front in order to induct Scott Lang into a heist Hank Pym wants to pull off," Winderbaum says.

Reed elaborates: "You get this sort of generational thing where Hank Pym was once Ant-Man, but really sort of put the costume in a vault. He created this technology to be used for the good of humankind, but as time went on he discovered that it was not being used that way—that it was going be weaponized, and it was going be used for a lot of bad things. So he decided the best thing was to sort of hide the technology away.

"In the intervening years, his company's been taken over, and it's not in his control anymore—so Hank has got to devise a way to get into PymTech and steal his technology away. He targets this guy, Scott Lang, who's really a thief—who he lets break into his house—and may be the last guy you'd think could pull off a thing like this. But Hank sees something in Scott that says, 'Against all logic and reason, this is the guy I'm going with.' And that's part of the fun of the movie."

Hank helps Scott escape from jail using the Ant-Man suit, and thus begins the passing of the torch. But Hank's daughter, Hope van Dyne, isn't so keen on the idea. She doesn't trust Scott—and she can't understand why Hank won't let *her* wear the suit. Hank assures her there will be a time when she can—but for now, he can't risk losing his daughter.

But Scott needs to learn to be a hero. To truly become Ant-Man, he must harness the power of Hank's inventions: the suit itself, the Pym Particles that enable it to shrink and grow, and the ability to communicate with ants through the marriage of a mental connection and elaborate technology. Reed was eager to explore how these unique abilities would add to the film's spectacle. "Ant-Man's powers are interesting because it's not just the matter of a guy shrinking down," Reed says. "When he shrinks down to become Ant-Man, he retains his power that he would have at normal size, because he becomes very dense when he's small. So I could be a bad guy sitting here holding a gun on somebody and suddenly, 'Wham!'—something flies in and knocks my tooth out. Well, it's Ant-Man flying through the air and launching into my tooth, but it has the power of a guy actually punching you. So that's something kind of new and interesting. It separates it from *The Incredible Shrinking Man* or *Honey, I Shrunk the Kids* or something because he's like a bullet.

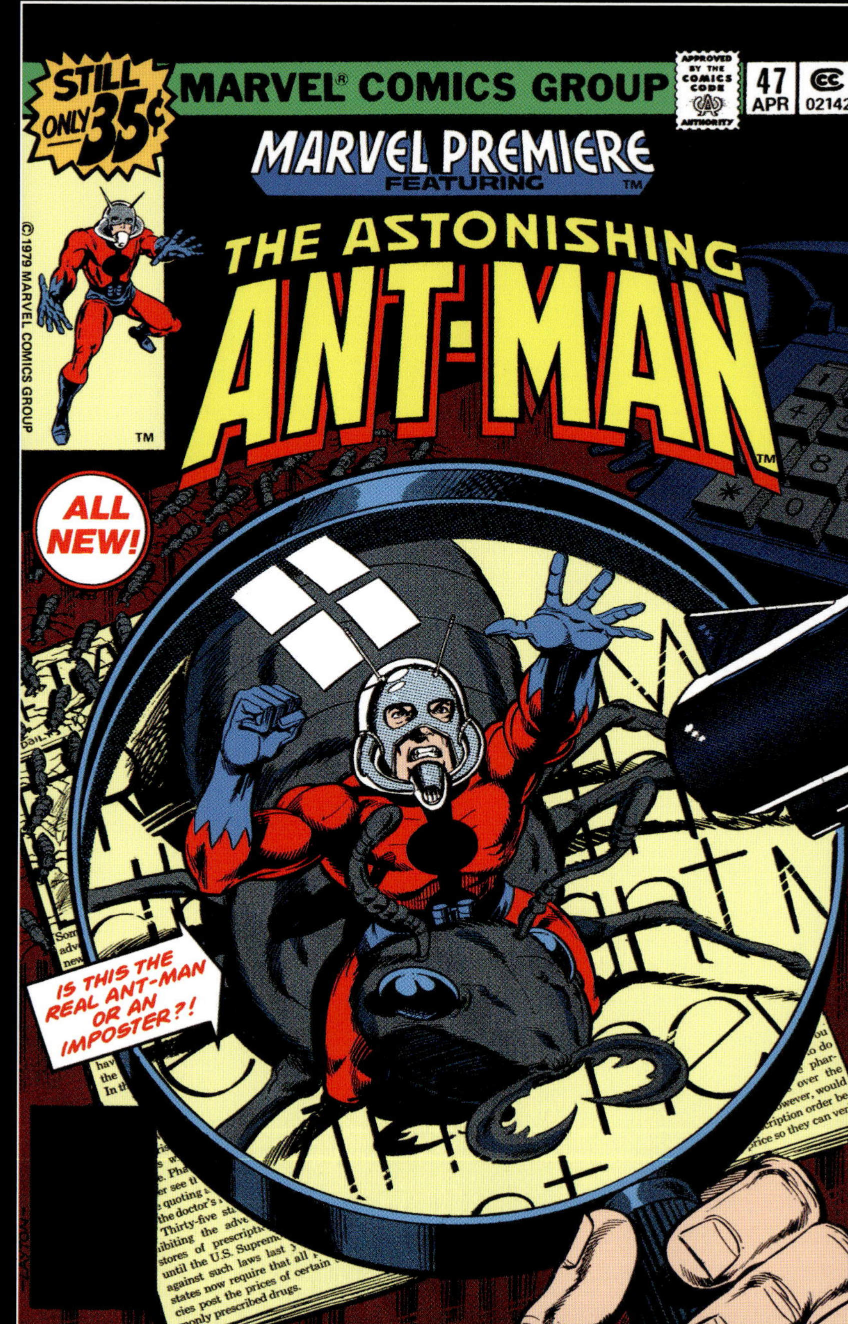

Cover to *Marvel Premiere (1972) #47*, by Bob Layton.

"The other thing about him is it's not just that he shrinks and he's done. He can change sizes very quickly. So really in the middle of an action scene, in the middle of a fight sequence, part of his power is really sort of keeping the enemy off-guard because he can change sizes with this suit at will."

By now, Marvel fans know to expect the unexpected. "I think film audiences are well-versed in the notion of shrinking," Feige says. "You know, it's been around for decades and decades—the notion that you can get really small, and crawl between the couch cushions, and go under a chair, and try to reach up and dial a phone. We've all seen those in movies before. What we want to do with the Pym Particles—the invention that Hank Pym had many years ago that can shrink himself, but also shrink other objects—is to see what happens when we use it in unexpected ways. One unexpected way is to give it to somebody who doesn't know how to use it, like Scott Lang."

Aside from the ability to shrink and grow, Ant-Man is aided and abetted by an army of surprisingly powerful friends. "You will see ants doing amazing things in this movie—all of it based in science and fact, things that ants actually do in nature," Winderbaum explains. "But when they're controlled with Hank Pym's invention, they're able to do things such as take down buildings."

His training complete, Scott prepares to take down Hank's old company and steal back the Ant-Man technology from Hank's former protégé, Darren Cross. In the comics, Cross first appeared opposite Scott Lang in *Marvel Premiere #47* as the head of Cross Technological Enterprises. In the film, Cross dons the helm of the Yellowjacket, one of Hank's many comic-book alter egos. The identity represents a period of instability for Hank, who takes the new name after an experiment gone wrong temporarily alters his personality. "Hank Pym has some questionable behavior when he's taken on the mantle of Yellowjacket in the comics," Winderbaum says. "As we build the Marvel Cinematic Universe, we can cherry-pick the best moments from the comics. And in a way we see a spiritual kinship between the Yellowjacket costume, and what it represents in Hank's life as being kind of the negative version of his creation to be able to shrink and grow. And for that reason, we are using the Yellowjacket design as the basis of our villain."

Bringing Ant-Man to the big screen was no small feat, and the filmmakers faced their share of raised eyebrows. "I really feel that all of our films have been forged in skepticism," Feige says. "When people hear the term Ant-Man, they go, 'What is this one now? Ant-Man? What, he's a little ant? How is he gonna save anybody? He's a super hero?' We love that kind of skepticism at Marvel Studios because we've encountered that kind of skepticism on almost every

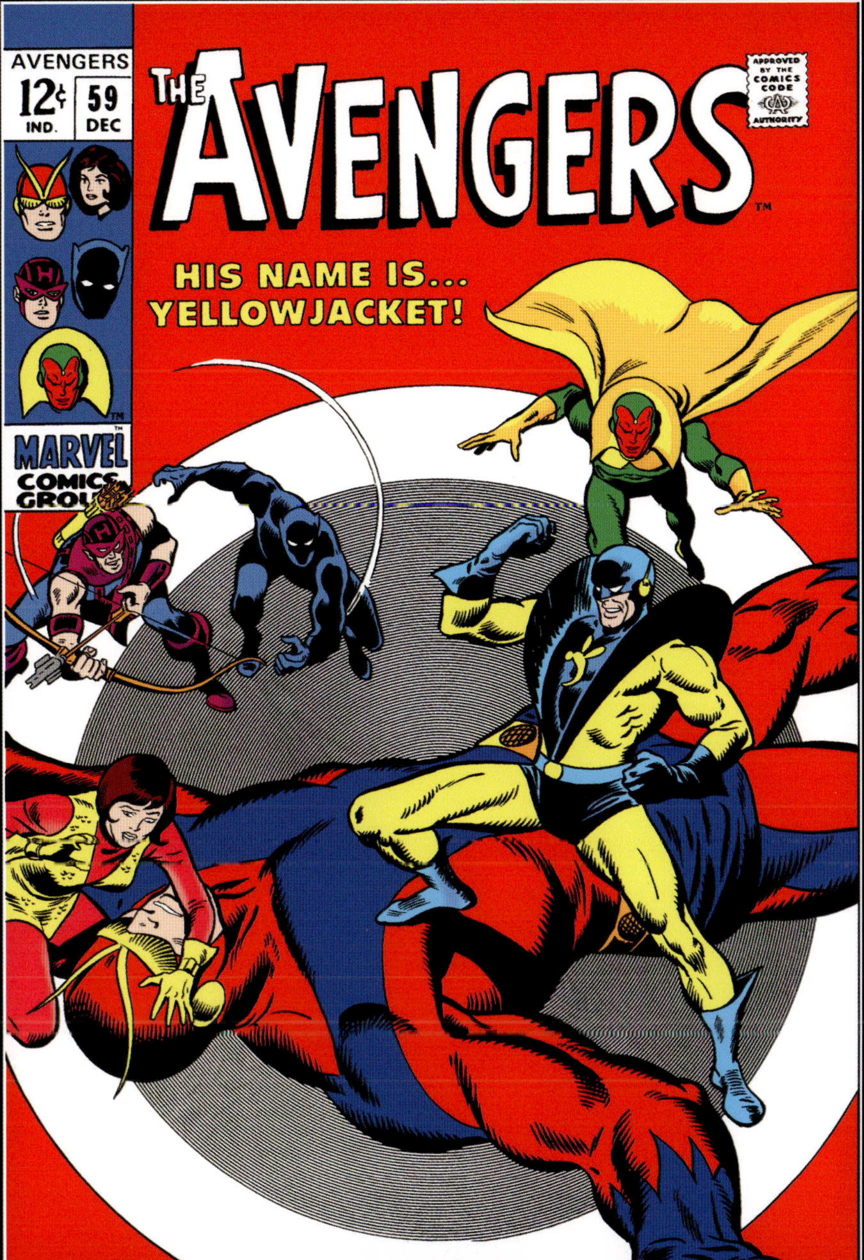

Cover to *Avengers (1963) #59*, penciled by John Buscema and inked by George Klein.

movie we've ever done, and people forget that after the movie comes out and is a big success. But a period-piece Captain America film, a Thor film, an Iron Man film—all of them were met with skepticism. Even putting them all together, people thought, 'Good luck. That hasn't been done before.' That's what excites us about it."

Armed with his unbridled passion for the subject matter, Reed was the perfect choice to strip away the skepticism and bring the story to life. "I've been a lifelong Marvel fan. I'm the kid who grew up with Silver Age Marvel Comics and spent untold hours in my bedroom just poring through Marvel comics—like, all of them. I was always an *Avengers* fan—and in the early issues, Ant-Man was one of the Avengers. So I've just always been drawn to those stories. They're just amazing tales, and the stories that those guys created in that period have really lasted. I mean, here we are in 2015, and these stories still have their power."

Reed's love for Marvel Comics resulted in some uncanny foreshadowing for his future work. At 2014's Comic-Con, fans saw that lucky obsession firsthand as Reed displayed a piece of his personal history. "I used to play drums in a punk band called Johnny Quest in the '80s," he explains. "I would also draw all the flyers for the band, and the flyer I showed at Comic-Con was from 1988, where I had ripped off the *Avengers #1* cover with each of the bandmates. I had drawn myself as Ant-Man, flying around on drums."

Marvel's *Ant-Man* moves those stories forward. Executive Producer Louis D'Esposito sums up: "We have a fresh film. New characters. You have Paul Rudd, Michael Douglas, Evangeline Lilly, Corey Stoll, Bobby Cannavale, Michael Peña—a great cast coming together to tell a fresh story where you're going see the world from a really unique perspective."

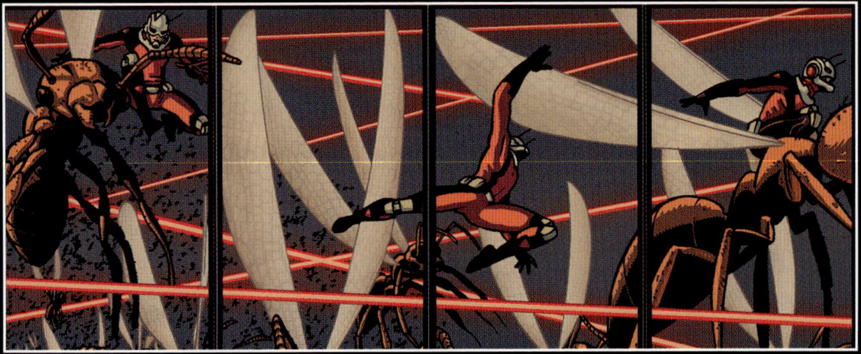

Ant-Man gets by with a little help from his friends, from *Ant-Man (2015) #1*—written by Nick Spencer, penciled and inked by Ramon Rosanas, and colored by Jordan Boyd.

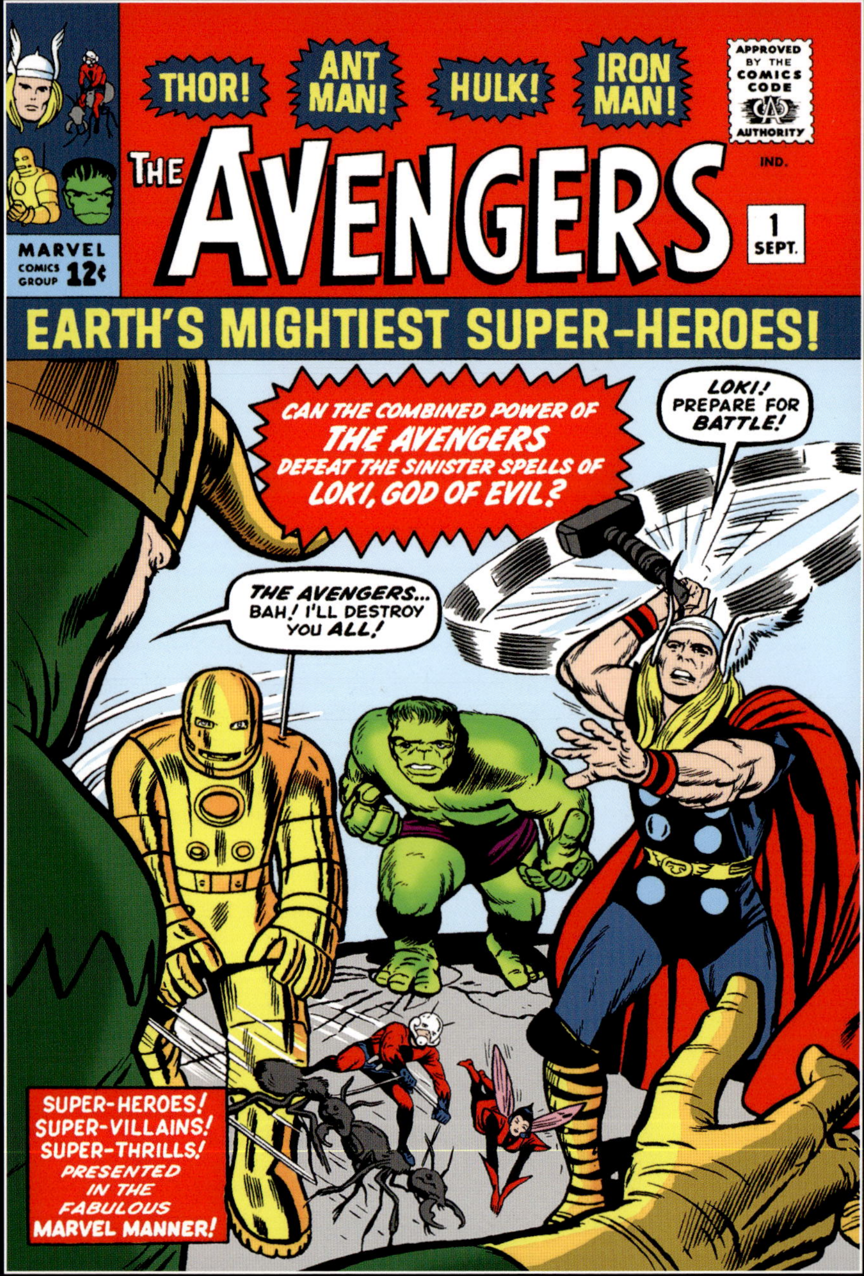

Cover to *Avengers (1963) #1*, penciled by Jack Kirby and inked by Dick Ayers.

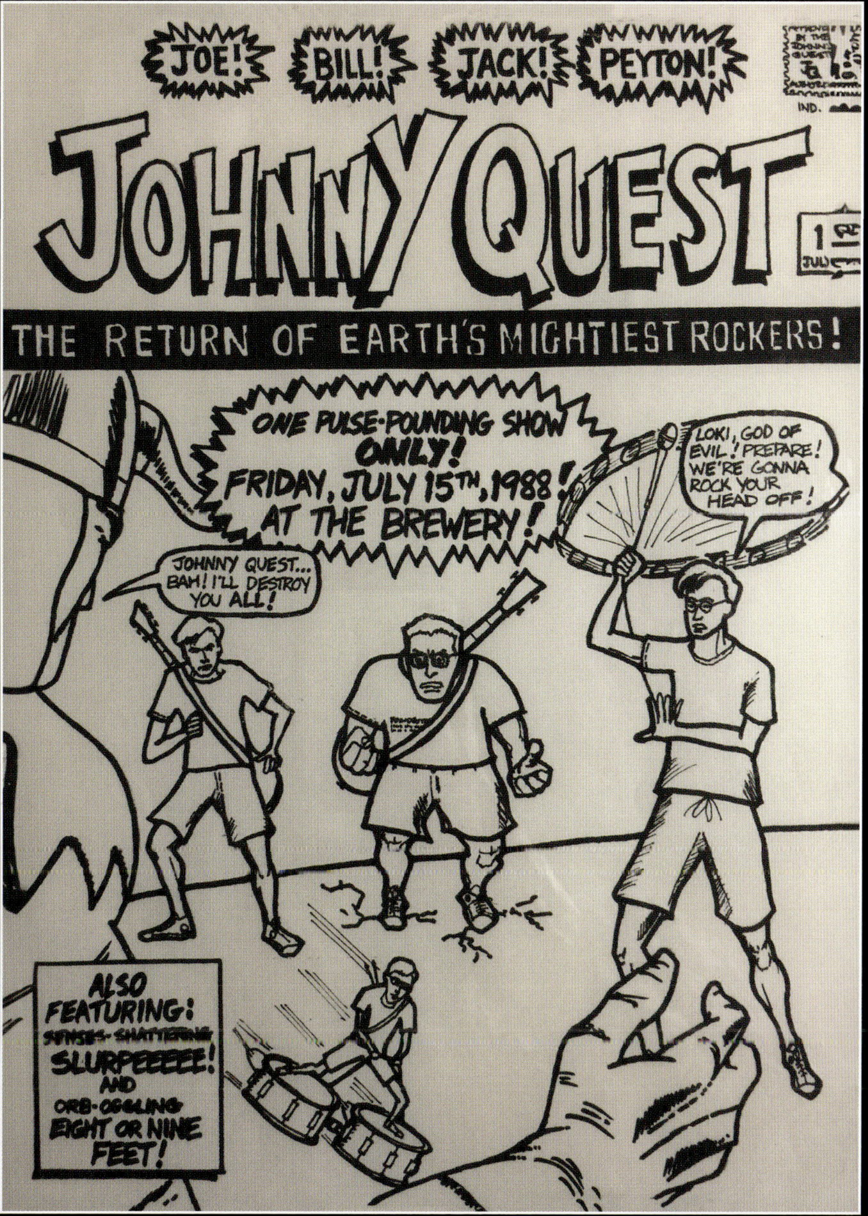

Peyton Reed drew this flyer for his band, Johnny Quest, in 1988. A riff on the cover to *Avengers (1963) #1*, it fittingly casts the director in the role of Ant-Man.

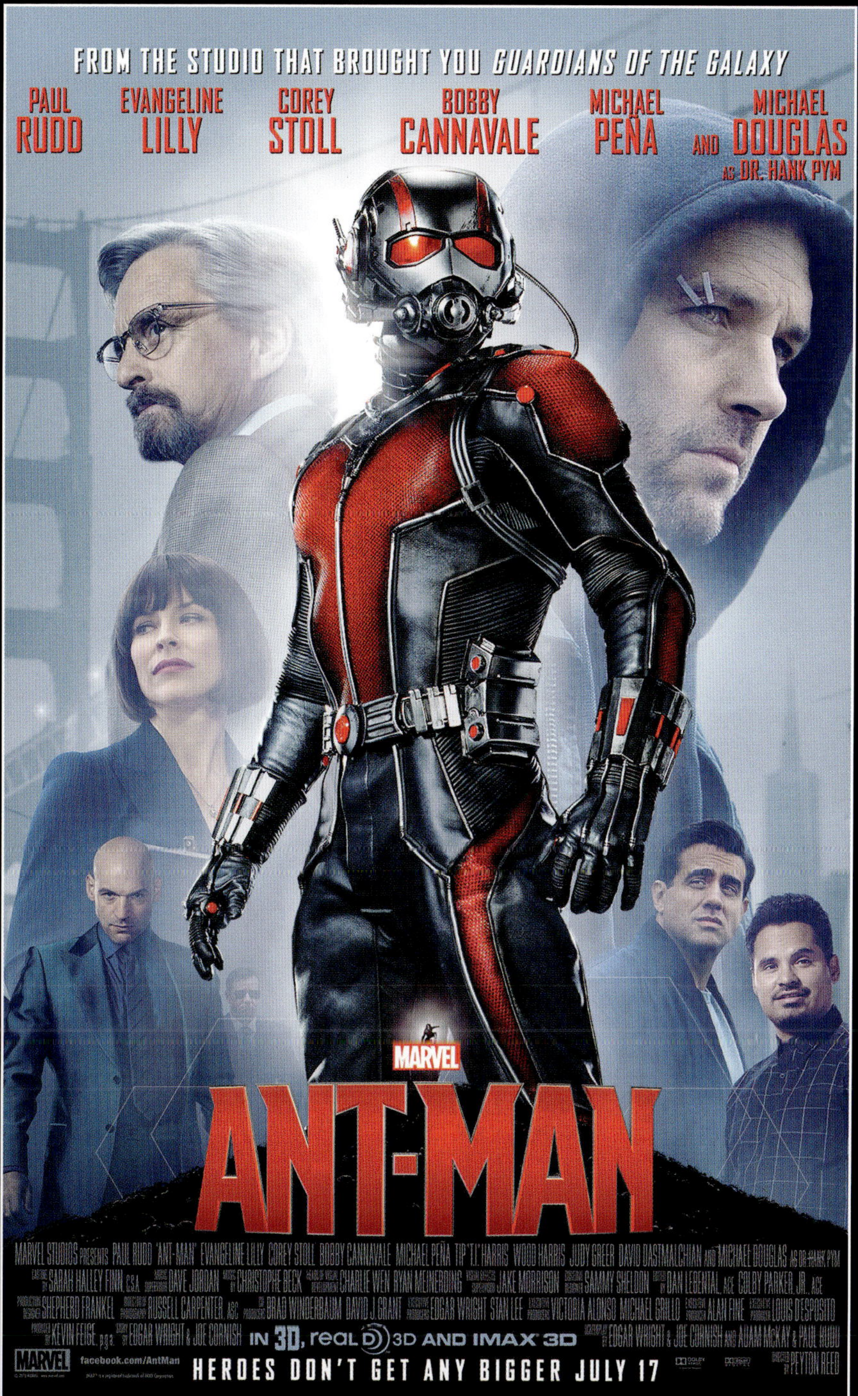

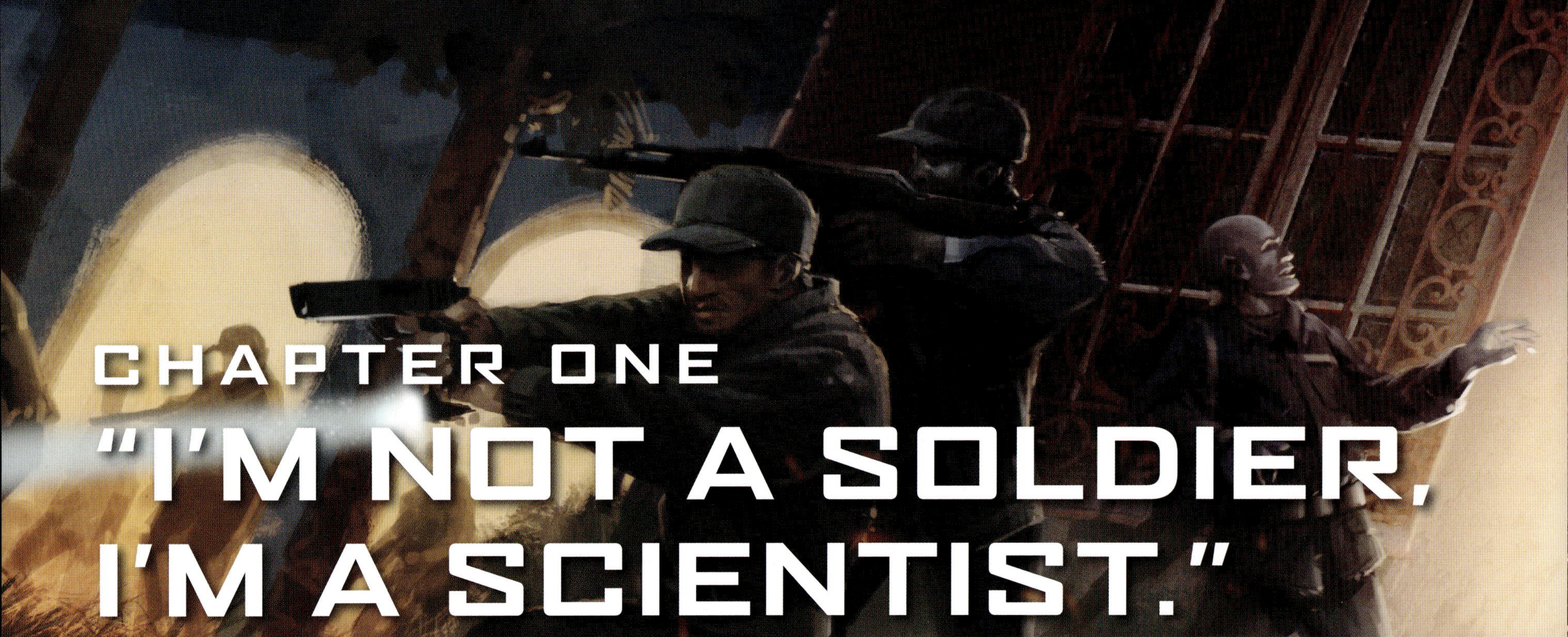

CHAPTER ONE

"I'M NOT A SOLDIER, I'M A SCIENTIST."

Every hero, big or small, starts somewhere. For Hank Pym, the adventure begins with S.H.I.E.L.D. There, Hank worked alongside Howard Stark, a fellow member of S.H.I.E.L.D. and the brilliant father of Tony Stark. Pym's breakthrough creation, the Pym Particle, revealed a genius that rivaled even Stark's. Using Pym Particles, Hank created a suit capable of minimizing the space between atoms, allowing him to shrink uniformly to about half-an-inch tall. For Paul Rudd, who portrays Scott Lang and co-wrote the script, it's not just the science or the spectacle that make Ant-Man unique—it's characters like Hank. "I think that making any kind of character human is what keeps you interested," Rudd says. "I think that you can have the most amazing fight sequence, or you could have the most dazzling special effects, and they could be pretty cool to look at, and it could make for an exciting way to pass some time, but it doesn't have any kind of depth—it doesn't stay with you really in any way unless you connect to those characters. The film certainly has amazing action sequences—some of the fights and things are just nuts—and then visually there are things in this movie you've never seen before. I think that's going to be really striking. But what I hope will be the thing that really resonates with people will be what's happening with the characters and their relationships with each other."

Despite his idealism, Hank recognizes his creation's potential for abuse. Moved to safeguard his legacy—and the world—Hank leaves S.H.I.E.L.D., taking with him both the Pym Particles and his brilliant mind. Over time, his heroic legacy as Ant-Man fades into the obscurity of urban legend...until its revival by the most unlikely of heroes: a former con artist named Scott Lang.

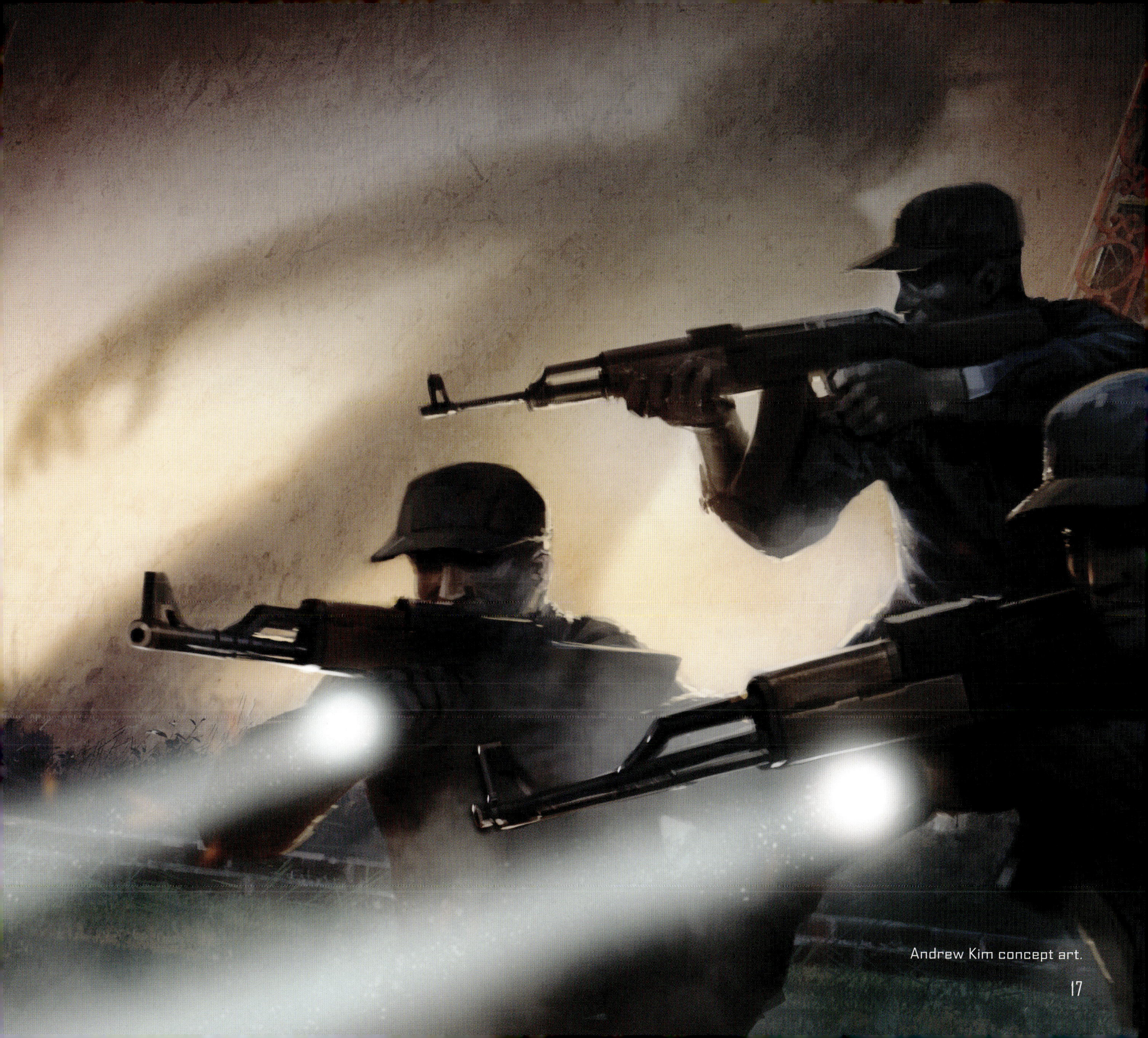

Andrew Kim concept art.

ANT-MAN

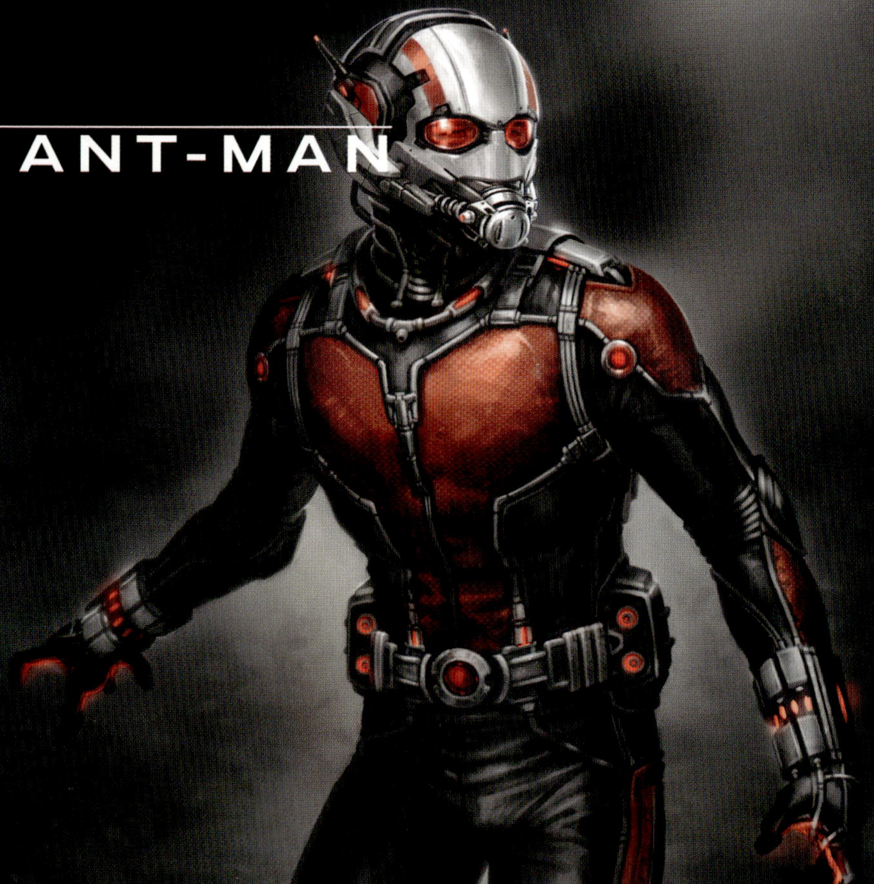

The Visual Development team began trying to crack Ant-Man's design early in the film's development. As with any hero in the Marvel Cinematic Universe, the Ant-Man costume needed to incorporate a sense of practicality amid the iconic elements of the character's comic-book counterpart. "Designs for characters in the Marvel Cinematic Universe all have their unique challenges," Concept Artist Andy Park explains. "Sometimes all we have to go off of is the look from the comic book. But besides the original comic-book look, I believe the best designs come when there is a clear story and purpose to that look. Ant-Man was certainly one of those cases with that kind of specificity. The mandate was to design a retro-looking costume, since it was created by the original Ant-Man, Hank Pym, in the 1960s and would also be worn in modern times by Scott Lang. So the challenge was to design a suit that reflected this dated look, but was still cool enough to be worn in modern times and not be laughed at—despite the fact that his super-hero name is 'Ant-Man.'"

Andy Park concept art.

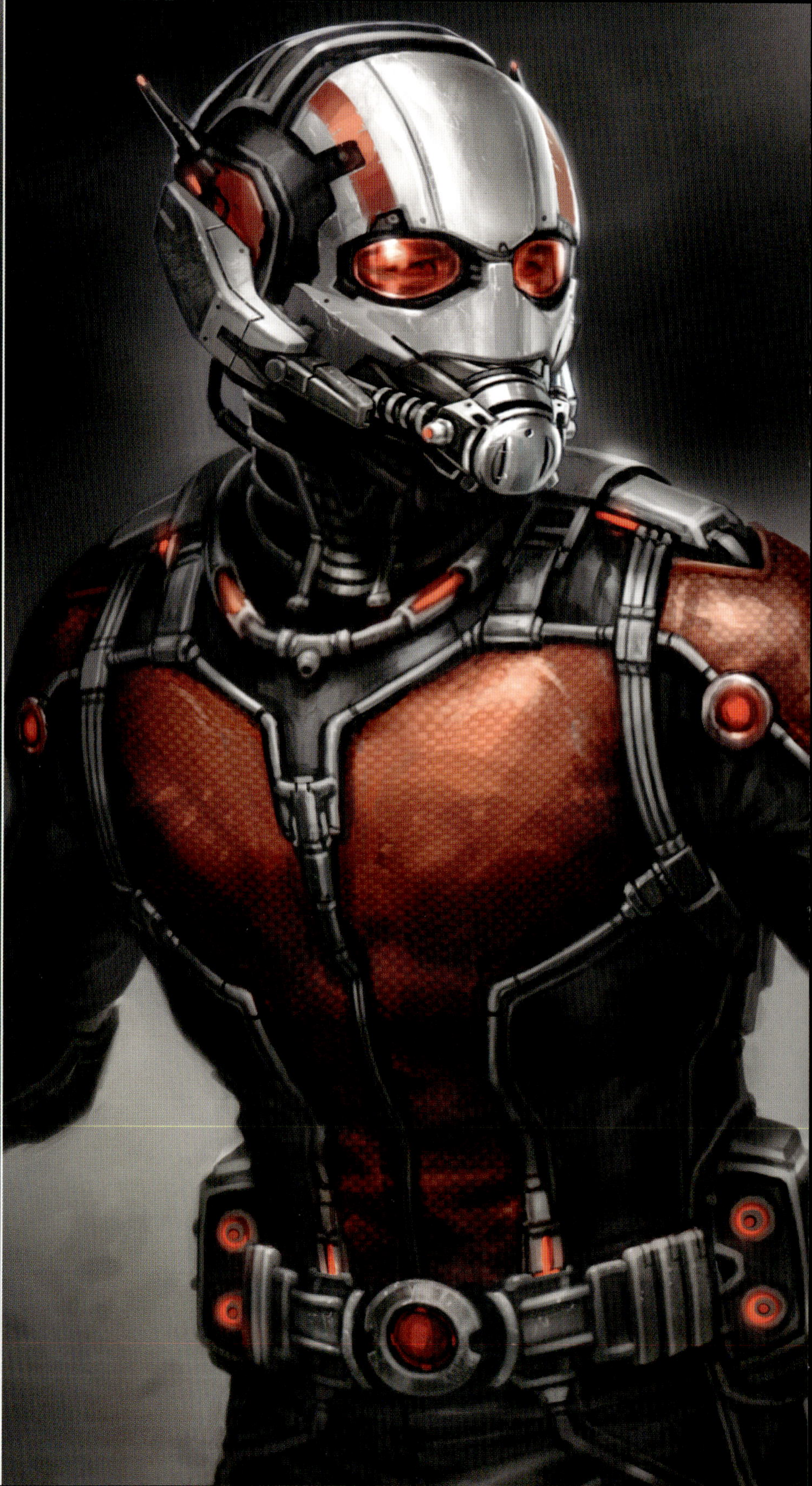

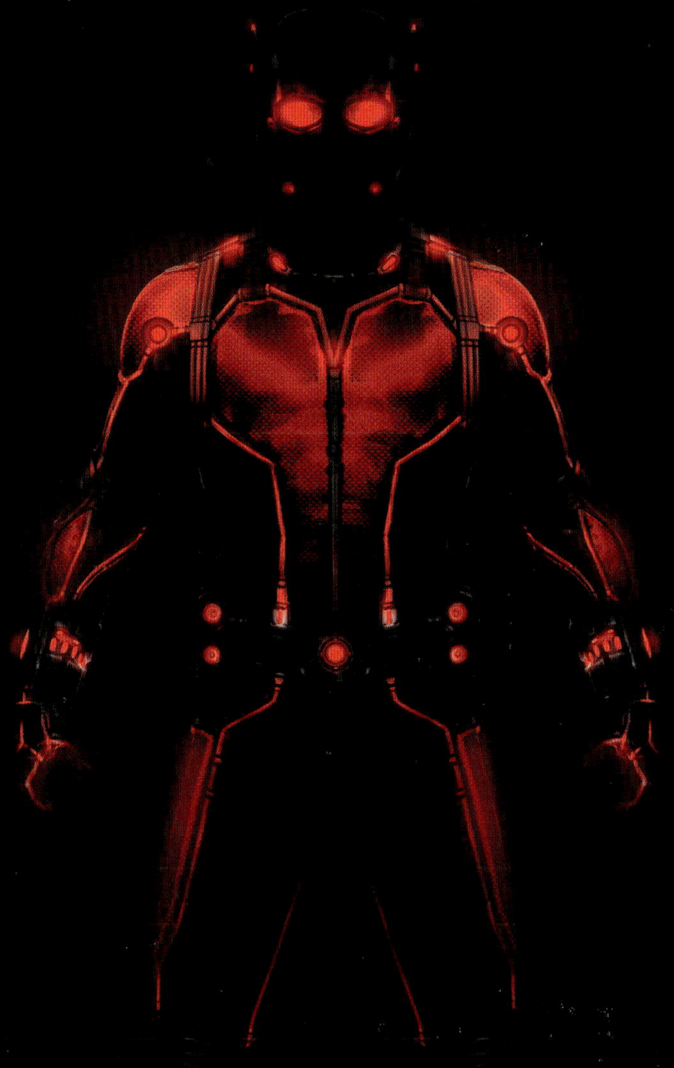

"We took inspiration from the old '60s-style spacesuits seen both in reality and in old sci-fi films," Park continues. "The idea was to design a costume that was not too sleek and modern. I wanted it to be a little bit clunky with obvious exposed tubing and wiring. The helmet needed to show that it had advanced technology, especially for that time, but couldn't be to the point of looking like highly advanced Stark or other modern technology. Our team did many variations with all this in mind, and ultimately I was honored to be able to come up with his final look you see in the movie."

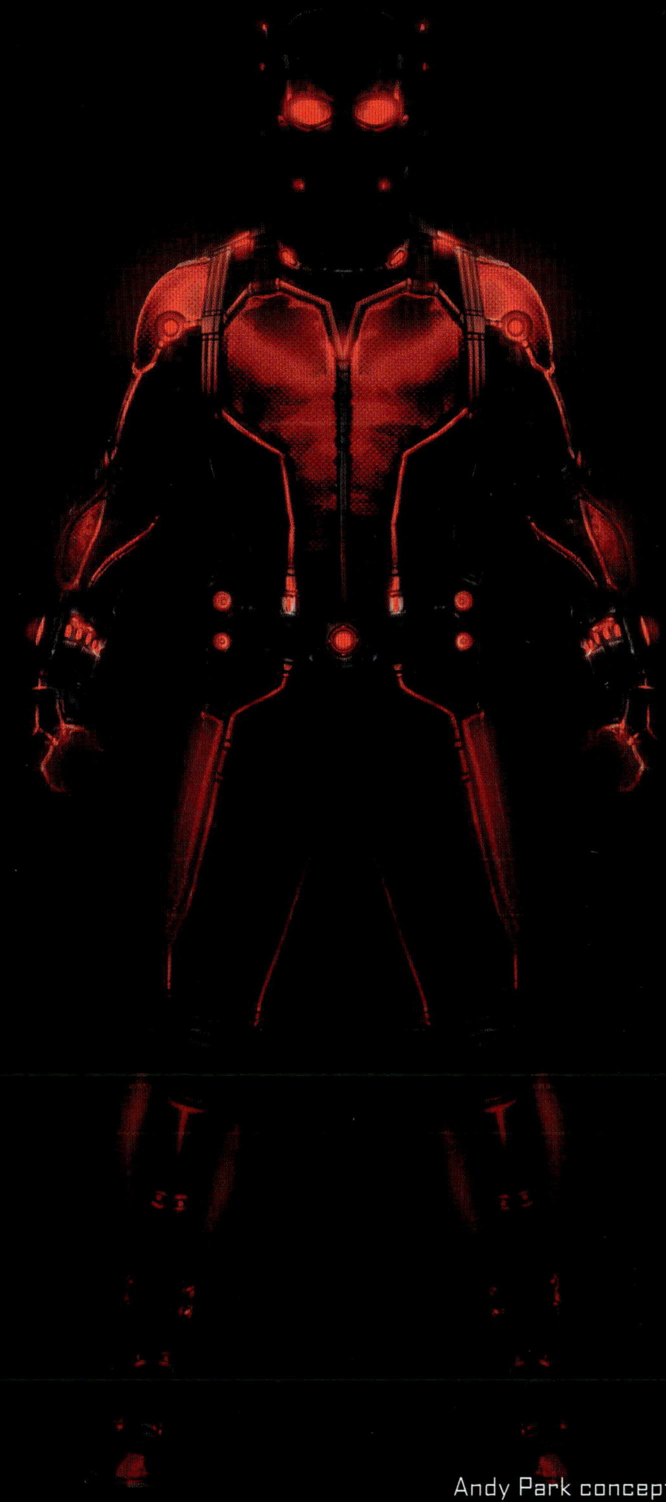

Andy Park concept art.

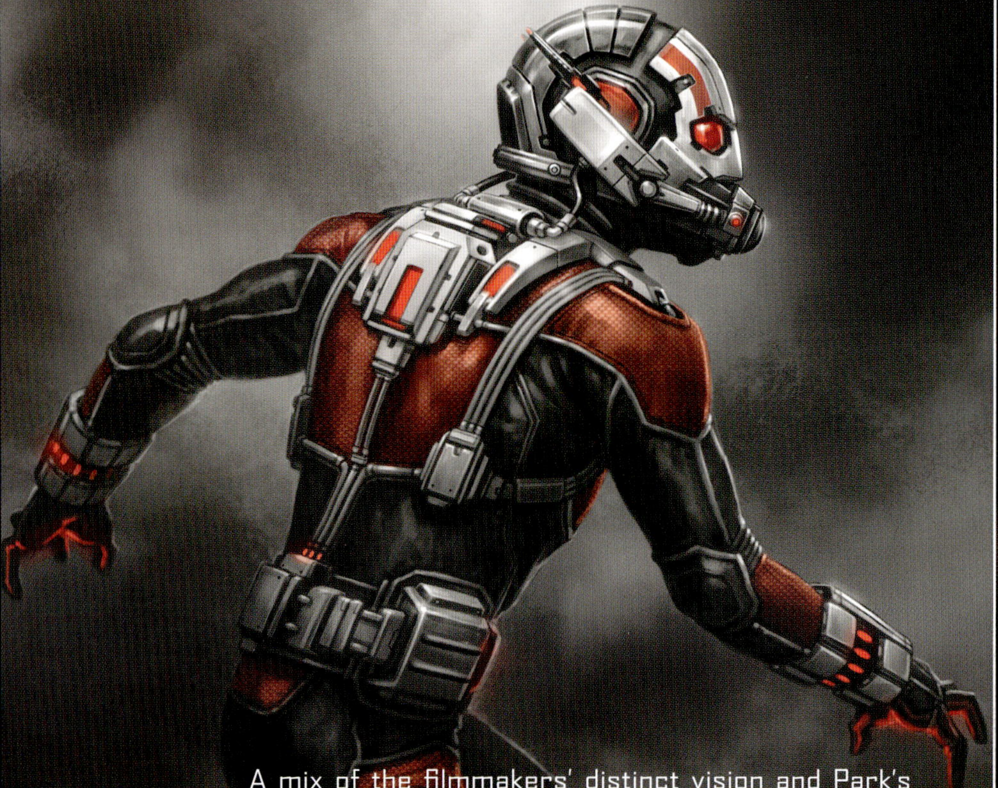

A mix of the filmmakers' distinct vision and Park's own adoration for the subject matter offered a clear direction for the suit's design. "Apart from being a concept artist on Marvel's Visual Development team, I am first a comic-book fan," Park says, "so when I design these characters, I do so with the desire to please the fans who are expecting a level of accuracy in terms of looking like the comic books. I do that because I, too, desire that. But of course my main job is to help the director and executives at Marvel find their vision for the character I am working on; it is definitely a collaborative endeavor. With Ant-Man in particular, I knew that some liberties would need to be taken in comparison to his comic-book look. Mainly his helmet needed to be a bit more streamlined and less bulbous. The antennas needed to look a bit more functionally integrated rather than the literal ant antennas sticking out of his forehead he has in the comic book. And lastly his mouth needed to be fully covered to make sense of the gas coursing through his costume that allows him to shrink in size. But I did all this while trying to maintain Ant-Man's overall essence and feel from the comic book."

Andy Park concept art.

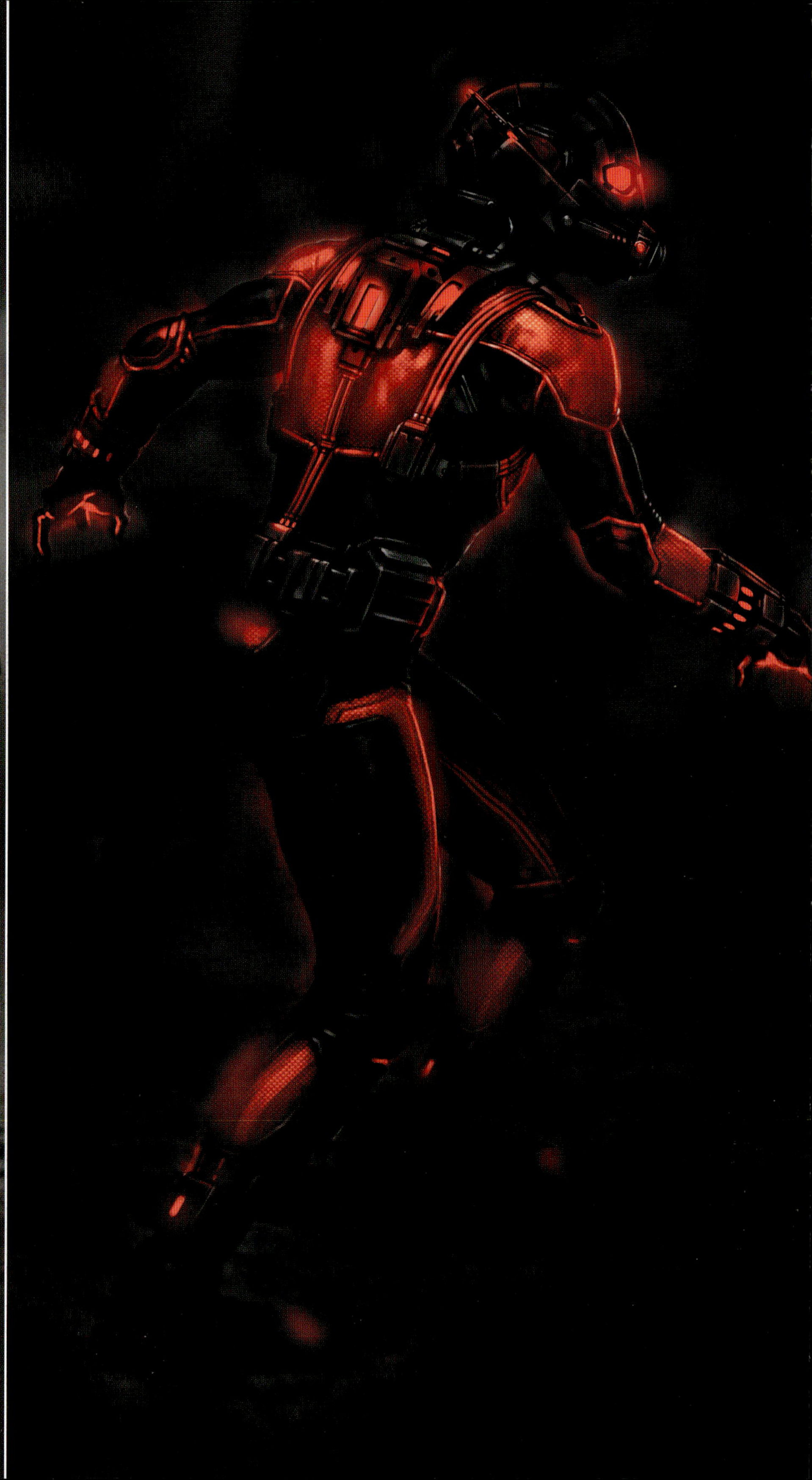

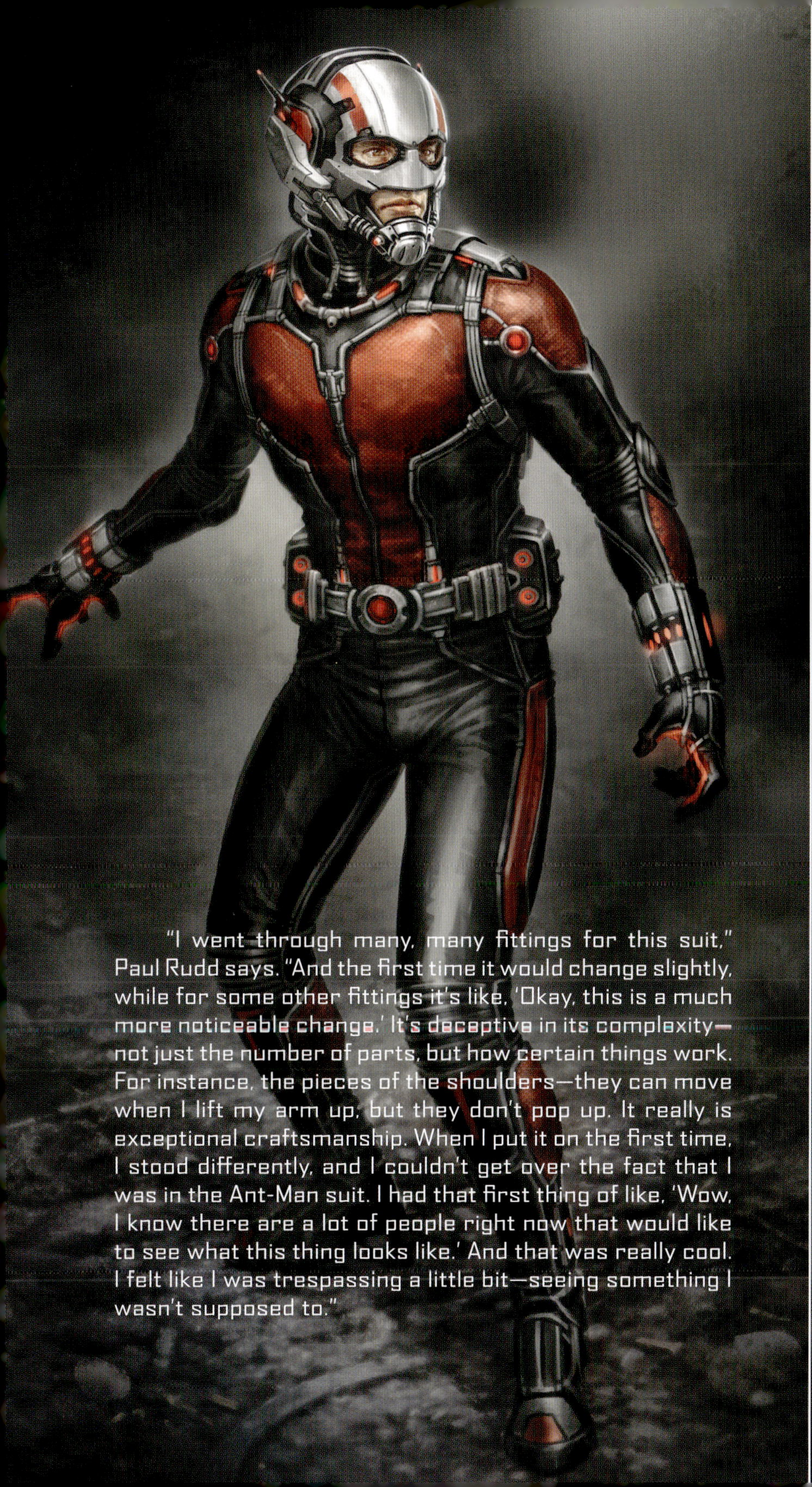

"I went through many, many fittings for this suit," Paul Rudd says. "And the first time it would change slightly, while for some other fittings it's like, 'Okay, this is a much more noticeable change.' It's deceptive in its complexity—not just the number of parts, but how certain things work. For instance, the pieces of the shoulders—they can move when I lift my arm up, but they don't pop up. It really is exceptional craftsmanship. When I put it on the first time, I stood differently, and I couldn't get over the fact that I was in the Ant-Man suit. I had that first thing of like, 'Wow, I know there are a lot of people right now that would like to see what this thing looks like.' And that was really cool. I felt like I was trespassing a little bit—seeing something I wasn't supposed to."

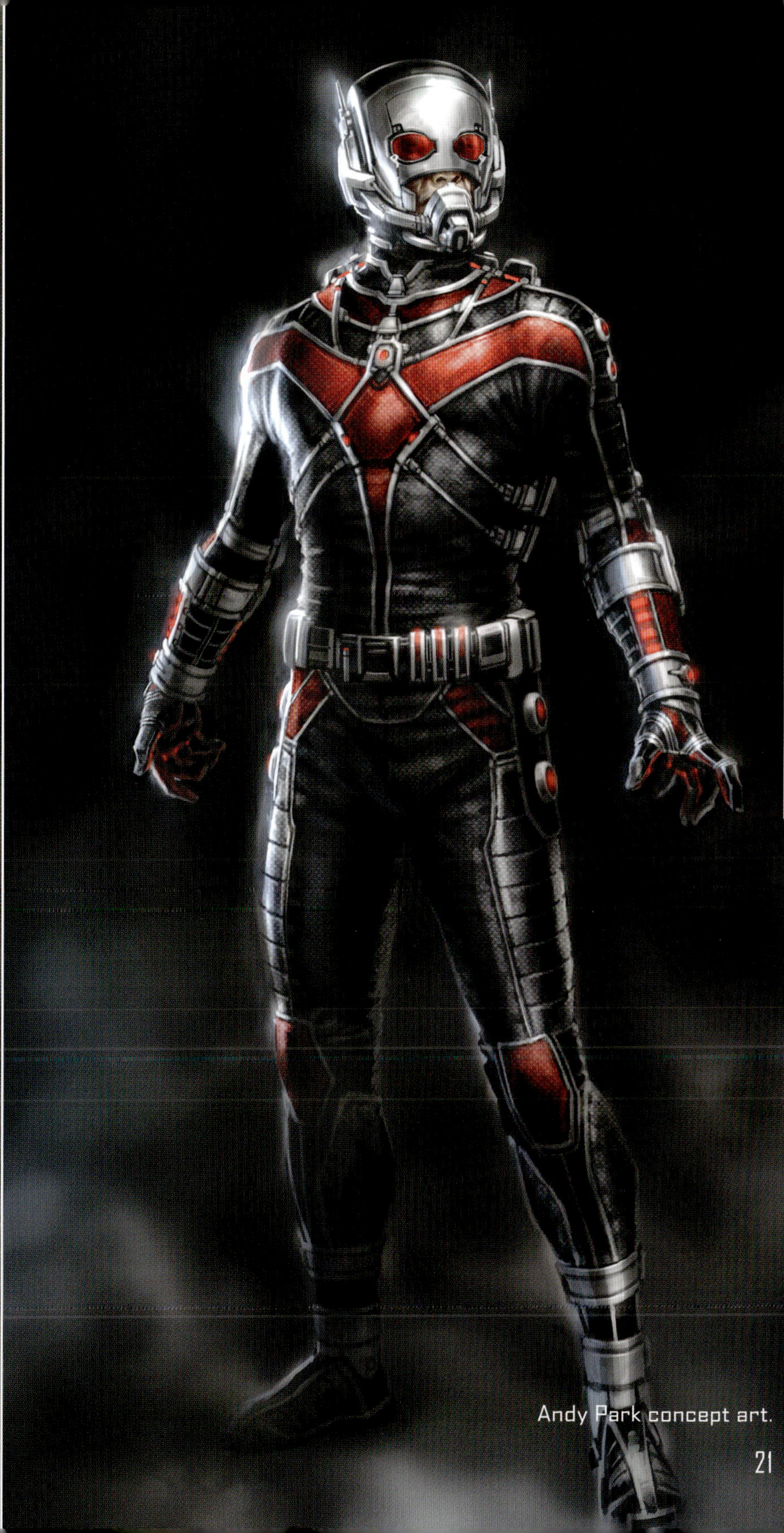

Andy Park concept art.

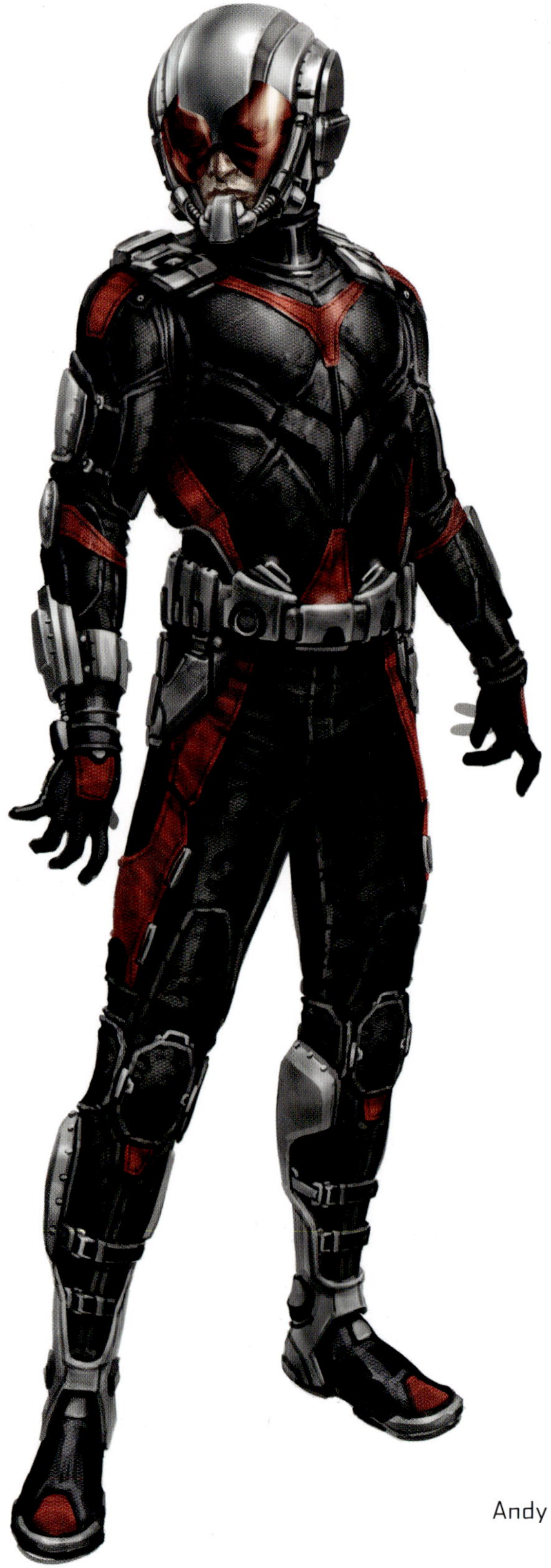

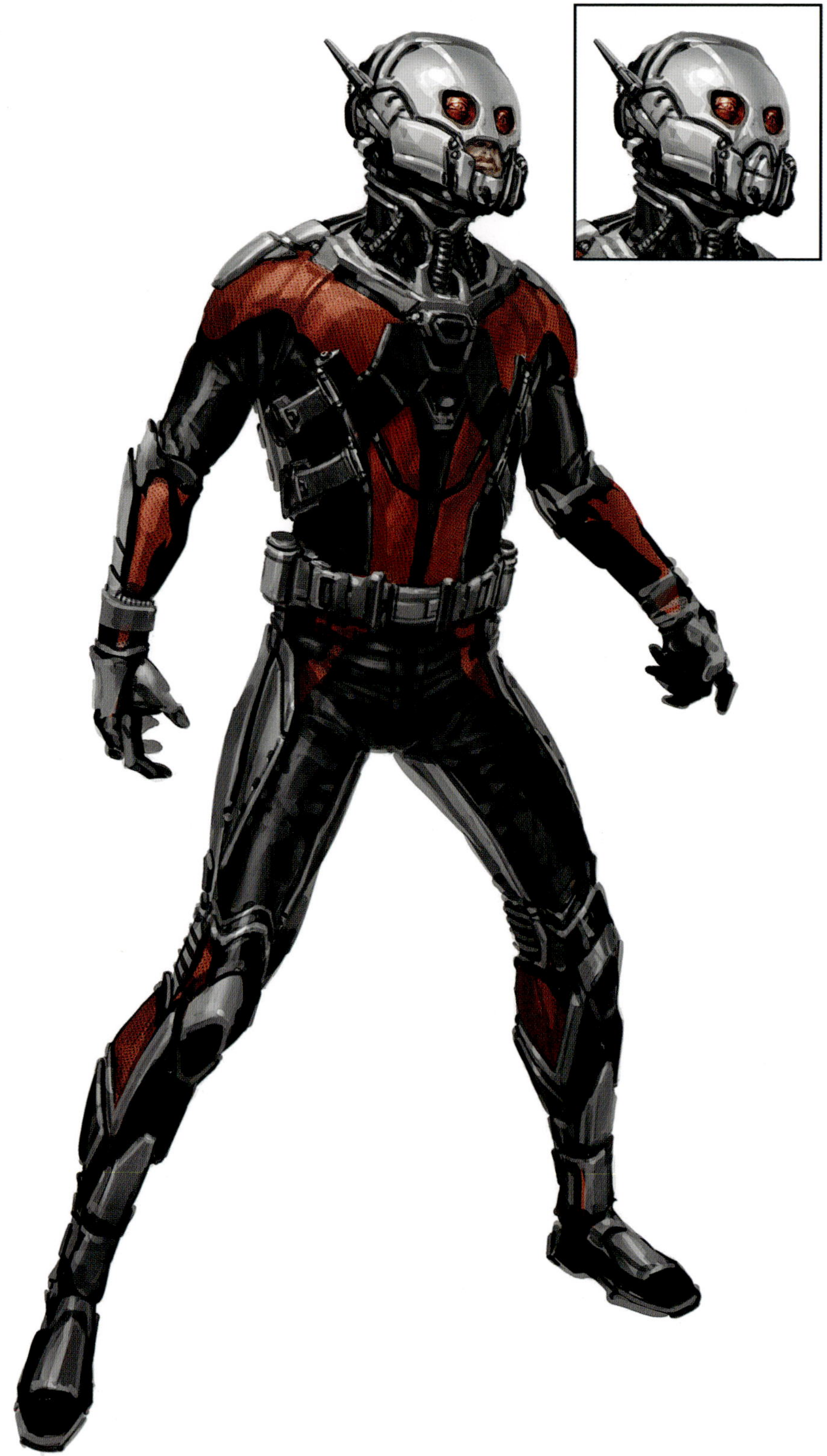

Andy Park concept art.

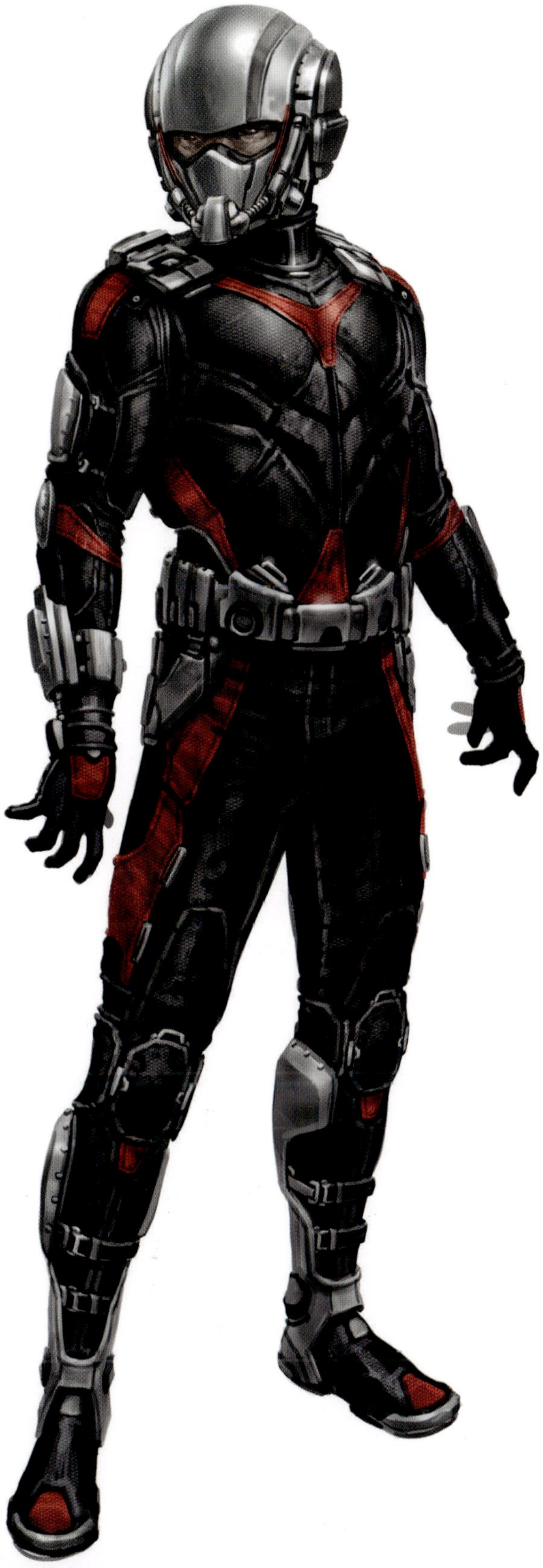

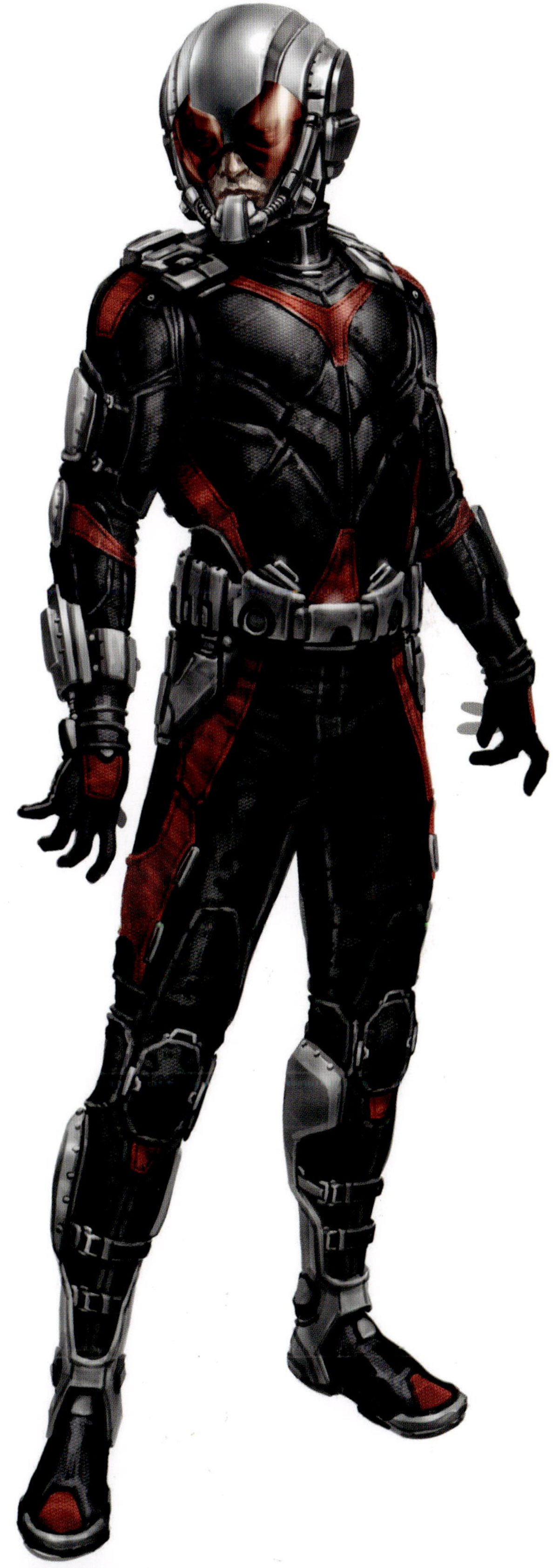

Andy Park concept art.

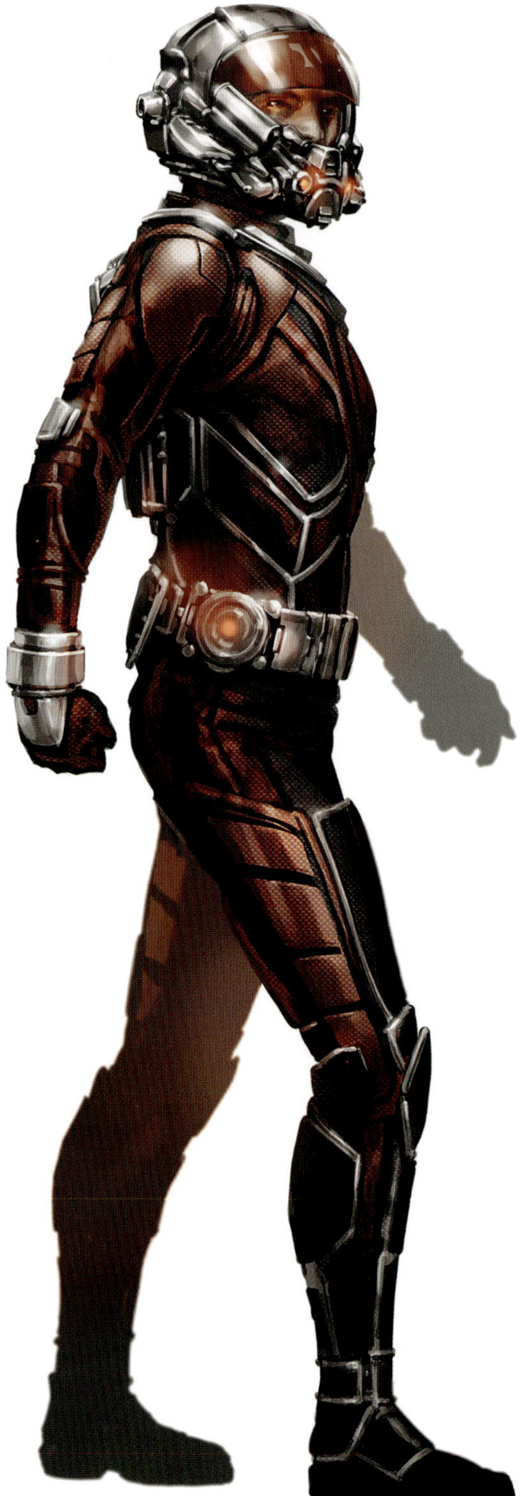

Andy Park
concept art.

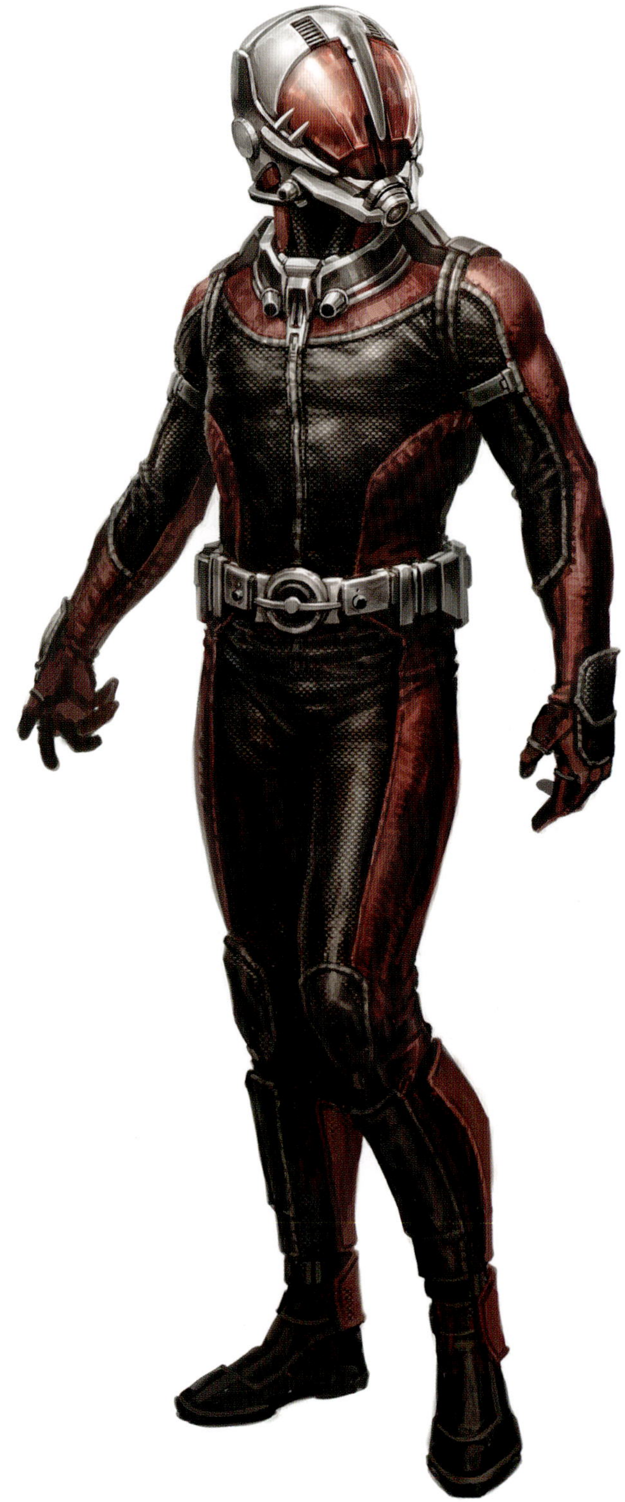

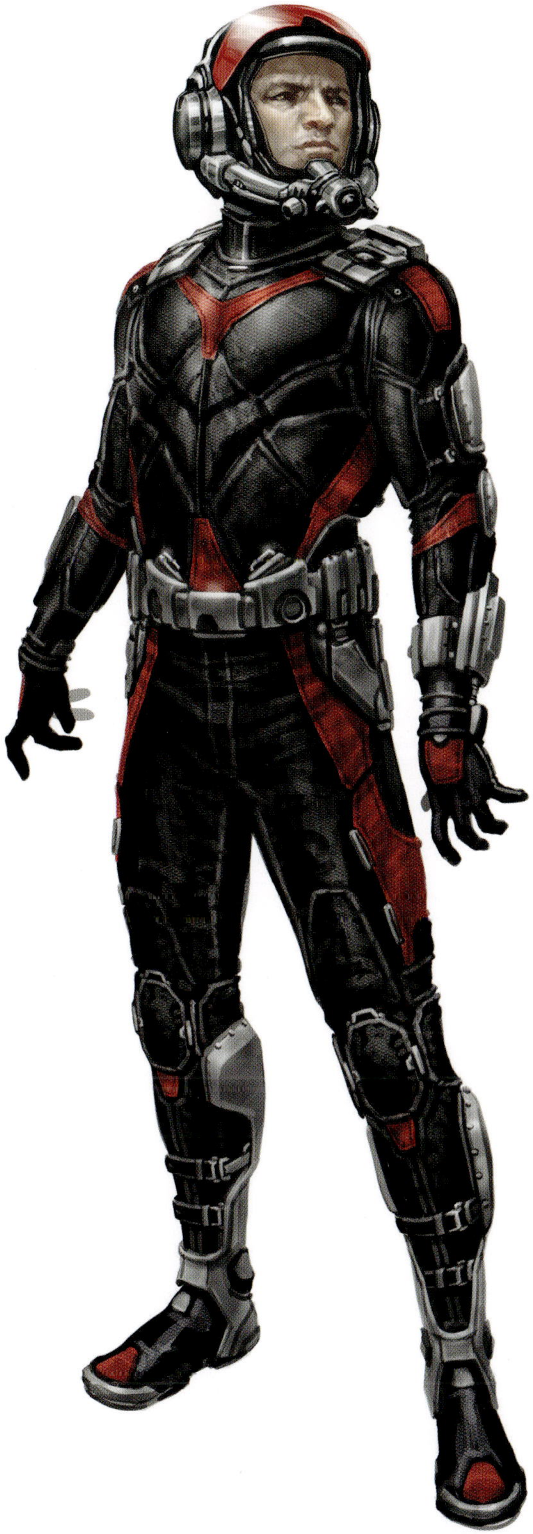

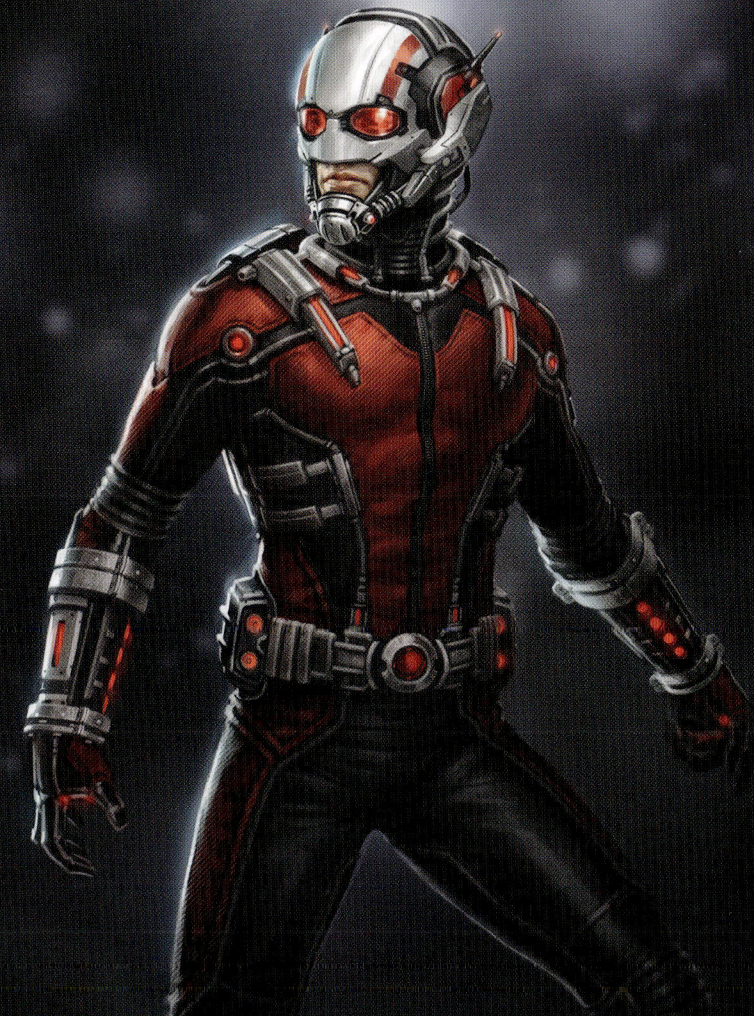

For Costume Designer Sammy Sheldon Differ, the suit proved deceptively complex due to its many moving parts. "The suit as a whole was a challenge to make! Trying to create all the tiny elements of technology that would work with the movement of the body was tricky. Especially around the shoulder area—those pieces took a long time to work out, as it needed to be multi-hinged to not hinder movement. Making the suit stunt-friendly was also a challenge. We made panels in the design of the suit so it stretched with the body. The suit was made from a black pearlized leather with metallic red panels of a stretch fabric with tiny rubber squares printed on to create an insect-eye texture. The belt had around 52 pieces, the suit had around 68 hard pieces, and each glove had 46 pieces; the total hard pieces are 268, plus the soft panels of around 200—making a grand total of over 468 pieces per suit."

Andy Park concept art.

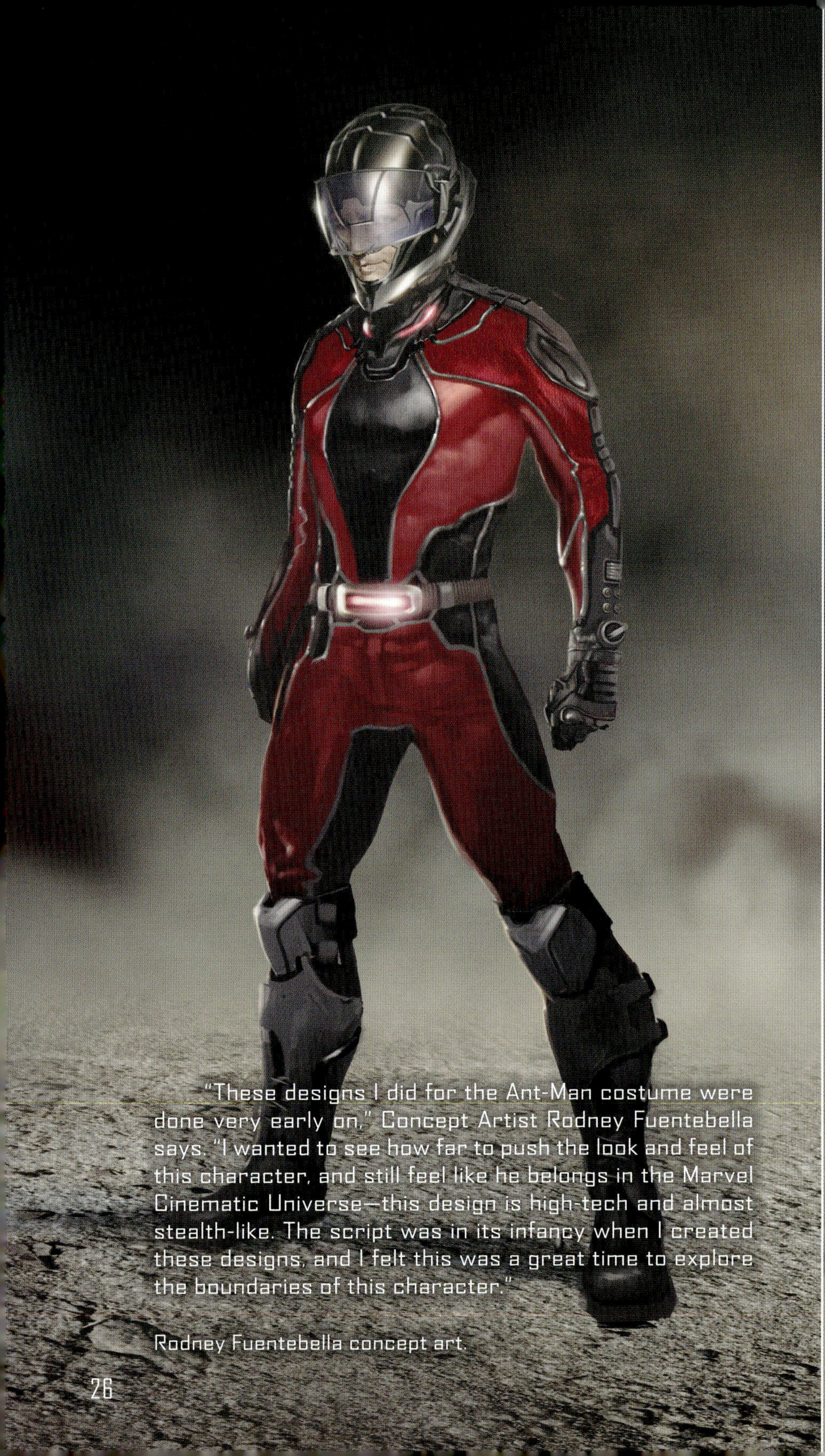

"These designs I did for the Ant-Man costume were done very early on," Concept Artist Rodney Fuentebella says. "I wanted to see how far to push the look and feel of this character, and still feel like he belongs in the Marvel Cinematic Universe—this design is high-tech and almost stealth-like. The script was in its infancy when I created these designs, and I felt this was a great time to explore the boundaries of this character."

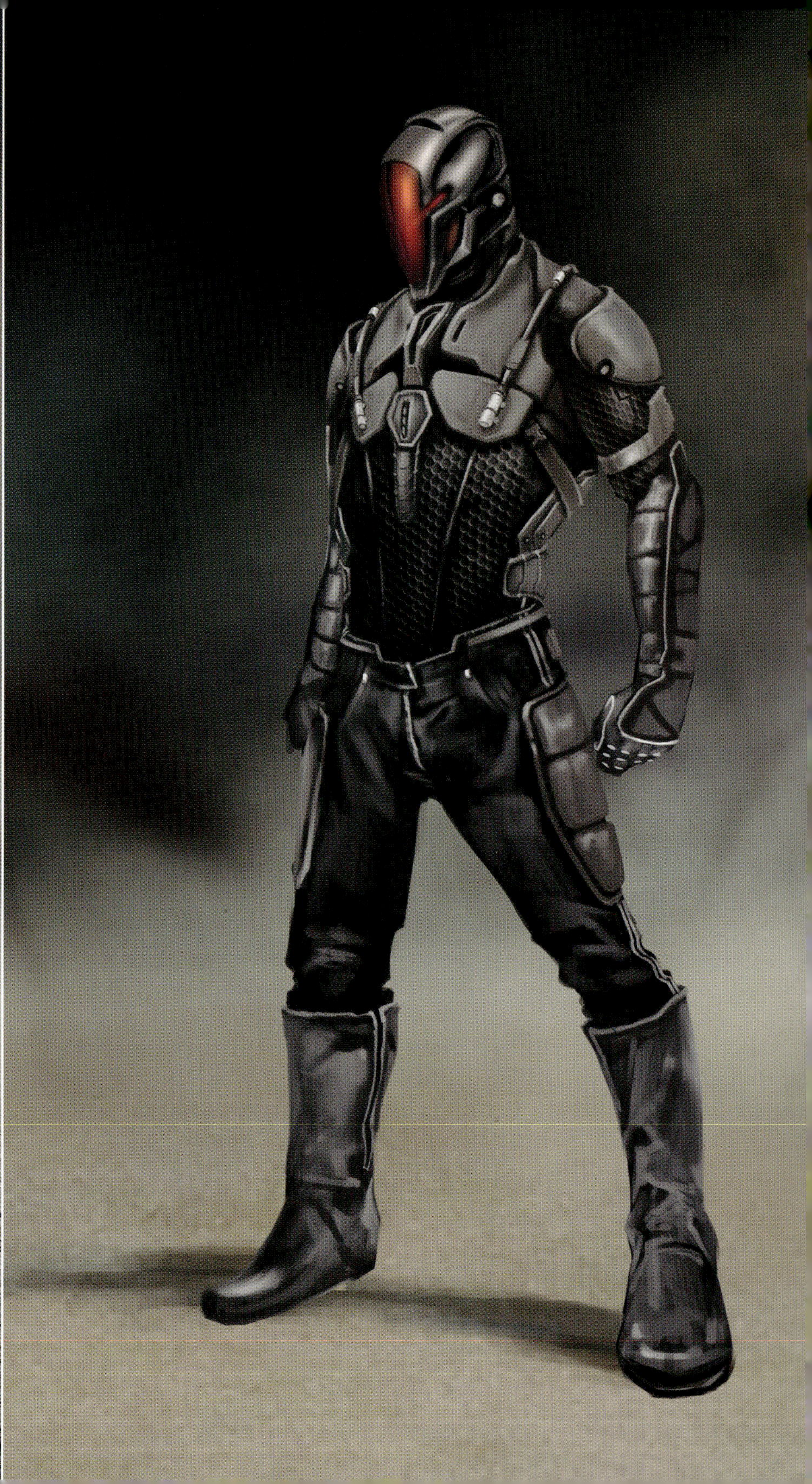

Rodney Fuentebella concept art.

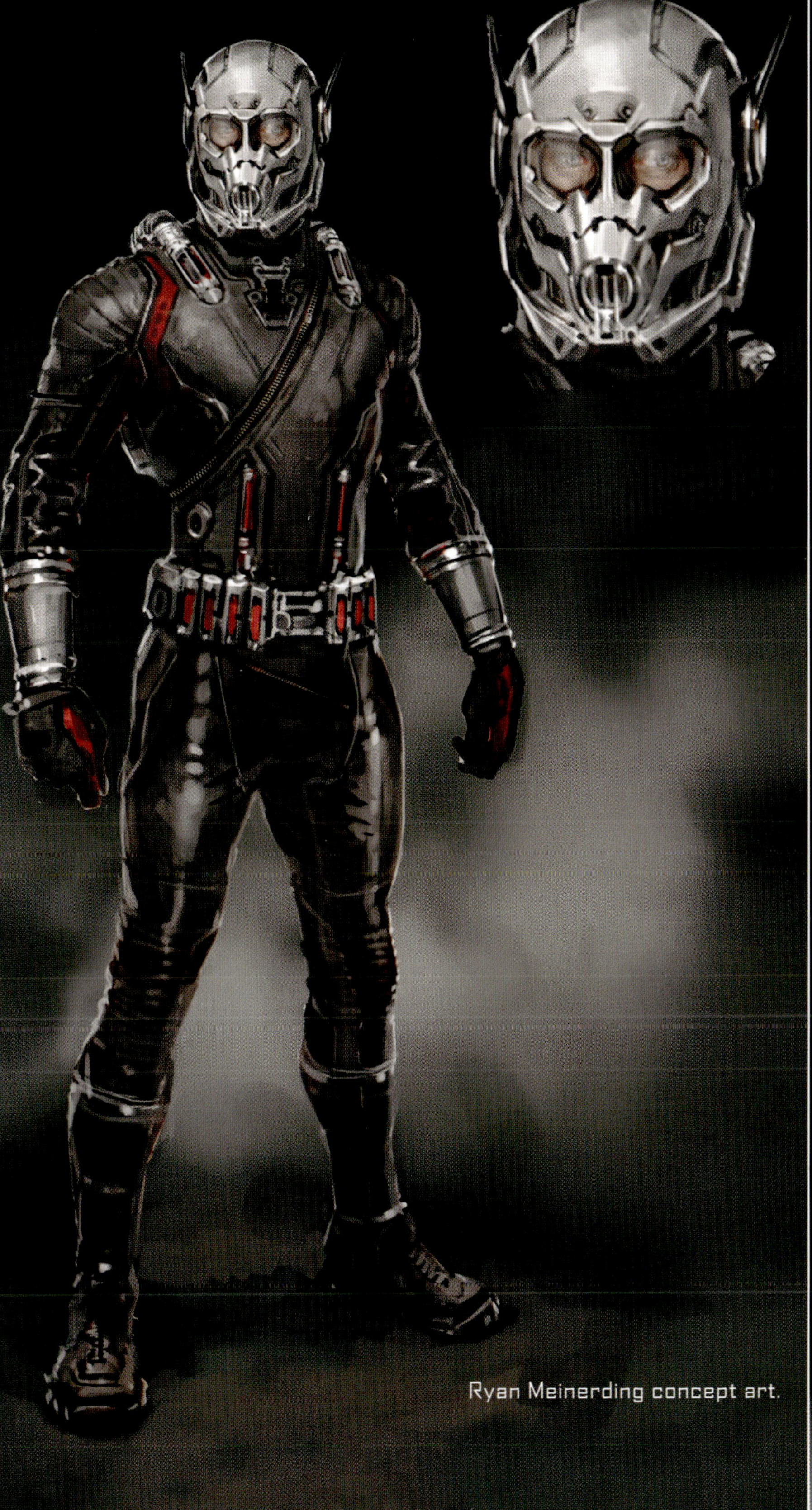

Ryan Meinerding concept art.

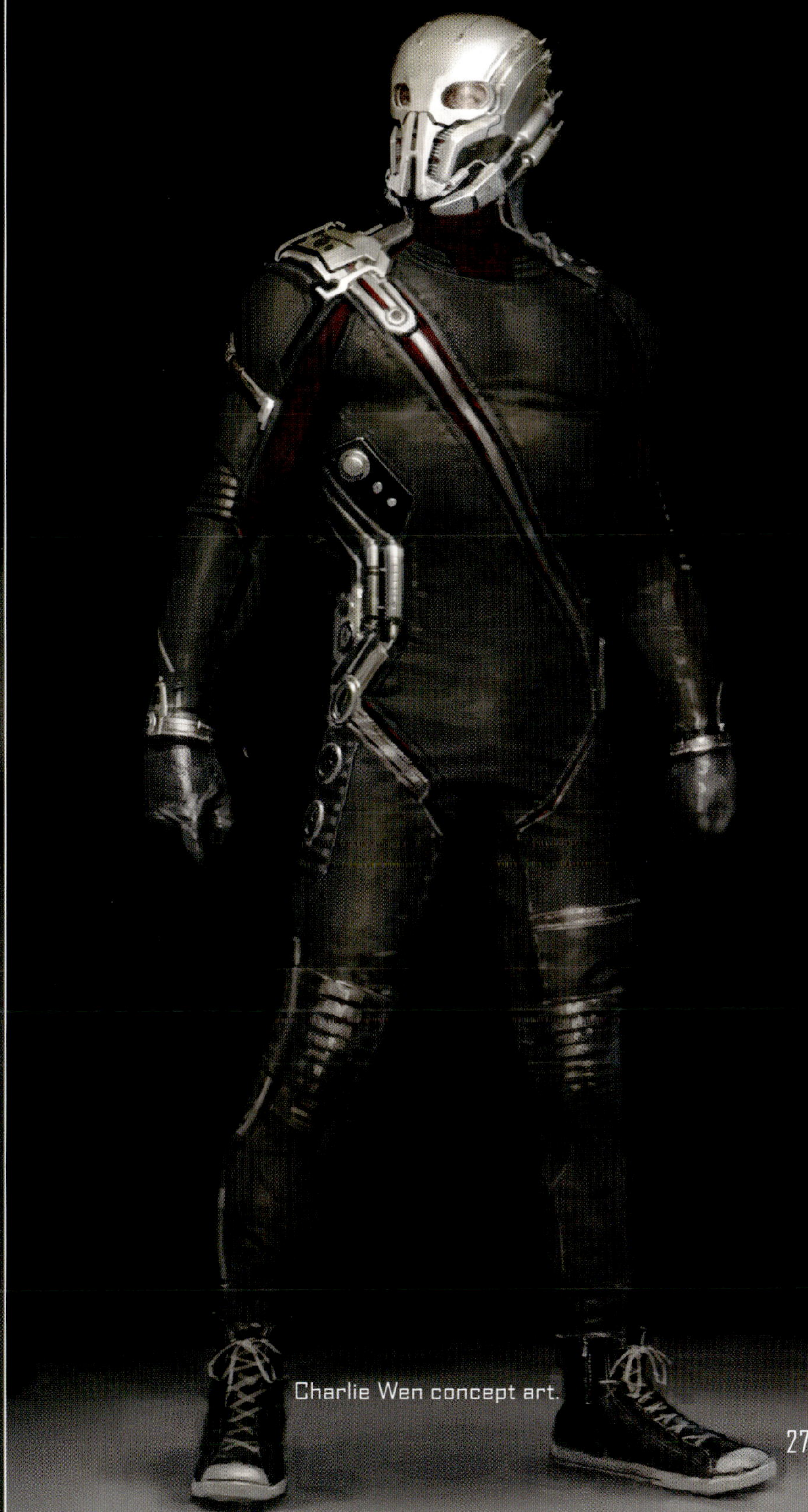

Charlie Wen concept art.

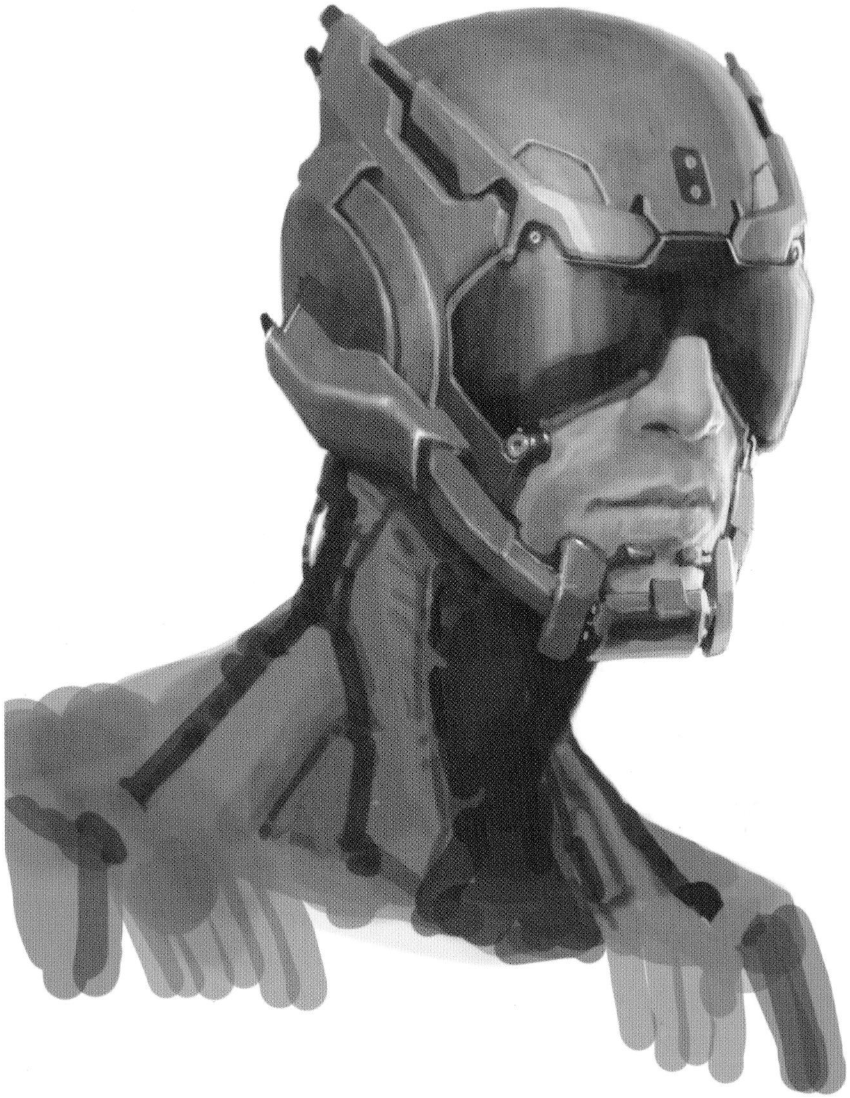

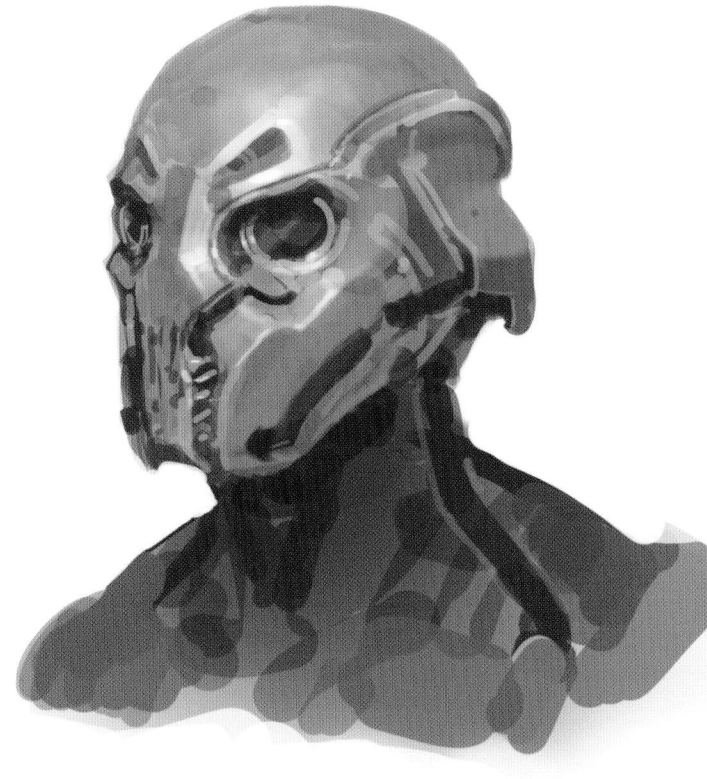

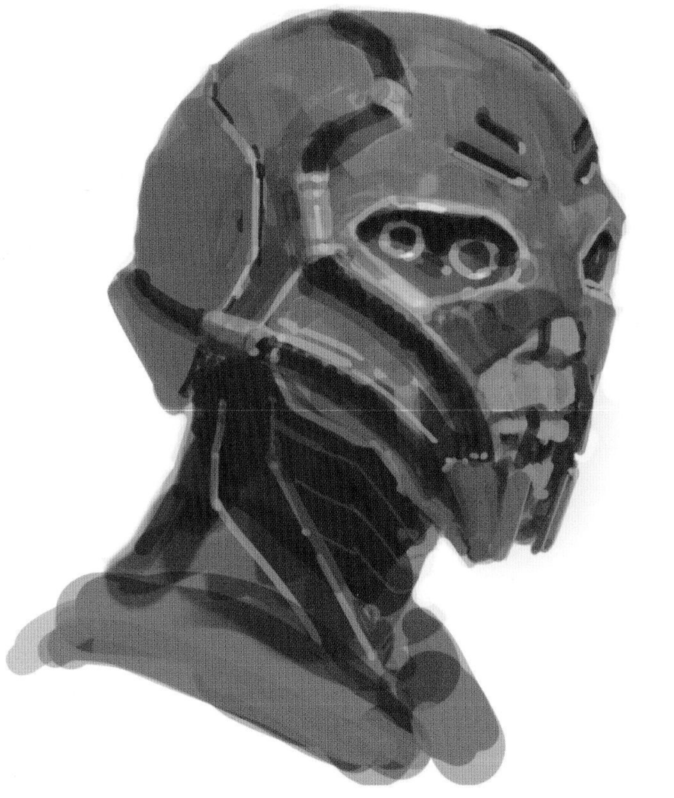

In the project's early stages, the Visual Development team created an array of helmet studies ranging from bug-like to sci-fi to high-tech. The final helmet's relatively simple appearance was considerably complex in its construction, just like the suit itself. "There are over 50 parts—50 pieces just to make one helmet—and we made 16 helmets," Mold Shop Supervisor Michael McFarlane reveals. "Each of those pieces has to be sculpted, molded, cast, and then repeated."

Charlie Wen concept art.

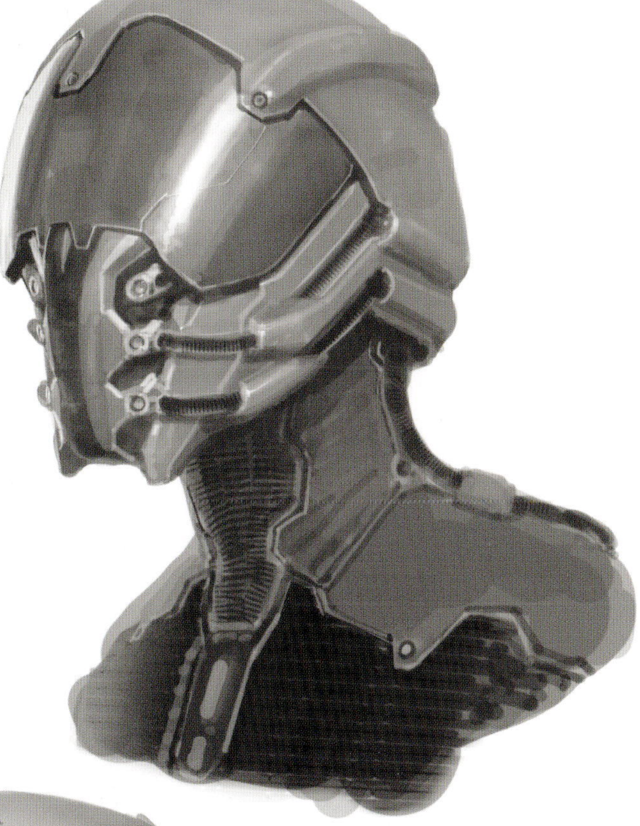

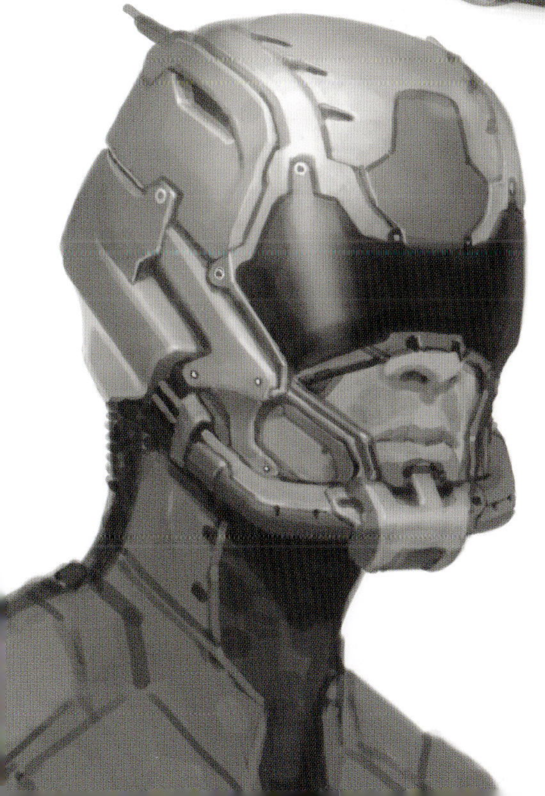

Charlie Wen concept art.

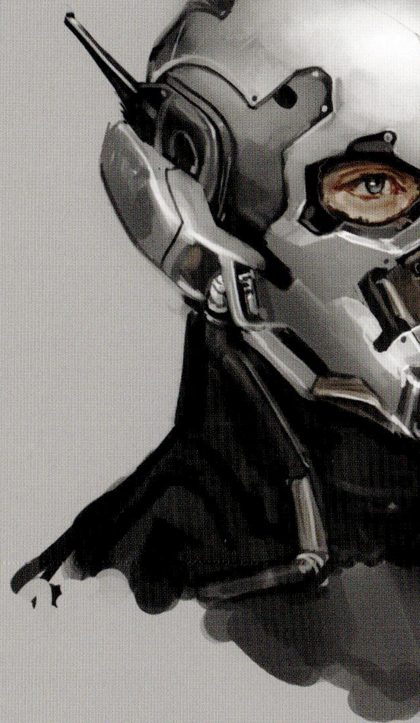

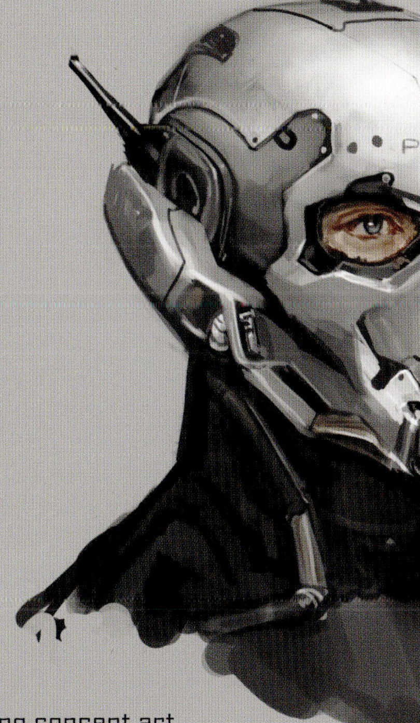

Ryan Meinerding concept art.

HANK PYM

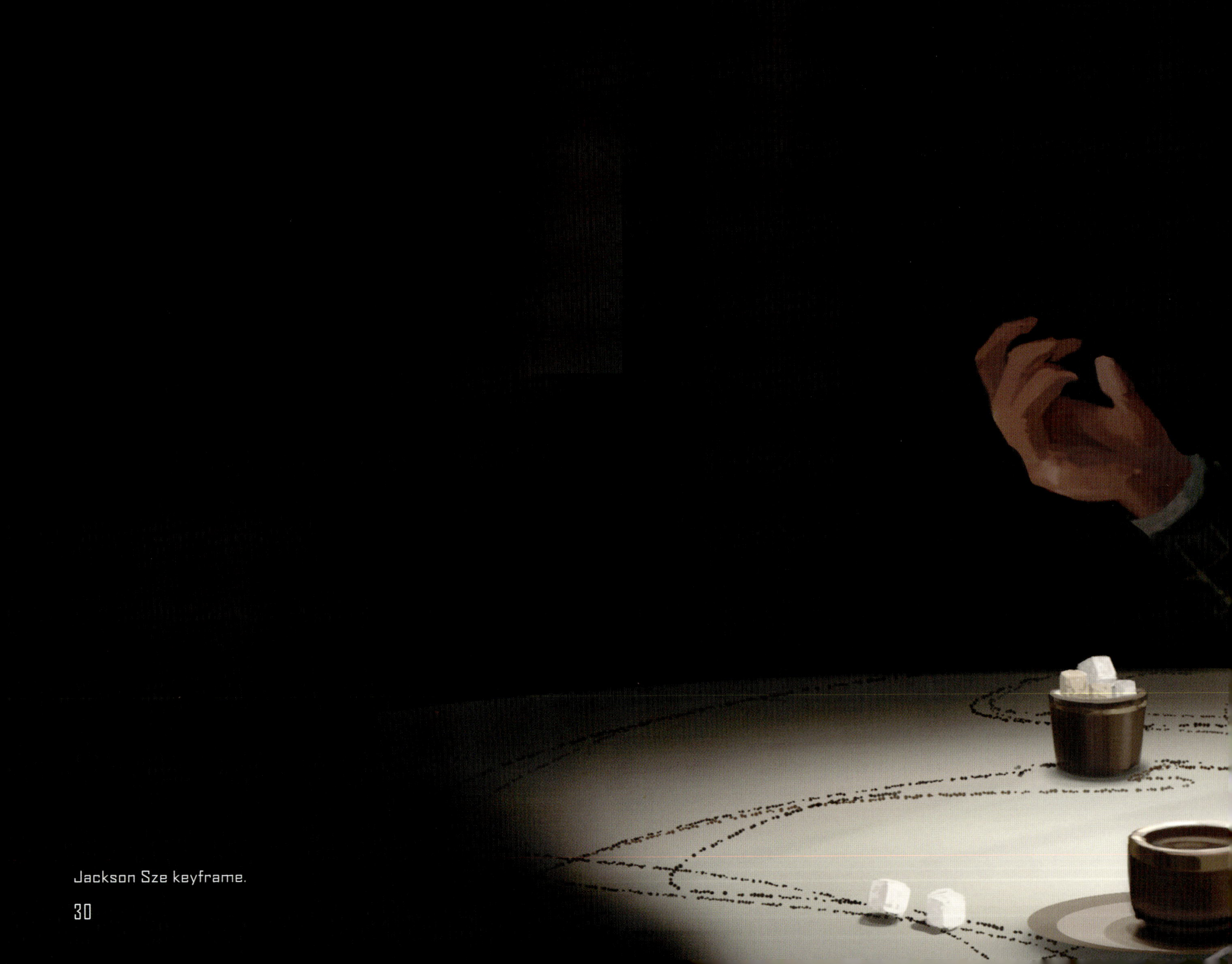

Jackson Sze keyframe.

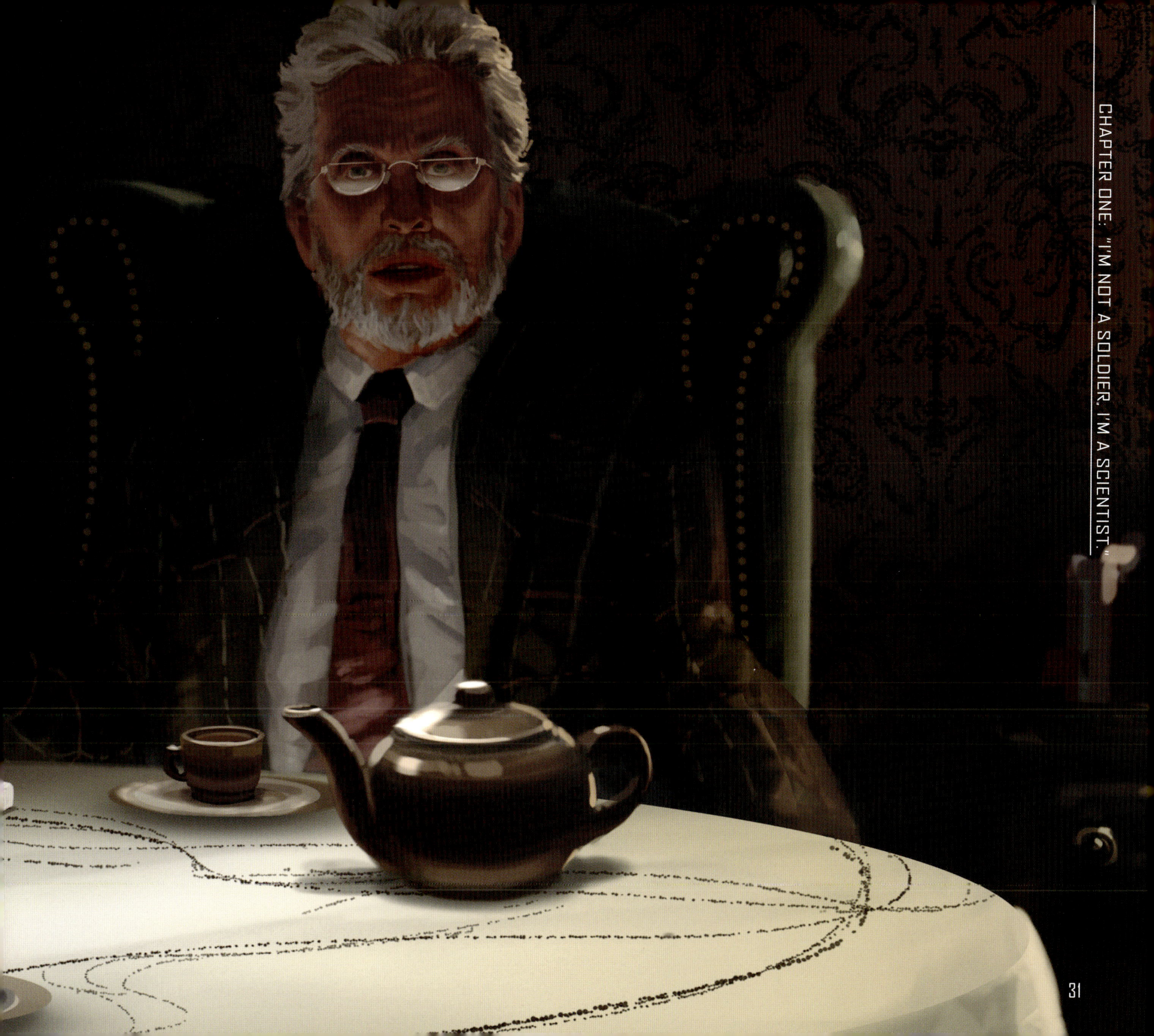

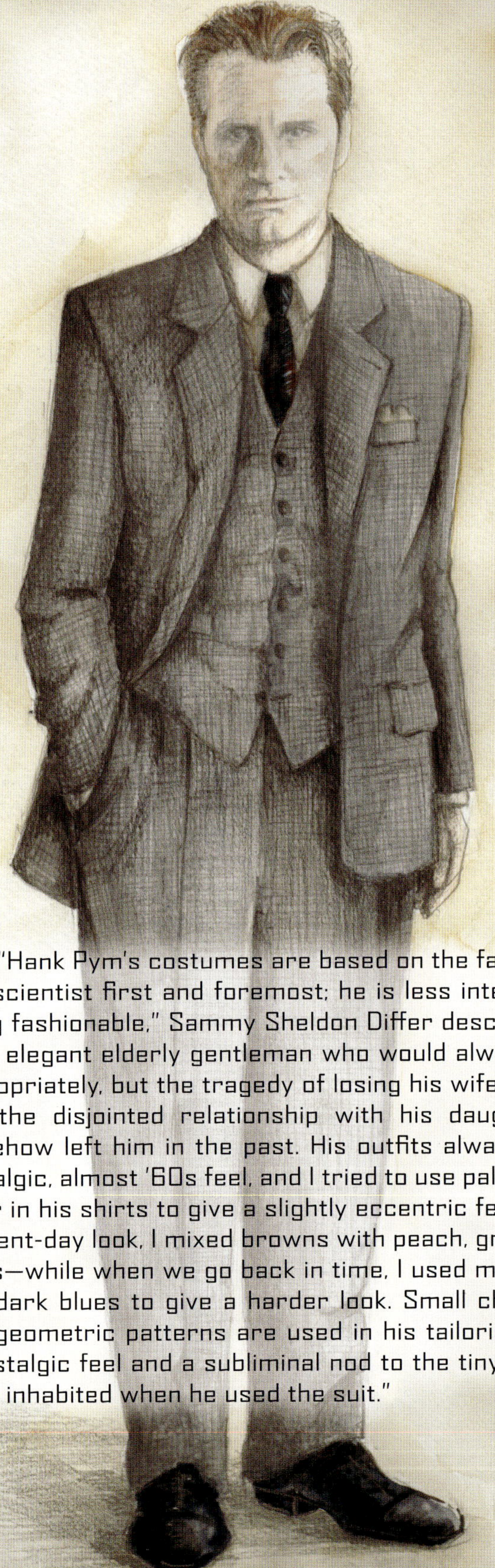

"Hank Pym's costumes are based on the fact that he is a scientist first and foremost; he is less interested in being fashionable," Sammy Sheldon Differ describes. "He is an elegant elderly gentleman who would always dress appropriately, but the tragedy of losing his wife so young and the disjointed relationship with his daughter has somehow left him in the past. His outfits always have a nostalgic, almost '60s feel, and I tried to use pale tones of color in his shirts to give a slightly eccentric feel. For his present-day look, I mixed browns with peach, greens, and blues—while when we go back in time, I used more grays and dark blues to give a harder look. Small checks and tiny geometric patterns are used in his tailoring to give a nostalgic feel and a subliminal nod to the tiny world he once inhabited when he used the suit."

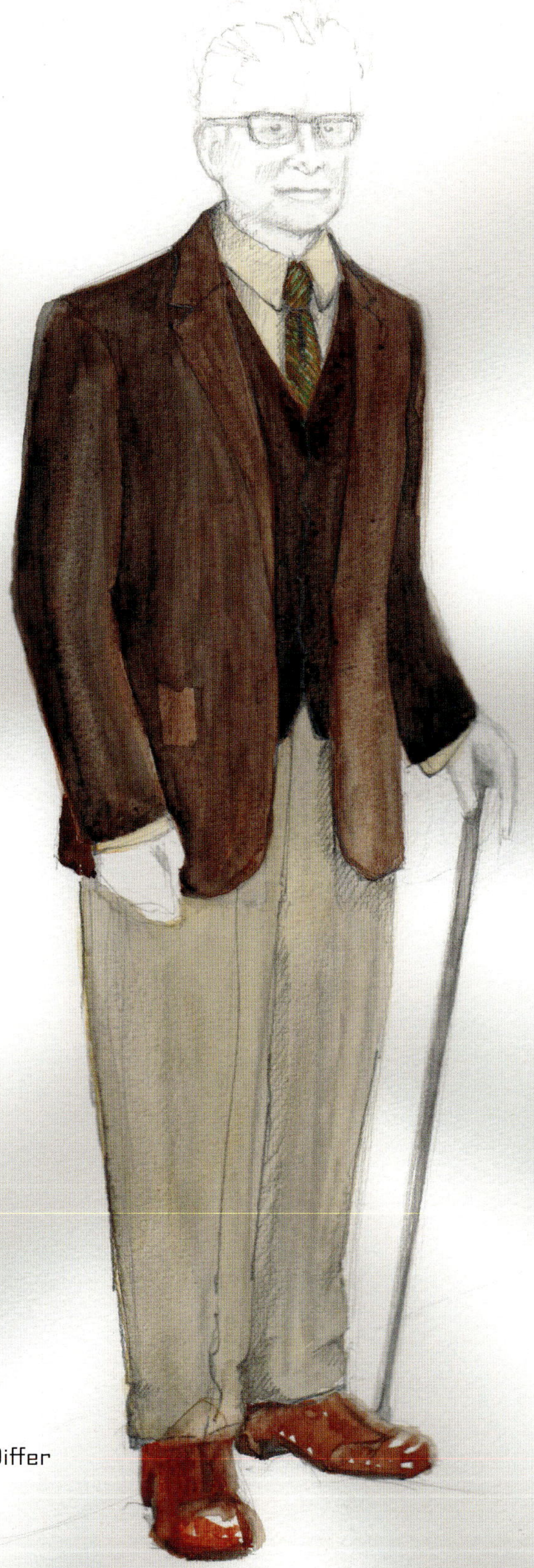

Sammy Sheldon Differ concept art.

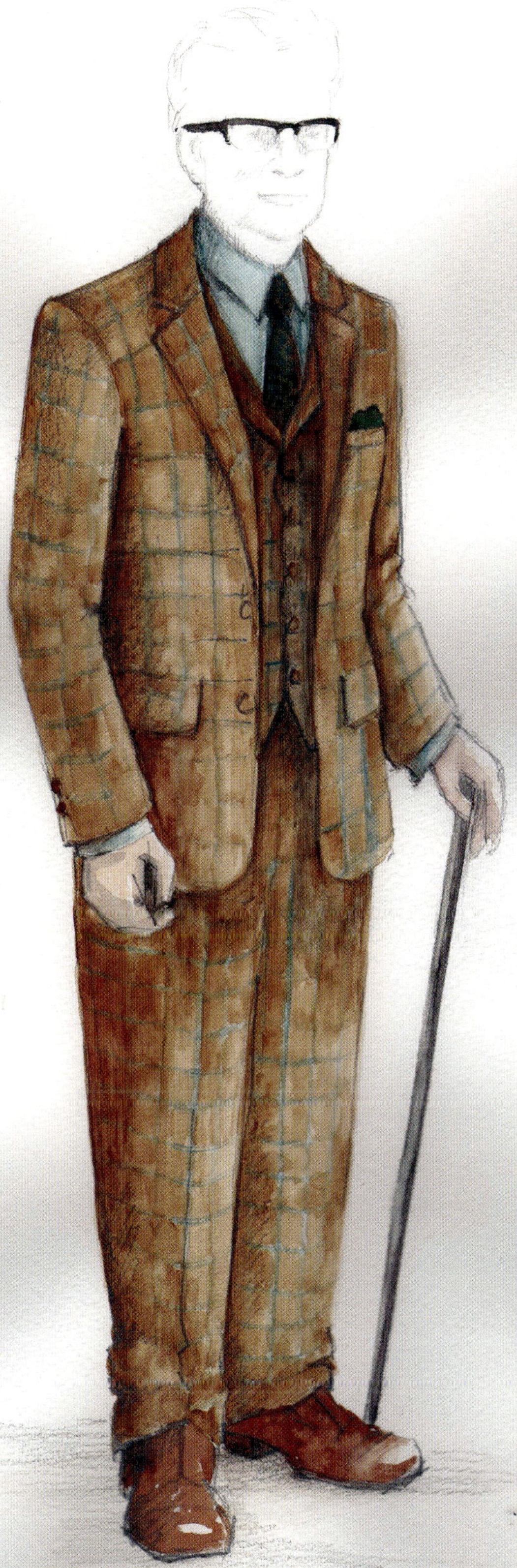

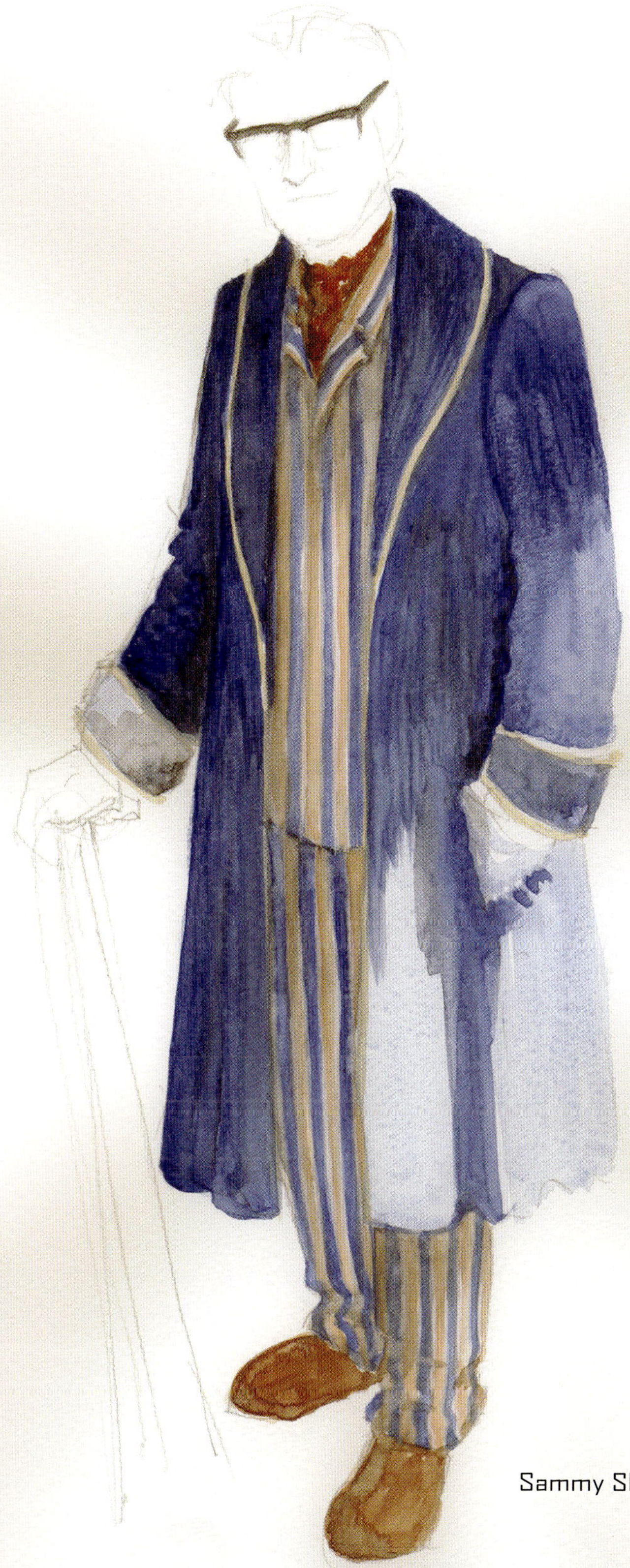

Sammy Sheldon Differ
concept art.

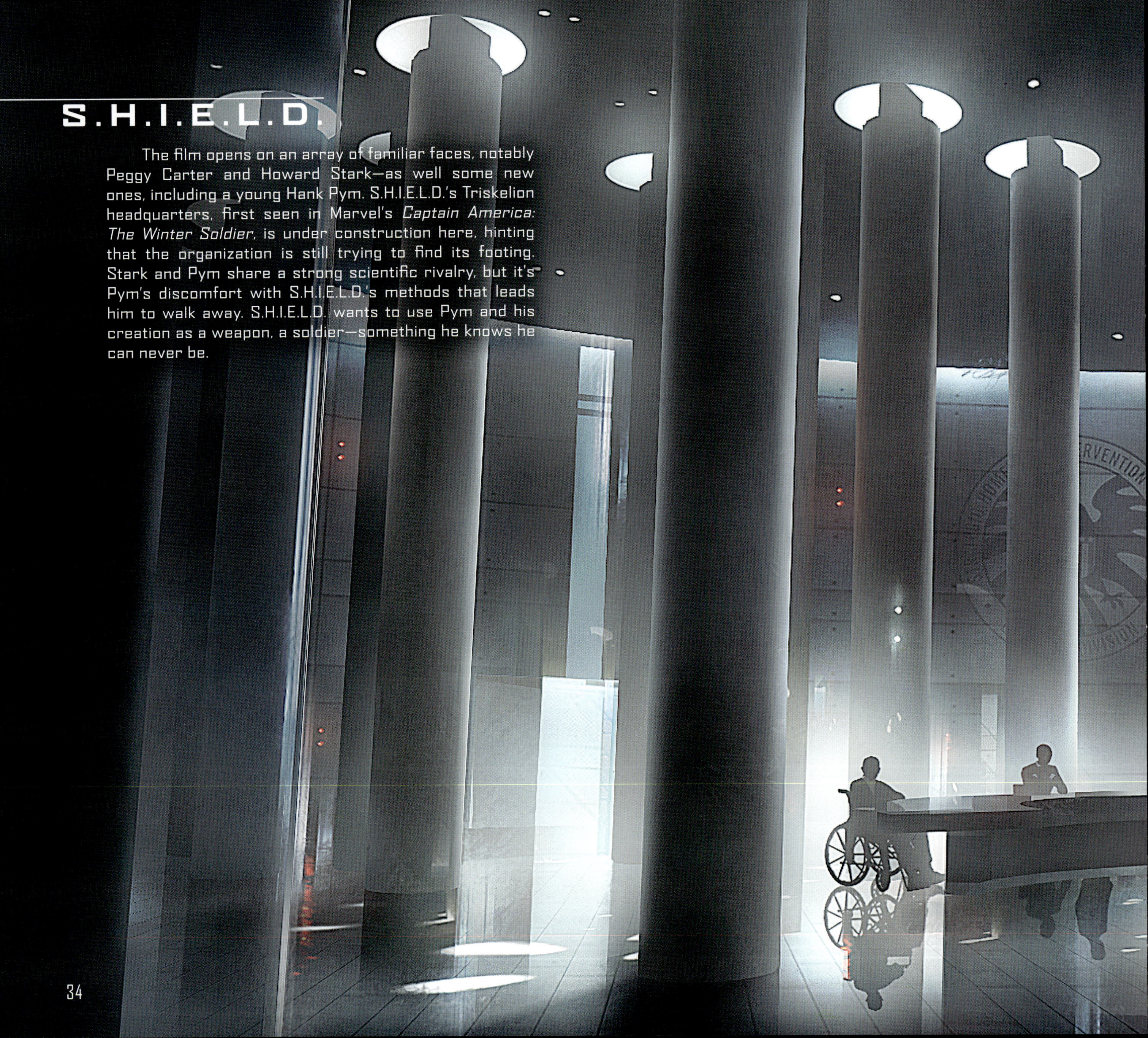

S.H.I.E.L.D.

The film opens on an array of familiar faces, notably Peggy Carter and Howard Stark—as well some new ones, including a young Hank Pym. S.H.I.E.L.D.'s Triskelion headquarters, first seen in Marvel's *Captain America: The Winter Soldier*, is under construction here, hinting that the organization is still trying to find its footing. Stark and Pym share a strong scientific rivalry, but it's Pym's discomfort with S.H.I.E.L.D.'s methods that leads him to walk away. S.H.I.E.L.D. wants to use Pym and his creation as a weapon, a soldier—something he knows he can never be.

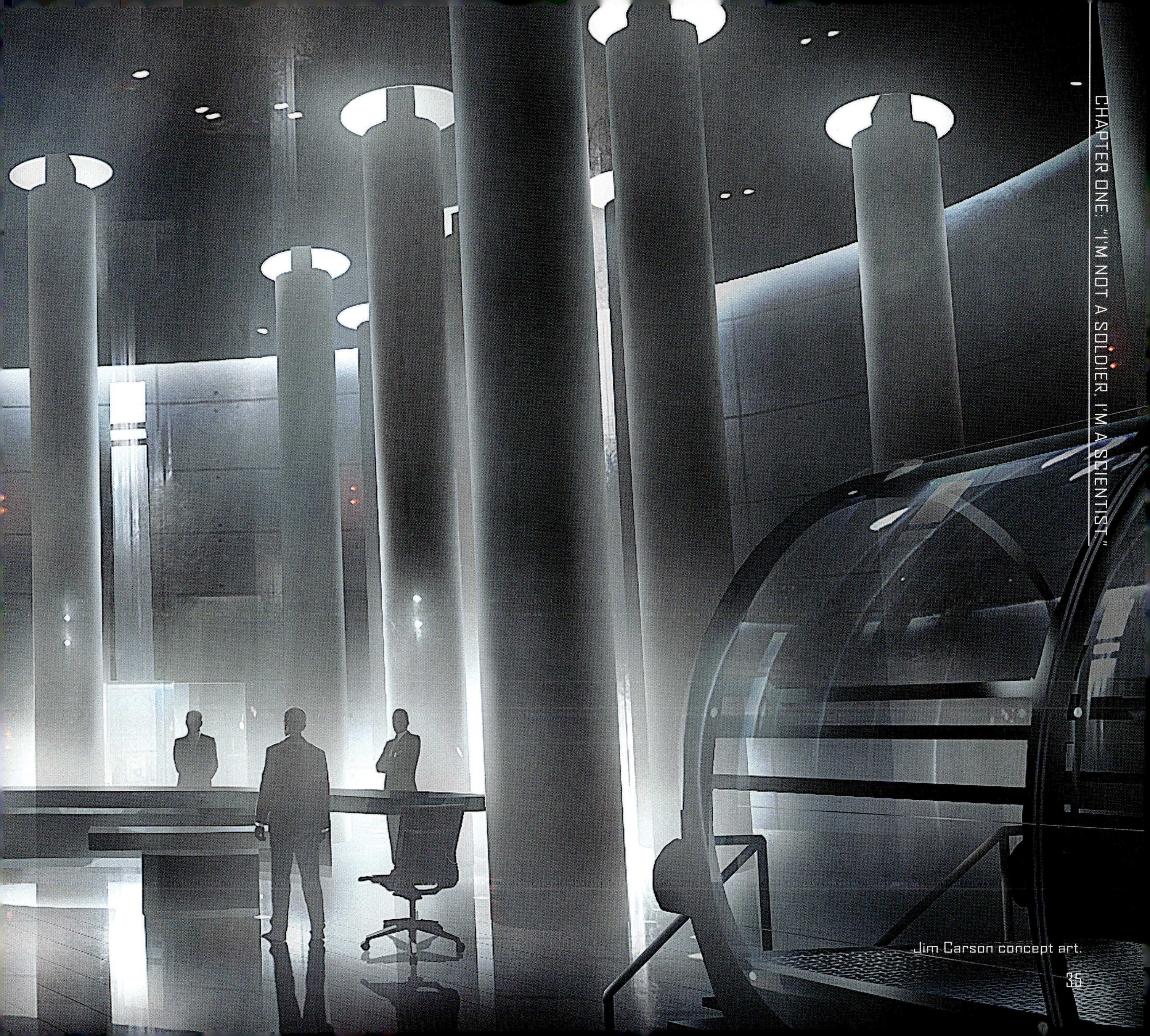

Jim Carson concept art.

To set the tone for Hank's resignation, Concept Artist Jackson Sze pre-visualized his departure in thumbnails. "At this point, Hank does not know Hydra has infiltrated S.H.I.E.L.D., but he does sense that something is amiss. For his parting scene, we wanted to convey a sense of foreboding, that something was not quite right at the highest level of S.H.I.E.L.D. Agendas were hidden, motivations shrouded in mystery—hence the heavy use of shadows and silhouetted faces."

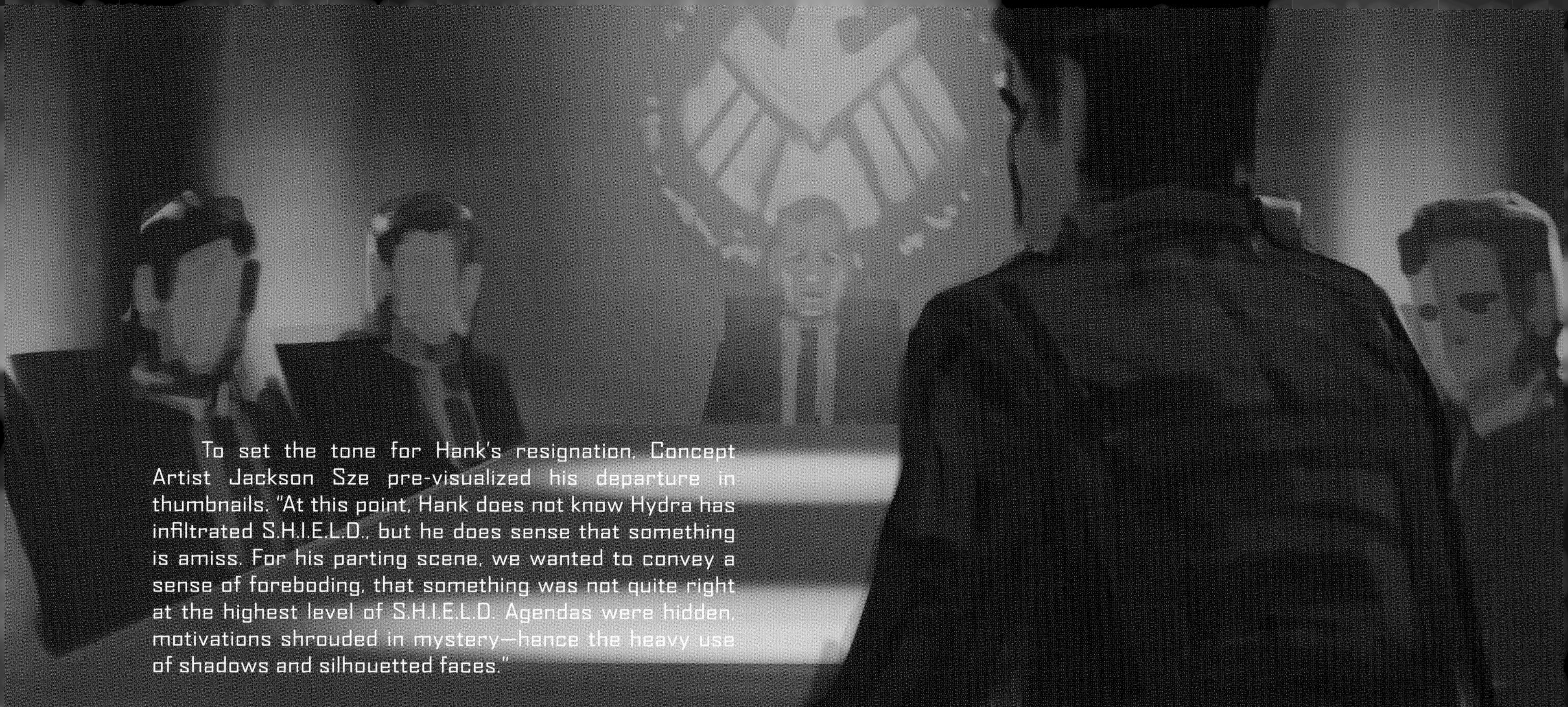

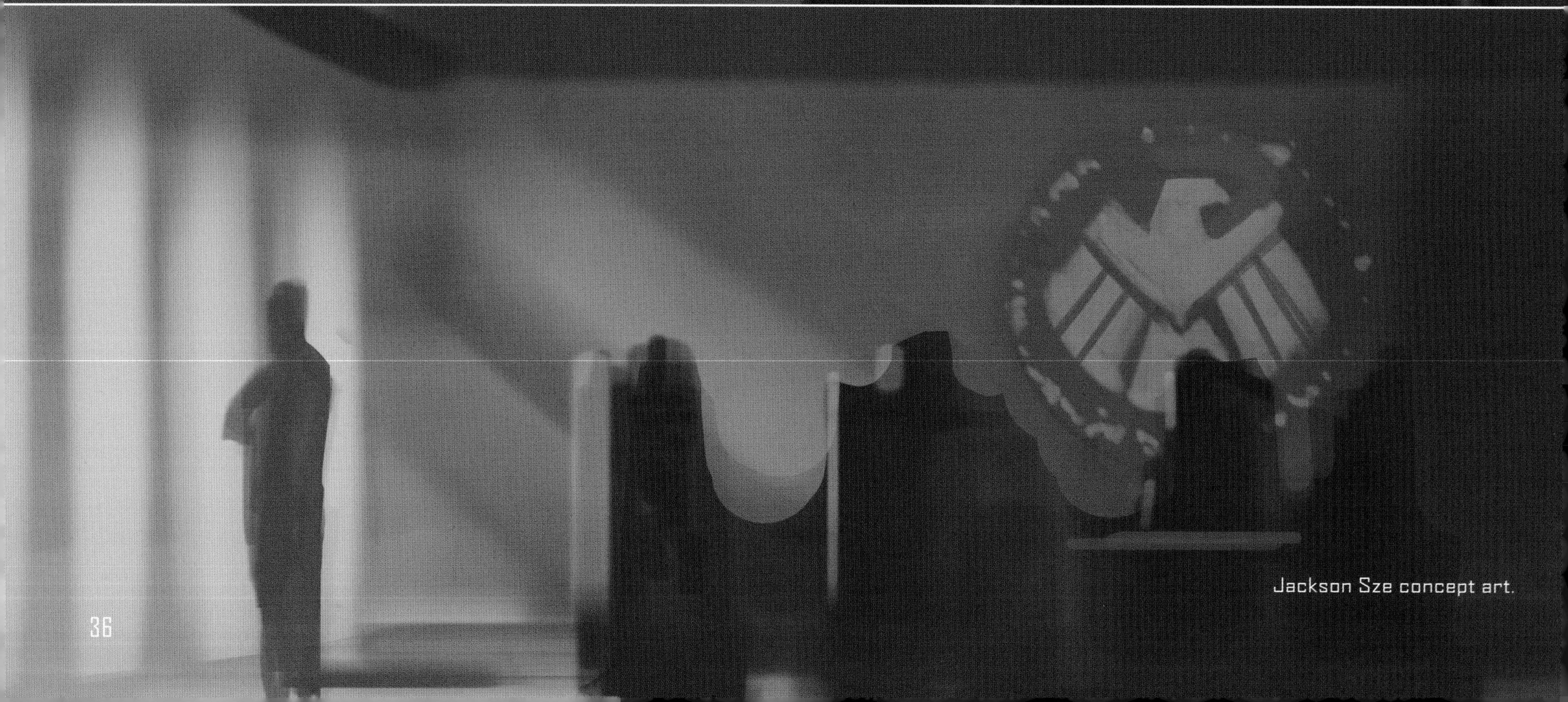

Jackson Sze concept art.

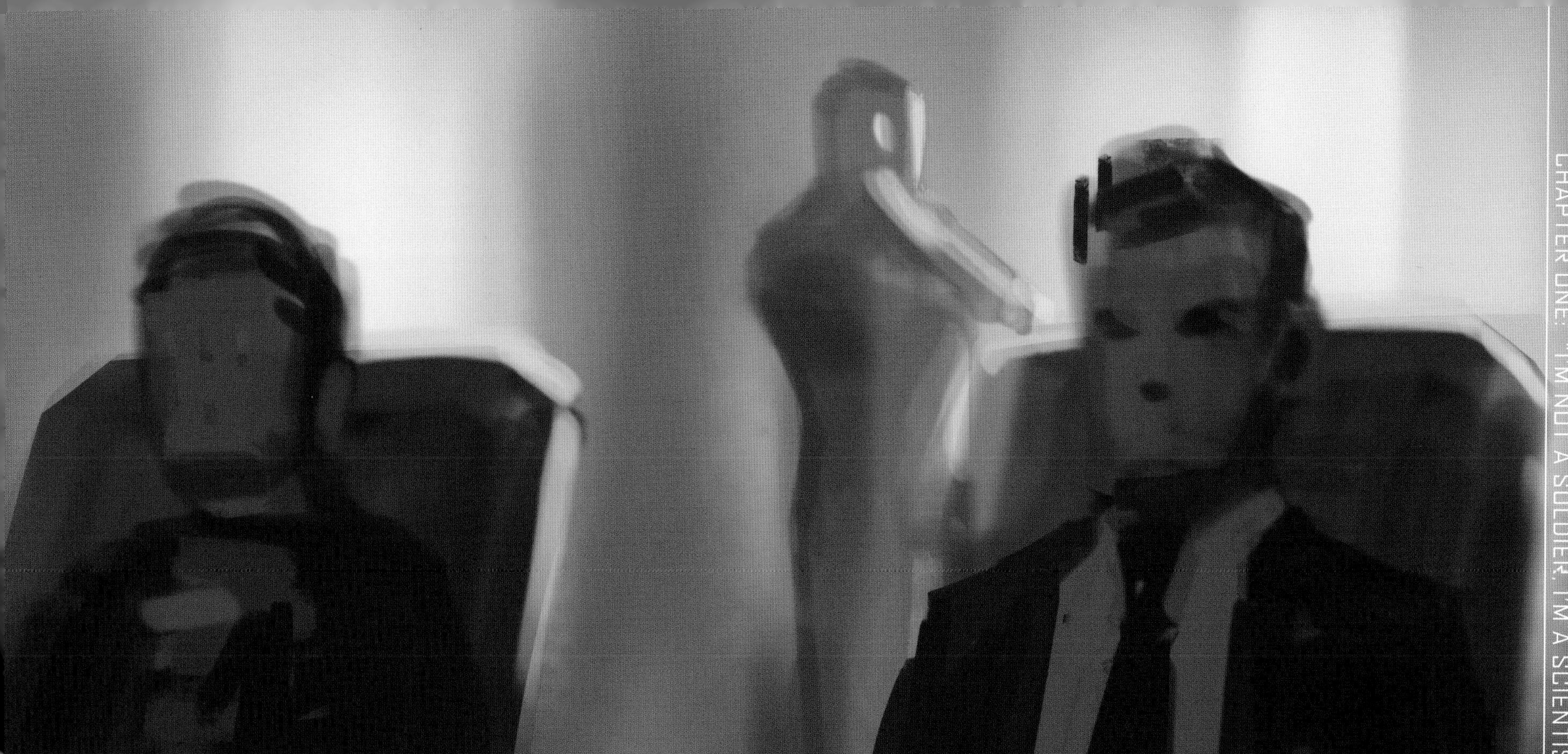

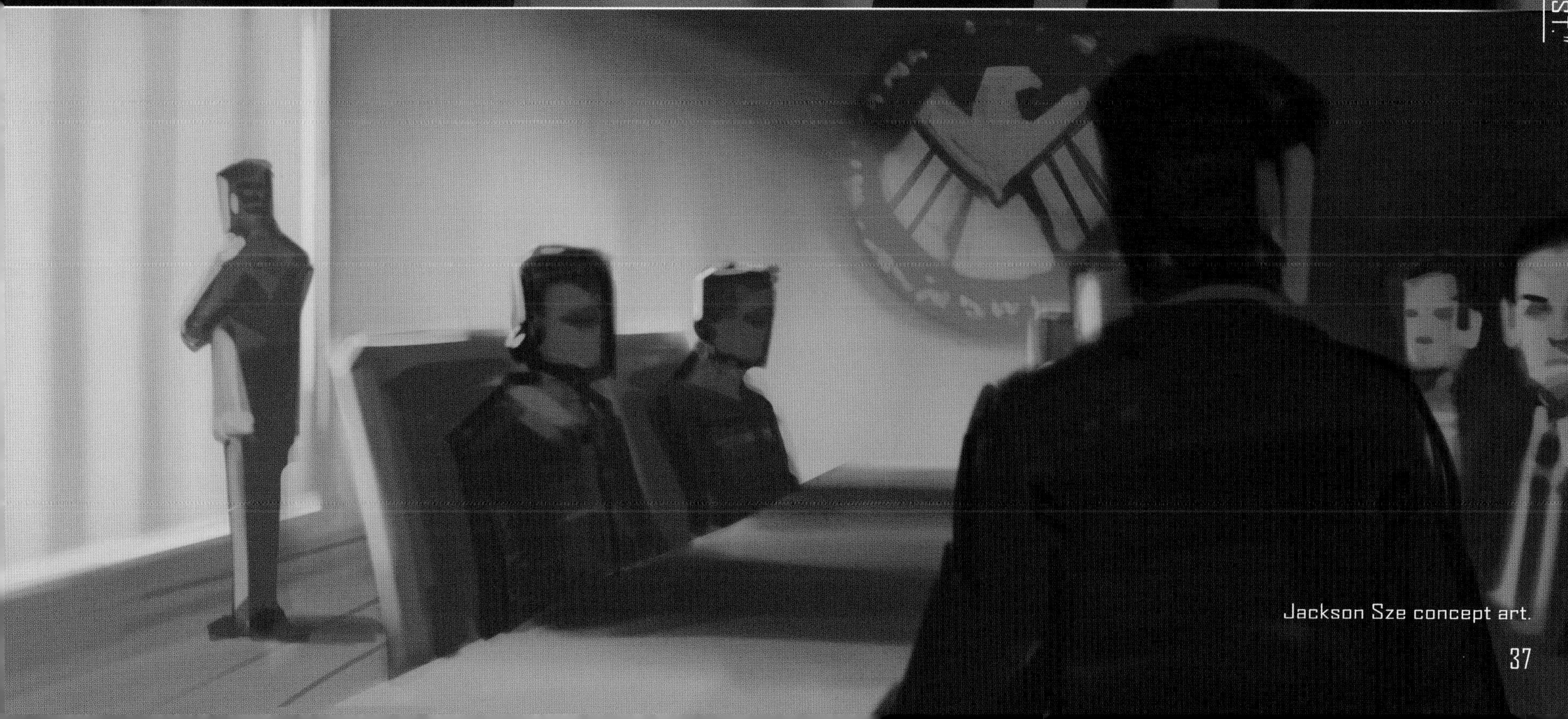

Jackson Sze concept art.

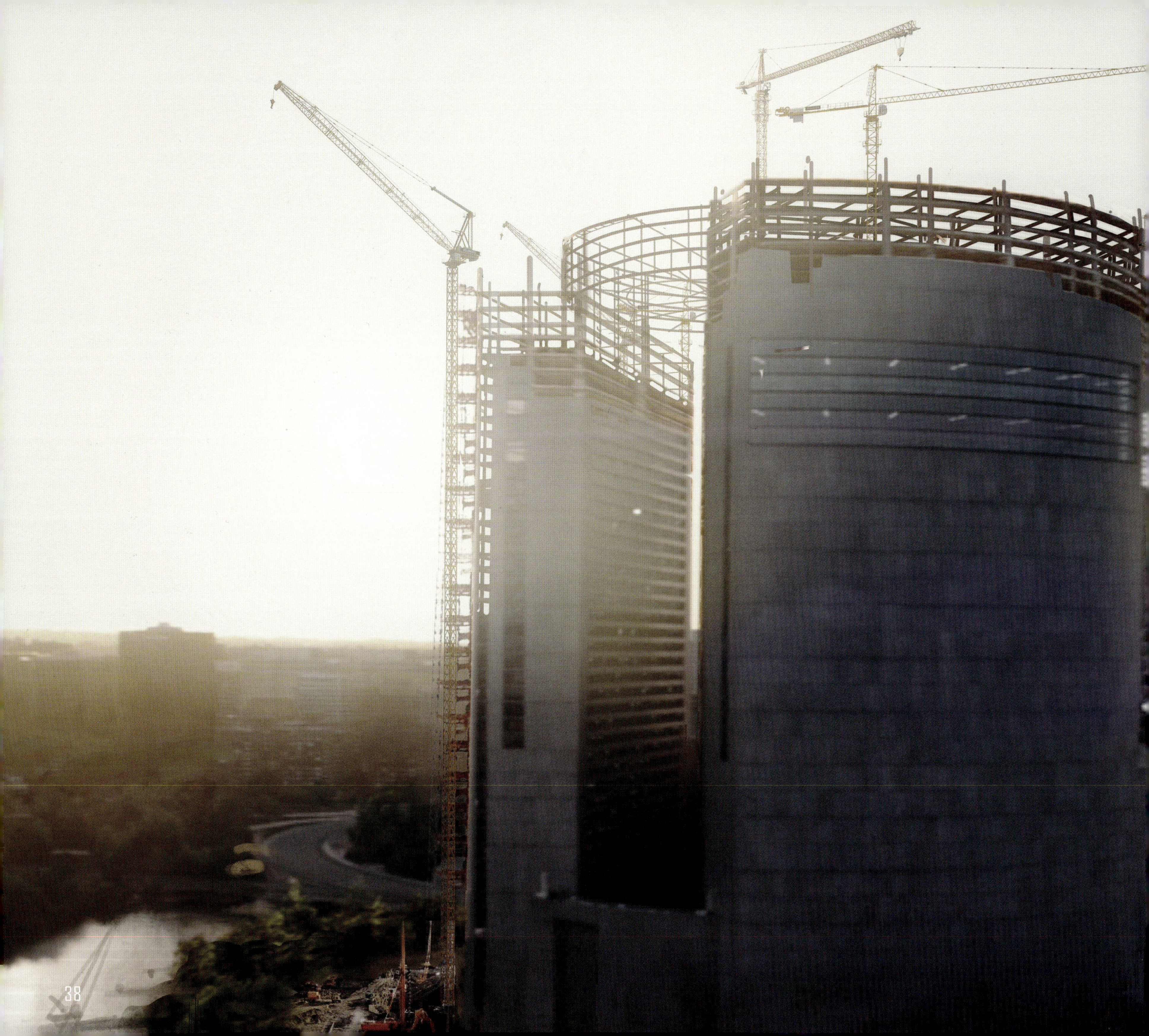

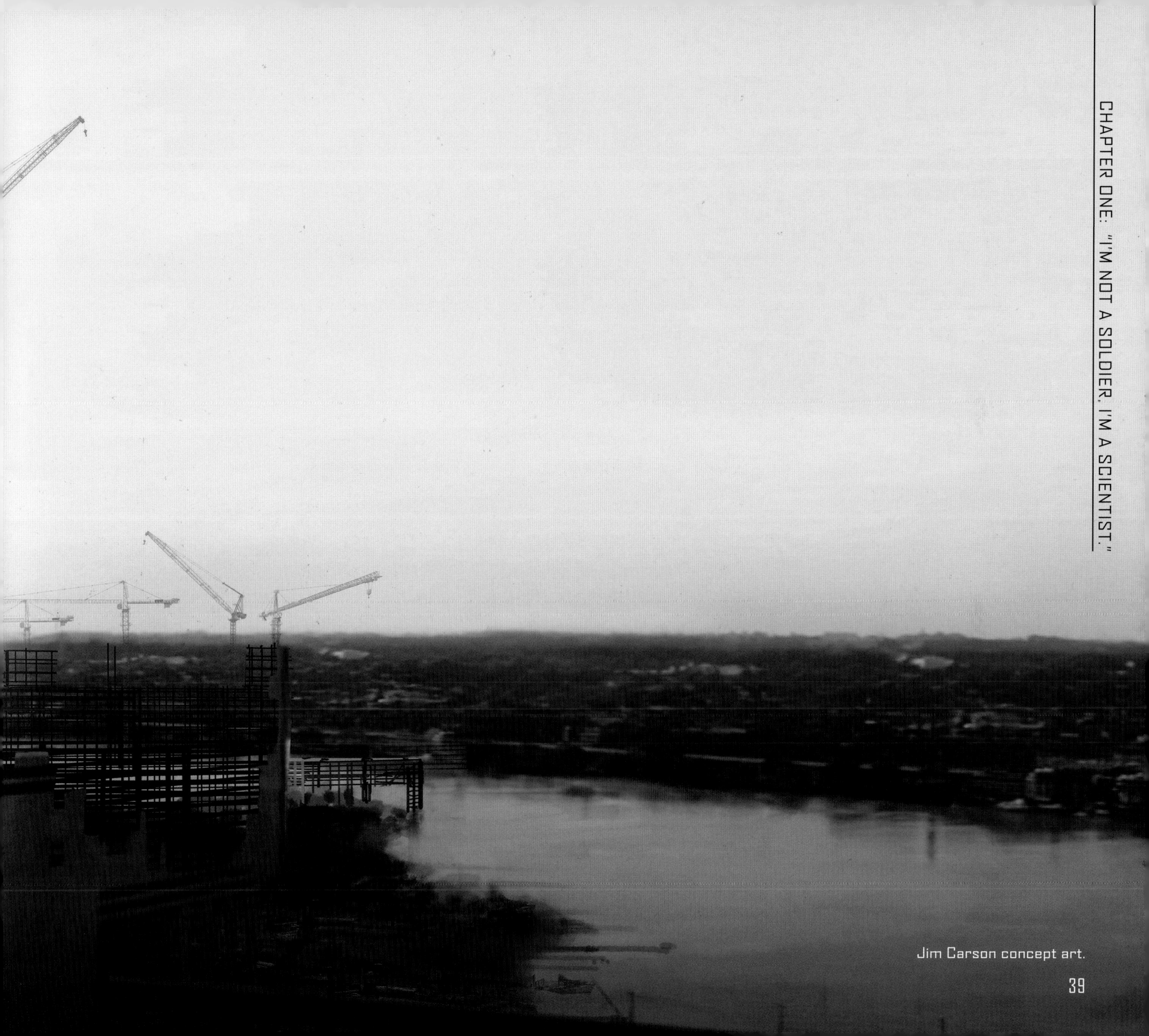

Jim Carson concept art.

CHAPTER TWO

"I BELIEVE THAT EVERYONE DESERVES A SHOT AT REDEMPTION."

Neither Hank Pym nor Scott Lang has been the best mentor or father, and that struggle is central to the film. "At Marvel, every movie has its own genre," Executive Producer Brad Winderbaum says. "It's not like we make super-hero movies just for the sake of making super-hero movies. Each film in and of itself is part of a bigger genre in cinematic history. *Captain America: The Winter Soldier* was a 1970s espionage movie, *Incredible Hulk* was a monster movie, and *Iron Man* was a technological thriller. *Ant-Man*, as conceived, was both a heist movie and something we've never explored before, which was a kind of mentor-mentee movie—a passing-of-the-baton film. By making Hank Pym a now-retired super hero from the '70s and '80s, and introducing Scott Lang, we could really explore the themes of what it takes to be a mentor, what it means to be a student, and what it means to be a father."

While it's apparent in the film that Hank is the teacher and Scott is the student, they both have a lot to learn. "Both are fathers to daughters," Winderbaum continues. "Scott is emotionally there for his daughter and really feels like he's a good dad in the emotional sense, but he's a terrible dad when it comes to providing a stable environment for her. Hank has the opposite problem. He's this brilliant scientist who started a business and, it is implied, has saved the world on occasion, but is completely ill-equipped to emotionally provide for his daughter. The thing that each of them has is the thing that the other needs to learn."

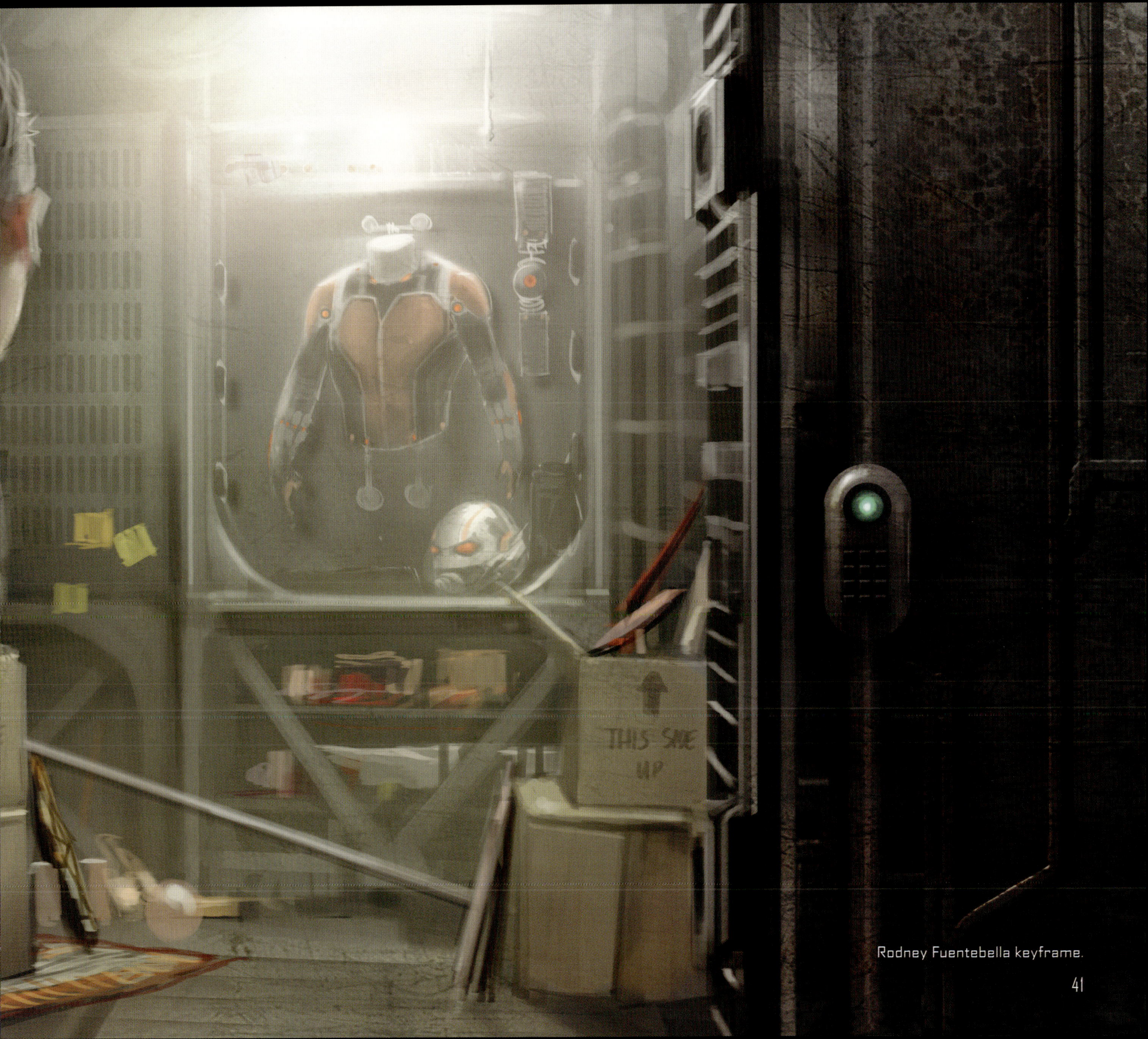

Rodney Fuentebella keyframe.

PYM RESIDENCE

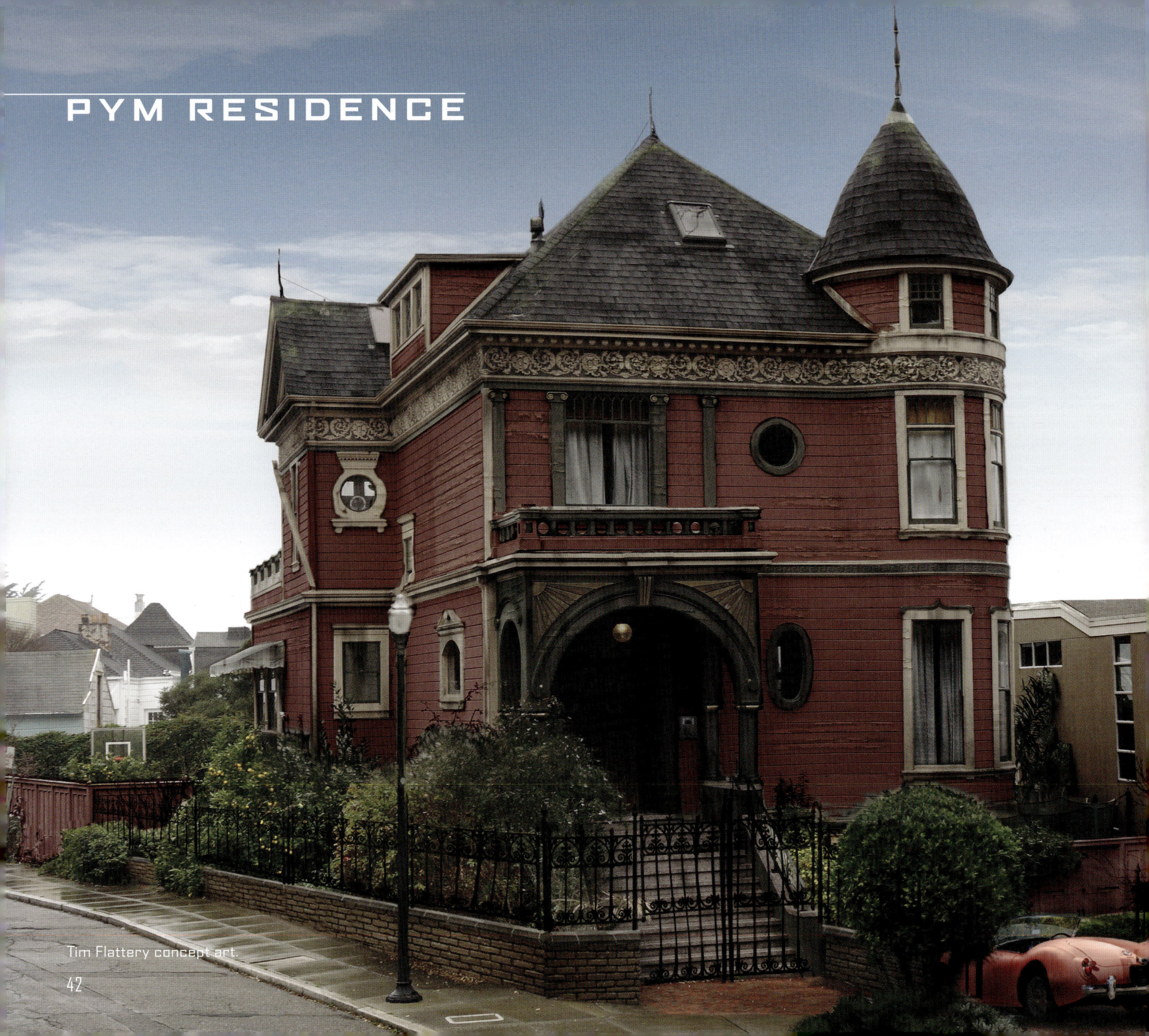

Tim Flattery concept art.

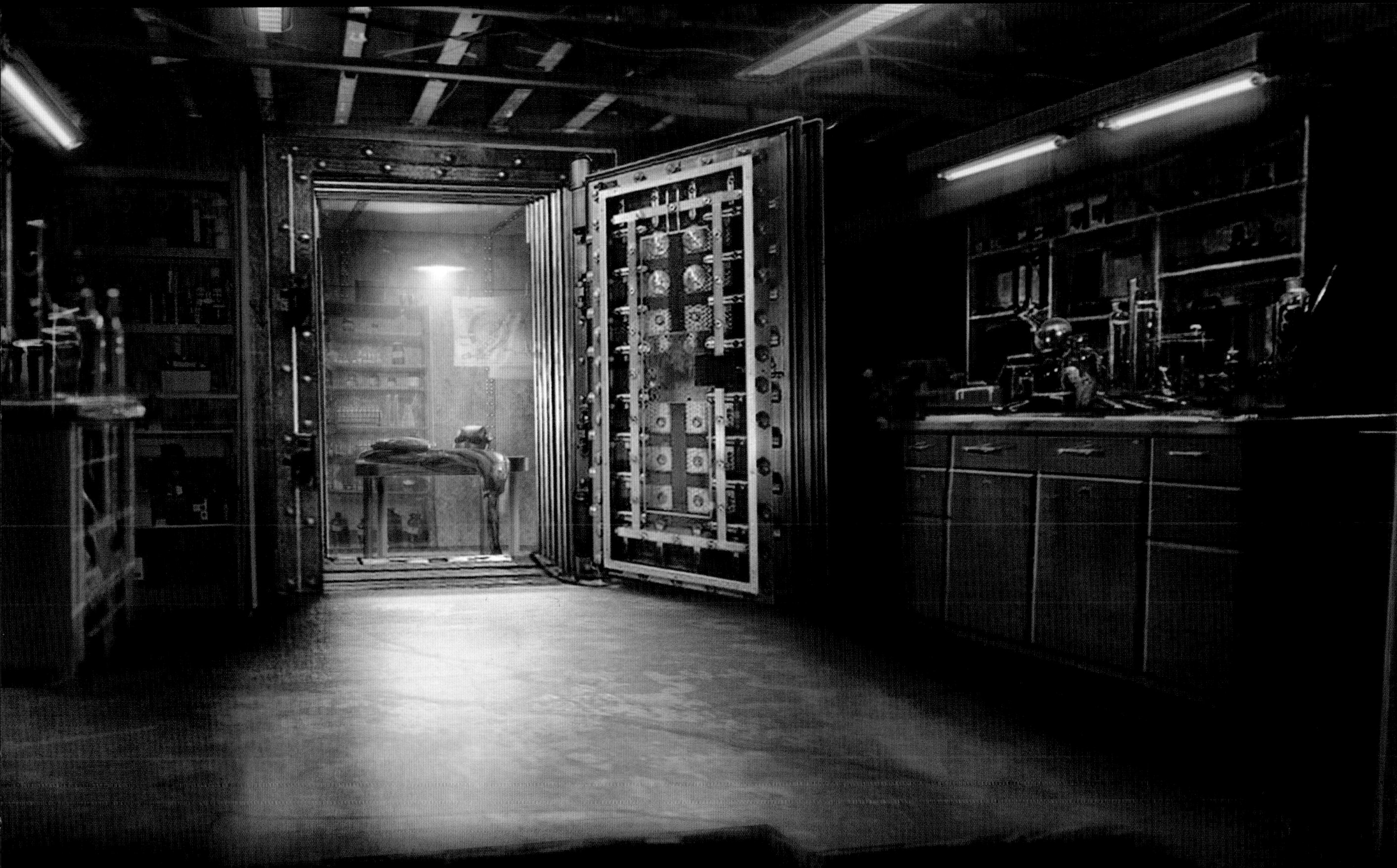

"Pym's house is a layered history of his character and life," Production Designer Shepherd Frankel explains. "The bones of the house, a grand old Victorian, are a classic San Francisco residence once lovingly curated and shared by Pym and his wife, Janet, and later their daughter, Hope. The house is rich in botanical prints and motifs, recalling his and Janet's love of the studies of the natural world: botany, zoology, and entomology. On top of these bones, Pym's personality is reflected throughout the house in his work, which has—over the course of several decades, since Janet's disappearance—taken over the house. It is seen in the piles of books—journals and entomology studies—and the miniaturized objects piled and placed haphazardly everywhere. As a single man driven by an intense need to continue his research, his work has built up to eclipse everything else in his home.

"Despite having every available surface in the house serve as an impromptu desk space, we were careful to withhold any overly scientific information, objects, or events. The purpose of this theme was to have Pym's house visually reflect an old scientist whose work was available to see out in the open—so as to not create curiosity about where else in the house his current scientific efforts were taking place. If Pym has any visitors, he does not want his work to be seen or stolen by prying eyes."

Jim Carson concept art.

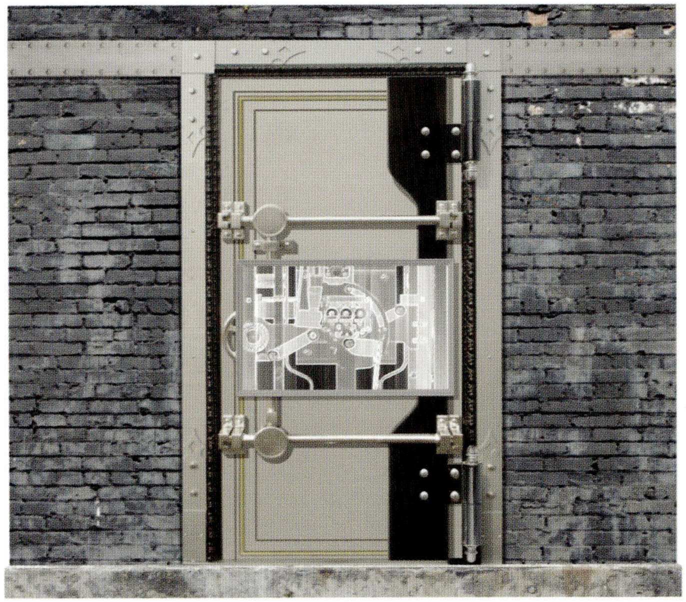

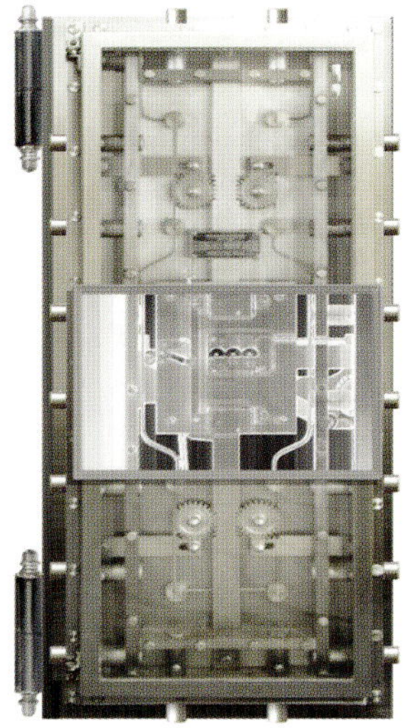

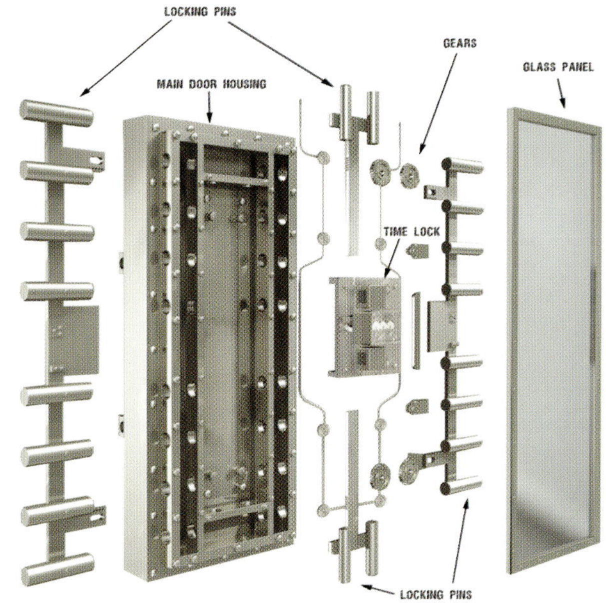

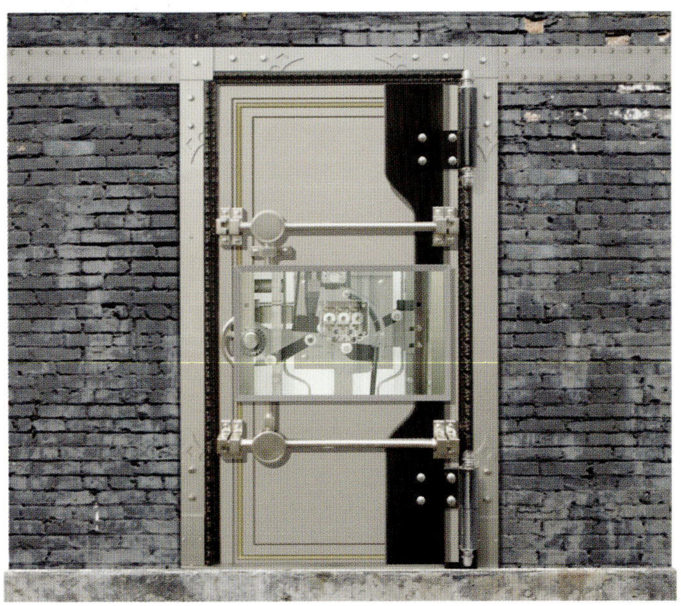

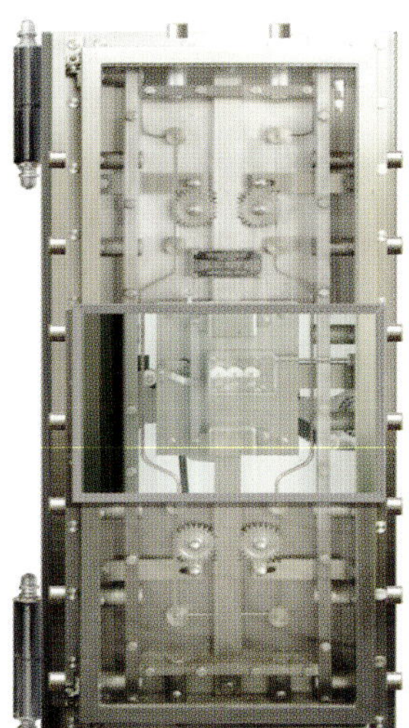

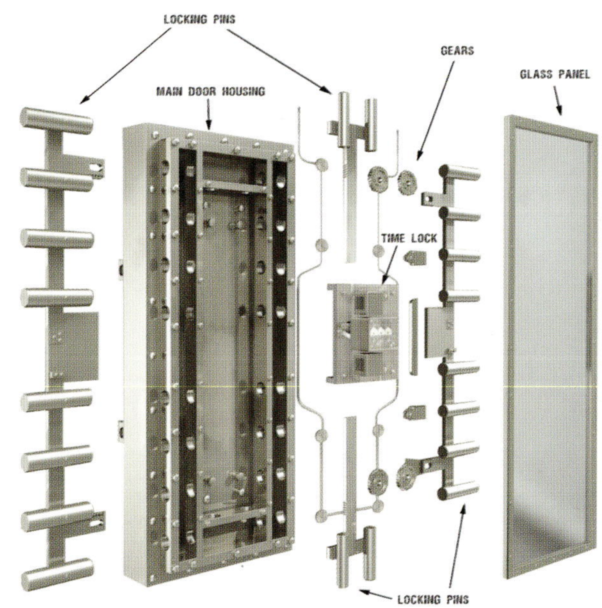

Jamie Rama concept art.

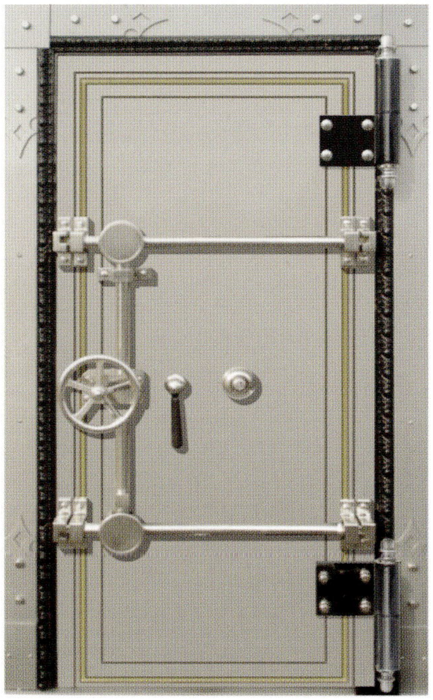

FRONT

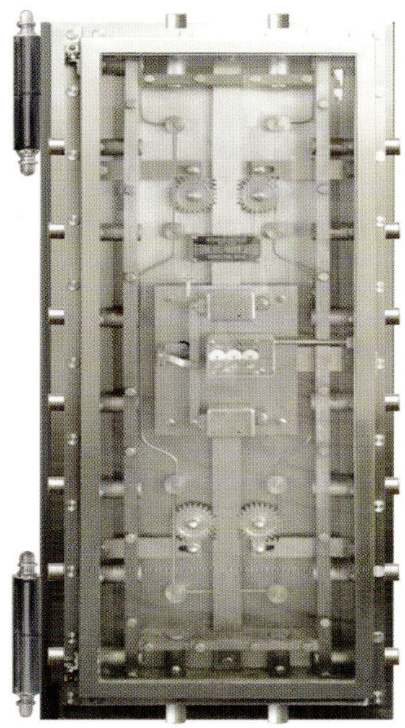

BACK

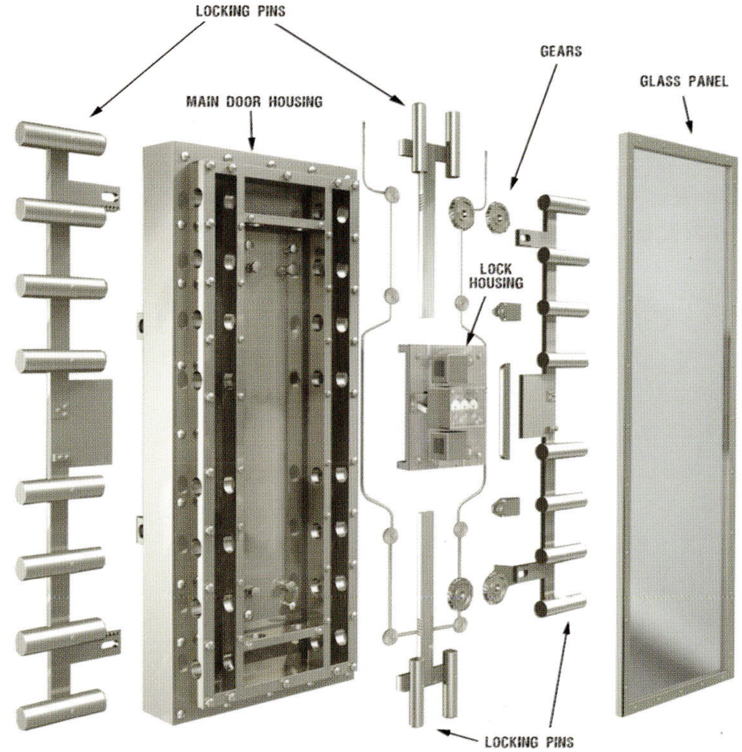

EXPLODED PARTS

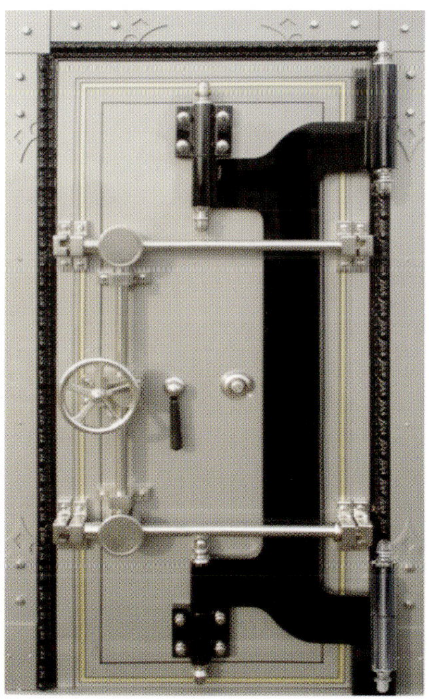

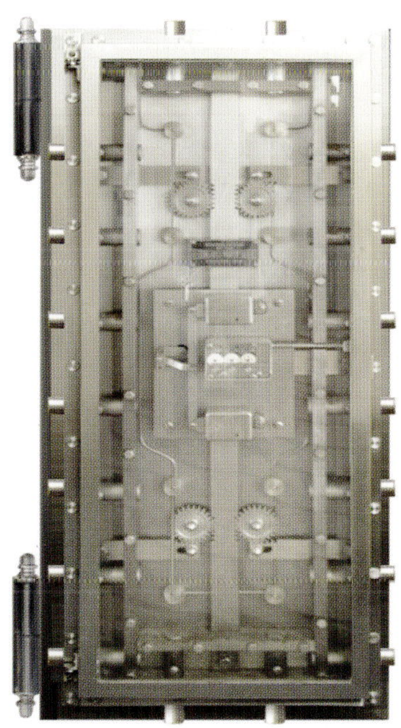

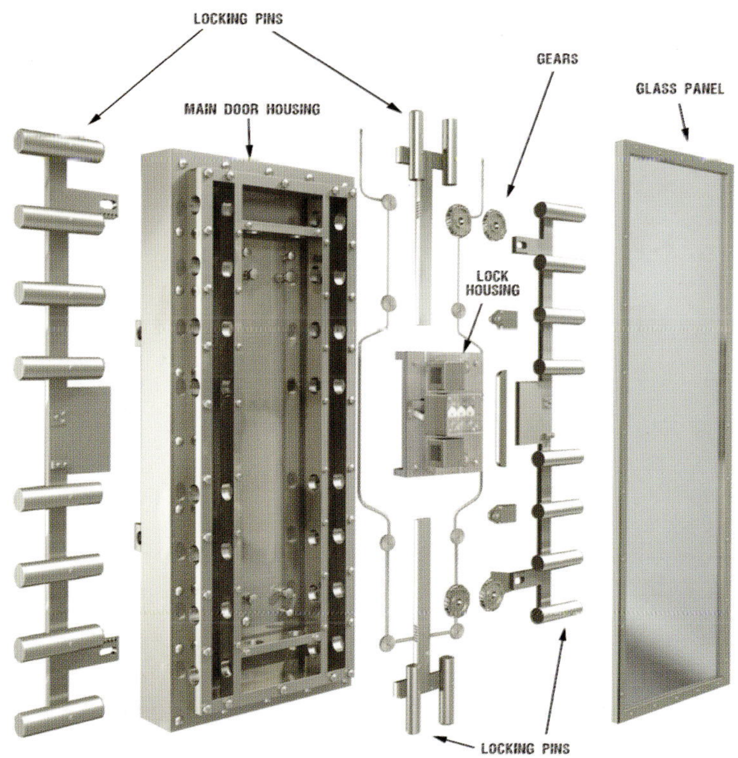

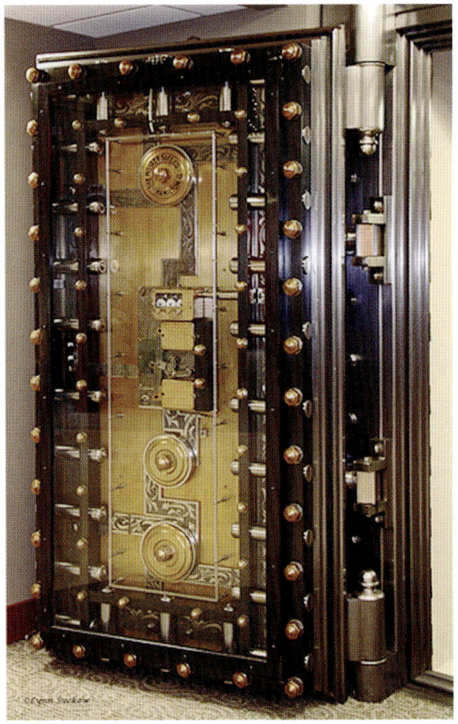

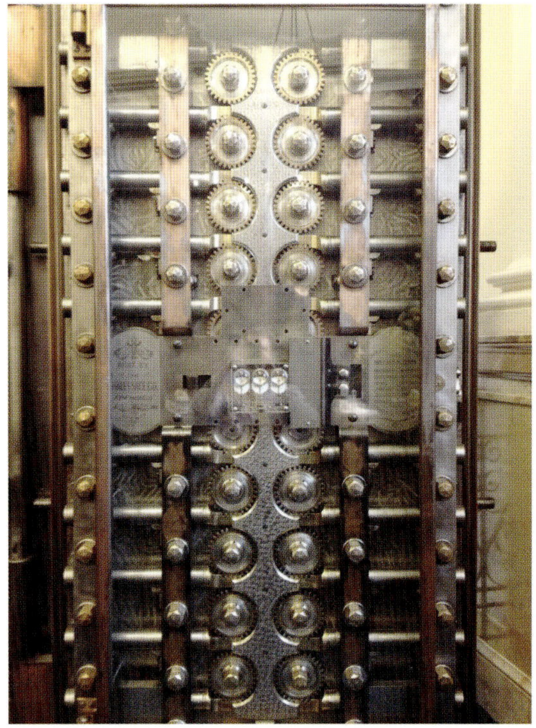

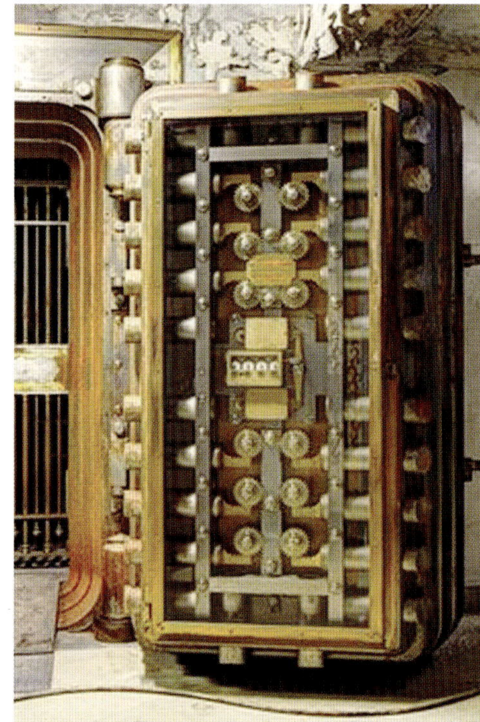

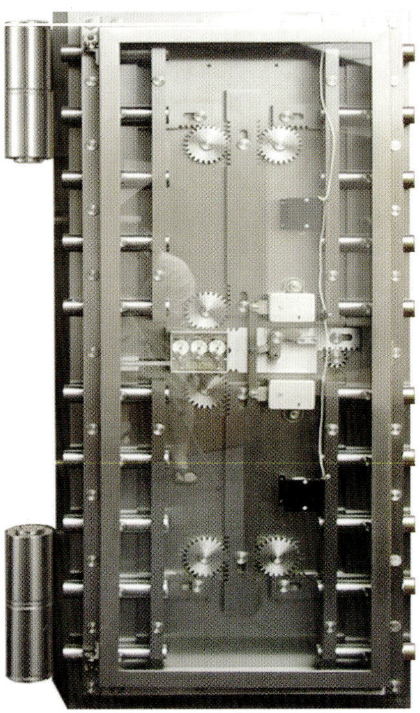

Josh Nizzi concept art.

"The door of the actual vault was extensively researched," Frankel continues. "This was a critical set piece and story beat where the script introduces the various skill sets and troubleshooting expertise of Scott Lang. His ability to be fast on his feet in the moment of breaking into the vault is a critical character point in the film that needed to be developed with real solutions to real problems. The goal was to find a door that not only looked right, but also functioned and felt like a real bank-vault door. Our shooting requirements dictated that we needed the exterior, interior mechanisms, and interior door to all look correct and function properly—and have been developed in the proper time period. We needed metal from the same year the Titanic was built, 1912. To this end, we researched period-appropriate doors, as well as paint and graphics for the exterior finish. We also researched and purchased actual time-lock mechanisms, which are the devices found inside bank-vault doors that prevent unauthorized entry between set times. Time locks were originally created to prevent criminals from holding bank employees hostage and torturing them for the combination. For us, it was a fascinating device that worked well for our inner-mechanism needs, with modifications to make it more cinematic.

"For the door itself, we ended up purchasing an actual bank-vault door from 1912, which weighed many tons. It was quite a process to strip it, paint it, and get it into place on the set, as well as create multiple duplicates for the FX work involved. We created a graphic that recalled the intricate hand-painted designs common to vault and safe doors from the 1910s. The finished piece was fully functional, on the set, and was swapped out with the rigged FX versions as needed."

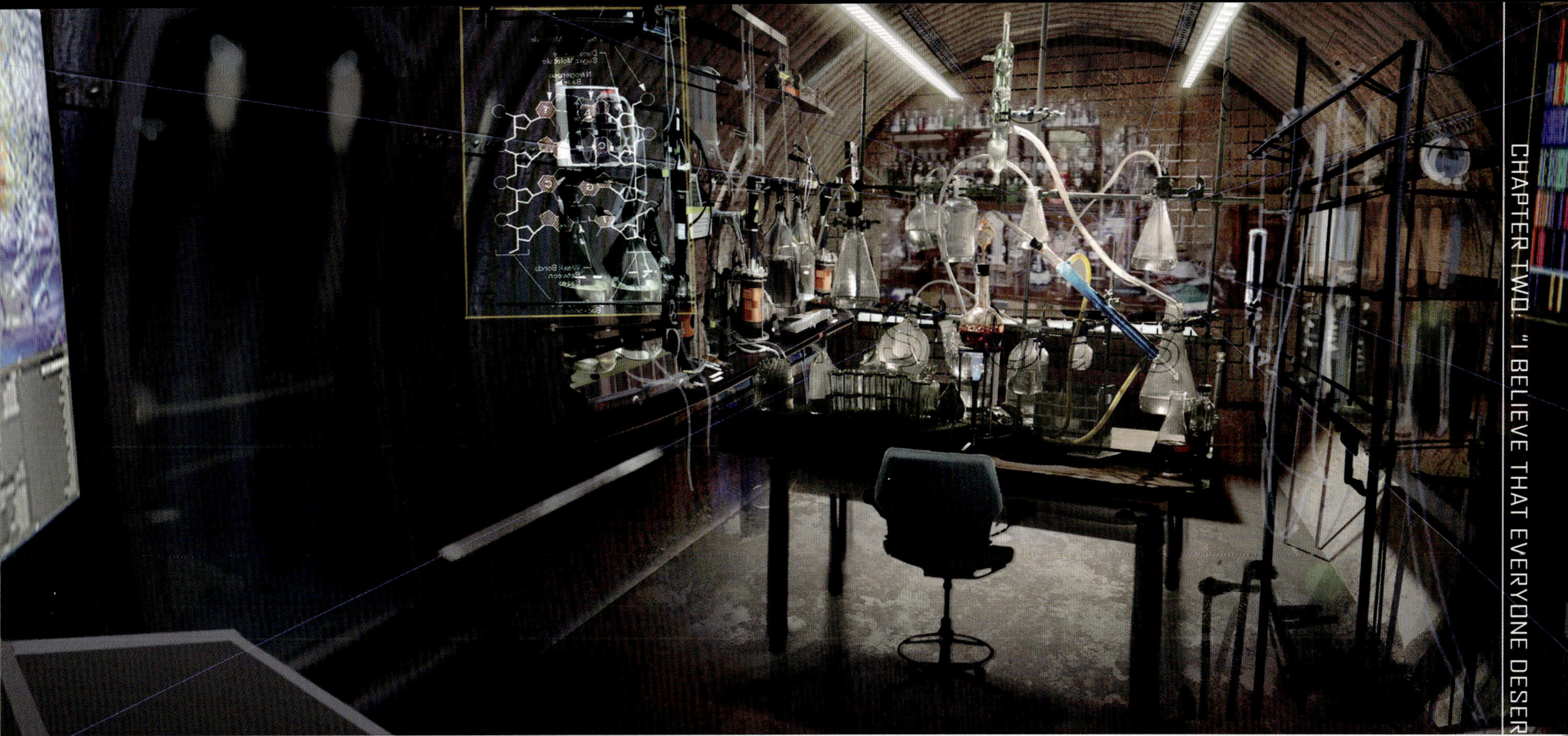

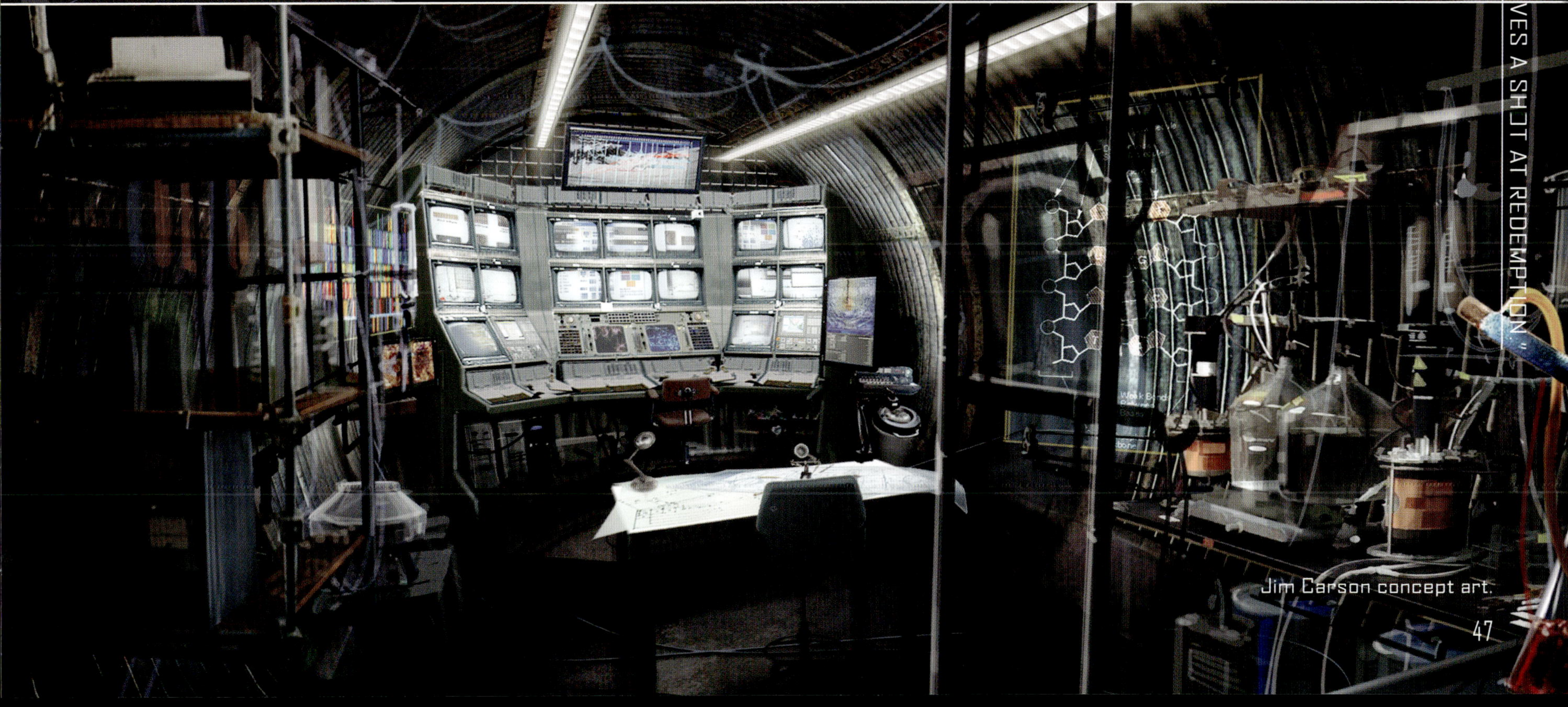

Jim Carson concept art.

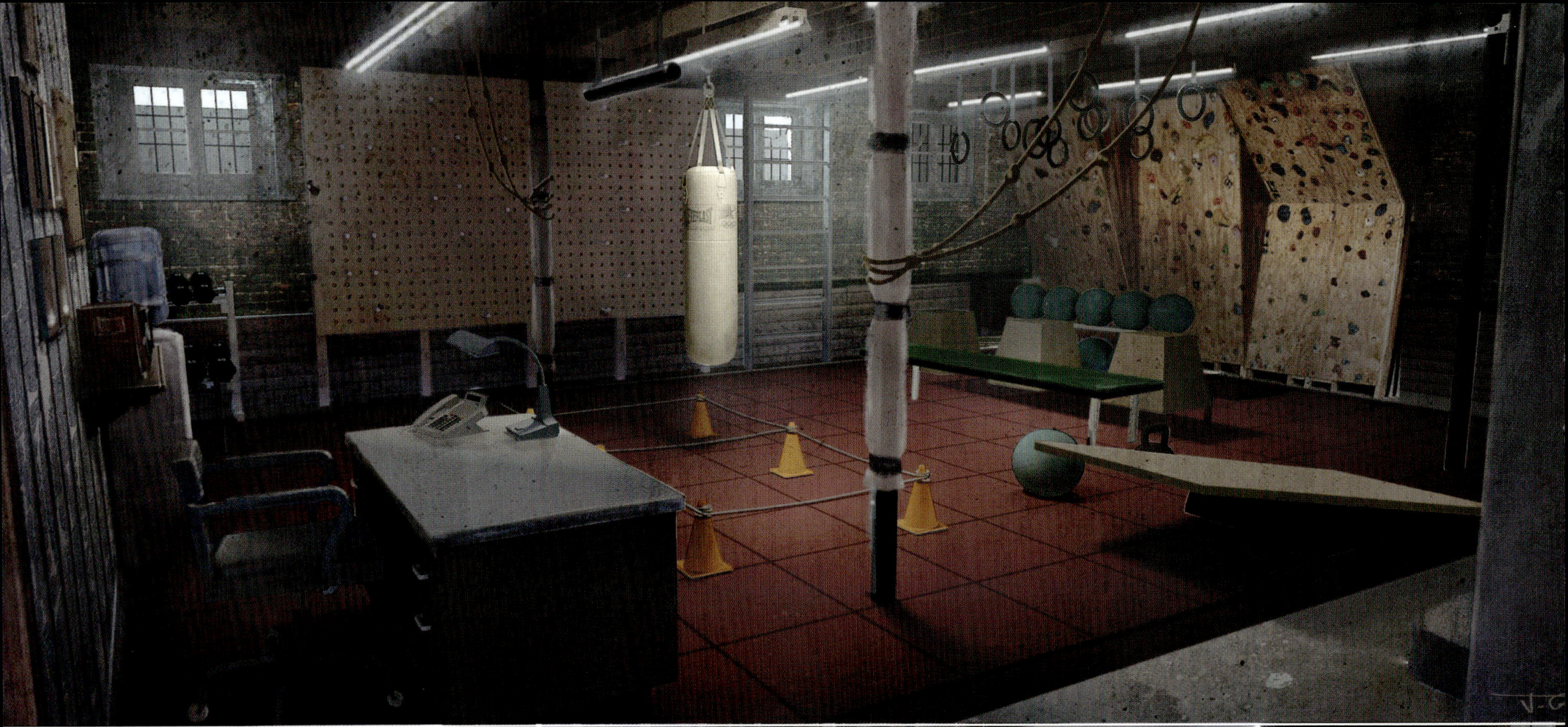

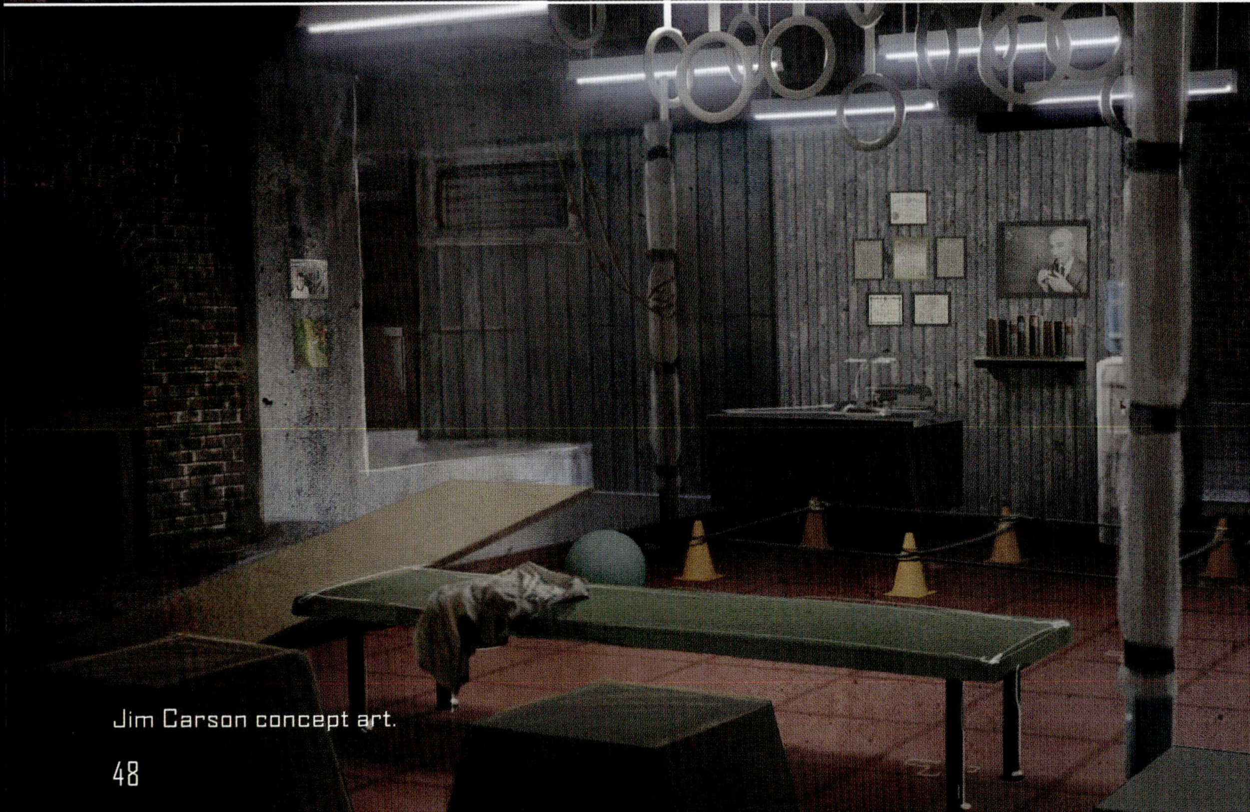

Jim Carson concept art.

Hidden in Pym's basement is his secure room, a high-tech juxtaposition against the house's Victorian elements. Filled with monitors and other surveillance equipment, this is where Pym has been keeping an eye on Scott Lang. "The secure-room vault is based off a bomb shelter, a highly secure room common to the 1960s when Pym would have constructed his room and developed the Pym Particles," Frankel describes. "The vaulted interior was constructed of actual corrugated steel pieces cut into 20 pieces for filming purposes to create 270-degree cylinders 18 feet in diameter and 40 feet long. This required constructing a series of massive, arched steel frames to support the pieces, which were also all hung from the ceiling of the studio for support and safety. Many of the vintage elements in this room would have been cutting edge in their day, and therefore would have been what Pym would have used to construct the original room and base technologies.

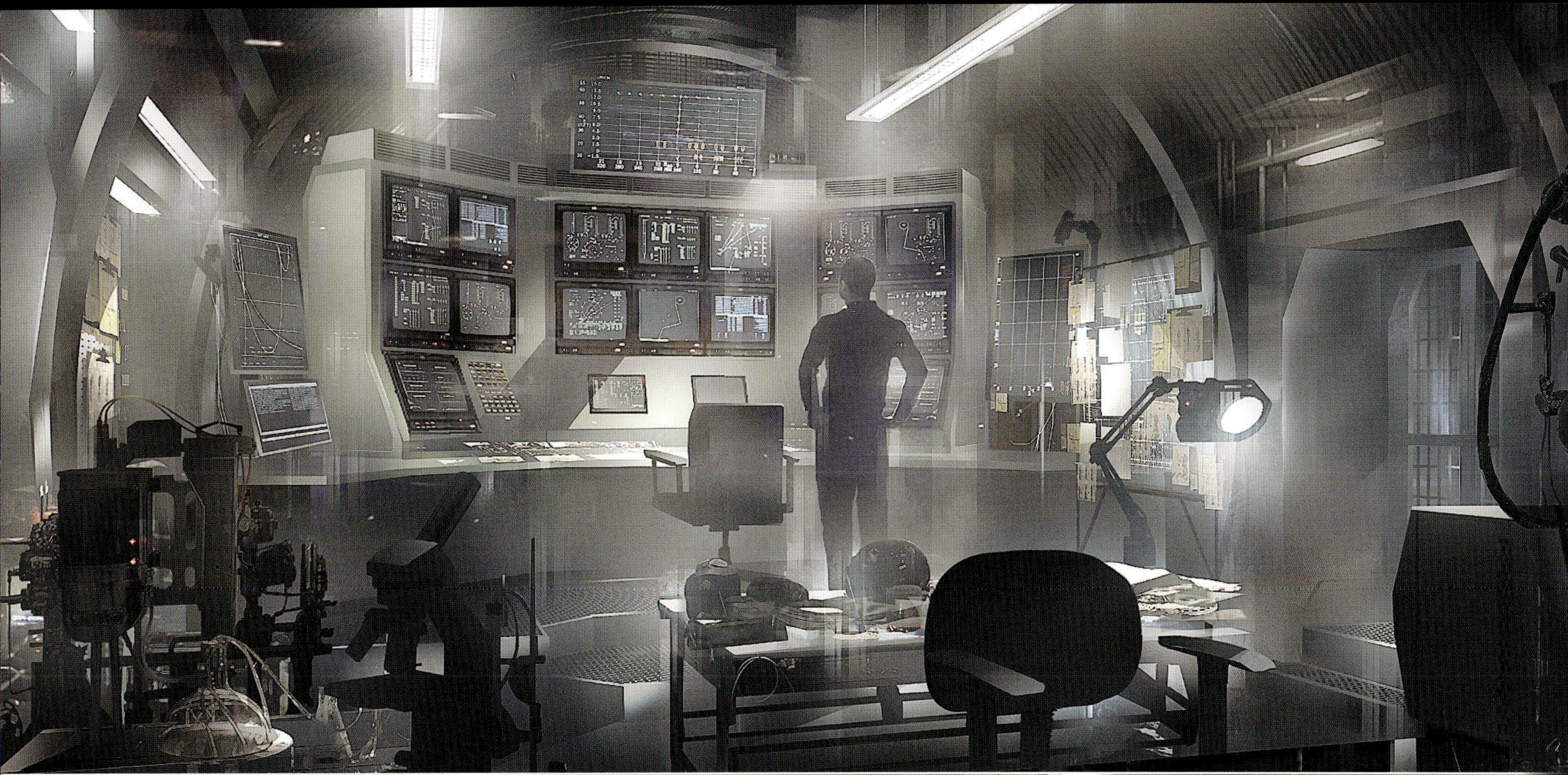

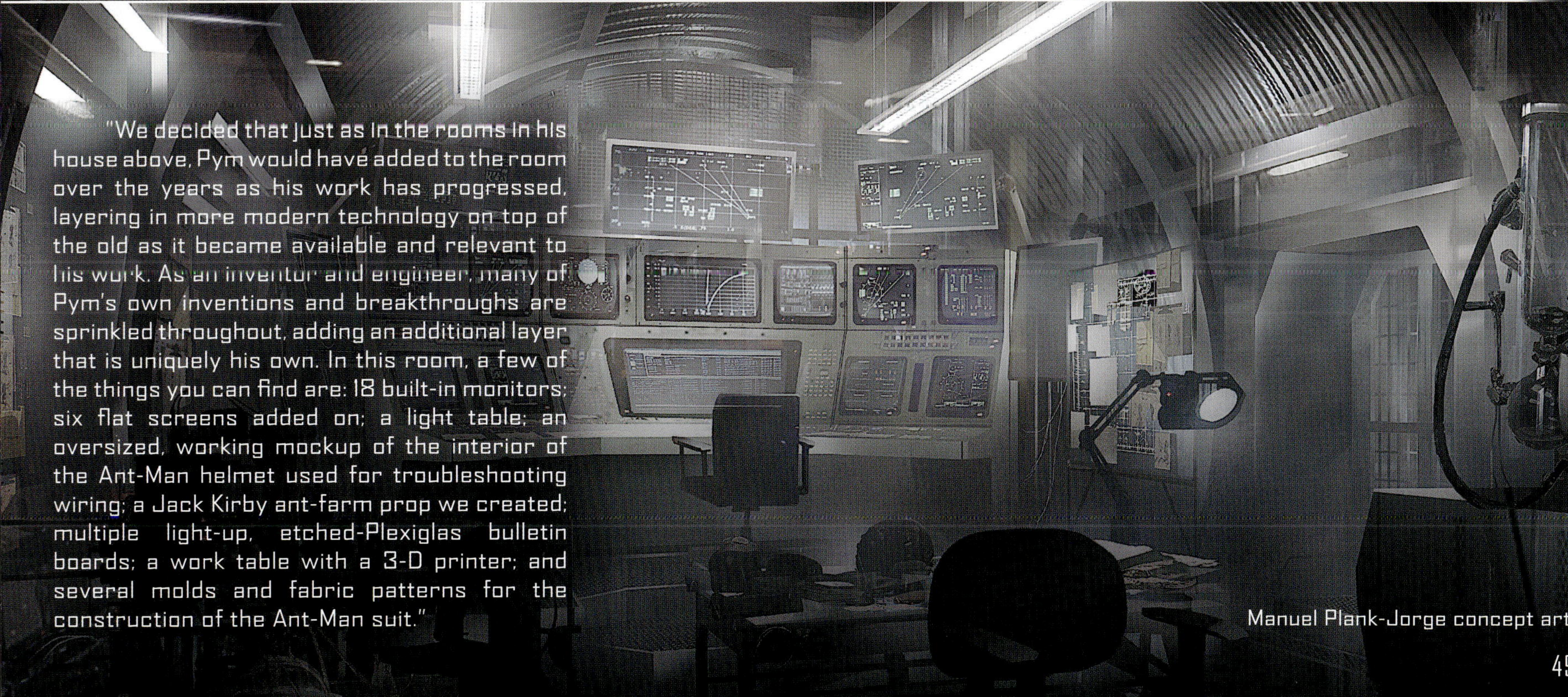

"We decided that just as in the rooms in his house above, Pym would have added to the room over the years as his work has progressed, layering in more modern technology on top of the old as it became available and relevant to his work. As an inventor and engineer, many of Pym's own inventions and breakthroughs are sprinkled throughout, adding an additional layer that is uniquely his own. In this room, a few of the things you can find are: 18 built-in monitors; six flat screens added on; a light table; an oversized, working mockup of the interior of the Ant-Man helmet used for troubleshooting wiring; a Jack Kirby ant-farm prop we created; multiple light-up, etched-Plexiglas bulletin boards; a work table with a 3-D printer; and several molds and fabric patterns for the construction of the Ant-Man suit."

Manuel Plank-Jorge concept art.

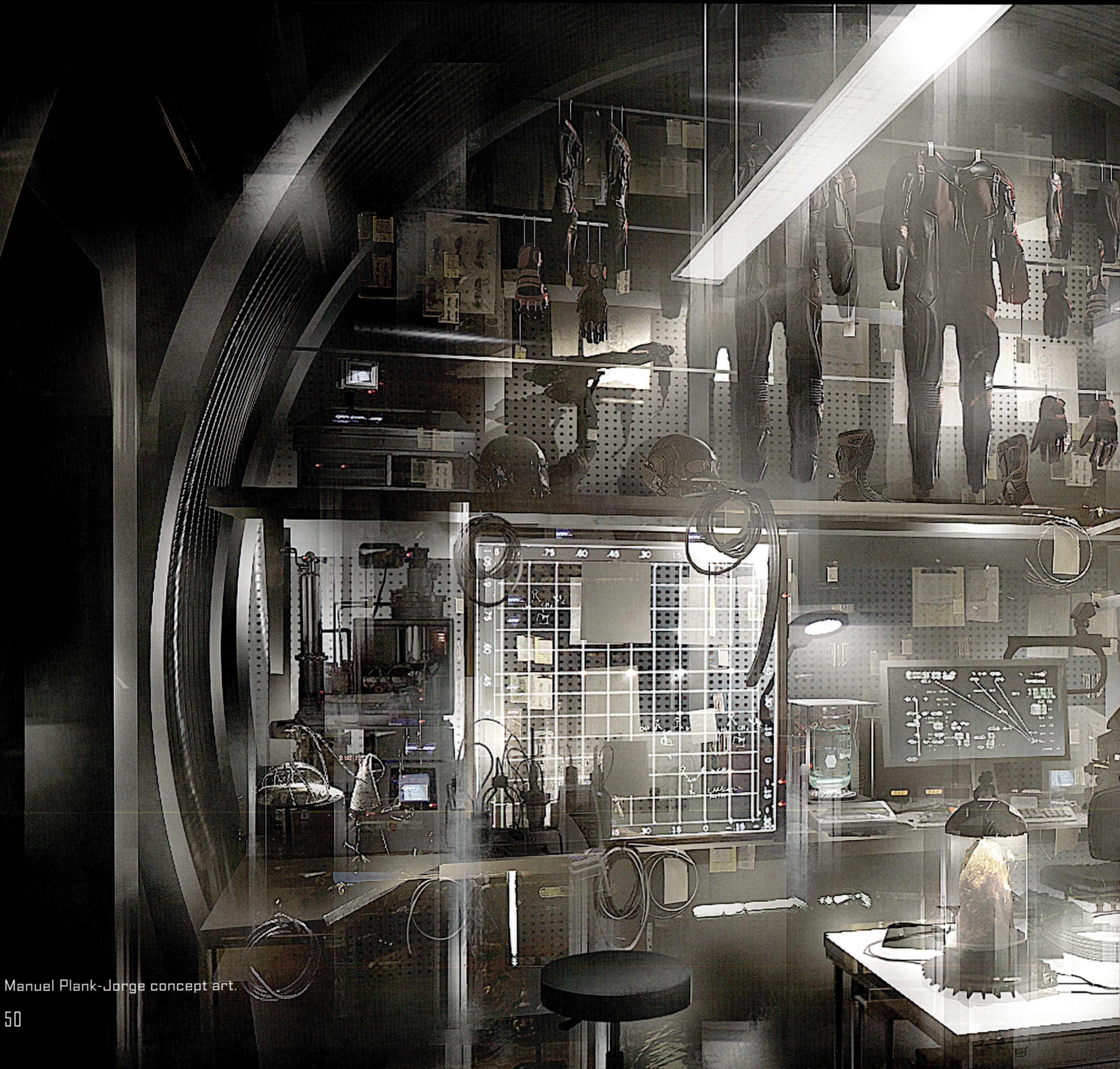

Manuel Plank-Jorge concept art.

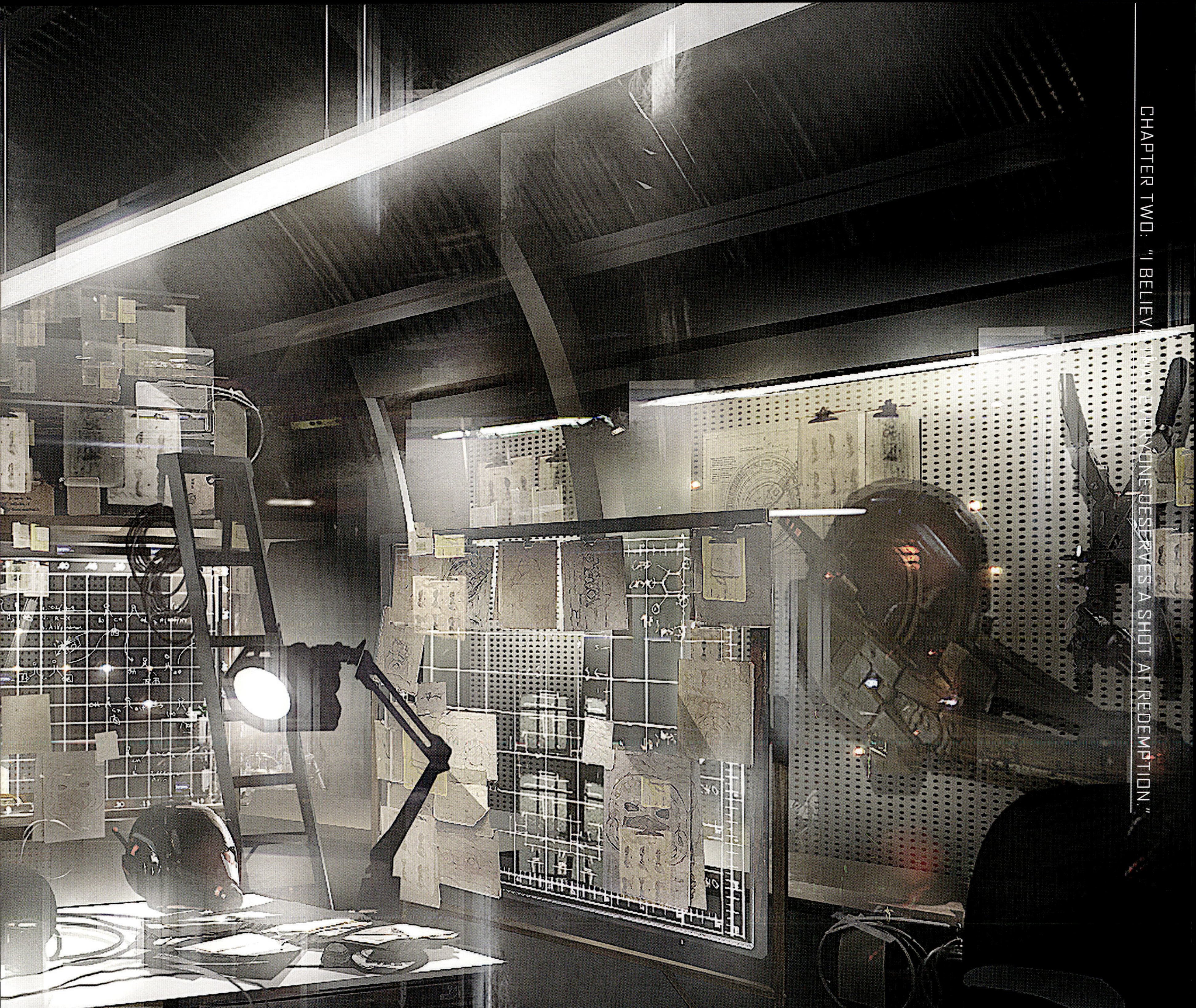

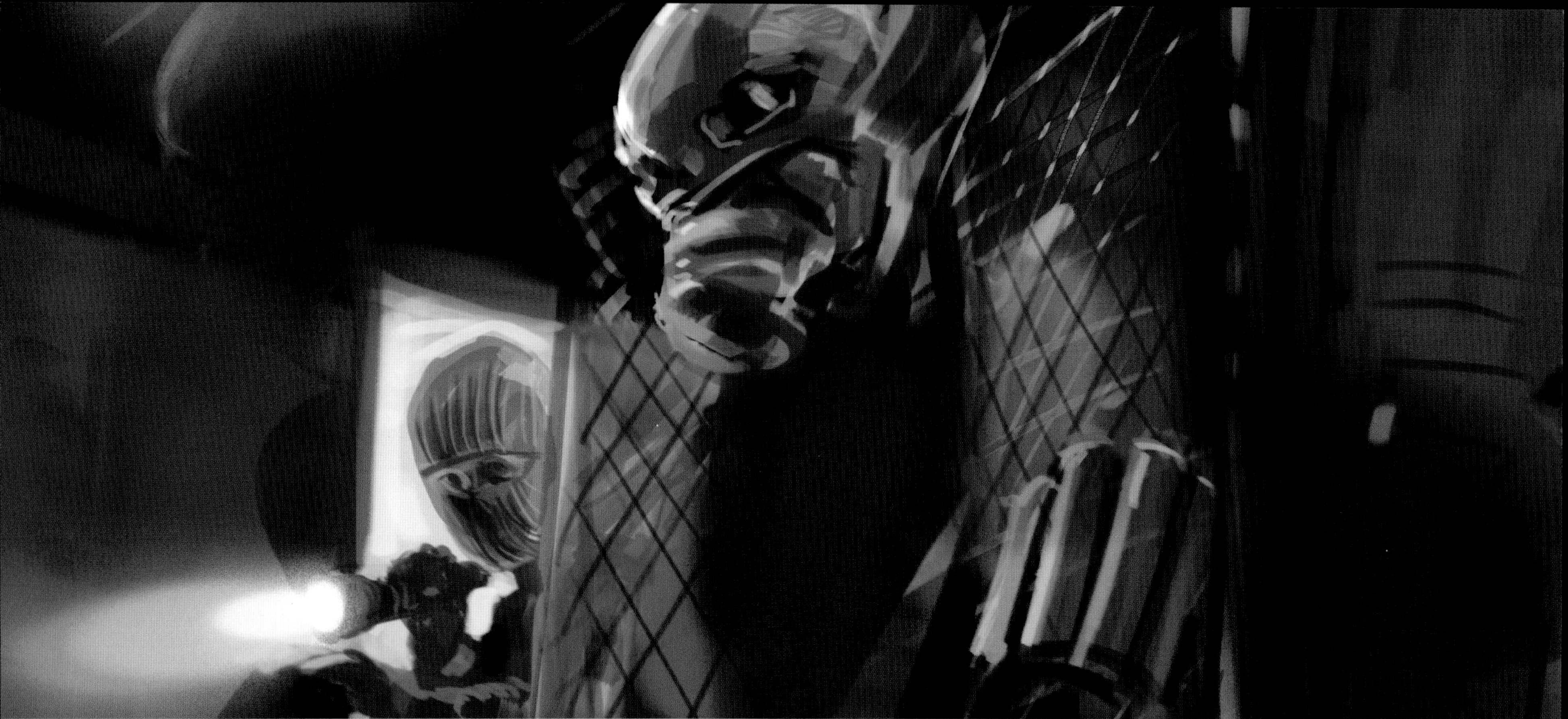

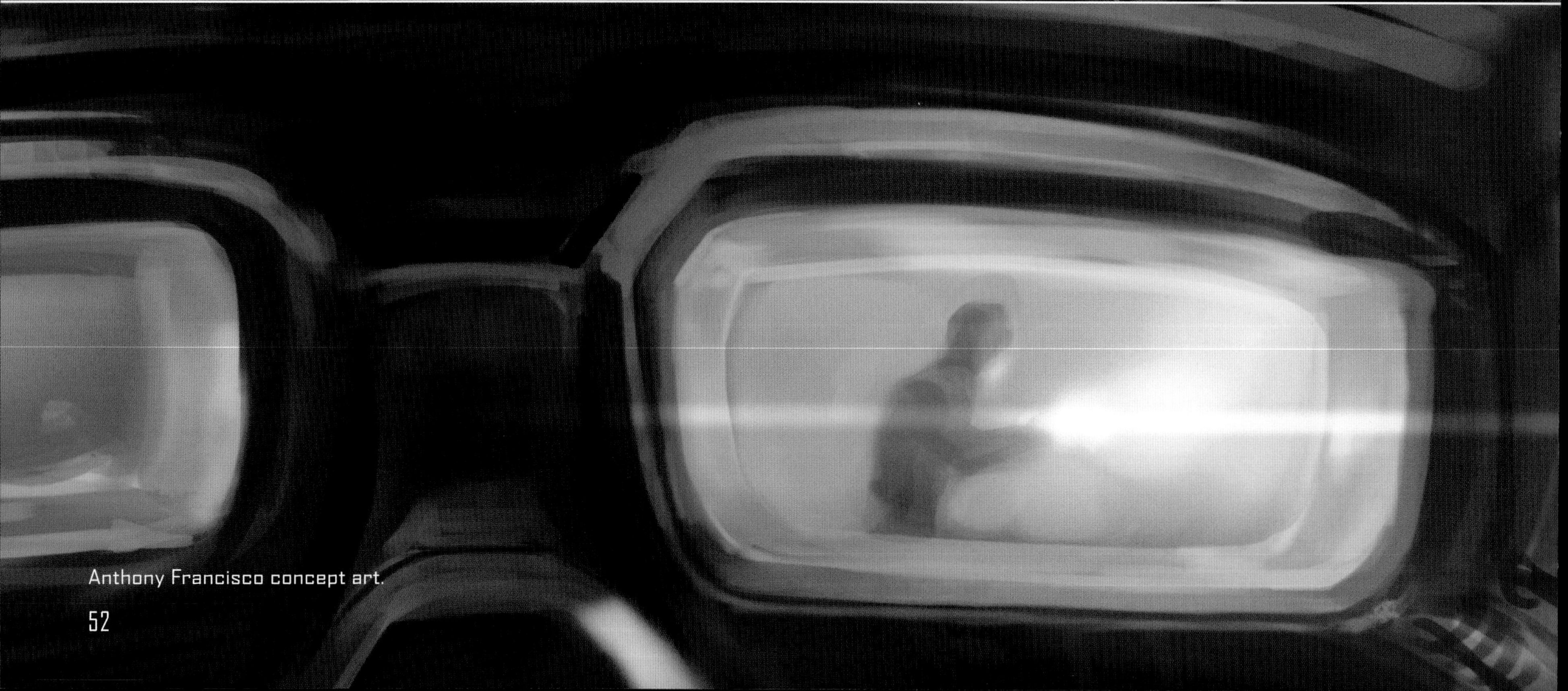

Anthony Francisco concept art.

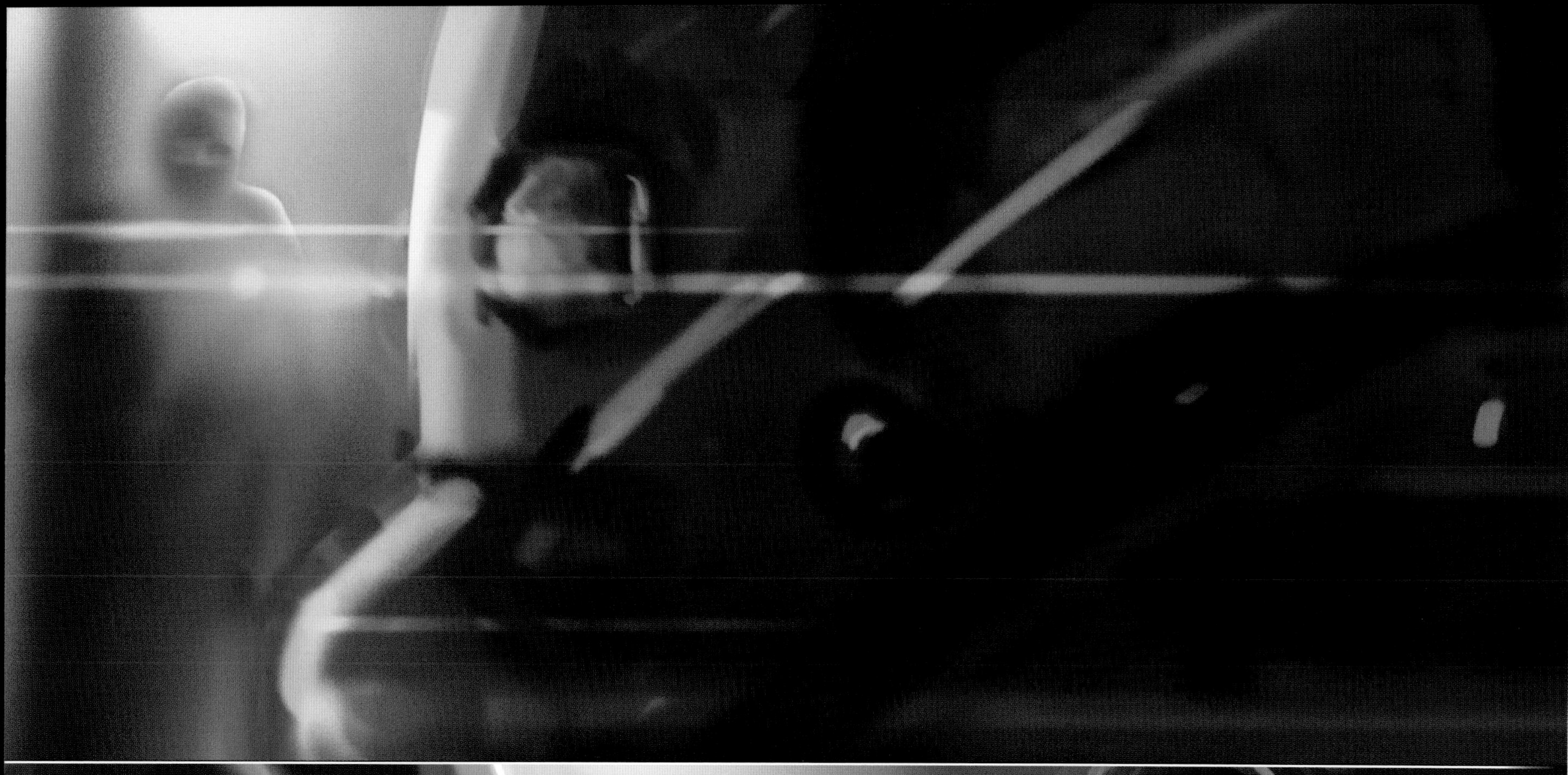

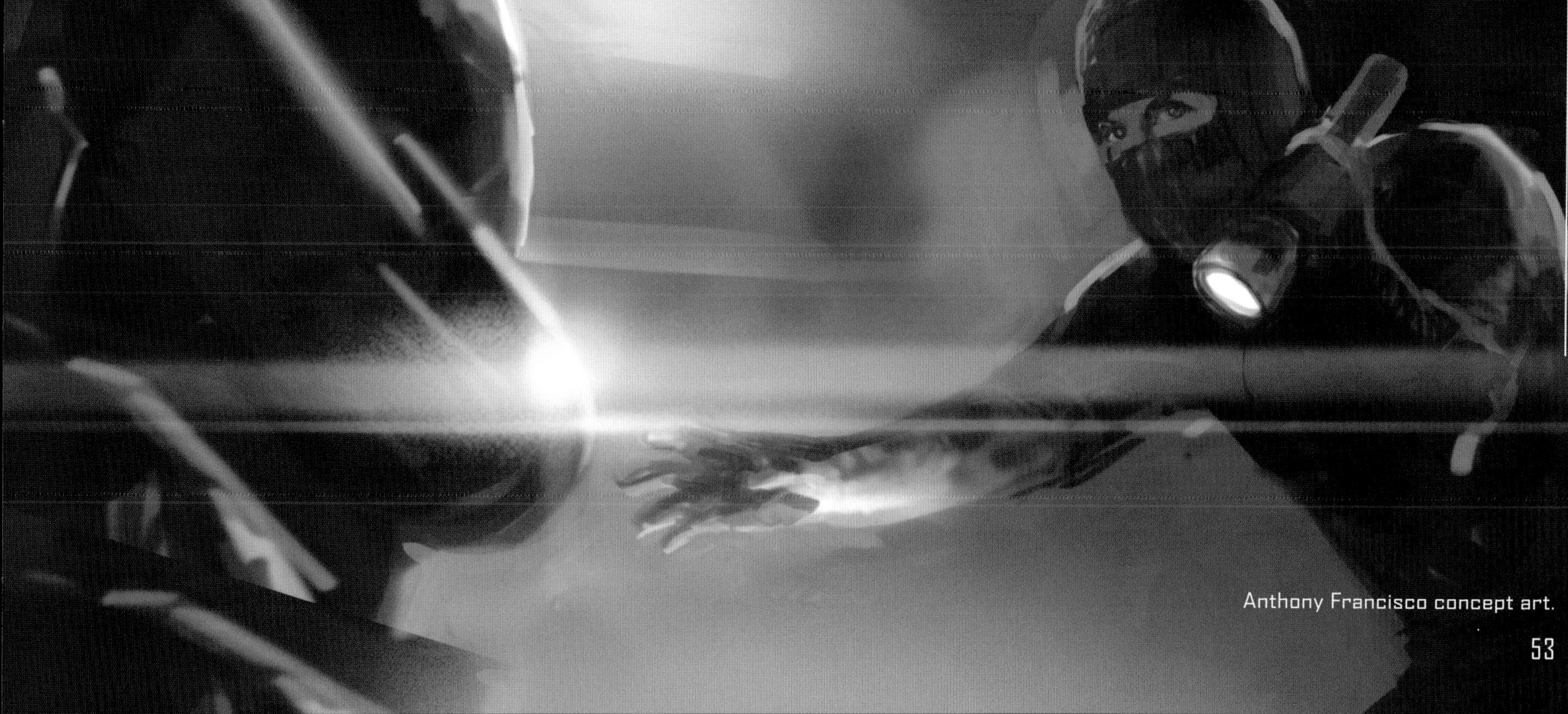

Anthony Francisco concept art.

"One of the biggest challenges with designing Pym's house was creating an architectural ecosystem that tells the complex story of Hank Pym's history as a hero, husband, father, scientist, inventor, engineer, entomologist, puppet master, and critical early member of S.H.I.E.L.D.," Frankel explains. "In the opening of the film, Pym's residence serves as a choreographed booby trap for Scott Lang to figure out. Pym is testing him and manipulating him throughout his break-in. Visually representing this history and these character traits was a delicate balance that required choreographing which parts of him were represented at different moments of the film.

"While the entire house was an engaging set to develop, one of the most compelling challenges was designing the secure room, the basement, the workout room, and the vault that hosts the Ant-Man suit, as well as the special room beyond that hosts the Wasp suit. This secure room was the true heart of the set—a dynamic culmination of the many layers of history: technological, architectural, and personal. Designing that set, combined with getting to design and create the evolution of Pym's own inventions with the collaboration of the Costumes and Props departments, was a real treat. Creating a visually engaging and story-appropriate architectural space—and then working with many departments to fulfill the dressing, props, lighting, and shooting needs—is always a joy."

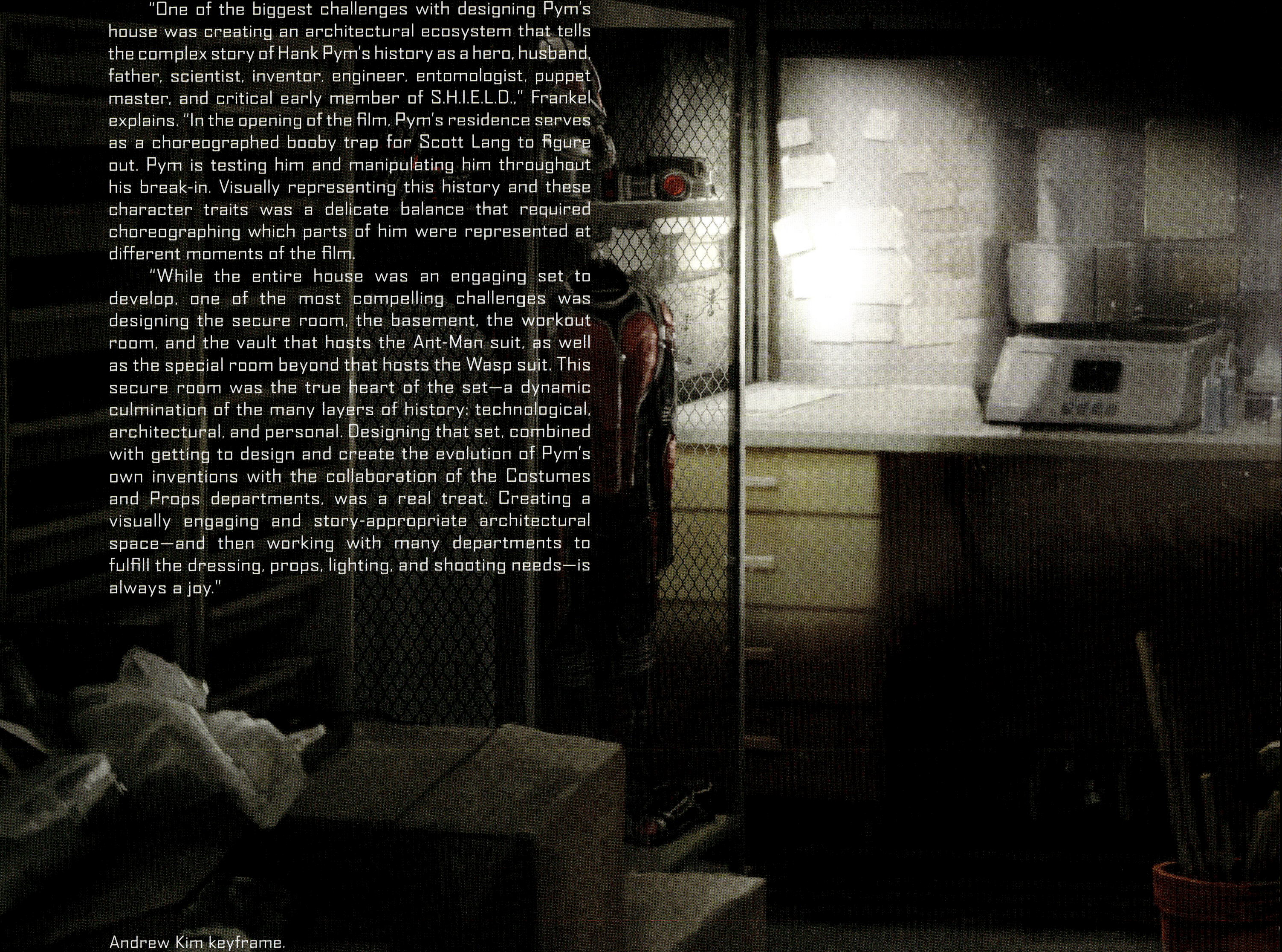

Andrew Kim keyframe.

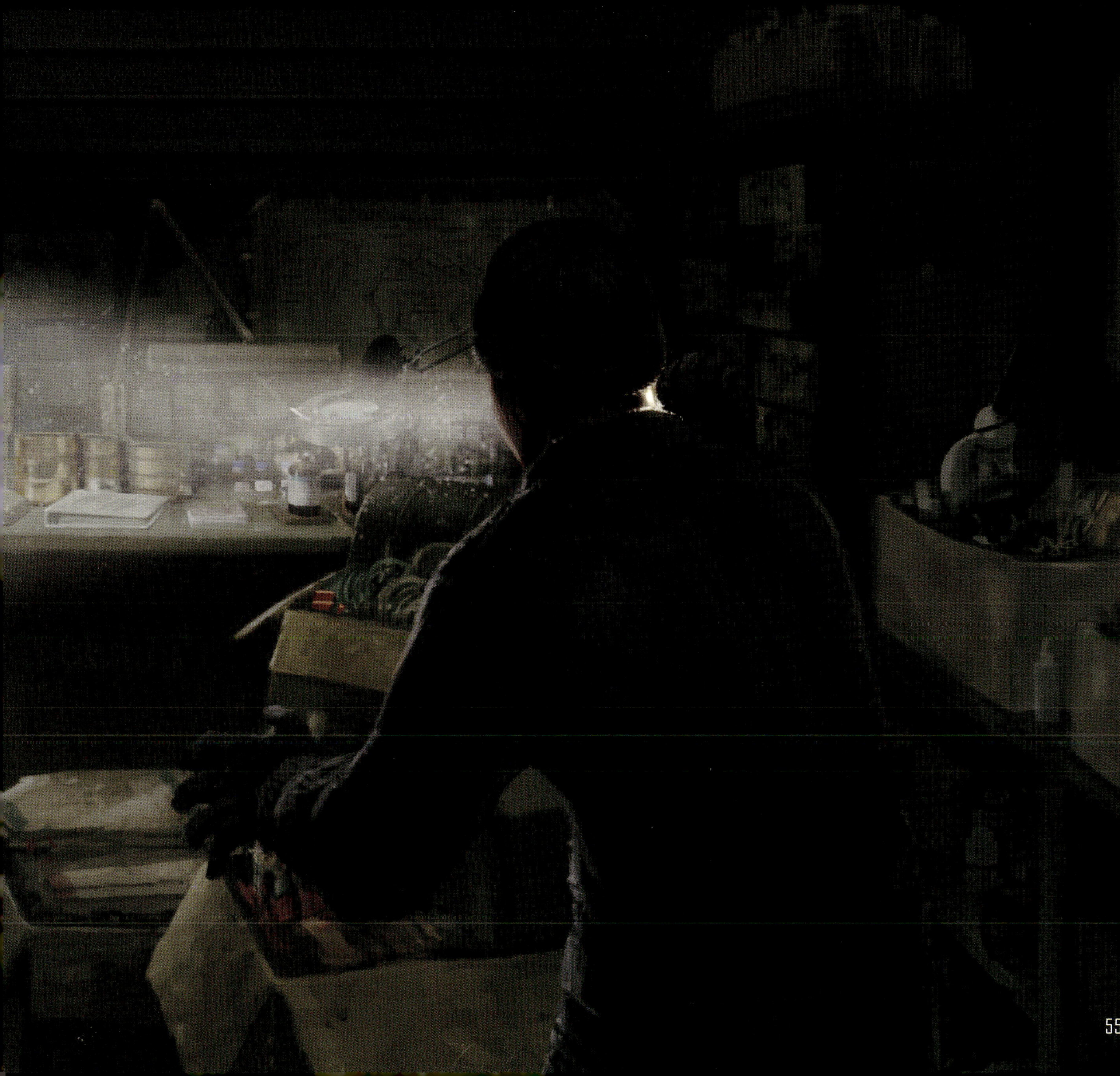

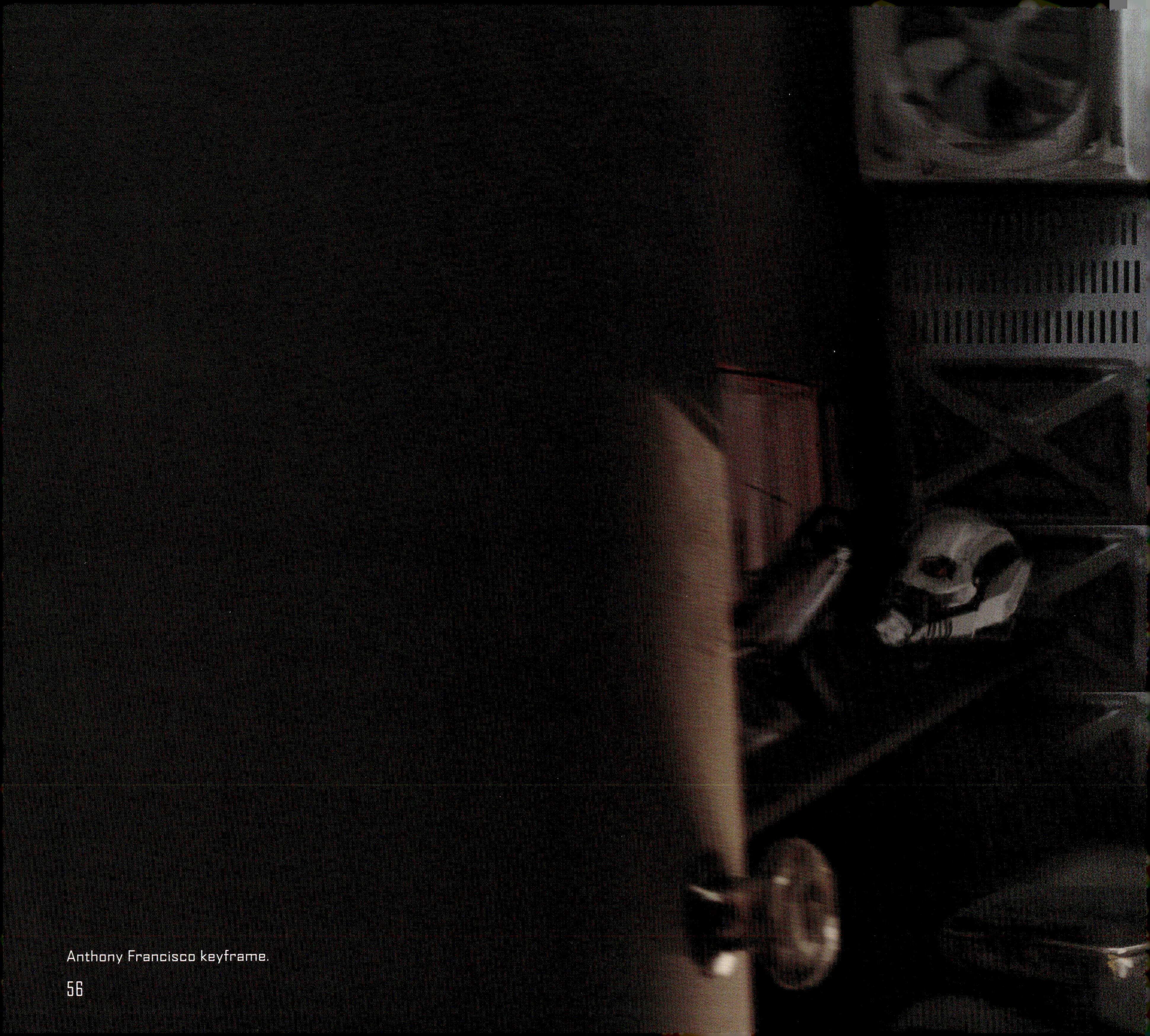

Anthony Francisco keyframe.

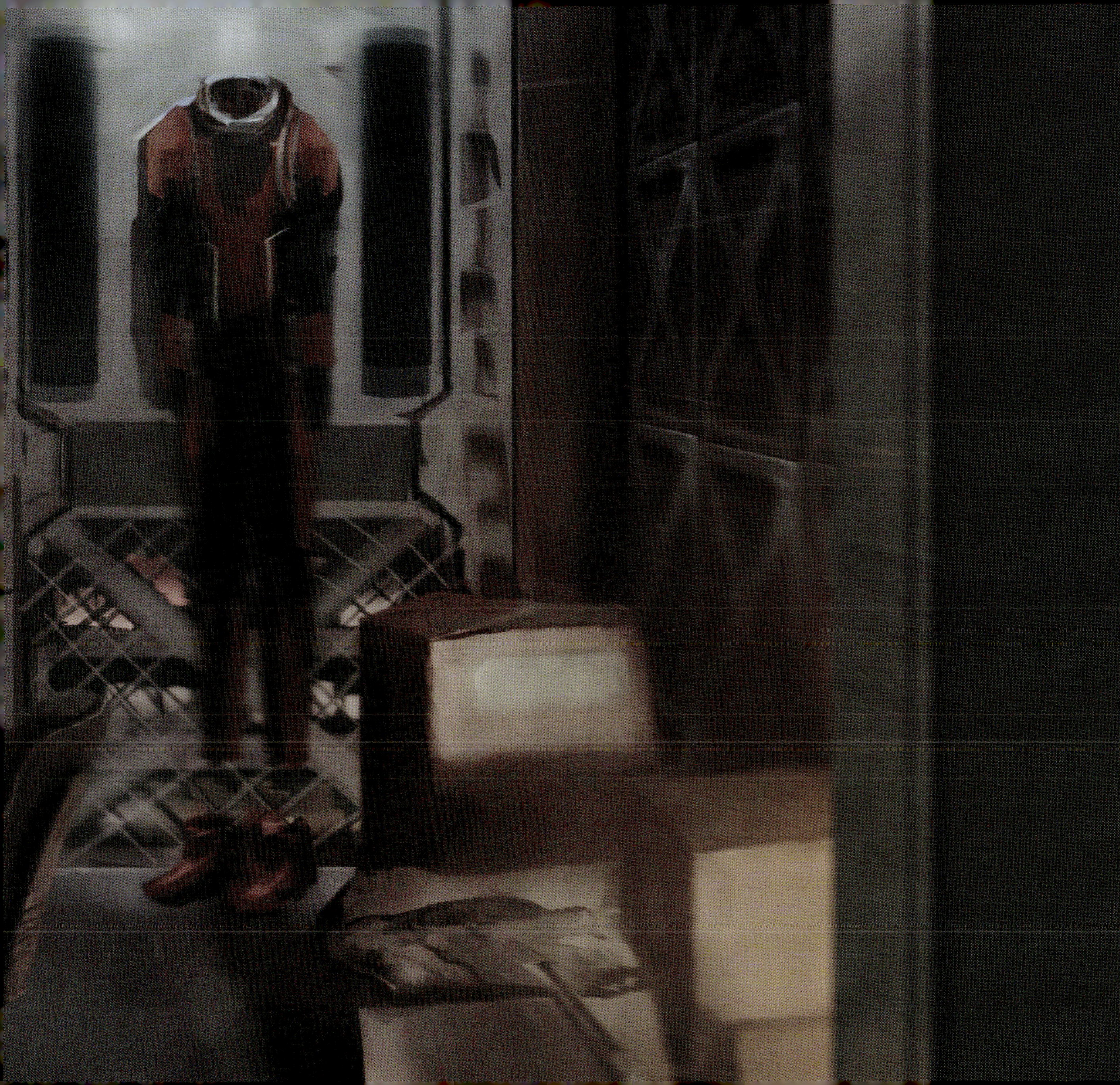

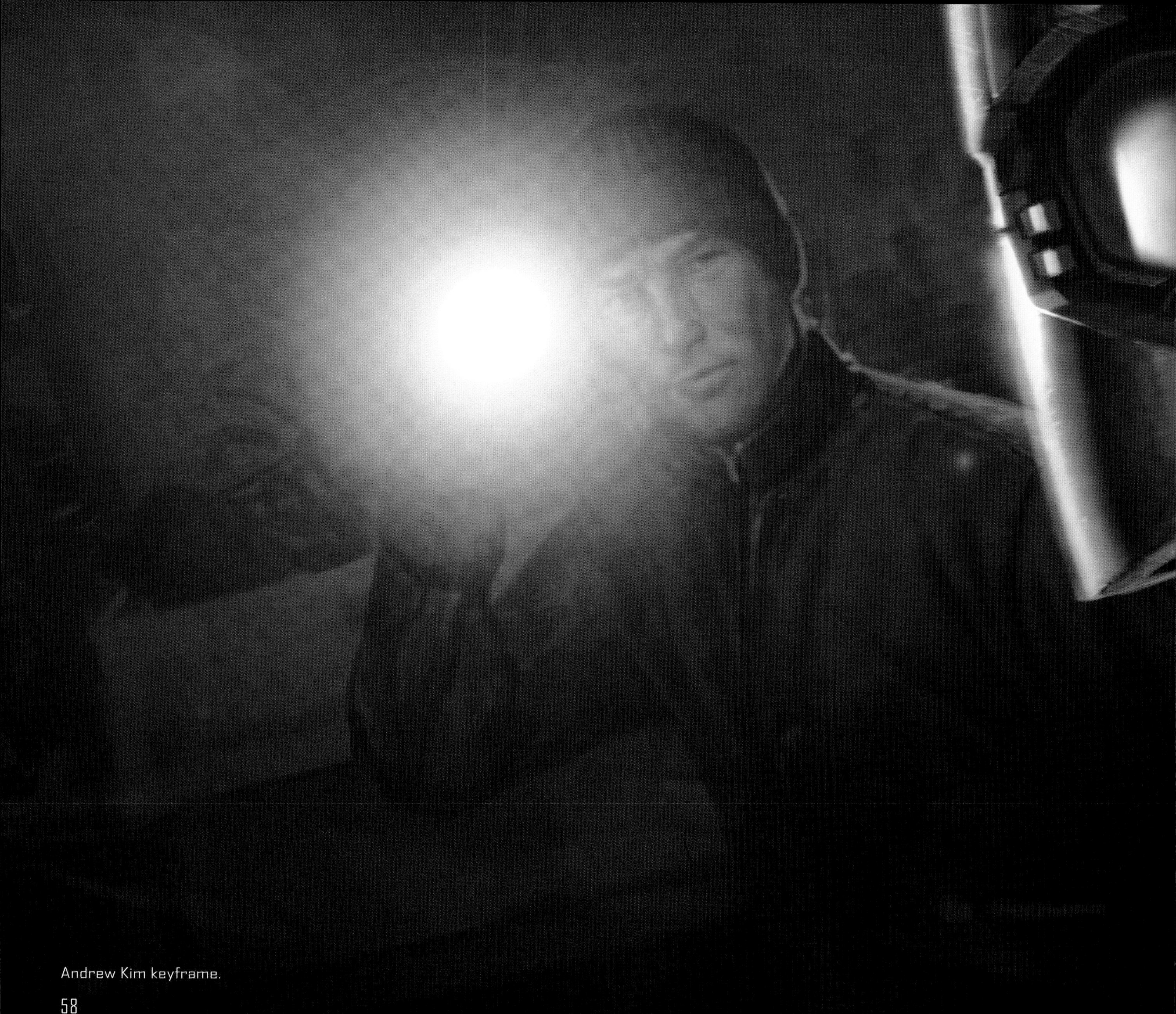

Andrew Kim keyframe.

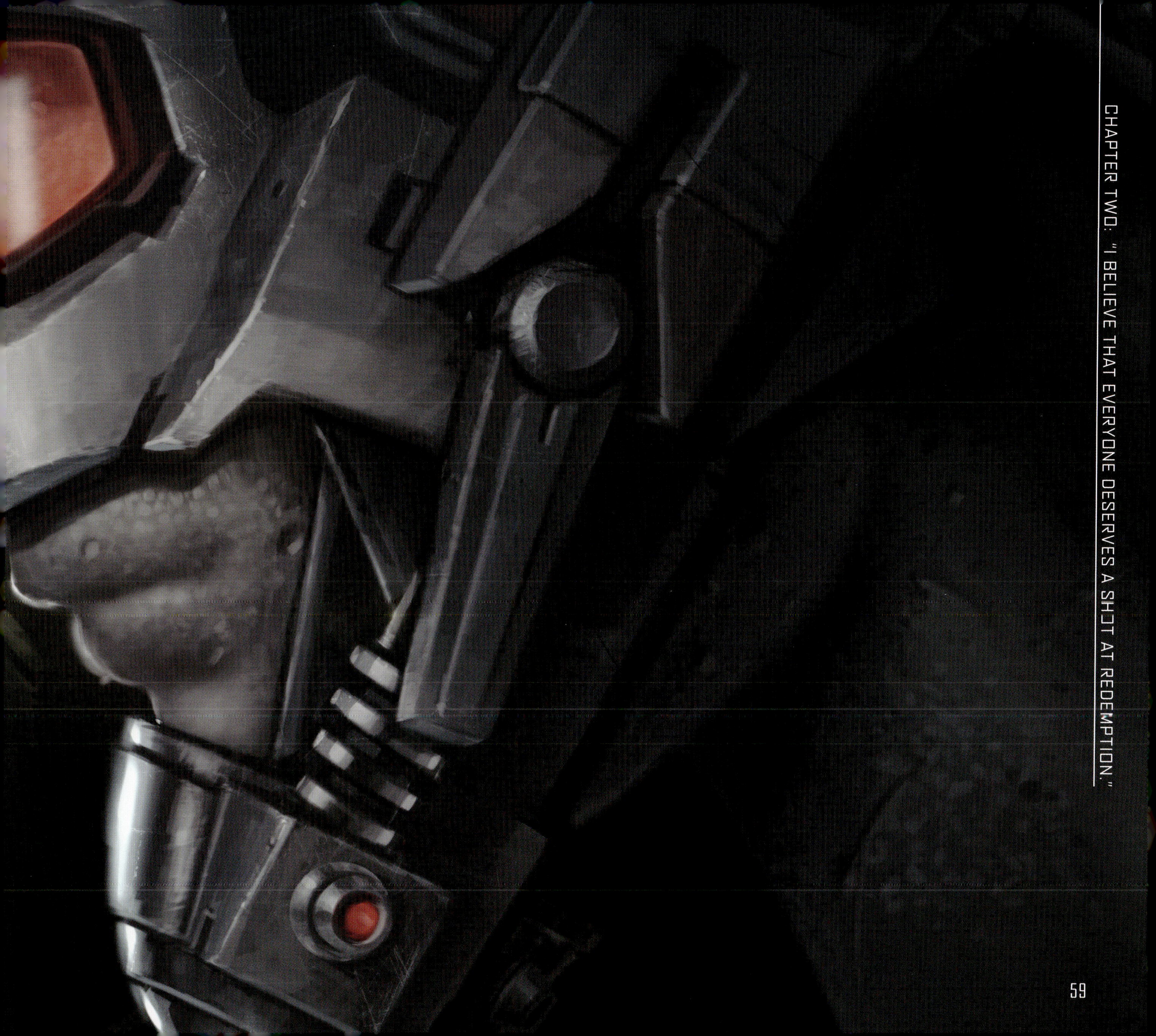

SCOTT'S FIRST SHRINK

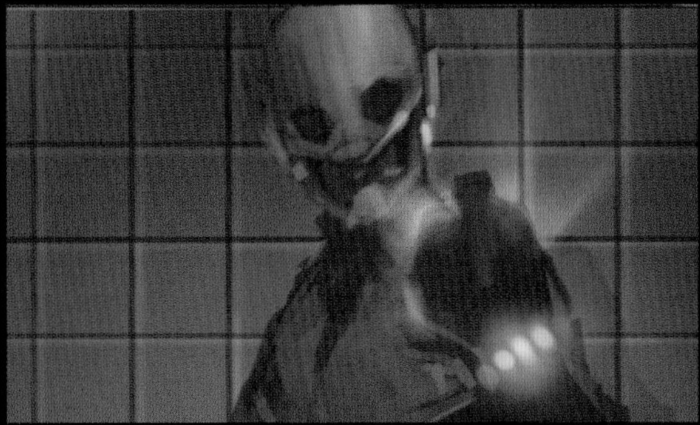

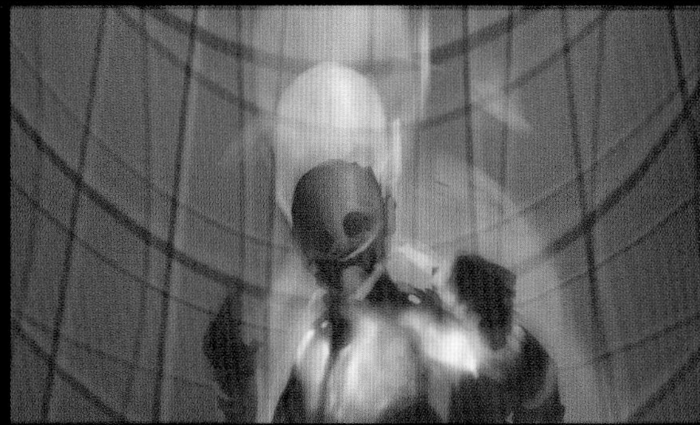

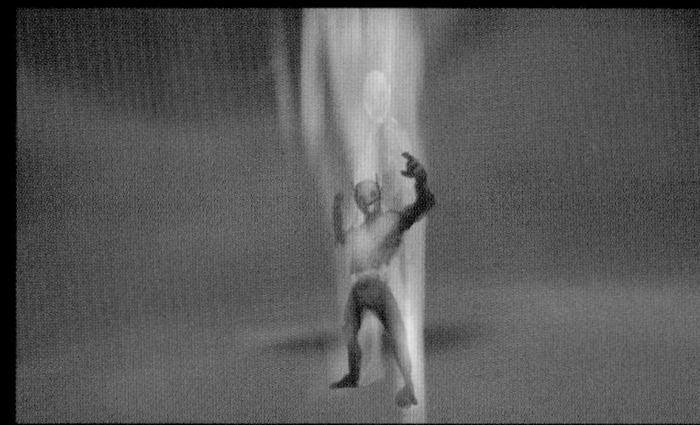

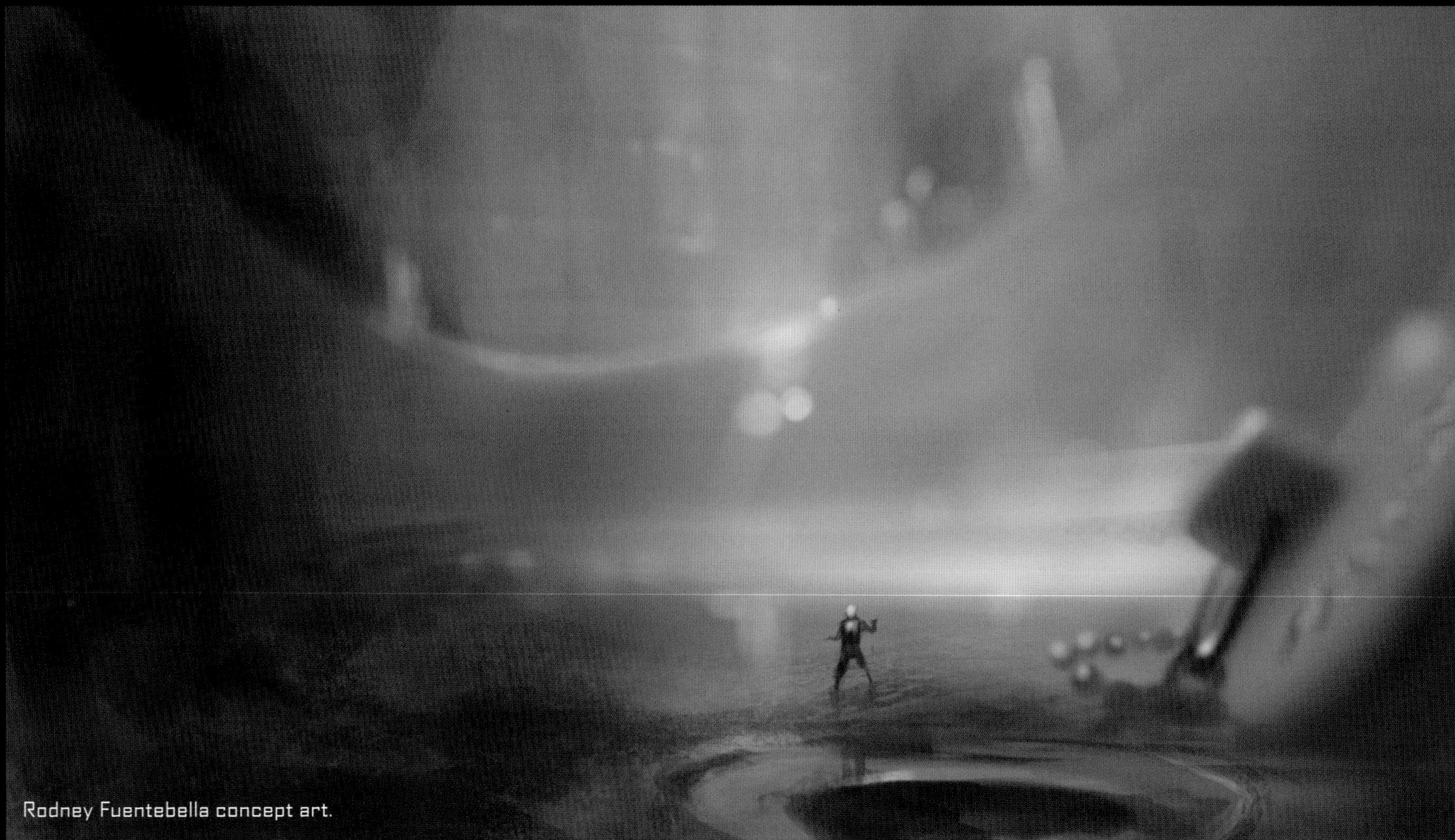

Rodney Fuentebella concept art.

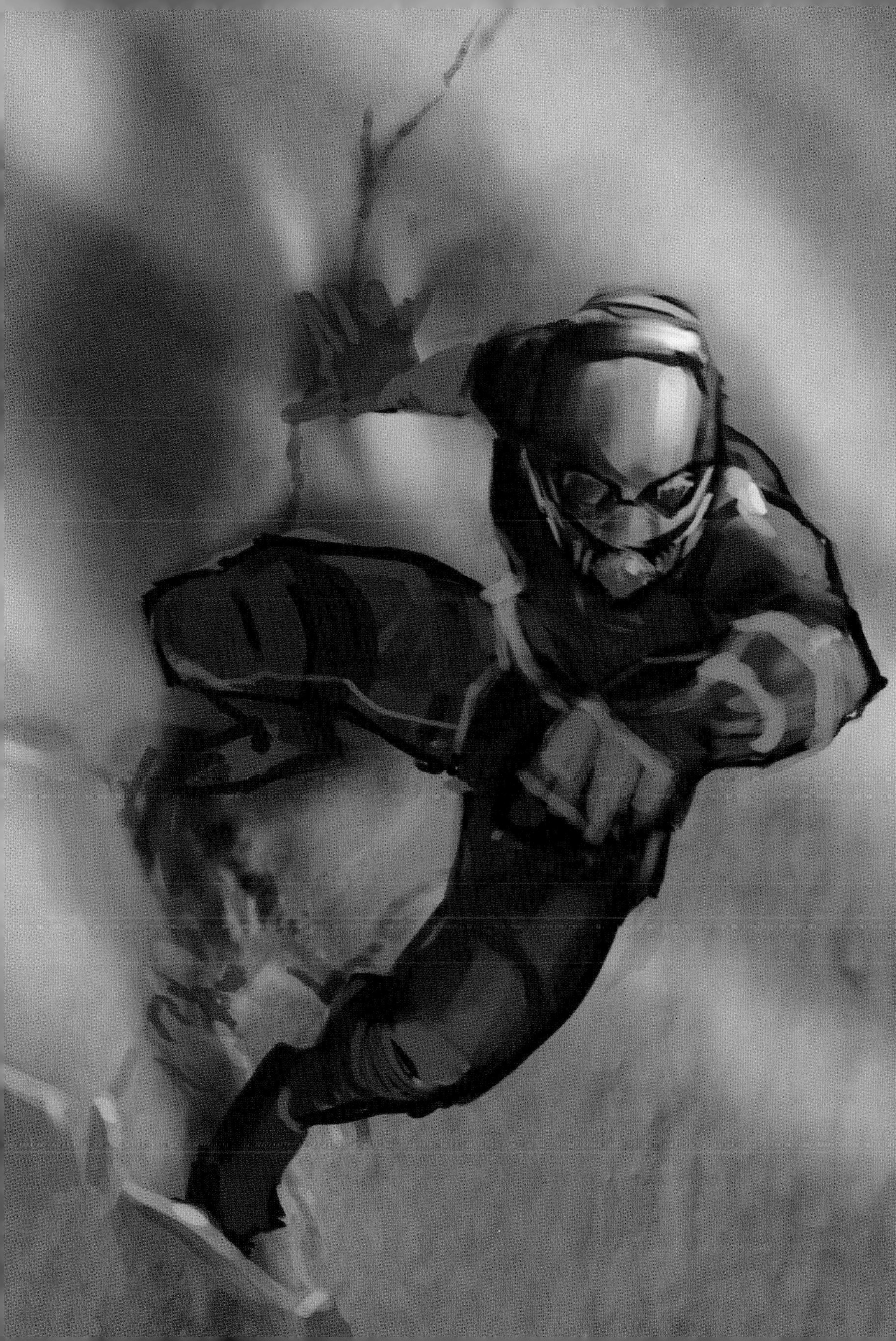

The more unassuming, the better—that was the filmmakers' breakthrough while creating and contextualizing the shrinking experience, Executive Producer Victoria Alonso explains. "What we wanted to create was something simple," Alonso says. "What you need to do is trick the eye into not thinking, trick the brain into not giving you too much time so the audience ends up going '...what?' It's in and out. 'What happened? Something happened? Oh, now he's little? Oh, okay.' The minute he lands, you're in the macro-world—and you're so into the 'Wow, I've never seen a bathtub like this before,' or any other environment he finds himself in, that you forget he's even shrunk. Simple, simple, simple. It doesn't take any more than five seconds. It's kind of streaky and leaves a little of what you might perceive as energy, like a shrinking/growing energy, but it's nothing that you can quantify or break apart."

Rodney Fuentebella concept art.

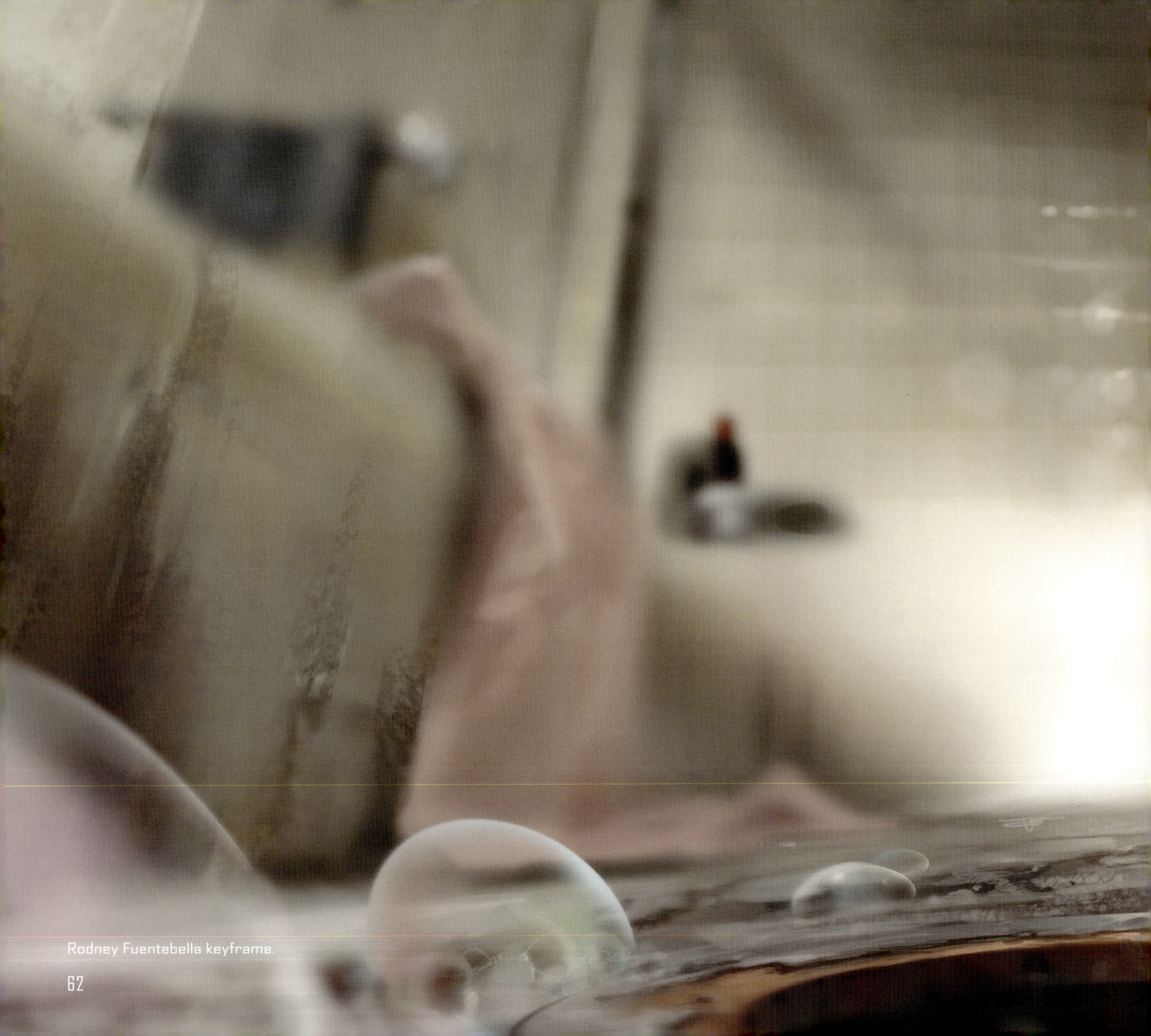

Rodney Fuentebella keyframe.

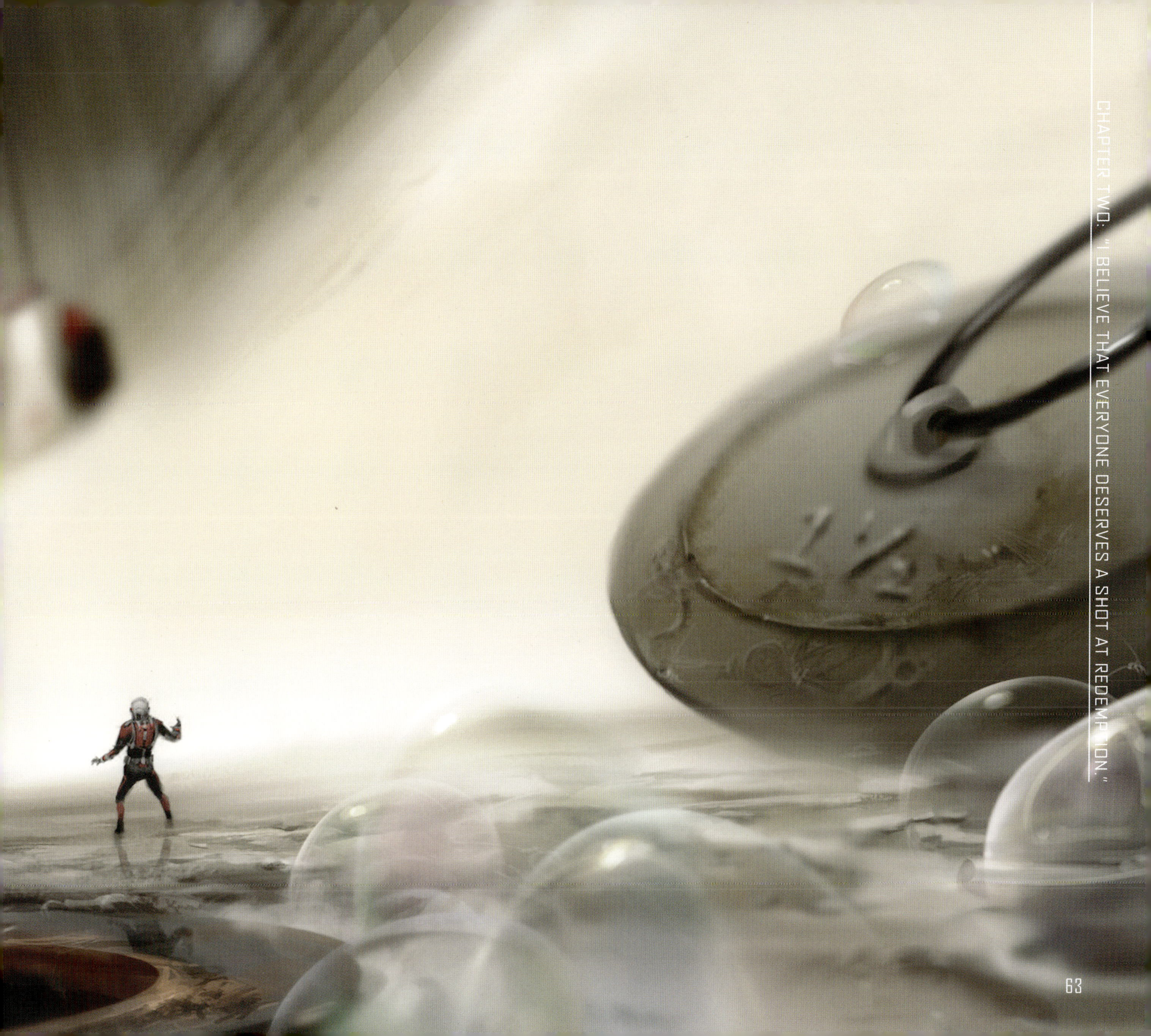

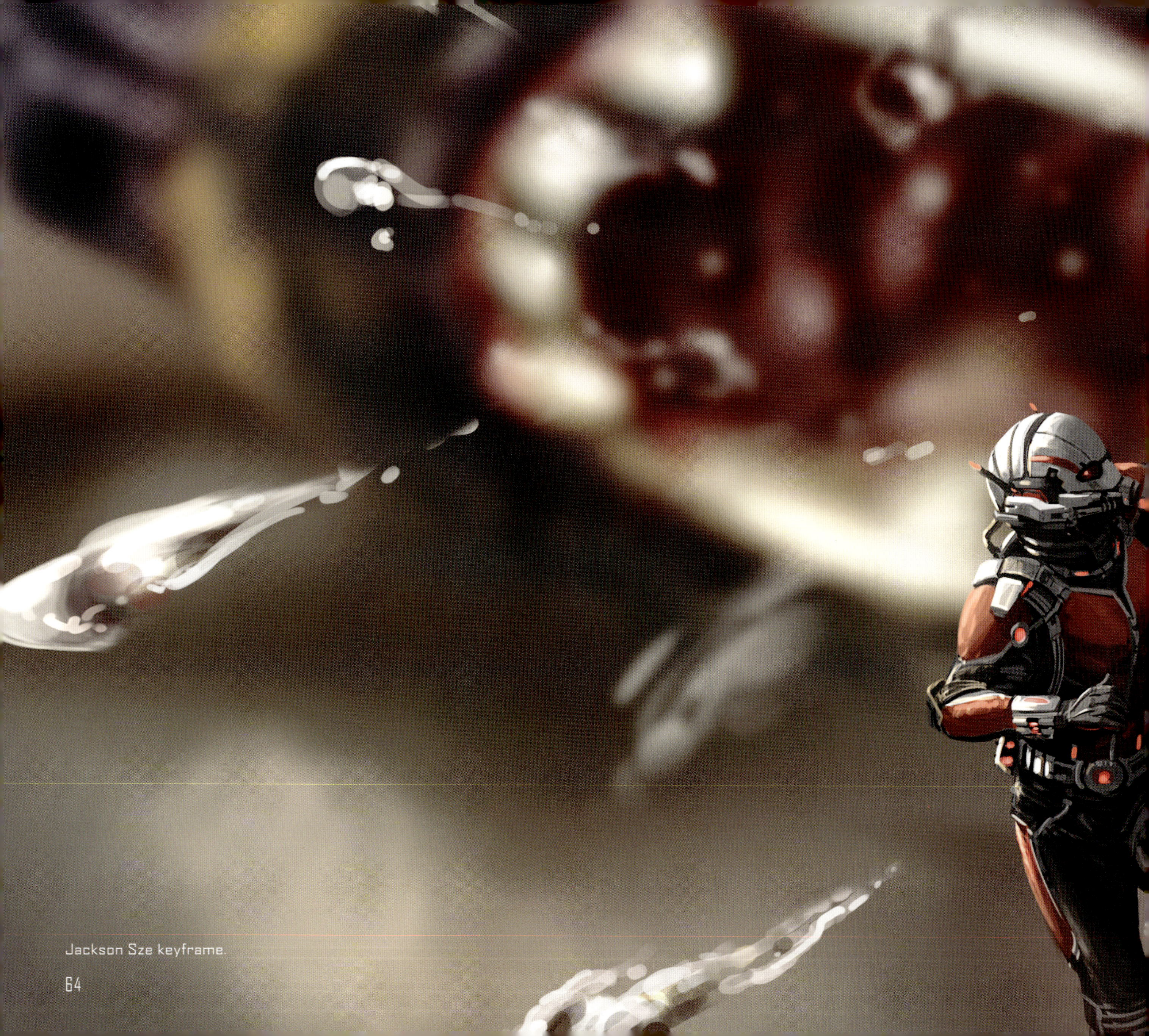

Jackson Sze keyframe.

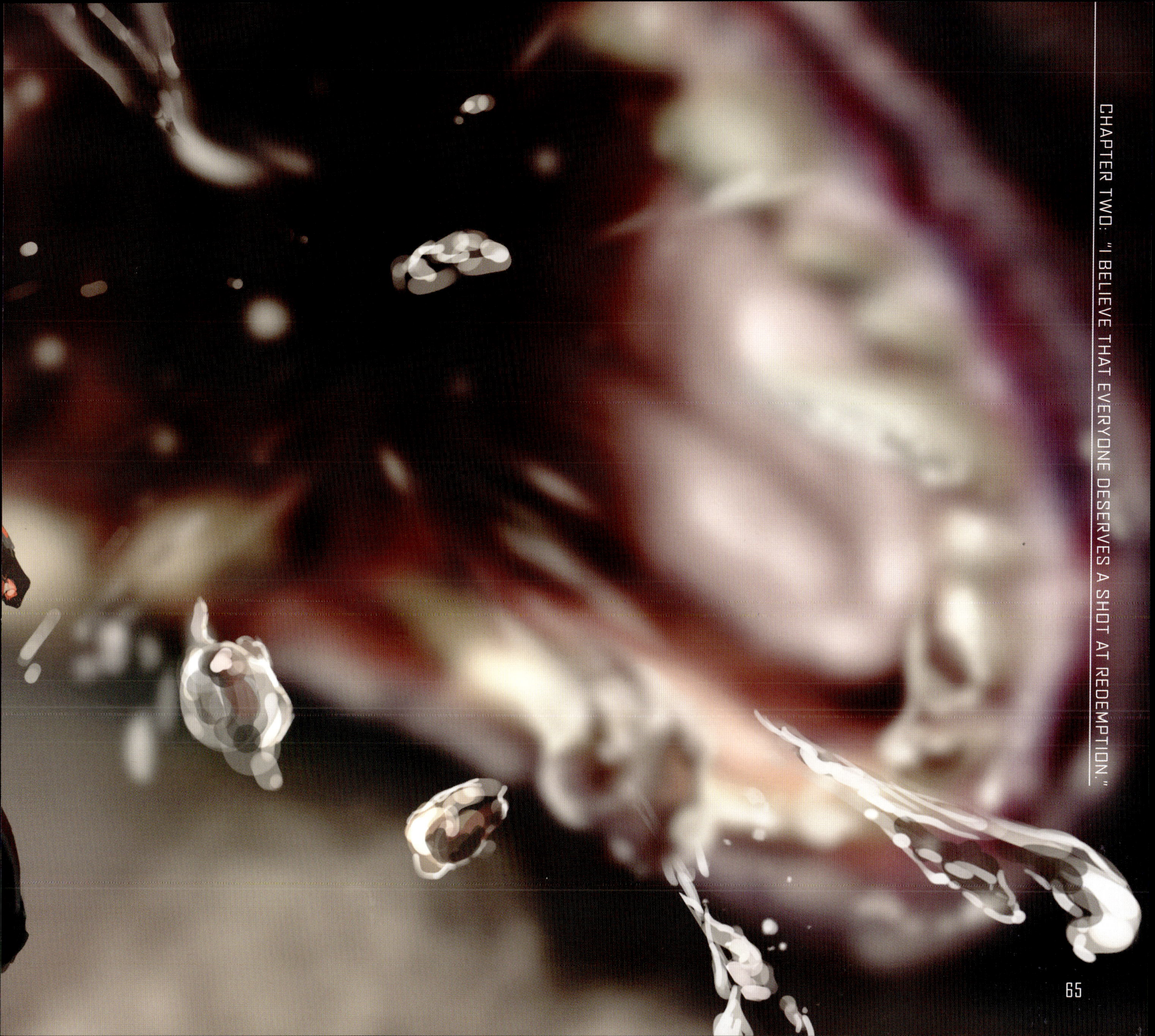

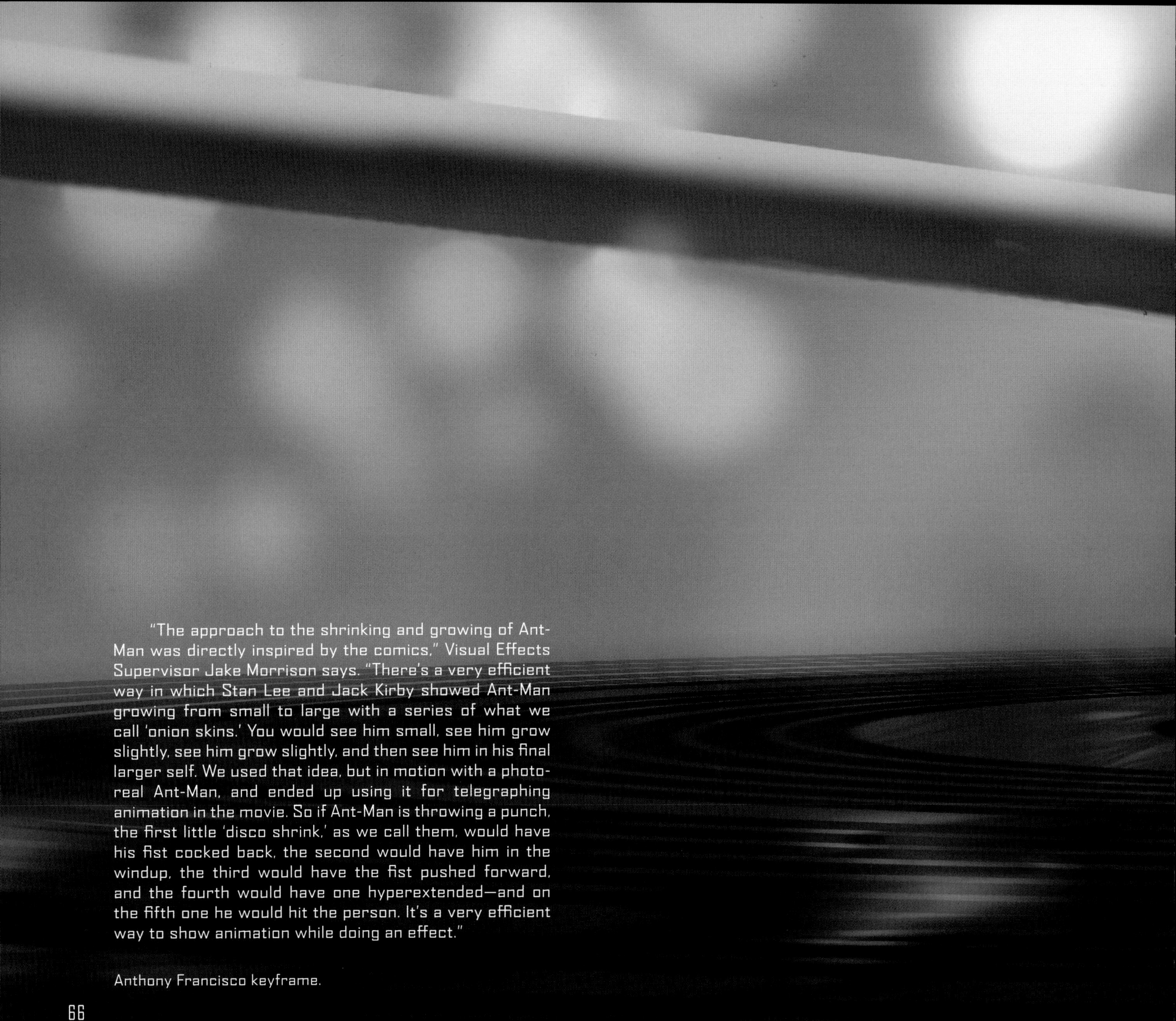

"The approach to the shrinking and growing of Ant-Man was directly inspired by the comics," Visual Effects Supervisor Jake Morrison says. "There's a very efficient way in which Stan Lee and Jack Kirby showed Ant-Man growing from small to large with a series of what we call 'onion skins.' You would see him small, see him grow slightly, see him grow slightly, and then see him in his final larger self. We used that idea, but in motion with a photo-real Ant-Man, and ended up using it for telegraphing animation in the movie. So if Ant-Man is throwing a punch, the first little 'disco shrink,' as we call them, would have his fist cocked back, the second would have him in the windup, the third would have the fist pushed forward, and the fourth would have one hyperextended—and on the fifth one he would hit the person. It's a very efficient way to show animation while doing an effect."

Anthony Francisco keyframe.

CHAPTER TWO: "I BELIEVE THAT EVERYONE DESERVES A SHOT AT REDEMPTION."

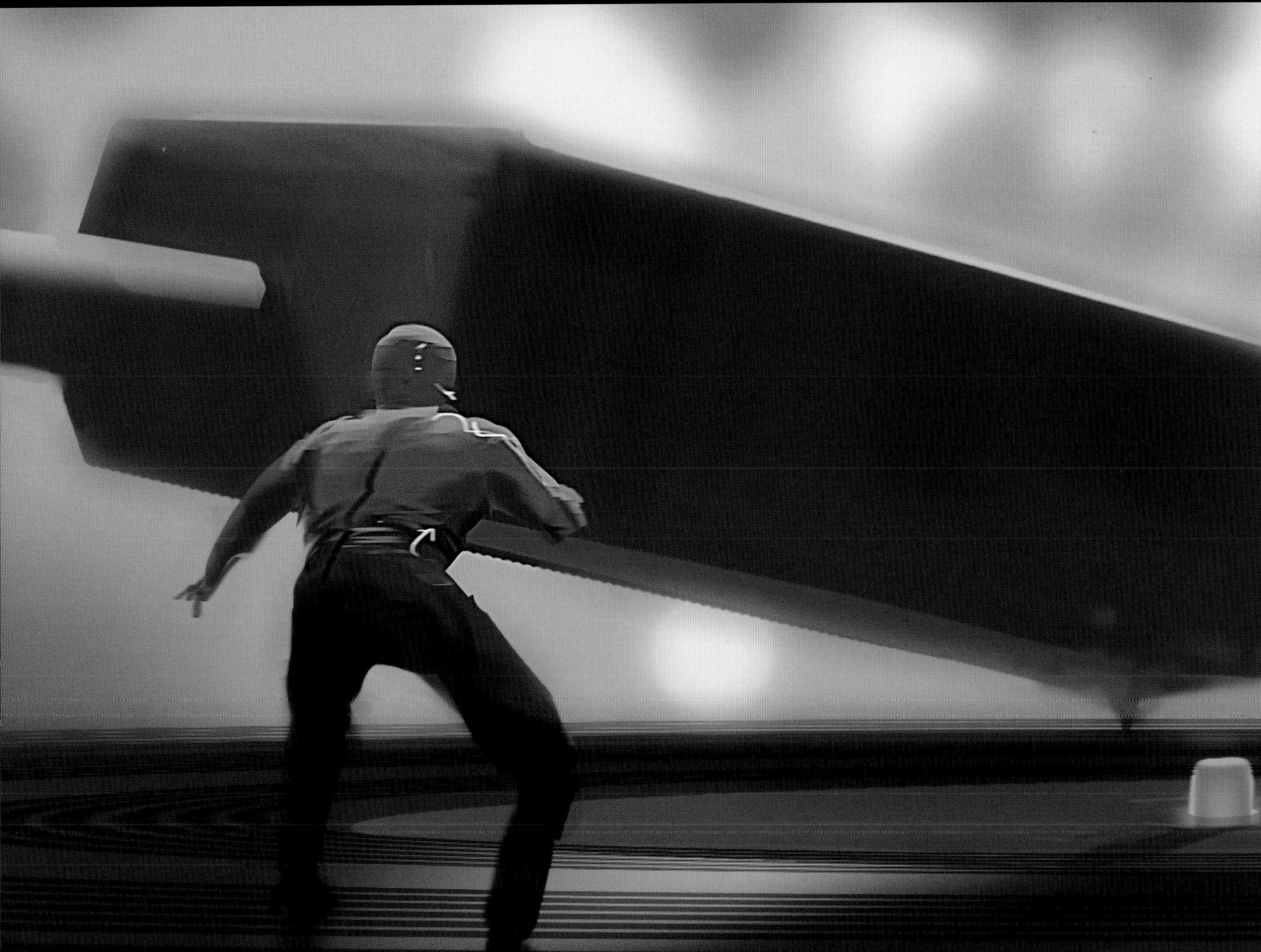

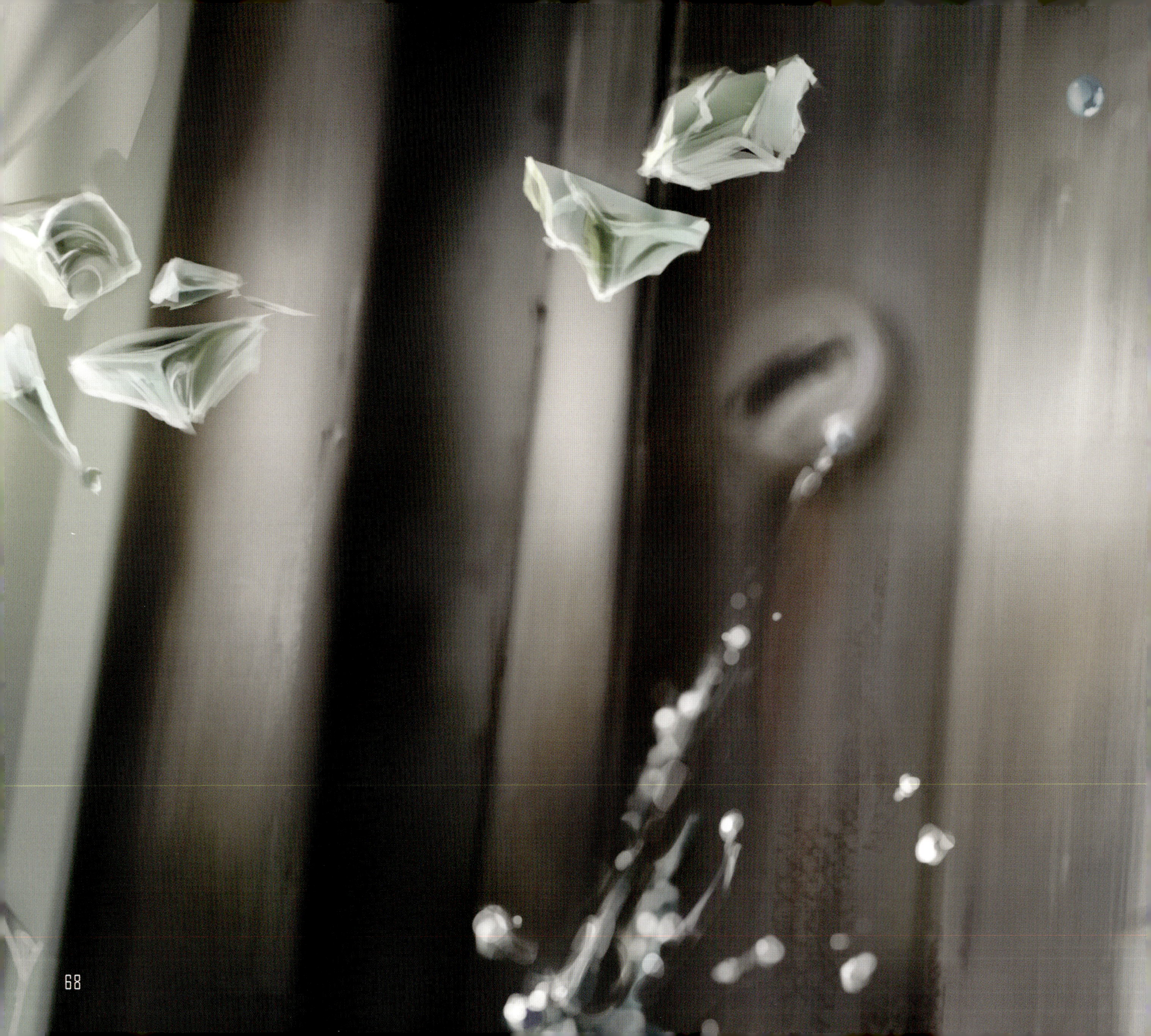

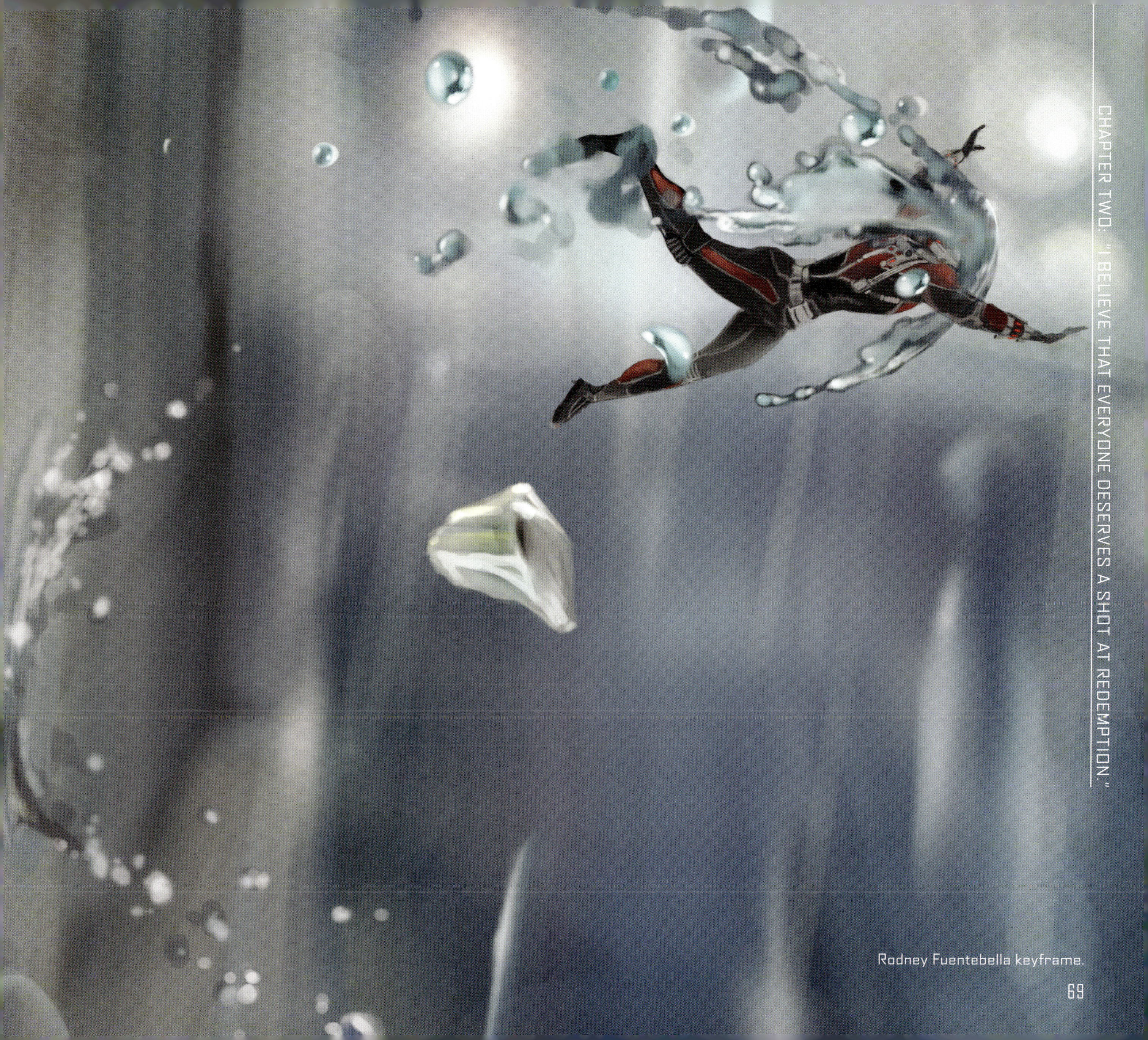

Rodney Fuentebella keyframe.

ANT-MAN SCALE EXPLORATION

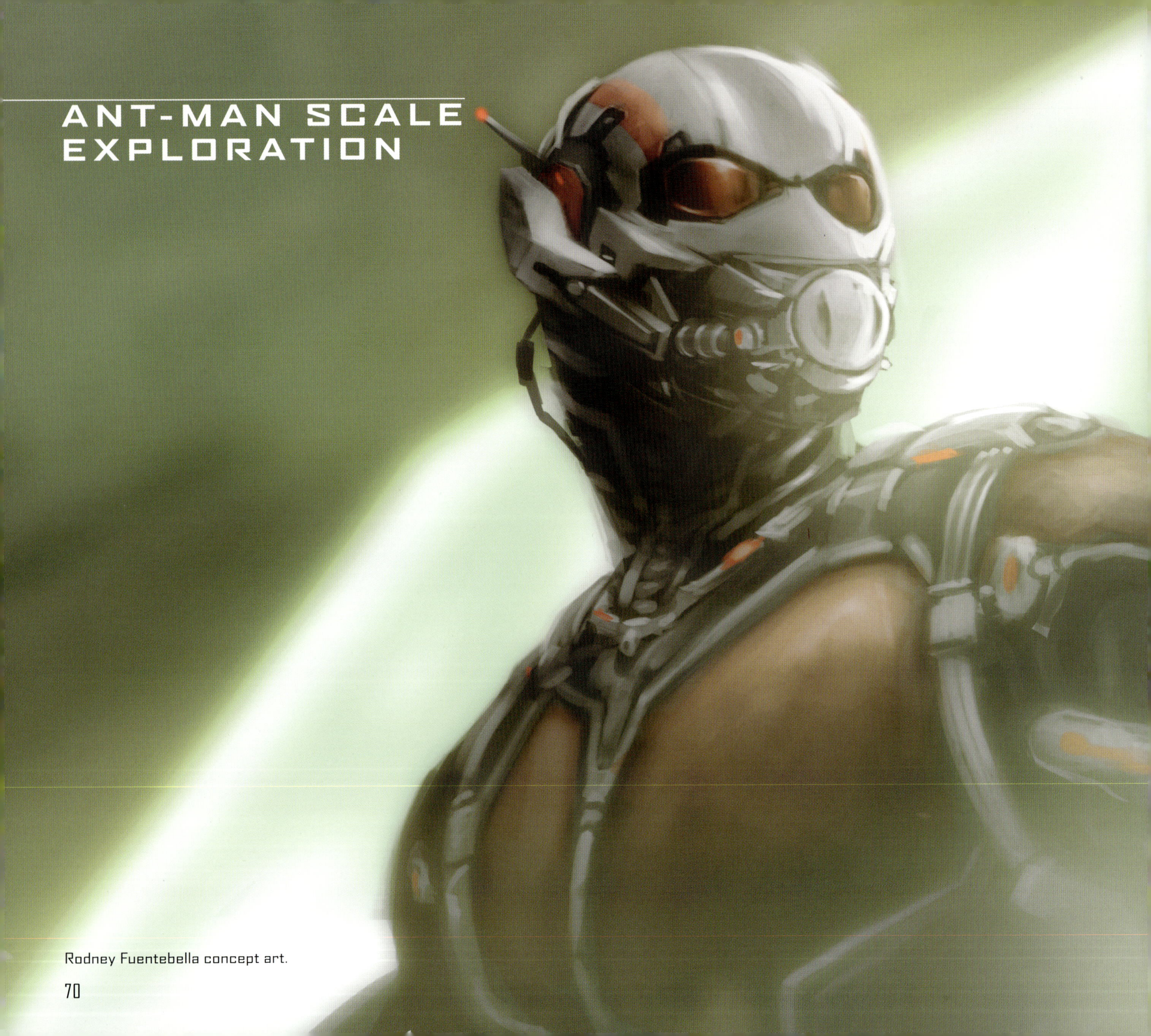

Rodney Fuentebella concept art.

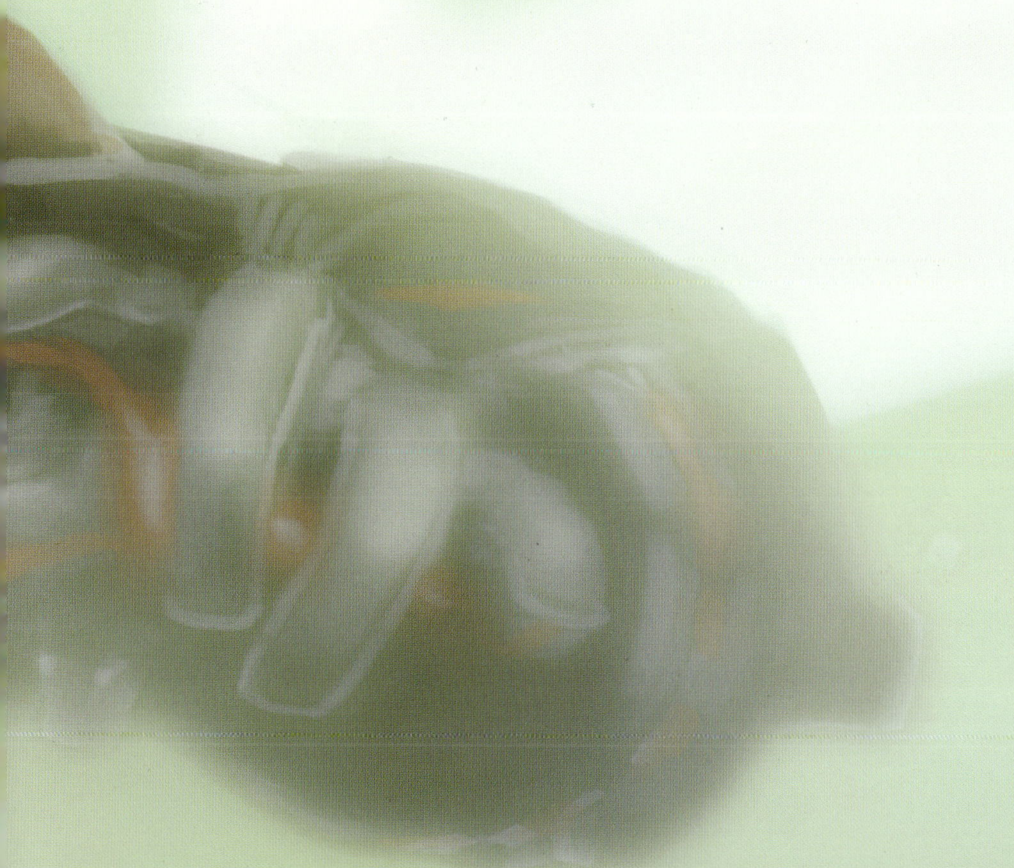

Early on, the Visual Development team explored various scenarios in which Ant-Man could use his powers, including escapades not seen in the script. What would a less-than-upright citizen such as Scott Lang do with the ability to shrink at will? Concept Artist Jackson Sze put himself in Scott's shoes. "Trying to think like a criminal, we explored different burglary and heist options: stealing jewelry, breaking into an ATM, using his powers to affect a lottery result, etc. The challenge was often to paint Ant-Man in an environment that was familiar, but at a scale that was foreign," Sze explains.

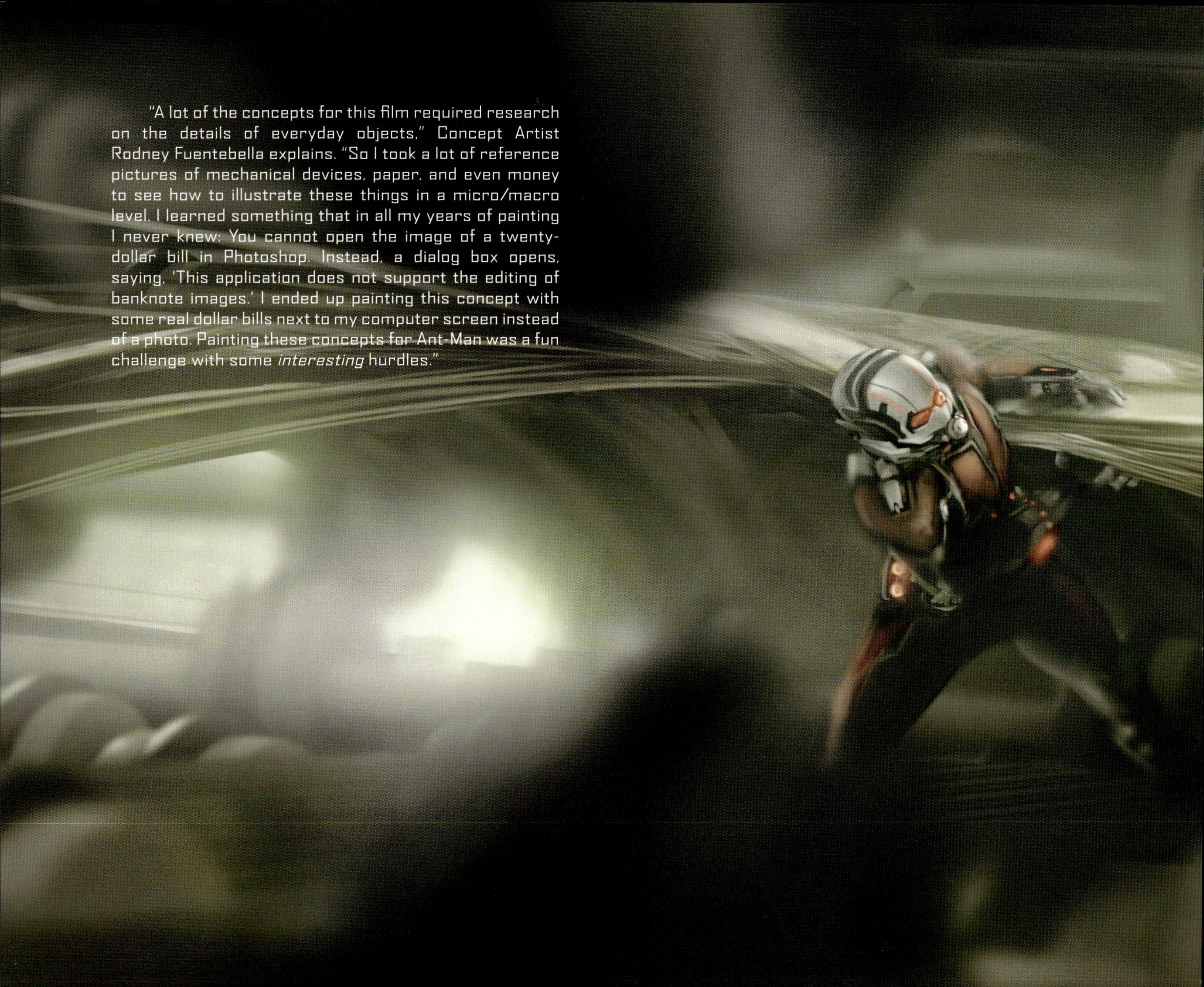

"A lot of the concepts for this film required research on the details of everyday objects," Concept Artist Rodney Fuentebella explains. "So I took a lot of reference pictures of mechanical devices, paper, and even money to see how to illustrate these things in a micro/macro level. I learned something that in all my years of painting I never knew: You cannot open the image of a twenty-dollar bill in Photoshop. Instead, a dialog box opens, saying, 'This application does not support the editing of banknote images.' I ended up painting this concept with some real dollar bills next to my computer screen instead of a photo. Painting these concepts for Ant-Man was a fun challenge with some *interesting* hurdles."

Rodney Fuentebella keyframe.

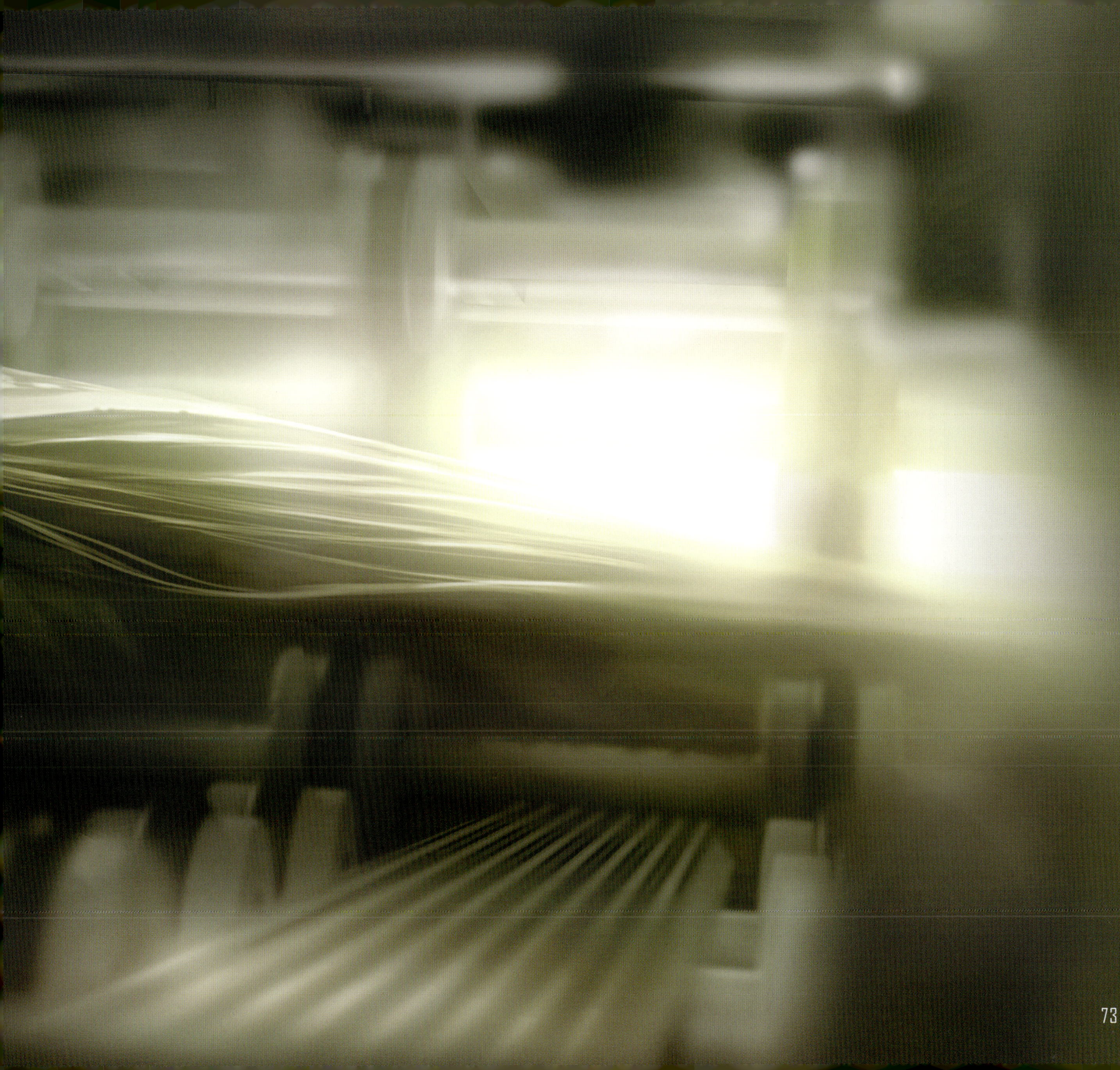

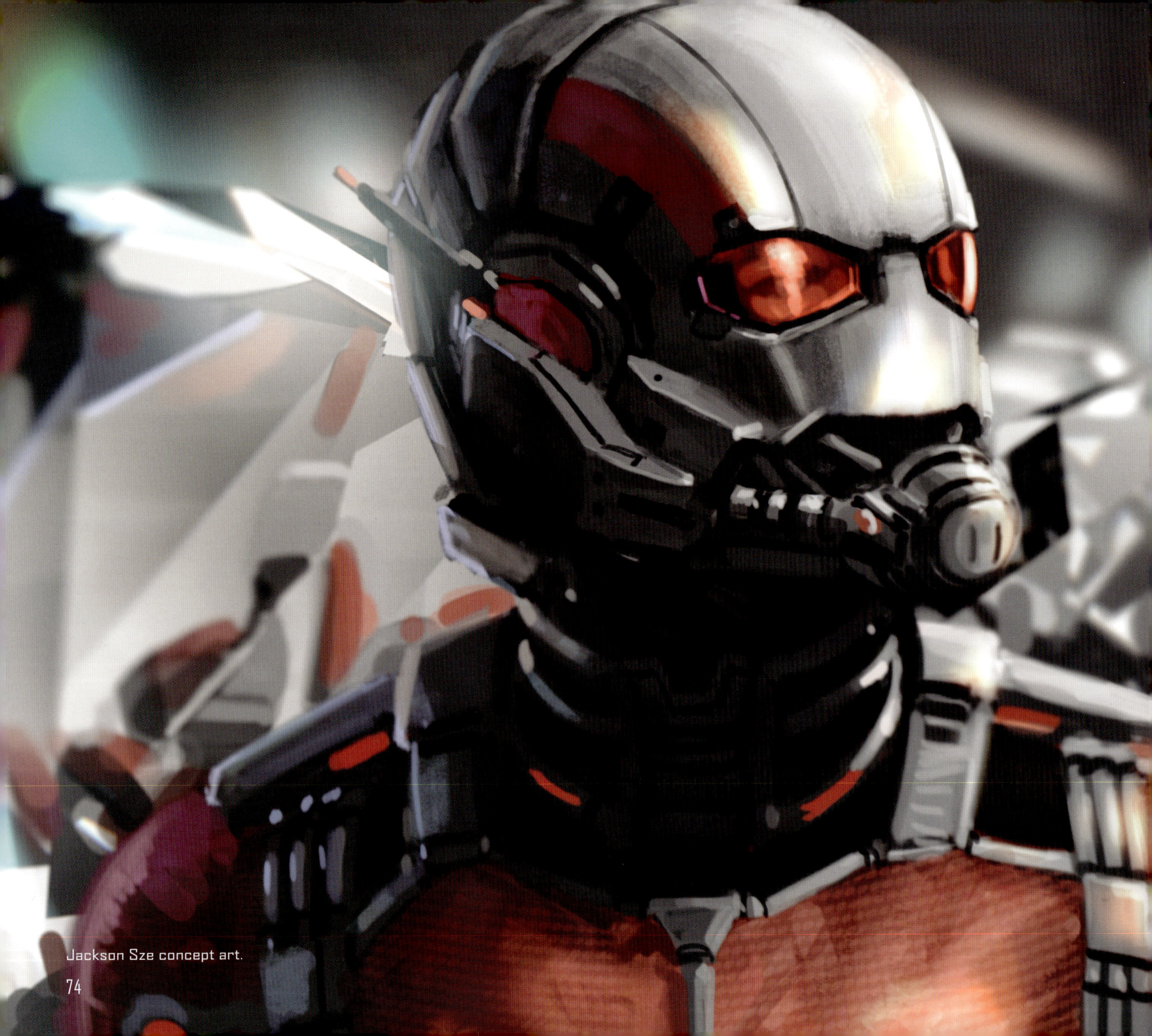

Jackson Sze concept art.

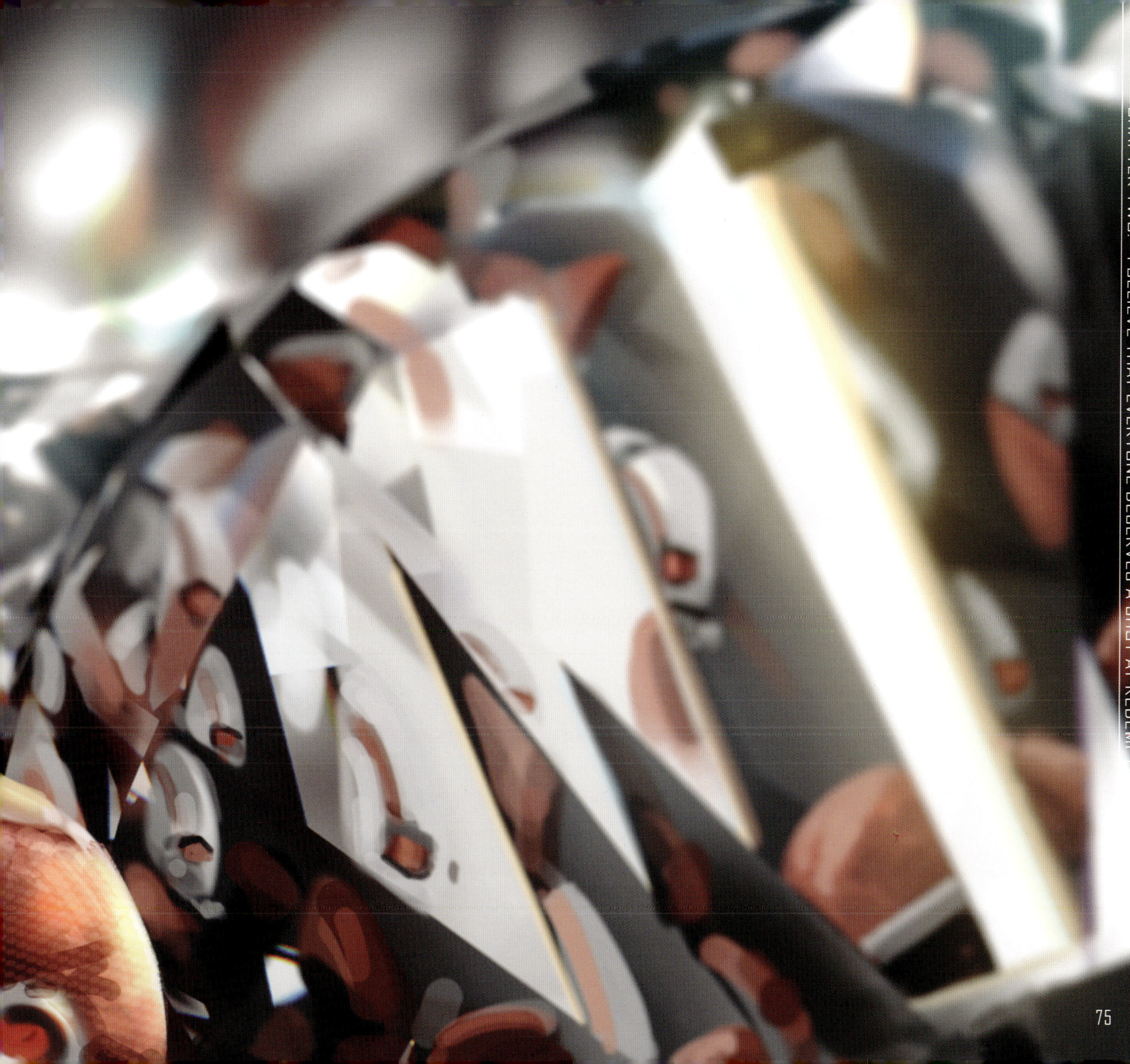

"The jewel-heist scenario was a good opportunity to showcase Ant-Man's reflections on the many facets of the surrounding diamonds," Sze recalls. "It was an homage to the iconic room-of-mirrors scene in Bruce Lee's *Enter the Dragon*. Again, the unique scale of Ant-Man provides infinite possibilities for rich visual storytelling."

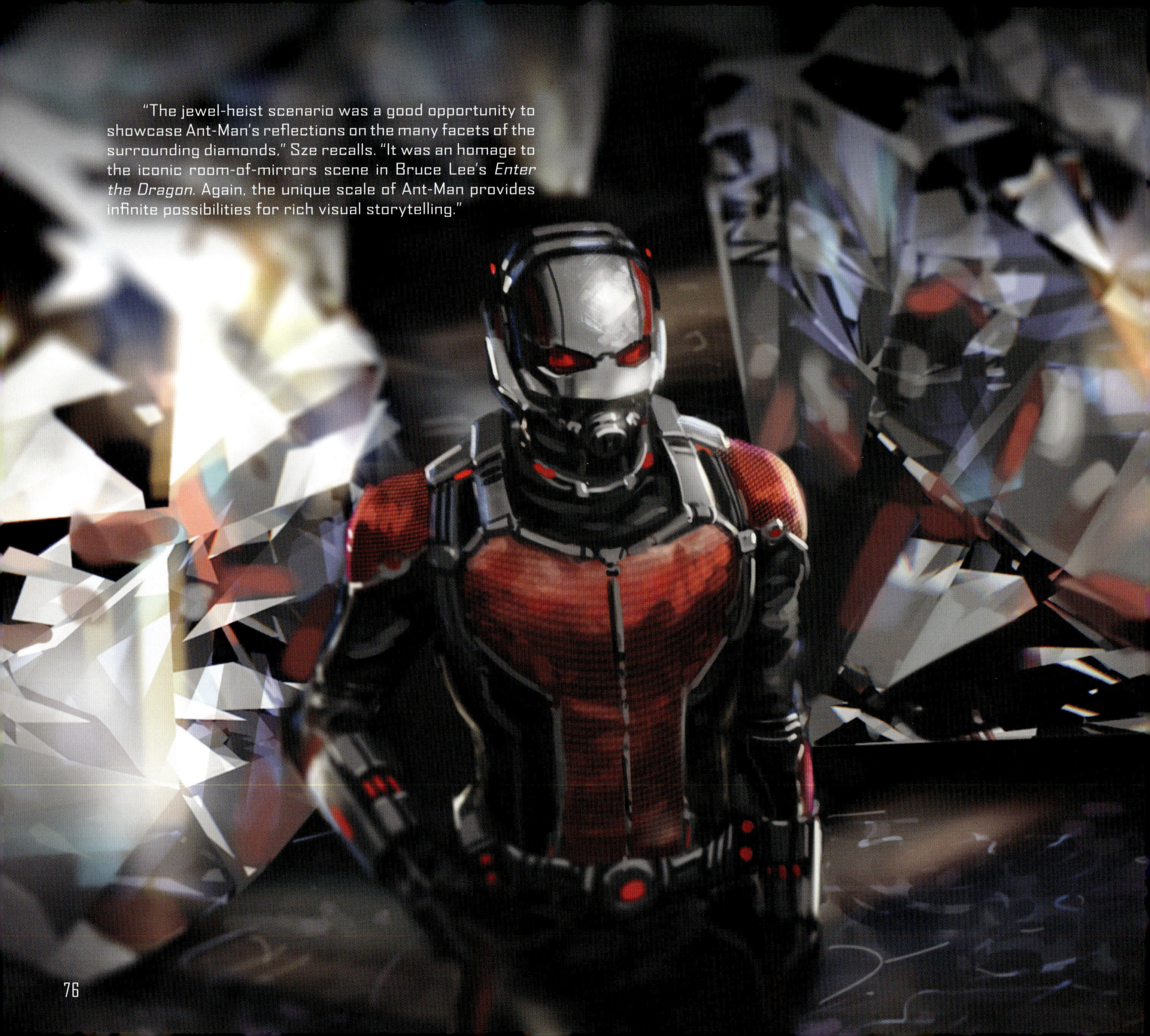

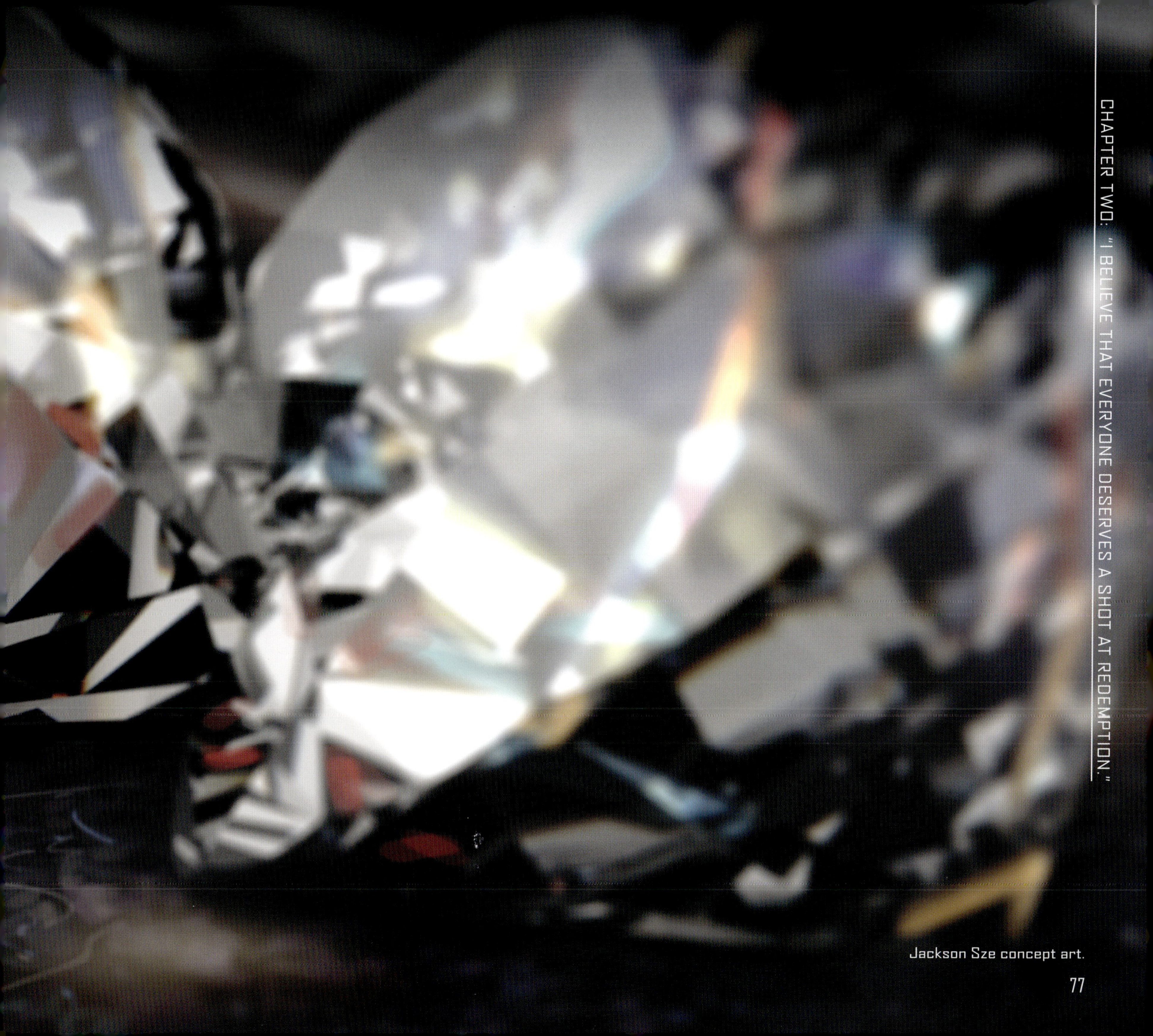

Jackson Sze concept art.

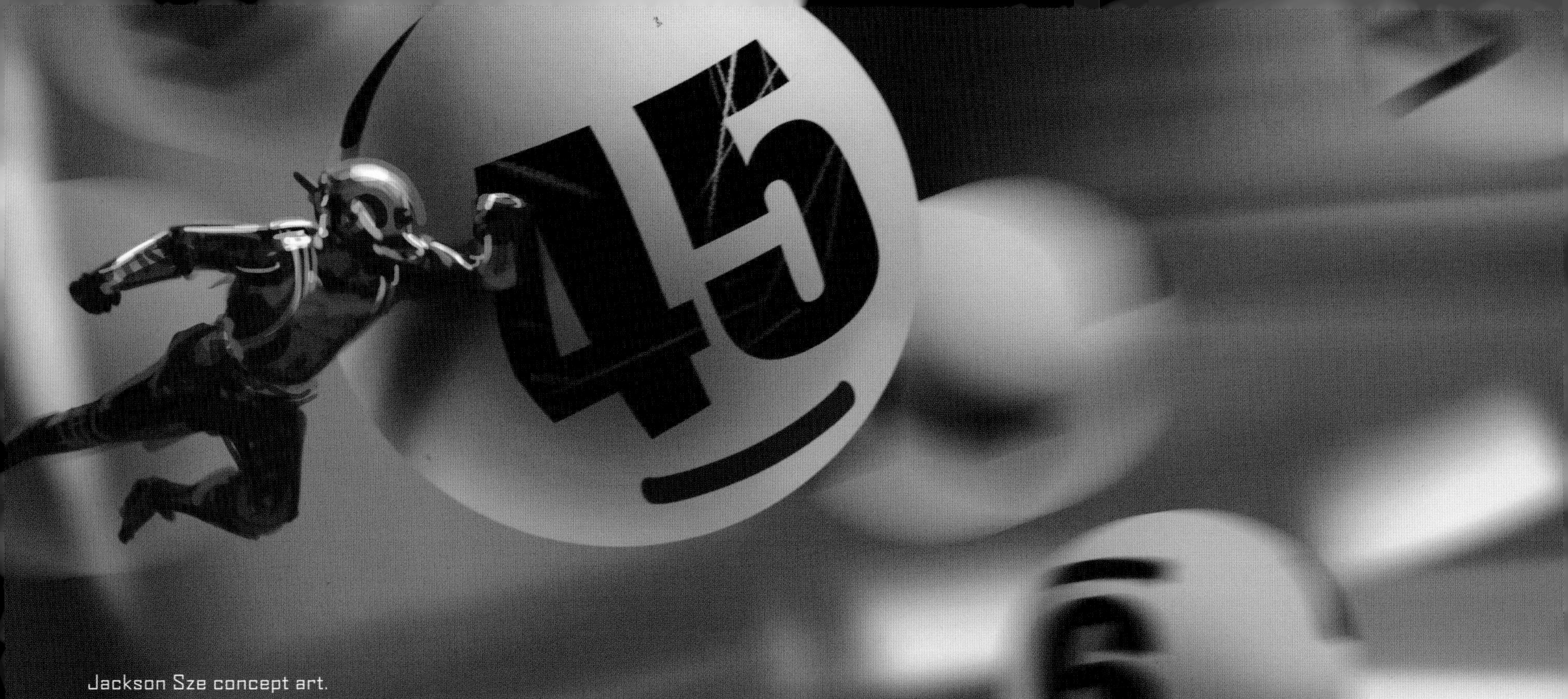

Jackson Sze concept art.

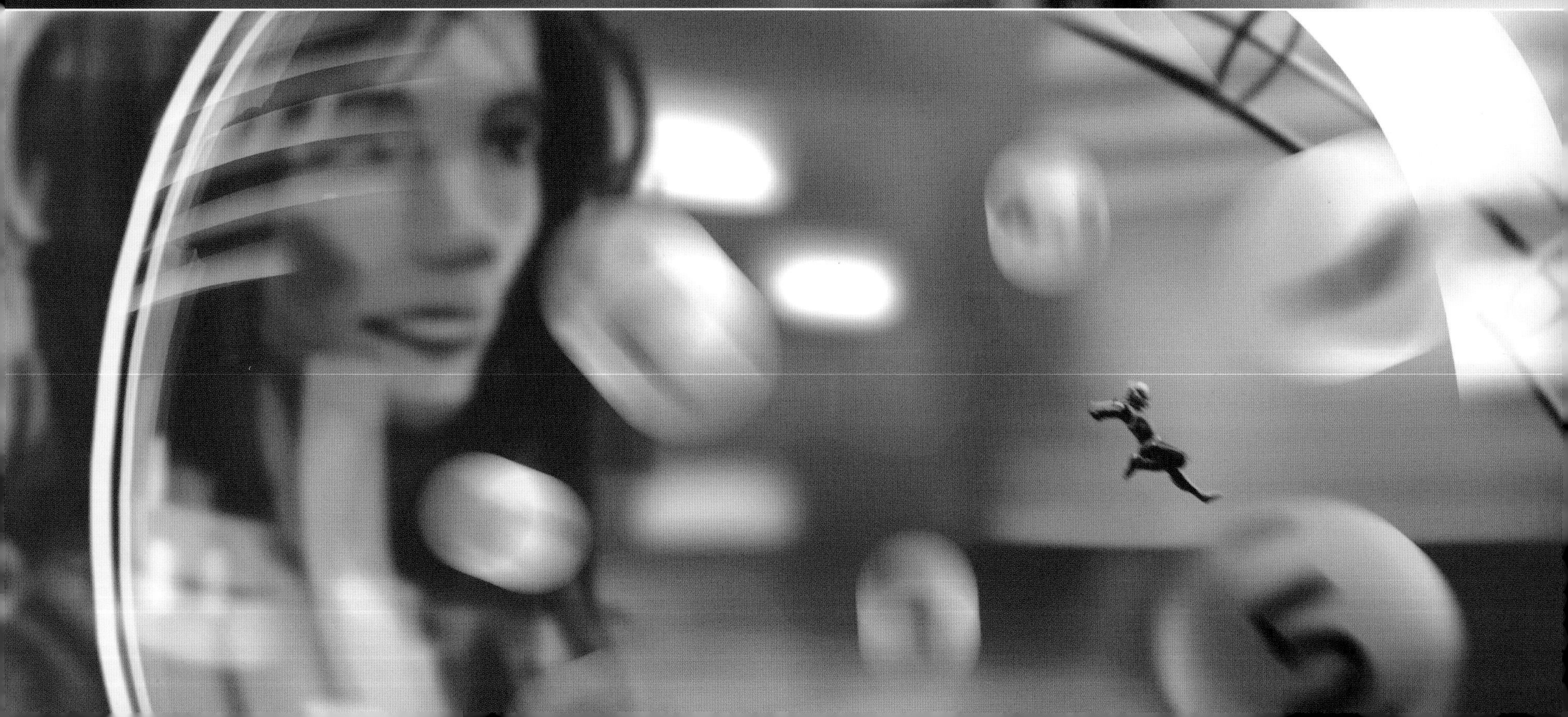

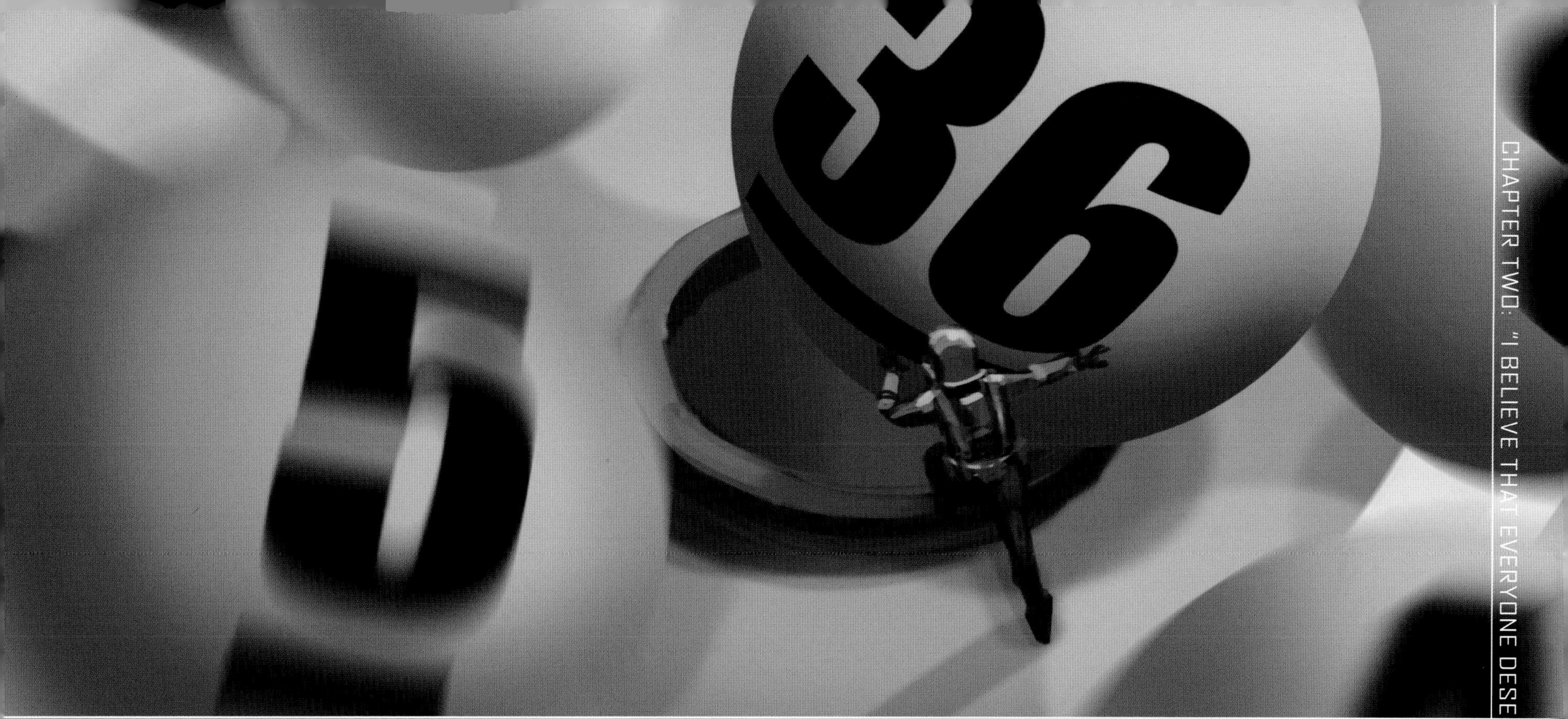

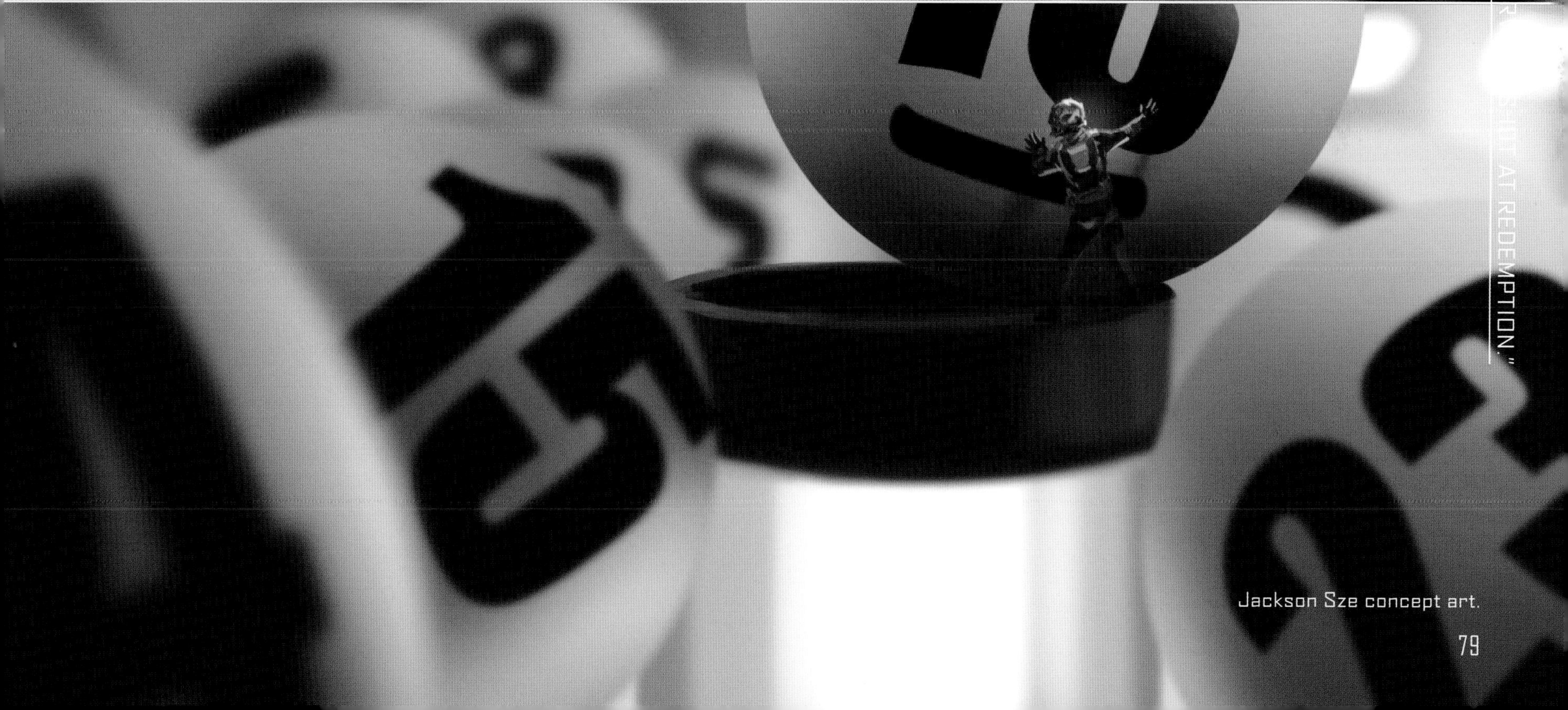

Jackson Sze concept art.

JAILBREAK!

STORYBOARDS BY JIM MAGDALENO

Scott's botched robbery of Hank Pym's house lands him back in the slammer. But this time, he isn't there for long. Storyboard Artist Jim Magdaleno worked with the filmmakers to conceive a tension-filled prison break using the Ant-Man suit. This would be the first time the ants, still controlled by Hank, have a chance to shine in the film. The sequence also serves as an introduction to Scott and Hank's mentor-mentee relationship.

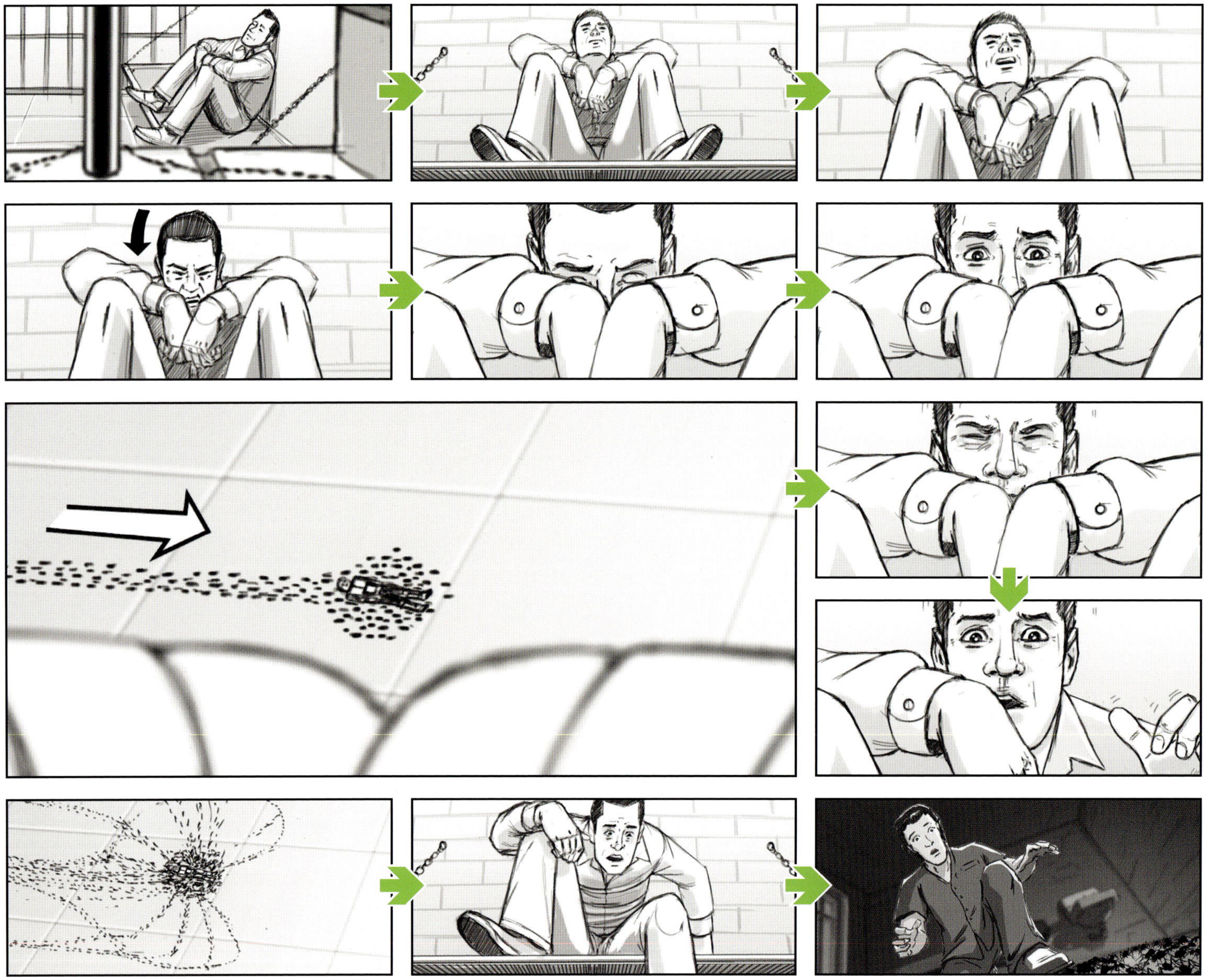

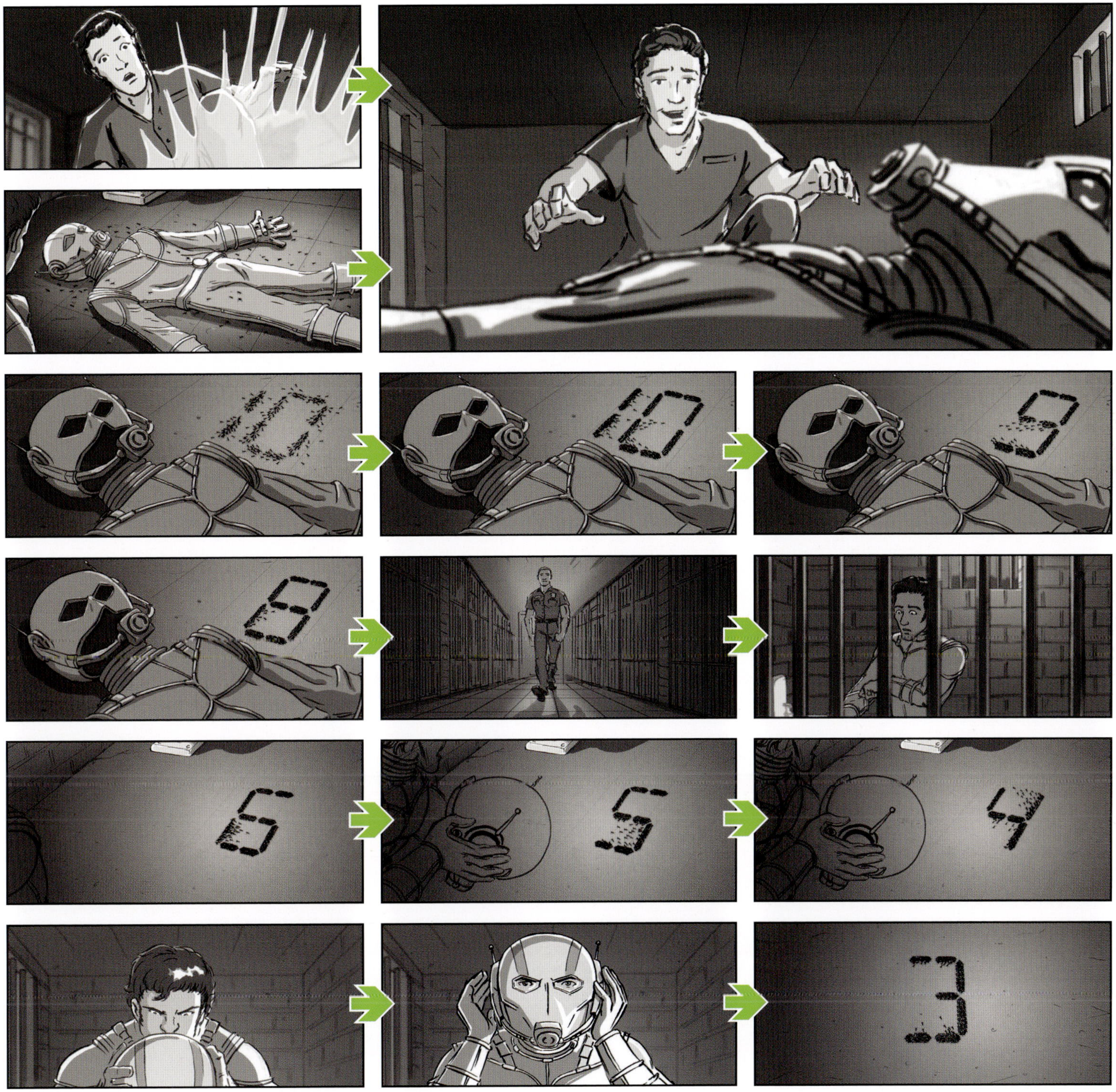

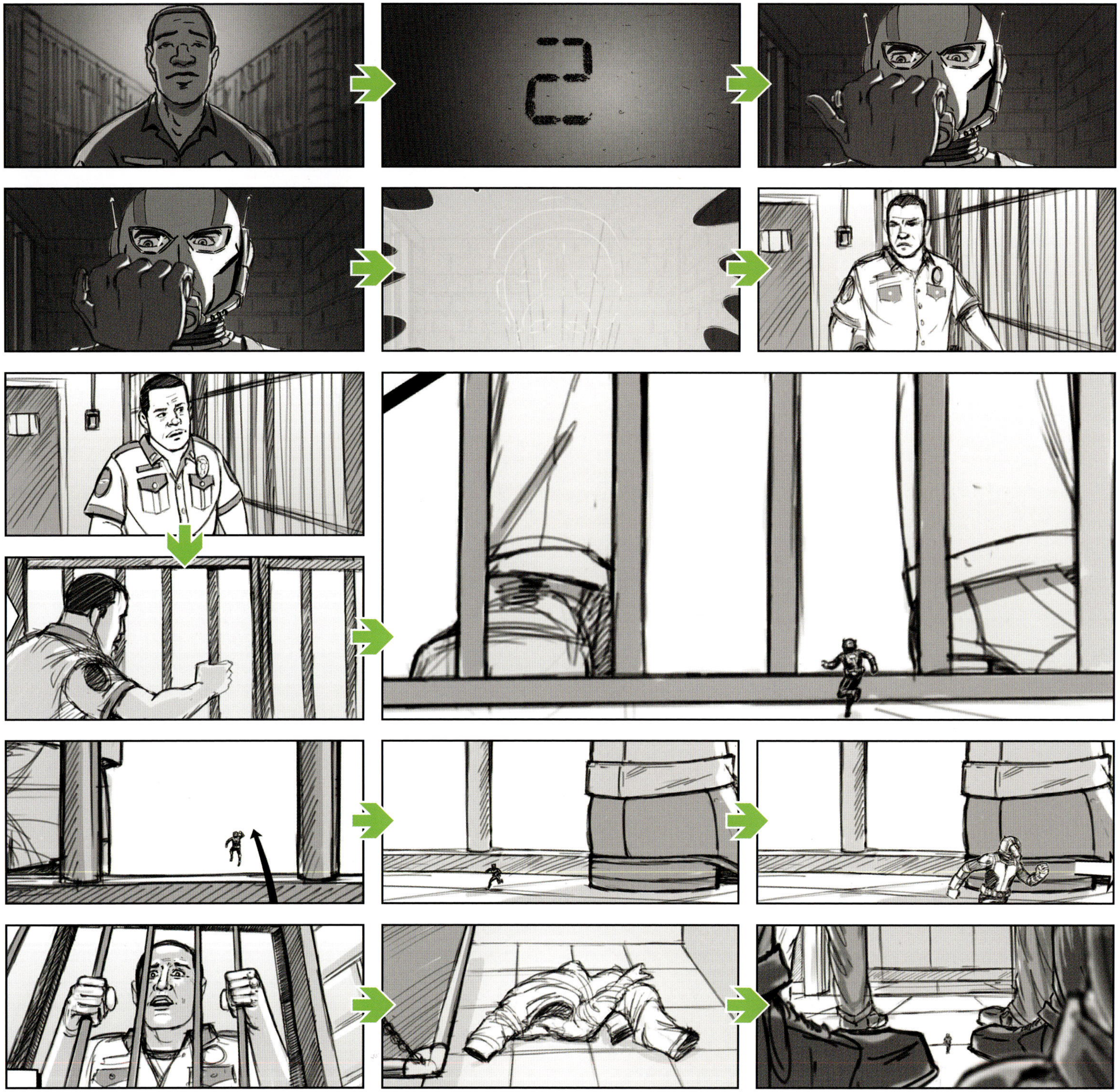

"The jailbreak sequence had been previously boarded by another artist so that Gale finds the empty cell and hits the alarm," Magdaleno says. "The cops run for the door, passing the Ant-Man-sized Scott as he escapes. When it was given to me, the scene had been rewritten so Scott runs out alone. So my job was to make this short sequence suspenseful as Gale walked to the cell and Scott got into the suit. But then Peyton Reed wanted to add some obstacles, so he came up with the cockroach and the rat. He gave me creative license on how that would happen. That's when work gets fun!"

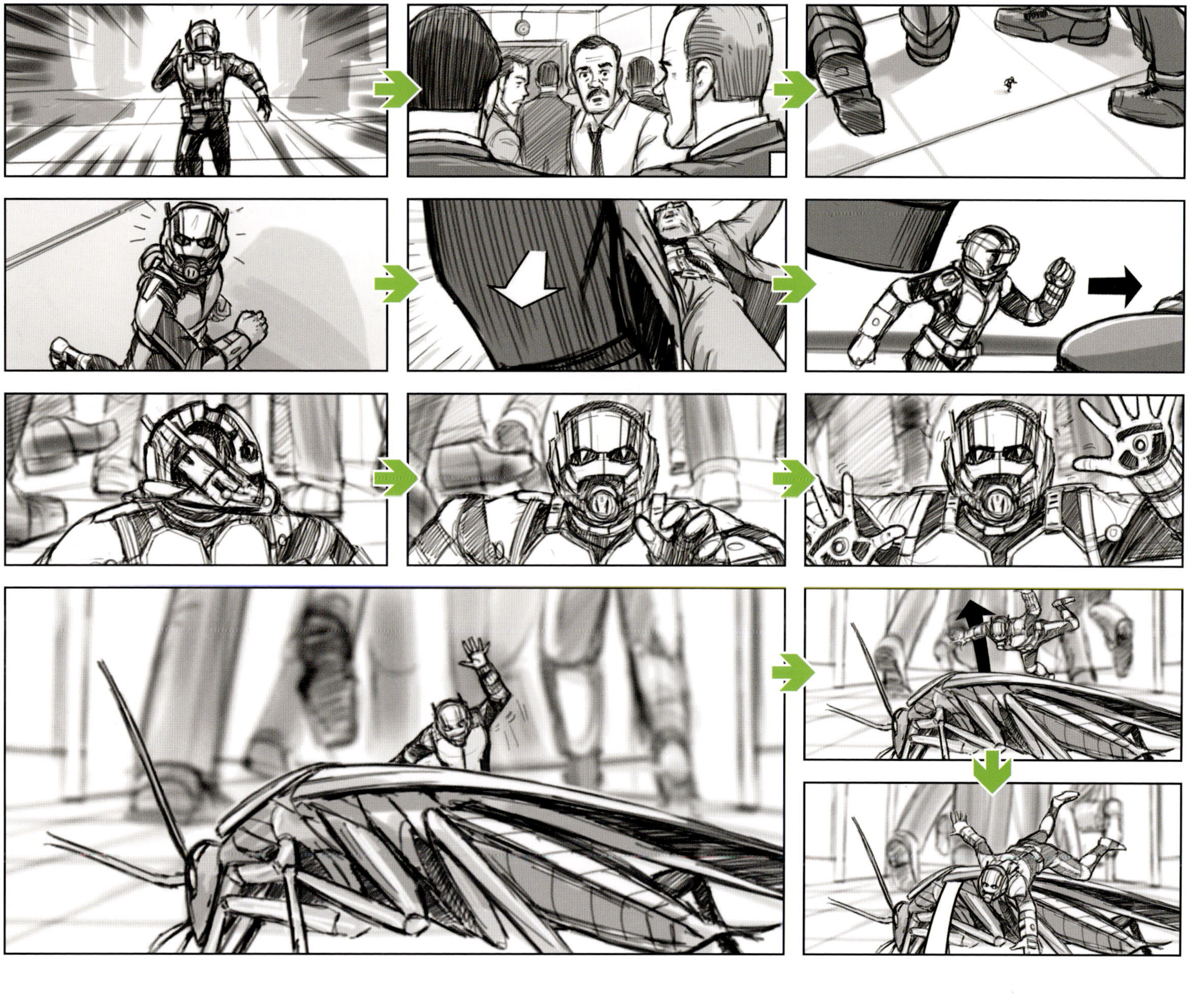

"This last bit was first given to me as notes," Magdaleno continues. "Peyton told me he wanted Scott to go through the police station, and encounter a cockroach and a rat. I enjoyed putting myself in Scott's perspective and trying to figure out how he would use the Ant-Man suit.

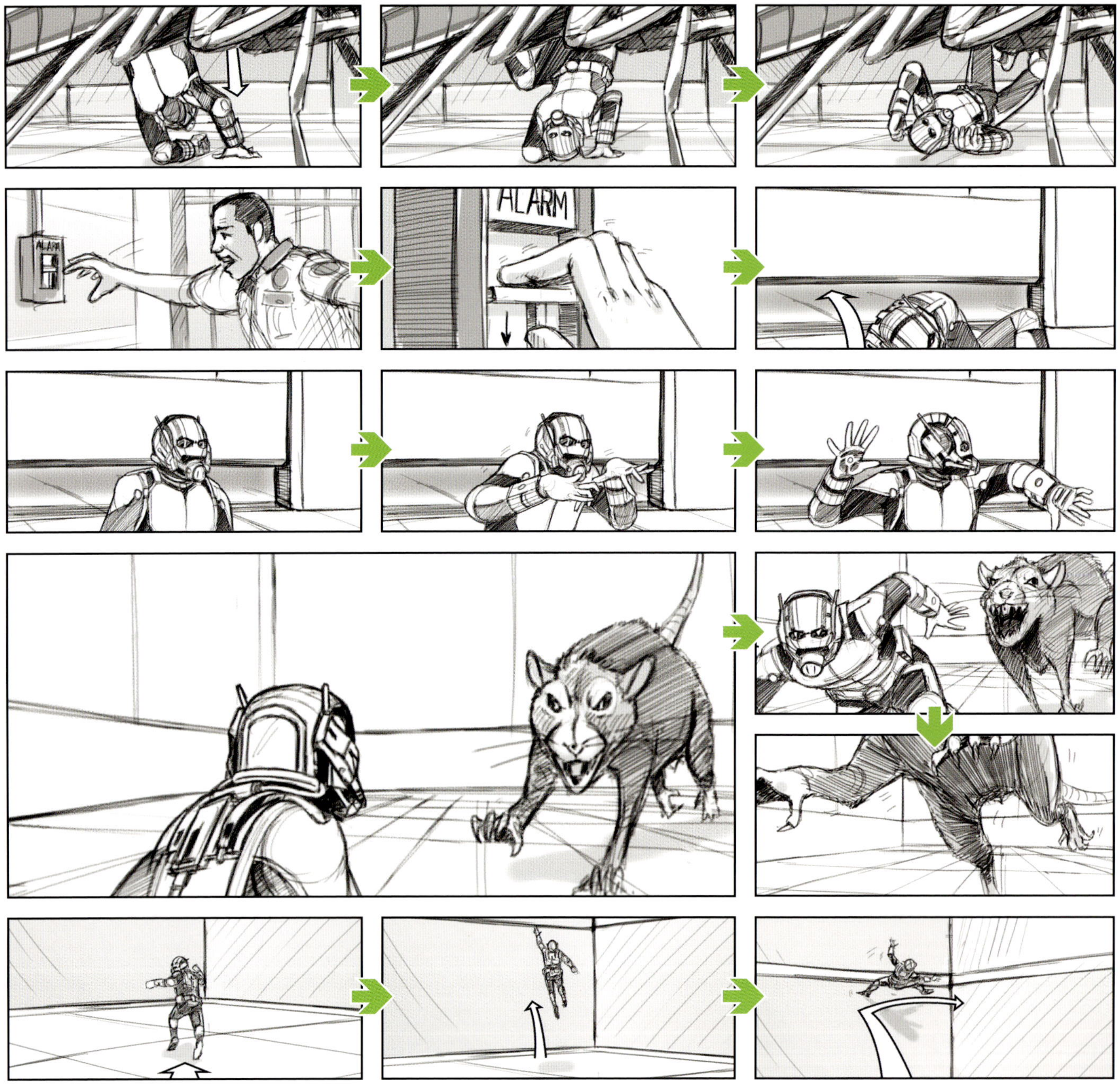

Who wouldn't?! The hardest part of this movie was trying to keep the scale of the Ant-Man suit in relation to the real world. How big is he compared to a cockroach and a rat?"

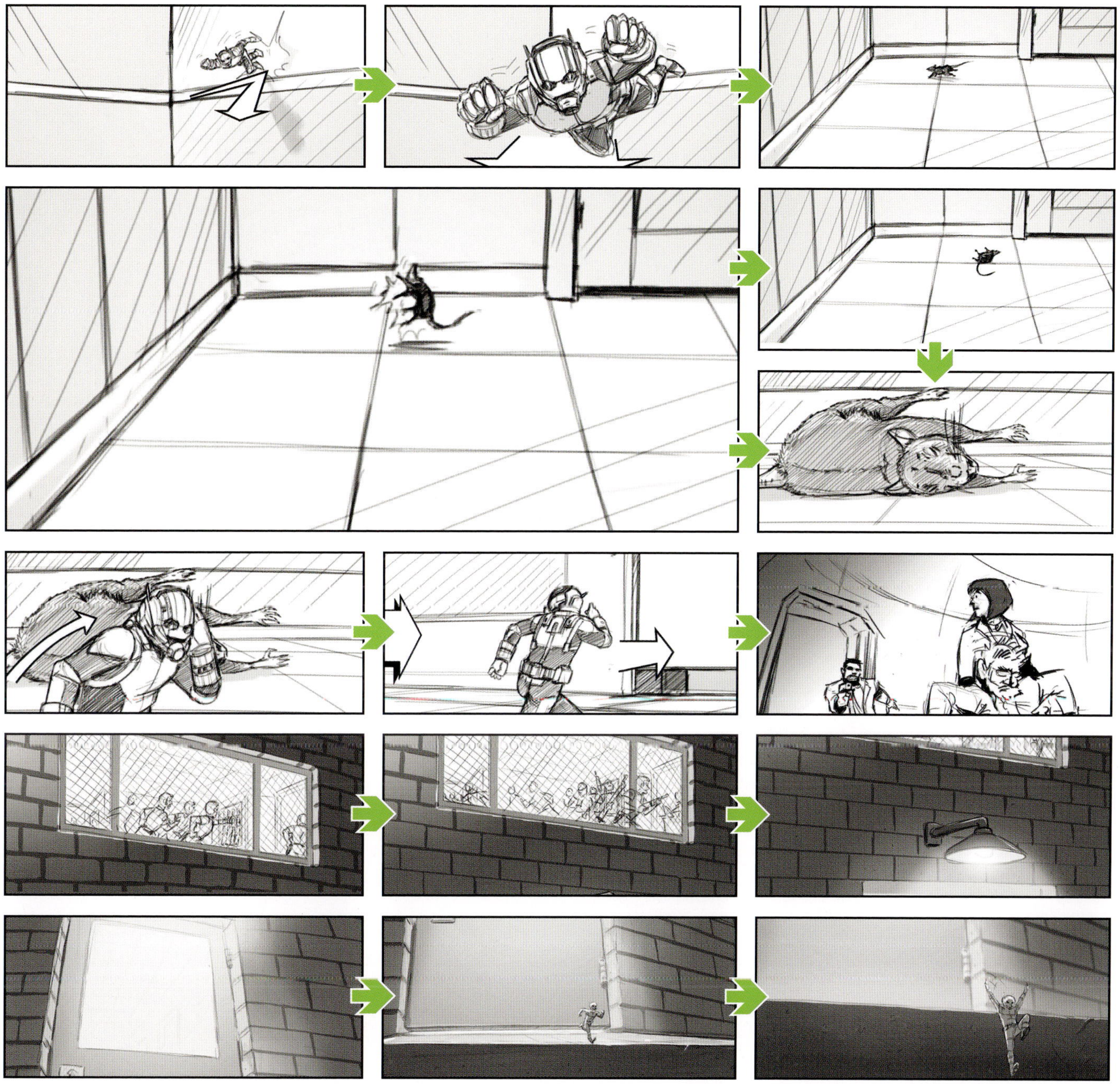

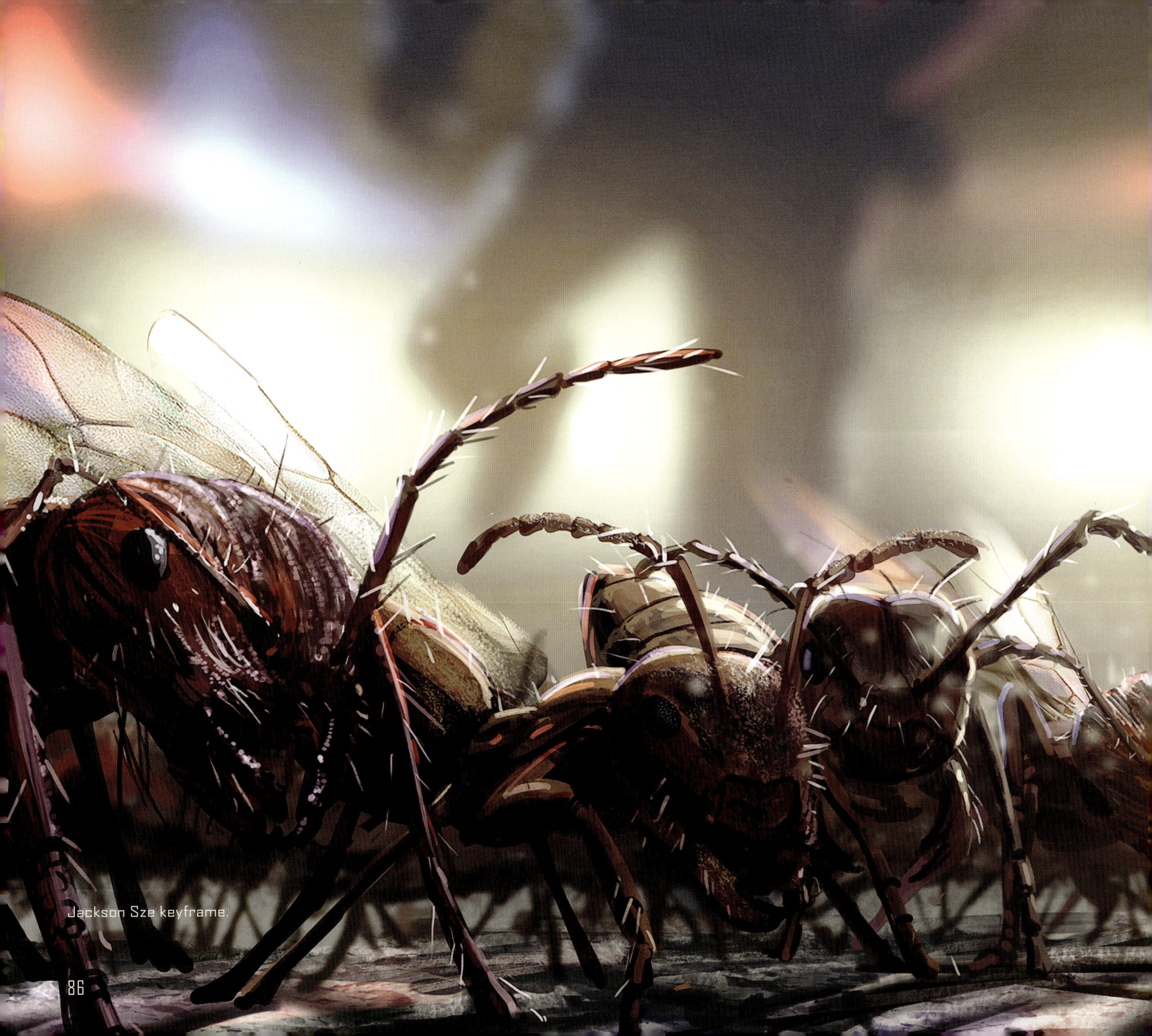

Jackson Sze keyframe.

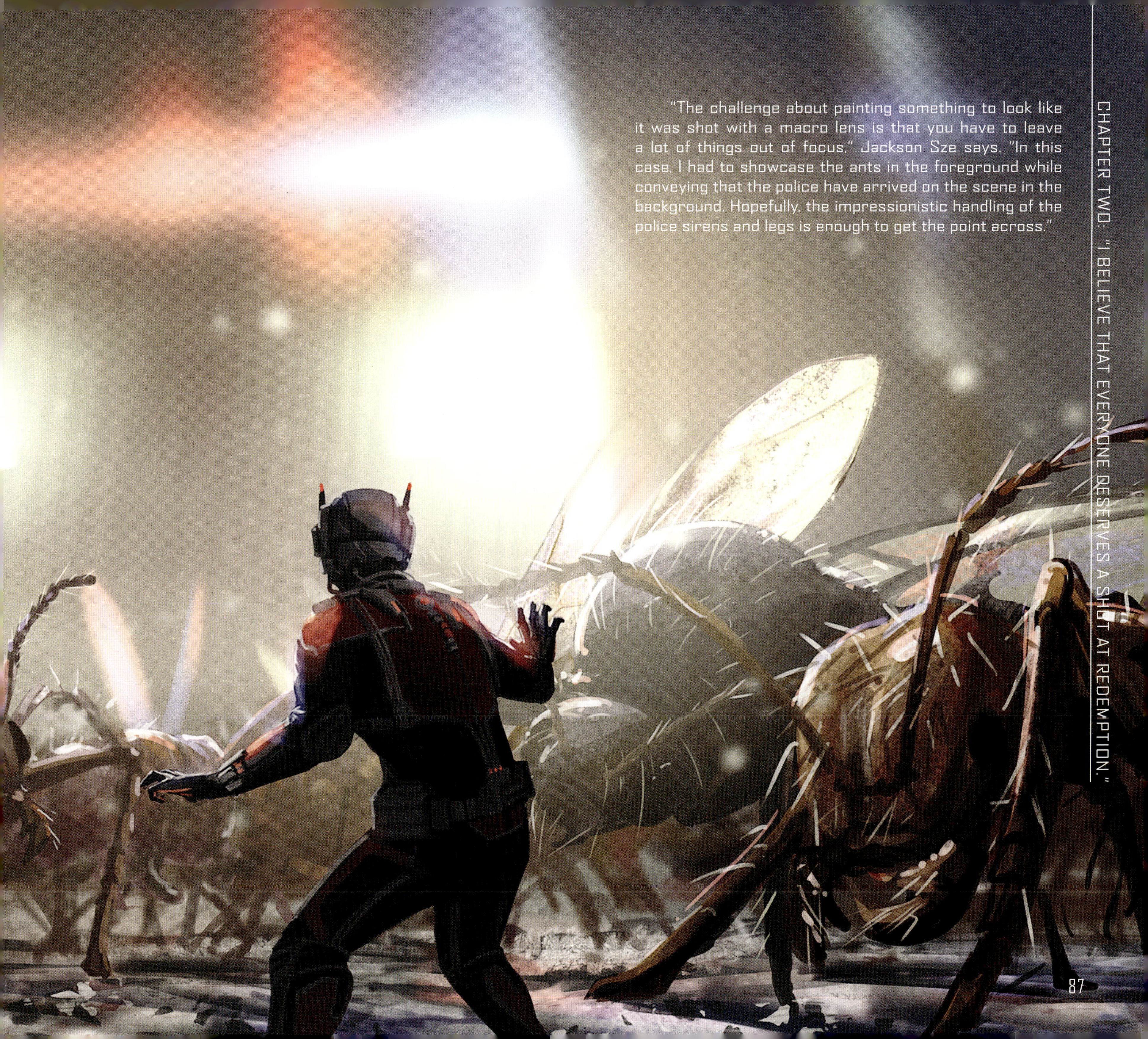

"The challenge about painting something to look like it was shot with a macro lens is that you have to leave a lot of things out of focus," Jackson Sze says. "In this case, I had to showcase the ants in the foreground while conveying that the police have arrived on the scene in the background. Hopefully, the impressionistic handling of the police sirens and legs is enough to get the point across."

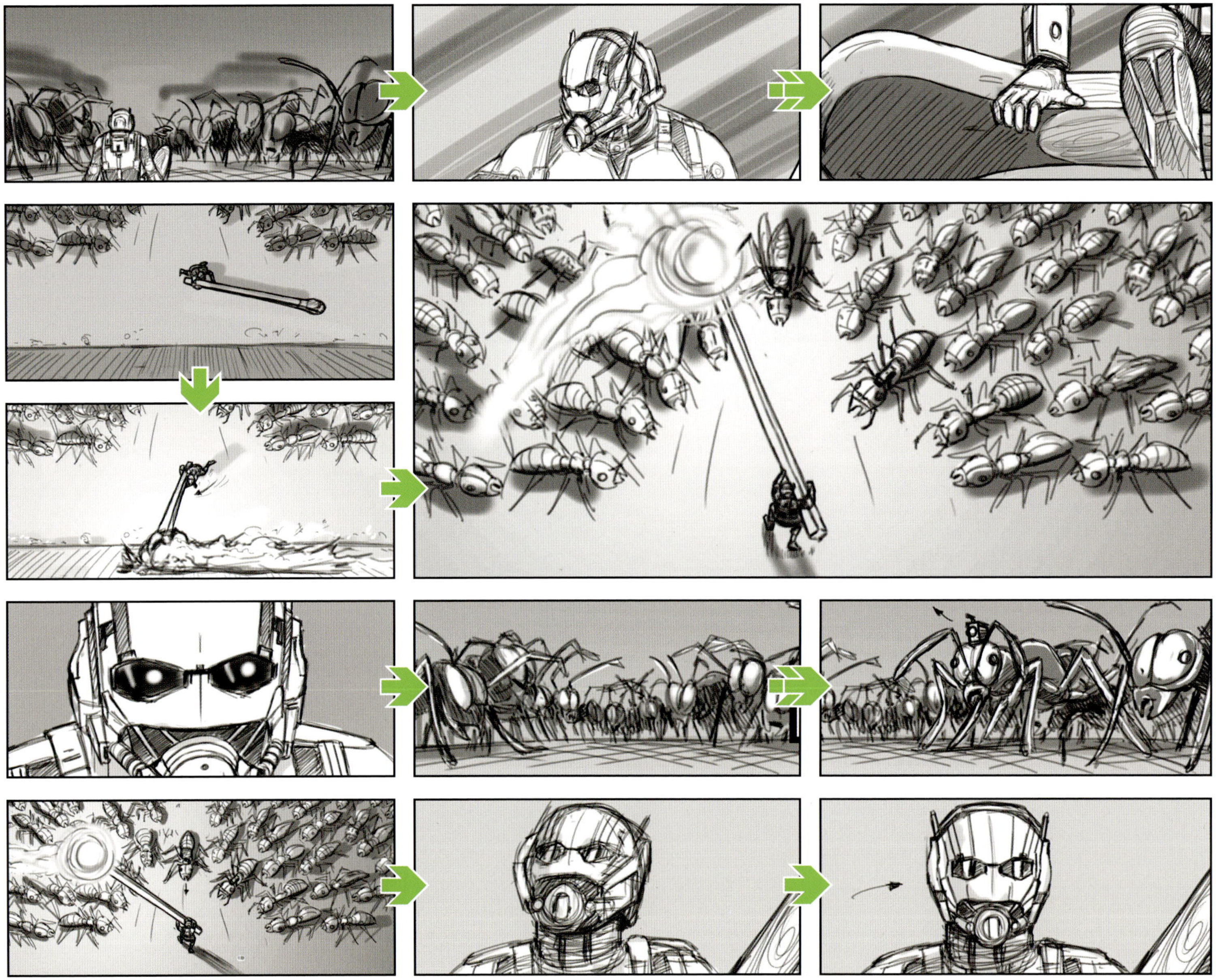

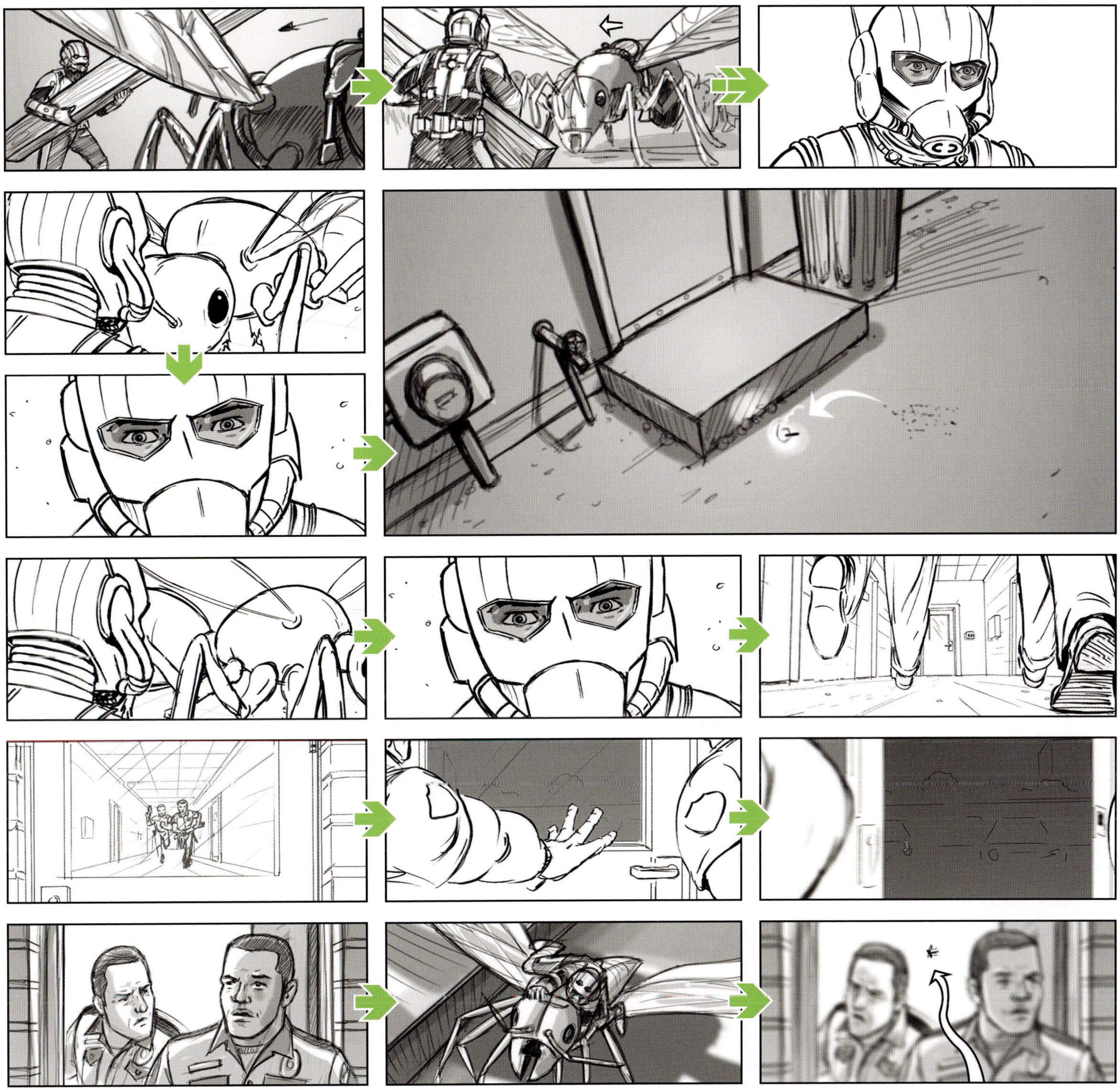

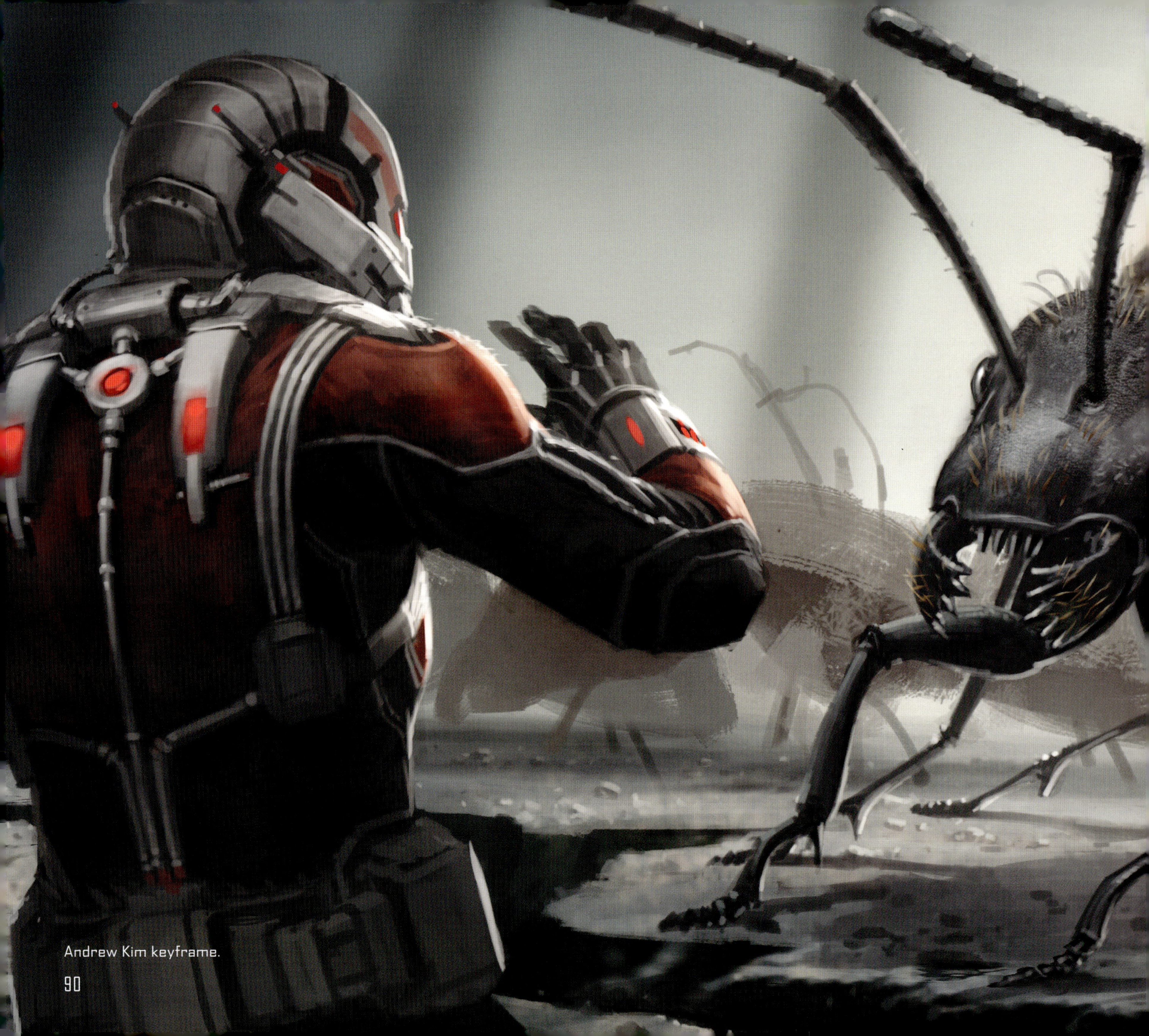

Andrew Kim keyframe.

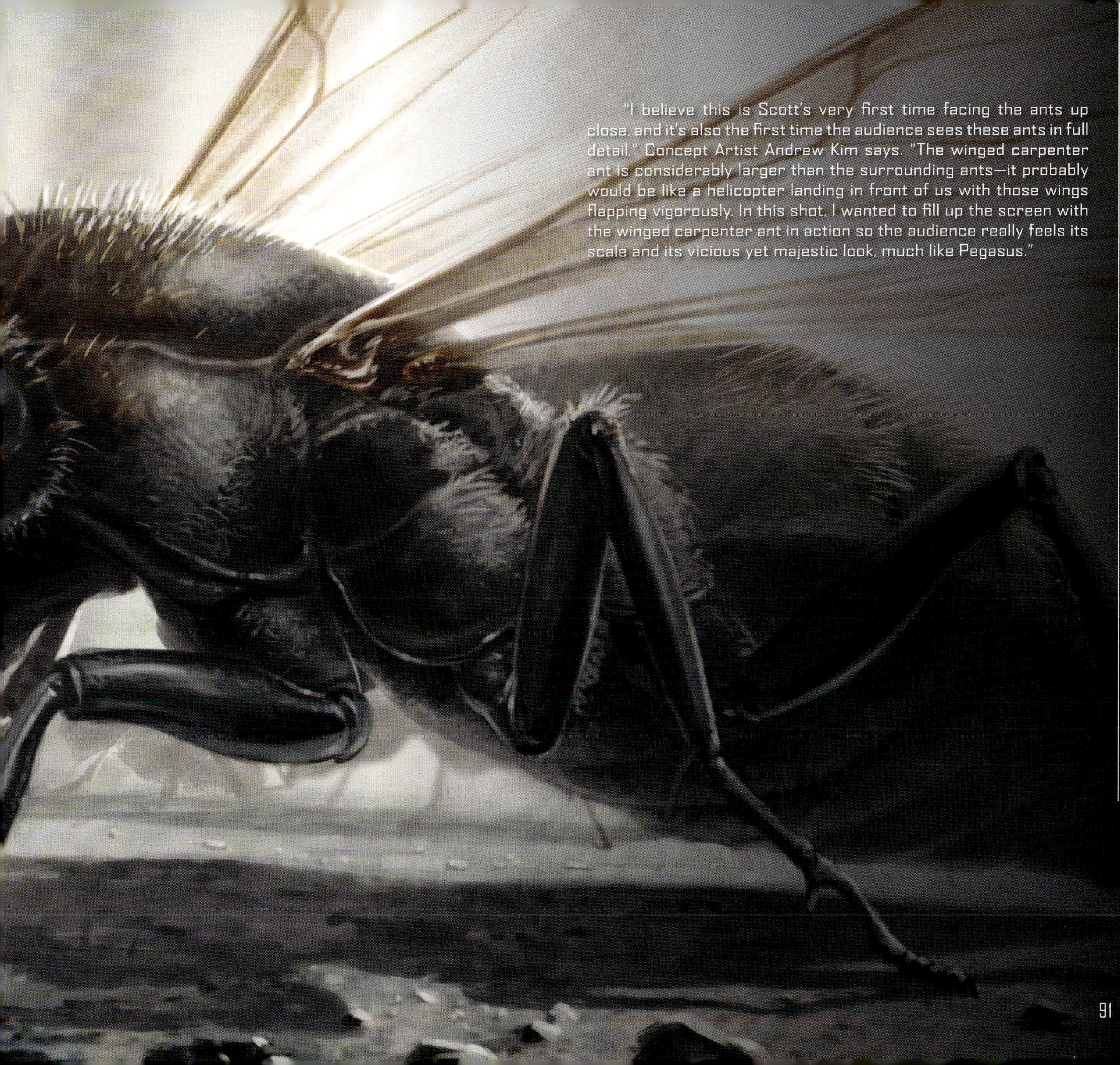

"I believe this is Scott's very first time facing the ants up close, and it's also the first time the audience sees these ants in full detail," Concept Artist Andrew Kim says. "The winged carpenter ant is considerably larger than the surrounding ants—it probably would be like a helicopter landing in front of us with those wings flapping vigorously. In this shot, I wanted to fill up the screen with the winged carpenter ant in action so the audience really feels its scale and its vicious yet majestic look, much like Pegasus."

With intensifying reservations but limited options, Scott decides to listen to Hank's voice inside his helmet. He mounts the winged carpenter ant's thorax and takes to the skies. "In this shot, now that the audience has come face-to-face with the flying carpenter ant and Scott together, it was time to show how Scott actually rides the ant," Kim says. "I explored different ways of how Scott would sit on top of the ant while maintaining the correct scale between the ant and Scott. Just take a look at the size comparison between Scott's head and the ant's head—it would be crazy to take a ride on that creature! Seriously..."

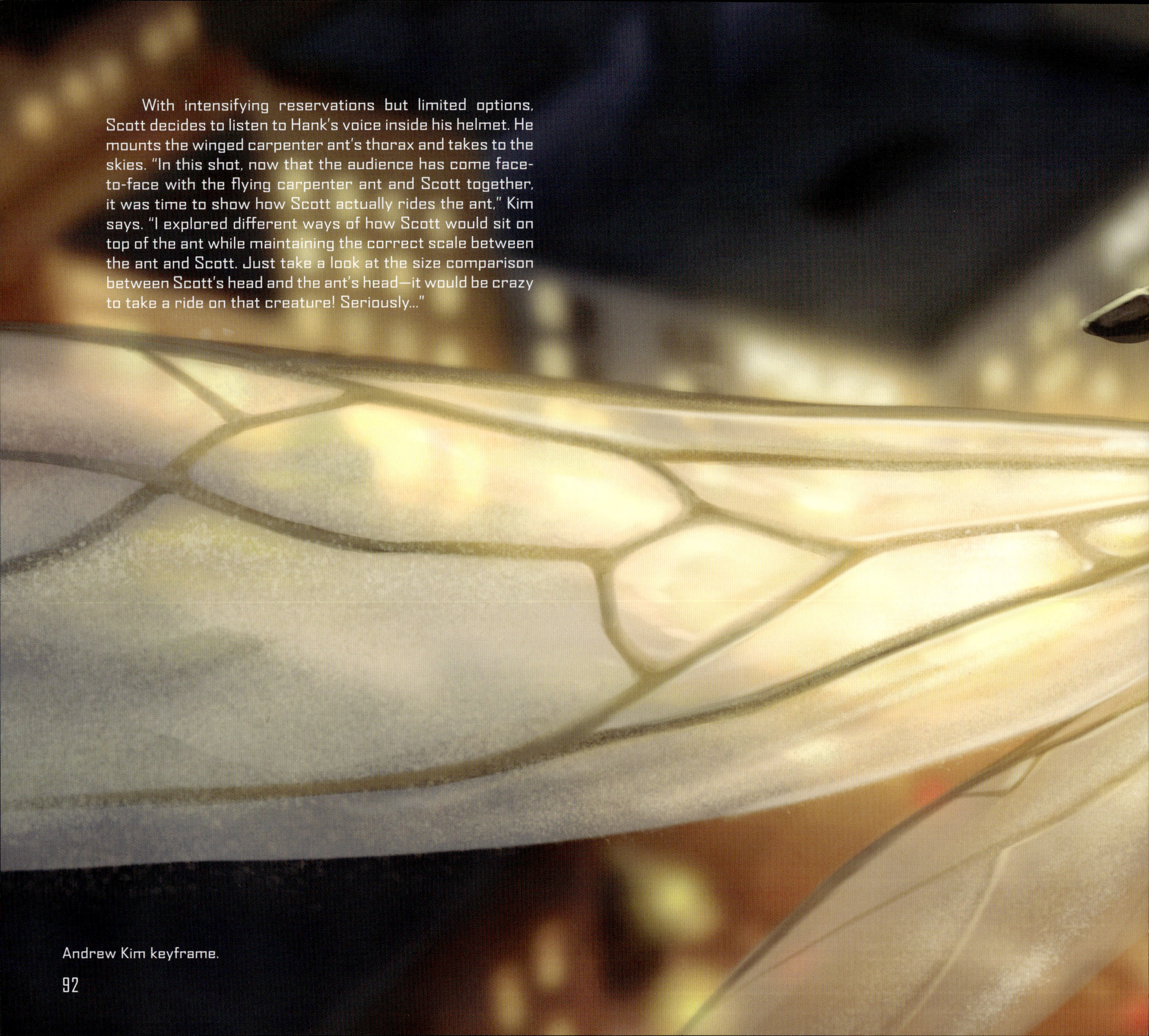

Andrew Kim keyframe.

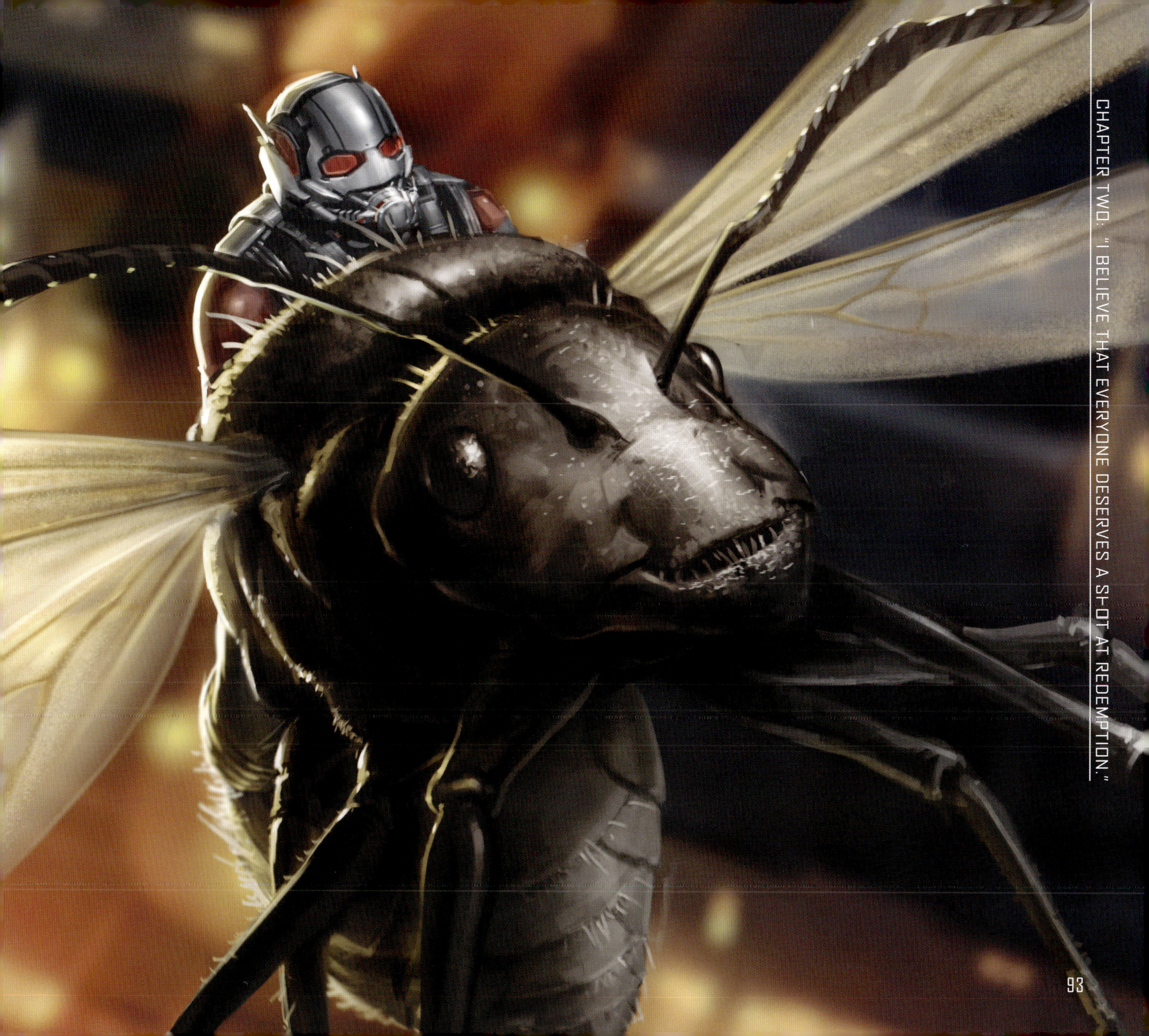

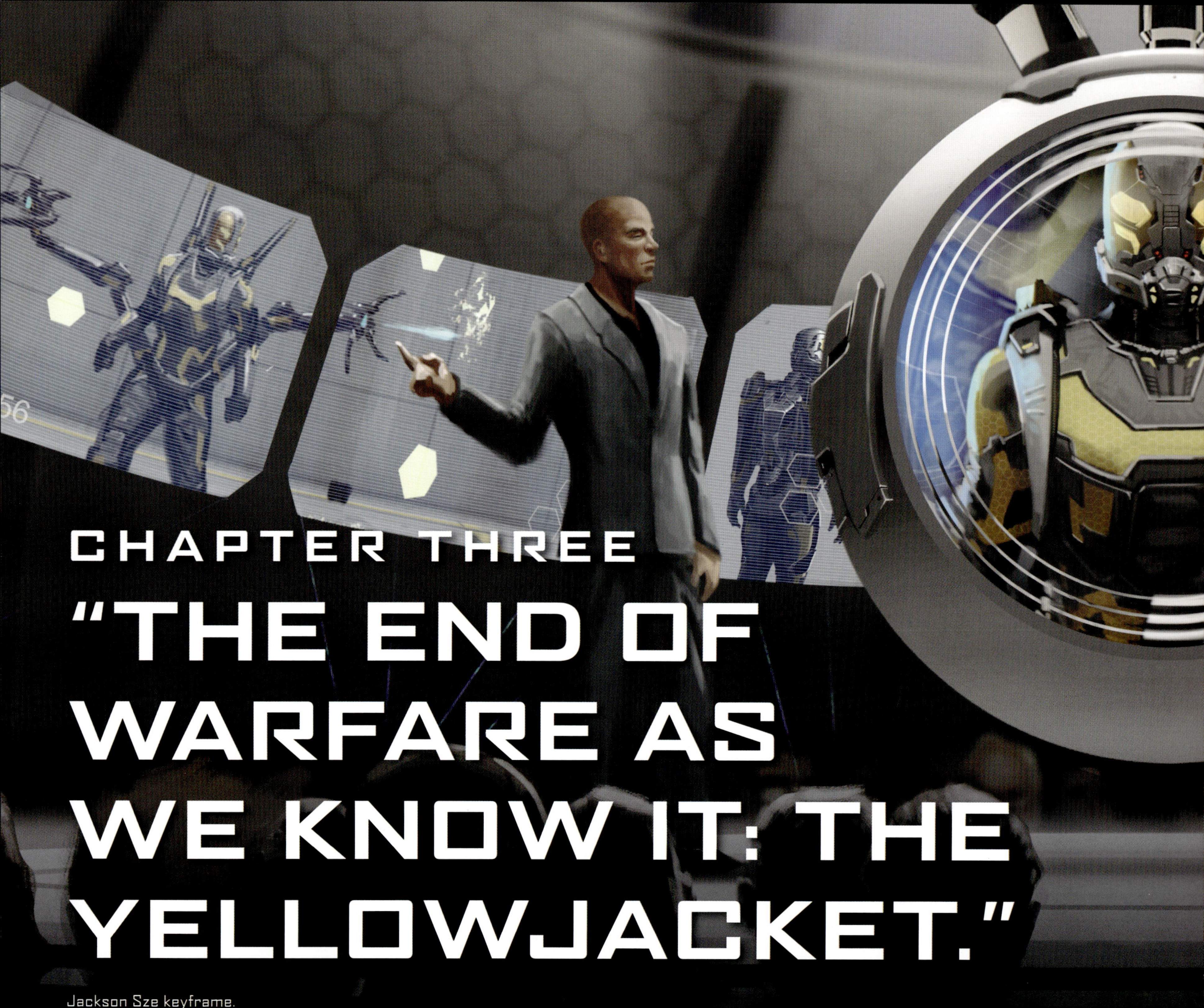

CHAPTER THREE

"THE END OF WARFARE AS WE KNOW IT: THE YELLOWJACKET."

Jackson Sze keyframe.

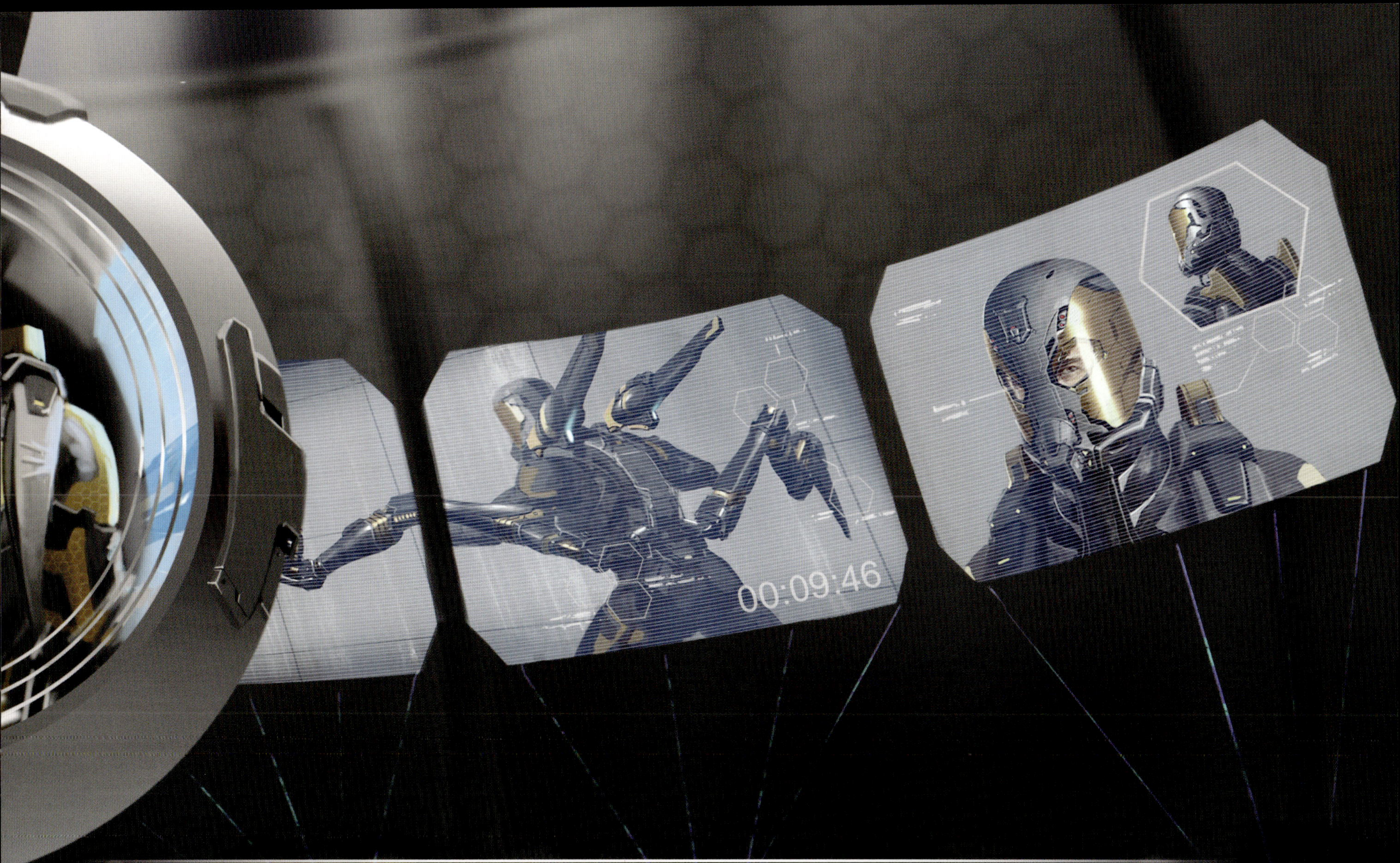

Keenly aware of the history of corporations like Stark Enterprises, Hank Pym establishes PymTech as a means to embrace science in a safe and contained environment—and prevent outside forces, such as S.H.I.E.L.D., from coopting his discoveries to develop advanced weaponry. As Hank grows older, he passes the company to his mentee, Darren Cross, a bright young pupil in whom he sees much of himself. But Cross's drive to uncover the secrets behind the Ant-Man suit and the creation of Pym Particles leads him down a dangerous path: He transforms PymTech into CrossTech, stripping away Hank's safeguards with the intent to use science as a destructive force.

The Yellowjacket is Cross's first innovation. "Cross has tried to replicate Pym's technology, but he's only replicated part of it, and he intends to sell it to the highest bidder—any sort of foreign country that needs an army," Director Peyton Reed explains. "The suit he's created is sort of a malevolent version of the Ant-Man suit called Yellowjacket."

Hank refuses to sit idly by. "There's a bit of a different spin on this because he's in business with Hank Pym, and Hank Pym is realizing he's gone into business with the wrong person," Executive Producer Kevin Feige adds. "Hank needs somebody to help him pull this business down and sabotage Pym's own business, because he's sort of lost control of it."

PYMTECH

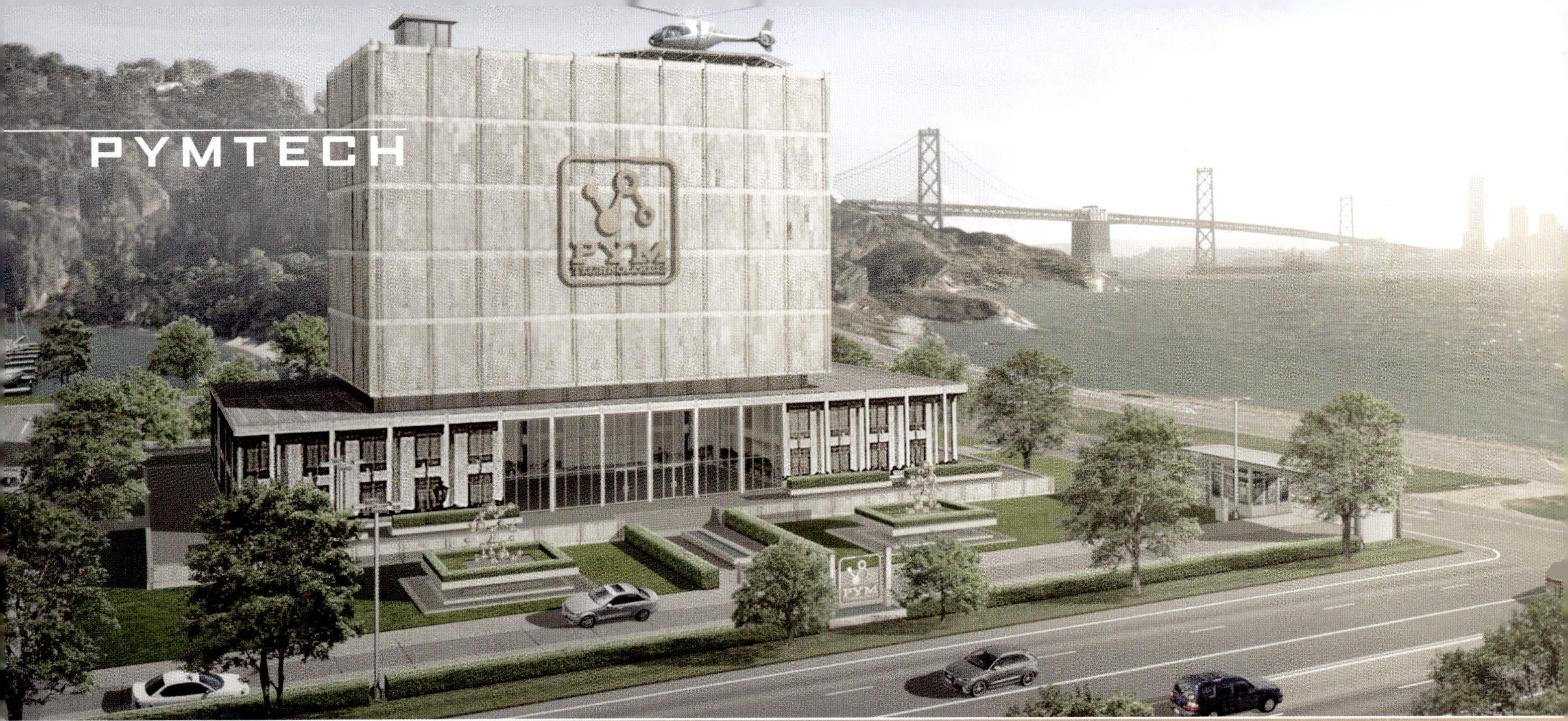

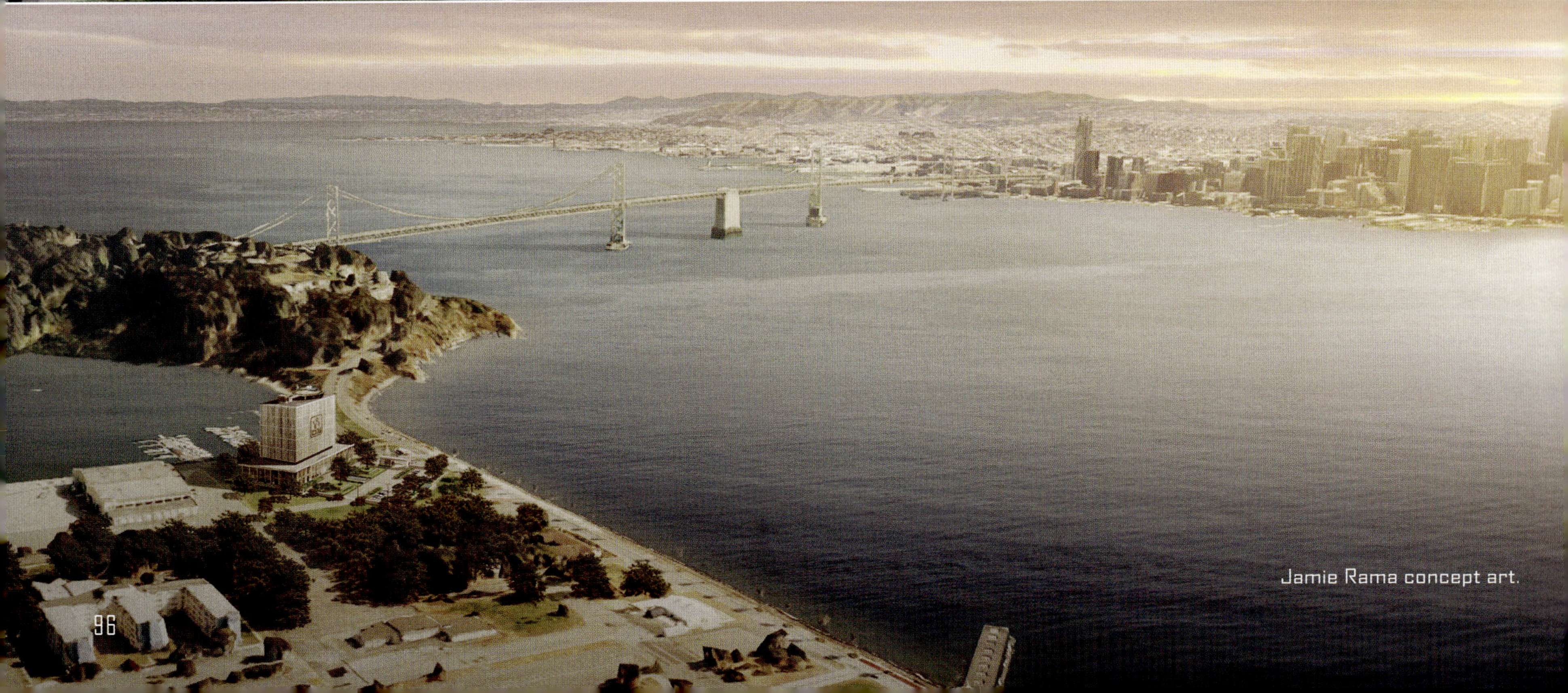

Jamie Rama concept art.

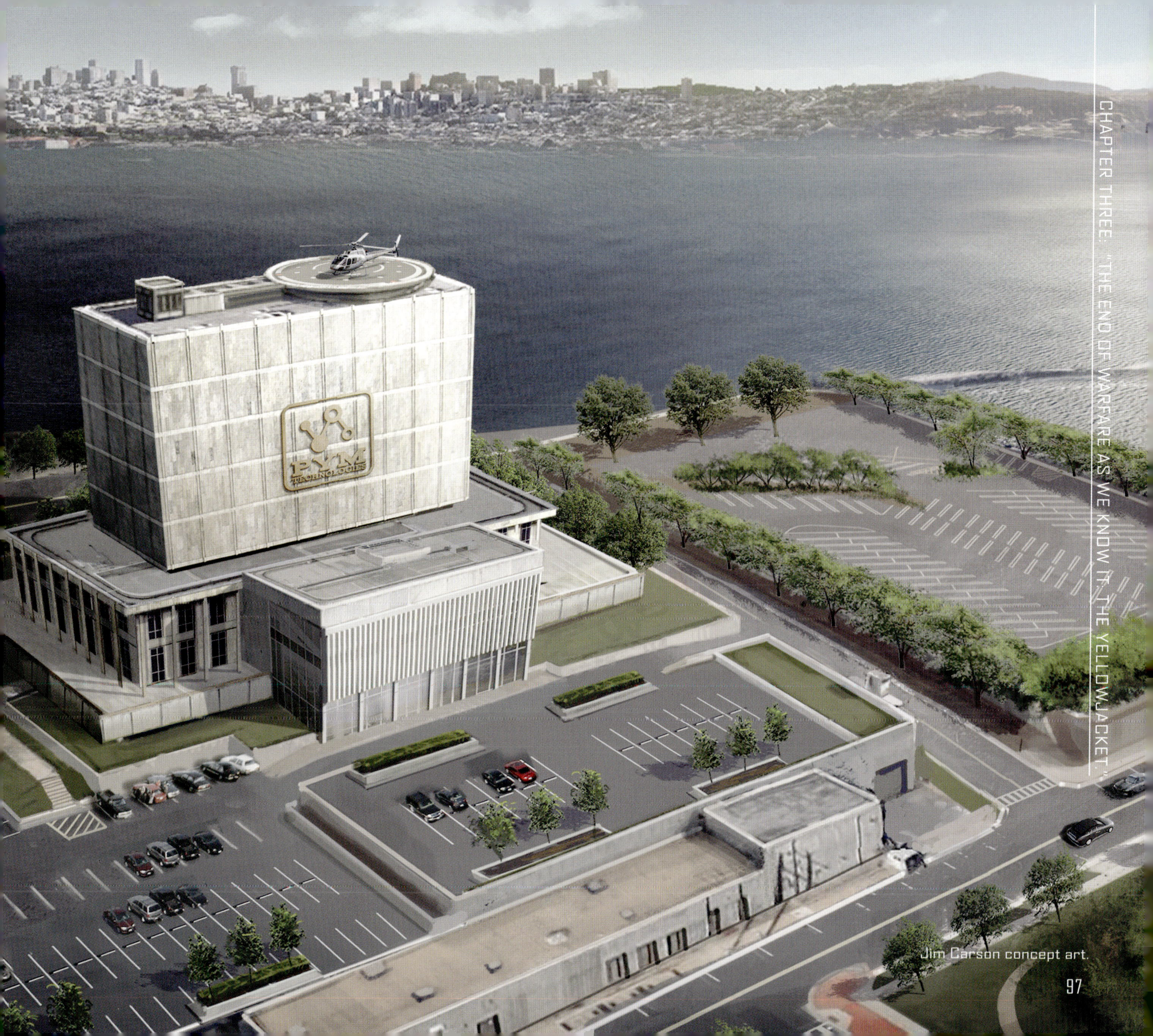

Jim Carson concept art.

Production Designer Shepherd Frankel faced the challenge of illustrating Hank's departure through interior design. "We wanted to visually connect the PymTech Futures lab, as well as the other rooms and corridors, to Darren Cross having taken over the company. So we had to tell that story. We wanted a space that made you feel that you were being engulfed by this character, like you were stuck in this mechanical ecosystem where everything is integrated—almost like you're in a machine. To exemplify this, we built in specialized, practical lighting within the set—which would also highlight the reflections, another key visual I wanted to explore. It really doubled the experience and made everything far more dynamic."

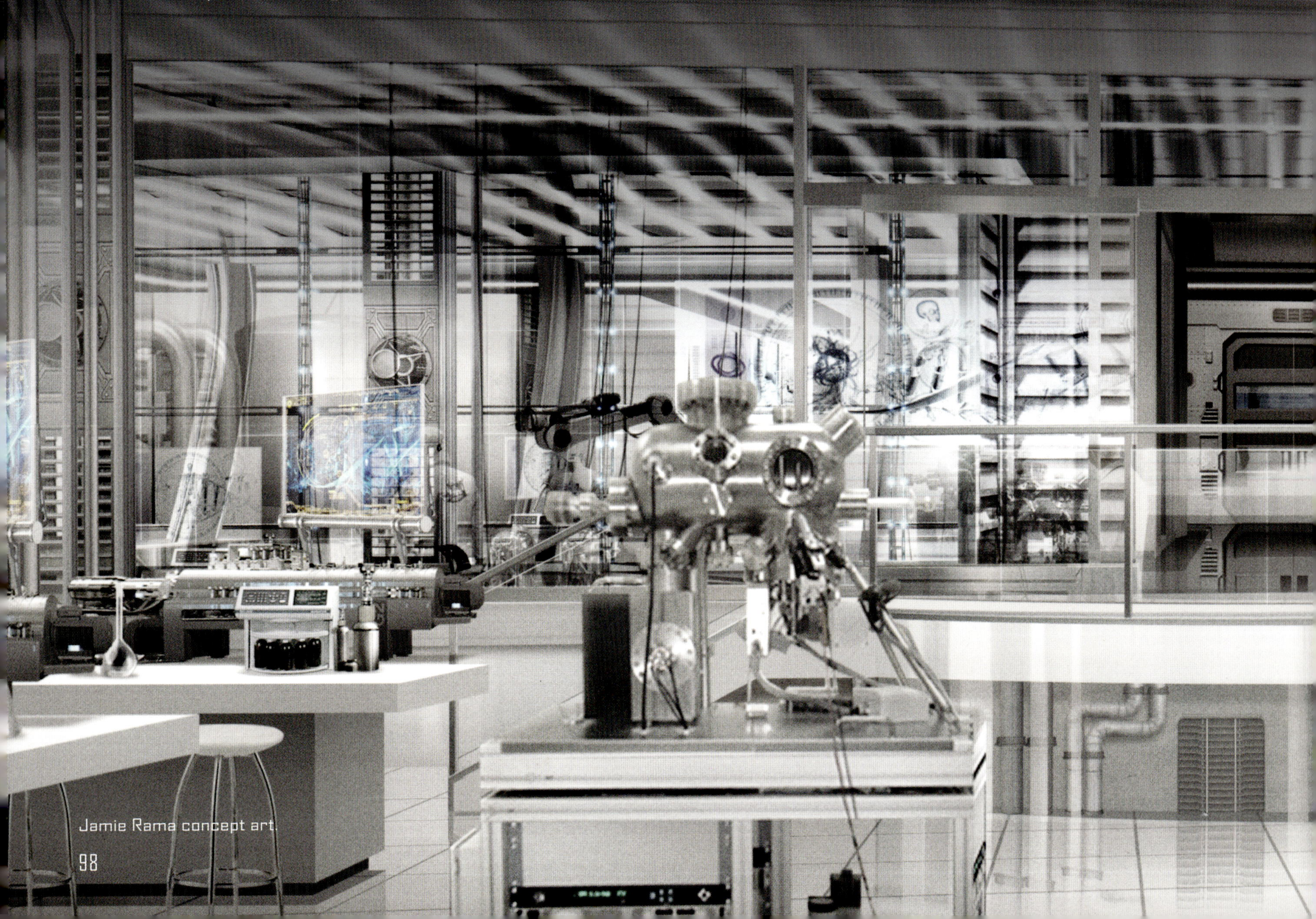

Jamie Rama concept art.

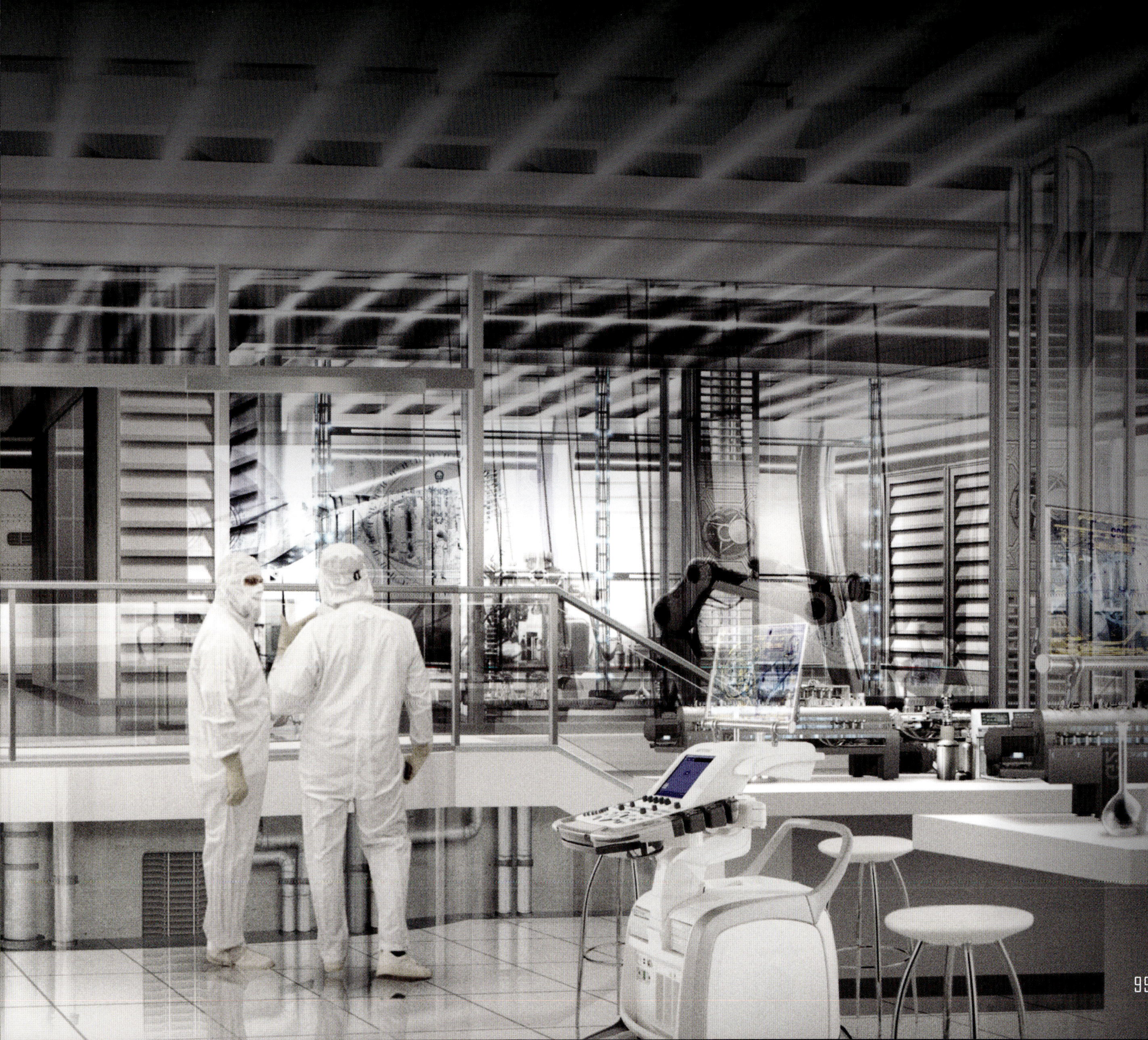

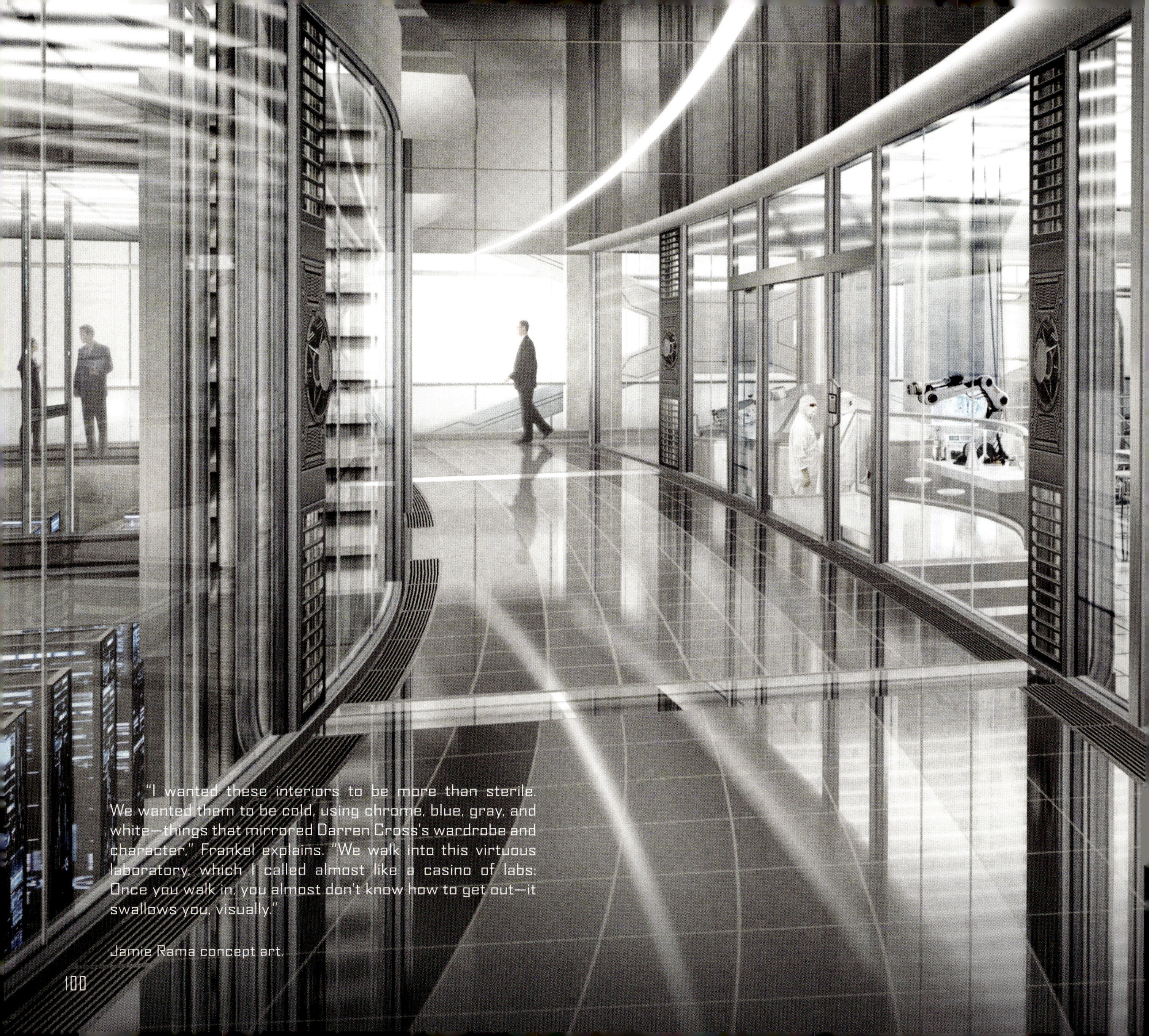

"I wanted these interiors to be more than sterile. We wanted them to be cold, using chrome, blue, gray, and white—things that mirrored Darren Cross's wardrobe and character," Frankel explains. "We walk into this virtuous laboratory, which I called almost like a casino of labs: Once you walk in, you almost don't know how to get out—it swallows you, visually."

Jamie Rama concept art.

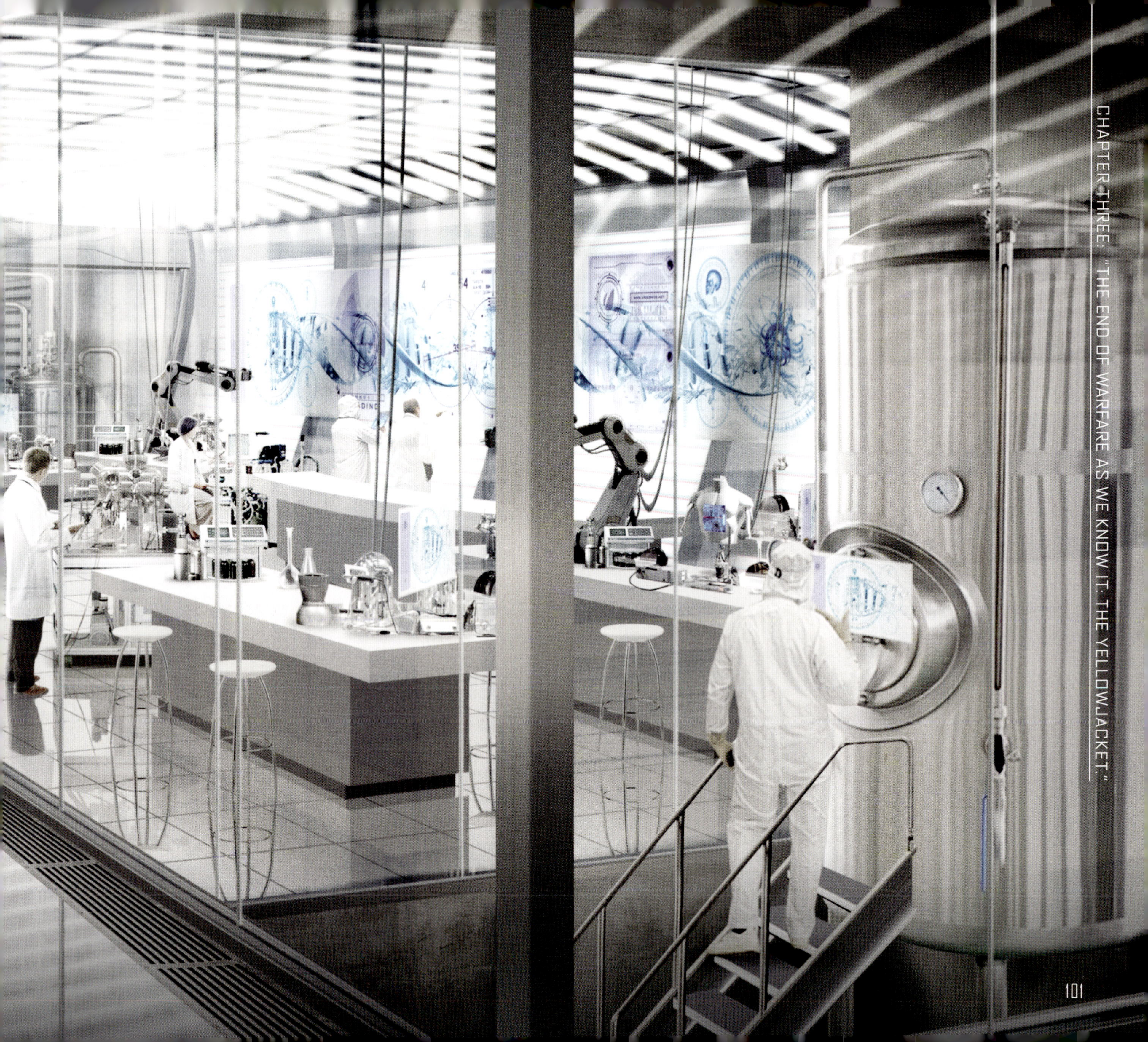

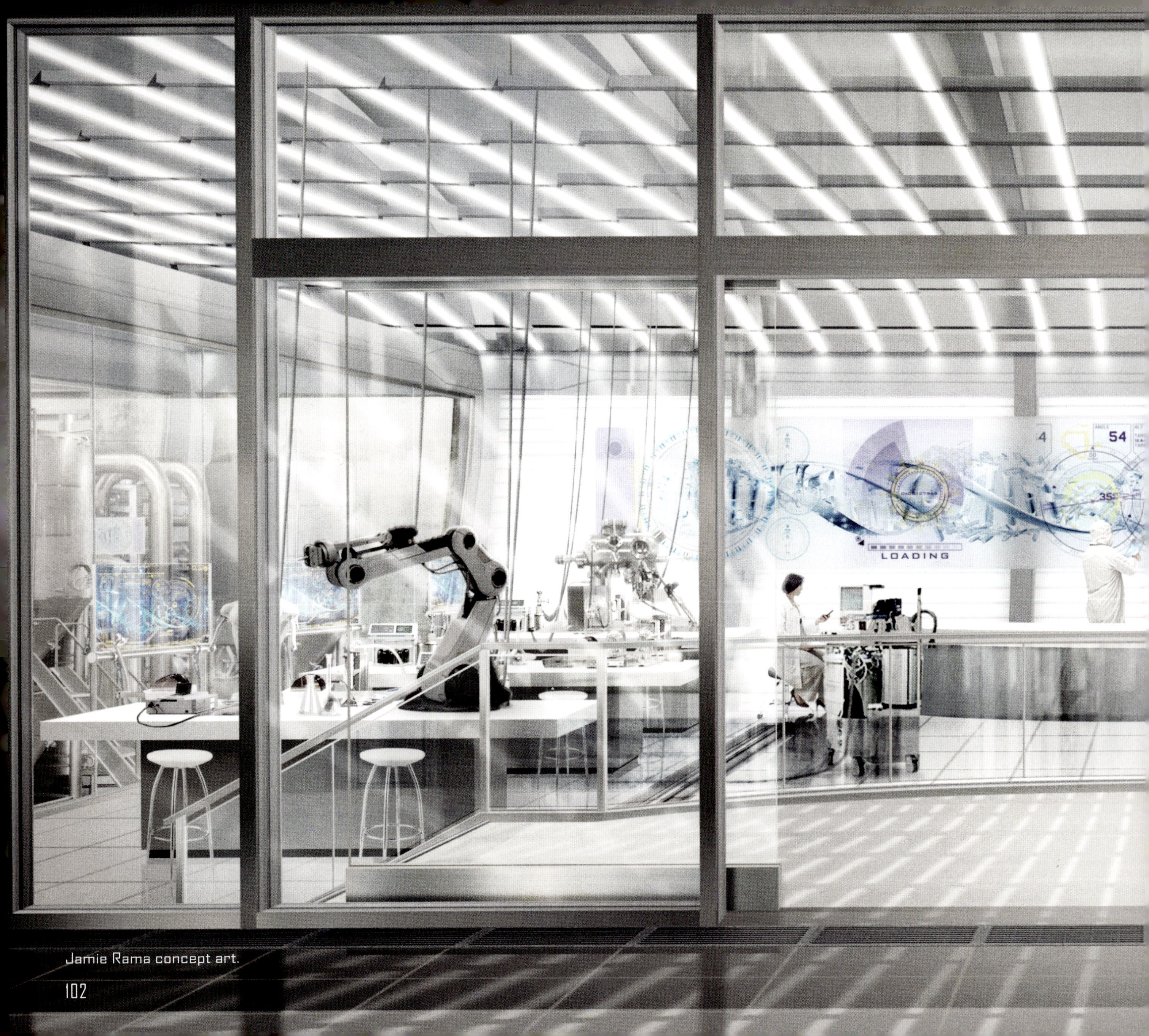

Jamie Rama concept art.

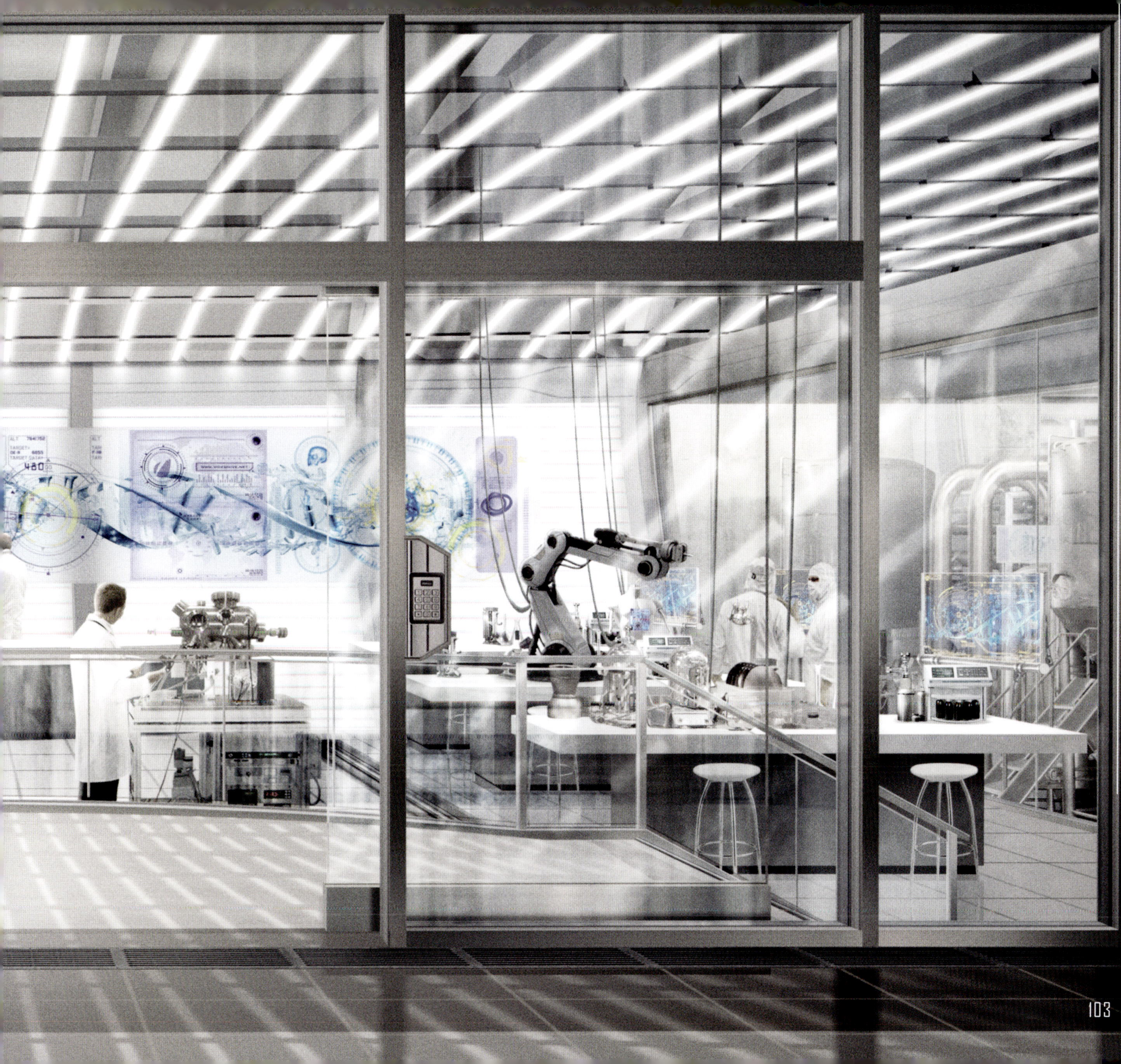

FUTURES VAULT

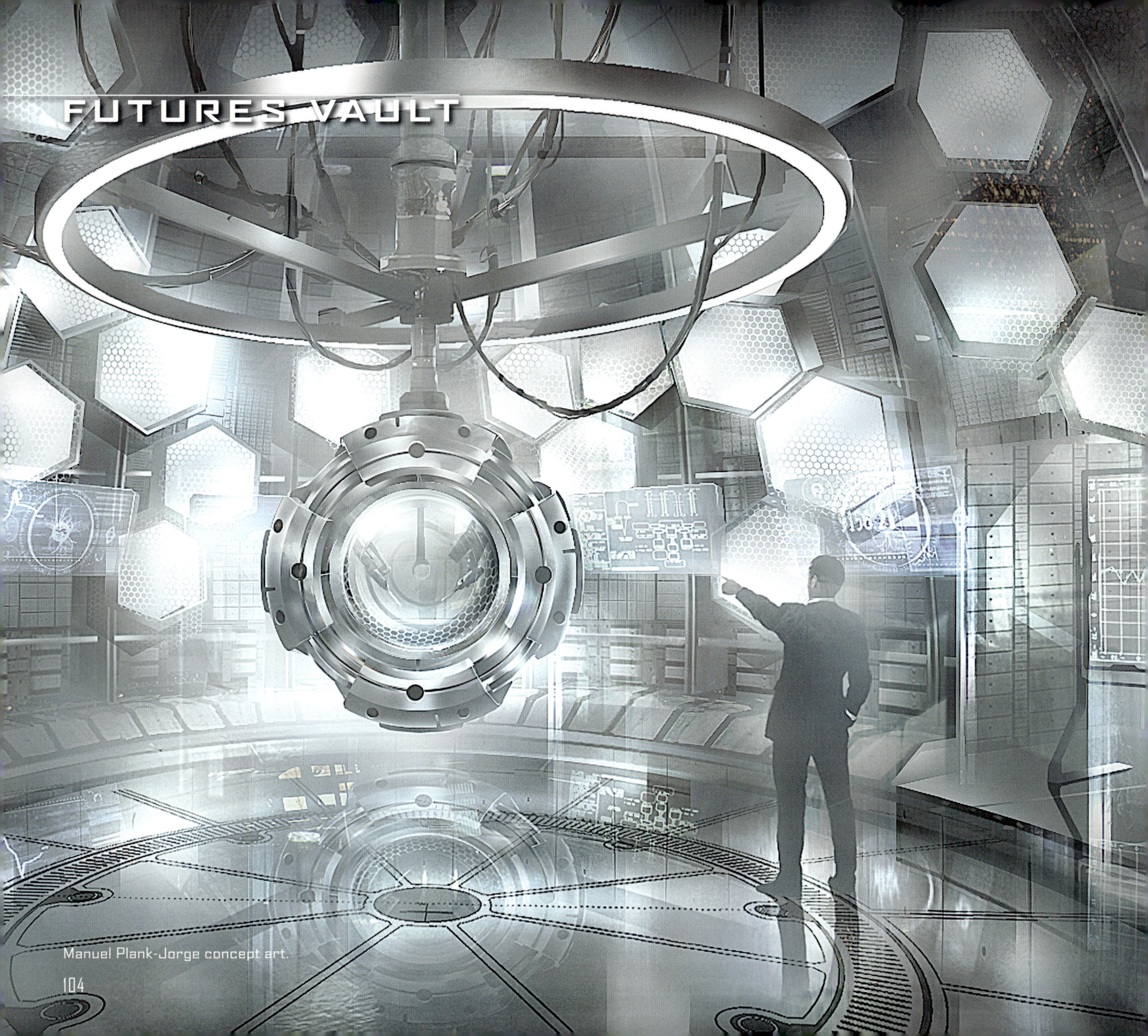

Manuel Plank-Jorge concept art.

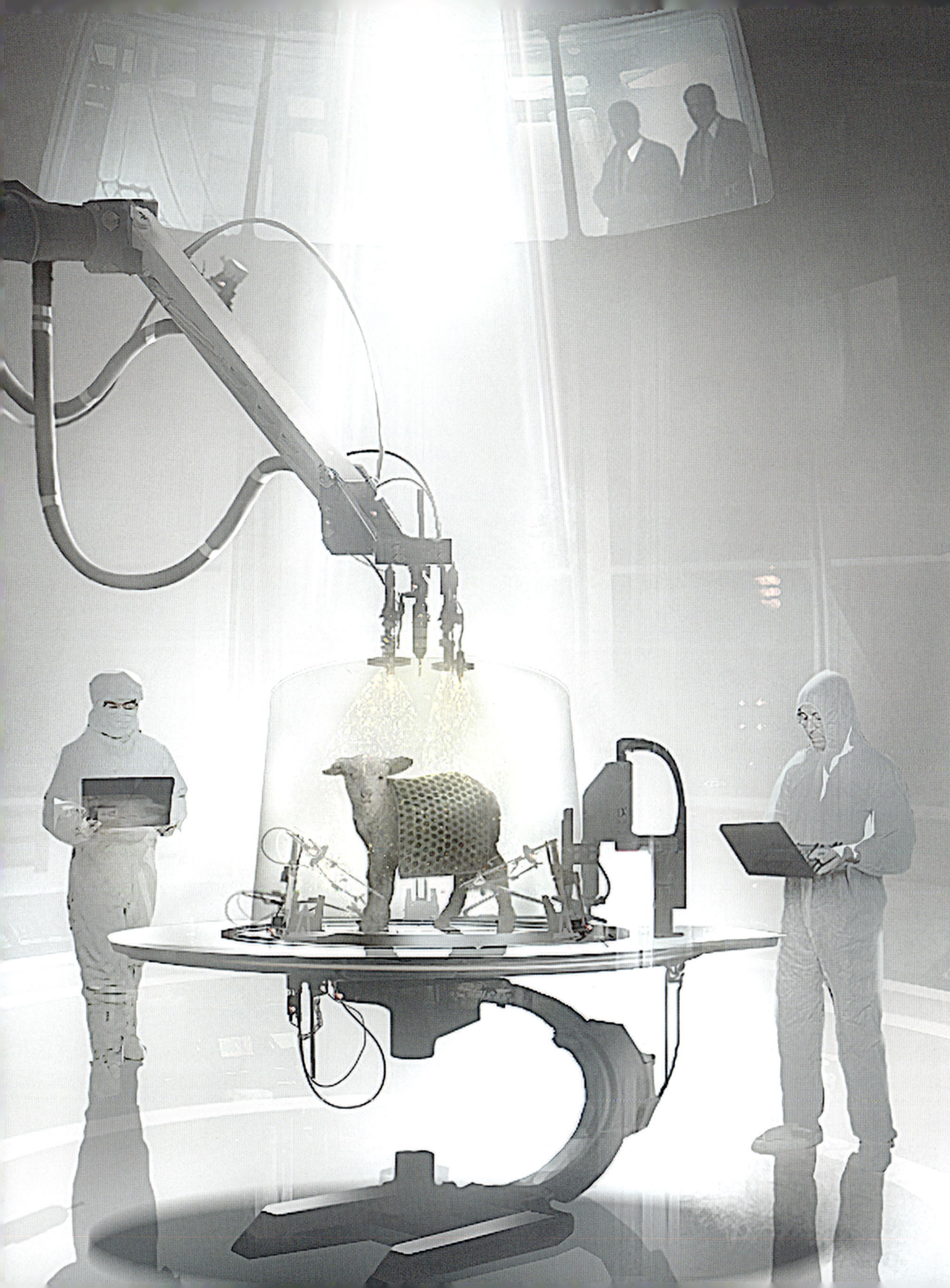

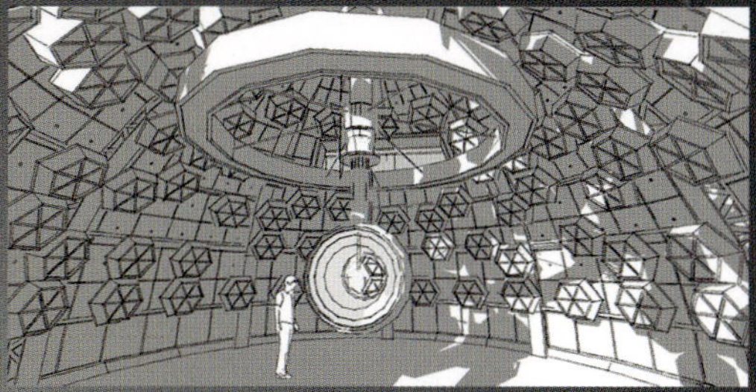

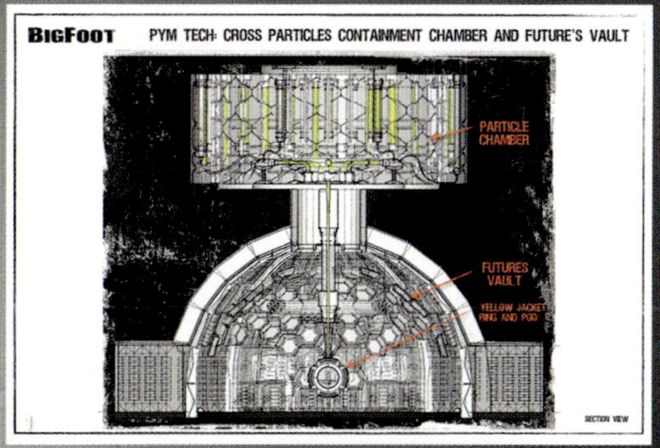

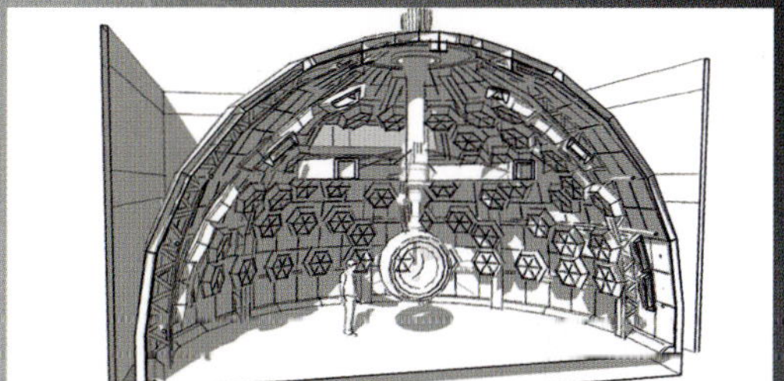

Manuel Plank-Jorge concept art with insets by Dean Wolcott (top), Austin Gorg (center), and Calla Klessig (bottom).

DARREN CROSS

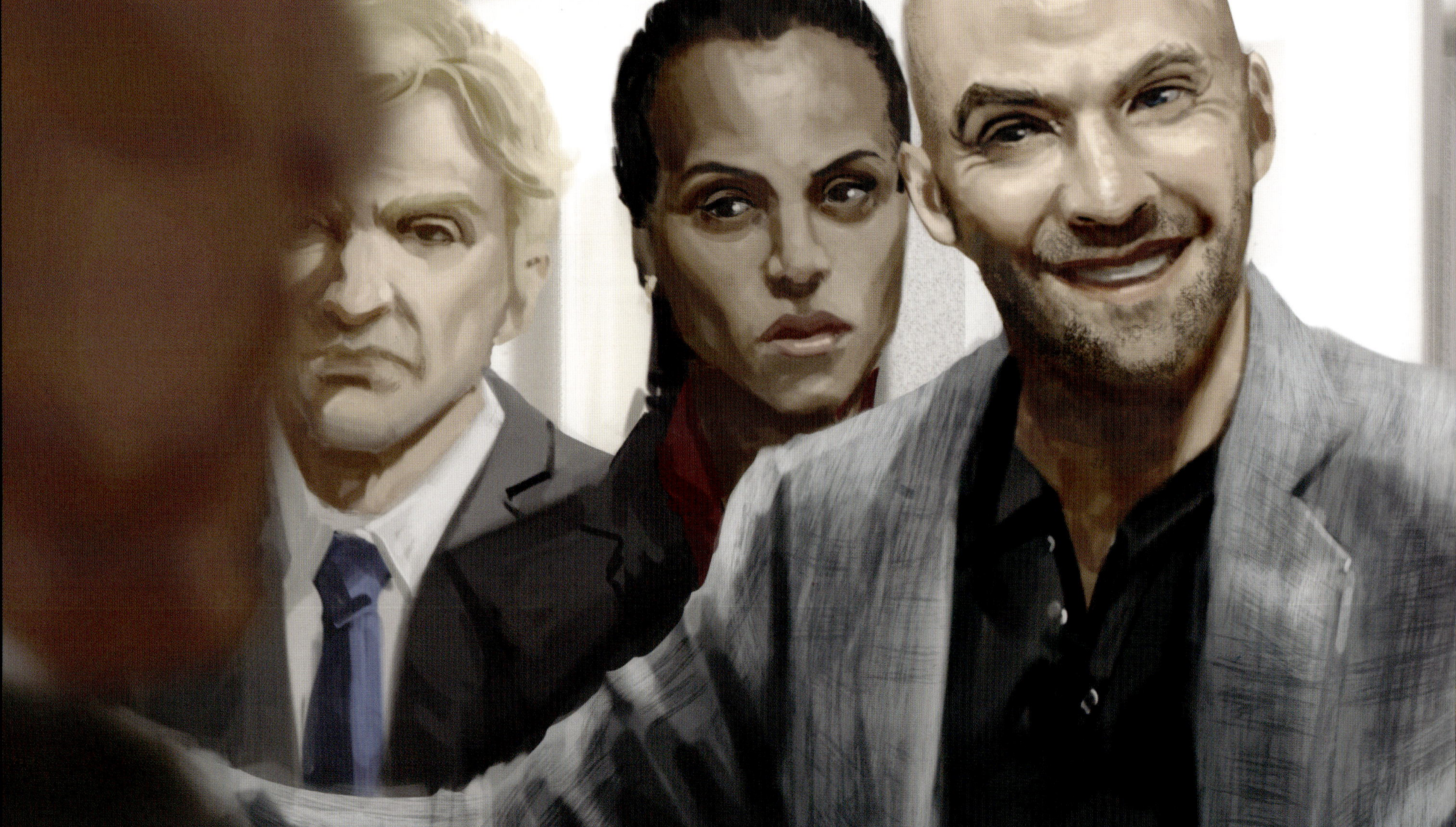

Darren Cross's rabid quest for knowledge and acceptance eventually corrupts him and his work, leaving little room for ethical considerations. "Darren Cross was Hank Pym's mentee. Pym found him at a very young age," says actor Corey Stoll, who plays Cross. "As Darren spent time at PymTech, he got a whiff of this incredible technology to be able to shrink to half an inch tall, and he became enthralled and obsessed with it."

Fearing he had opened Pandora's Box with his Pym Particle, Hank Pym buried his research. Not even Cross, the protégé who would come to see Hank as a father, could be trusted with its power. "Hank is not the warmest father figure possible, and really broke Darren's heart," Stoll explains. "Darren took over the company and is now the CEO, and is full-steam-ahead trying to pursue that technology."

Jackson Sze keyframe.

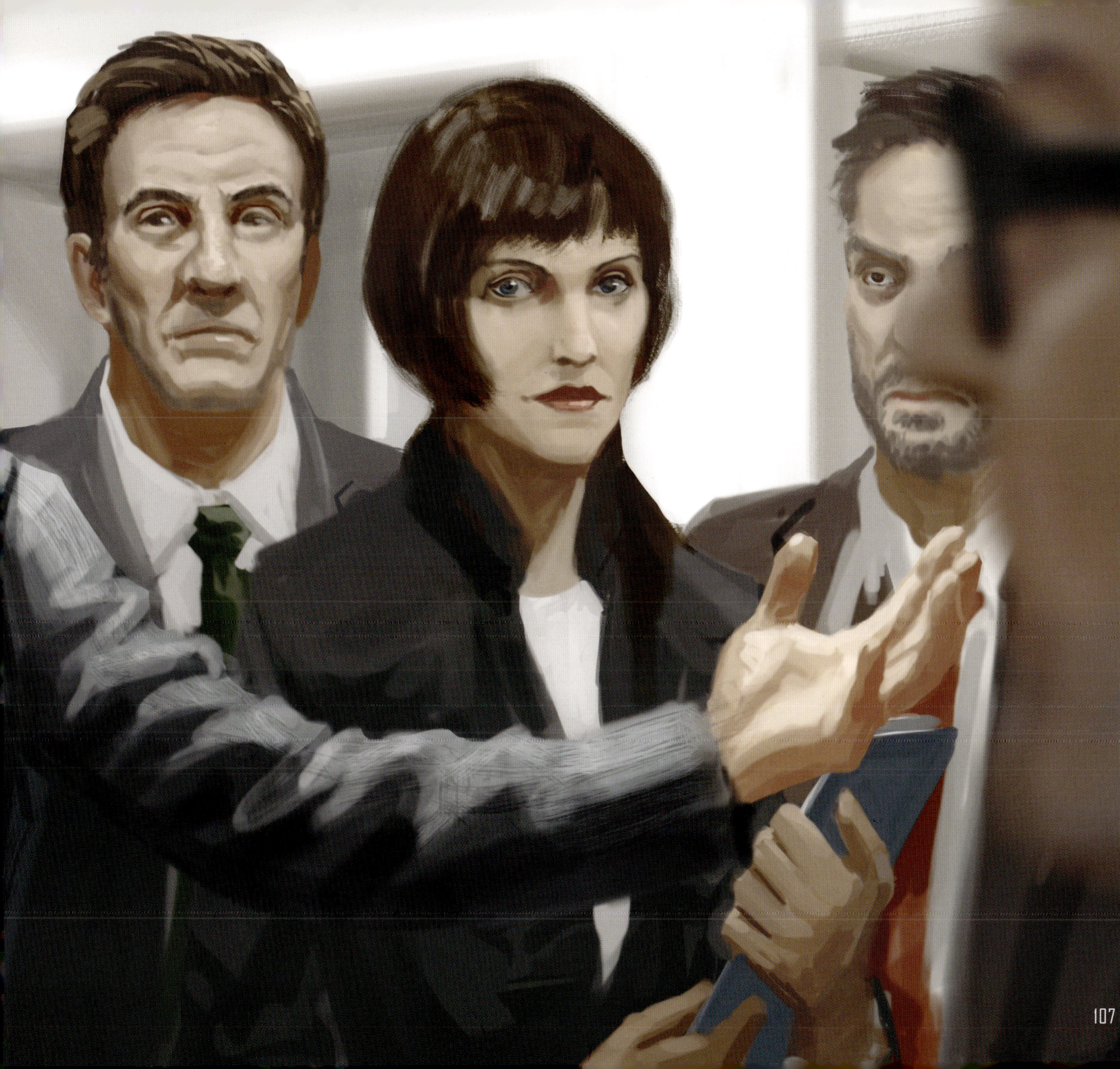

YELLOWJACKET

Concept Artist Jackson Sze was among the first artists to begin crafting the Yellowjacket look. "As with designing any of our characters, we start by looking at what has been done in the comics," he explains. "From there, we assess how much is translatable or feasible in a live-action setting. In the movie, Yellowjacket is not Hank Pym, as he was in the comics. The suit is meant to be a high-tech, soldier version of the Ant-Man suit, and is worn by the movie's villain. With those parameters in mind, Yellowjacket will have to be quite different in look from his comic counterpart. It had to be advanced, aggressive, and intimidating."

Sze was eager to incorporate Darren Cross's personality into the suit's design. "Darren Cross harbors quite a bit of emotional baggage with regards to his former mentor, Hank Pym," he says. "His jealousy and anger fueled his pursuit of the Pym Particle technology. I imagined Cross would want to show up Hank's suit in every way. So a sleeker, more modern and sophisticated suit would be created. Having no qualms about militarizing the technology, Cross would make his suit deadlier and weaponized."

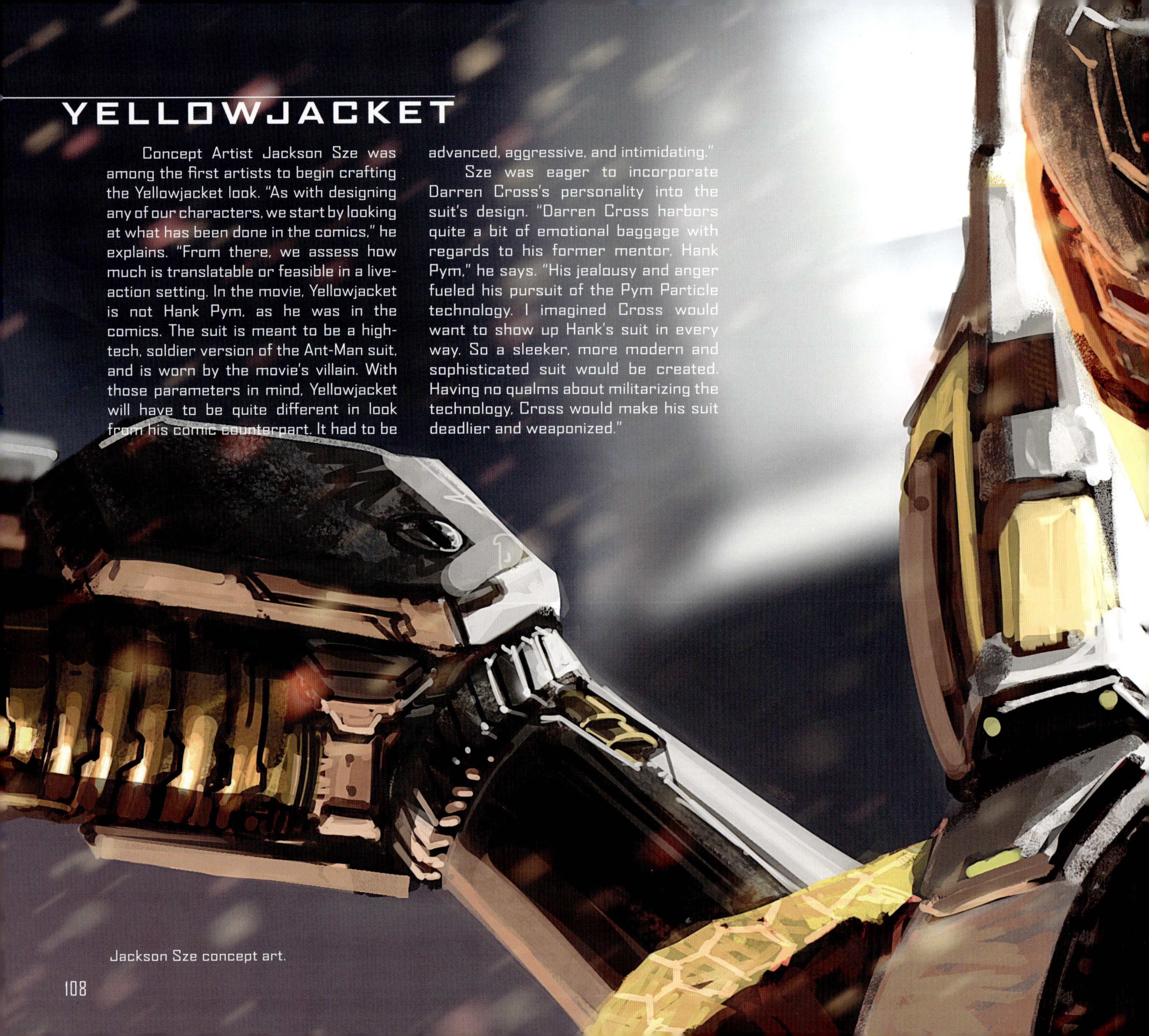

Jackson Sze concept art.

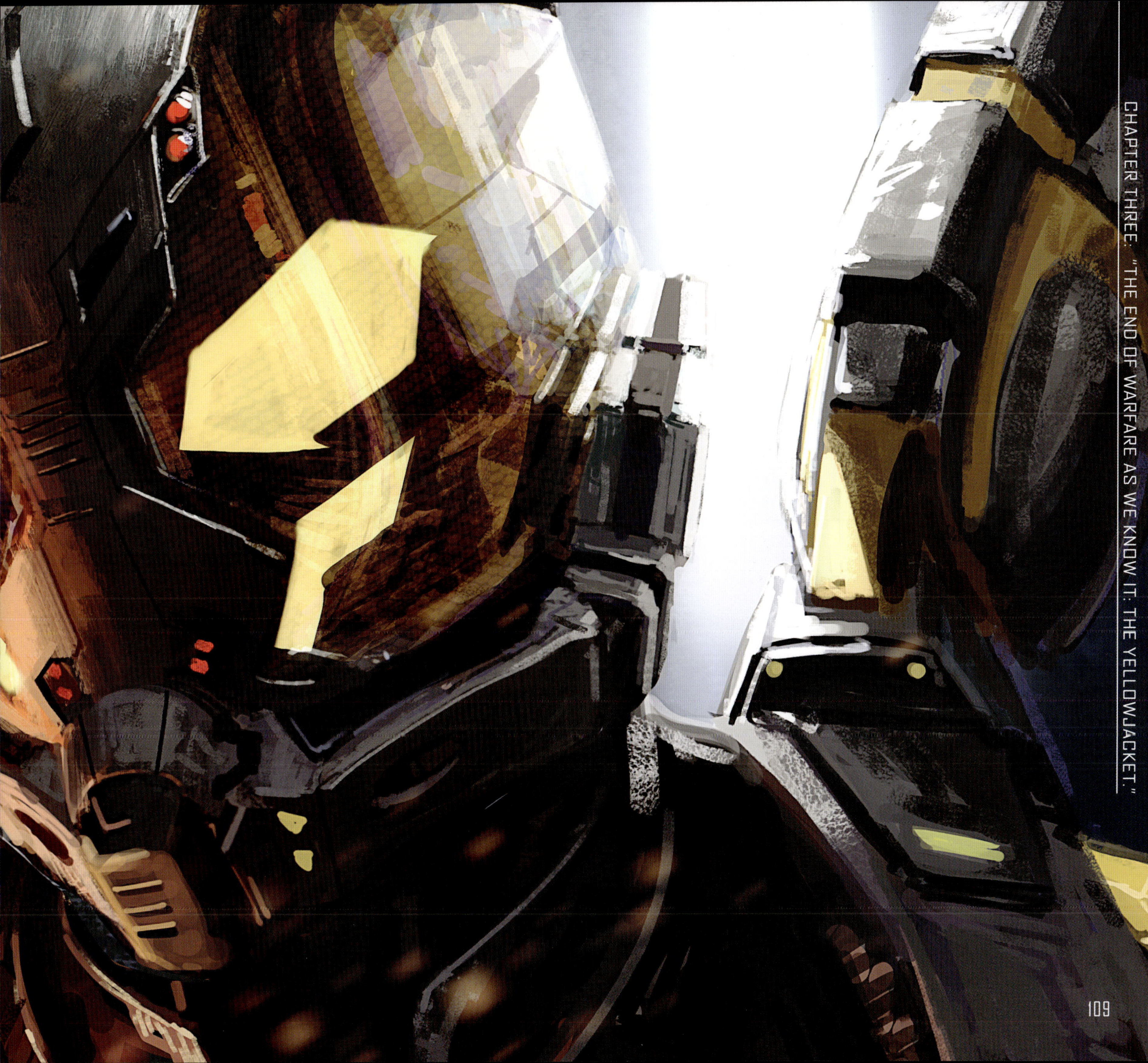

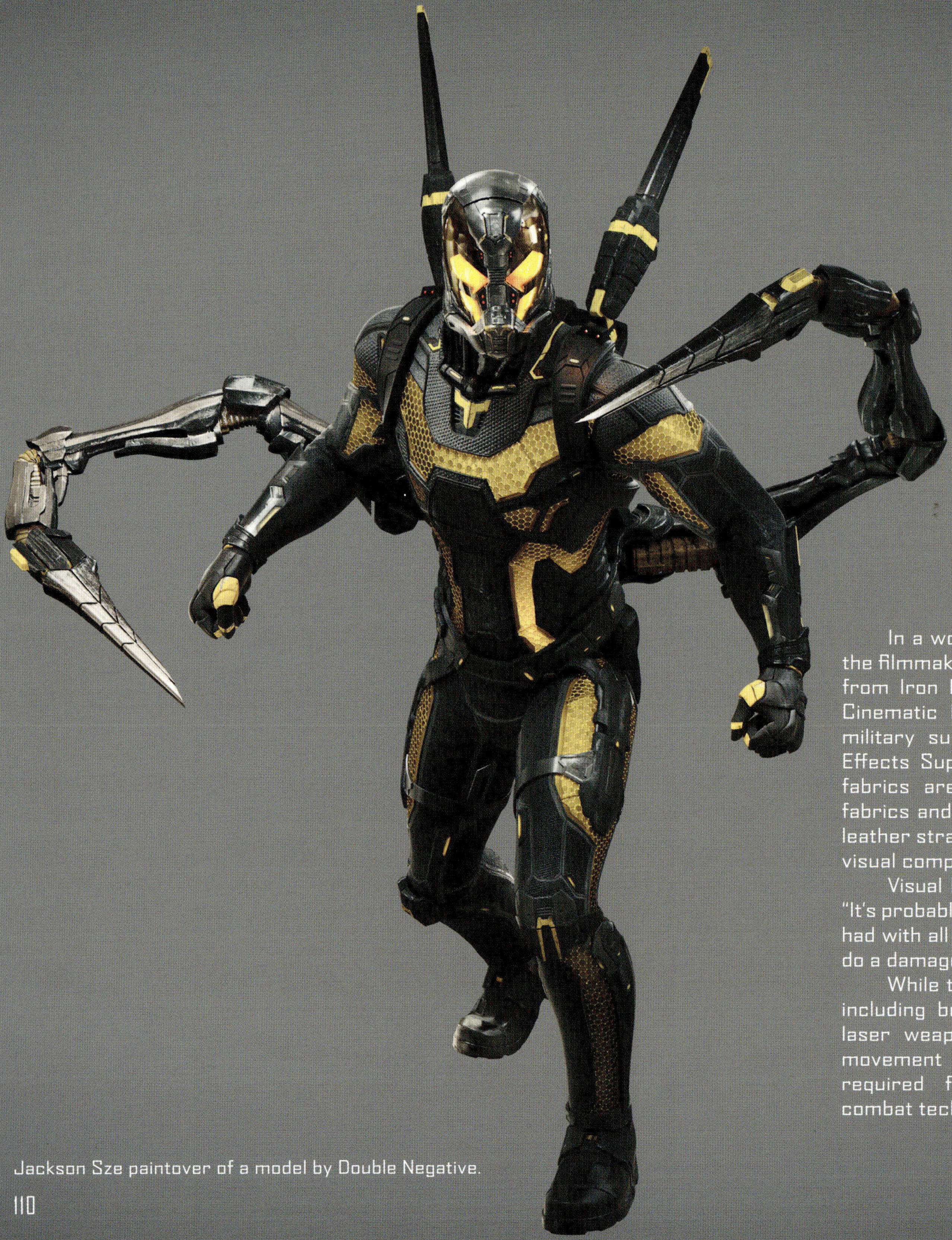

Jackson Sze paintover of a model by Double Negative.

In a world filled with cutting-edge technology, the filmmakers sought to differentiate Yellowjacket from Iron Man and other aspects of the Marvel Cinematic Universe. "It's a modern, light-weight military suit that a person could wear," Visual Effects Supervisor Jake Morrison explains. "The fabrics are Kevlar and other actual manmade fabrics and textures, dark metal bits in the chest, leather straps on the shoulders—it's a good deal of visual complexity."

Visual Effects Producer Diana Giorgiutti adds, "It's probably one of the most complex models we've had with all the bits and pieces, and then we had to do a damaged version of it, as well."

While the suit meets all the standard criteria, including bulletproof shielding and high-powered laser weapons, it offers far more freedom of movement than even the Iron Man armor—as required for Cross's advanced hand-to-hand combat techniques and acrobatics.

No practical Yellowjacket costume was created for the film, save a maquette that served as lighting reference. An open communication pipeline between the Visual Development and Visual Effects teams ensured the suit would retain all the details present in Sze's original. "It was a great collaborative process," Sze says. "After we sent them the approved Yellowjacket design, we got to see initial models and textures. I painted on those renders to clarify certain ideas, and also adjusted certain design details. There were a few rounds of modeling, paintovers, and feedback. The end result was a better version of Yellowjacket than any one department could do alone."

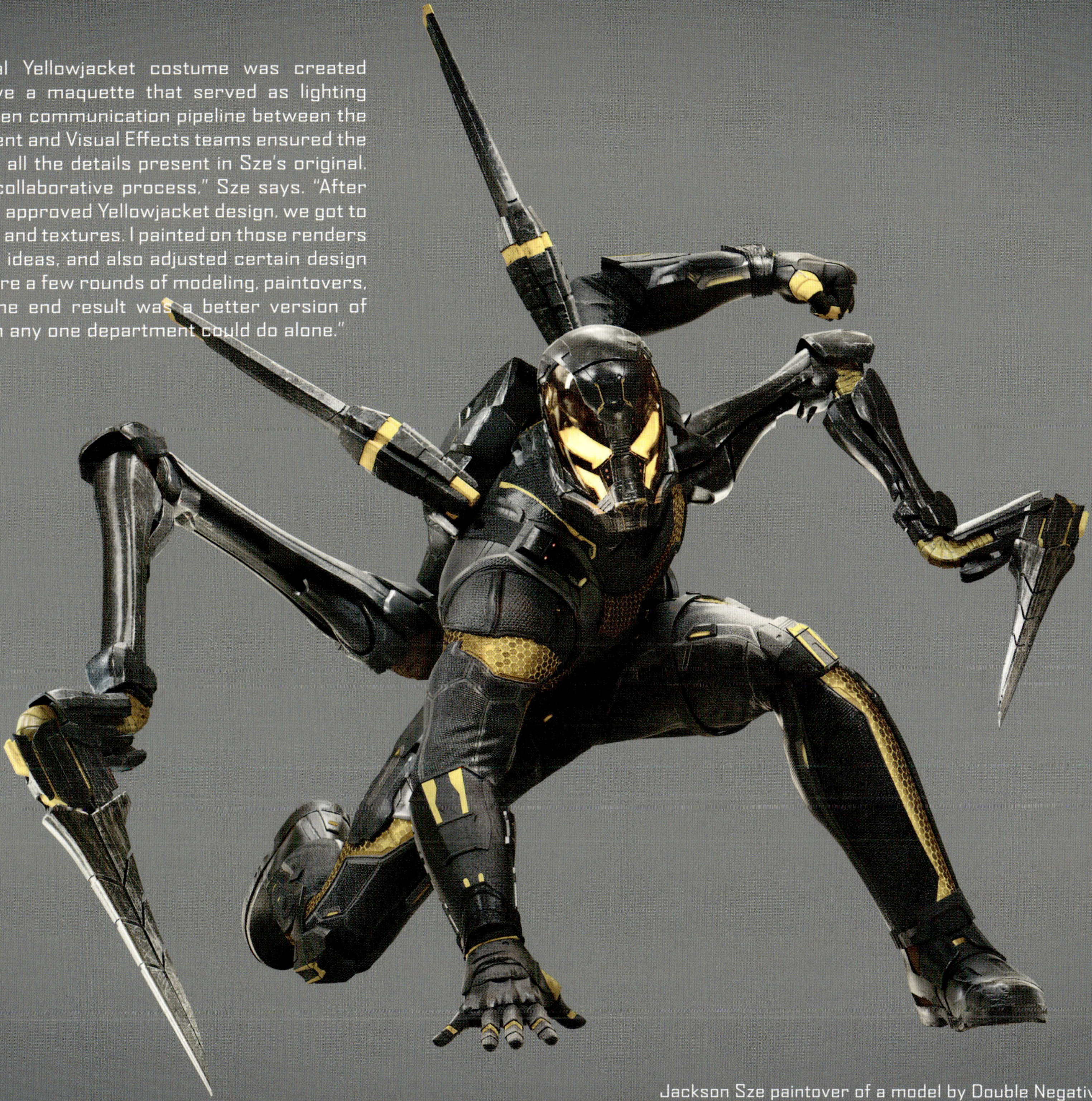

Jackson Sze paintover of a model by Double Negative.

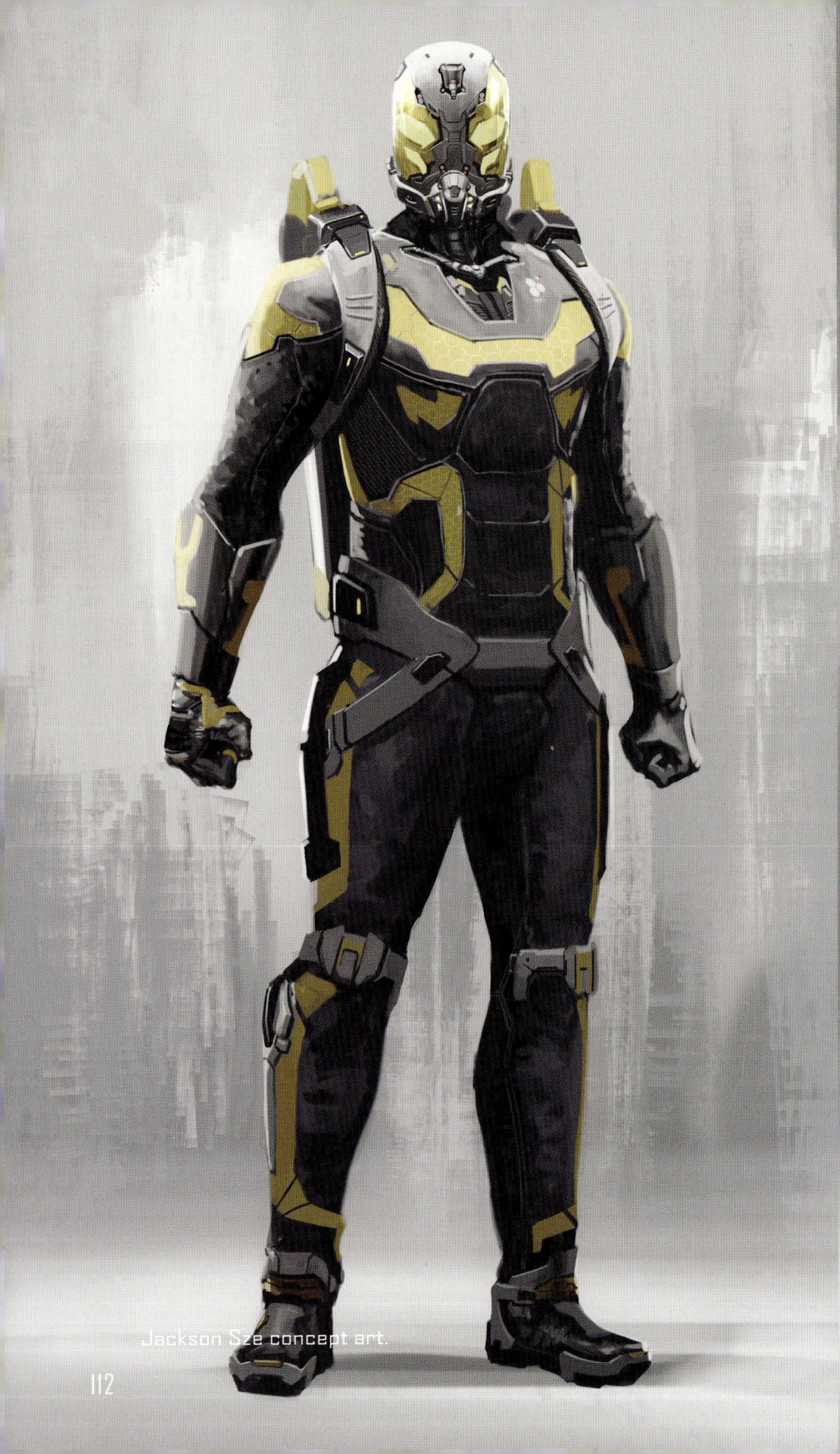
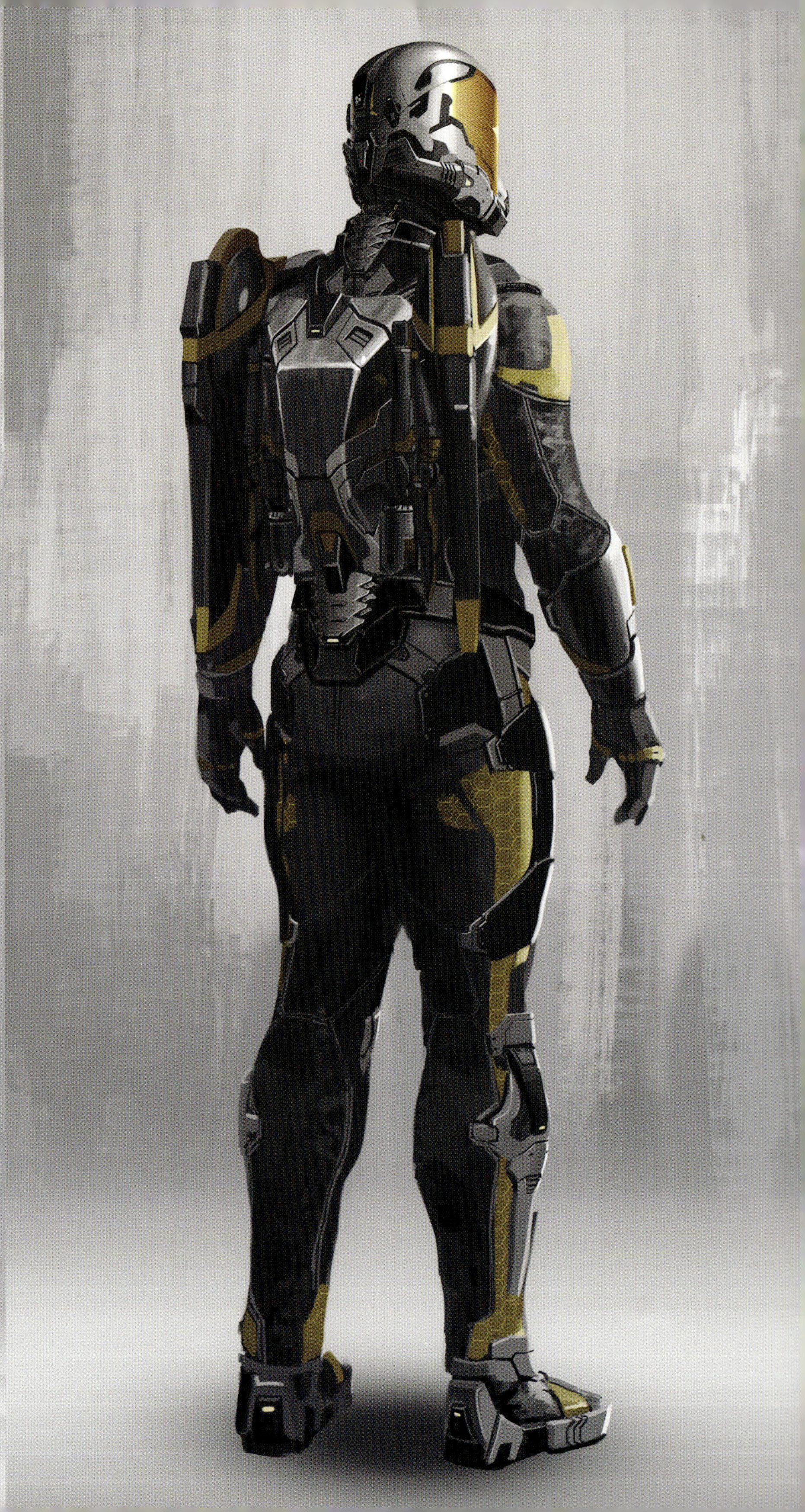

Jackson Sze concept art.

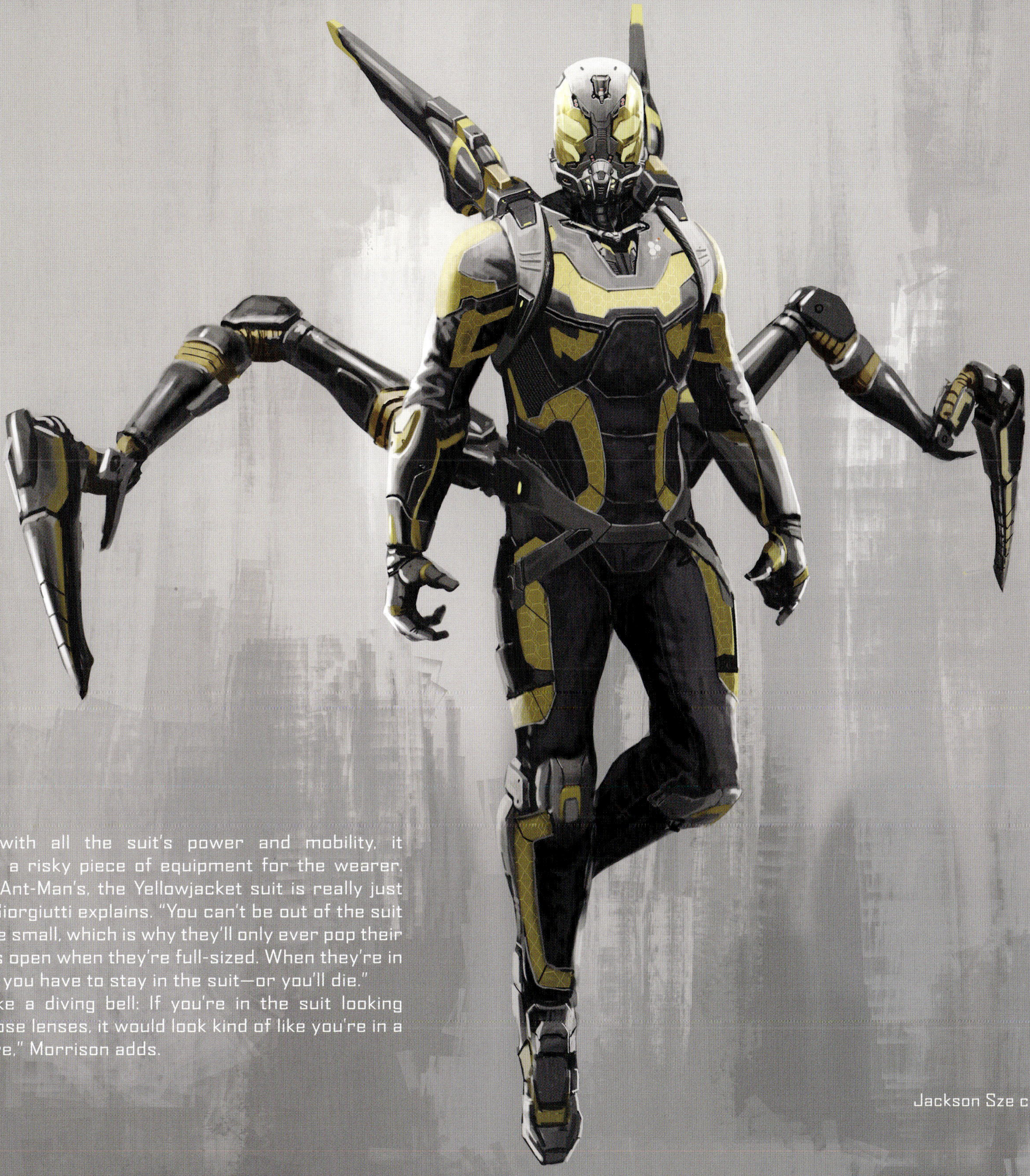

Even with all the suit's power and mobility, it represents a risky piece of equipment for the wearer. "Much like Ant-Man's, the Yellowjacket suit is really just a vessel," Giorgiutti explains. "You can't be out of the suit when you're small, which is why they'll only ever pop their face-masks open when they're full-sized. When they're in little mode, you have to stay in the suit—or you'll die."

"It's like a diving bell: If you're in the suit looking through those lenses, it would look kind of like you're in a bathysphere," Morrison adds.

Jackson Sze concept art.

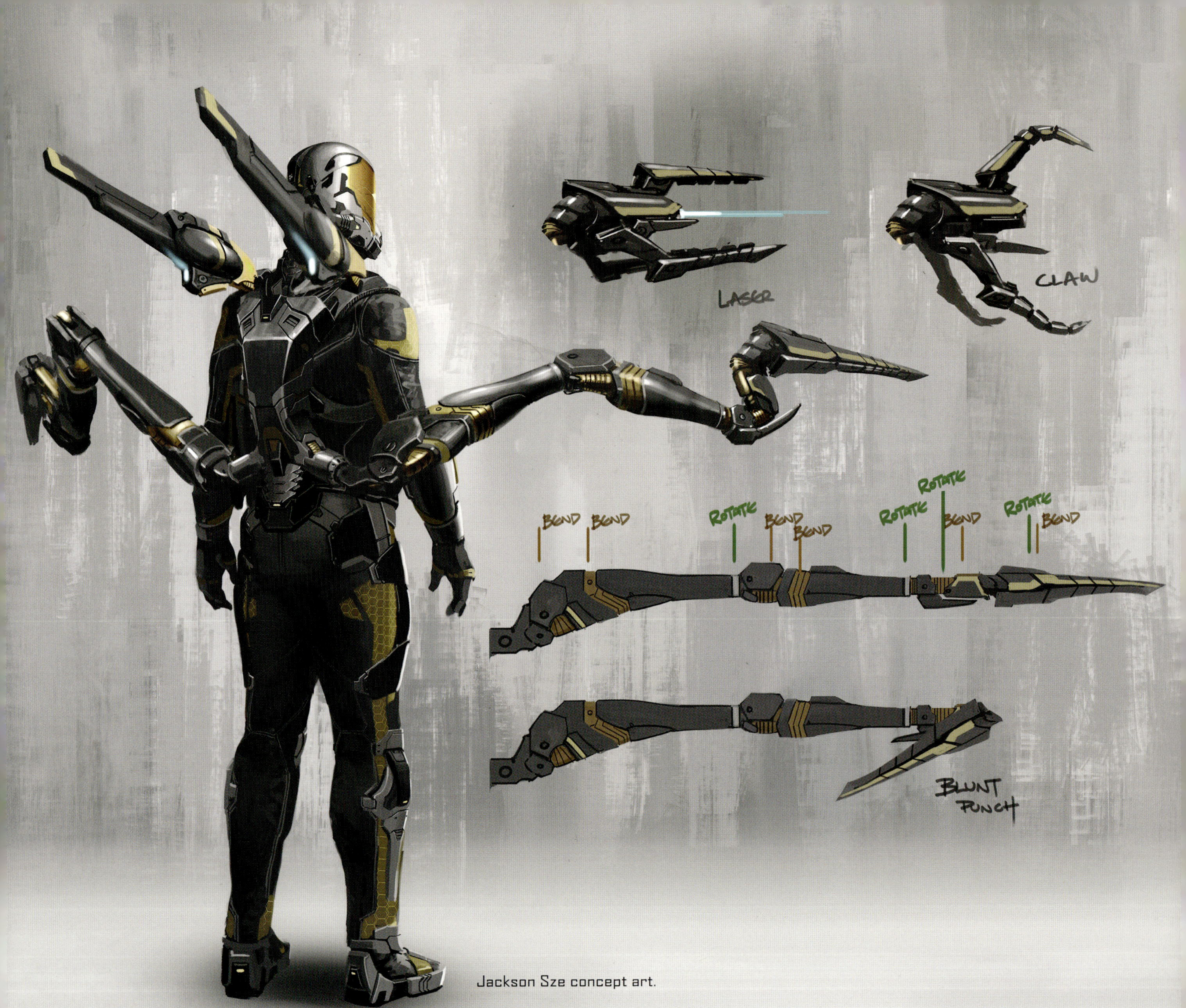

Jackson Sze concept art.

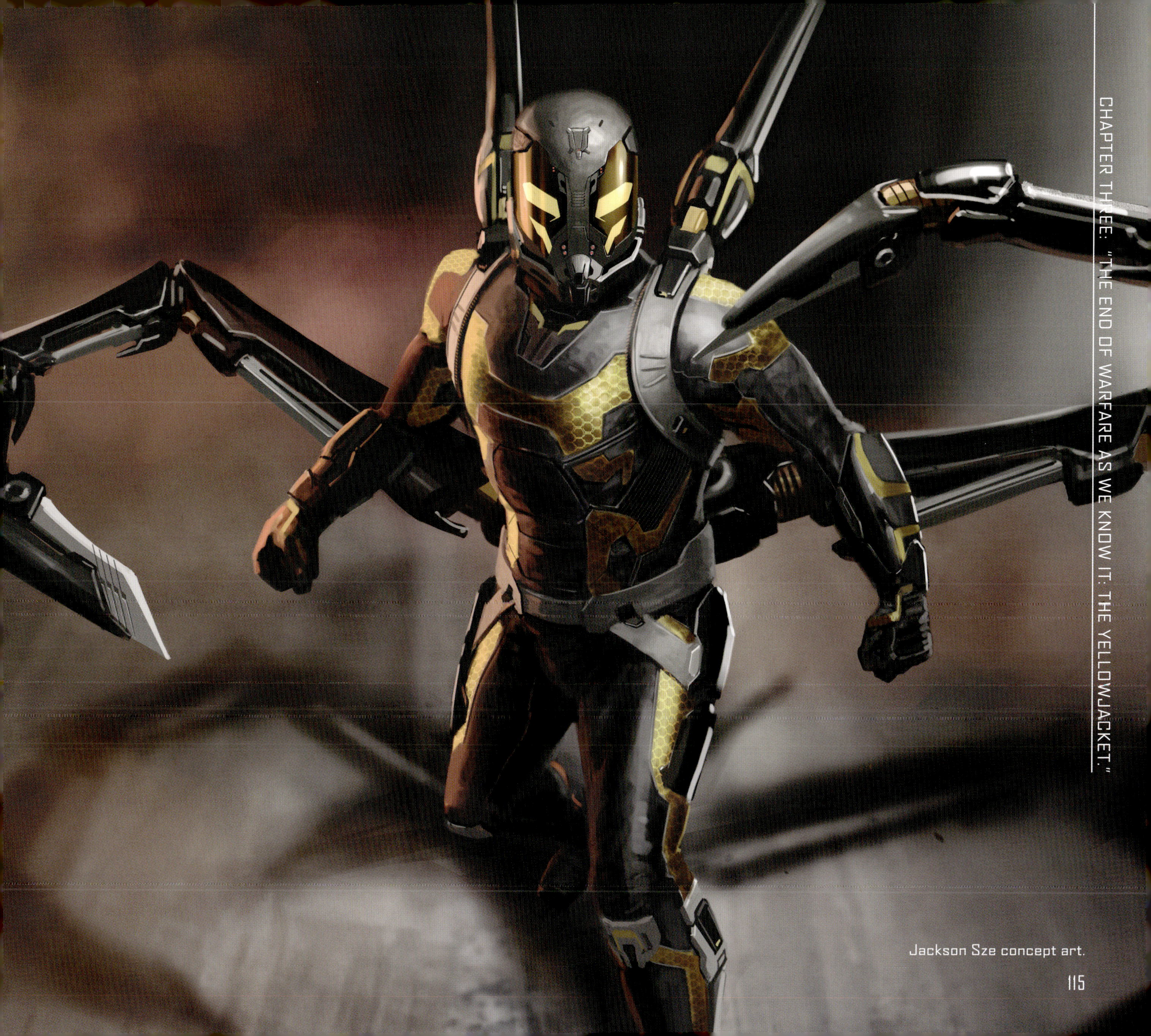

Jackson Sze concept art.

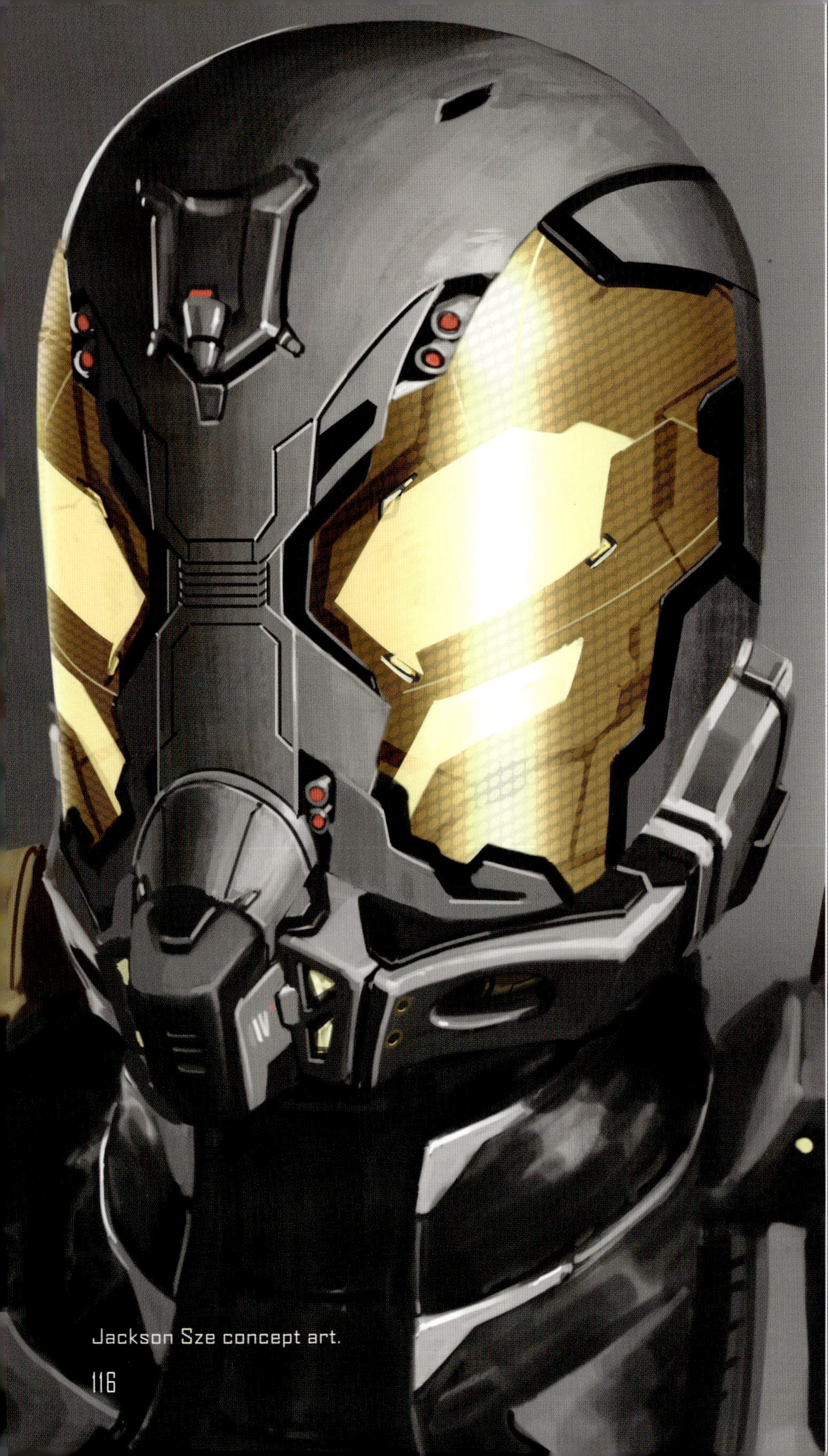

Jackson Sze concept art.

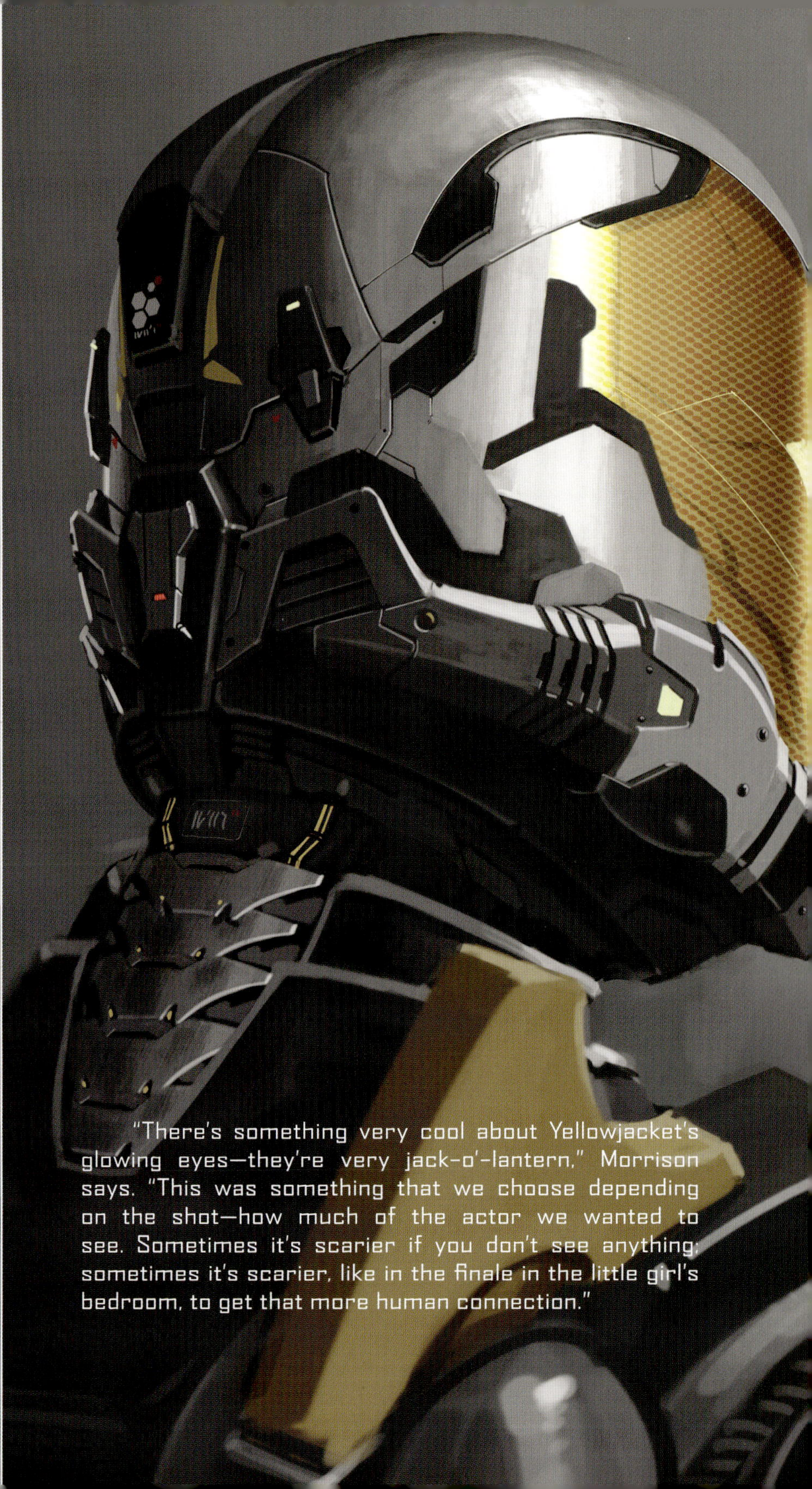

"There's something very cool about Yellowjacket's glowing eyes—they're very jack-o'-lantern," Morrison says. "This was something that we choose depending on the shot—how much of the actor we wanted to see. Sometimes it's scarier if you don't see anything; sometimes it's scarier, like in the finale in the little girl's bedroom, to get that more human connection."

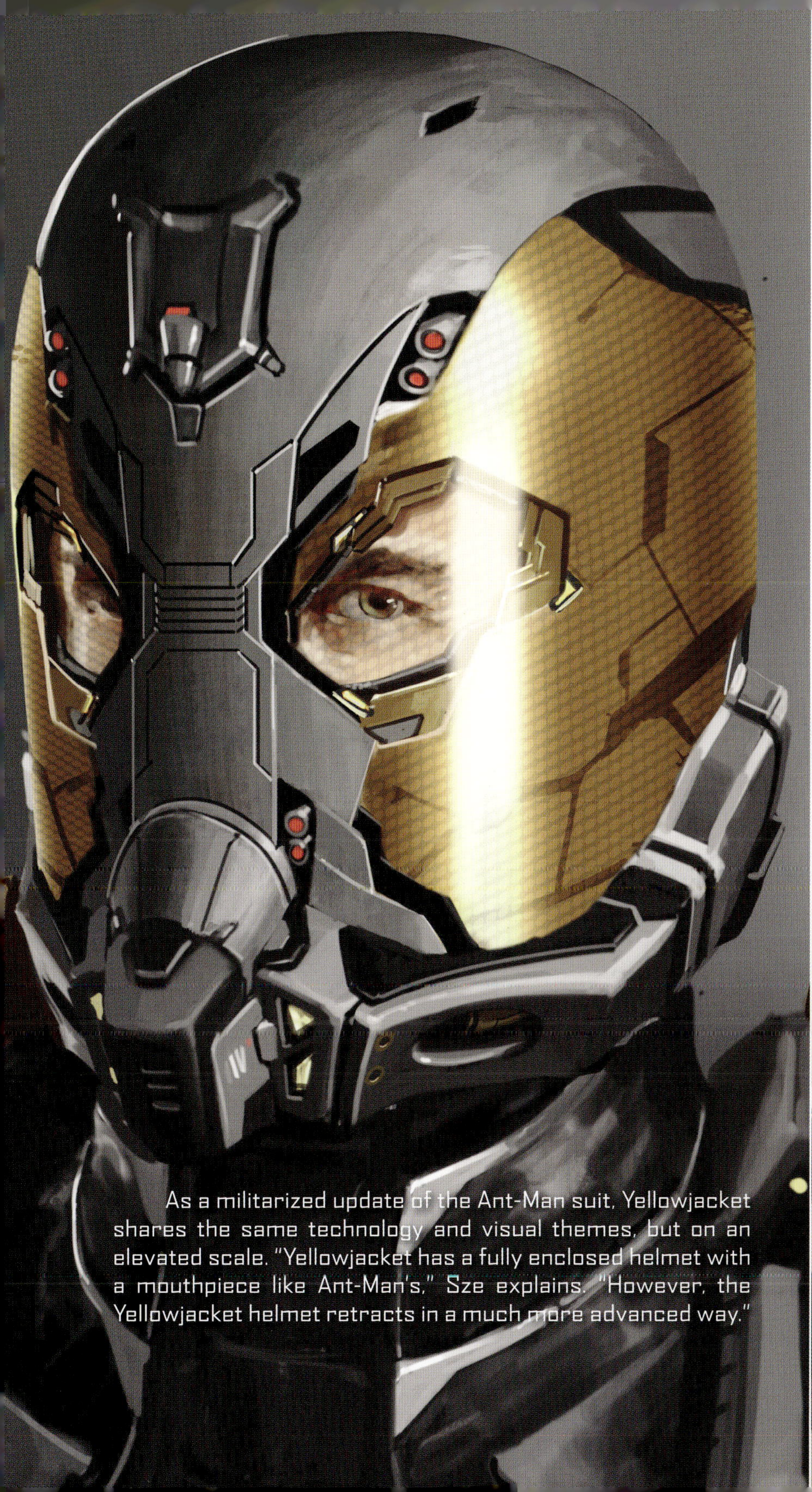

As a militarized update of the Ant-Man suit, Yellowjacket shares the same technology and visual themes, but on an elevated scale. "Yellowjacket has a fully enclosed helmet with a mouthpiece like Ant-Man's," Sze explains. "However, the Yellowjacket helmet retracts in a much more advanced way."

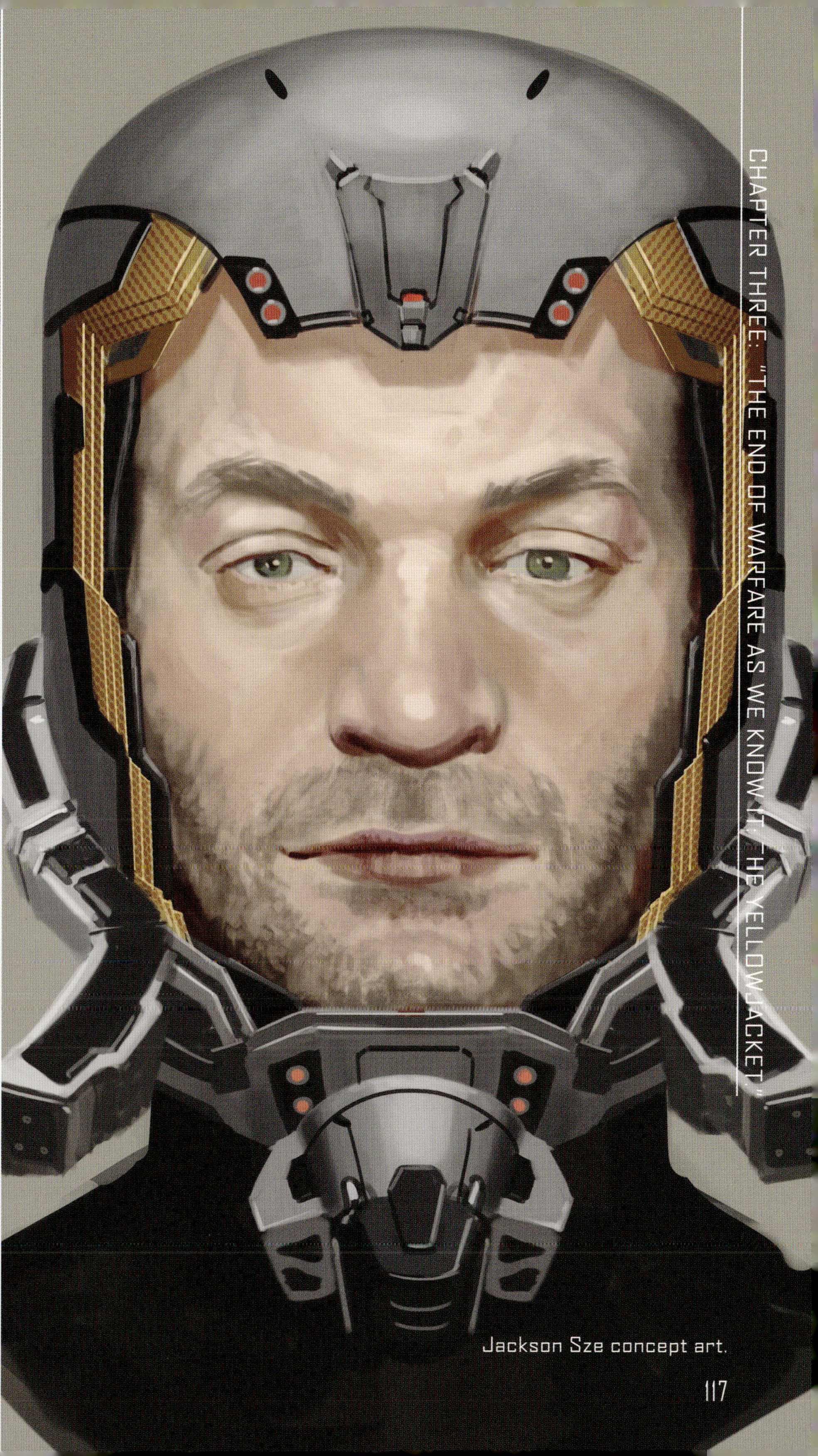

Jackson Sze concept art.

YELLOWJACKET COMBAT CONCEPTS

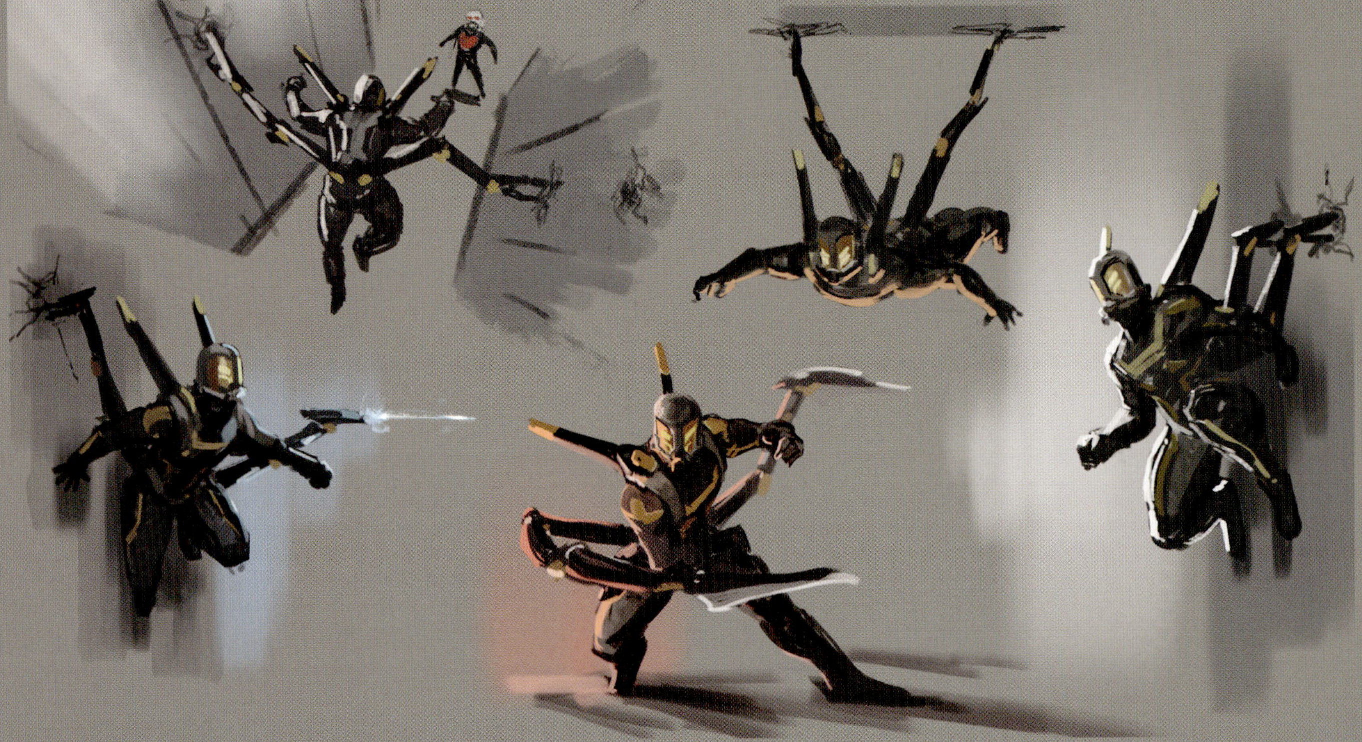

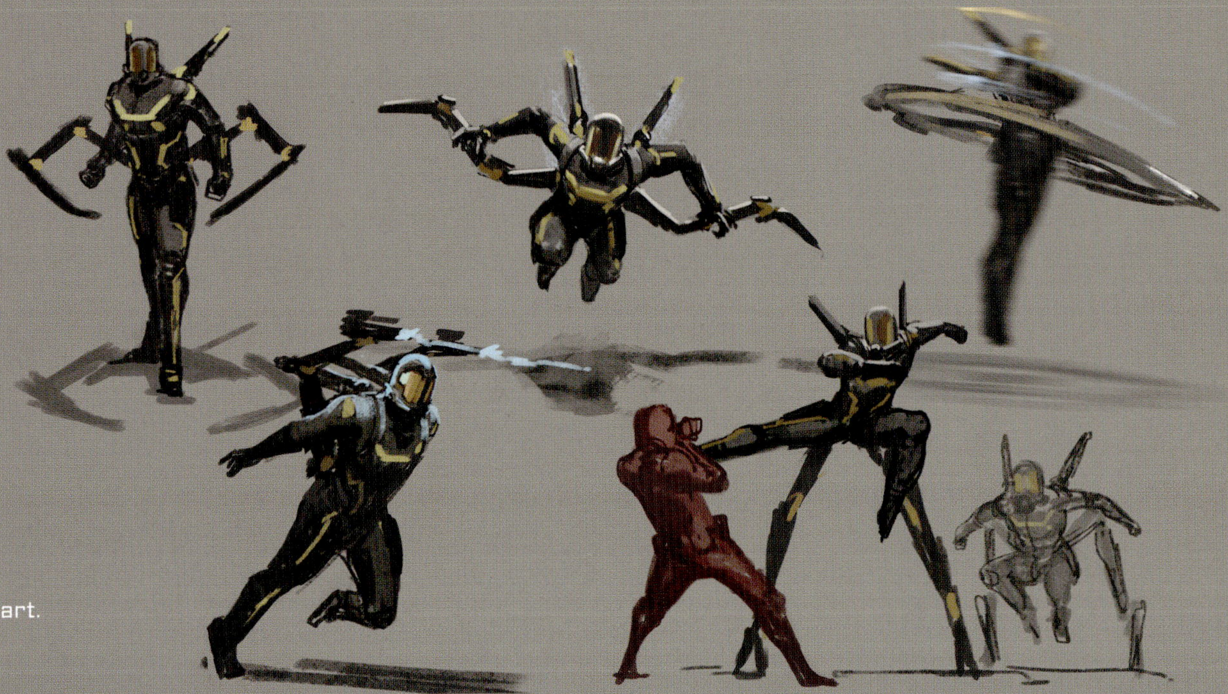

Jackson Sze concept art.

"With Yellowjacket having articulated robotic arms, we explored their functionality in terms of unique mobility and weaponry: What can Yellowjacket do, and how can he move in aggressive and unpredictable ways? By using the arms on his back creatively, we want to show the audience why Yellowjacket is a formidable threat to Ant-Man," Jackson Sze says.

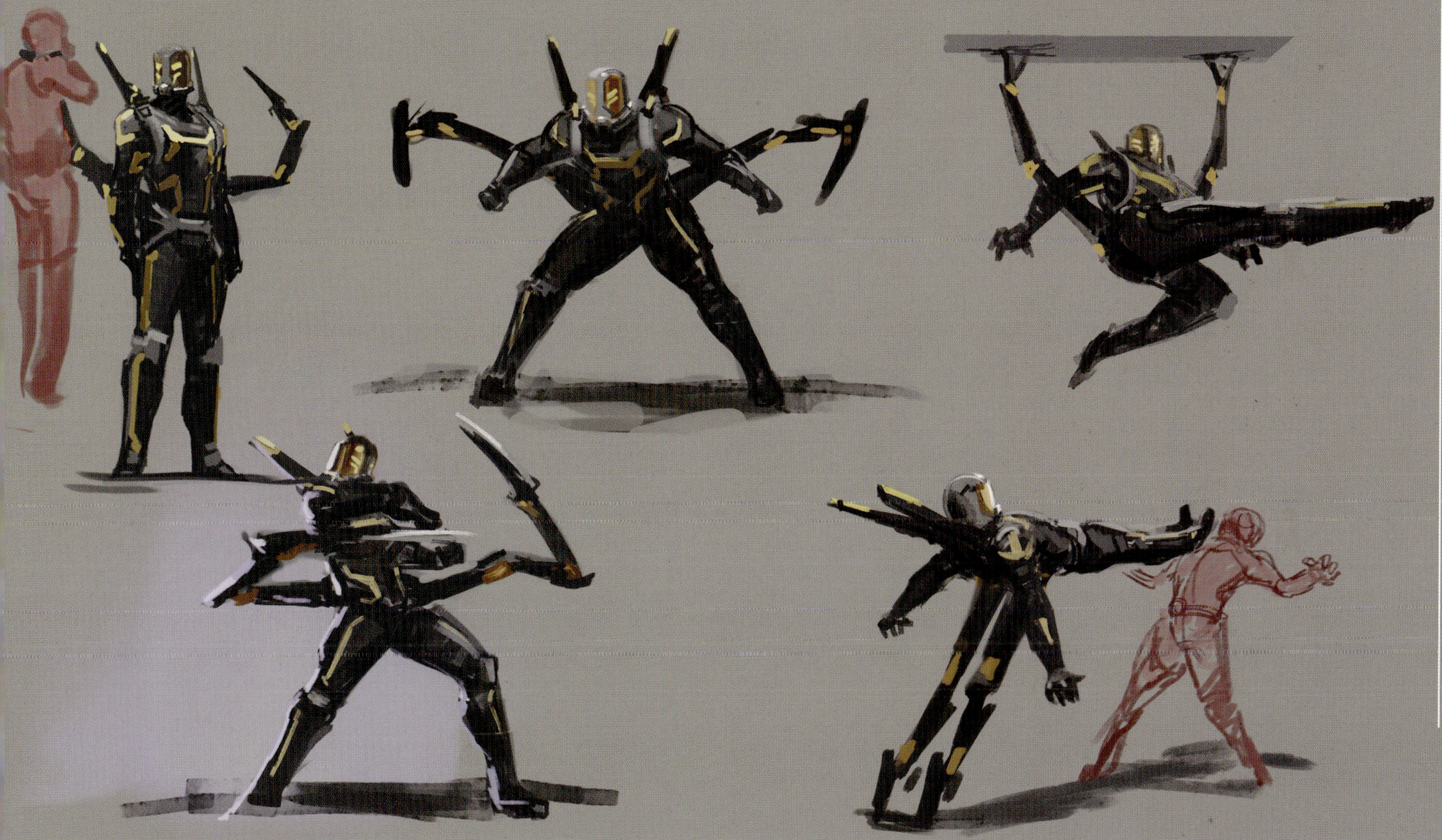

Jackson Sze concept art.

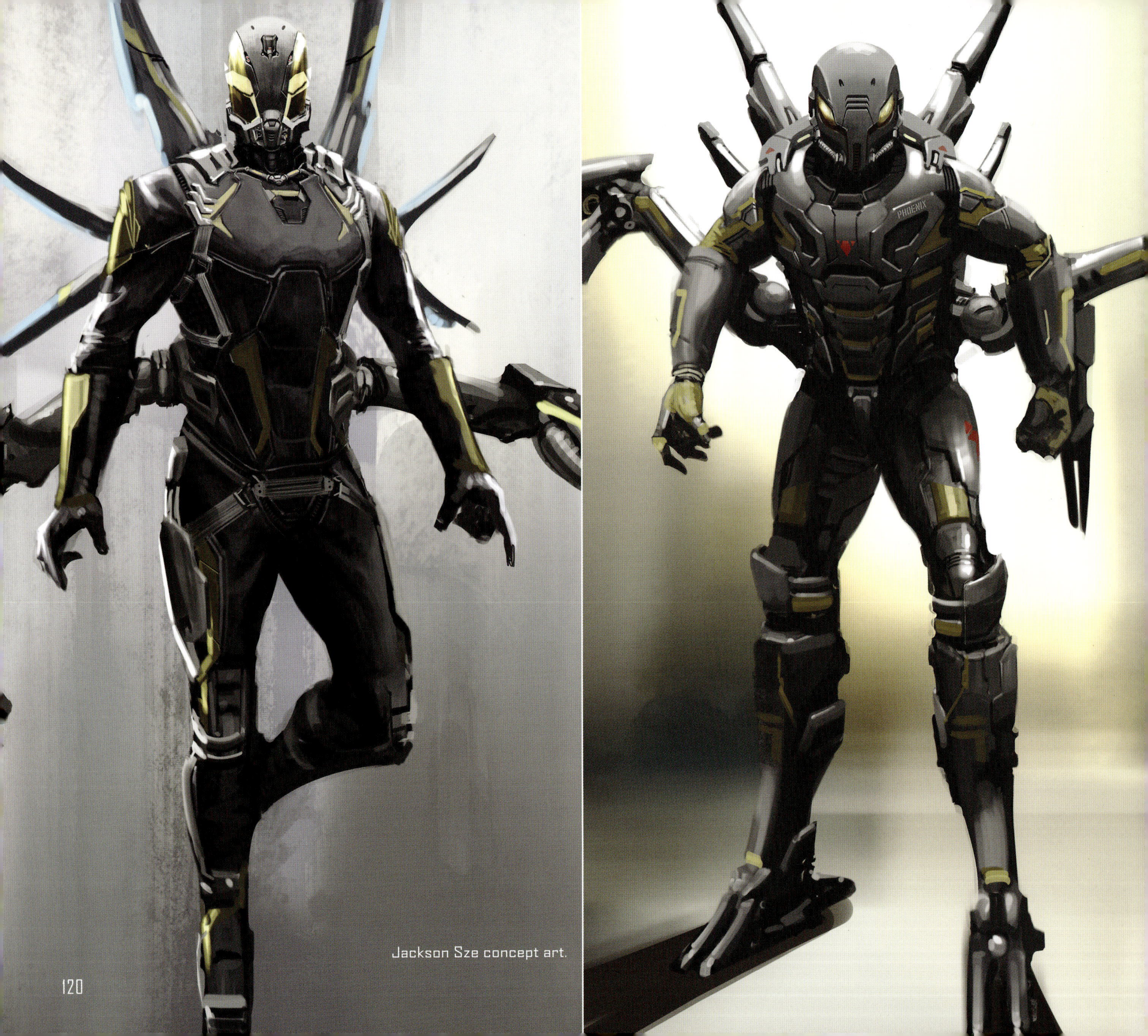

Jackson Sze concept art.

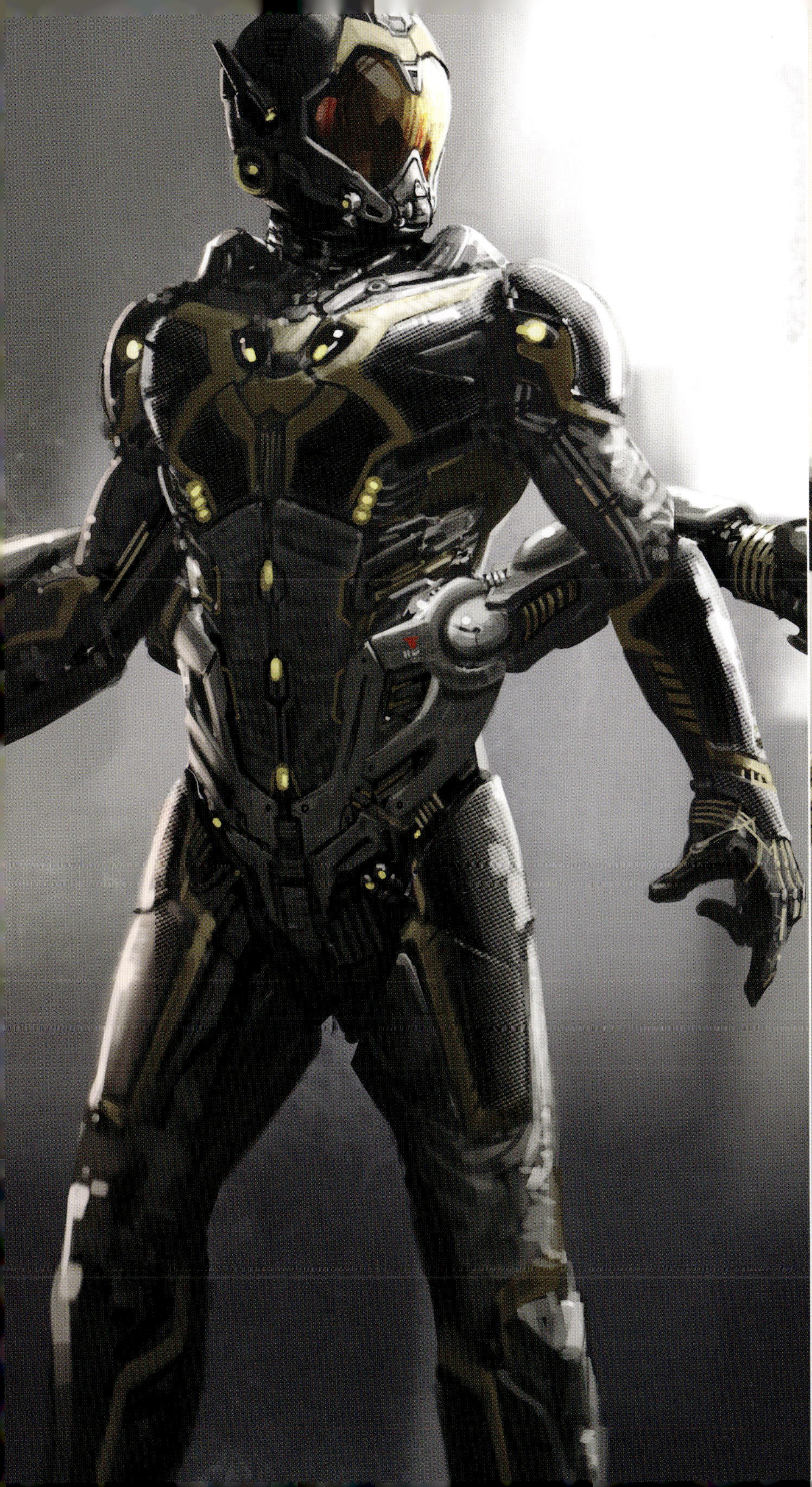

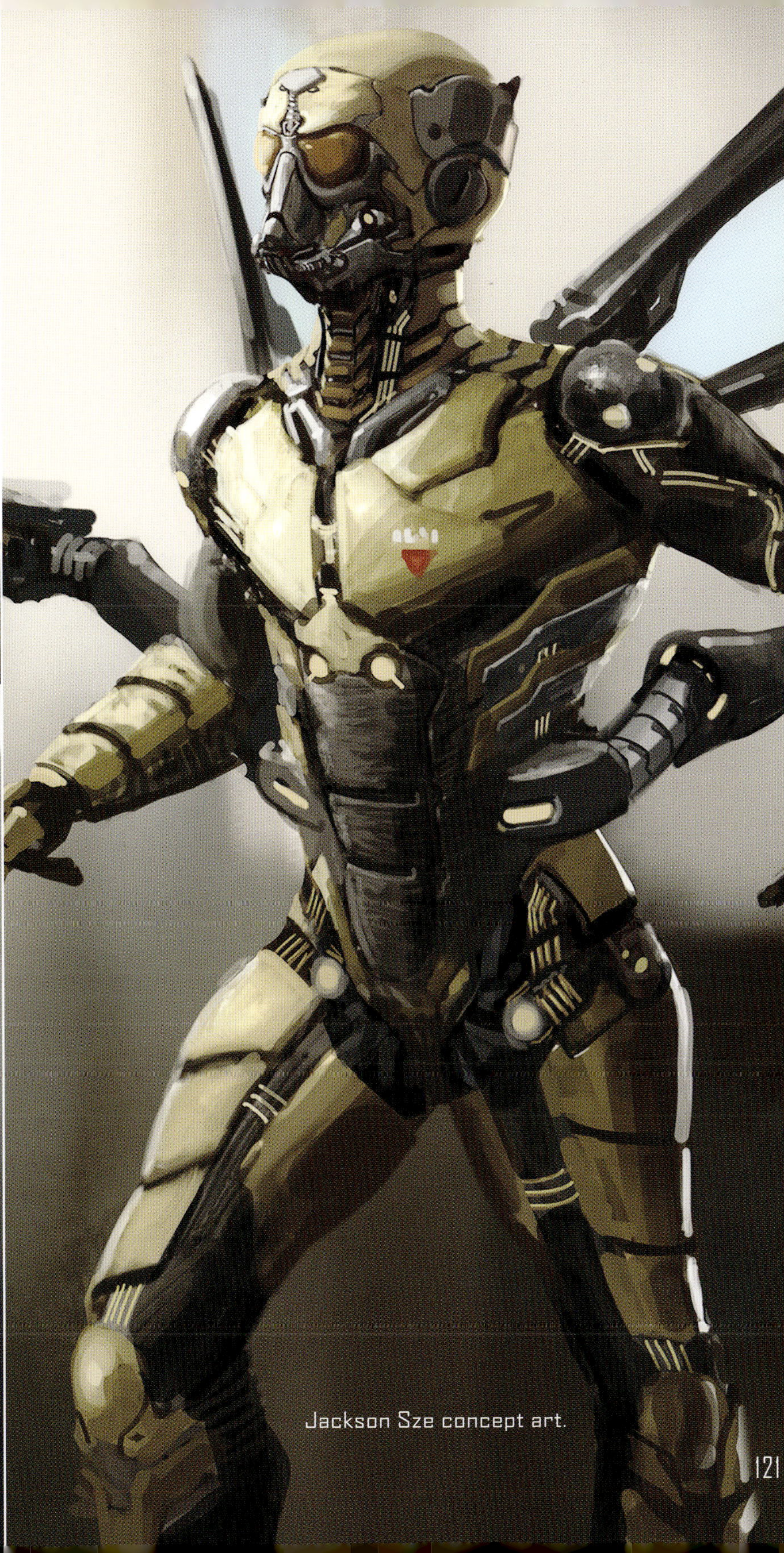

Jackson Sze concept art.

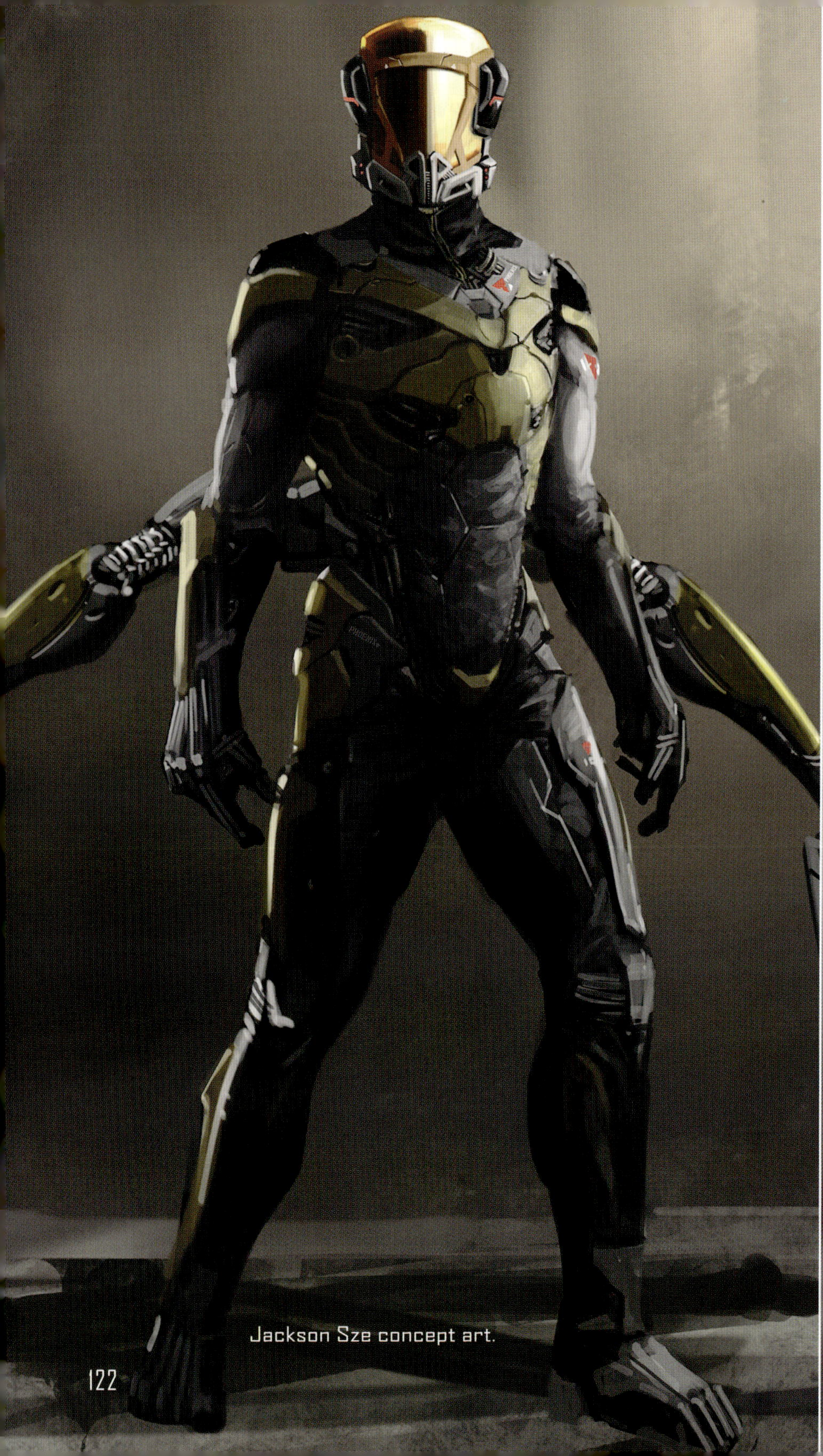

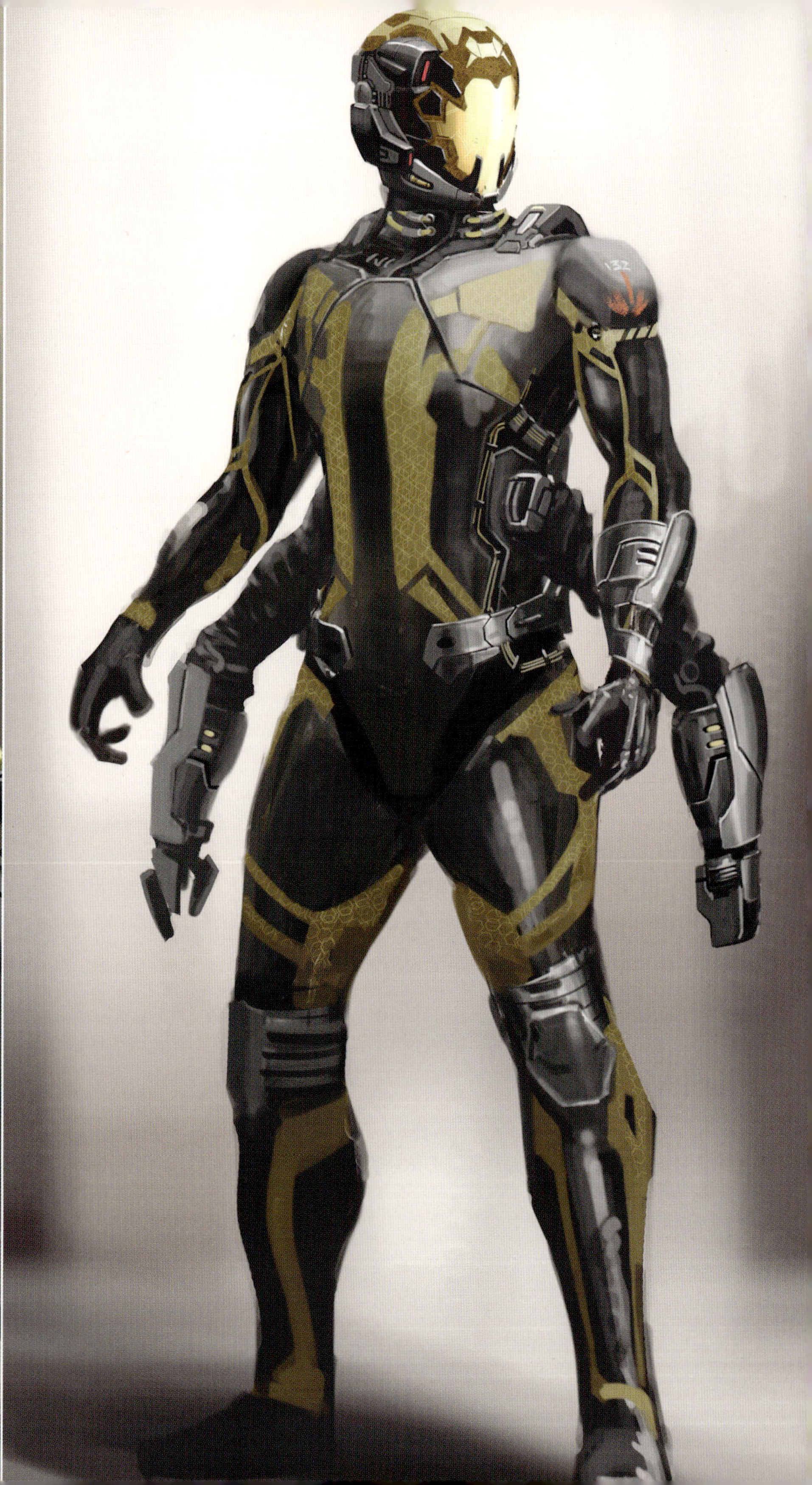

Jackson Sze concept art.

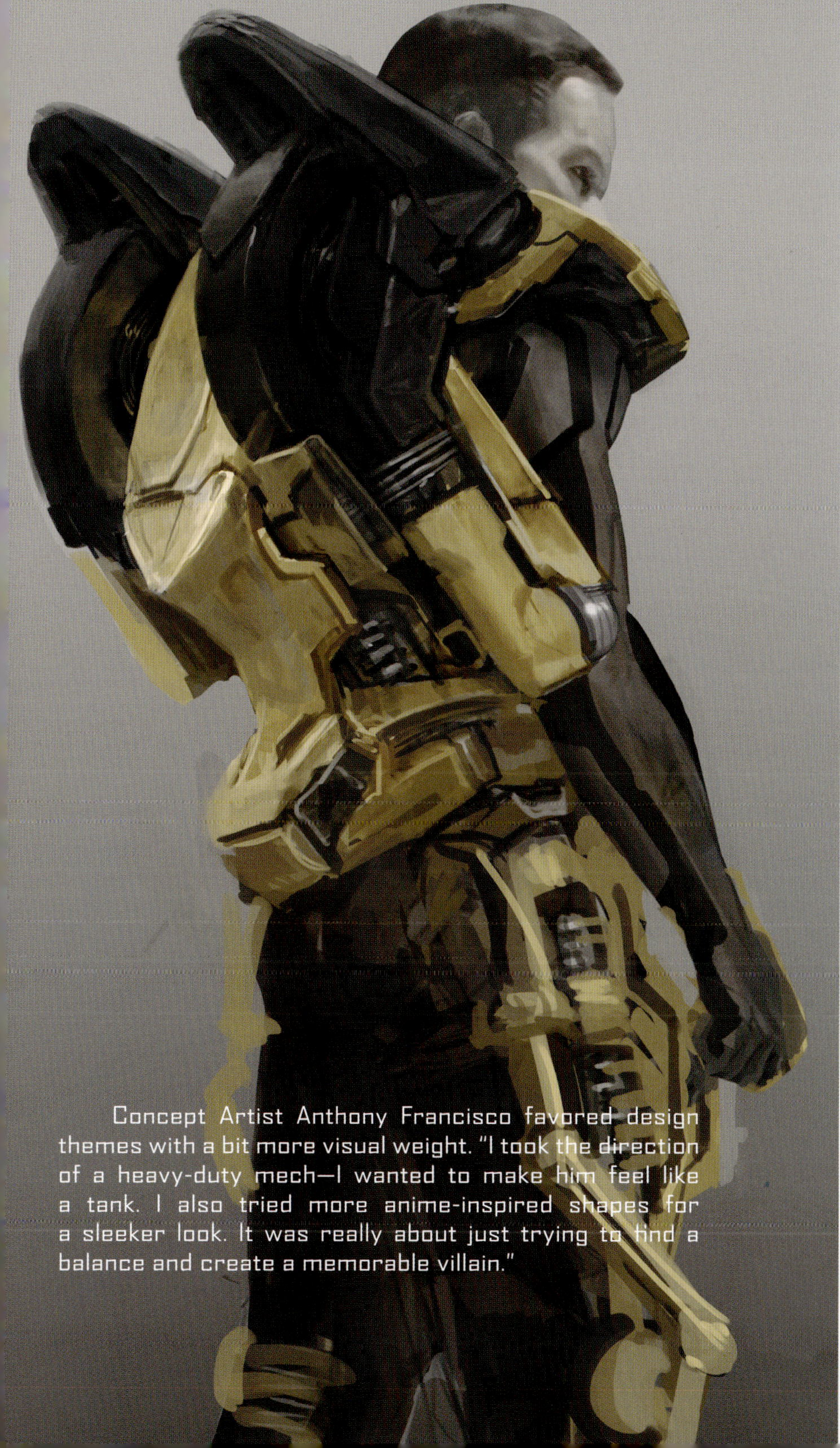

Concept Artist Anthony Francisco favored design themes with a bit more visual weight. "I took the direction of a heavy-duty mech—I wanted to make him feel like a tank. I also tried more anime-inspired shapes for a sleeker look. It was really about just trying to find a balance and create a memorable villain."

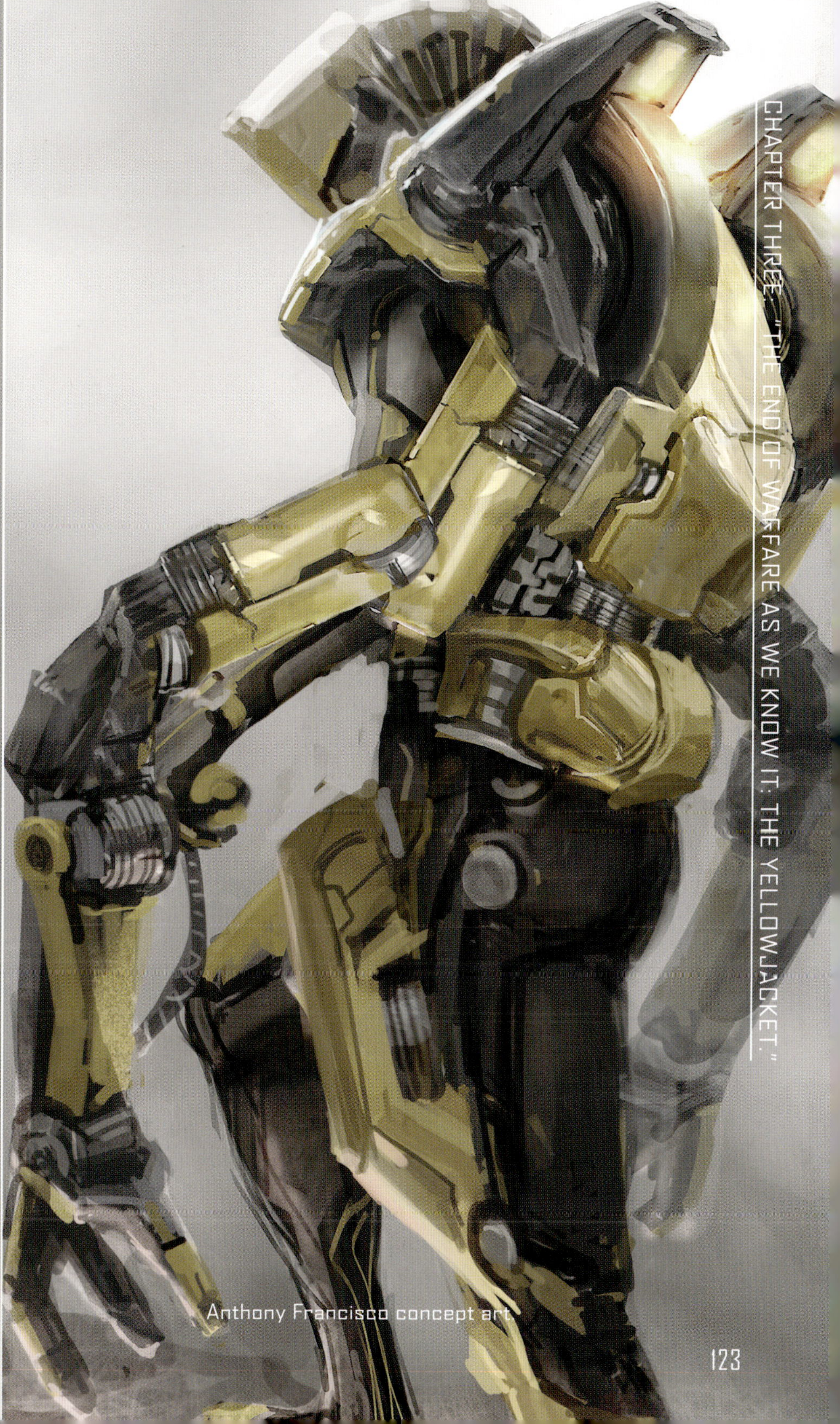

Anthony Francisco concept art.

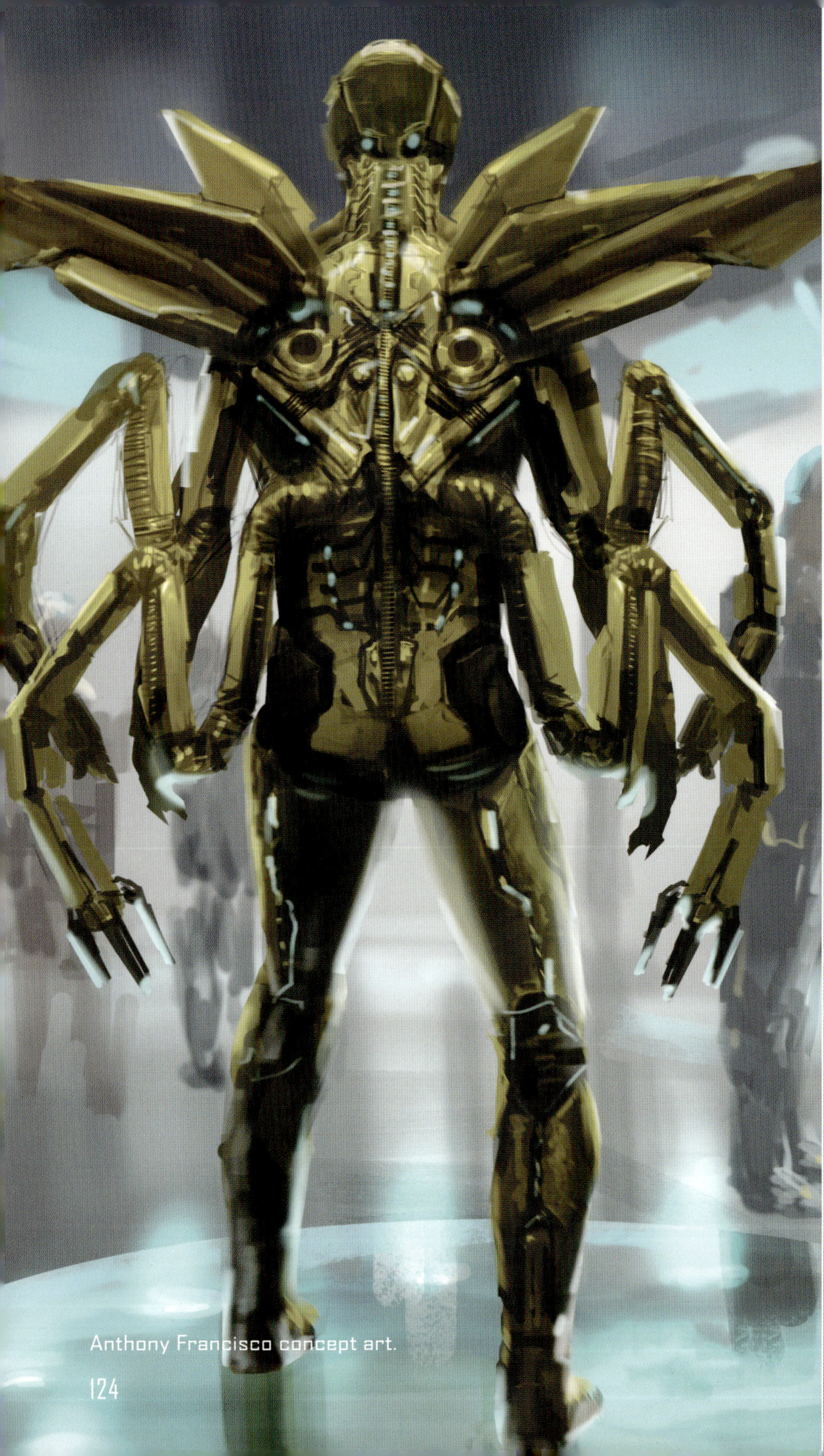

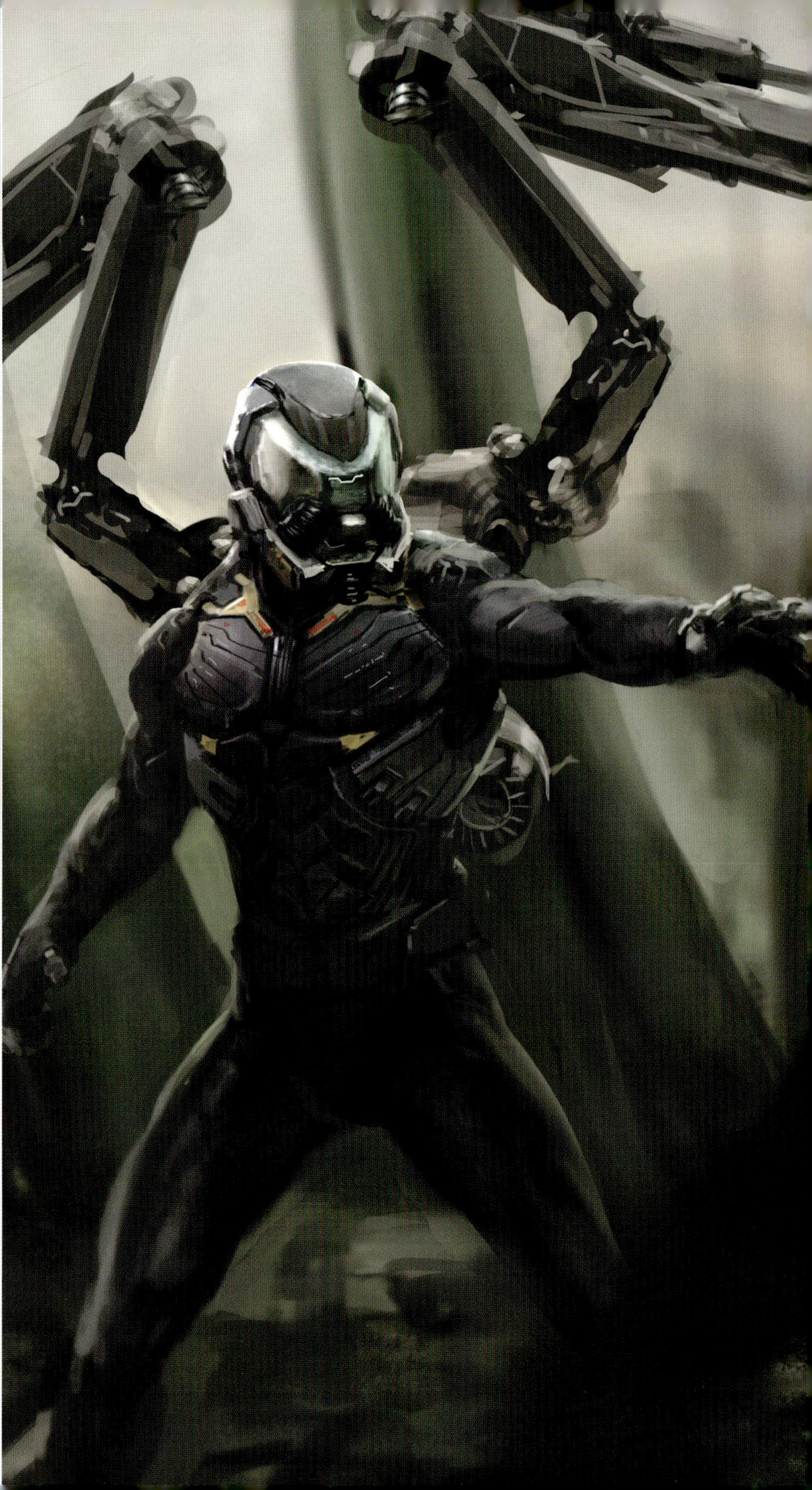

Anthony Francisco concept art.

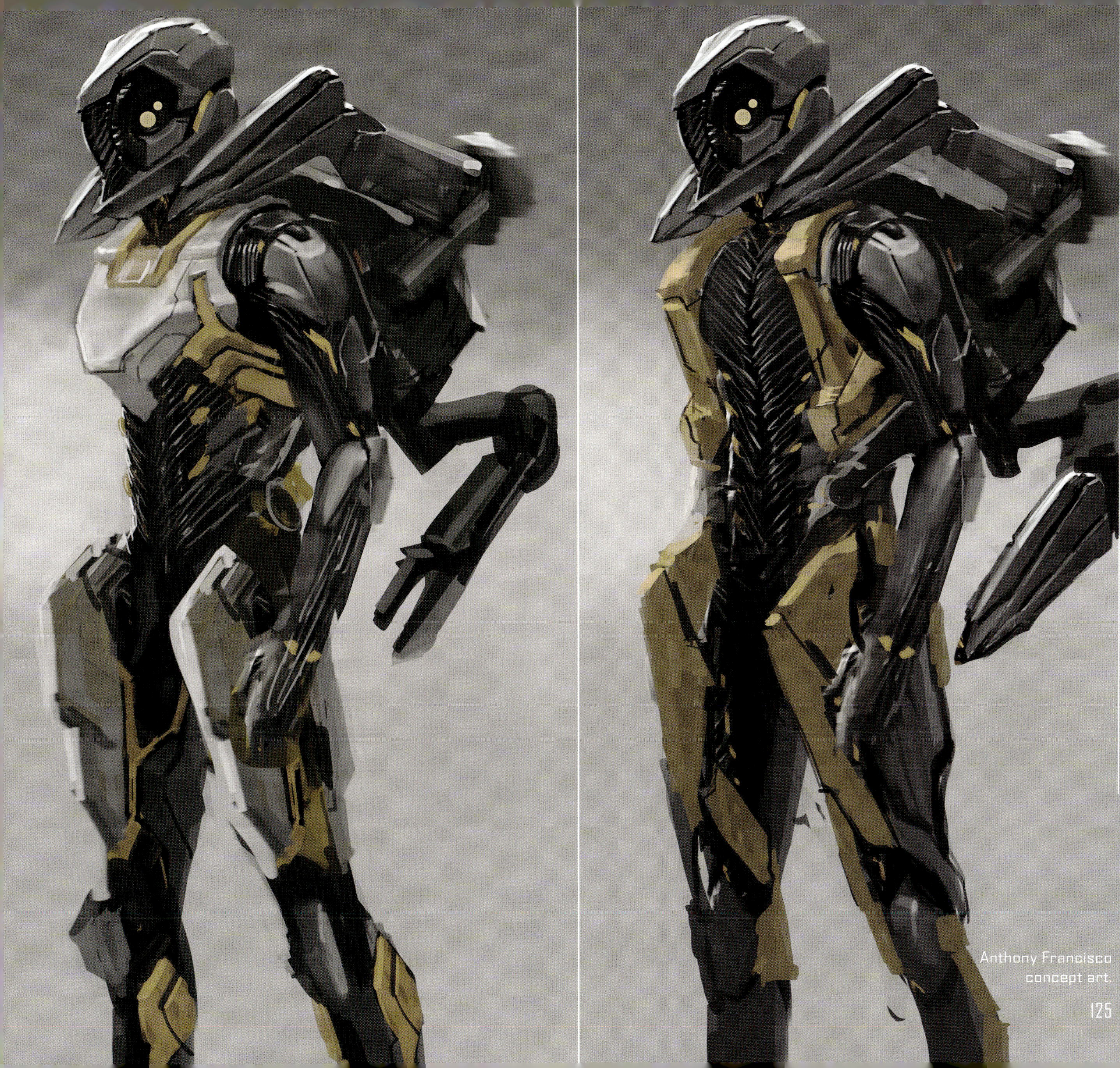

Anthony Francisco concept art.

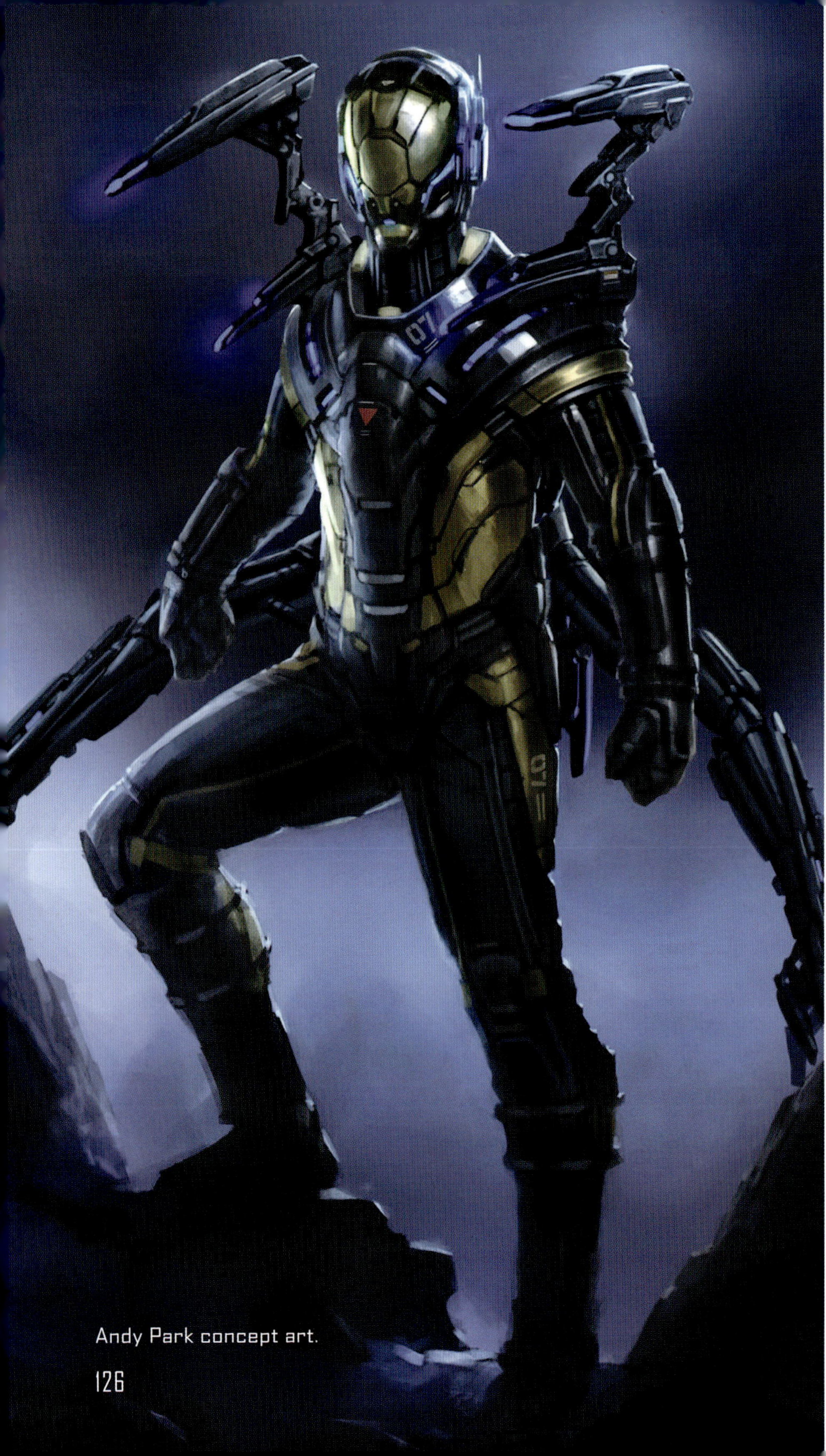

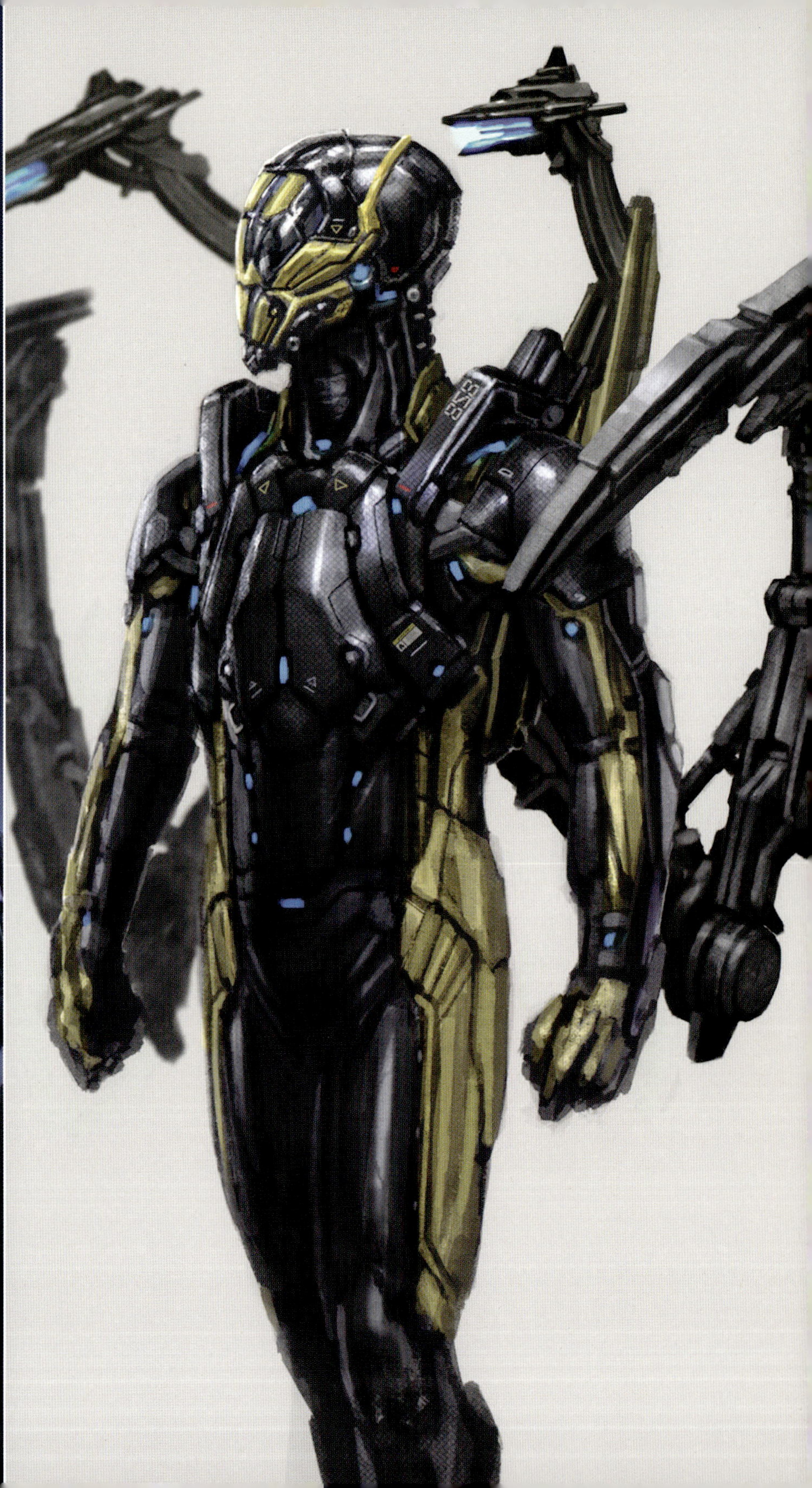

Andy Park concept art.

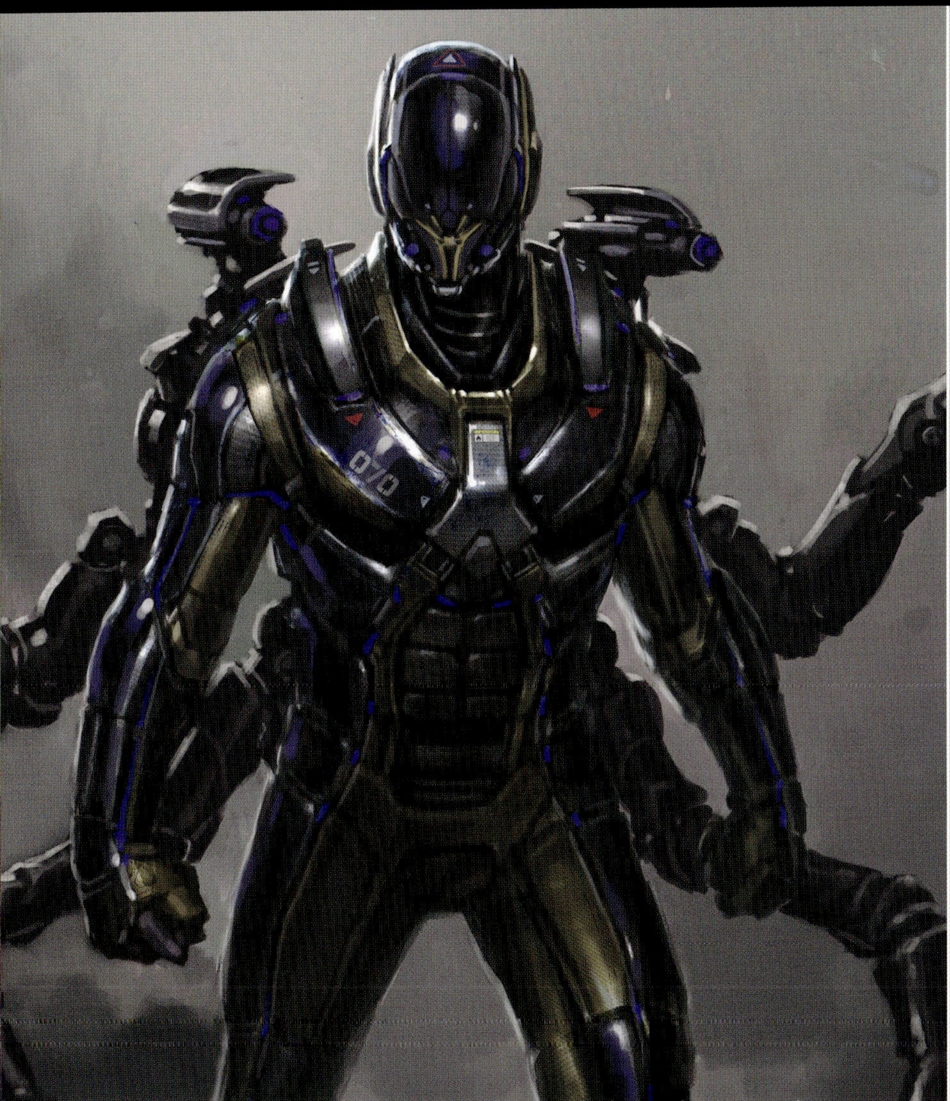

"In concept design, it always helps when you have a base to work off of," Concept Artist Andy Park says. "In this case, the base was Ant-Man. Ant-Man has the retro 'advanced for his time' look, but it's a bit clunky. In contrast, Yellowjacket is today's sleek, high-tech suit, with all the bells and whistles you could imagine. And given that this was one character who had no comic-book source material (beyond his name), we were free to really explore ideas. It's a rare opportunity to design a purely new character with no comic-book background. I explored various looks that showed a high-technology base, but something that was clearly different from an Iron Man suit. The most that I tried to integrate from the comic-book look was in his color scheme, with yellow jacket bee design themes and shoulder protrusions that essentially folded out to become his extra appendages."

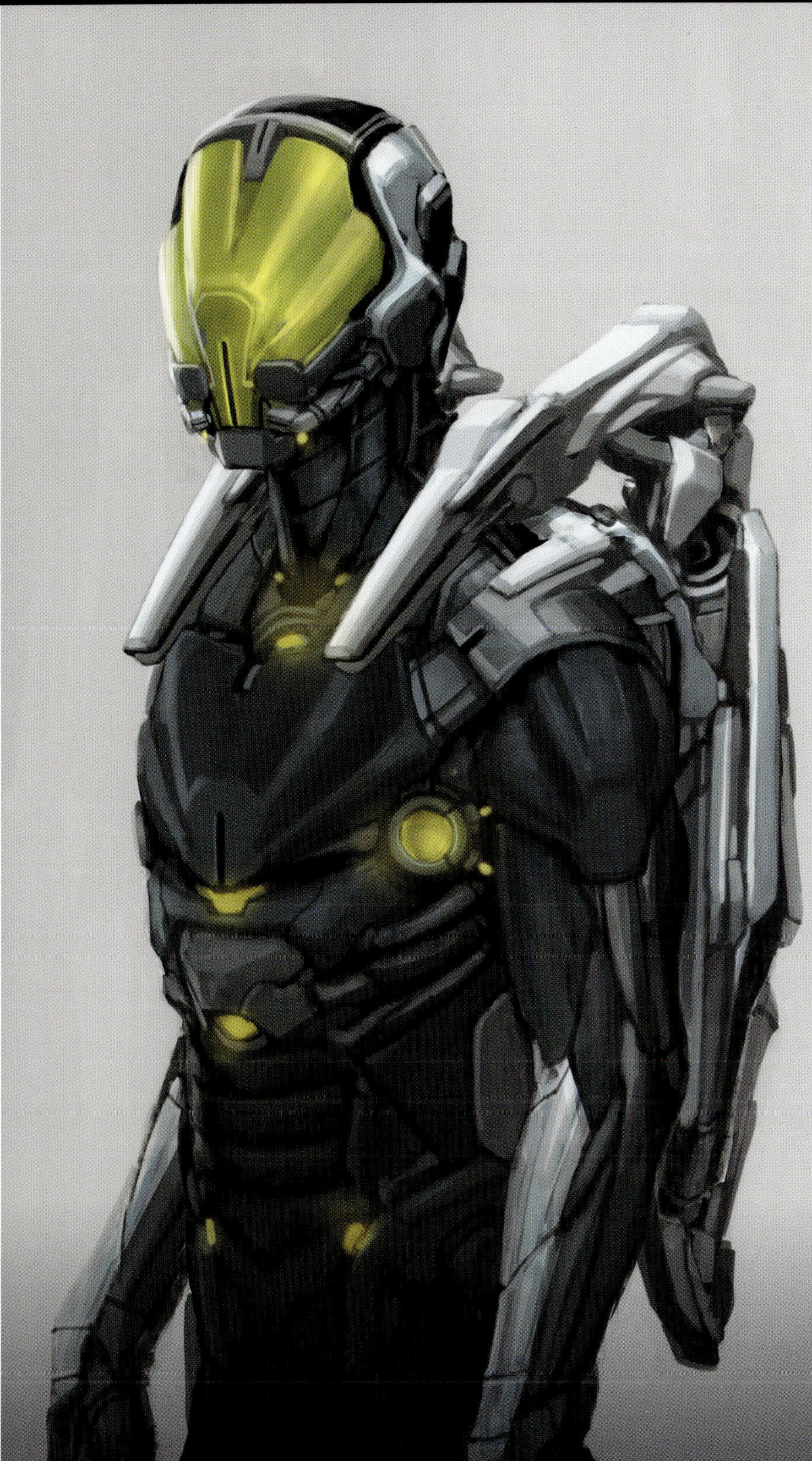

Andy Park concept art.

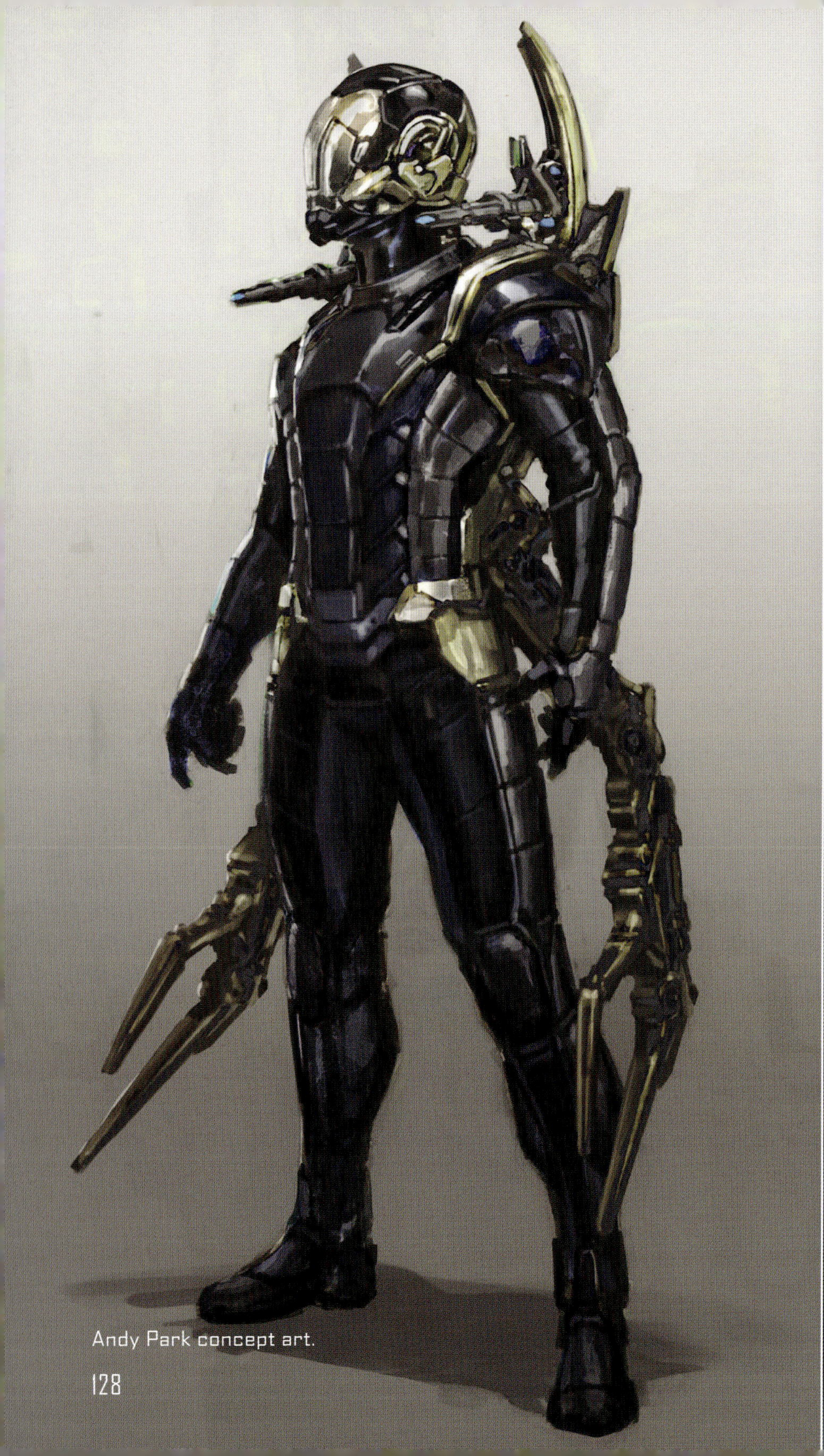

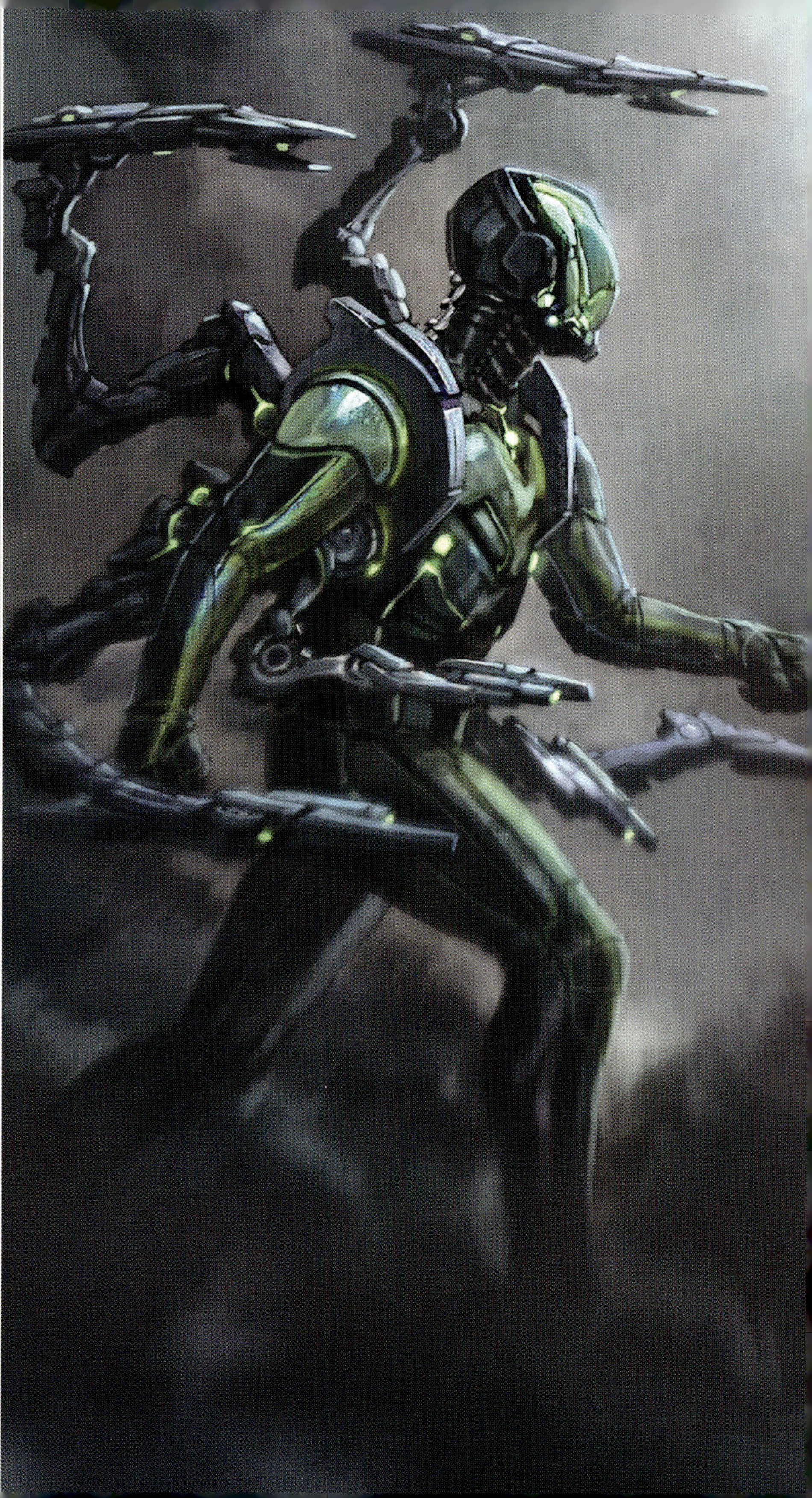

Andy Park concept art.

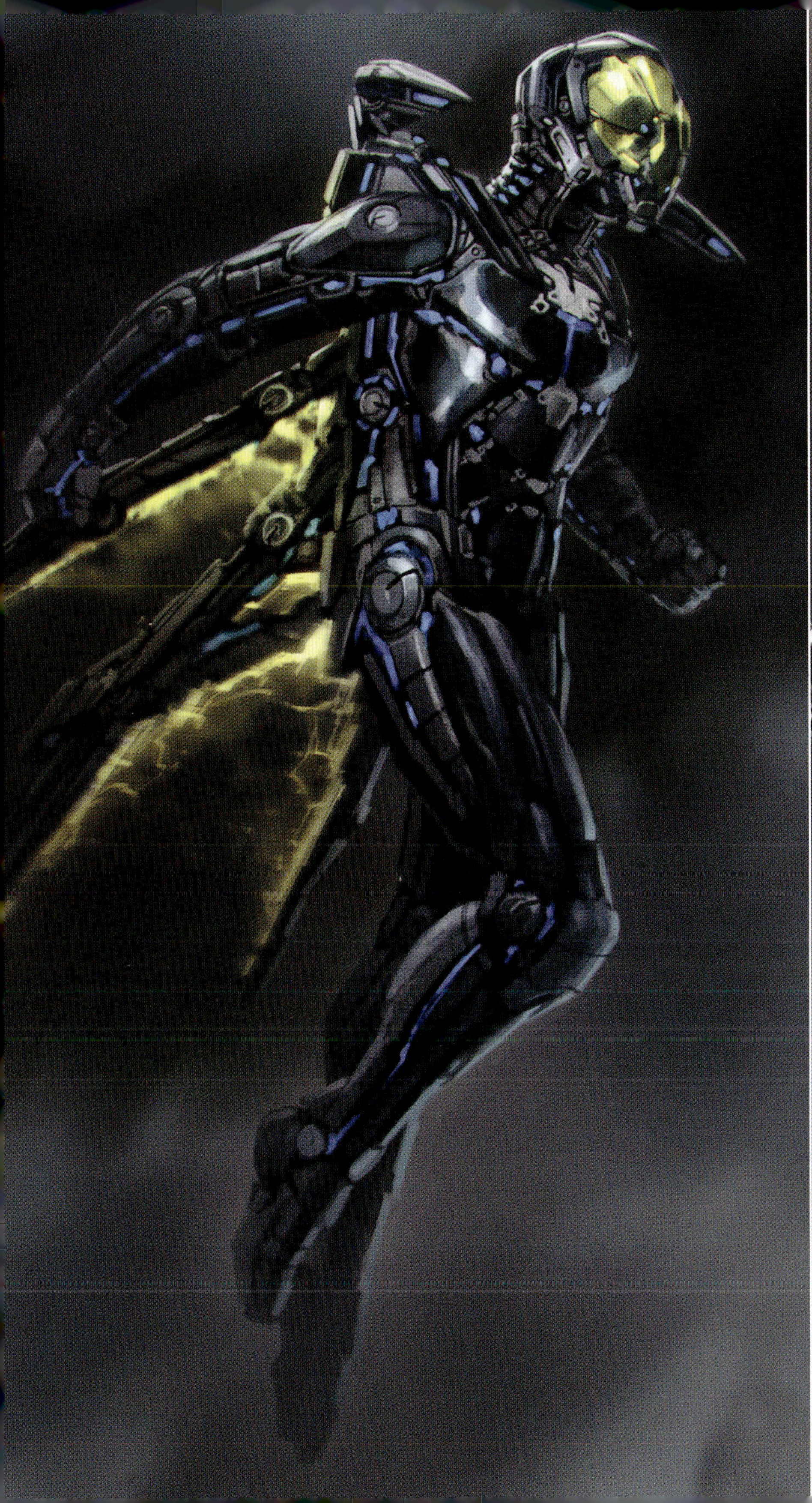

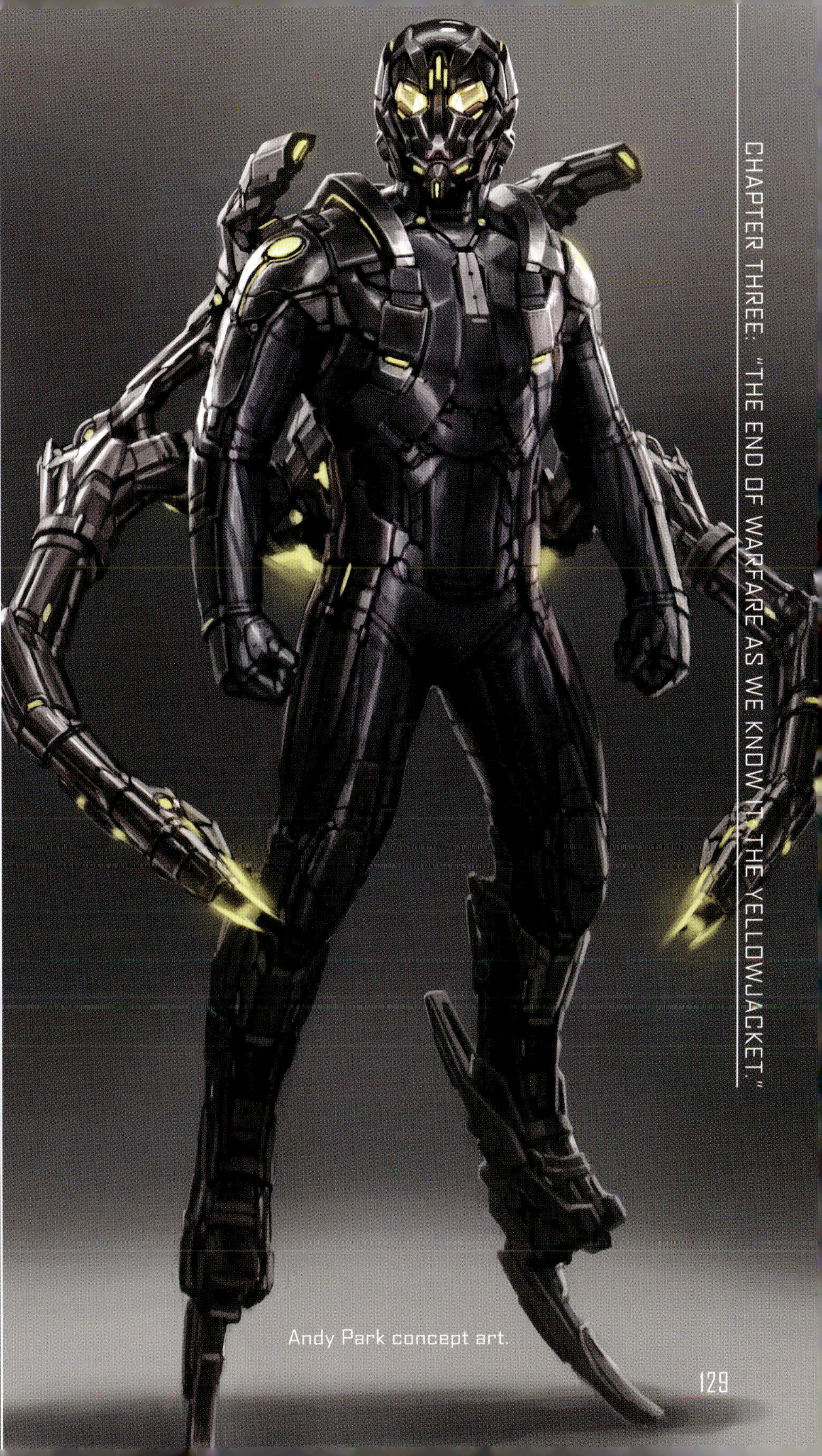

Andy Park concept art.

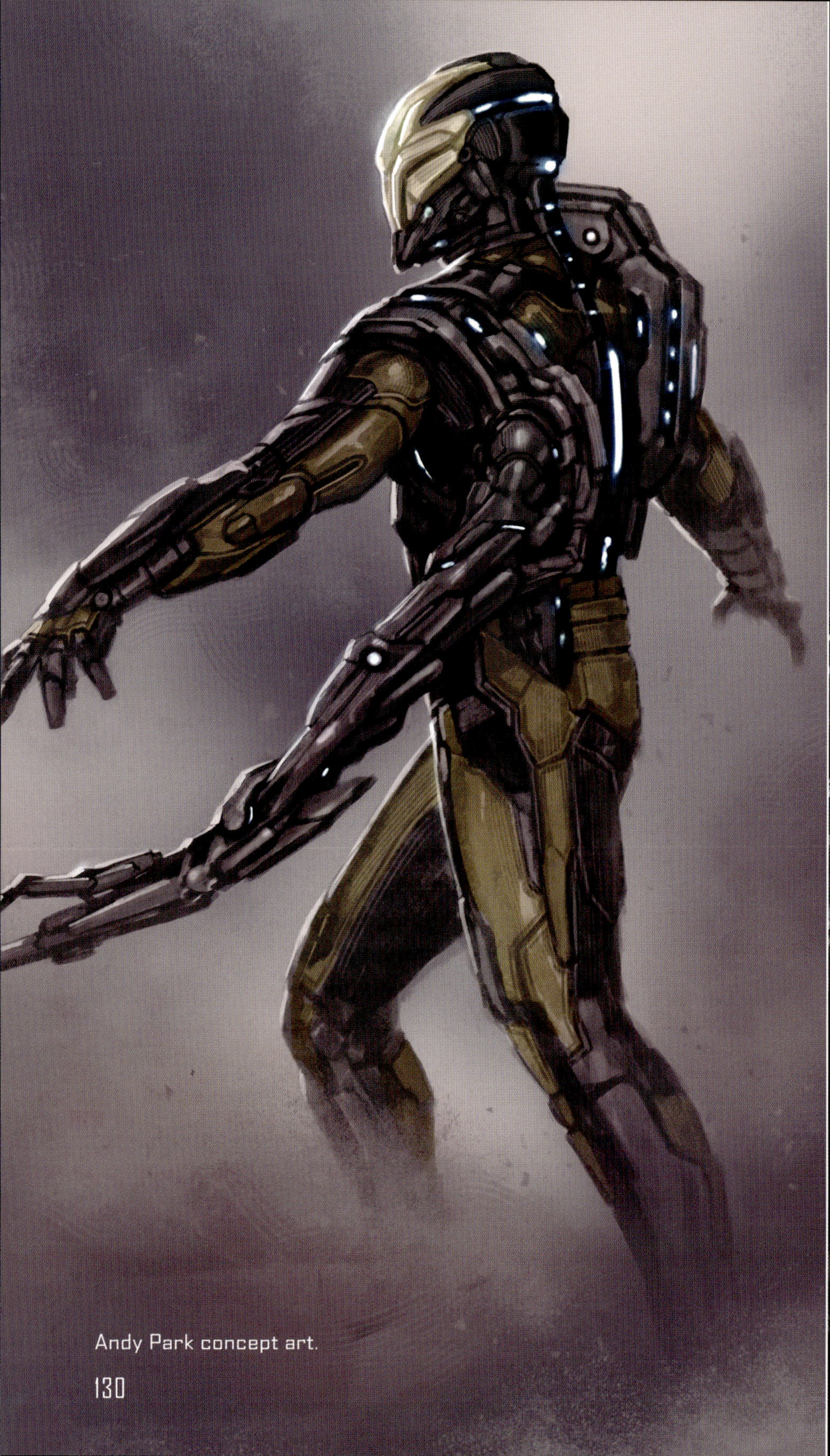

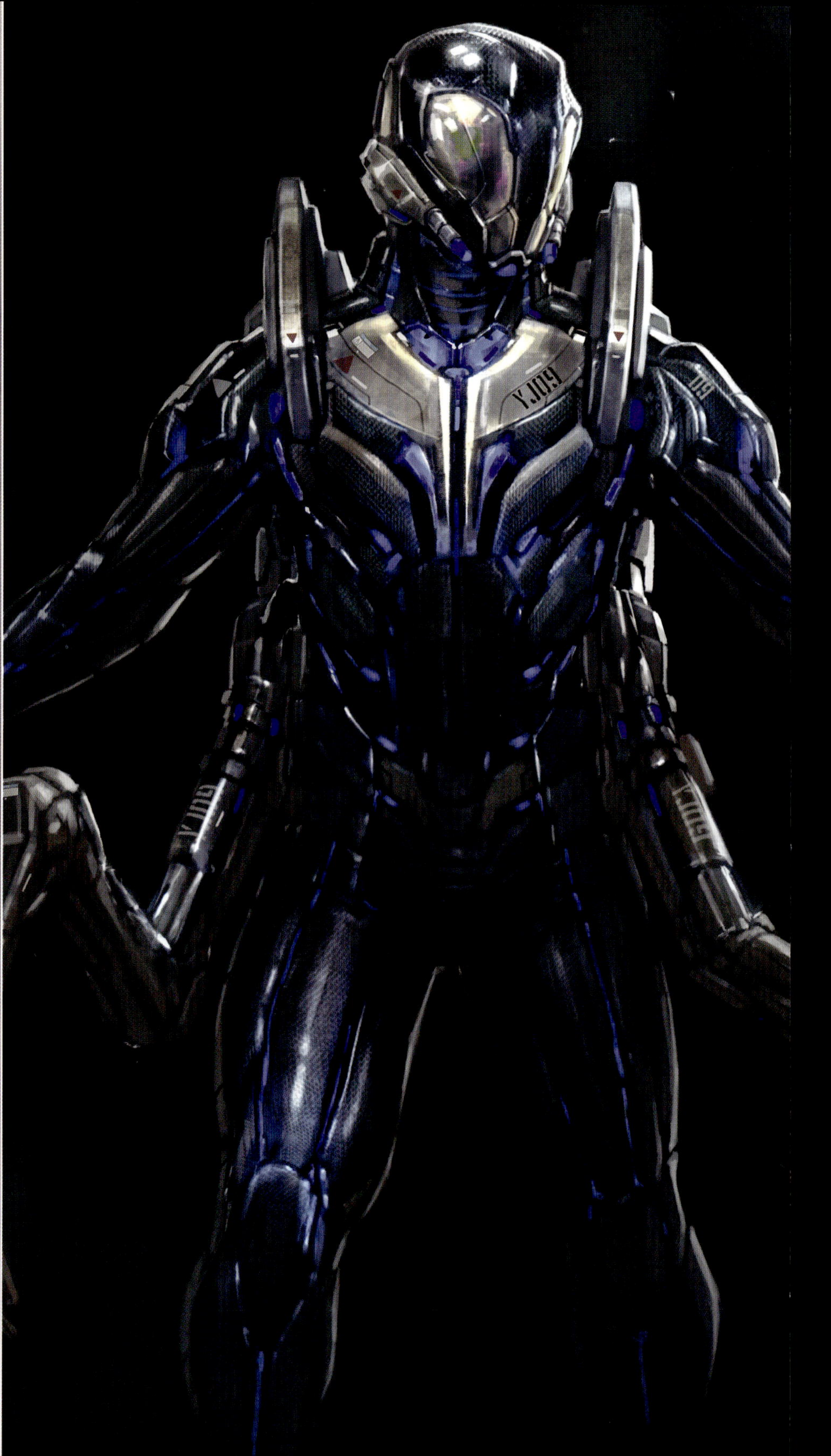

Andy Park concept art.

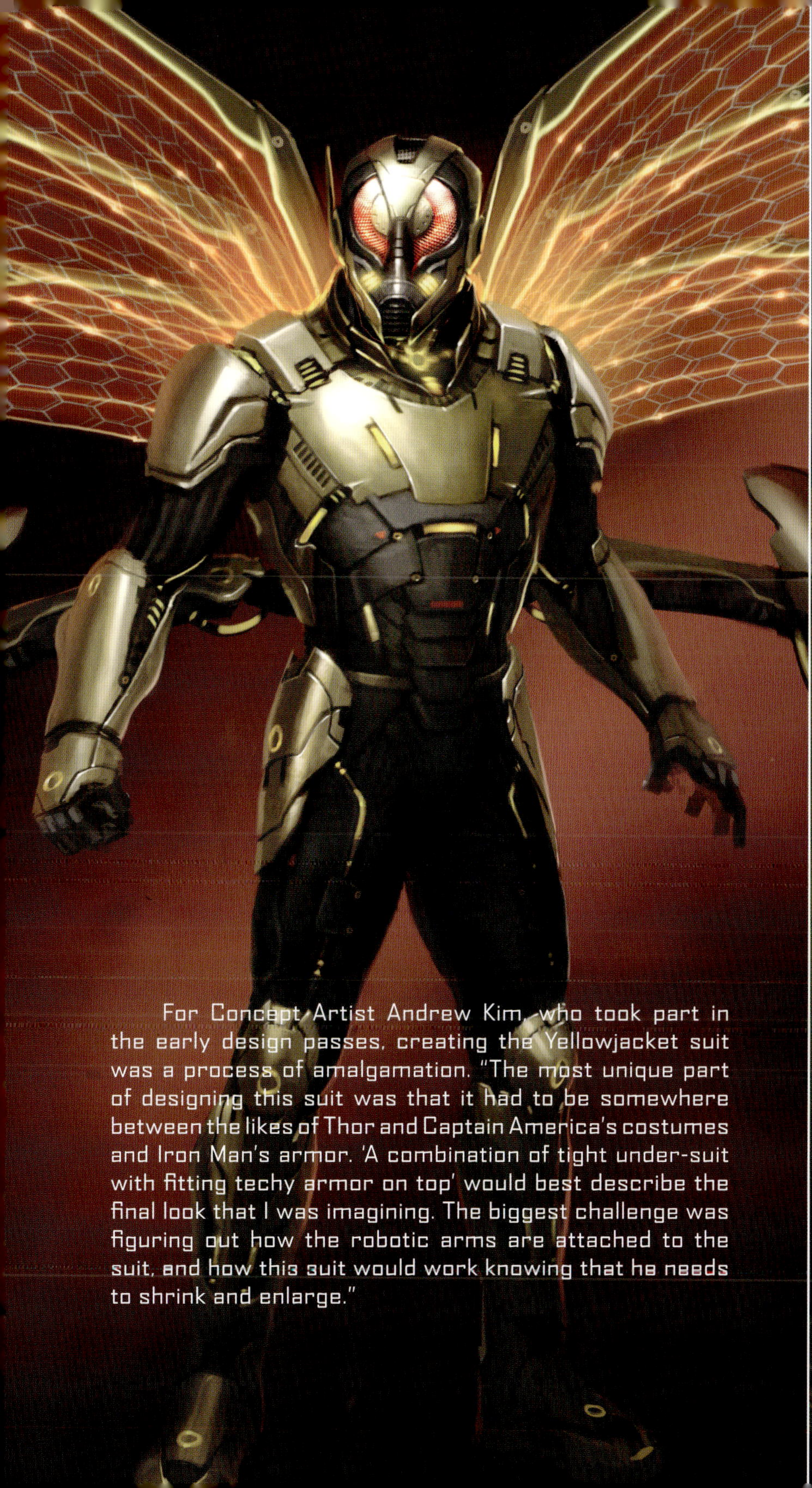

For Concept Artist Andrew Kim, who took part in the early design passes, creating the Yellowjacket suit was a process of amalgamation. "The most unique part of designing this suit was that it had to be somewhere between the likes of Thor and Captain America's costumes and Iron Man's armor. 'A combination of tight under-suit with fitting techy armor on top' would best describe the final look that I was imagining. The biggest challenge was figuring out how the robotic arms are attached to the suit, and how this suit would work knowing that he needs to shrink and enlarge."

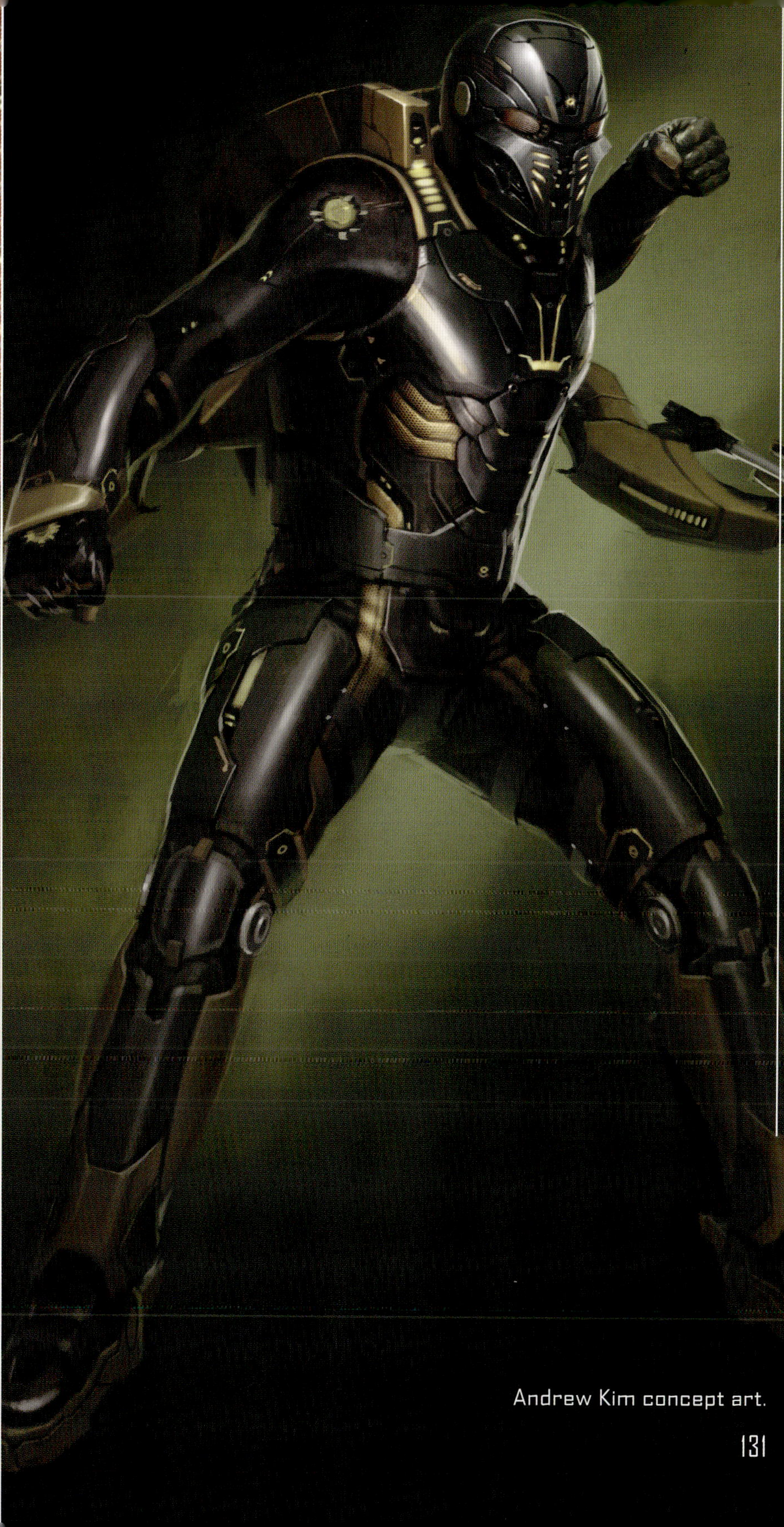

Andrew Kim concept art.

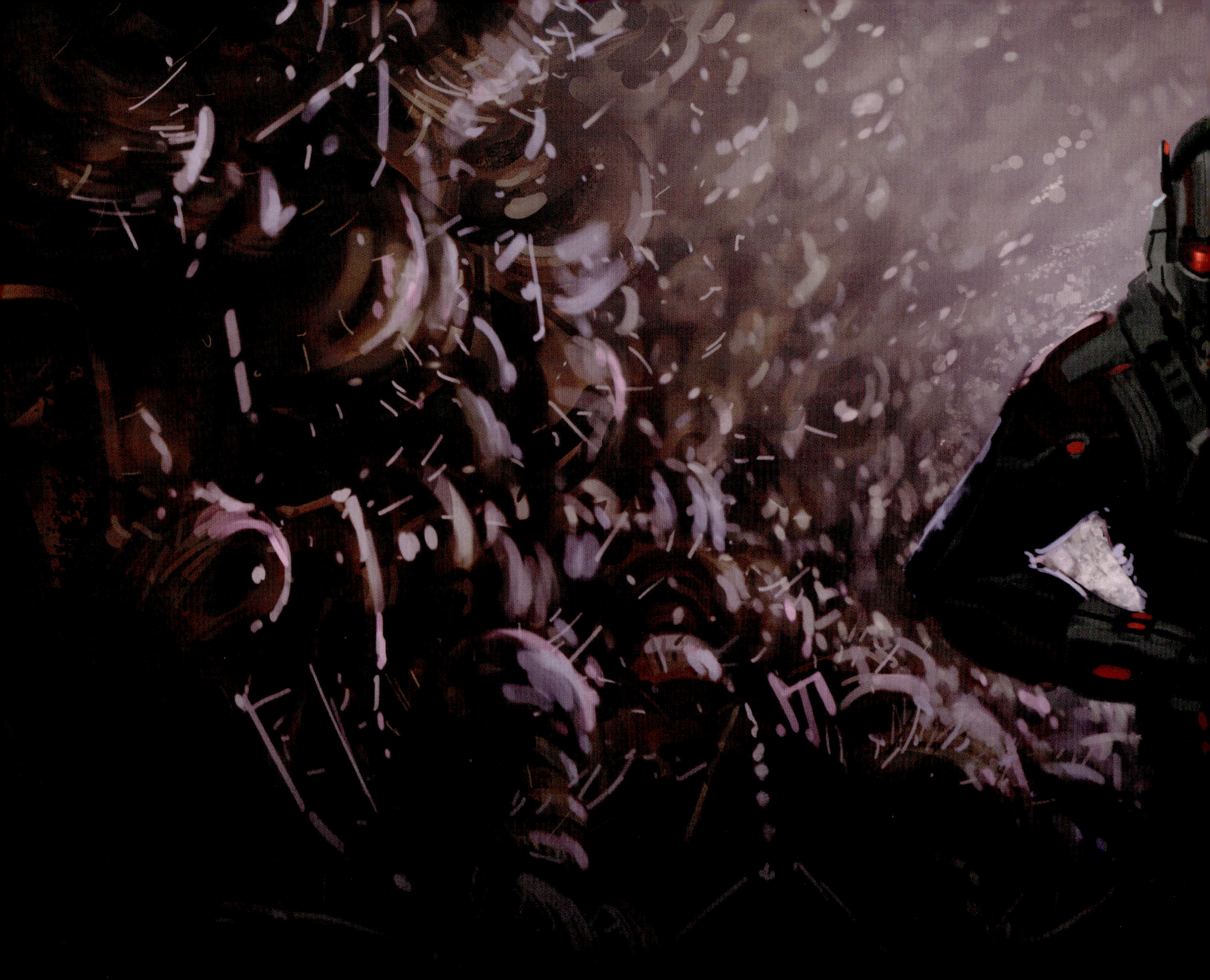

Jackson Sze keyframe.

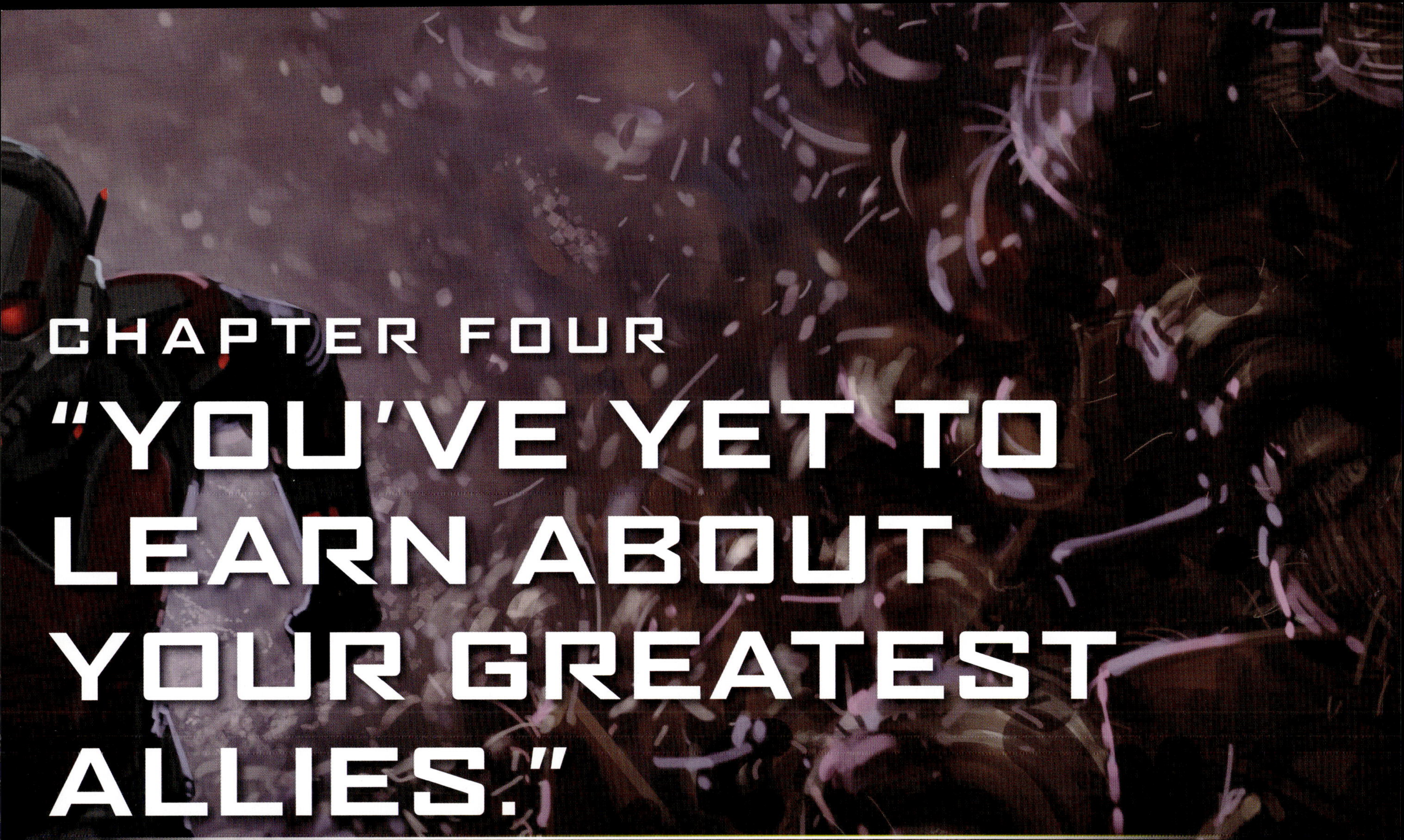

CHAPTER FOUR

"YOU'VE YET TO LEARN ABOUT YOUR GREATEST ALLIES."

As Scott Lang thrusts himself into rigorous training to become the new Ant-Man under Hank Pym and Hope Van Dyne's guidance, he begins to realize there's more to the suit than what's on the surface—much like an anthill. Underground, thousands of tiny allies await his command, but first he'll have to master the art of communicating with his six-legged soldiers. Scott must memorize the scientific names and characteristics of a spread of species with individualized specialties based on size and personality. The ants offer more than their technical services—they also bring personality and heart to the film. "They add a huge amount of character to the piece," Visual Effects Supervisor Jake Morrison explains. "Hopefully when the viewers finish watching the film, they feel for the ants—and they realize there is a world down there that they can't see, or don't experience, but it's full of life and full of character. We debated early on how we could give this anthropomorphic behavior to ants—clearly they don't behave that way when you look through a magnifying glass—and Kevin Feige looked at me and said, 'How do you know? Maybe you have to be half-an-inch tall to see this character.'"

The film's crew, much like Scott, underwent an educational excavation into the microscopic world of ants. "Ants are a lot like humans—they have their own world, and they're actually quite likeable," Visual Effects Producer Diana Giorgiutti says. "I have a lot of respect for them now—a lot more than I did before."

HOPE VAN DYNE

Hank Pym's daughter, Hope Van Dyne, is an employee at PymTech under Darren Cross. Her deep-rooted emotional issues—products of a tragic family history—are only exacerbated by Scott Lang's involvement with her father. Actress Evangeline Lilly, who portrays Hope Van Dyne in the film, elaborates: "Hope can't stand Scott. She thinks he's a useless idiot, and she thinks that Hank's wasting his time with him. She actually believes that he's detrimental to their mission to bring down PymTech. I think Hope is pretty convinced that there's nobody who would be better to complete this mission than her in the Ant-Man suit."

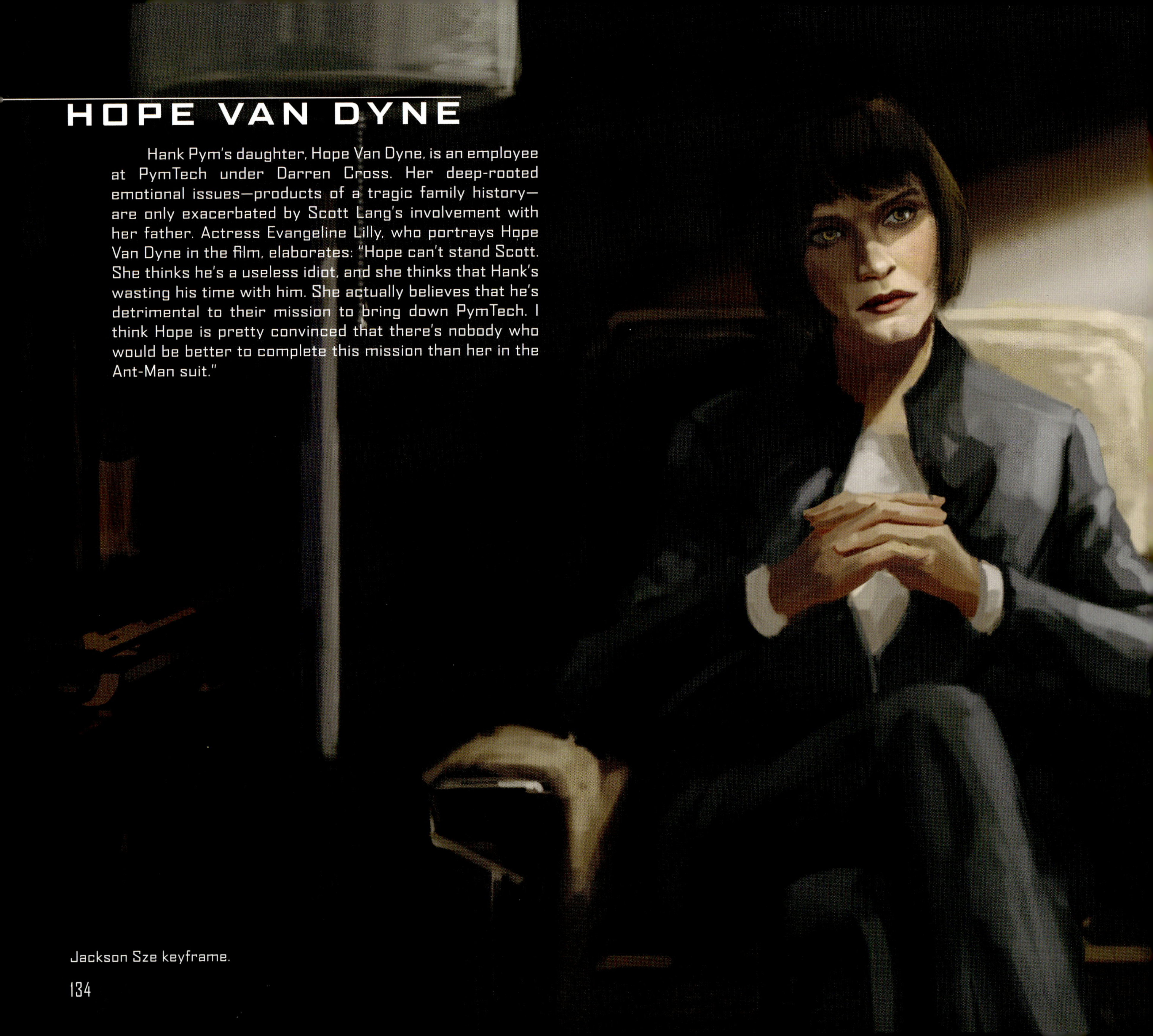

Jackson Sze keyframe.

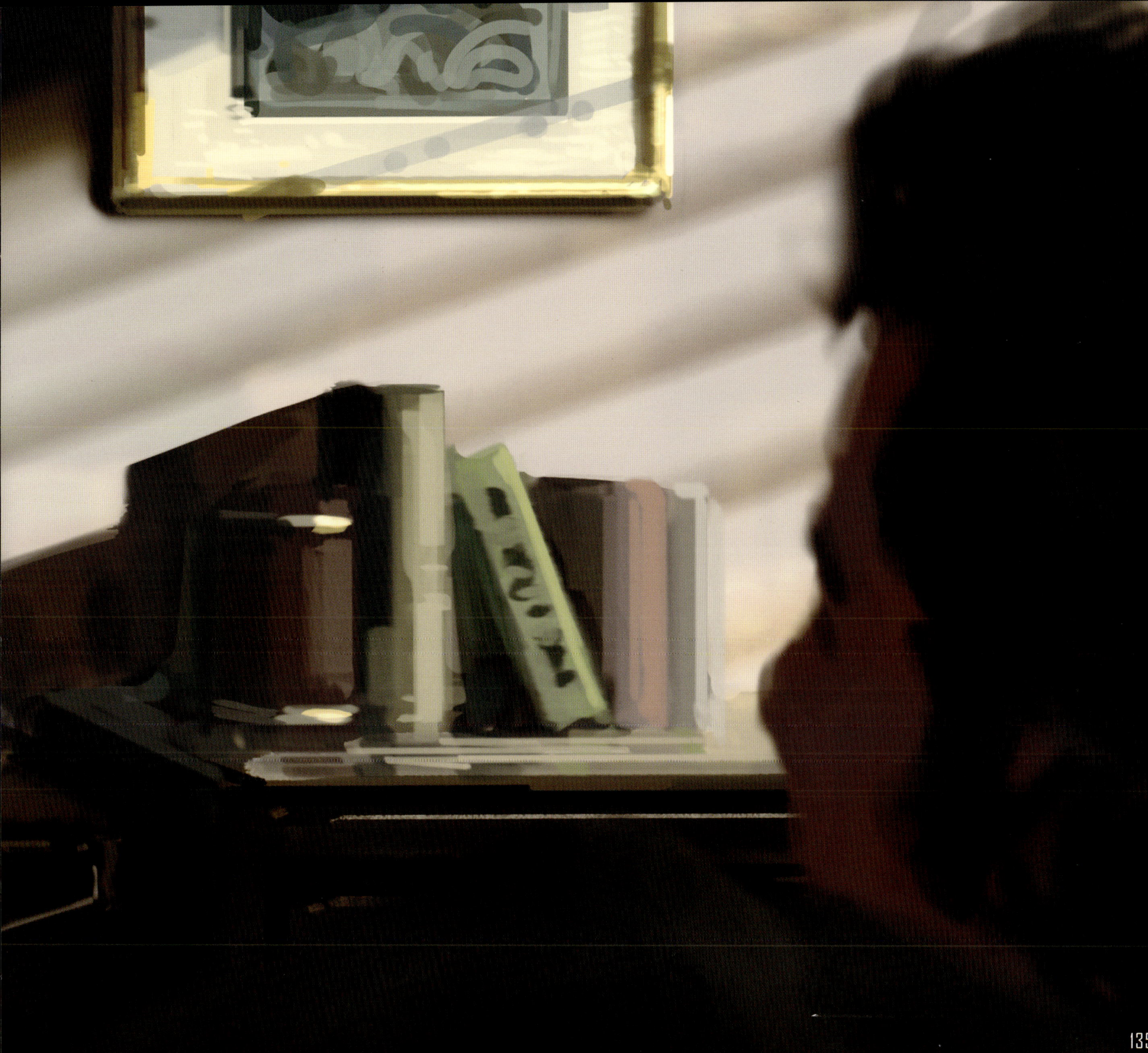

THE ROSTER

Ant-Man's army of ants includes five different species with equally distinct personalities. According to Executive Producer Victoria Alonso, the key to defining the ants was remaining as accurate to their natural selves as possible. "There was no hyper-characterization of the ants," she explains. "The idea was to stay true to how the ants are in real life, but to give it enough of a filmic look that—well, most people want to step on an ant. The idea was not to have that feeling. The key to doing this was to enter their world, go down to microphotography, and see how they live and what they really look like. The minute you see what they really look like, the minute you can enter their world, you almost find them endearing, and you can connect with them."

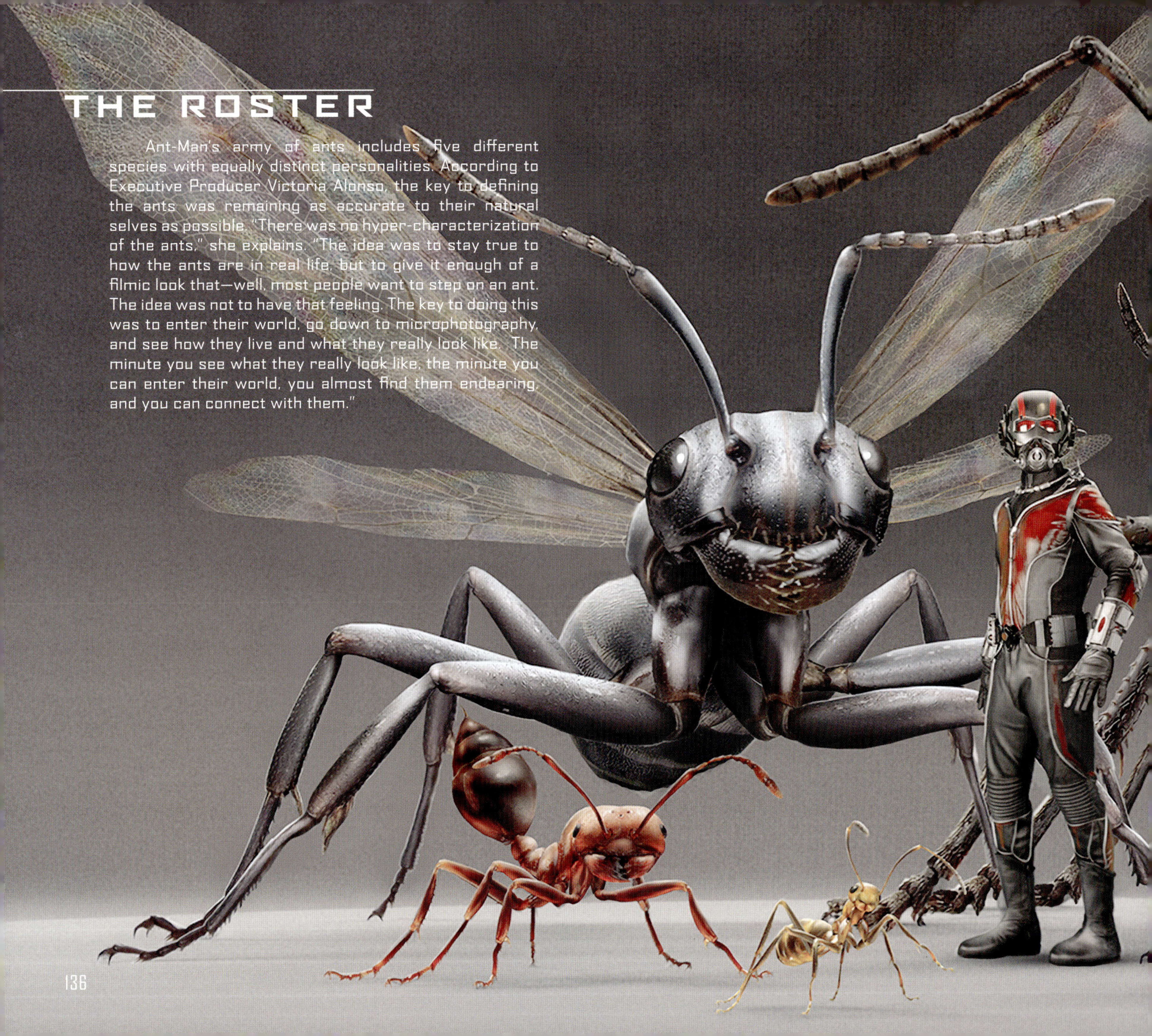

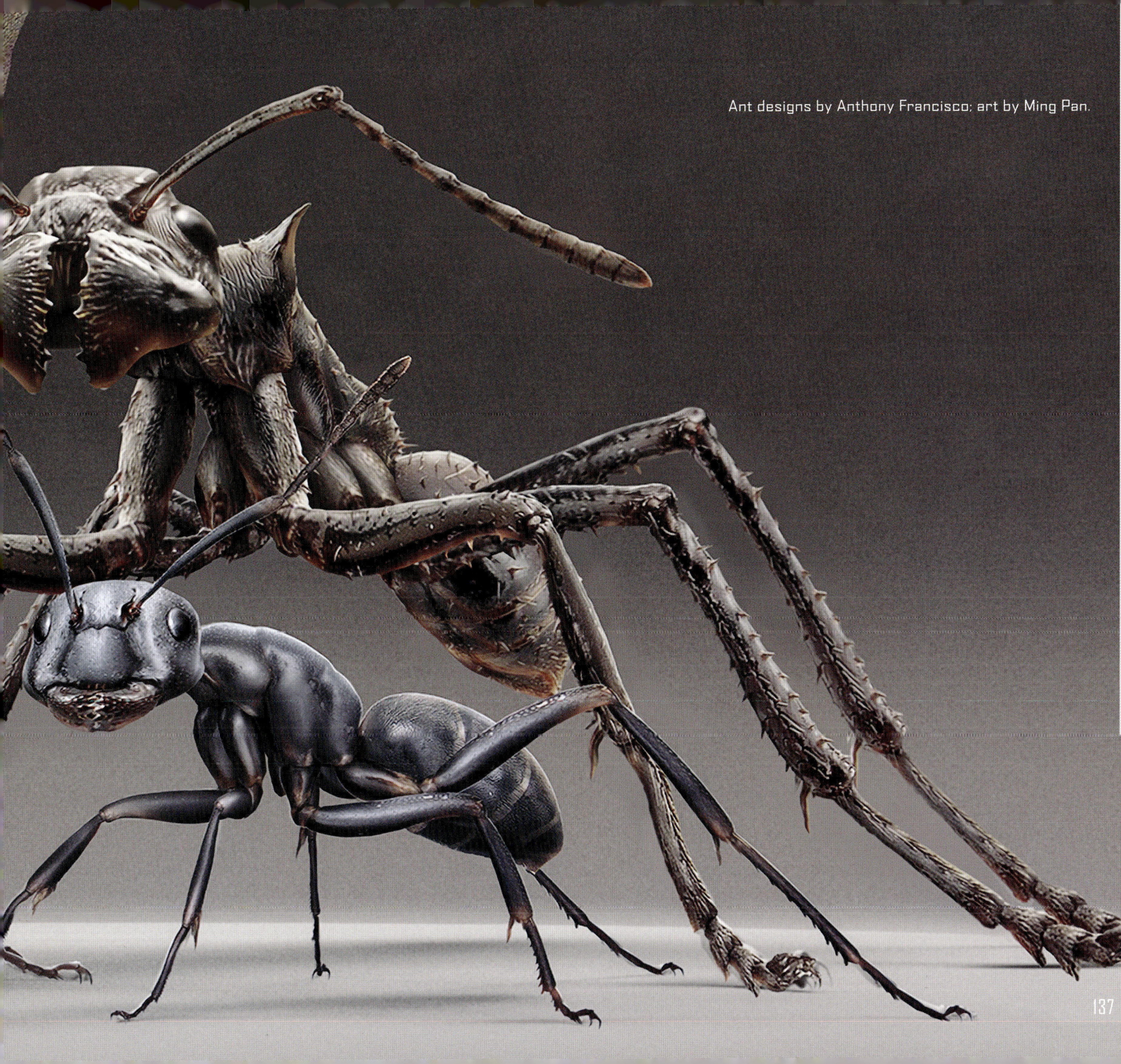

Ant designs by Anthony Francisco; art by Ming Pan.

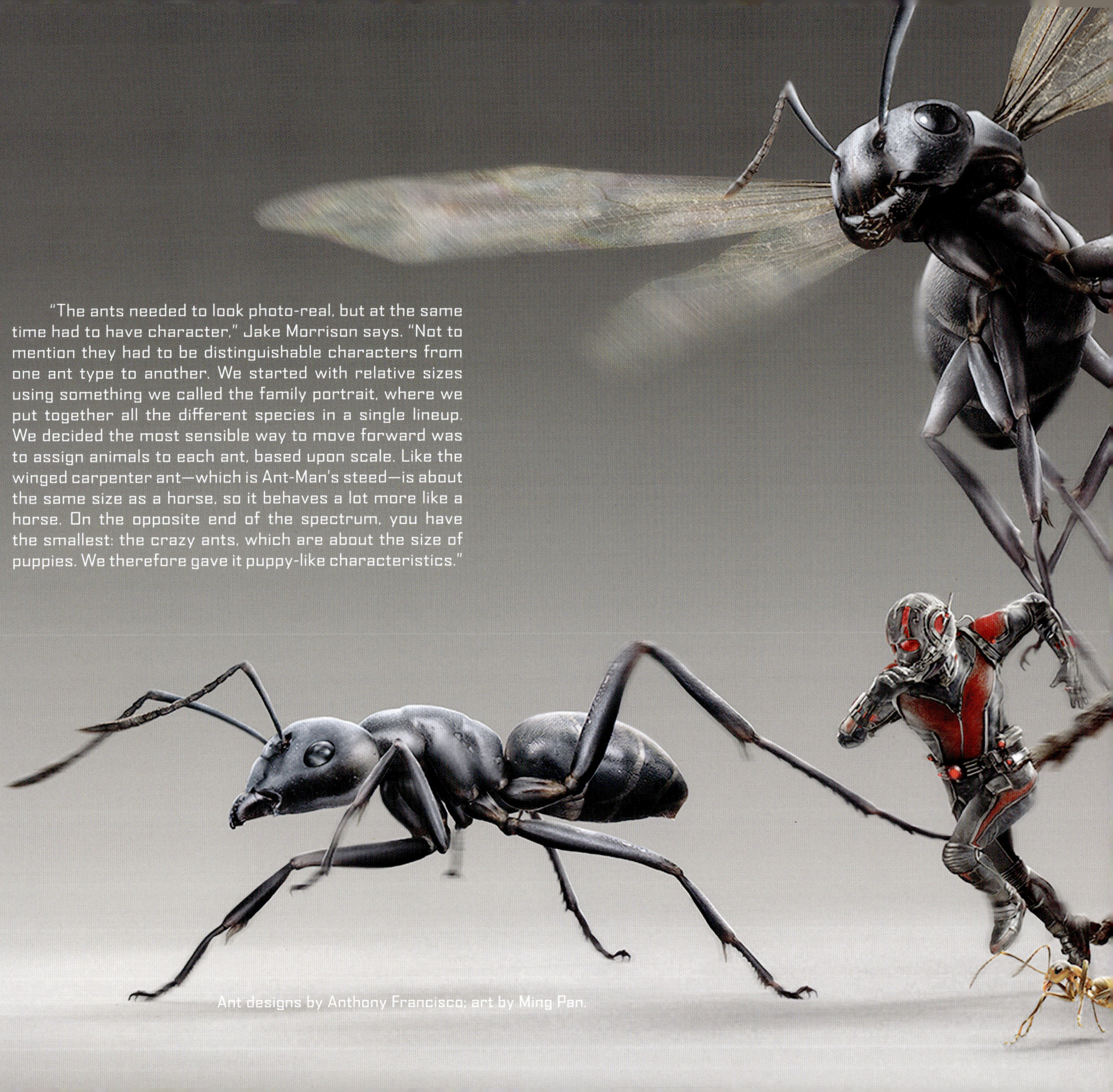

"The ants needed to look photo-real, but at the same time had to have character," Jake Morrison says. "Not to mention they had to be distinguishable characters from one ant type to another. We started with relative sizes using something we called the family portrait, where we put together all the different species in a single lineup. We decided the most sensible way to move forward was to assign animals to each ant, based upon scale. Like the winged carpenter ant—which is Ant-Man's steed—is about the same size as a horse, so it behaves a lot more like a horse. On the opposite end of the spectrum, you have the smallest: the crazy ants, which are about the size of puppies. We therefore gave it puppy-like characteristics."

Ant designs by Anthony Francisco; art by Ming Pan.

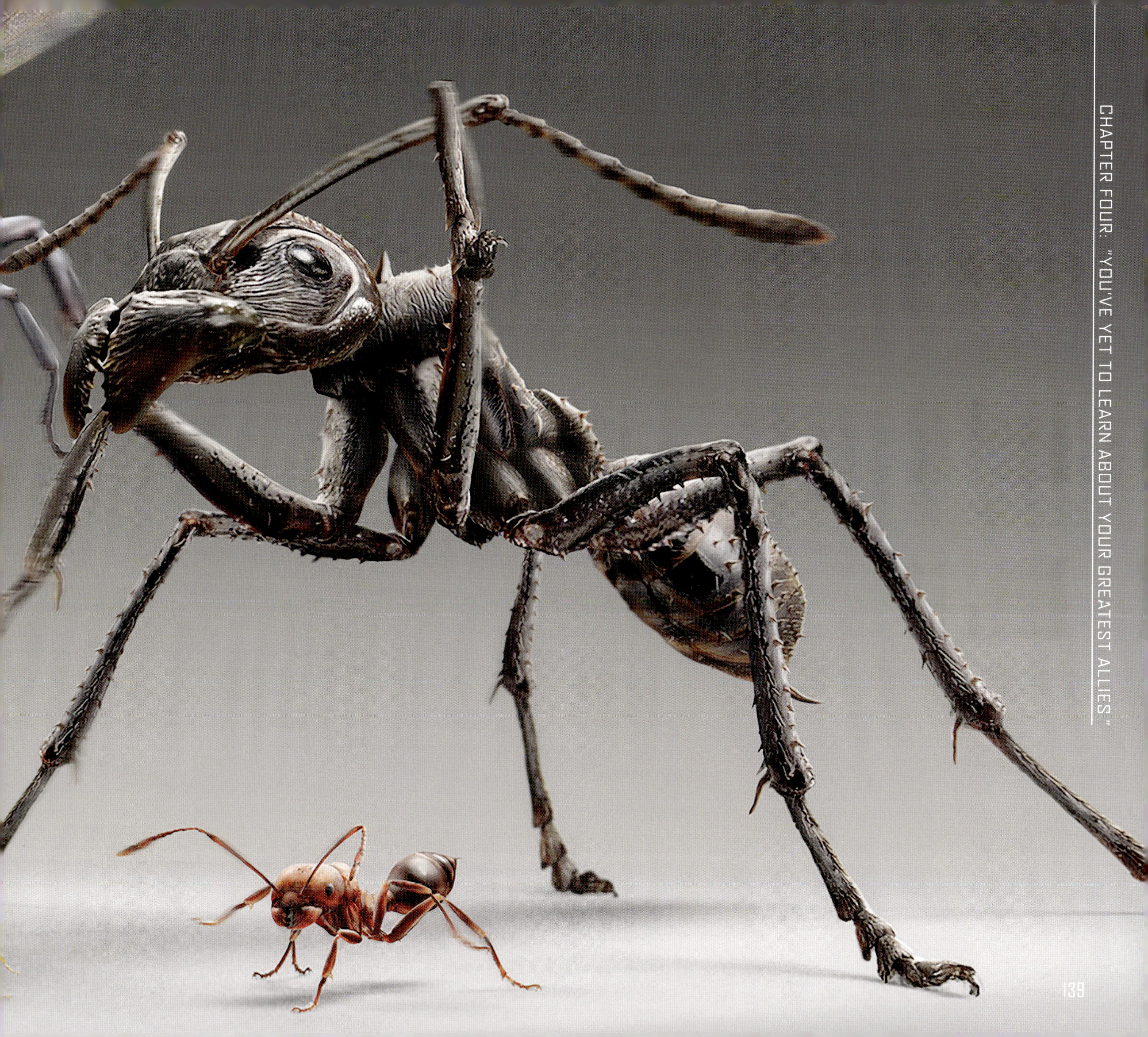

BULLET ANT

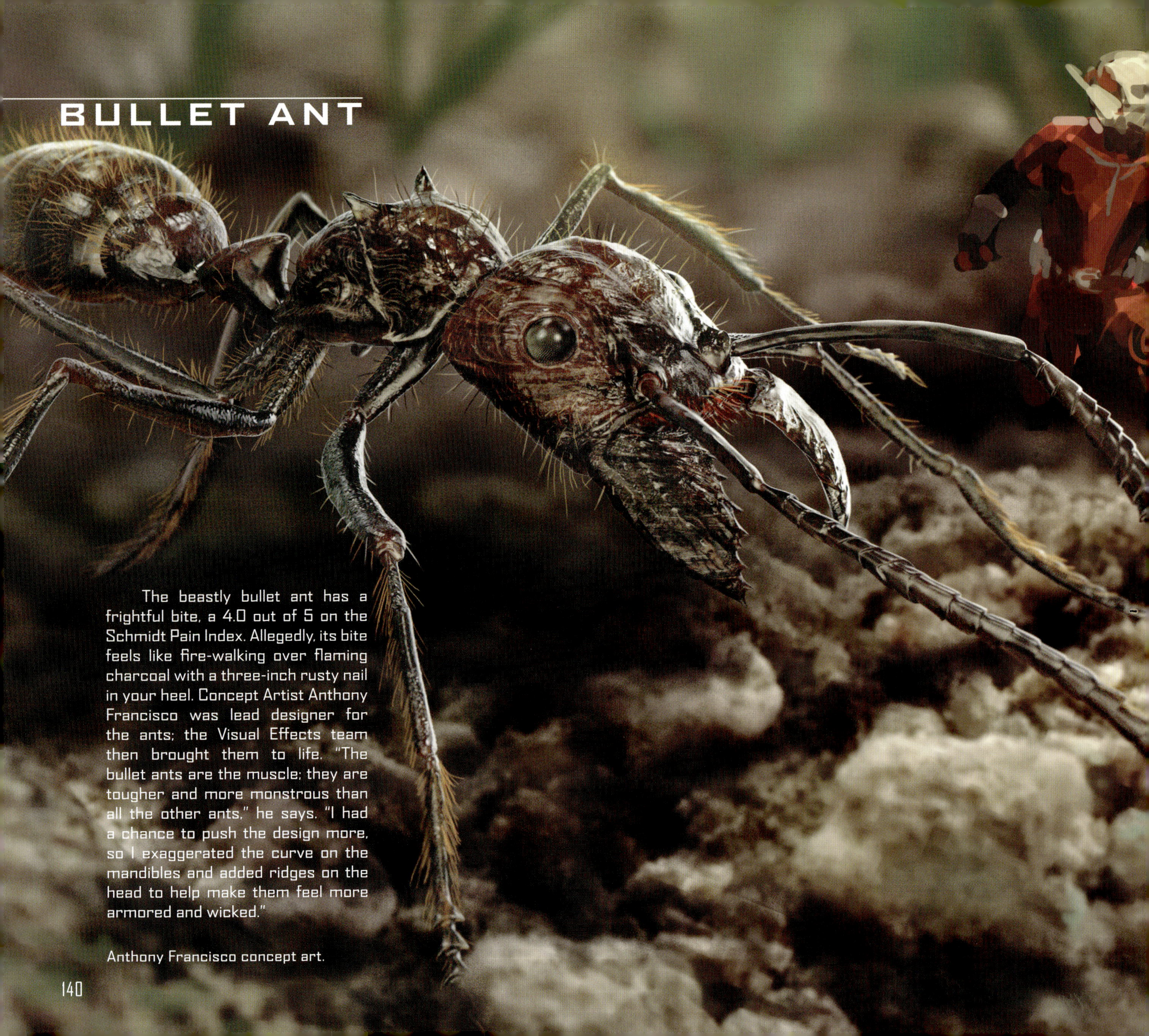

The beastly bullet ant has a frightful bite, a 4.0 out of 5 on the Schmidt Pain Index. Allegedly, its bite feels like fire-walking over flaming charcoal with a three-inch rusty nail in your heel. Concept Artist Anthony Francisco was lead designer for the ants; the Visual Effects team then brought them to life. "The bullet ants are the muscle; they are tougher and more monstrous than all the other ants," he says. "I had a chance to push the design more, so I exaggerated the curve on the mandibles and added ridges on the head to help make them feel more armored and wicked."

Anthony Francisco concept art.

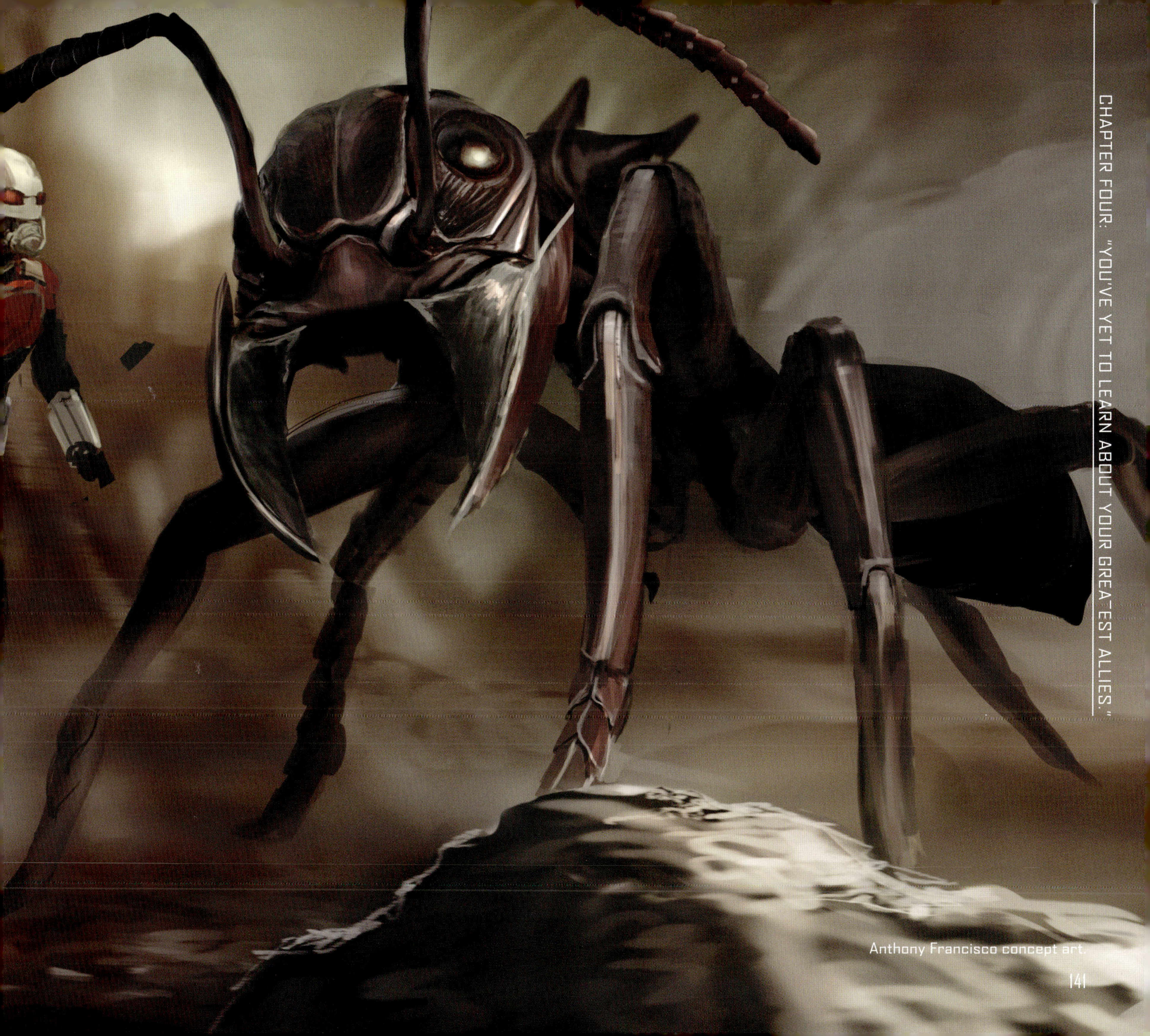

Anthony Francisco concept art.

CARPENTER ANT

"The carpenter ant is effectively the size of a St. Bernard, so it's more like a big dog," Jake Morrison explains. "Ant-Man brings in all the carpenter ants from the garden to lend a hand in the final battle—because in large groups, they're actually quite powerful."

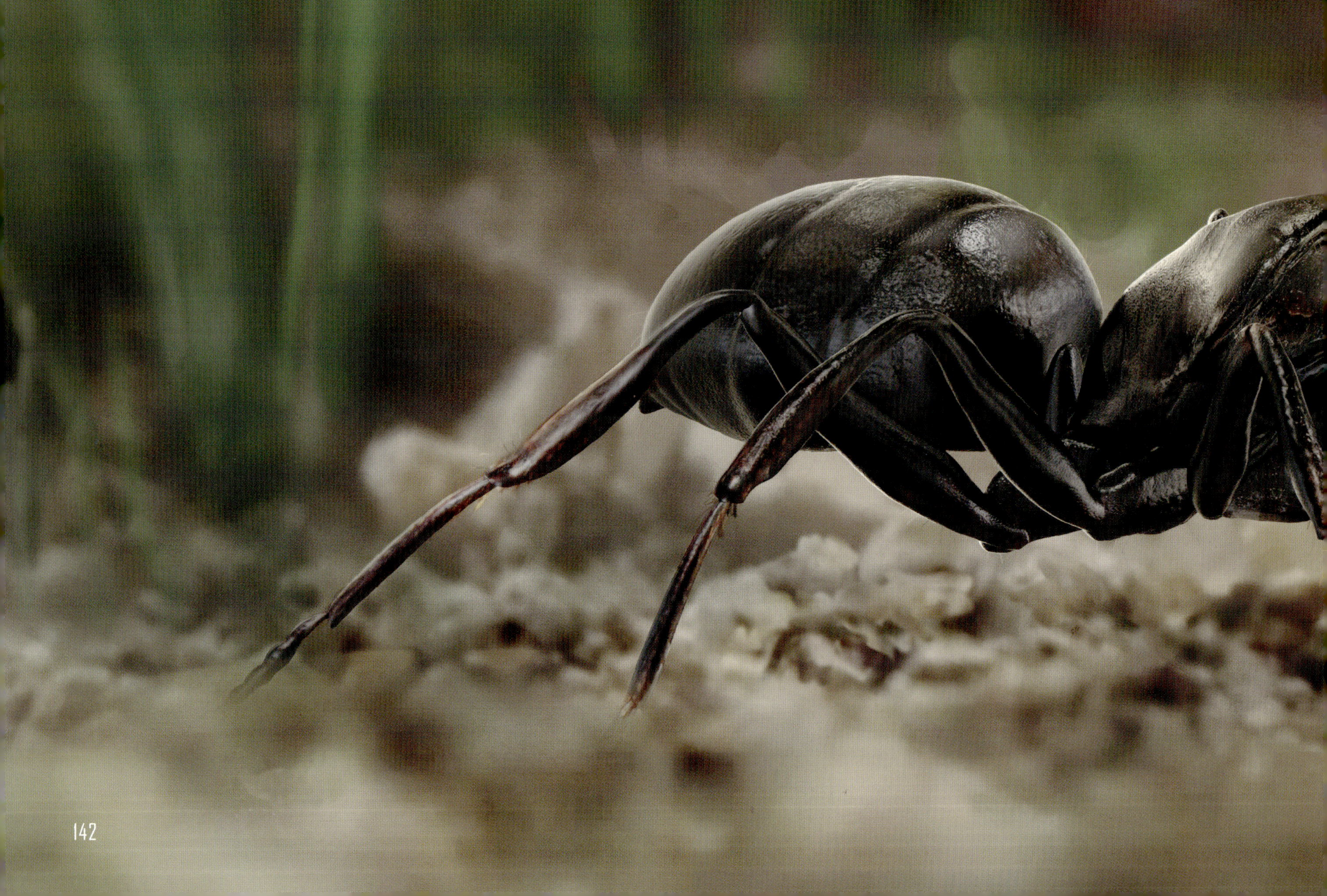

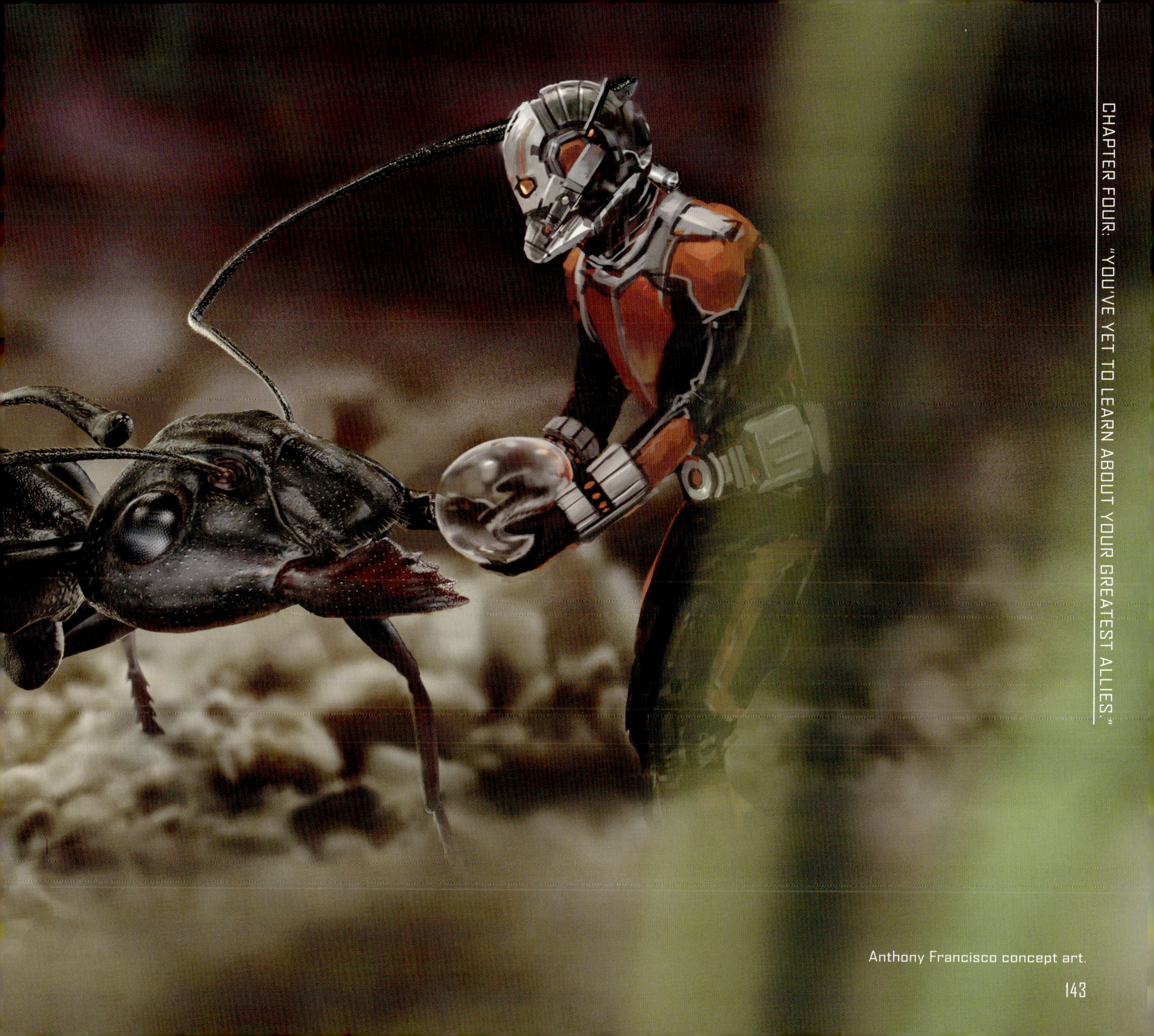

Anthony Francisco concept art.

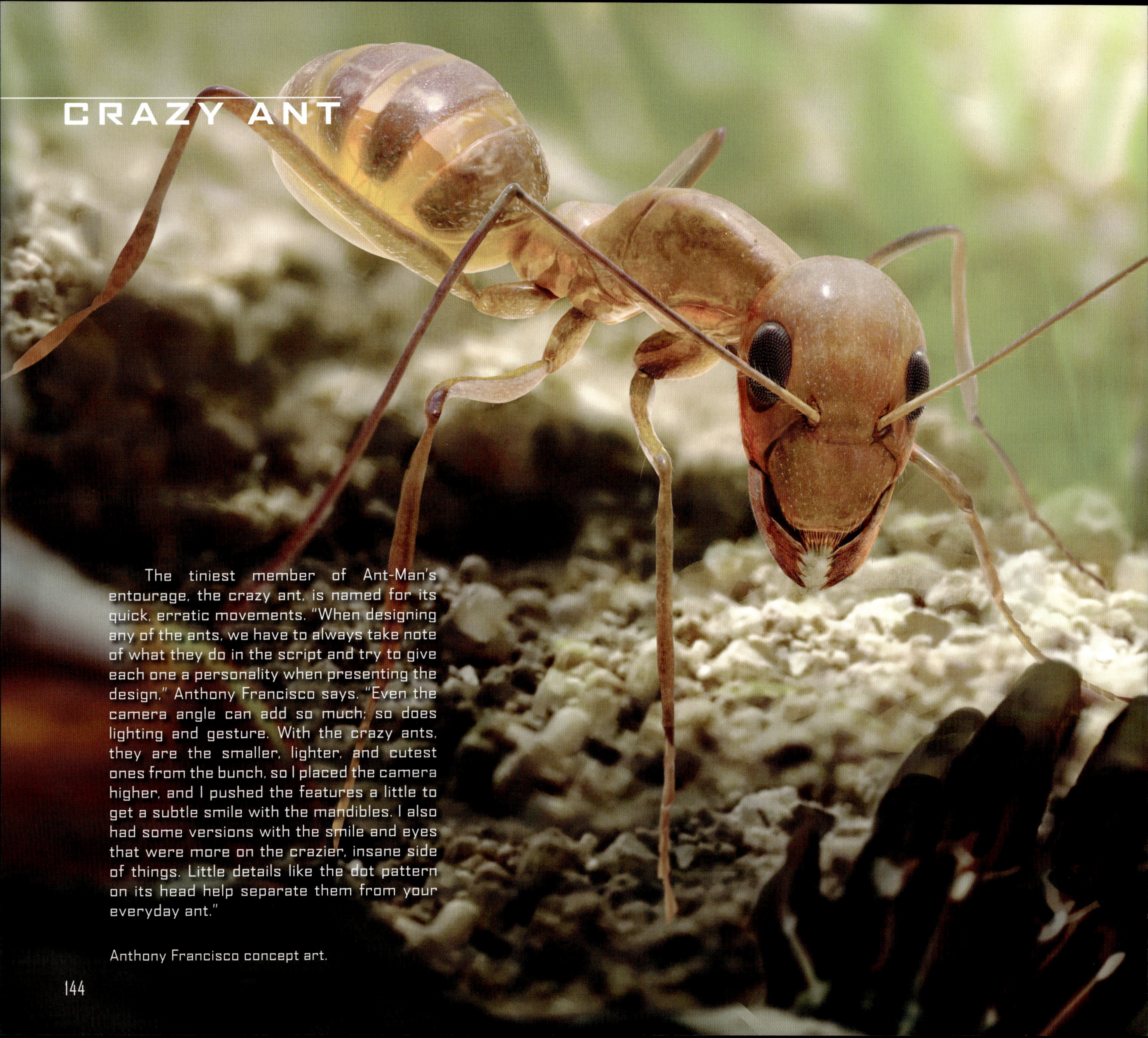

CRAZY ANT

The tiniest member of Ant-Man's entourage, the crazy ant, is named for its quick, erratic movements. "When designing any of the ants, we have to always take note of what they do in the script and try to give each one a personality when presenting the design," Anthony Francisco says. "Even the camera angle can add so much; so does lighting and gesture. With the crazy ants, they are the smaller, lighter, and cutest ones from the bunch, so I placed the camera higher, and I pushed the features a little to get a subtle smile with the mandibles. I also had some versions with the smile and eyes that were more on the crazier, insane side of things. Little details like the dot pattern on its head help separate them from your everyday ant."

Anthony Francisco concept art.

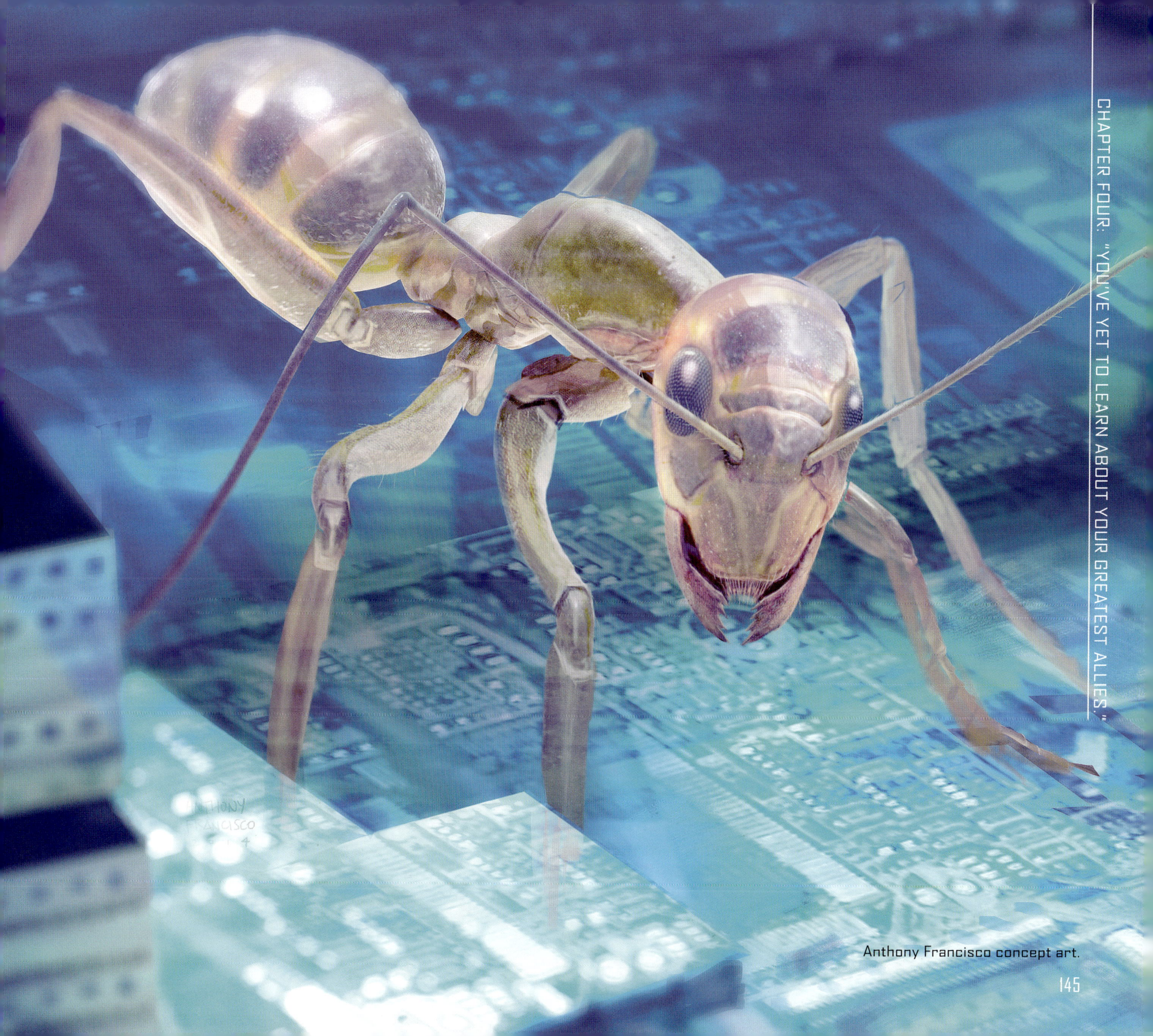

Anthony Francisco concept art.

FIRE ANT

While most people only associate fire ants with their painful bite, Jake Morrison says there's a lot more to these little guys than meets the eye. "The fire ants are interesting. They're technical, they're kind of the engineers, the builders—they're the ones who can create interlocking rafts and bridges, so they're more of a hive mind," he describes. "They behave much more like a touring circus. You call them in to solve a particular problem, and they'll build a way out of it for you." In that way, they're the grunts of the ant army. "The fire ants are real workers," Diana Giorgiutti says. "I mean, they're all worker ants, but these ones are like the center of the army."

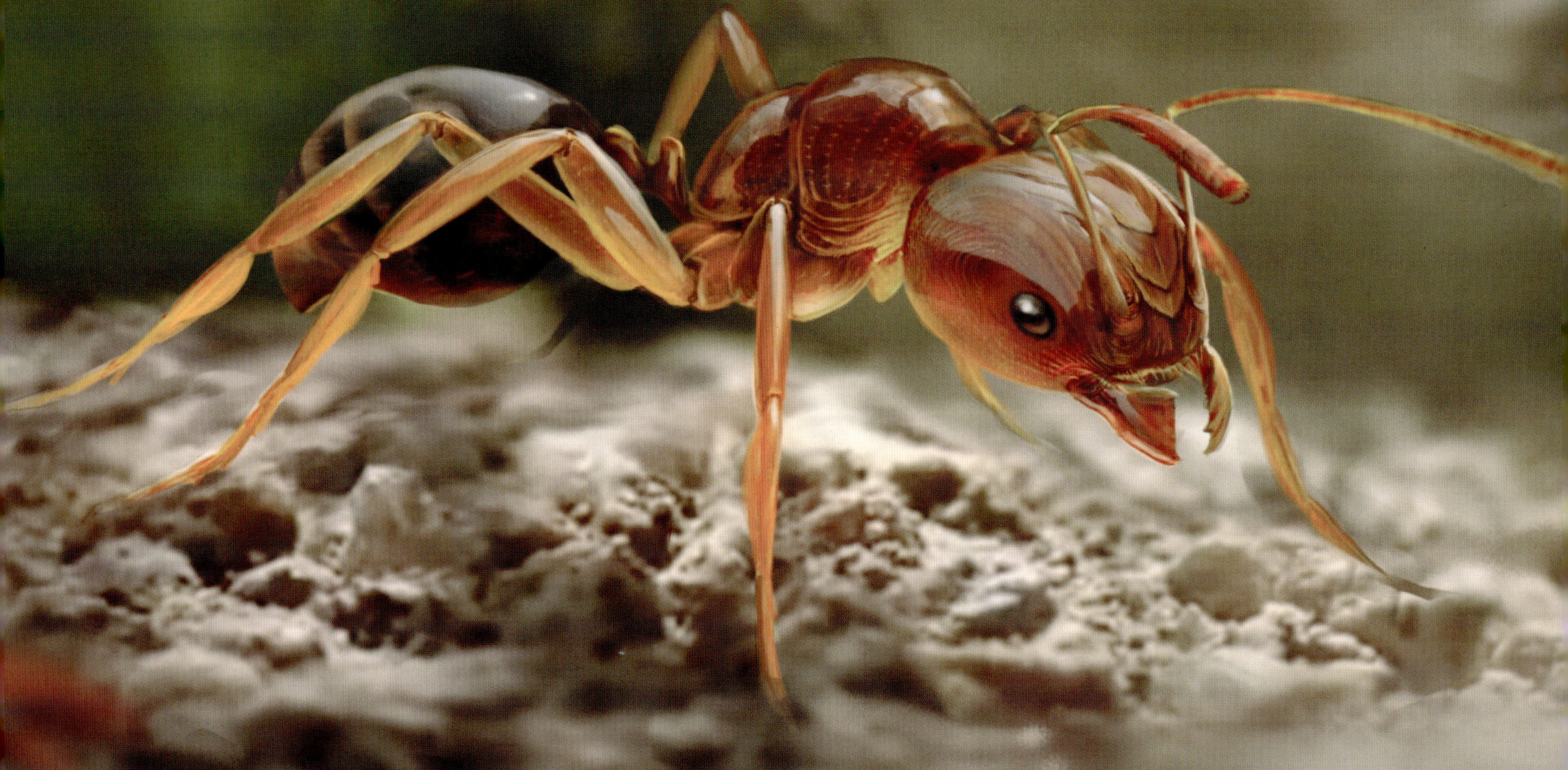

Anthony Francisco concept art.

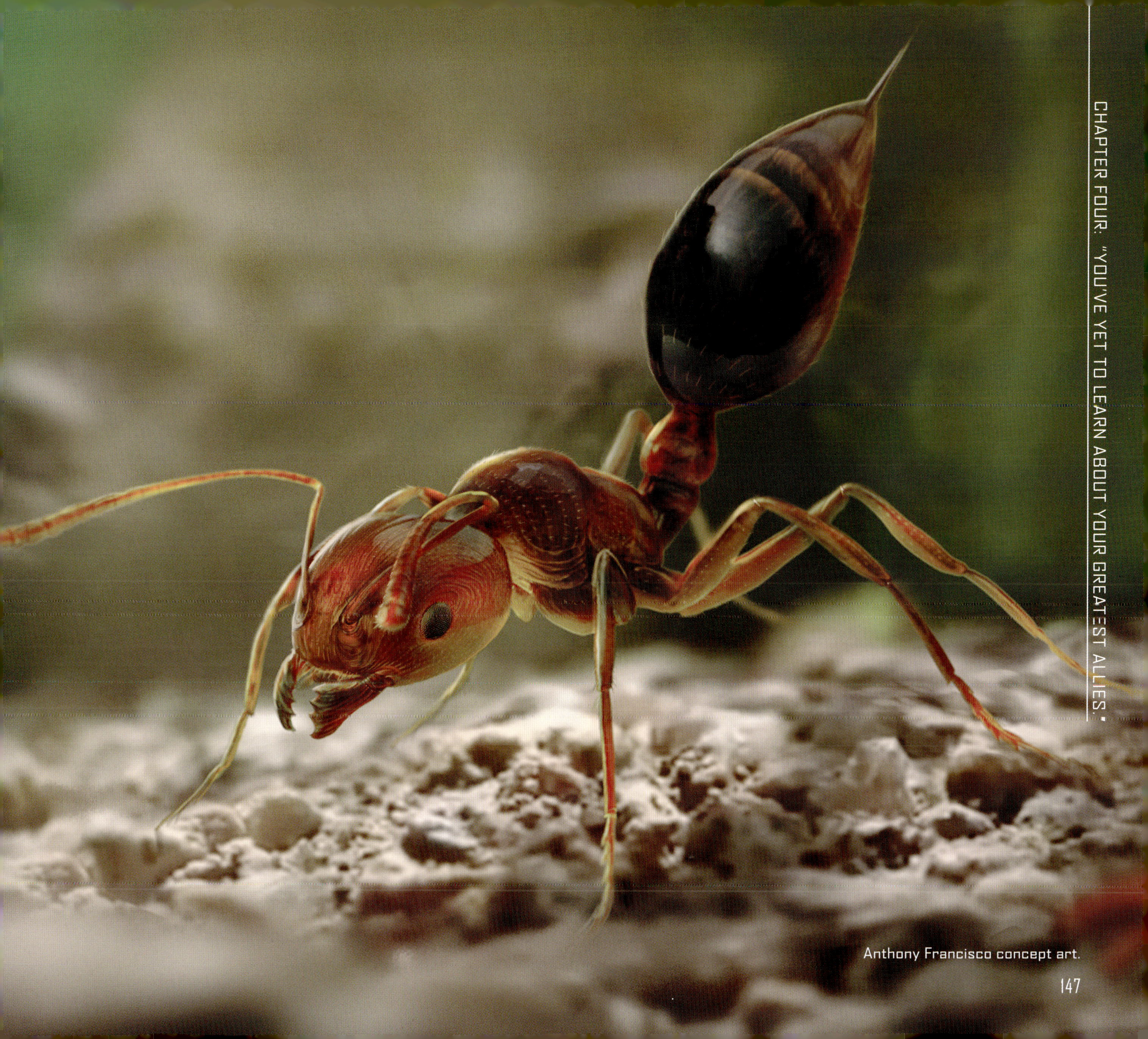

Anthony Francisco concept art.

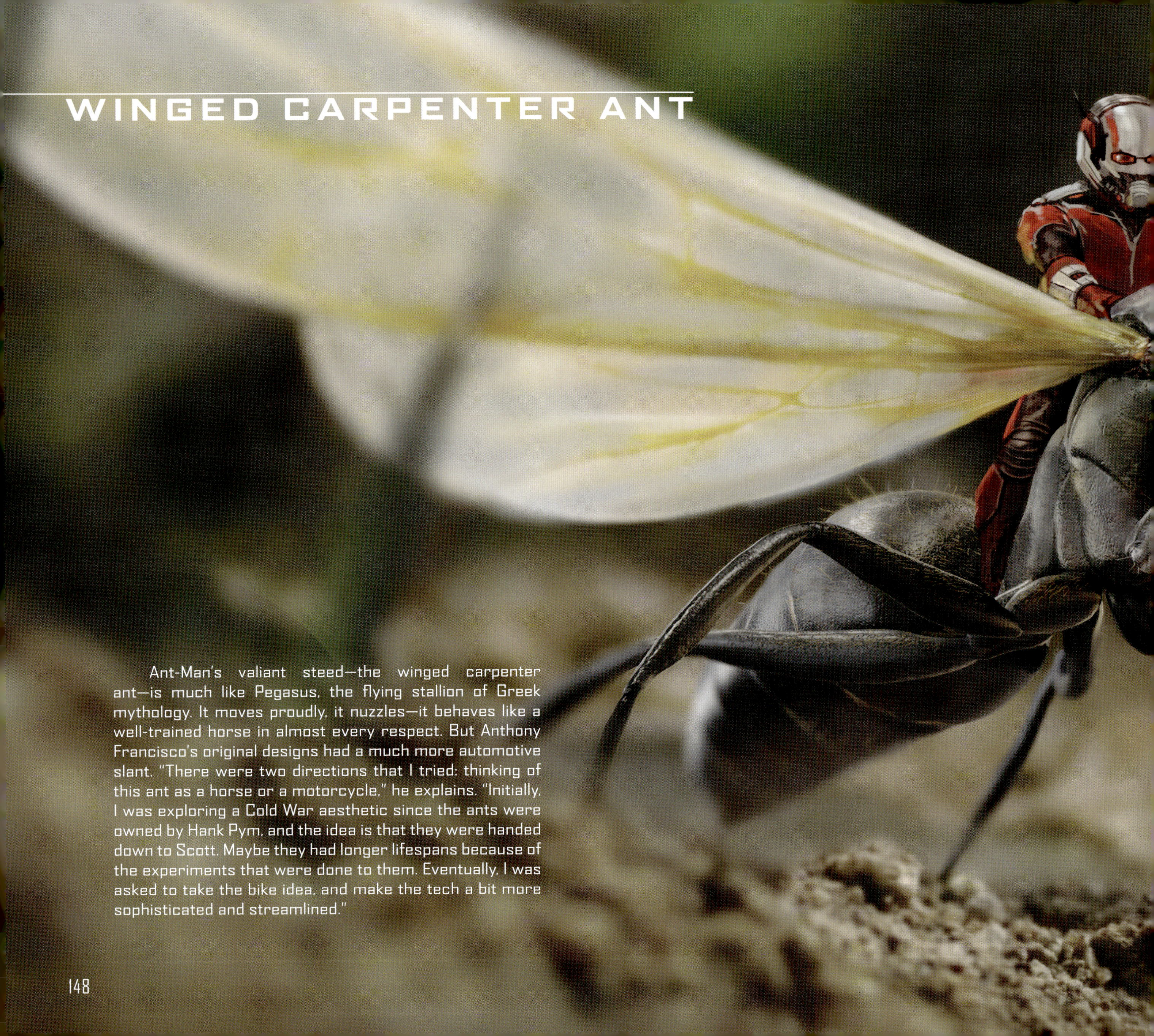

WINGED CARPENTER ANT

Ant-Man's valiant steed—the winged carpenter ant—is much like Pegasus, the flying stallion of Greek mythology. It moves proudly, it nuzzles—it behaves like a well-trained horse in almost every respect. But Anthony Francisco's original designs had a much more automotive slant. "There were two directions that I tried: thinking of this ant as a horse or a motorcycle," he explains. "Initially, I was exploring a Cold War aesthetic since the ants were owned by Hank Pym, and the idea is that they were handed down to Scott. Maybe they had longer lifespans because of the experiments that were done to them. Eventually, I was asked to take the bike idea, and make the tech a bit more sophisticated and streamlined."

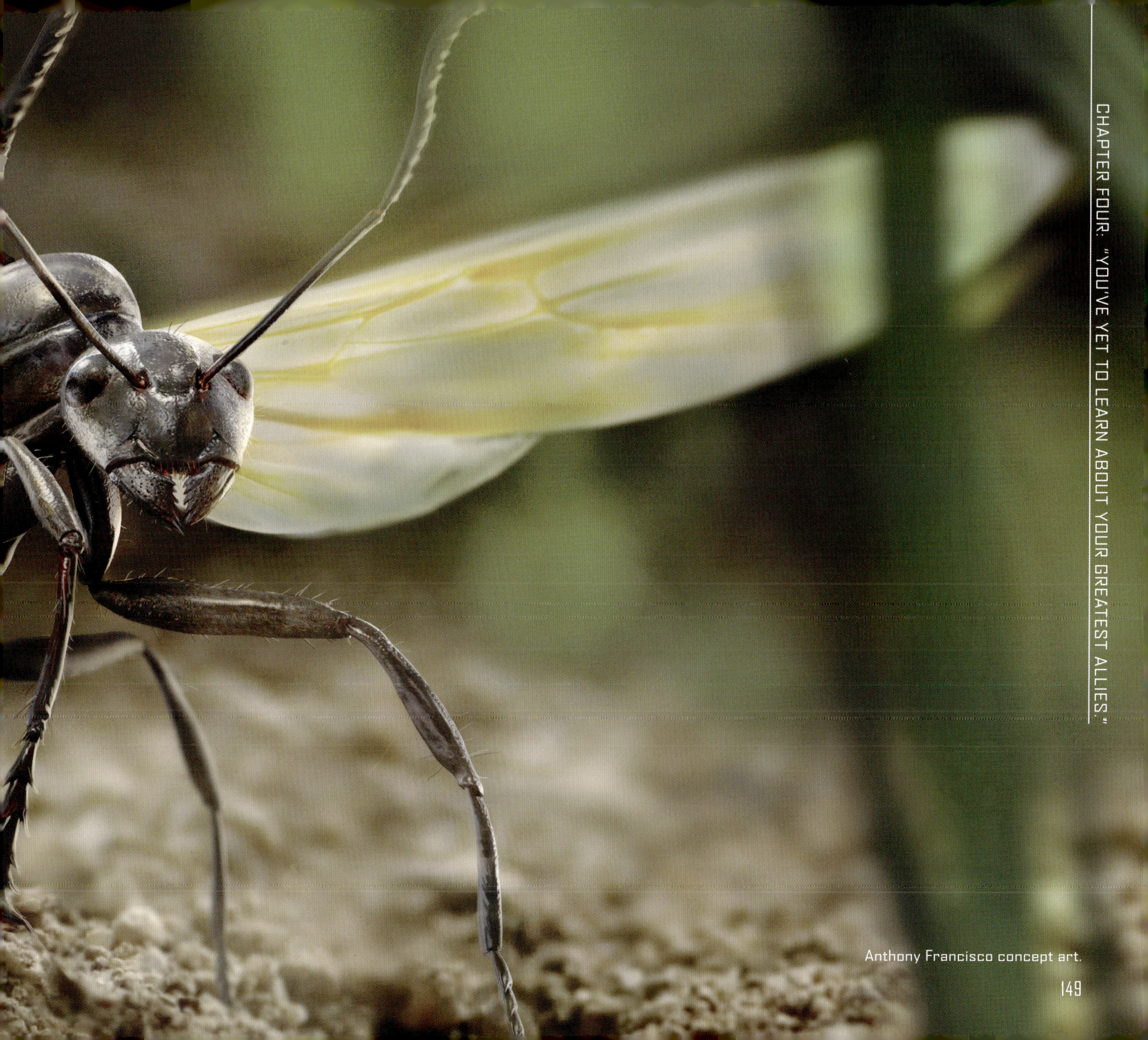

Anthony Francisco concept art.

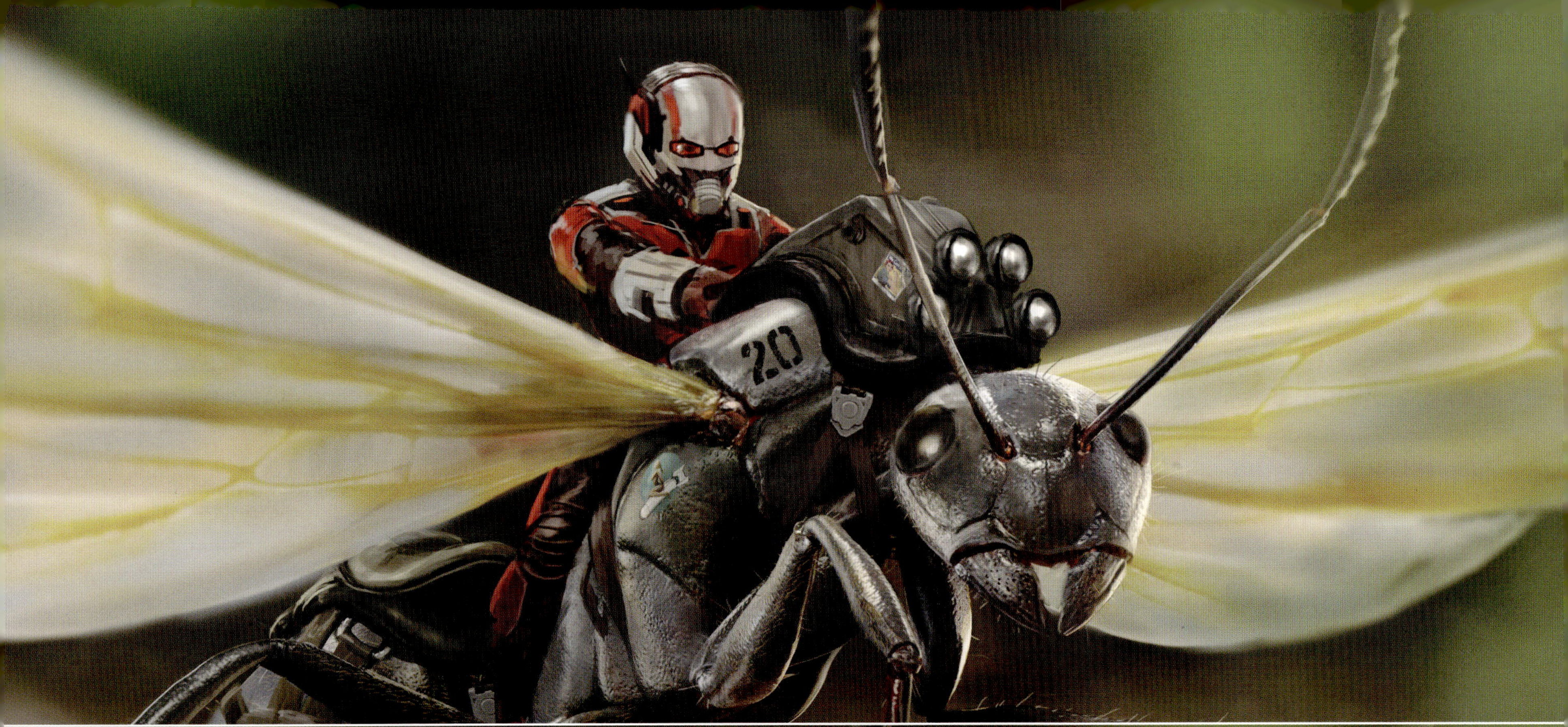

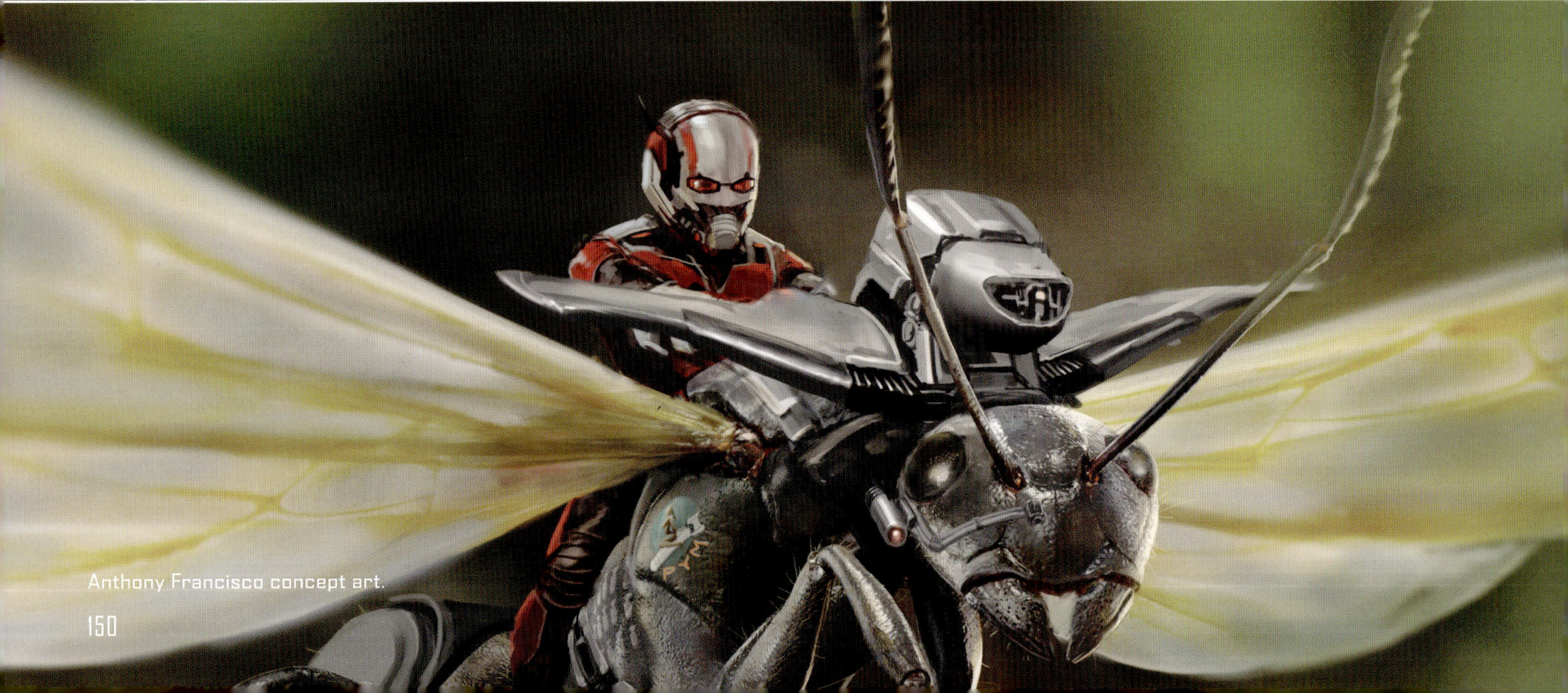

Anthony Francisco concept art.

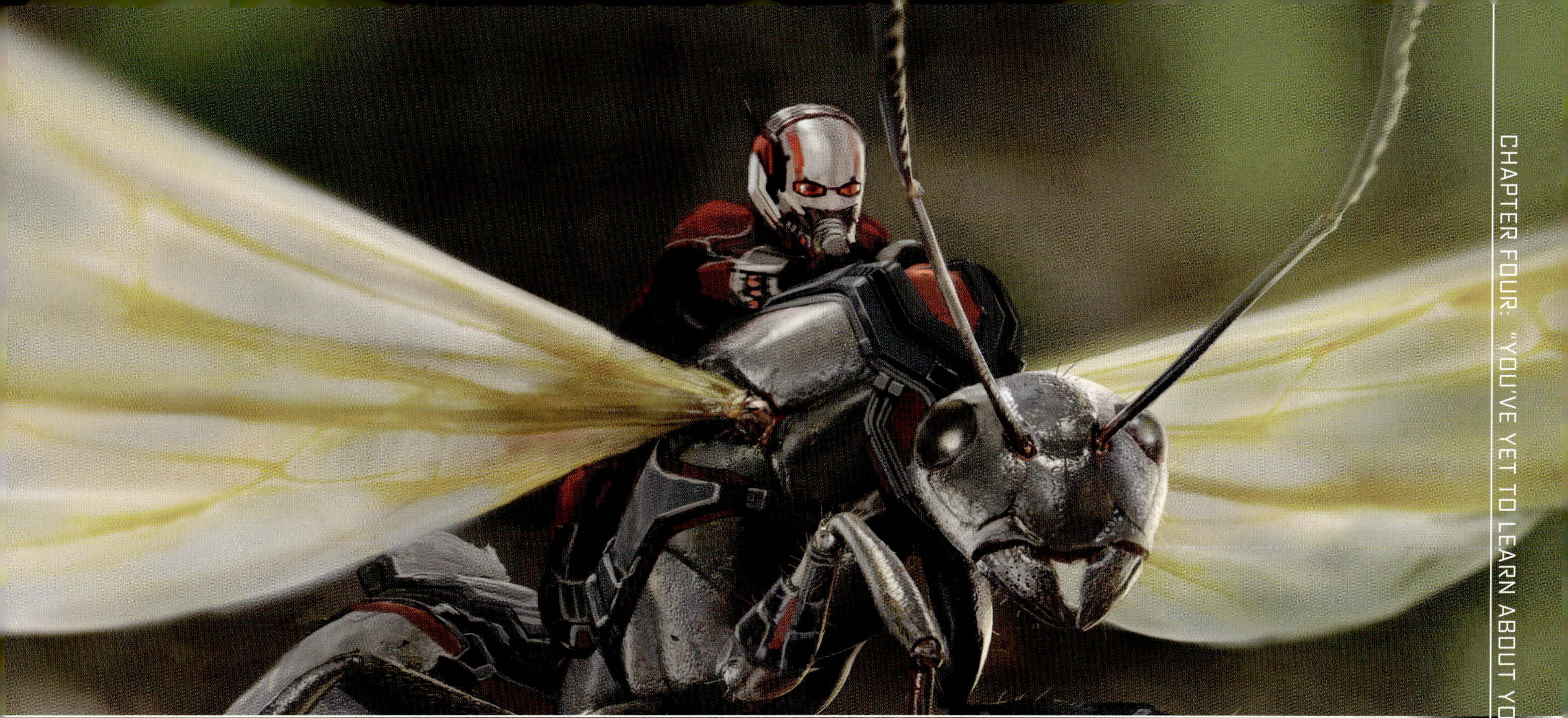

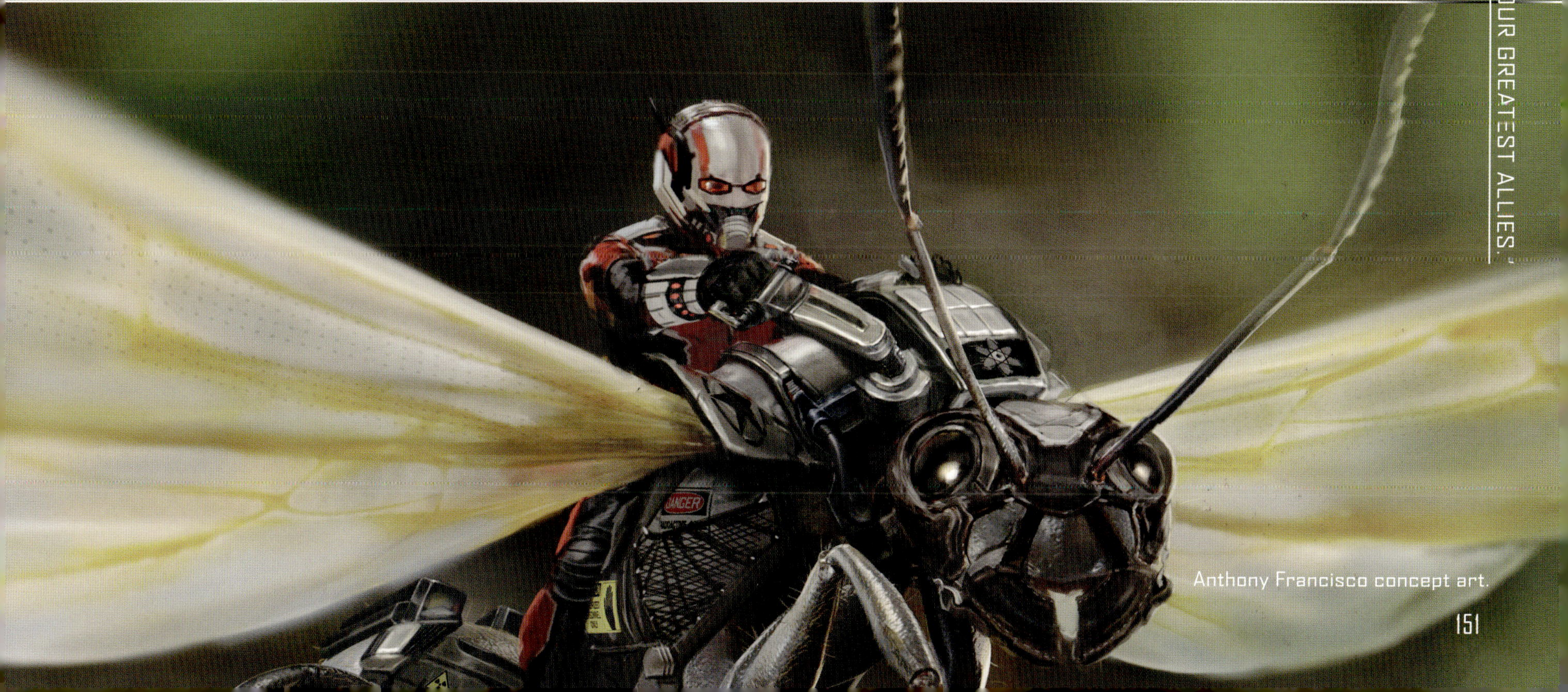

Anthony Francisco concept art.

ANT-TRAINING DEVICE

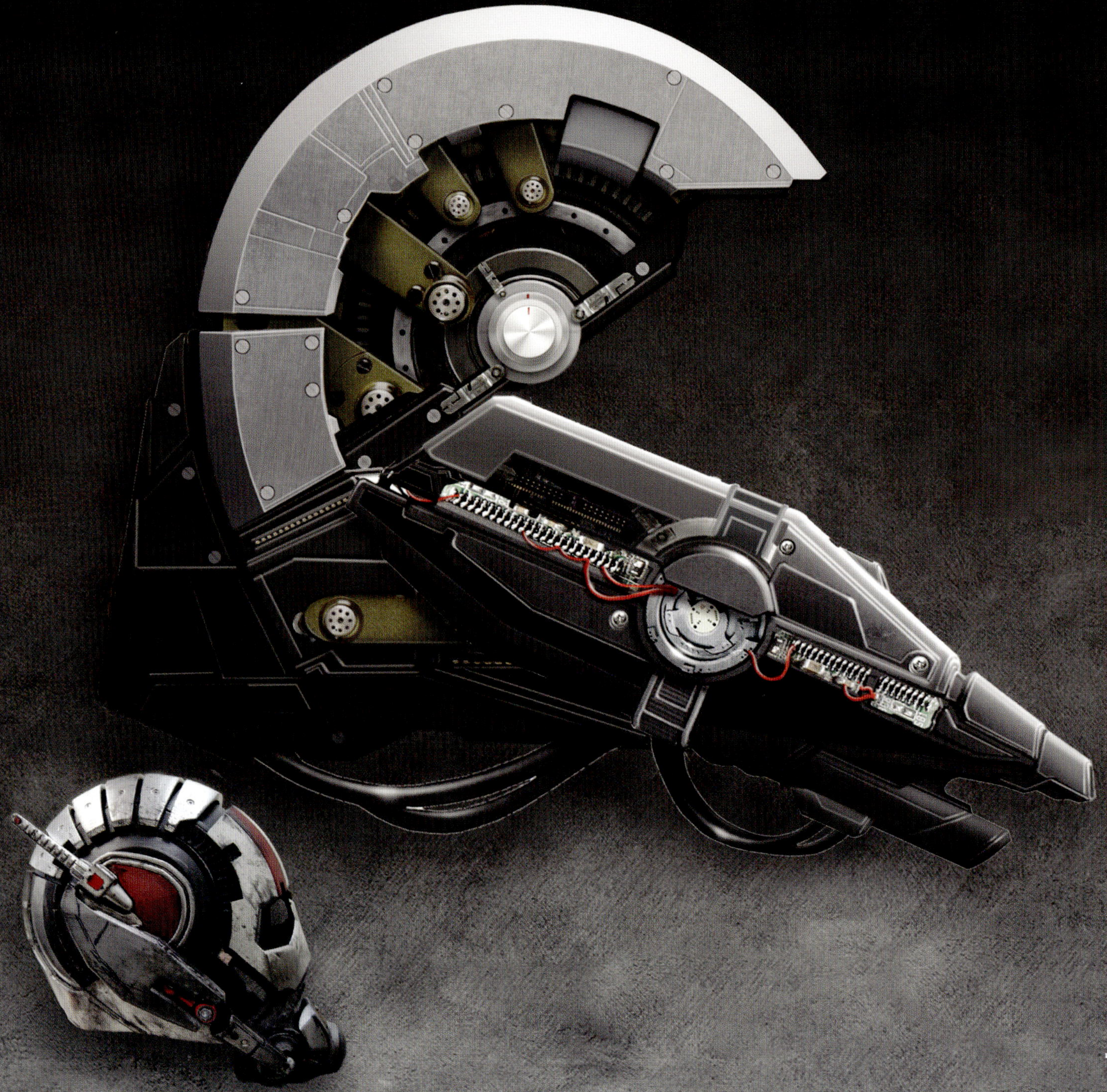

John Eaves concept art.

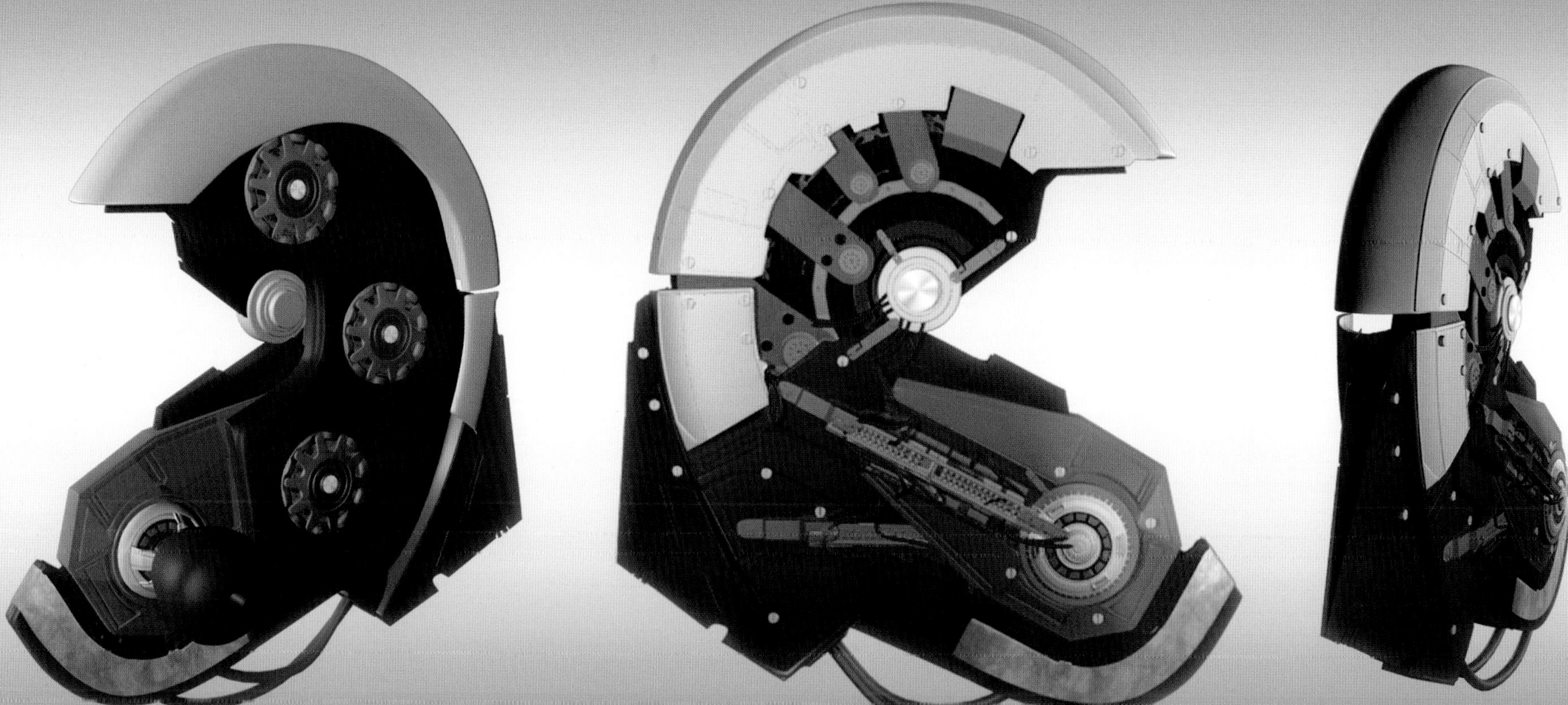

The ants are controlled via a small earpiece in the Ant-Man helmet. To help Scott learn to communicate with the ants, Hank gives him the earpiece to practice. The device functions much like the ants' antennas: It conveys information from the user, sharing thoughts and demands with the ants. The ants will only comply when the user is clear and focused—not Scott's strong points.

WINCH ANT

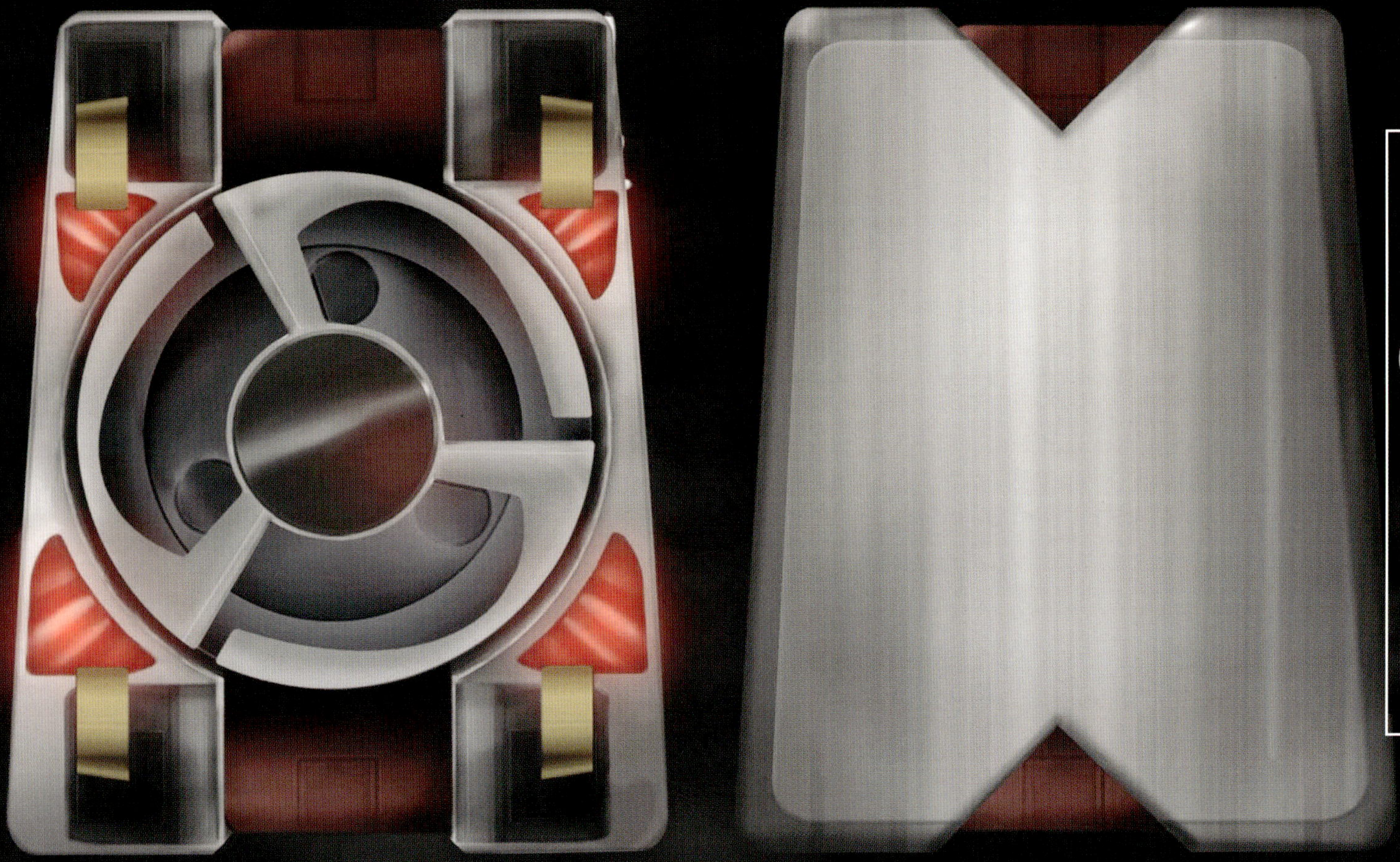

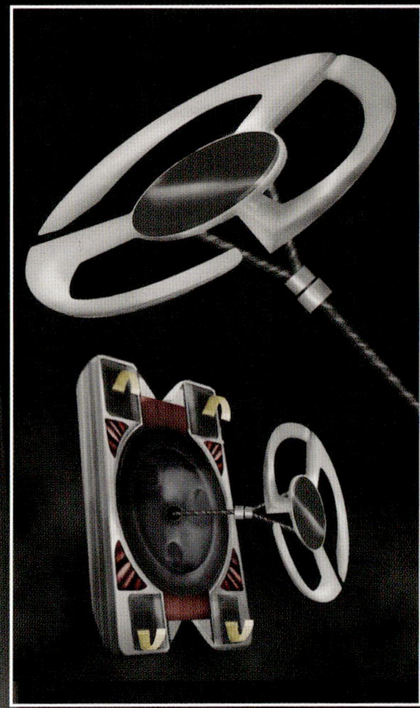

Props Department concept art.

For the mission, Ant-Man eschews traditional repelling gear in favor a winch system carried proudly on the abdomen of an ant. "In designing the winch ant, there were a number of questions that went through my mind," Anthony Francisco says. "Is this going to be a clunky gadget or sophisticated device? How many moving parts am I allowed to show? I ultimately decided it would be good to show the winch in motion, turning—that way it visually signaled to the audience that something was happening."

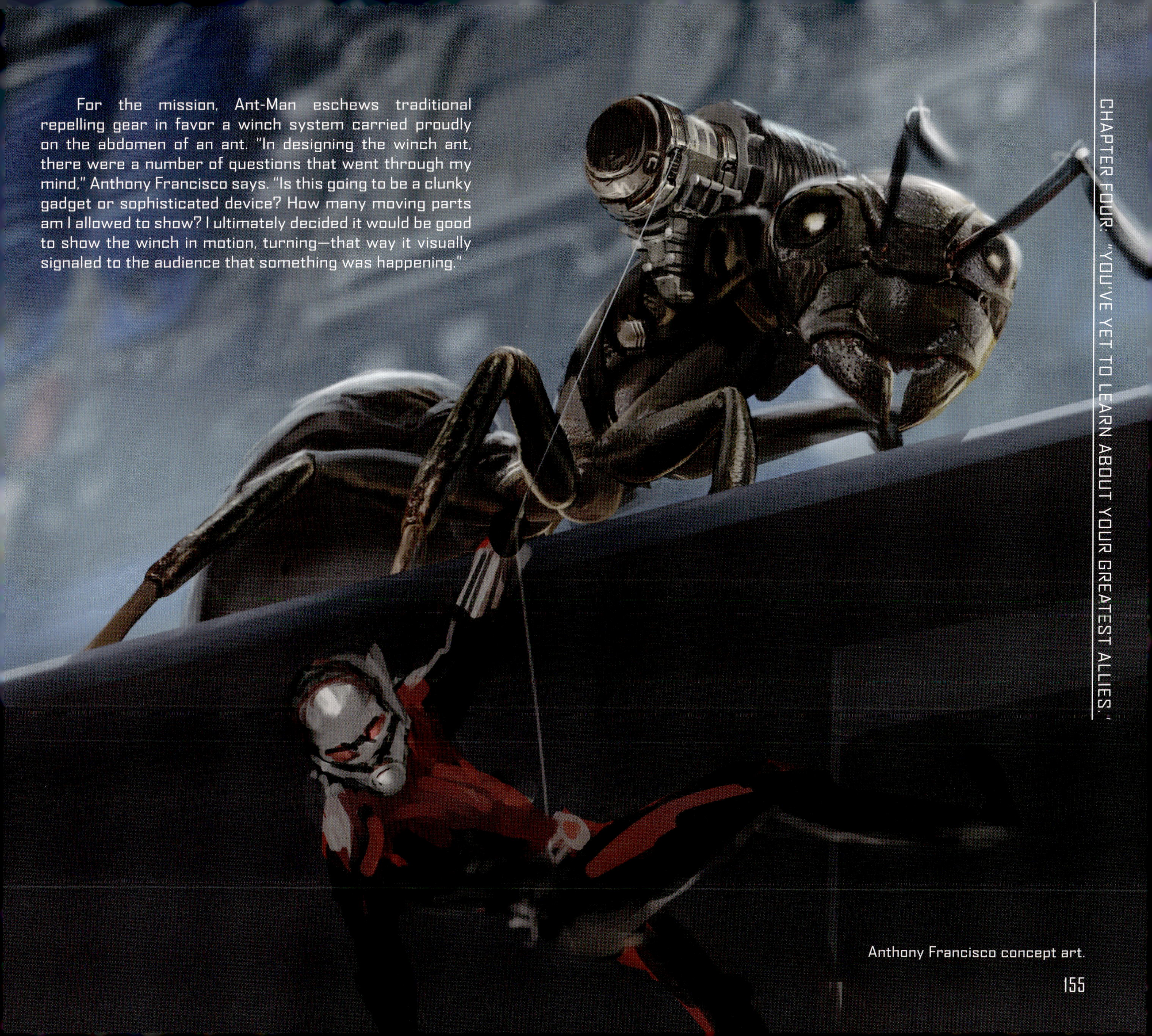

Anthony Francisco concept art.

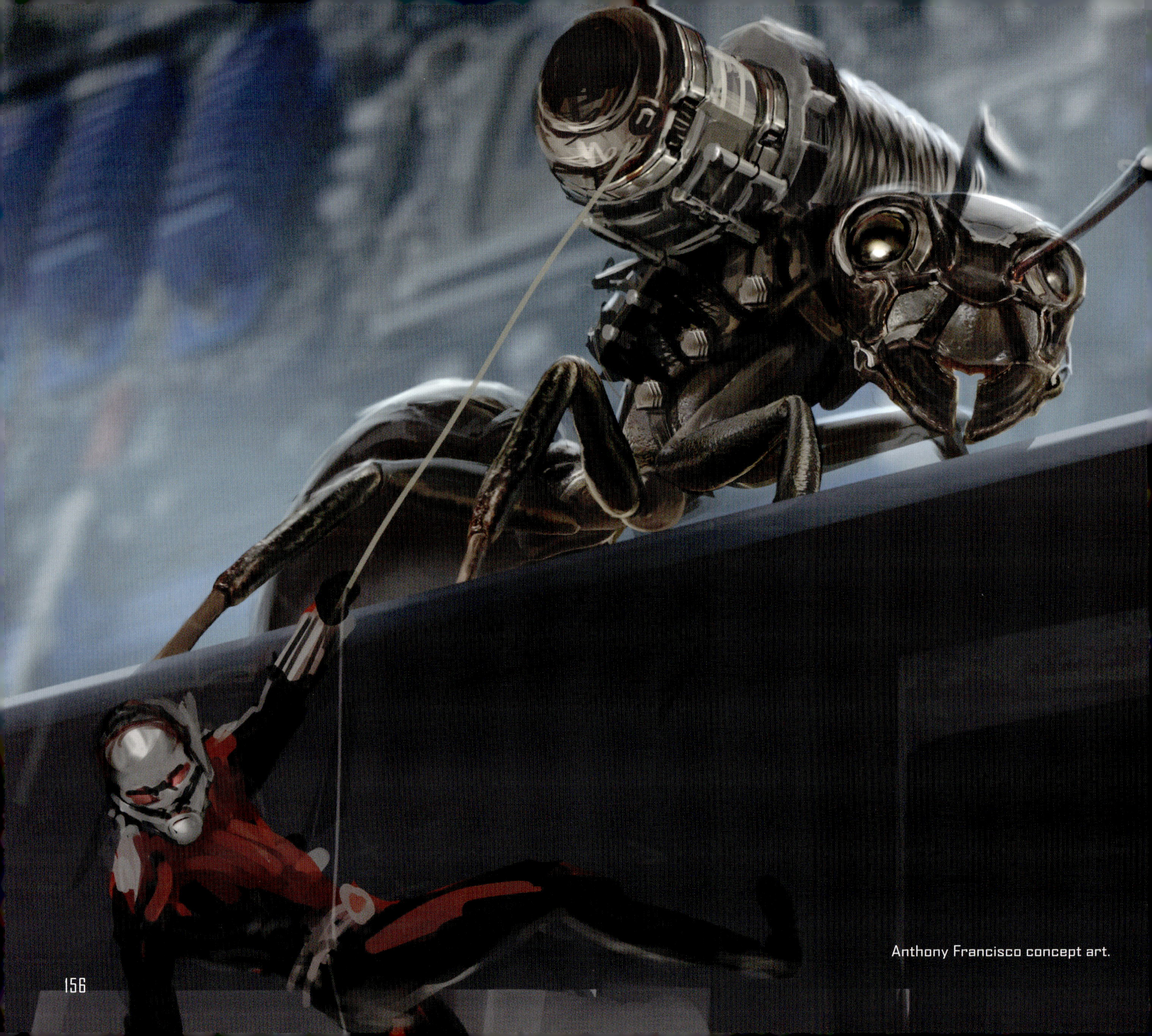

Anthony Francisco concept art.

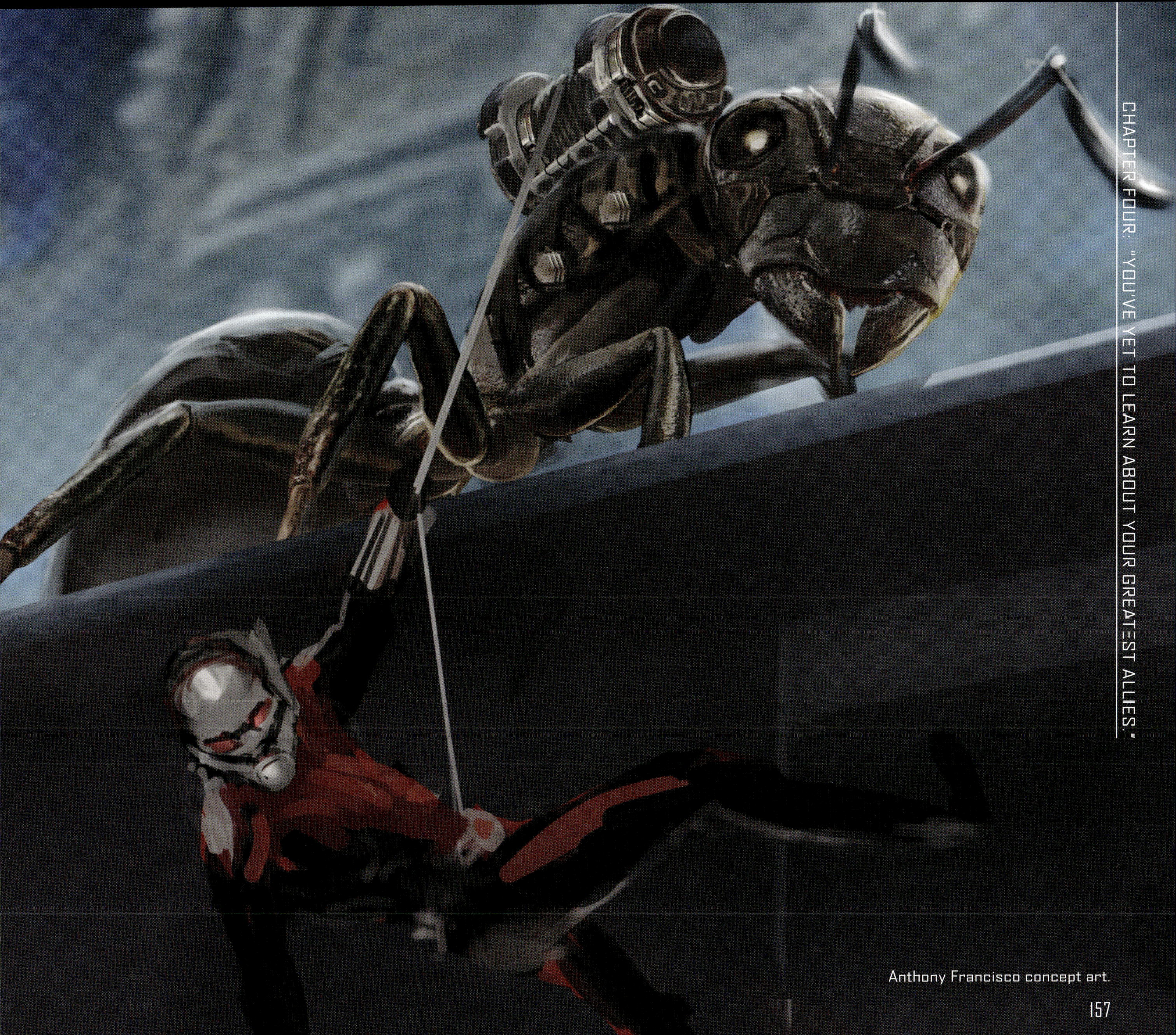

Anthony Francisco concept art.

CAMERA ANT

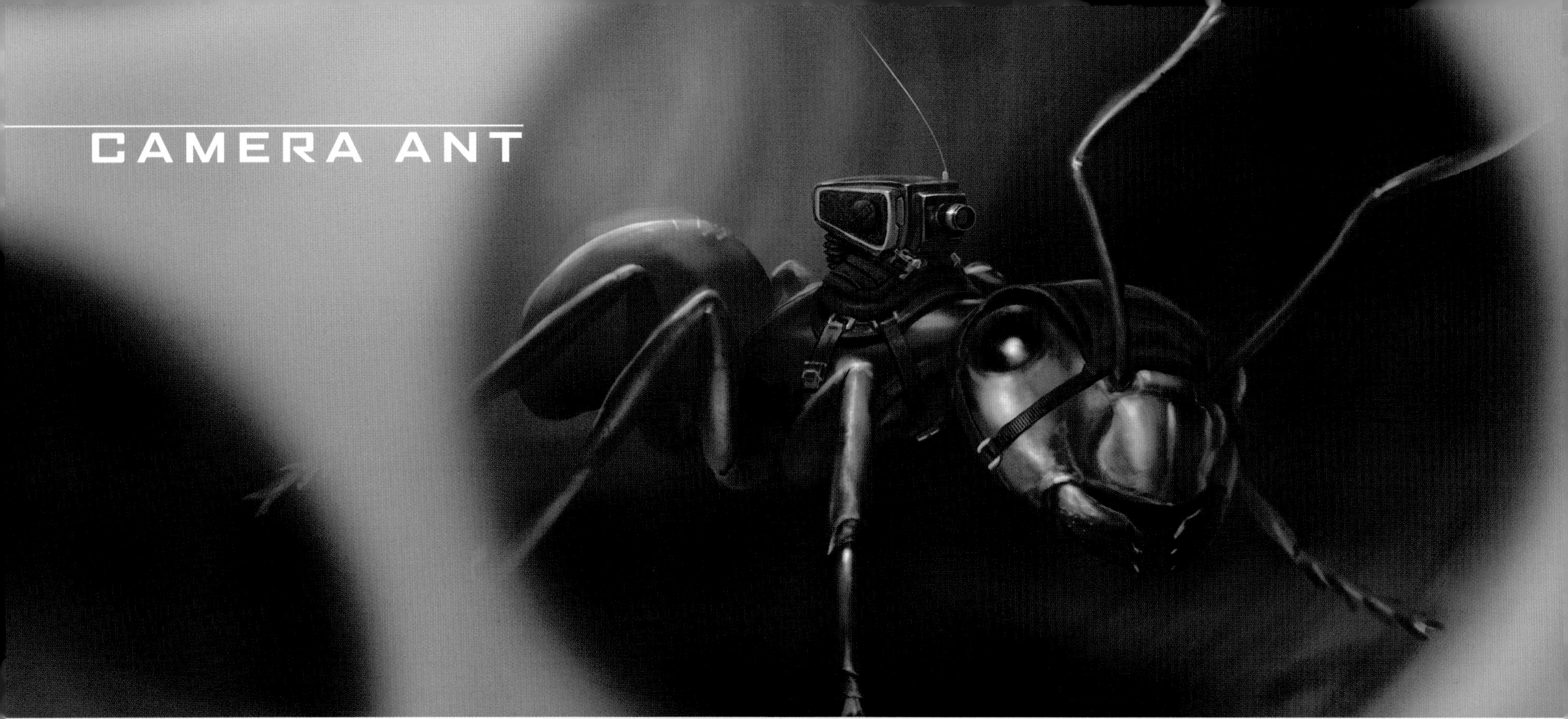

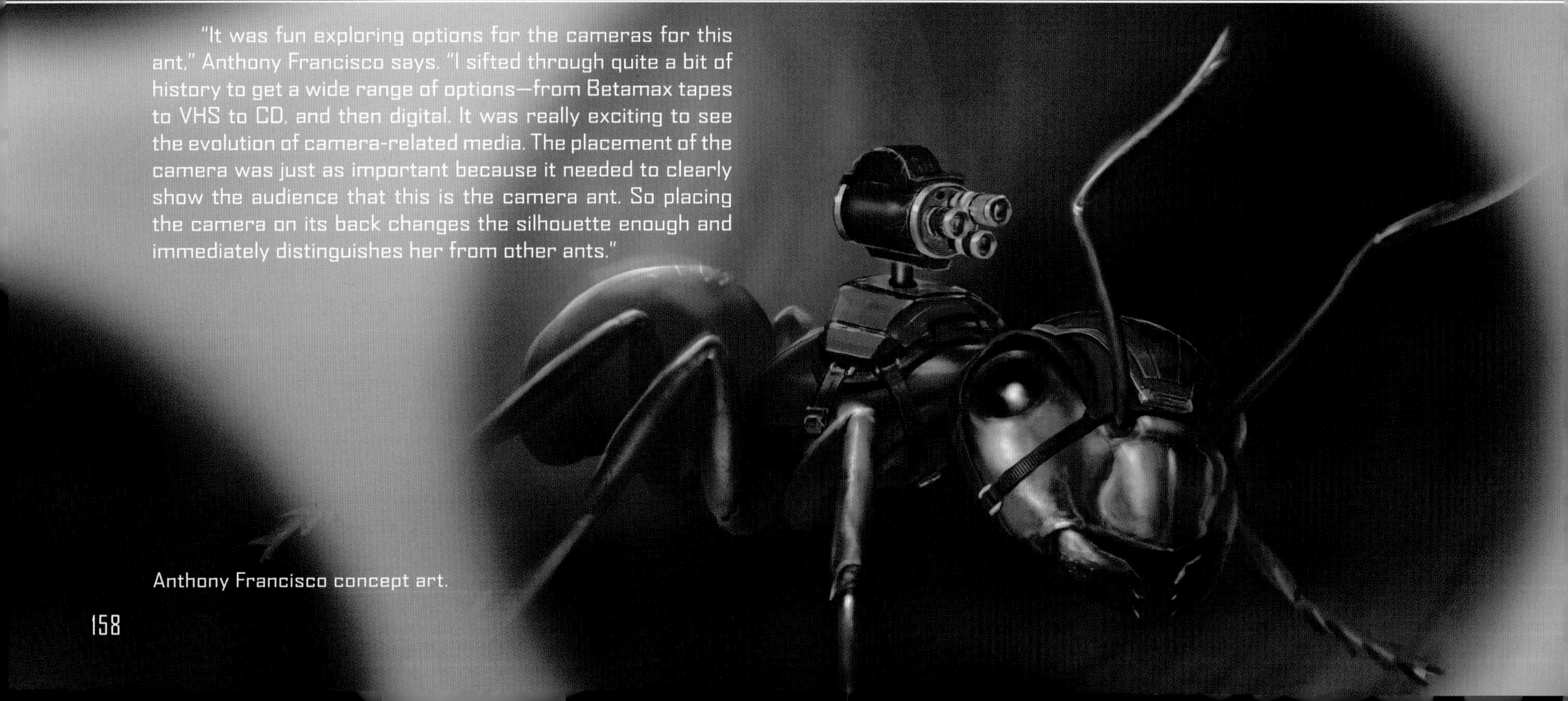

"It was fun exploring options for the cameras for this ant," Anthony Francisco says. "I sifted through quite a bit of history to get a wide range of options—from Betamax tapes to VHS to CD, and then digital. It was really exciting to see the evolution of camera-related media. The placement of the camera was just as important because it needed to clearly show the audience that this is the camera ant. So placing the camera on its back changes the silhouette enough and immediately distinguishes her from other ants."

Anthony Francisco concept art.

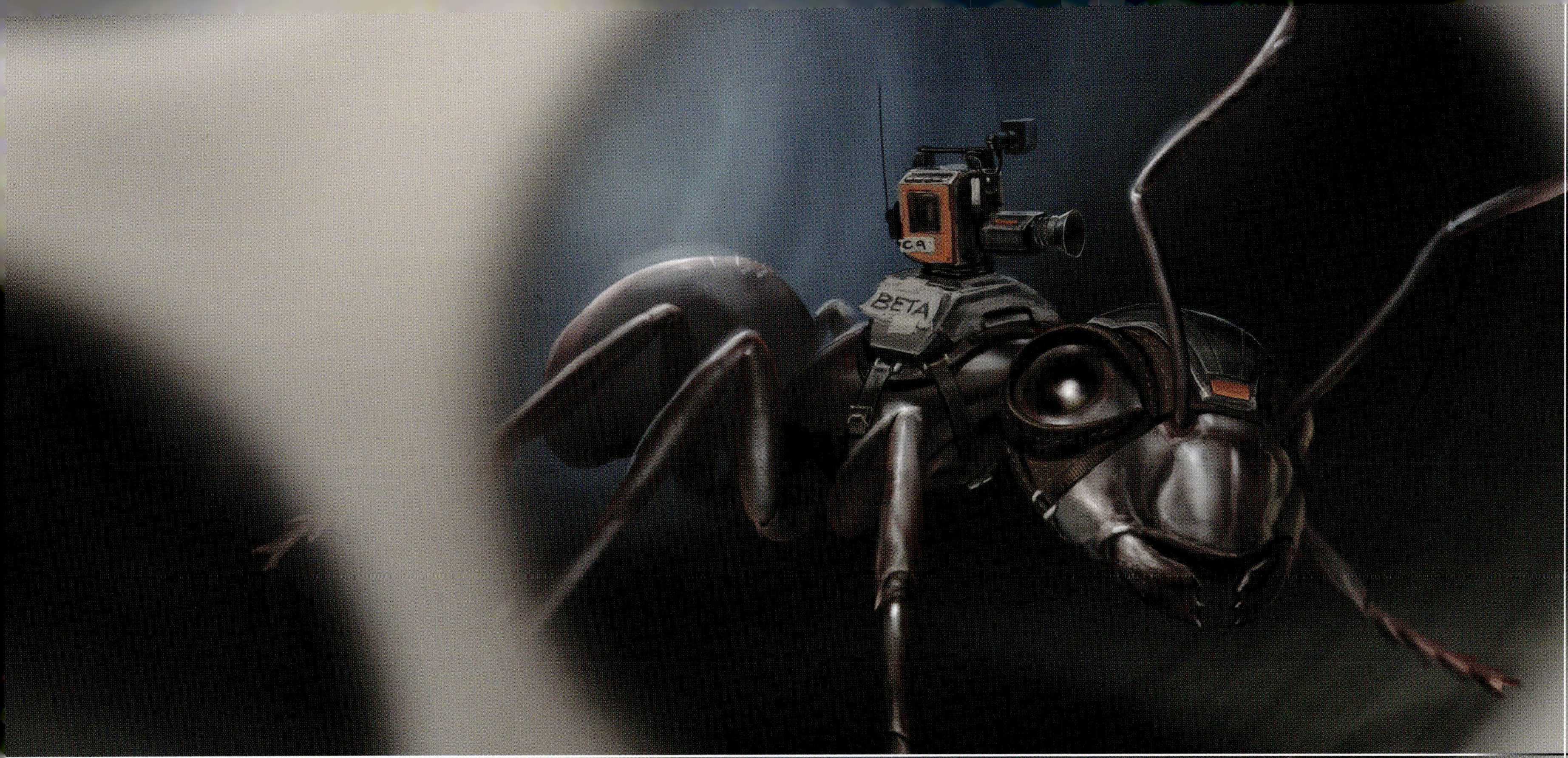

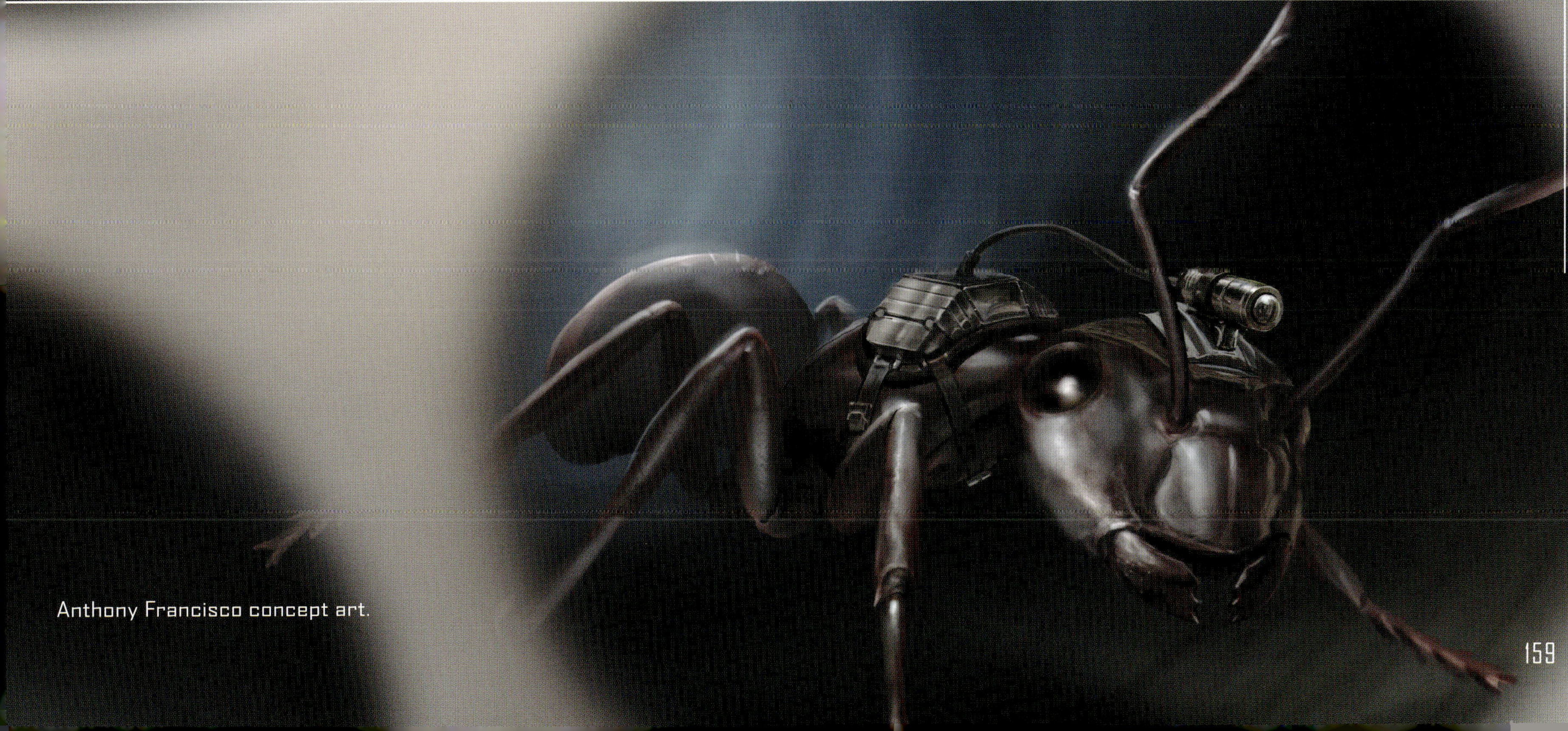

Anthony Francisco concept art.

ADDITIONAL ANT EXPLORATION

Early in production, Concept Artist Josh Nizzi explored a plethora of fun, sometimes outlandish, ideas for ant enhancements. Designs for ants carrying tanks of instantly freezing liquid nitrogen, portable flamethrowers, lasers, sonar equipment, and more were all explored during this preliminary phase. Ultimately, most of the concepts didn't work in the context of the story. The production team wanted to emphasize the ants' integrity and skills without enhancing them with excessive technology.

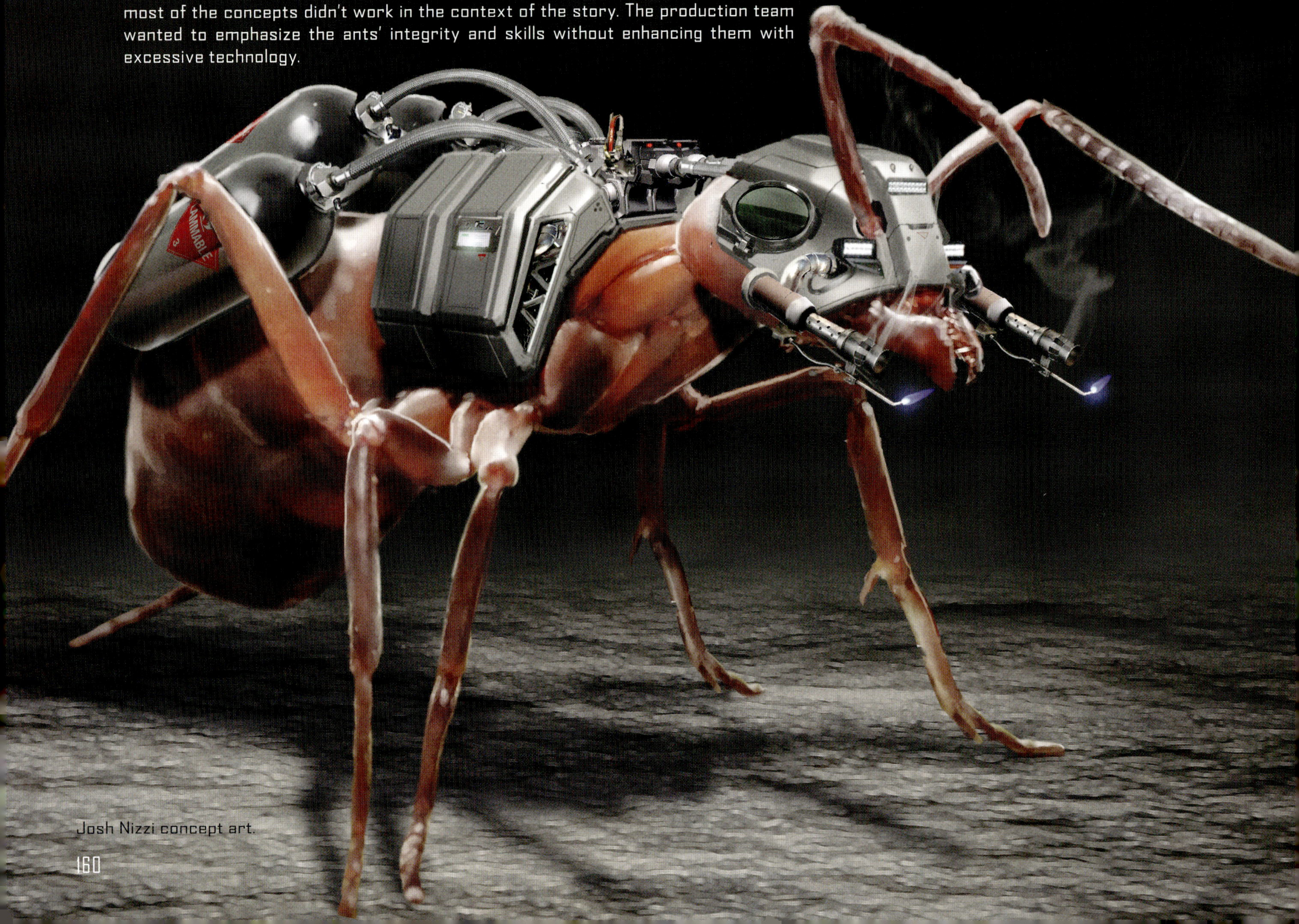

Josh Nizzi concept art.

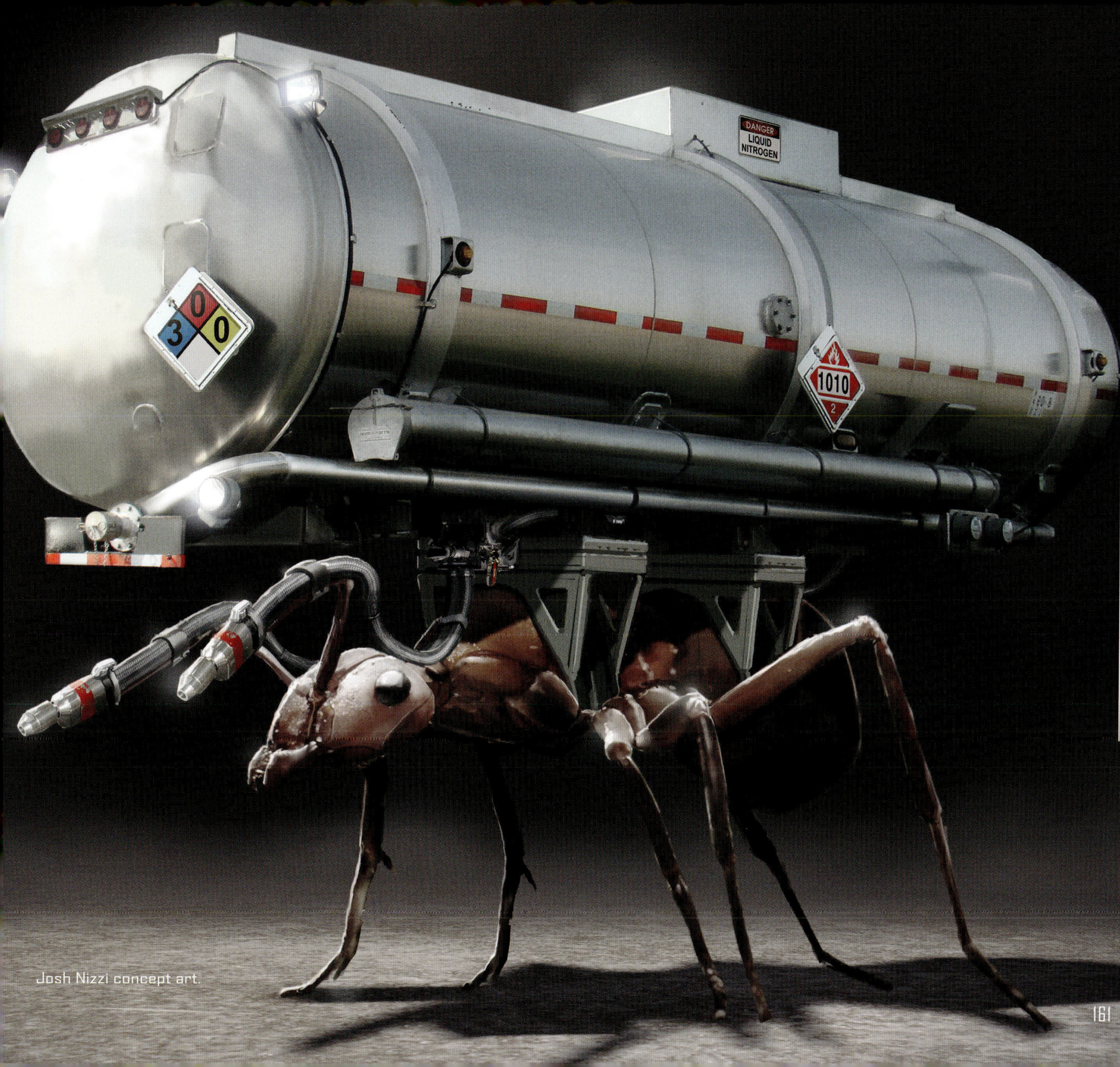

Josh Nizzi concept art.

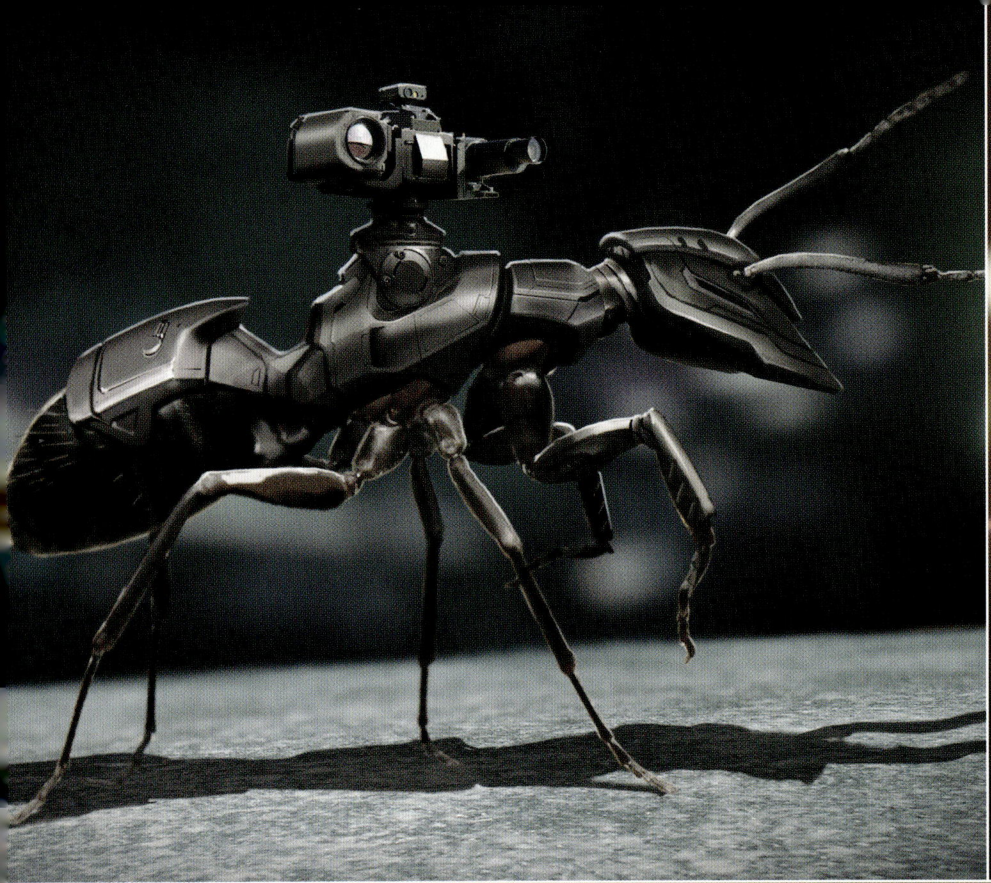

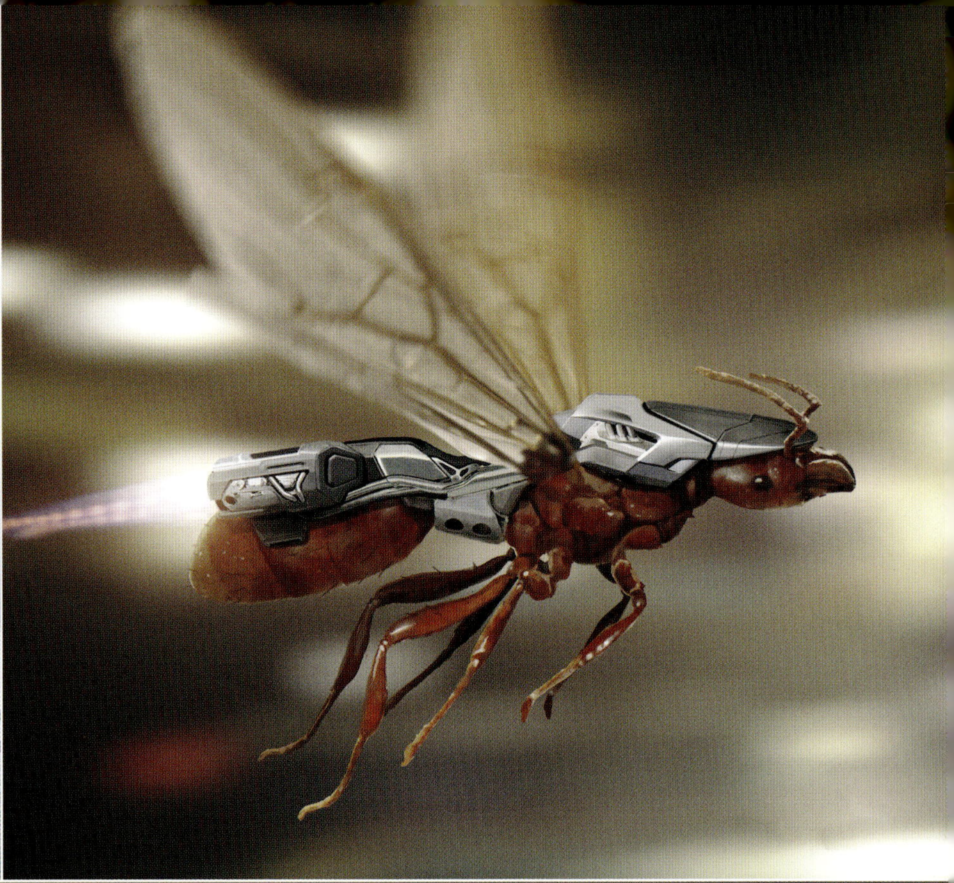

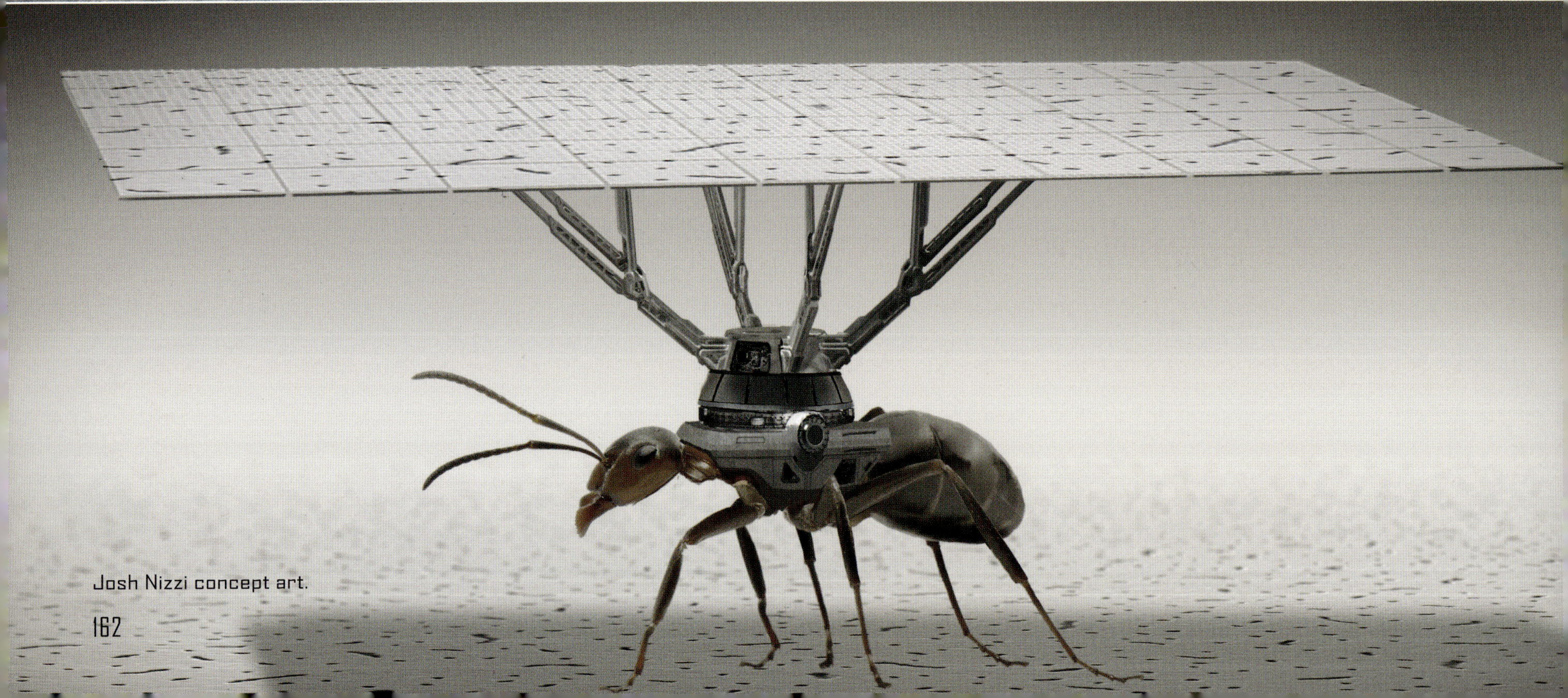

Josh Nizzi concept art.

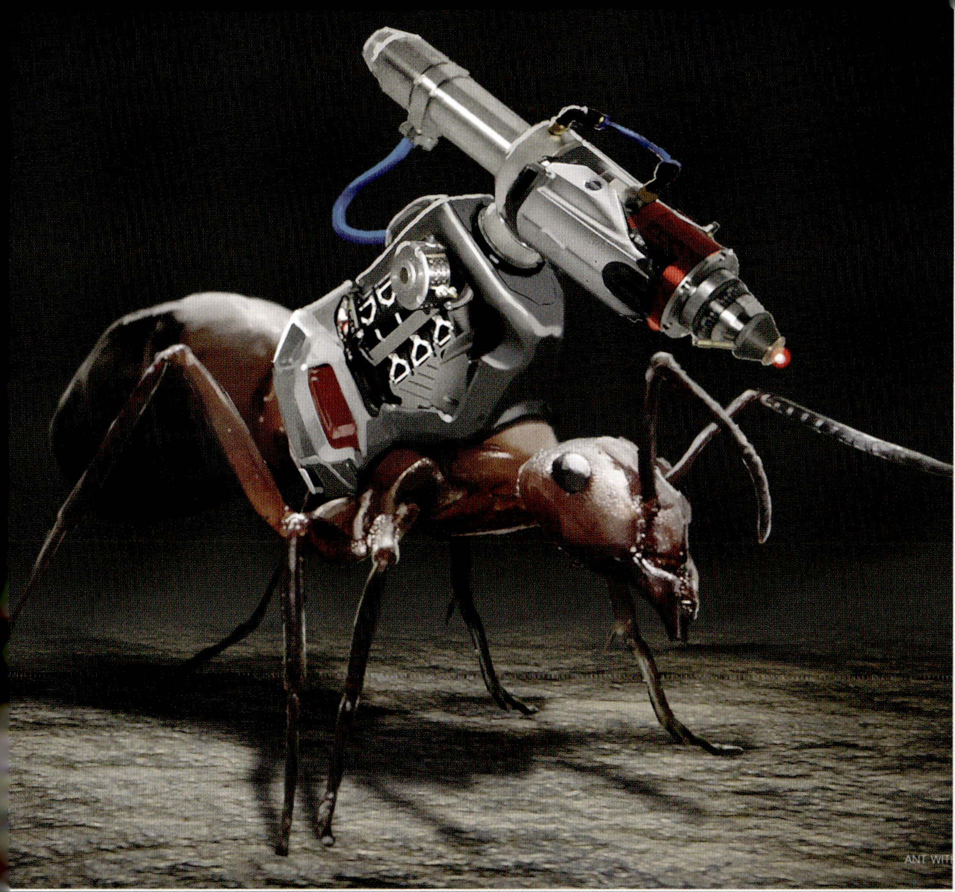

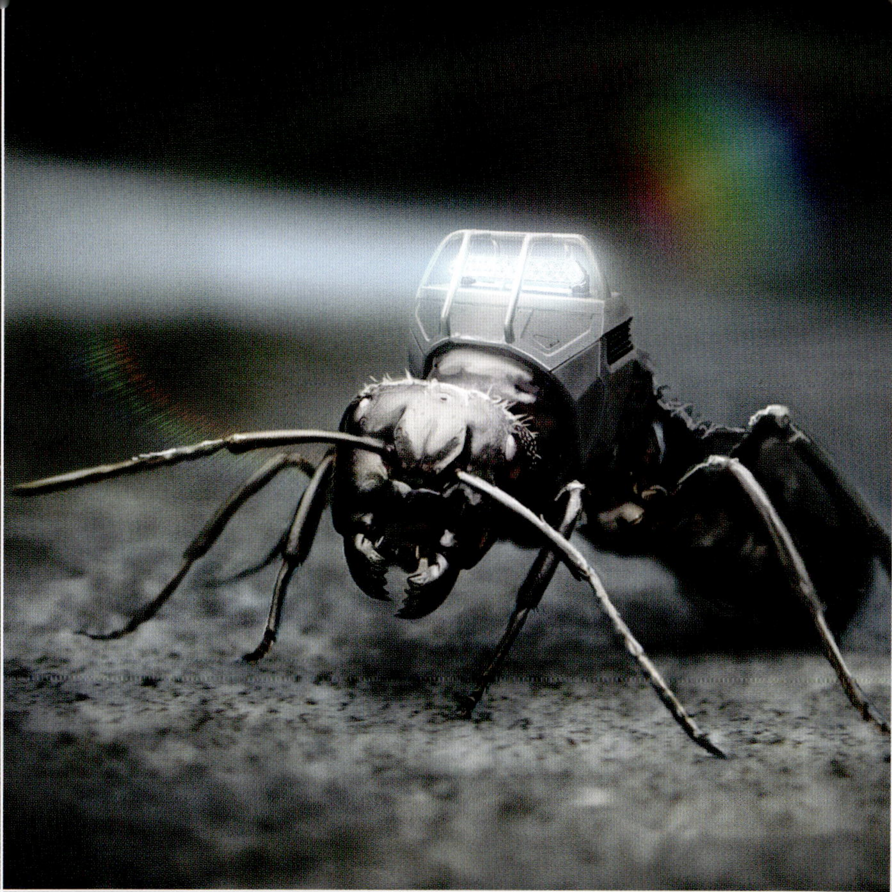

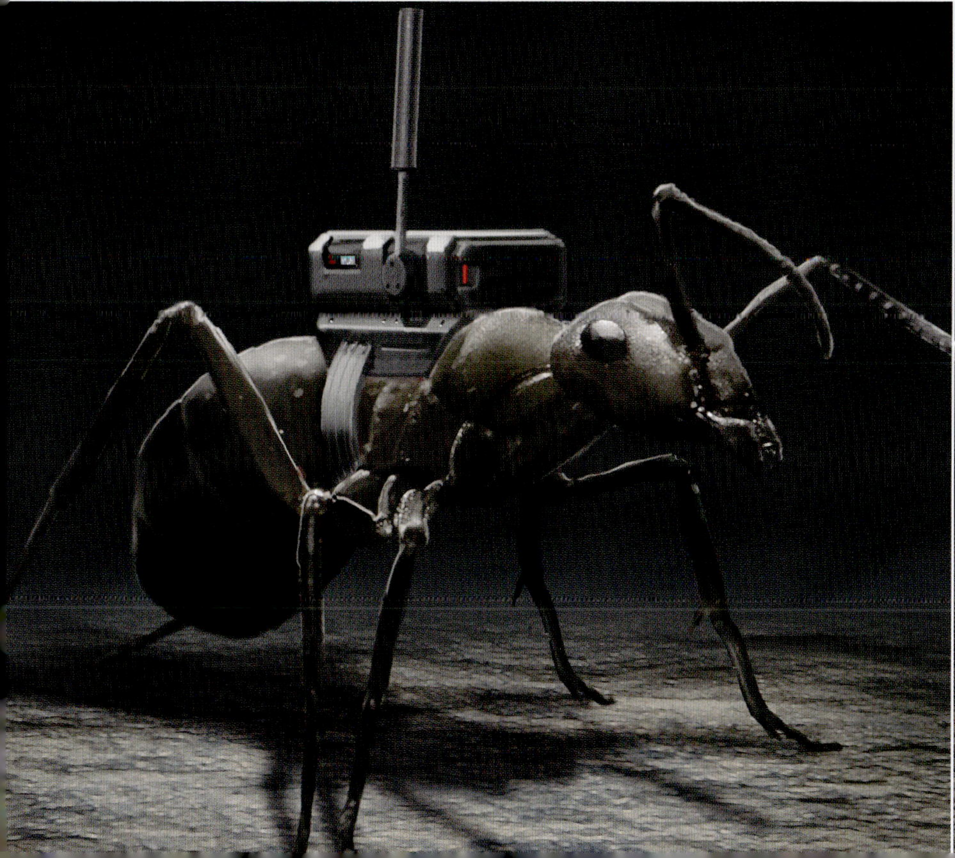

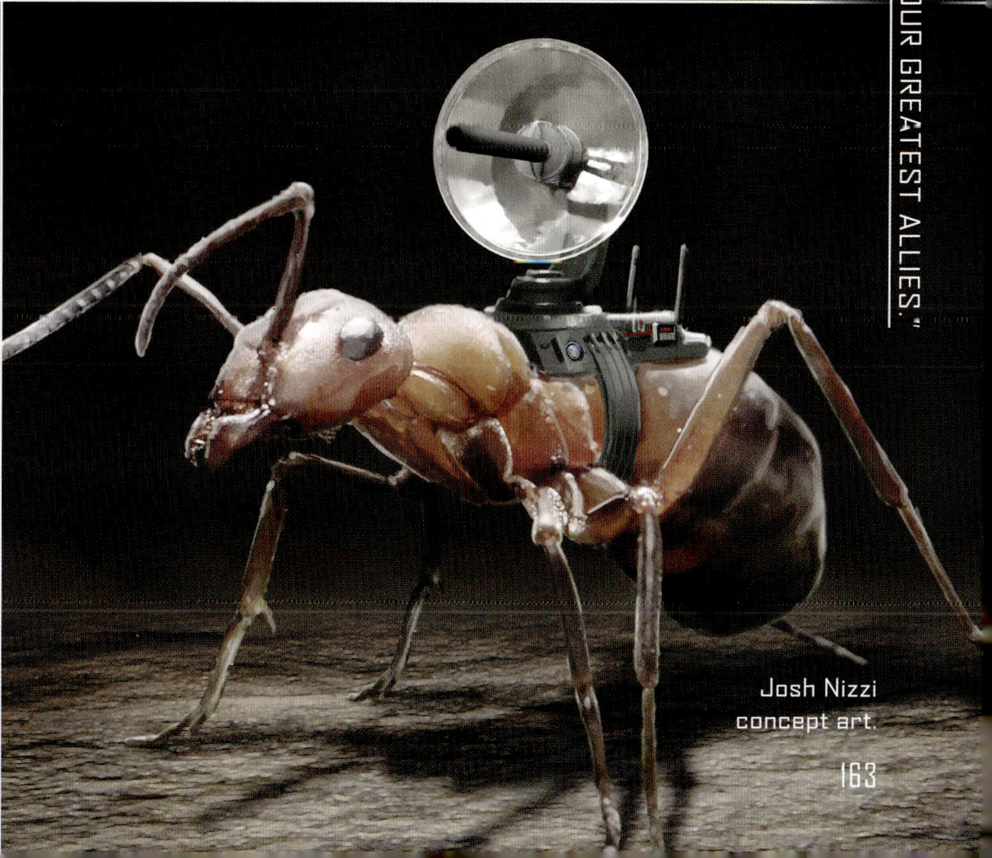

Josh Nizzi concept art.

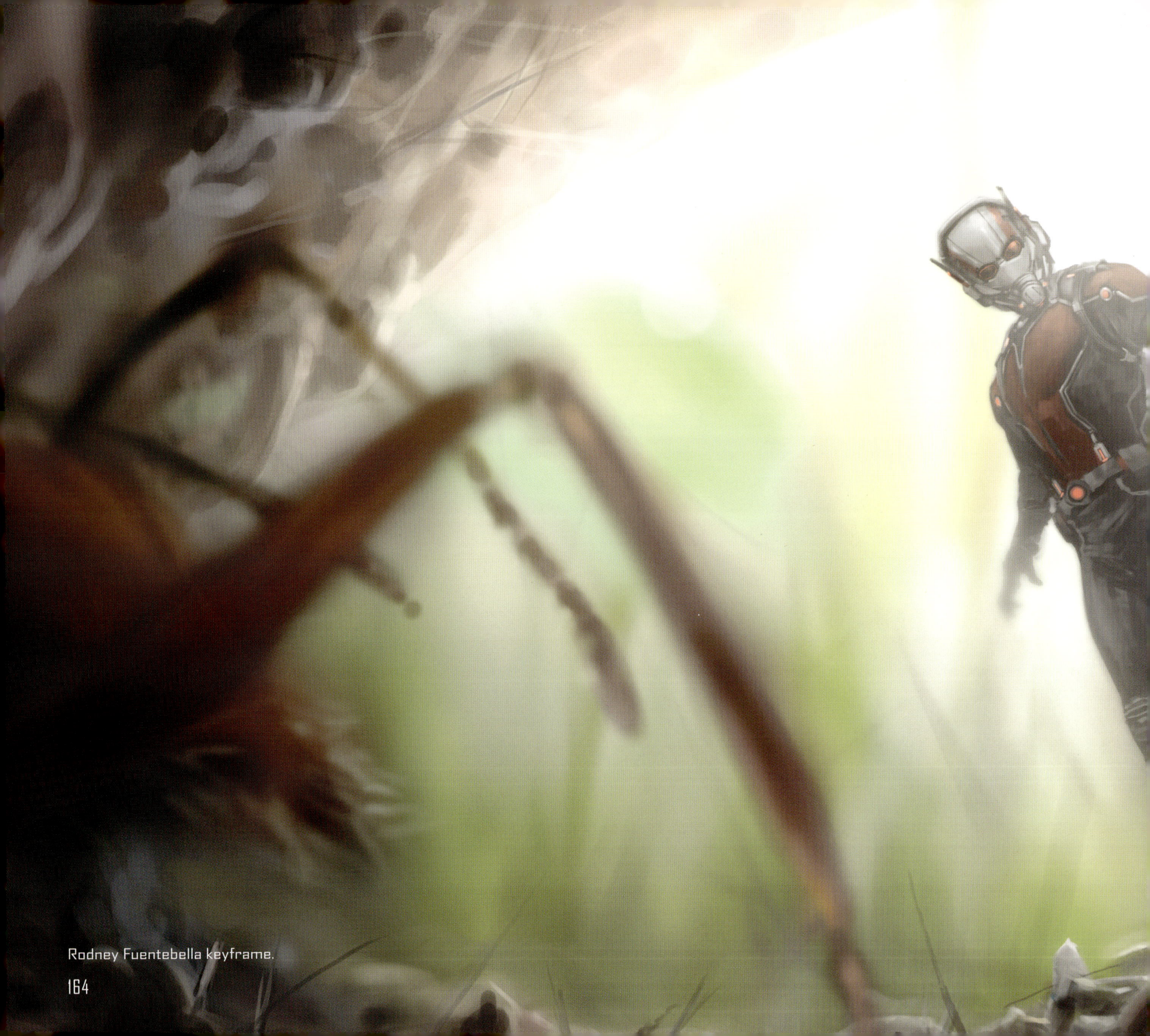

Rodney Fuentebella keyframe.

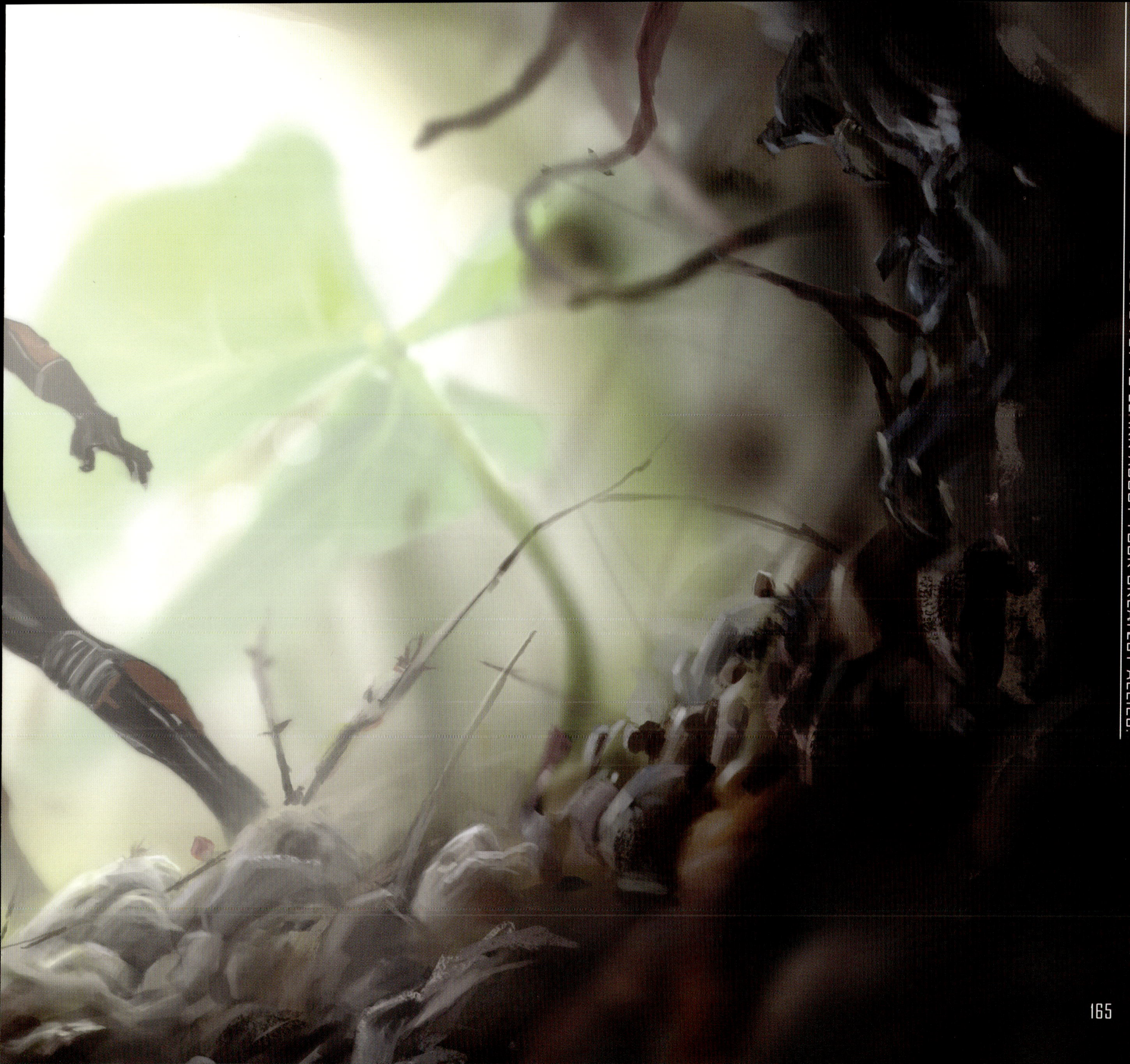

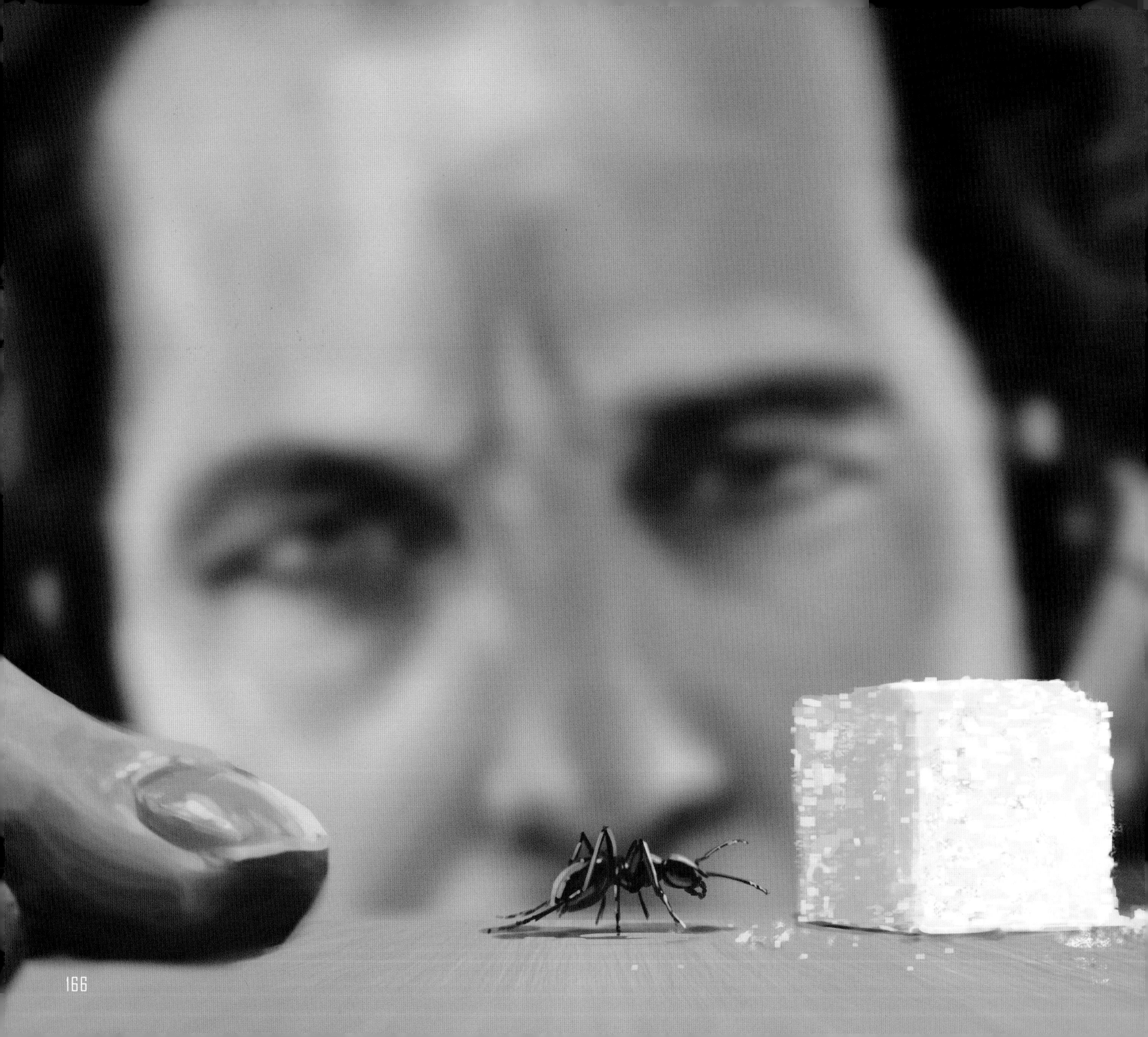

Concept Artist Jackson Sze worked closely with the filmmakers to execute many of the inspirational keyframes for the film—including this moment in which Scott finally communicates with the ants, instructing them to place a sugar cube into a cup of tea. "This beat came straight from the director," Sze recalls. "He had a very clear idea of how he wanted the shot composed, so my job was to sell the sense of scale and appropriate depth of field. I used both 3-D software and digital painting to help me realize the scene."

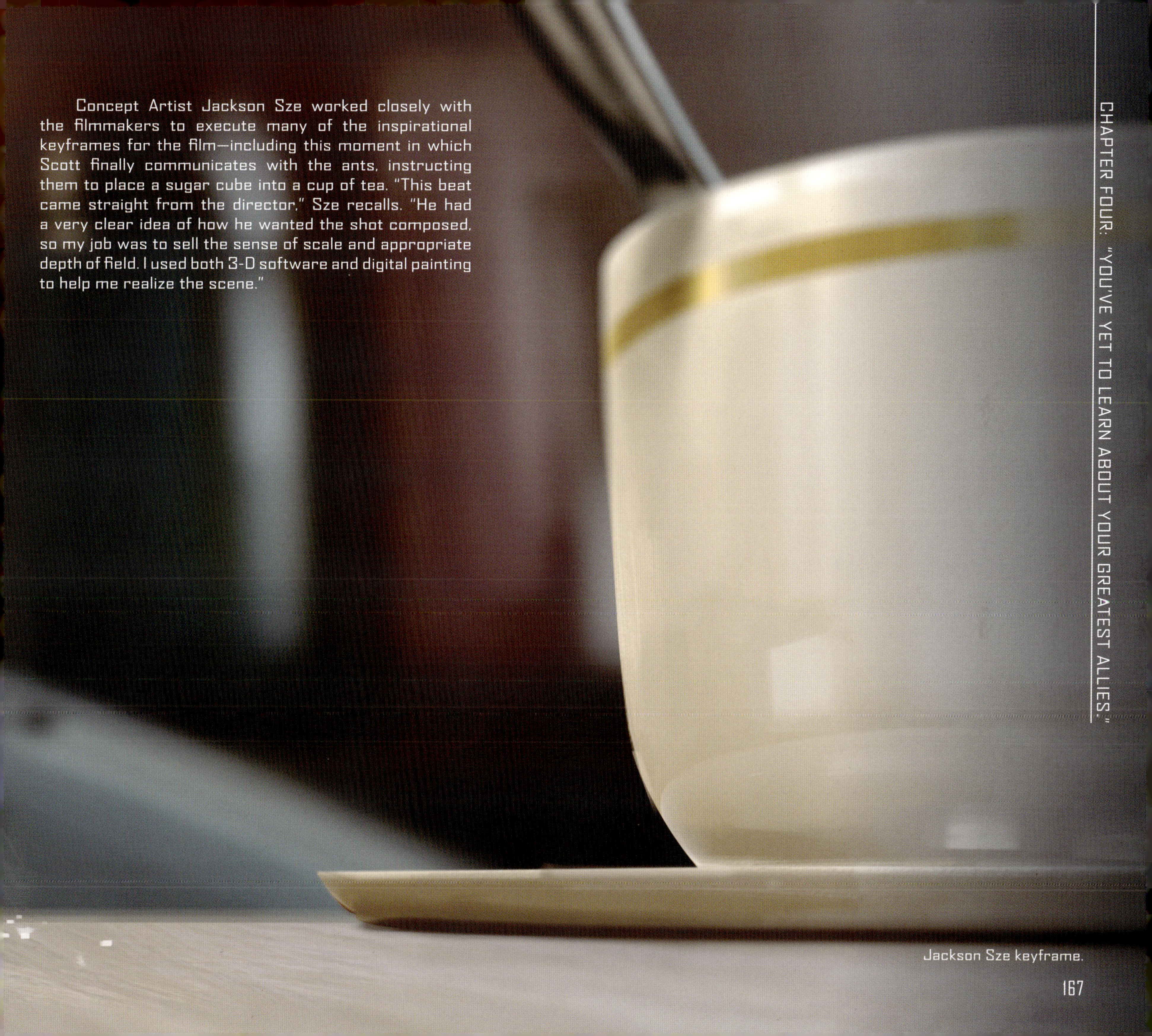

Jackson Sze keyframe.

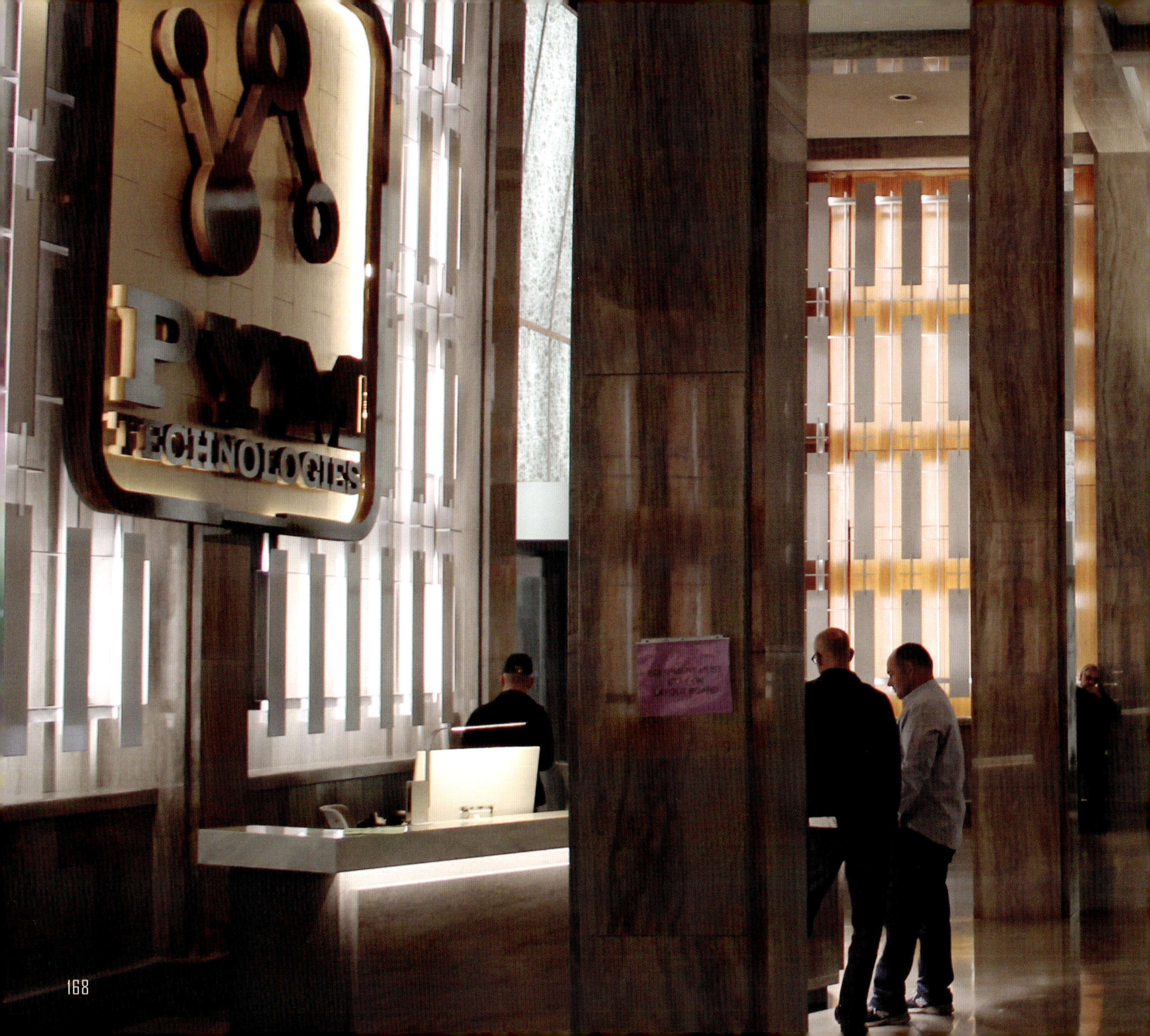
PYM
TECHNOLOGIES

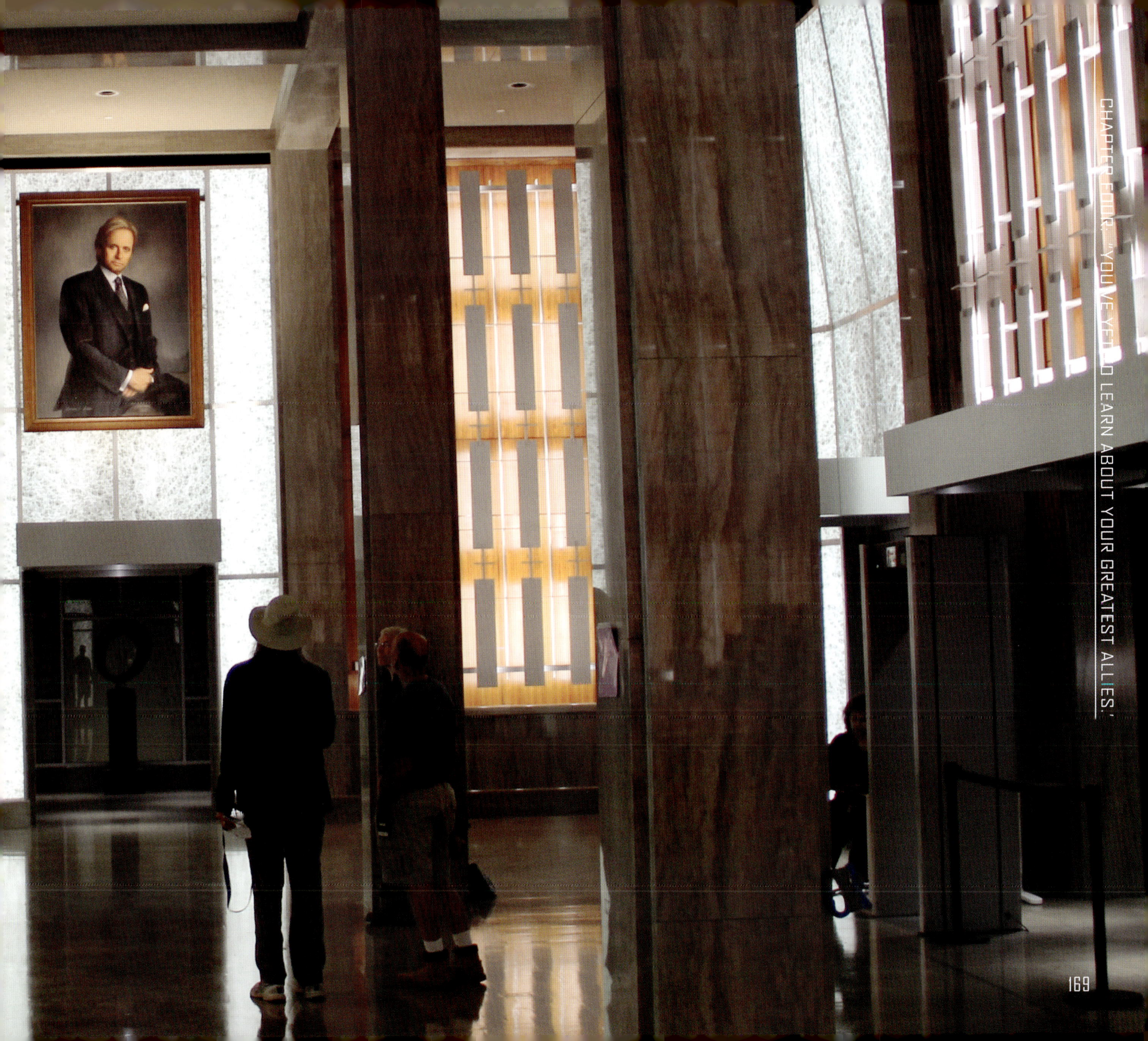

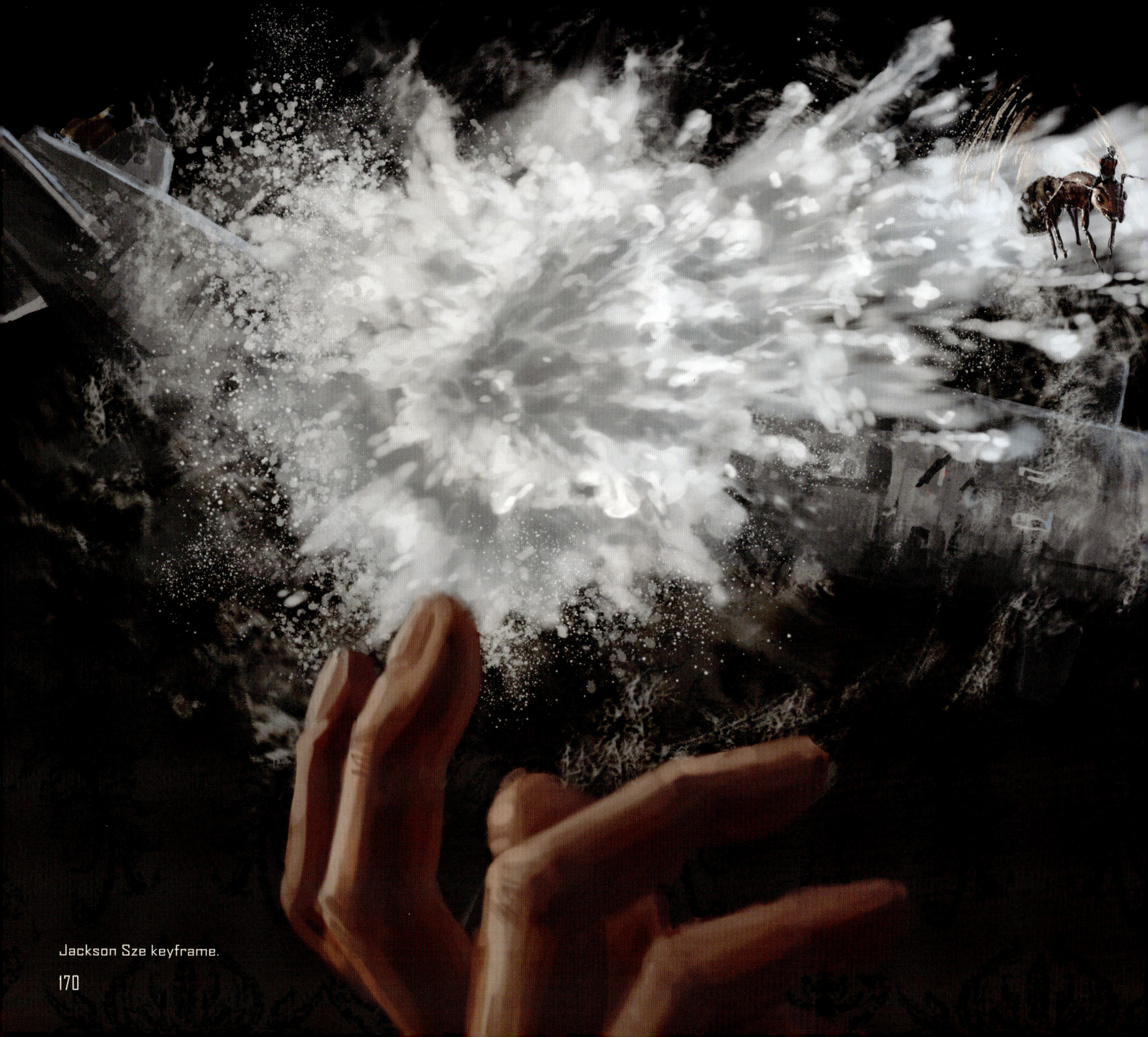

Jackson Sze keyframe.

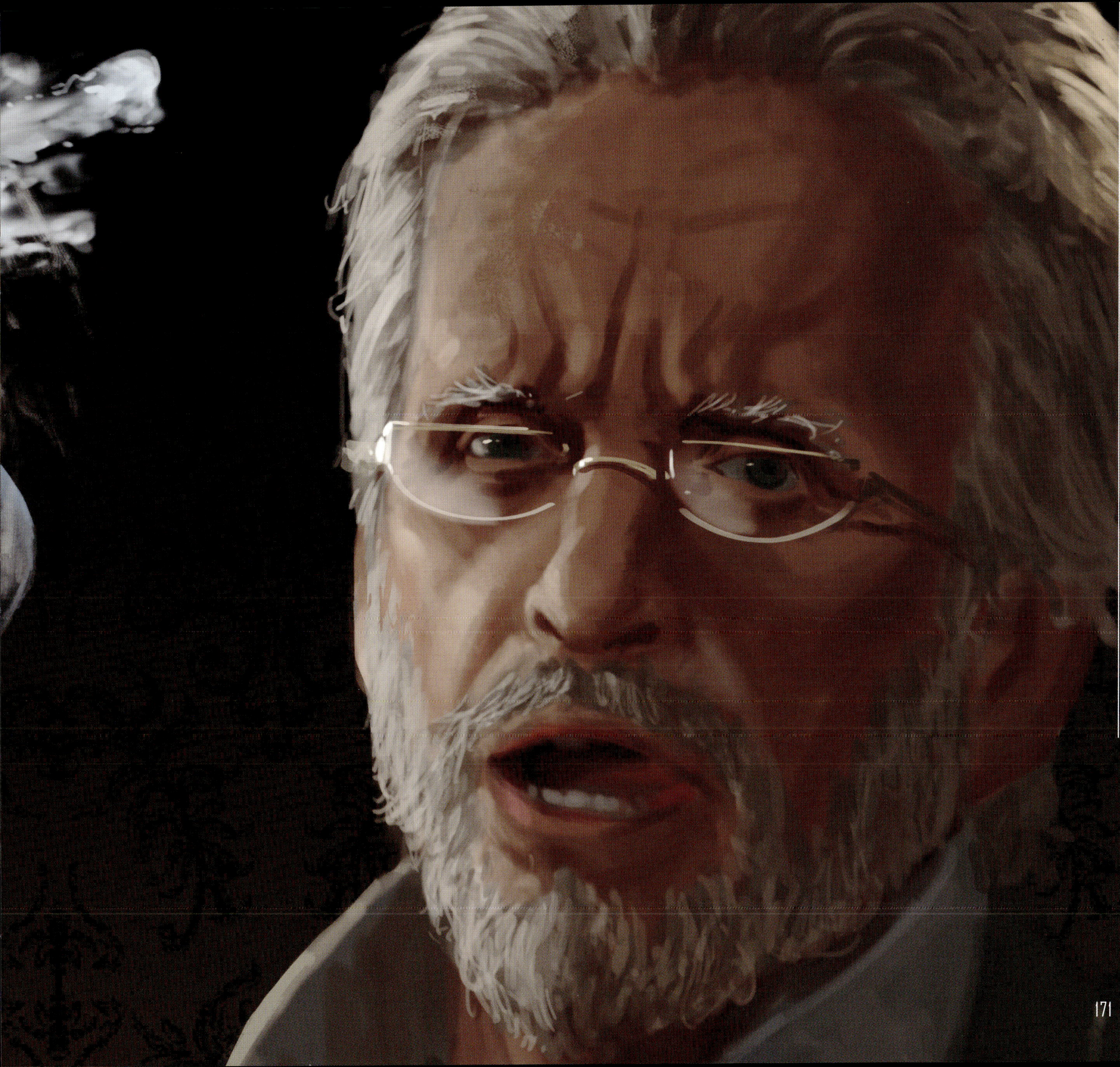

THE WASP

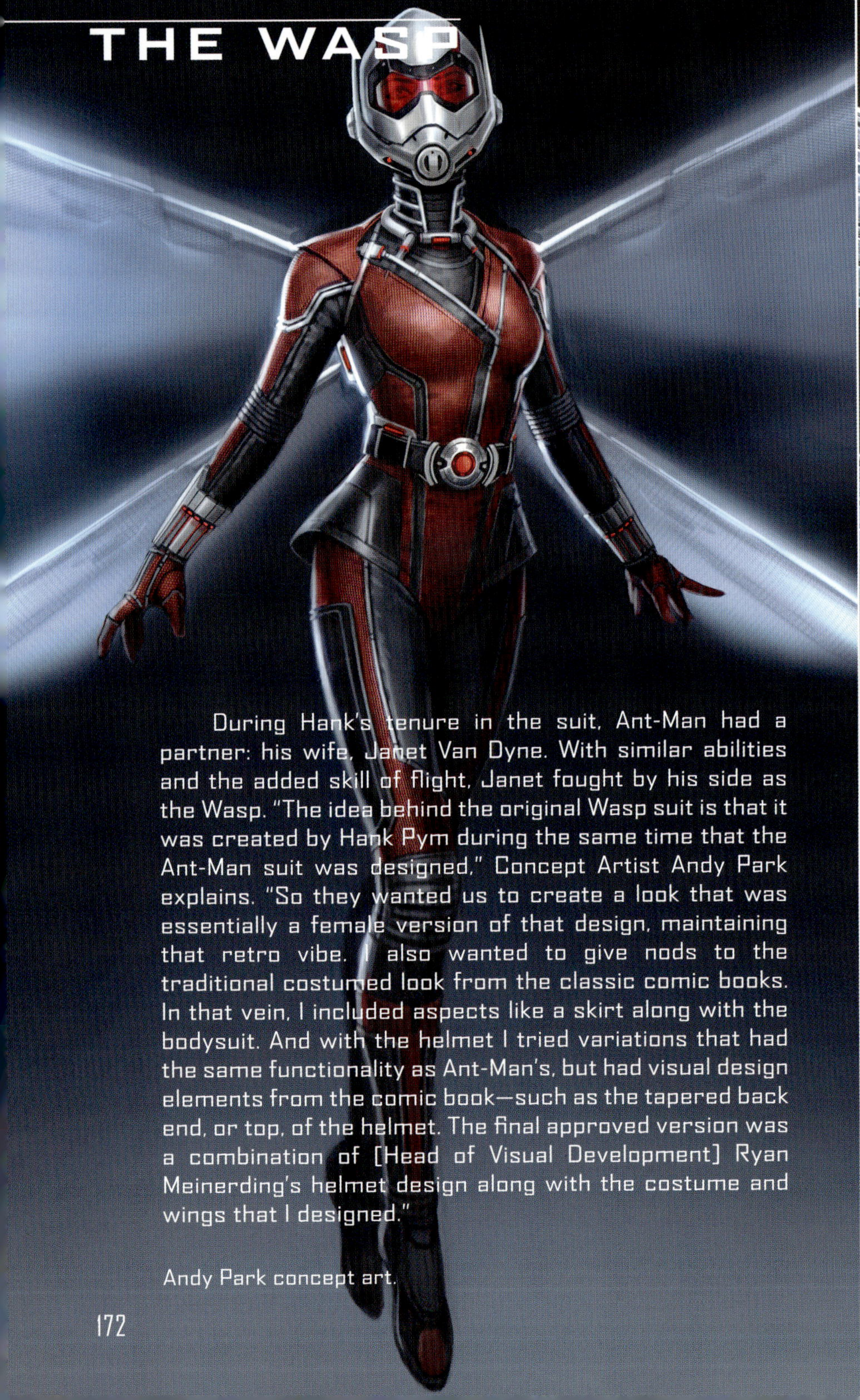

During Hank's tenure in the suit, Ant-Man had a partner: his wife, Janet Van Dyne. With similar abilities and the added skill of flight, Janet fought by his side as the Wasp. "The idea behind the original Wasp suit is that it was created by Hank Pym during the same time that the Ant-Man suit was designed," Concept Artist Andy Park explains. "So they wanted us to create a look that was essentially a female version of that design, maintaining that retro vibe. I also wanted to give nods to the traditional costumed look from the classic comic books. In that vein, I included aspects like a skirt along with the bodysuit. And with the helmet I tried variations that had the same functionality as Ant-Man's, but had visual design elements from the comic book—such as the tapered back end, or top, of the helmet. The final approved version was a combination of [Head of Visual Development] Ryan Meinerding's helmet design along with the costume and wings that I designed."

Andy Park concept art.

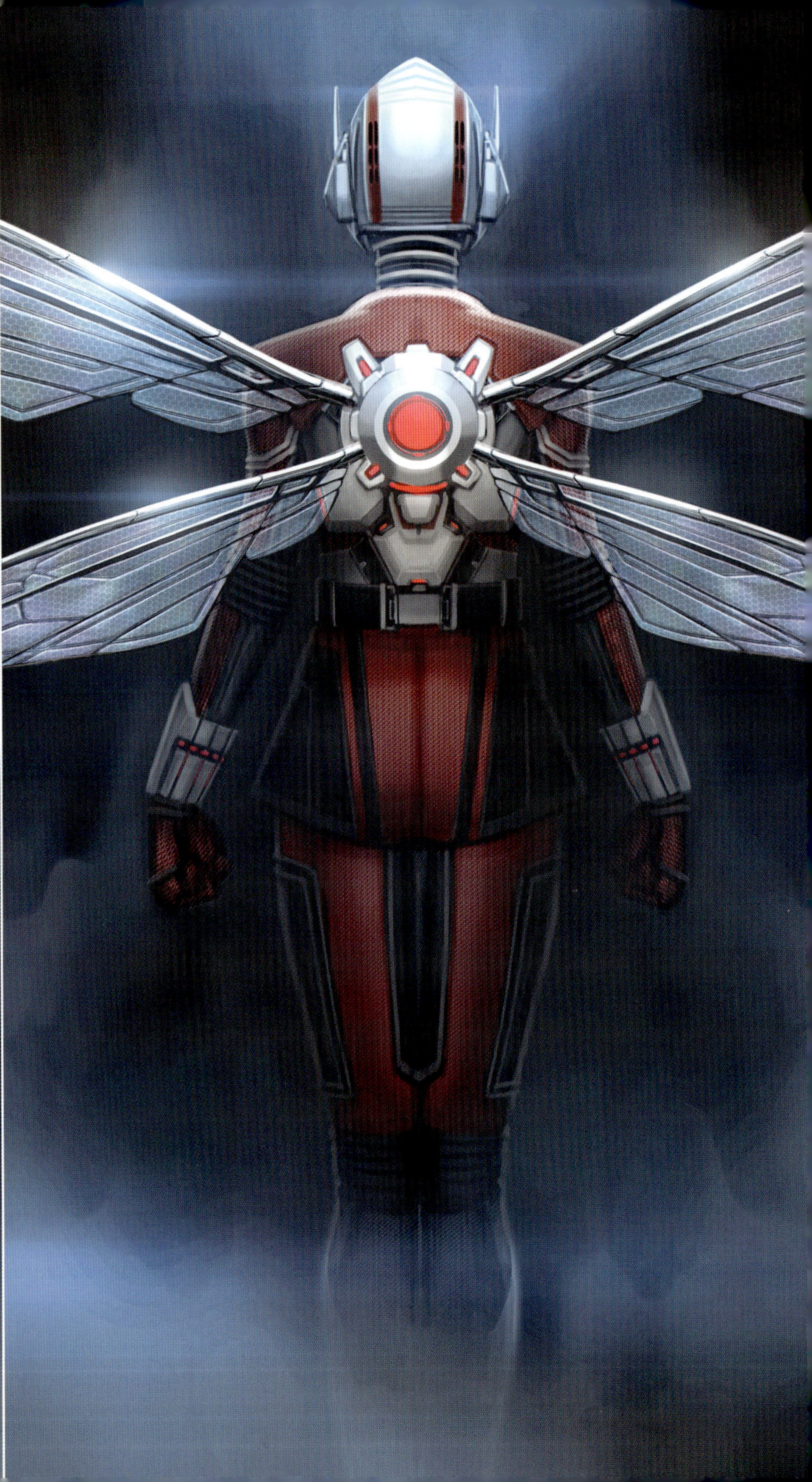

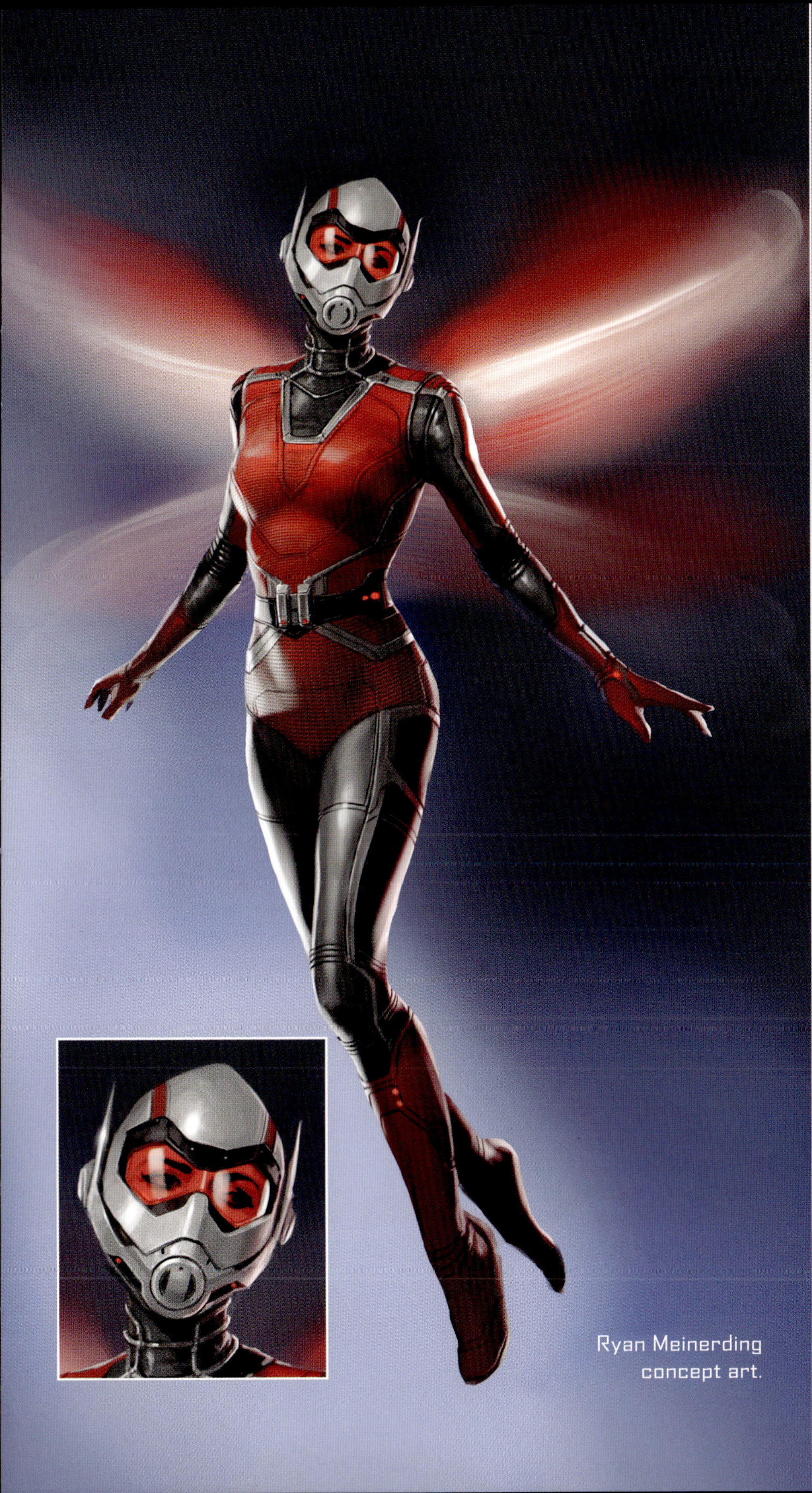

Ryan Meinerding concept art.

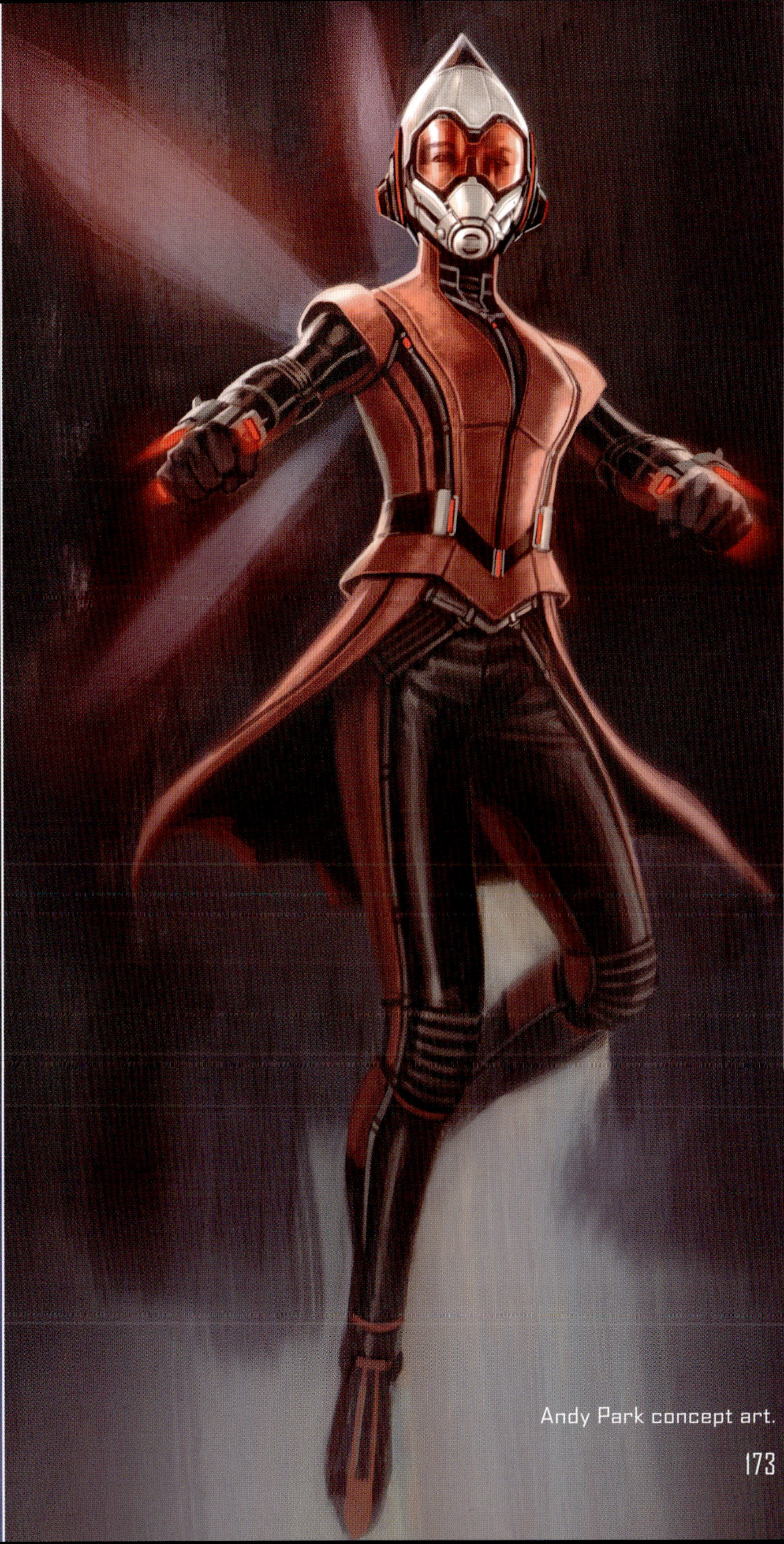

Andy Park concept art.

Concept Artist Rodney Fuentebella also created early designs for the Wasp: "I wanted to create a sleek, retro-inspired look for Wasp," he recalls. "I drew inspiration from motorcycle wear and gear, and vintage cartoons."

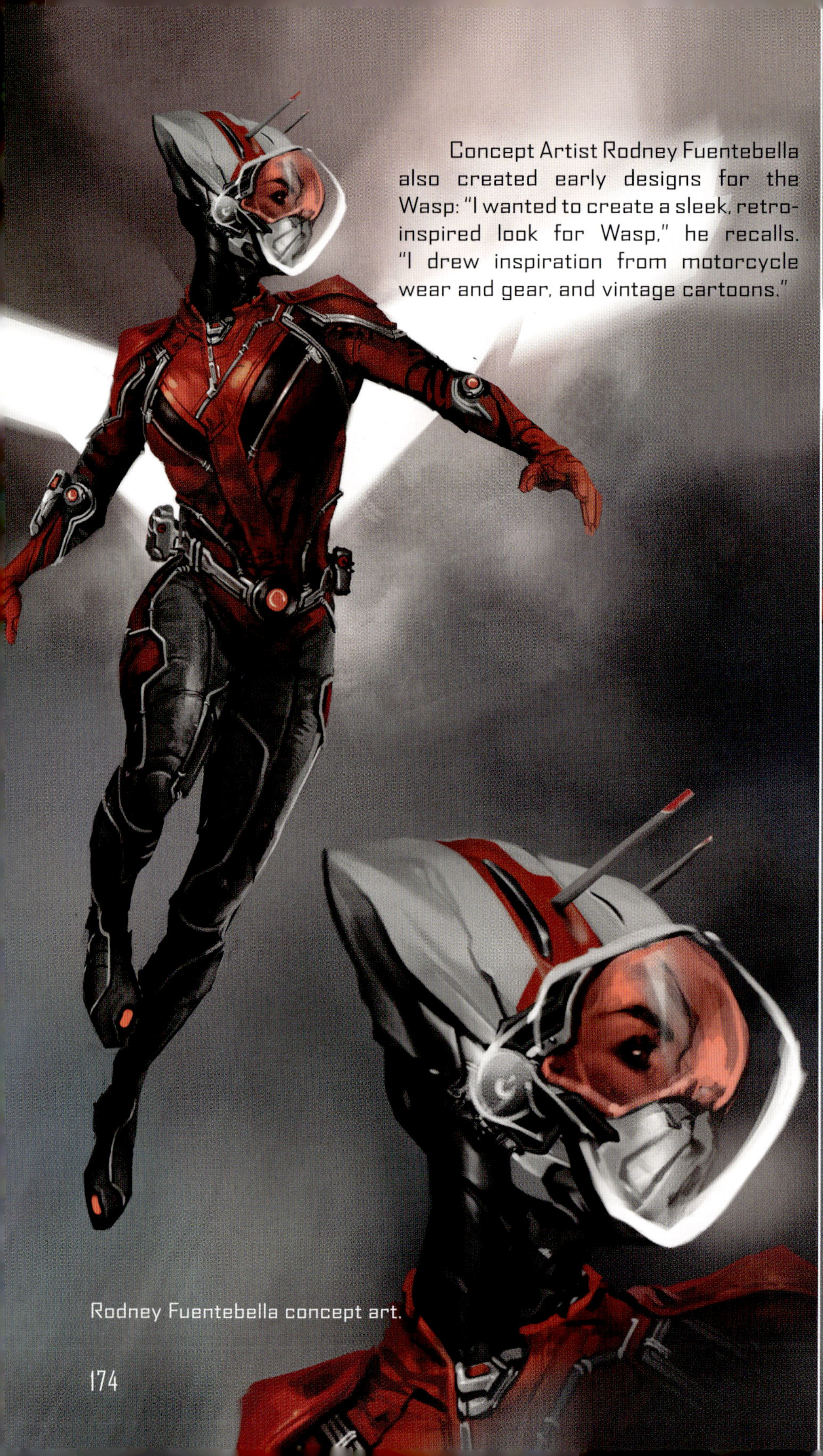

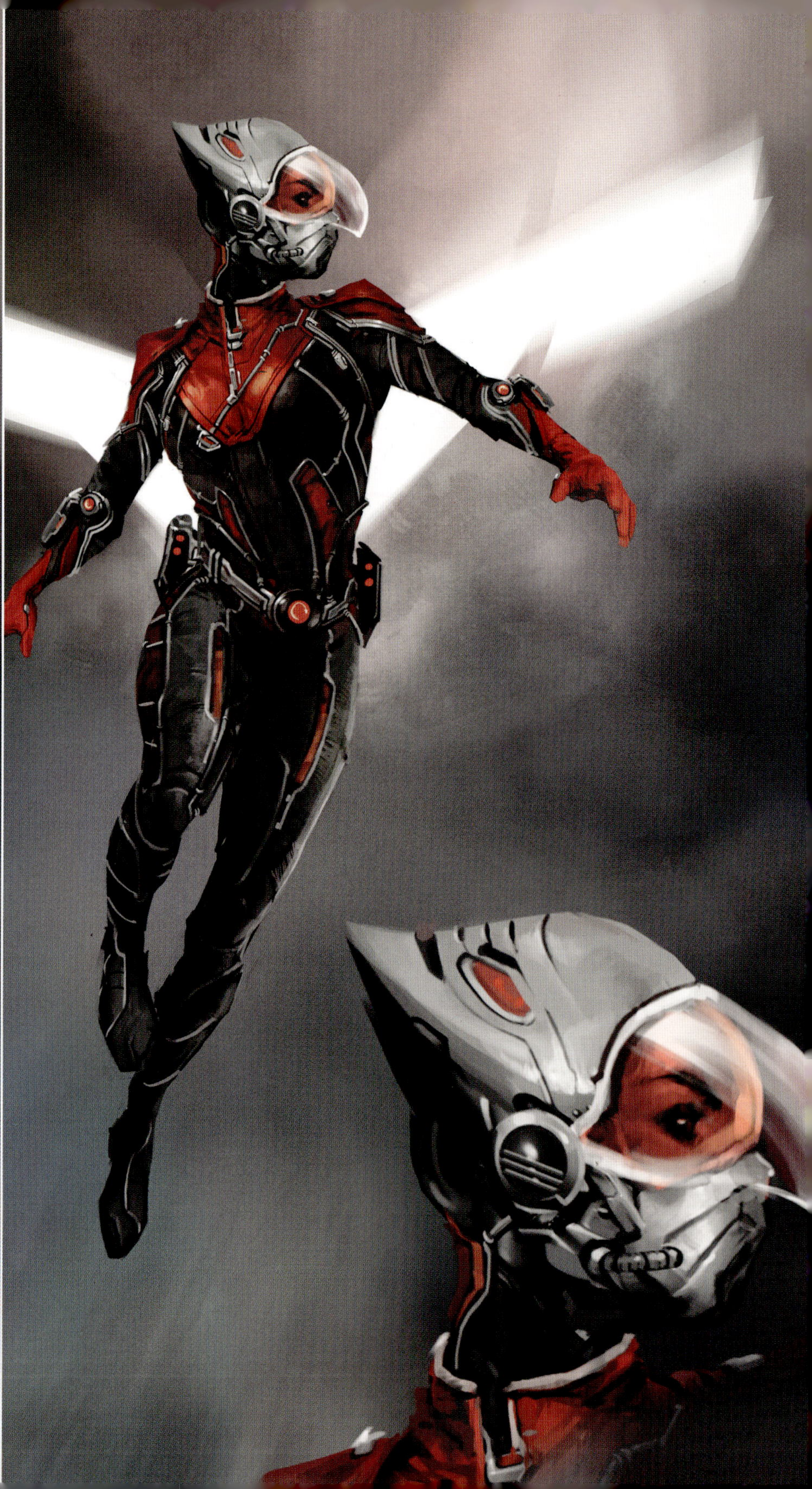

Rodney Fuentebella concept art.

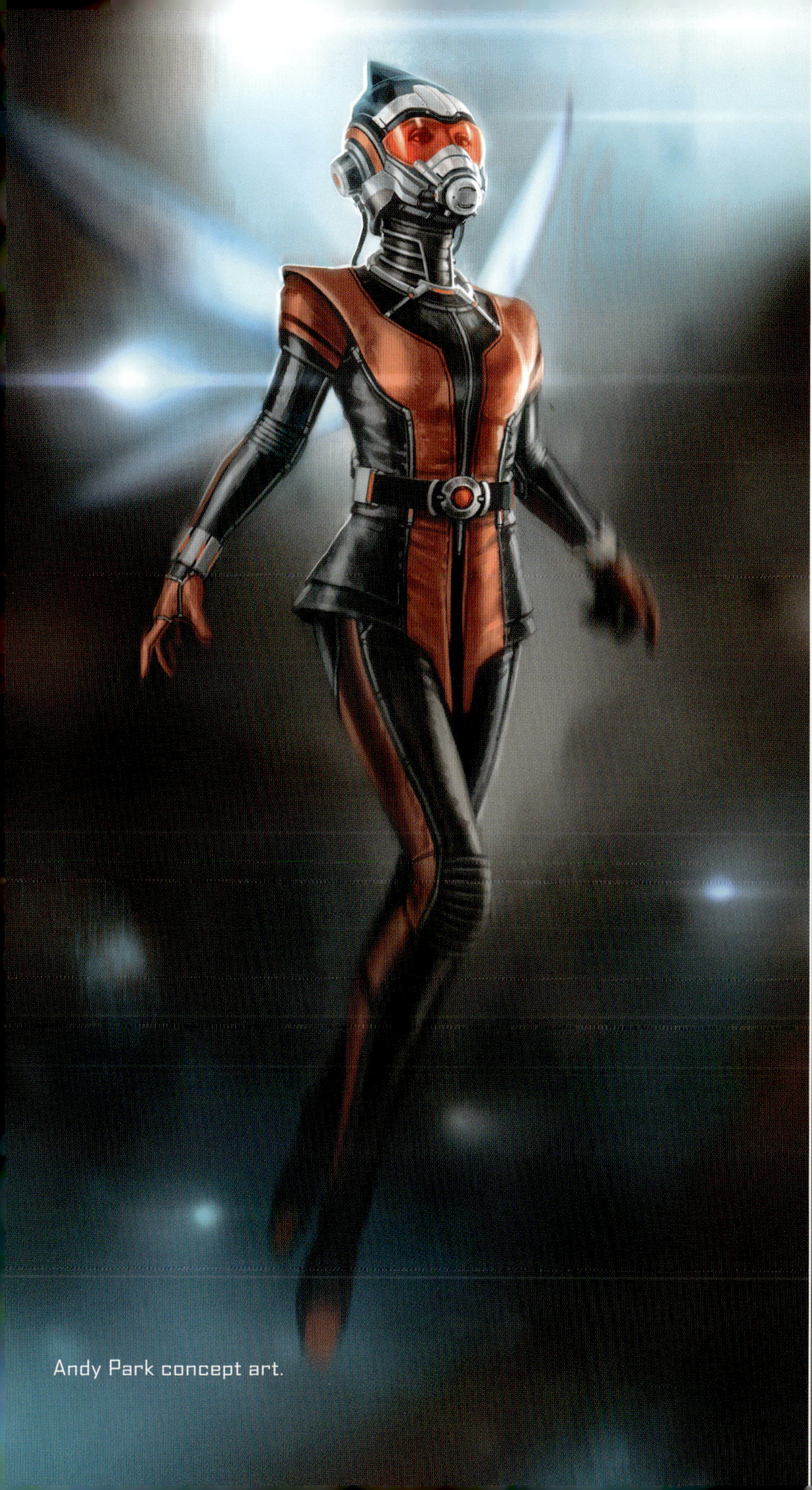

Andy Park concept art.

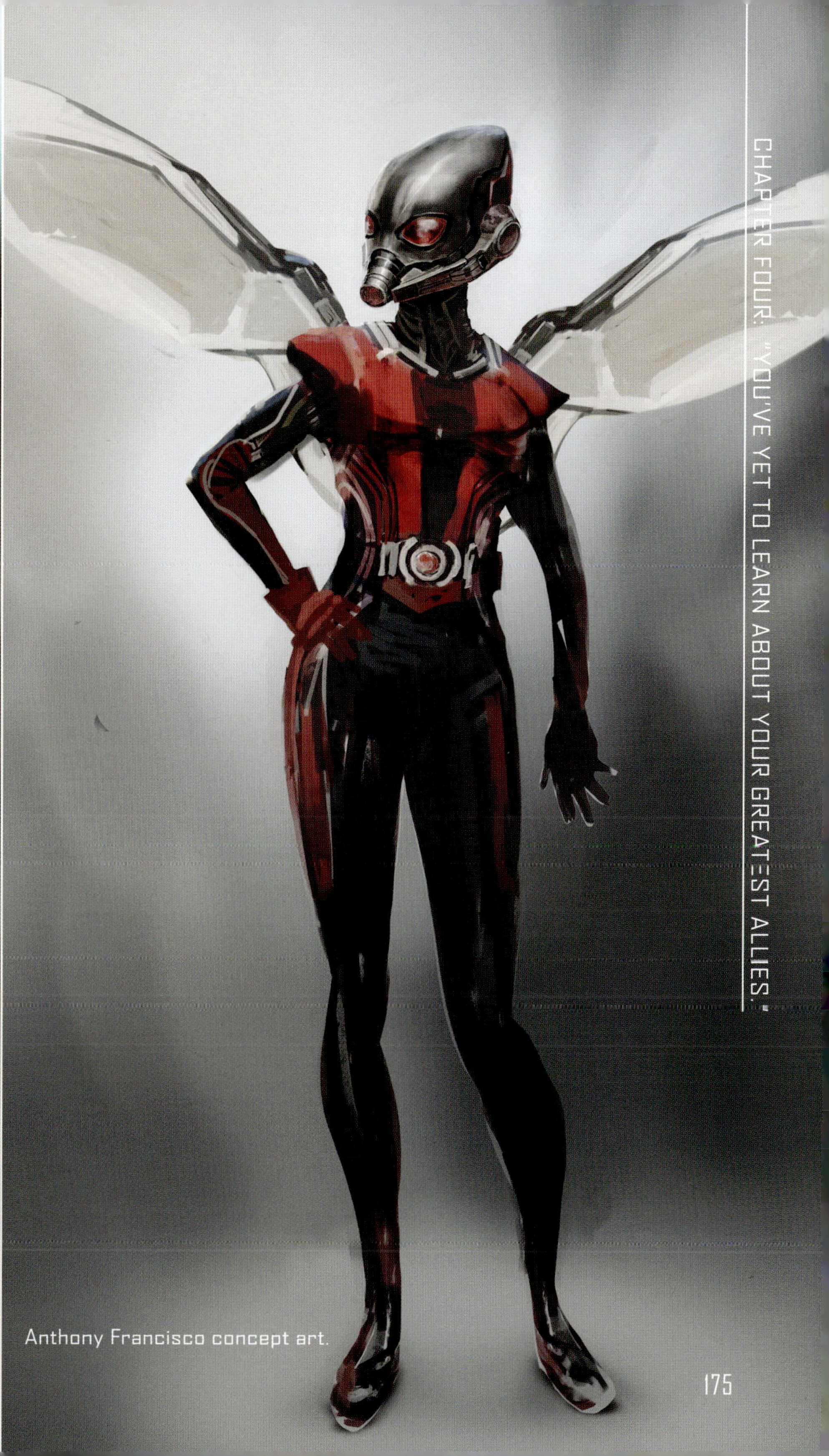

Anthony Francisco concept art.

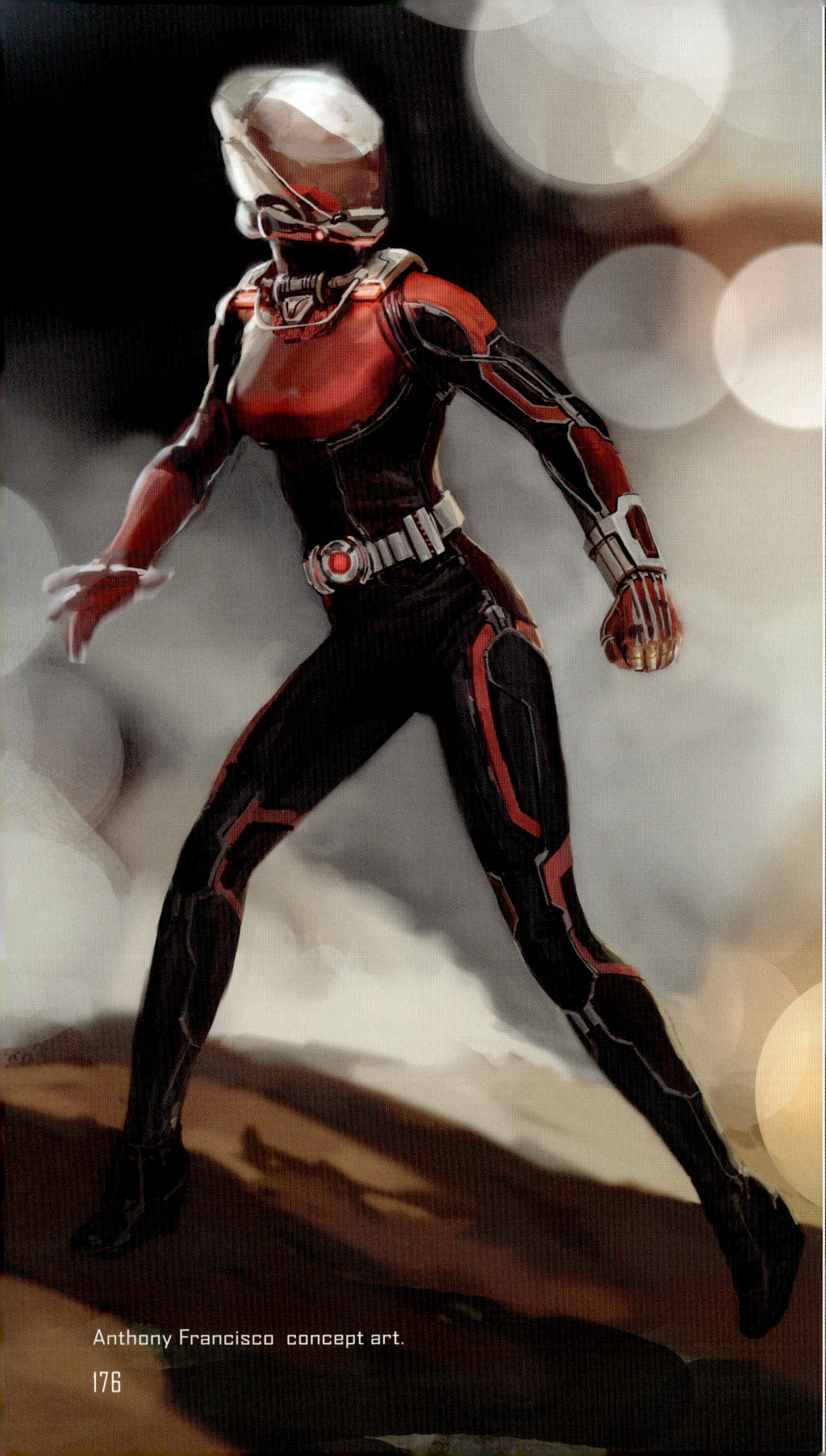

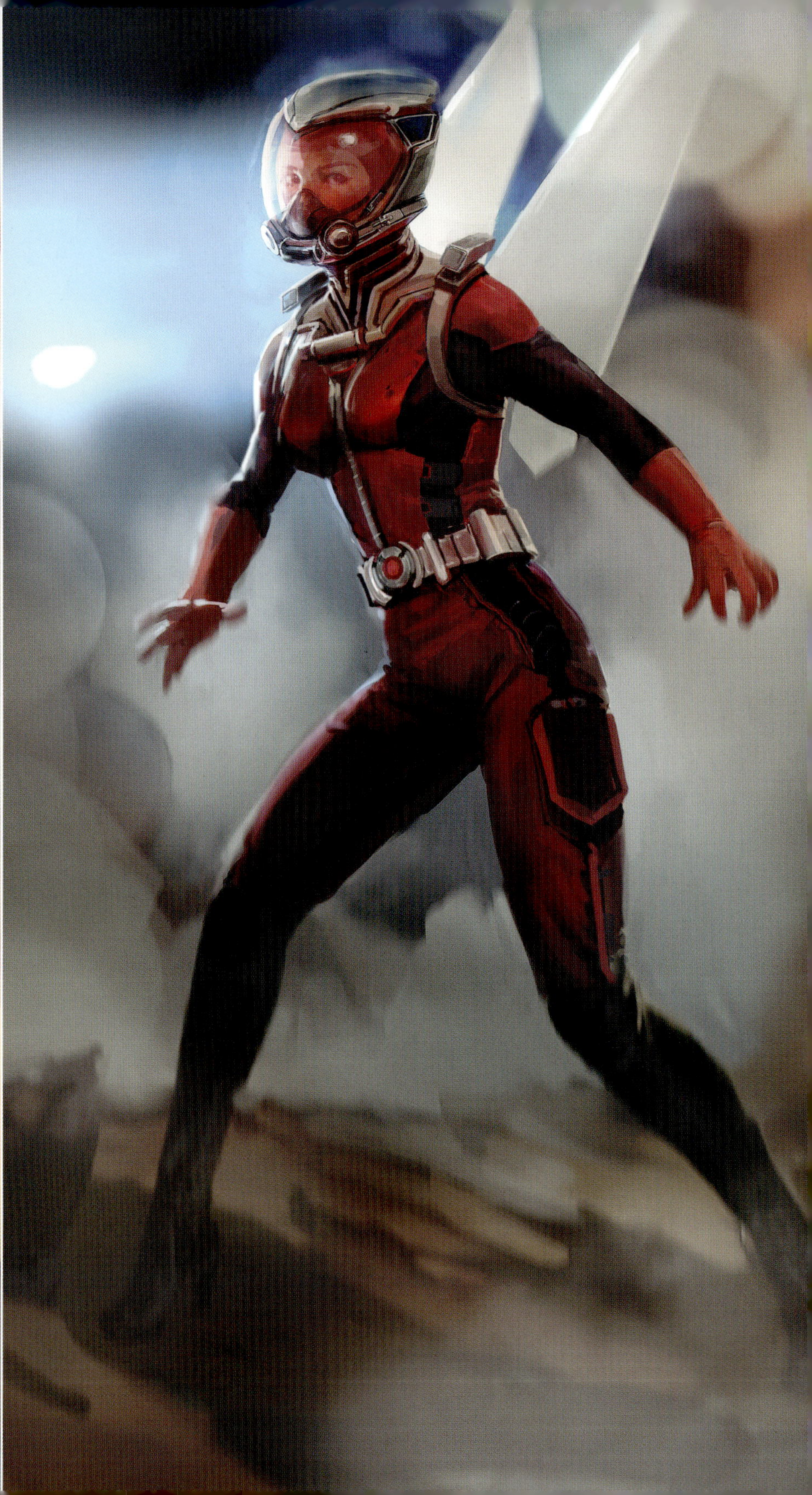

Anthony Francisco concept art.

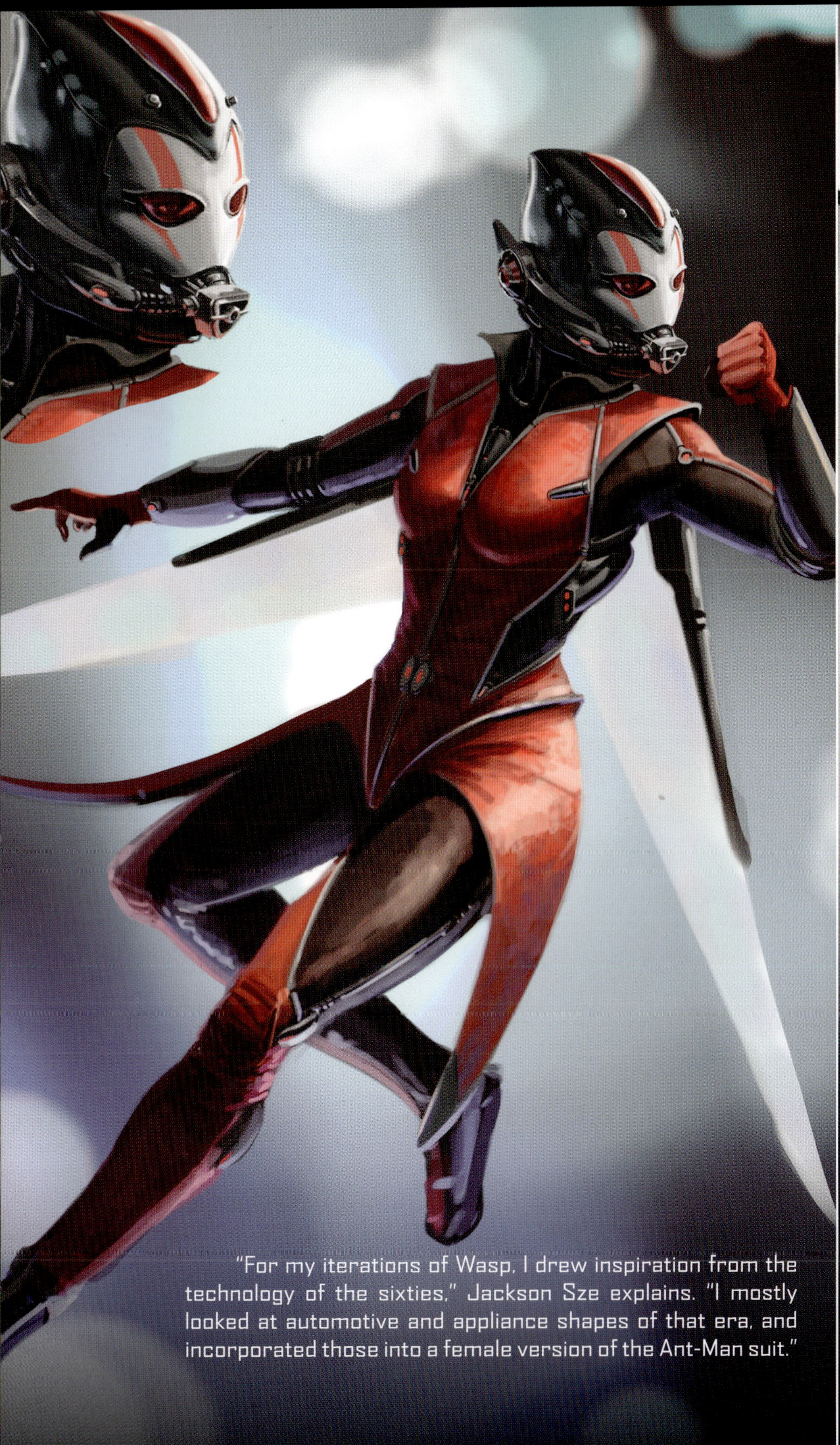

"For my iterations of Wasp, I drew inspiration from the technology of the sixties," Jackson Sze explains. "I mostly looked at automotive and appliance shapes of that era, and incorporated those into a female version of the Ant-Man suit."

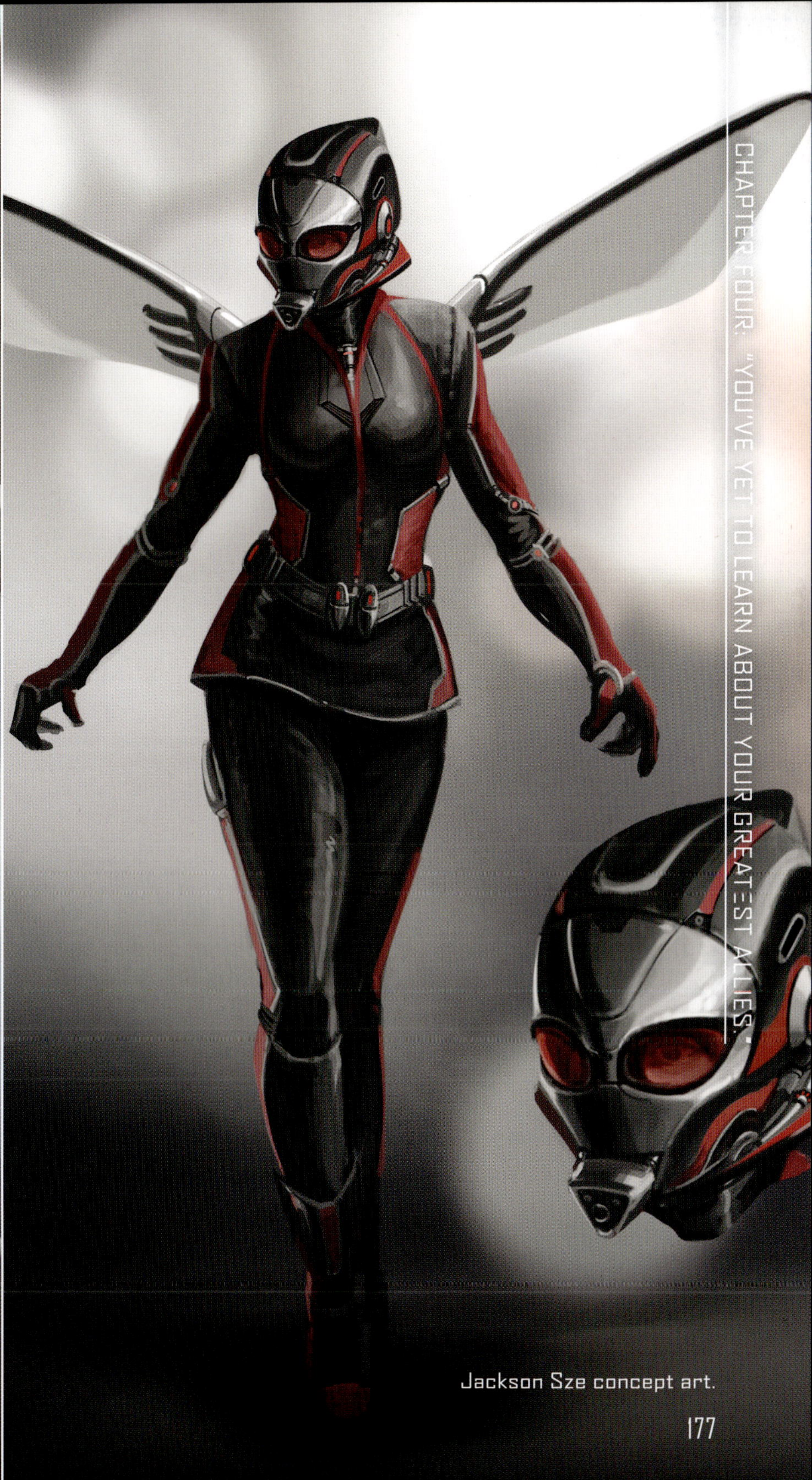

Jackson Sze concept art.

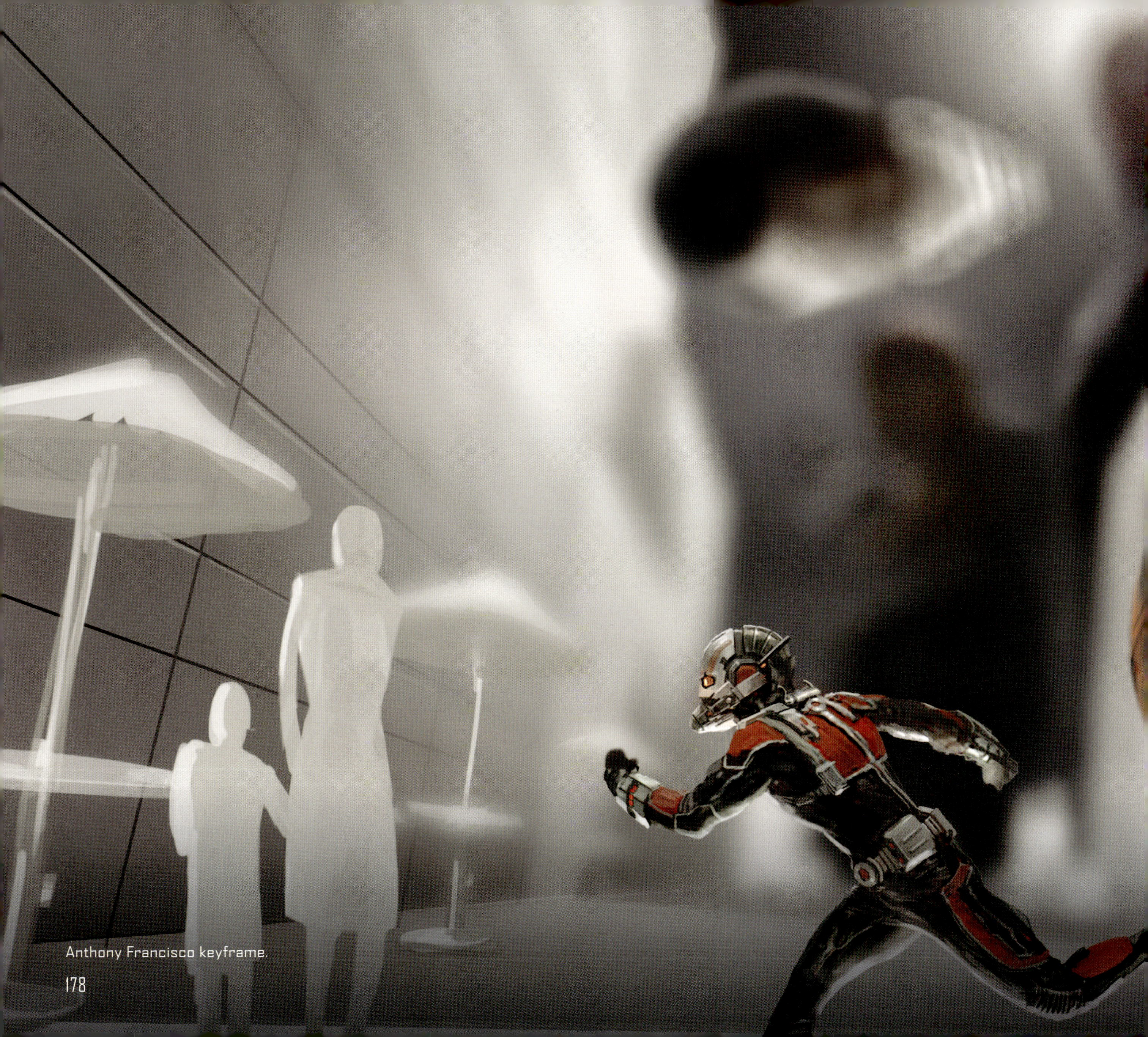

Anthony Francisco keyframe.

CHAPTER FIVE

"DID YOU THINK YOU COULD STOP THE FUTURE?"

His training complete, Scott Lang teams with Hank Pym, Hope Van Dyne, and a crew of ex-con friends to take down PymTech. It's a meticulous and ambitious plan with no margin for error. According to Director Peyton Reed, Scott's power set serves as a visual metaphor for David versus Goliath. "The focus of the training was to essentially get Scott to become Ant-Man, to learn how he can fight and move in the suit. Part of that is shrinking and growing on a dime so he can, for instance, run toward a door, shrink, use that momentum to catapult small Ant-Man through a keyhole, and come out the other side—which in the PymTech takedown translates to a bullet hole. Hope has also trained him to fight, but more specifically how to punch. When you shrink down to Ant-Man's size, your density increases, so a punch can become like a bullet: If you do it too hard, you could actually penetrate skin and potentially kill someone."

Scott faces this gargantuan task with help from his insect army. The ants not only form a raft that allows Lang to penetrate PymTech via its water pipes, but also shuttle miniature bombs to crucial points in the building to weaken its infrastructure. "This is what I think one of the secret weapons of the movie is," Reed says. "People think, 'Oh, he can control ants? That's ridiculous! How could that possibly come into play in a battle?' I think what the movie does really well is show the audience, 'Wow, that's really badass.' It adds a level of charm and excitement we haven't really seen before."

PYMTECH ESCAPE

STORYBOARDS BY DAVID KRENTZ, JIM MAGDELENO & THE THIRD FLOOR

The PymTech escape reveals the full range of Ant-Man's abilities. While the script described the sequence in great detail, storyboard artists David Krentz and Jim Magdeleno came together with pre-visualization team The Third Floor to help visualize the escape. "I had many script pages to board in a relatively short time," Krentz says. "It was evident that these were not going to be pretty boards, so they had to be clear. I would turn off all distractions, read a chunk of the script, and then sit back and close my eyes. In my head, I would imagine I was watching the finished movie, then I would quickly start banging out the boards before what I just conceived in my head went away. Marvel allowed me a lot of freedom interpreting

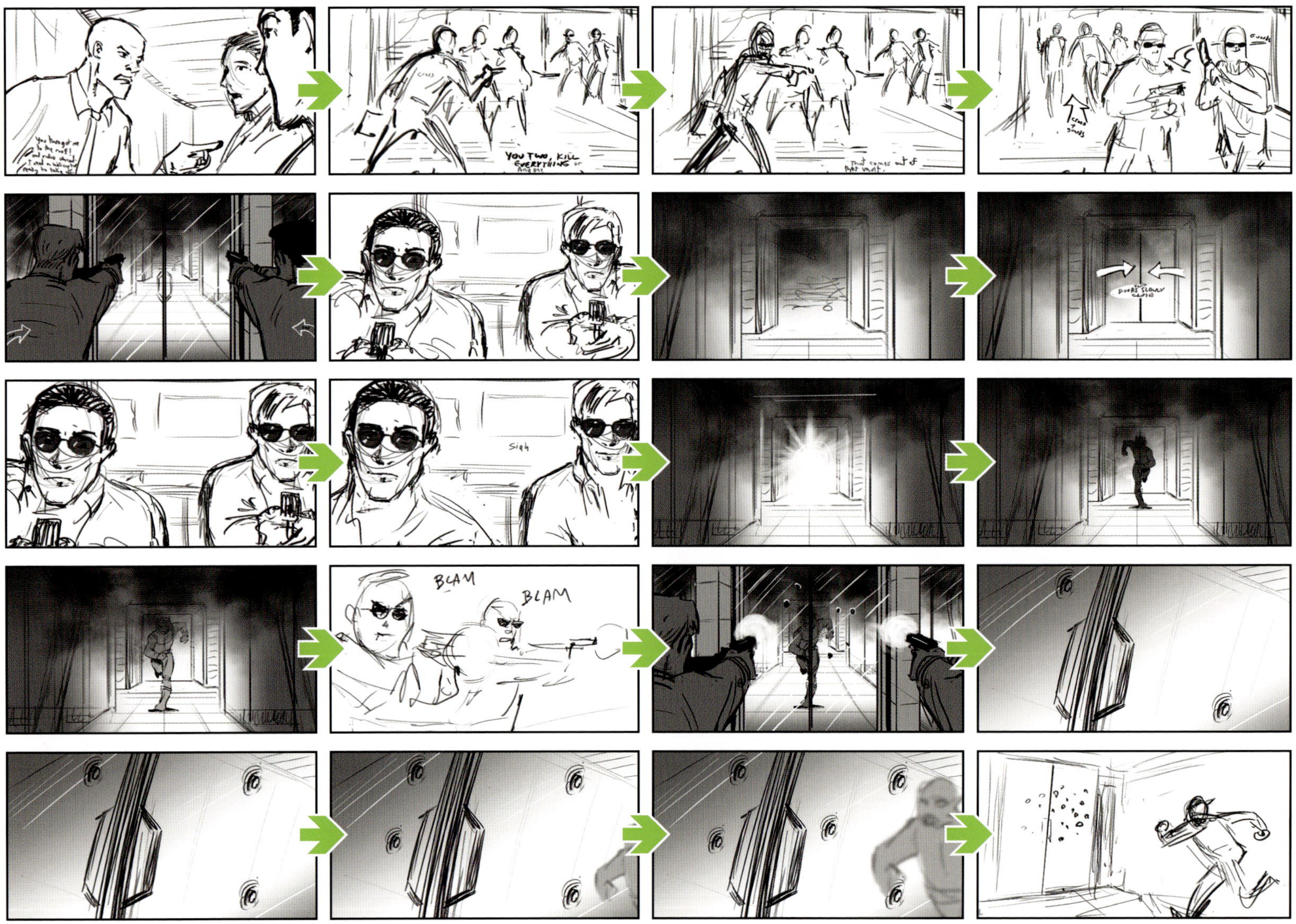

the script—it's one of the main reasons I love working for them. It's a very collaborative process, and often scenes were conceived by just sitting in editing with the editors, the writers, and the director, trying to figure out how we could make a great scene even better."

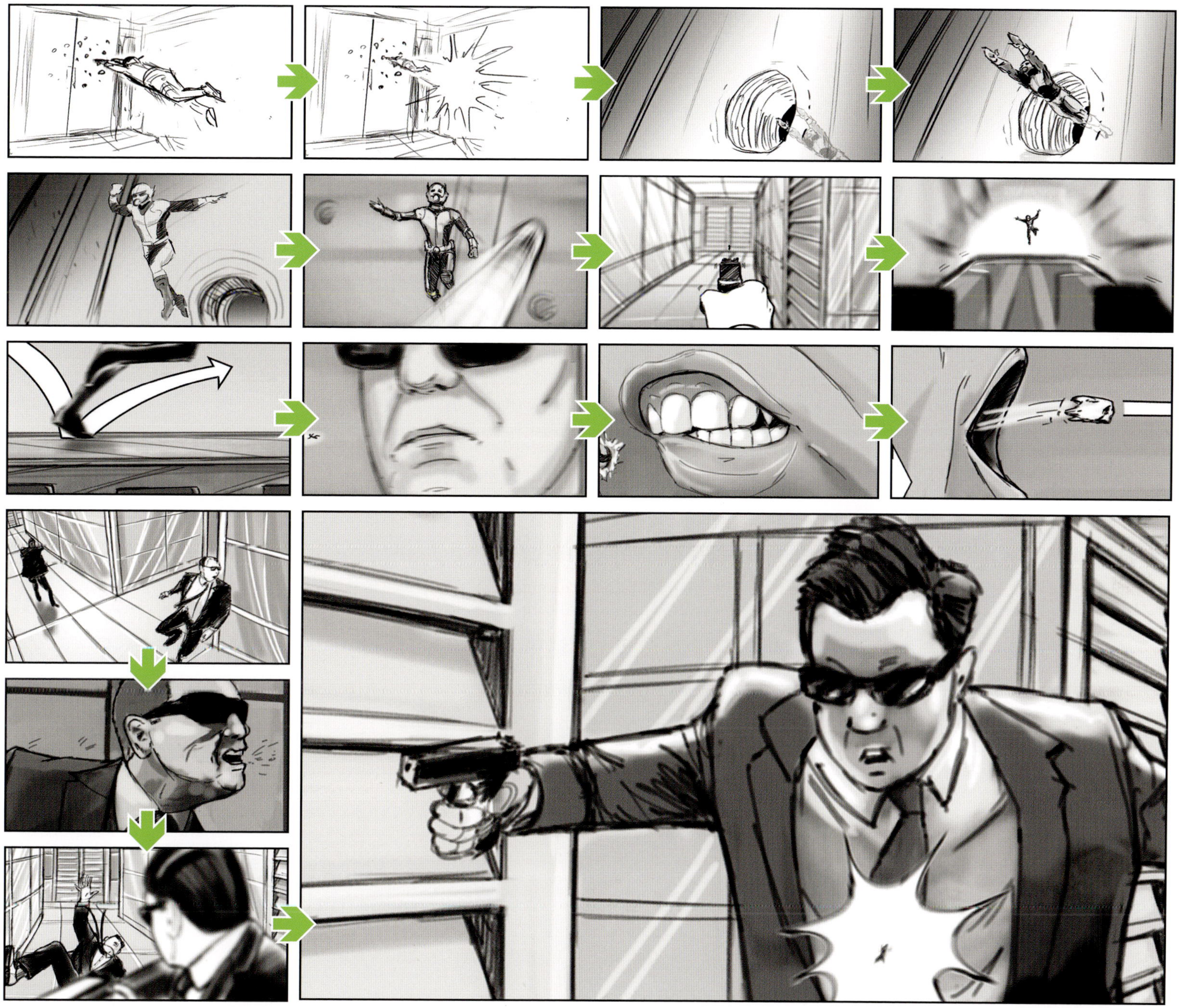

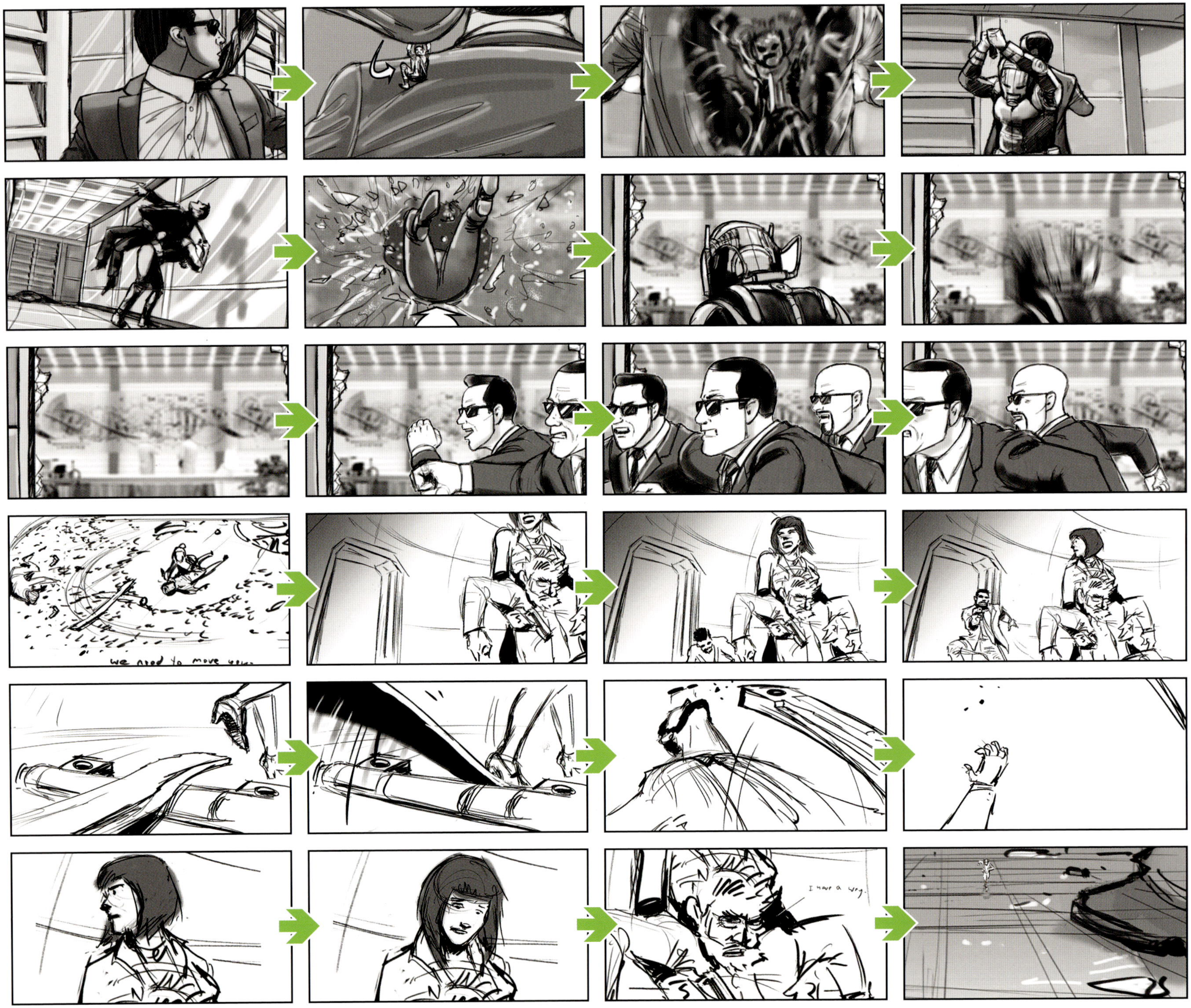
we need to move you..
I have a way.

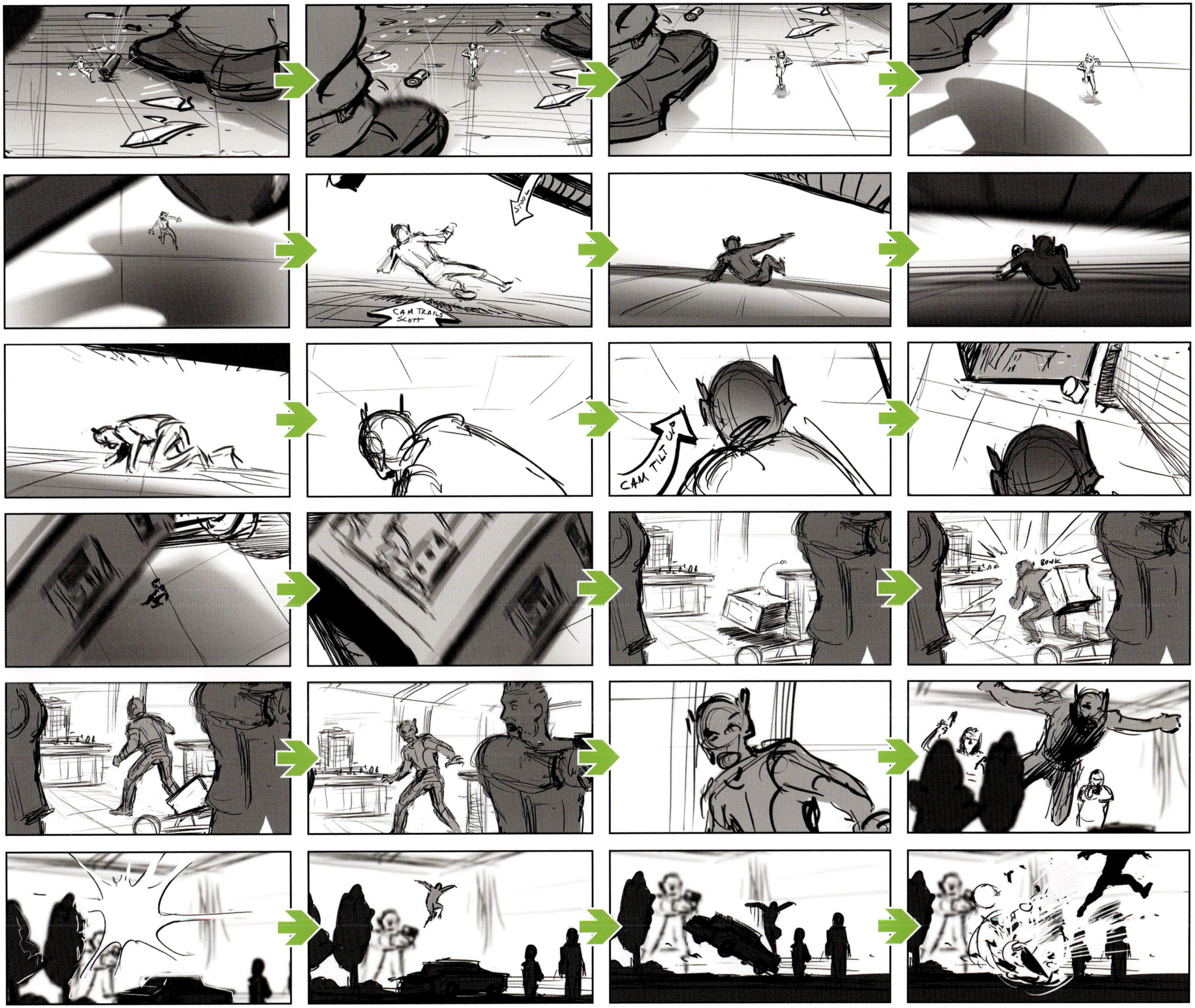
CAM TRAILS SCOTT
CAM TILT UP
BONK

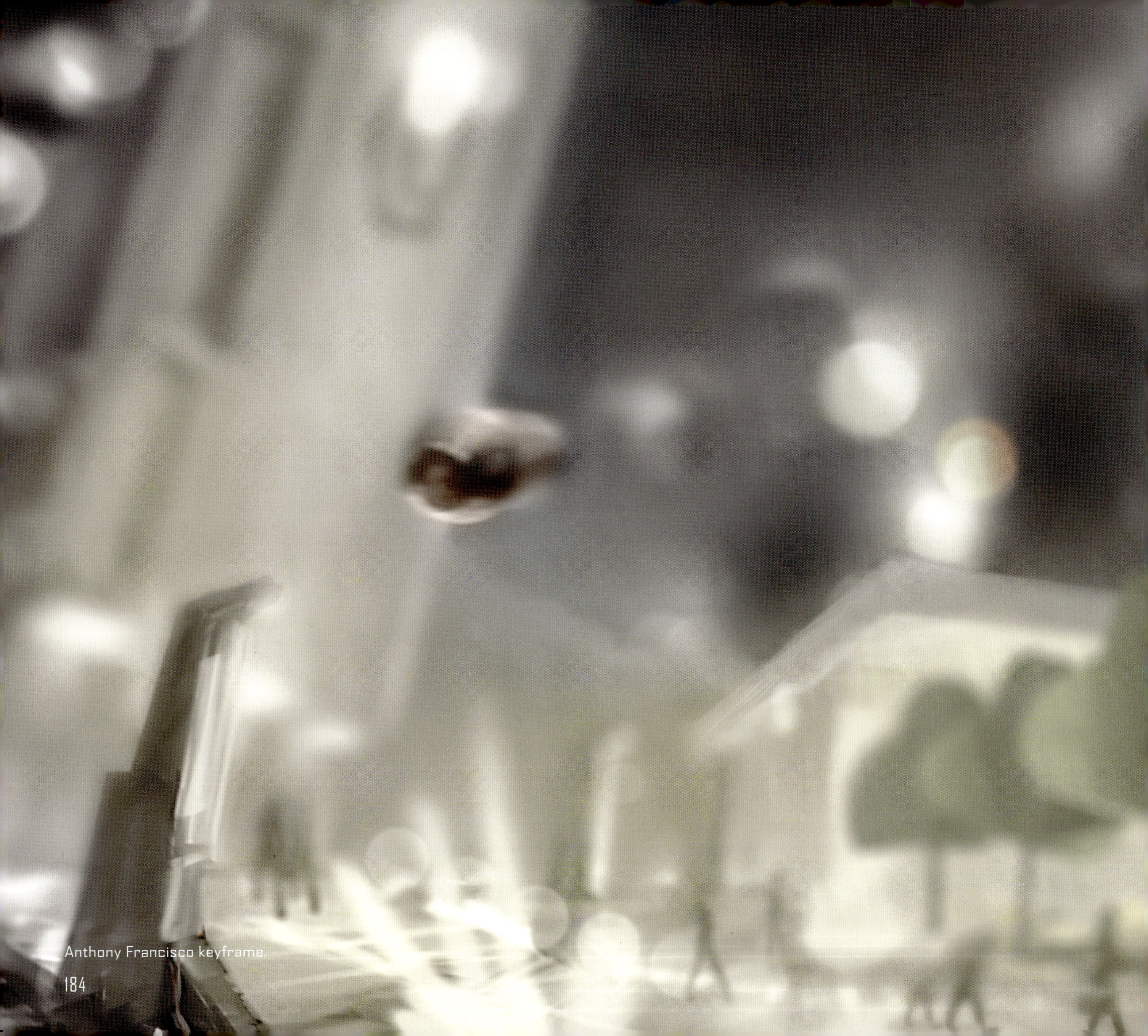

Anthony Francisco keyframe.

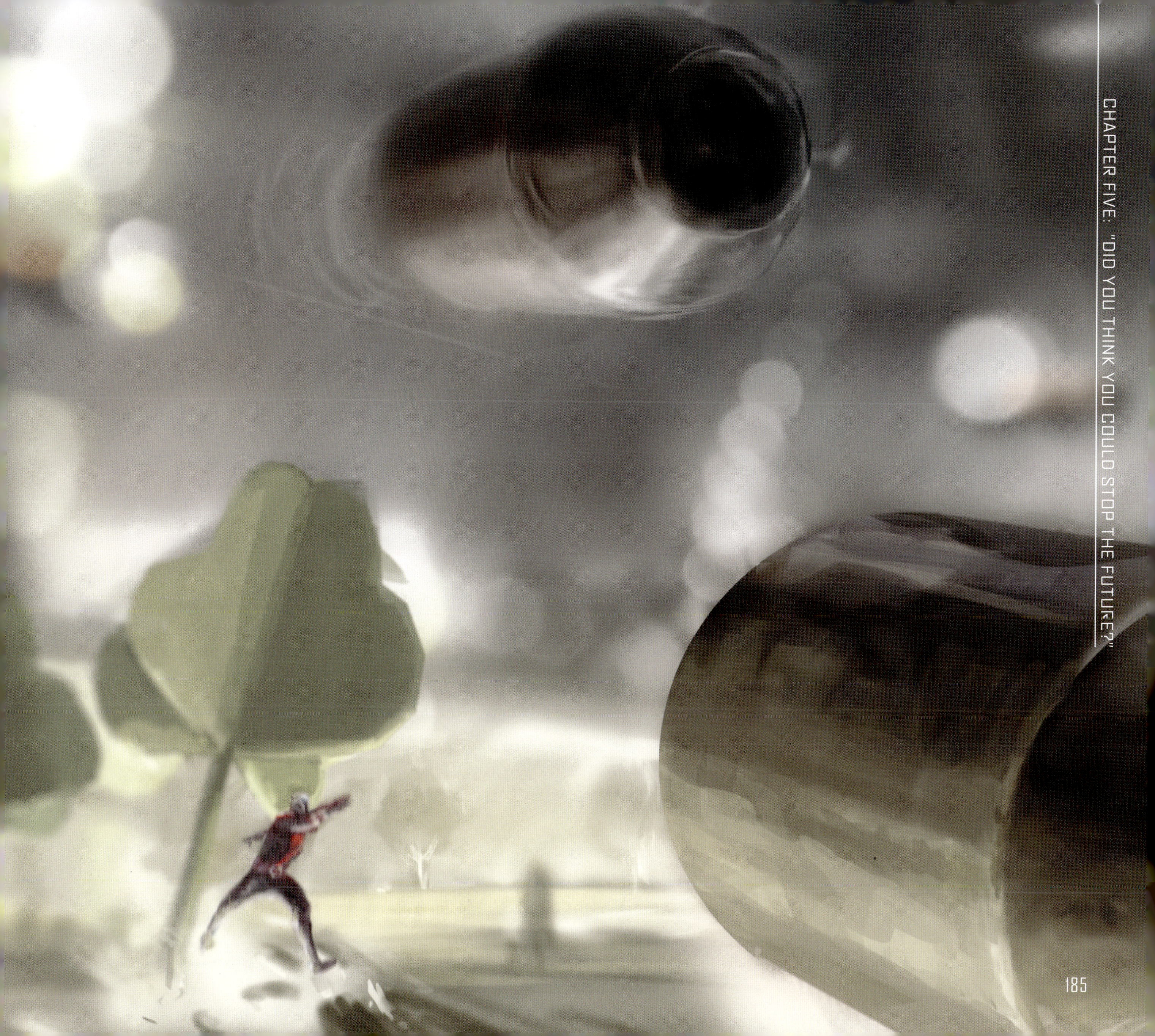

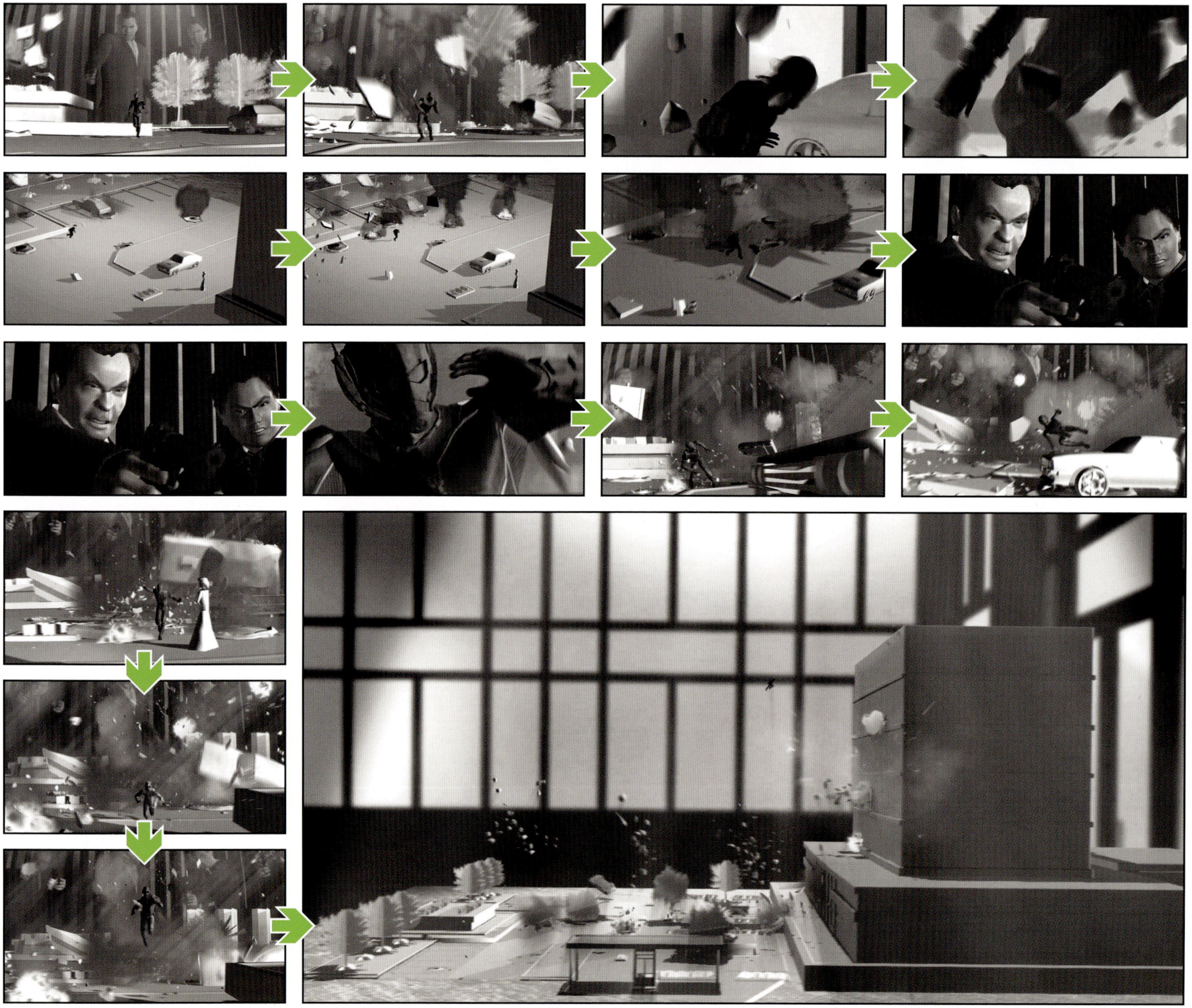

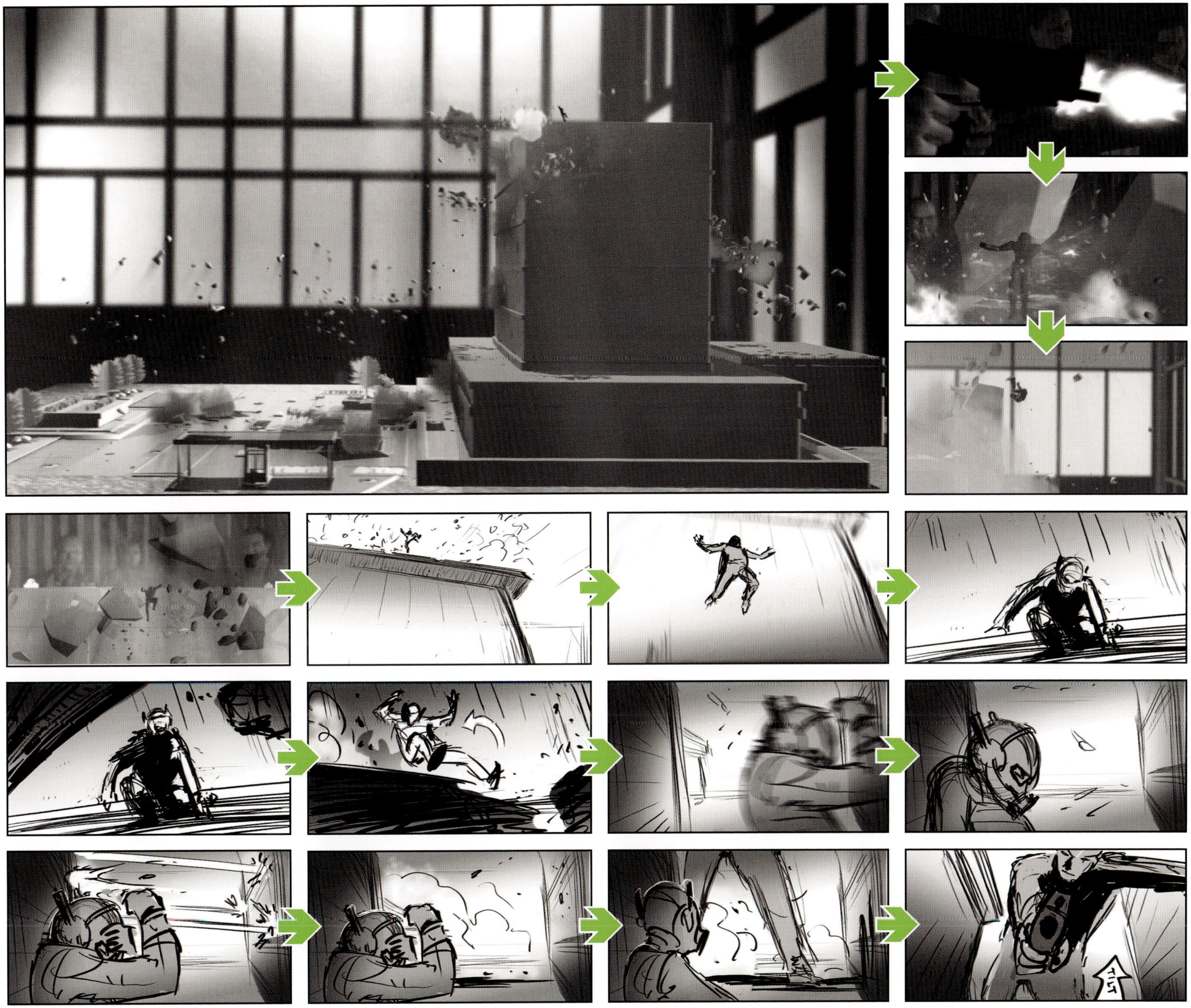
TILT

"It was important to always enter the scene mid-action to keep things moving quickly and maintain the tension," Krentz continues. "I loved playing with Scott's scale change; it was the highlight of the whole movie for me. Deciding when it was beneficial for Scott to be large or small was a challenge. For instance, when Scott is running through the lab, he needs to be small because he is outnumbered and outgunned. But by being small, things like falling shell casings and lab stools prove to be dangerous. I thought it would be cool for him to save his skin by suddenly turning big so the falling hard drive didn't crush him, and in doing so give his position away to the bad guys. Scott would be on an epic journey in a world of giants, and then you could pull back to human scale and just see how ridiculous it looked. Moments like that were dubbed 'the gift that keeps on giving.'"

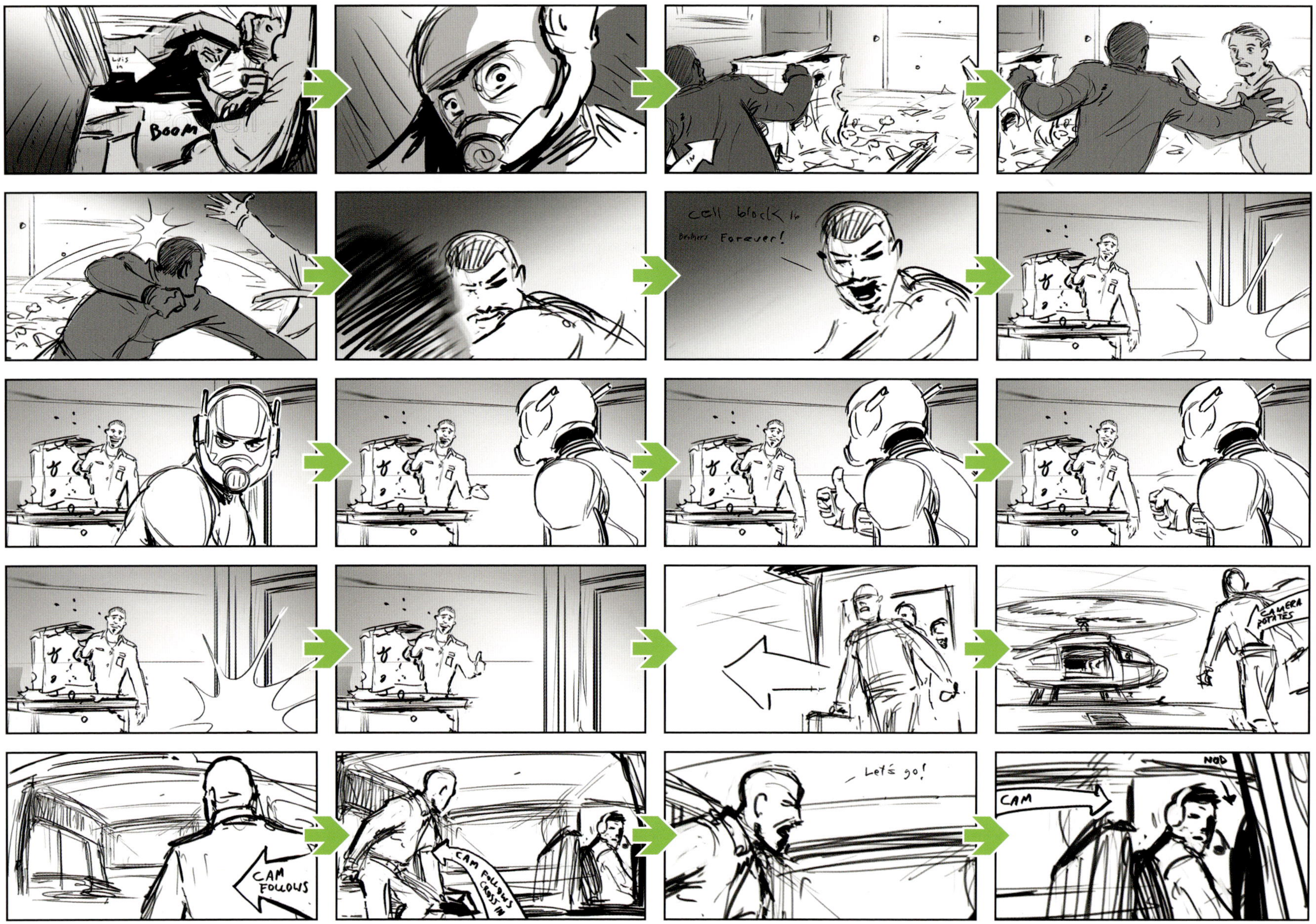

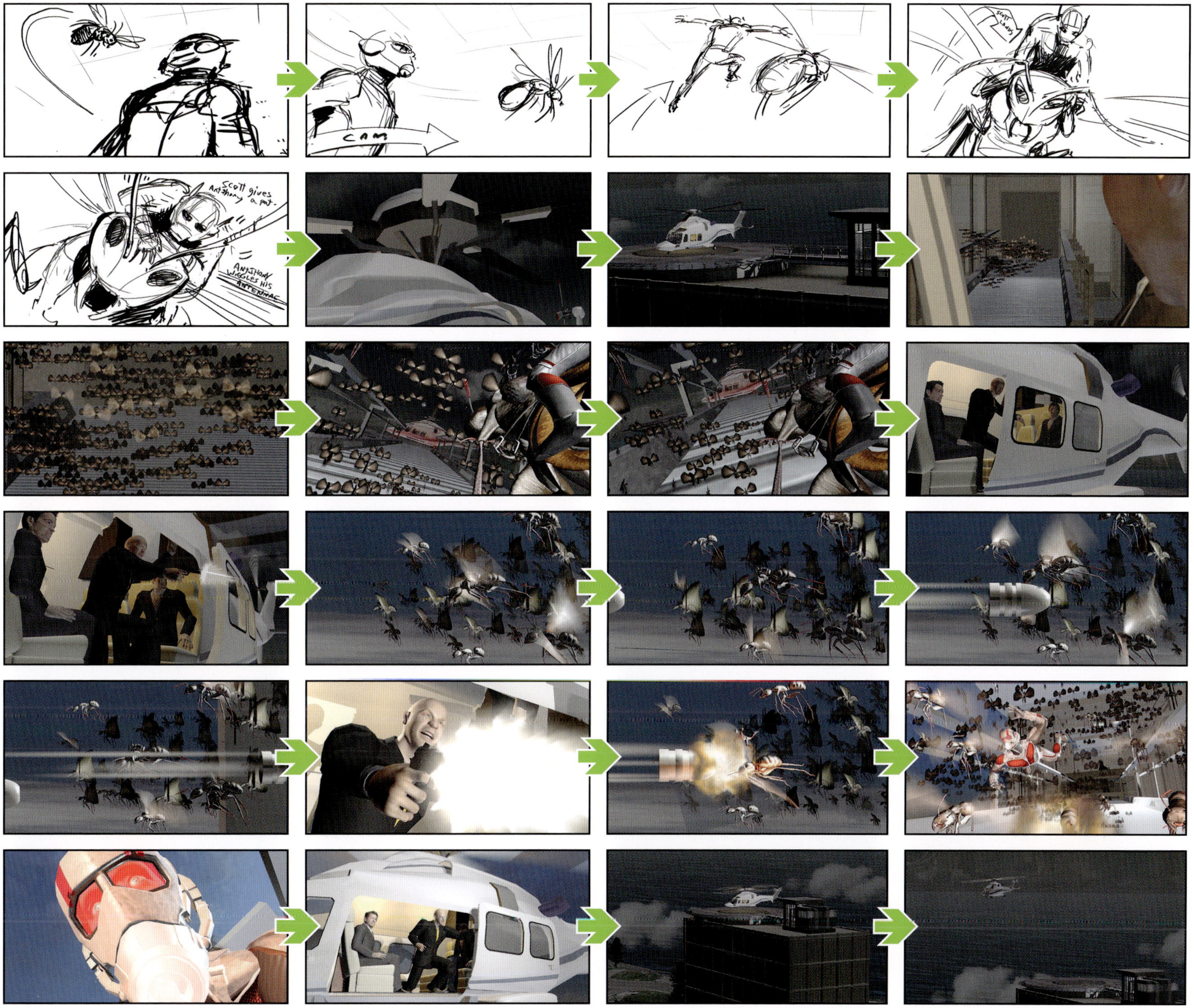
CAM
SCOTT LANDS
Scott gives Antthony a pat.
ANTHONY WIGGLES HIS ANTENNAE

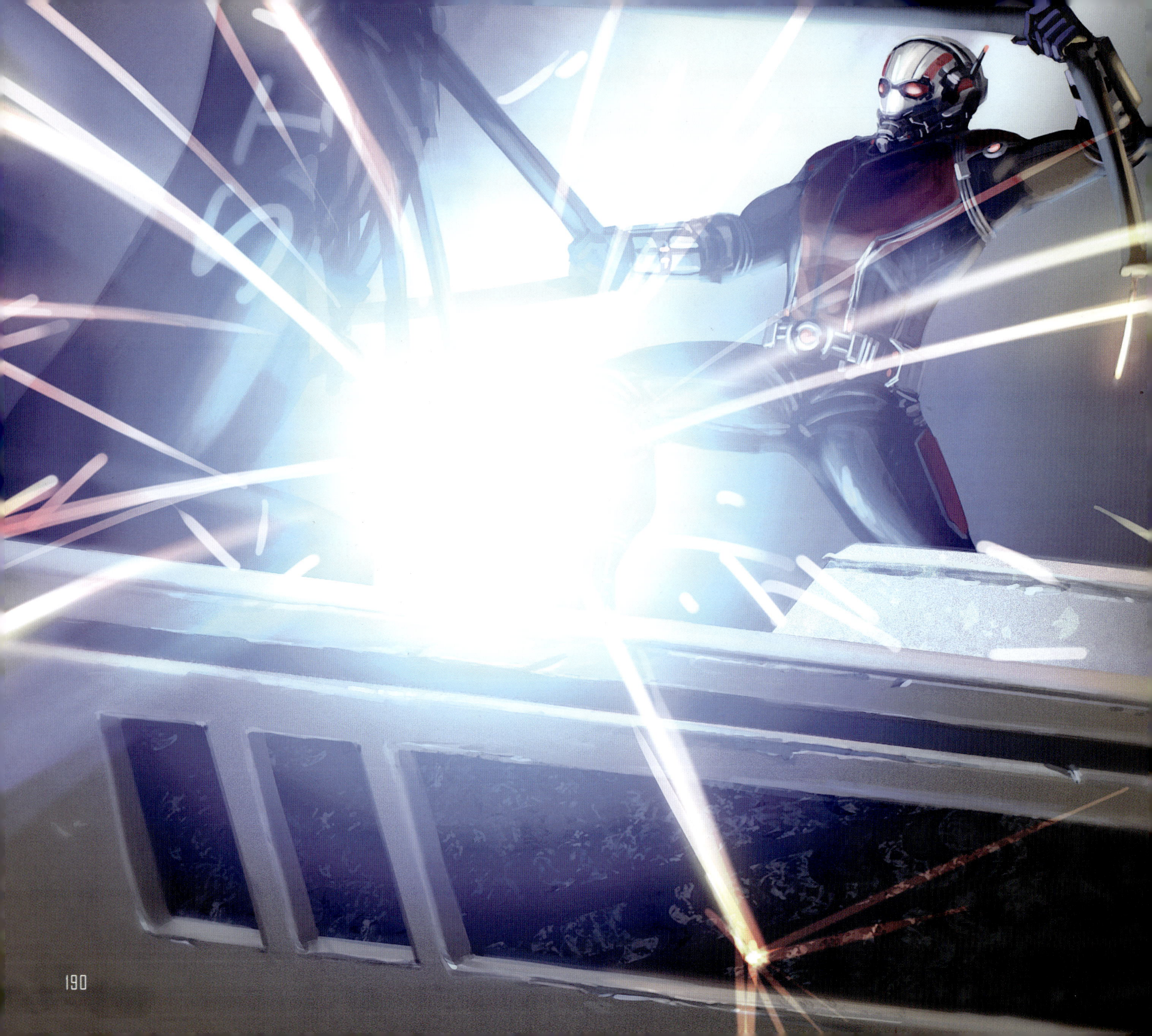

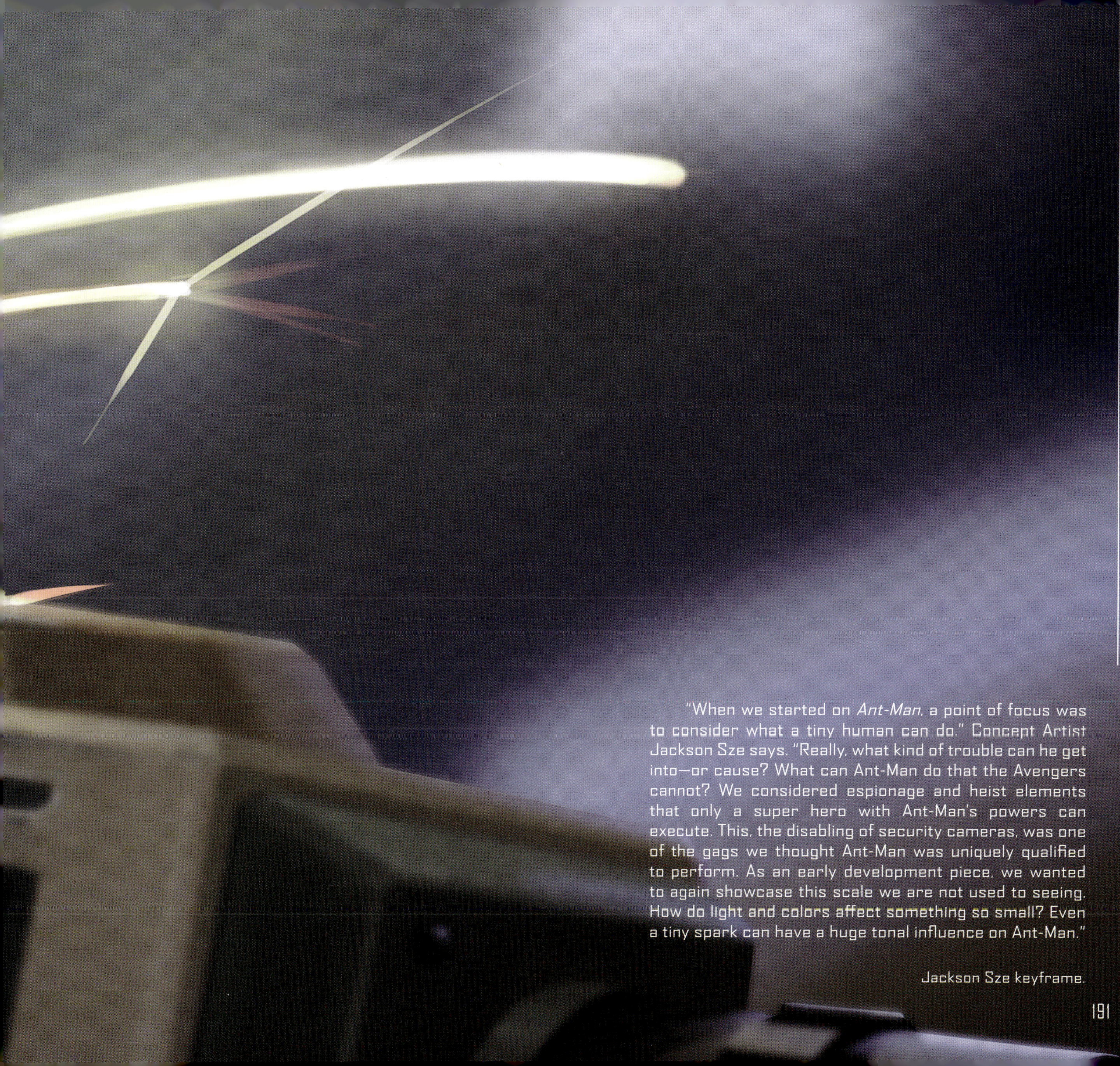

"When we started on *Ant-Man*, a point of focus was to consider what a tiny human can do," Concept Artist Jackson Sze says. "Really, what kind of trouble can he get into—or cause? What can Ant-Man do that the Avengers cannot? We considered espionage and heist elements that only a super hero with Ant-Man's powers can execute. This, the disabling of security cameras, was one of the gags we thought Ant-Man was uniquely qualified to perform. As an early development piece, we wanted to again showcase this scale we are not used to seeing. How do light and colors affect something so small? Even a tiny spark can have a huge tonal influence on Ant-Man."

Jackson Sze keyframe.

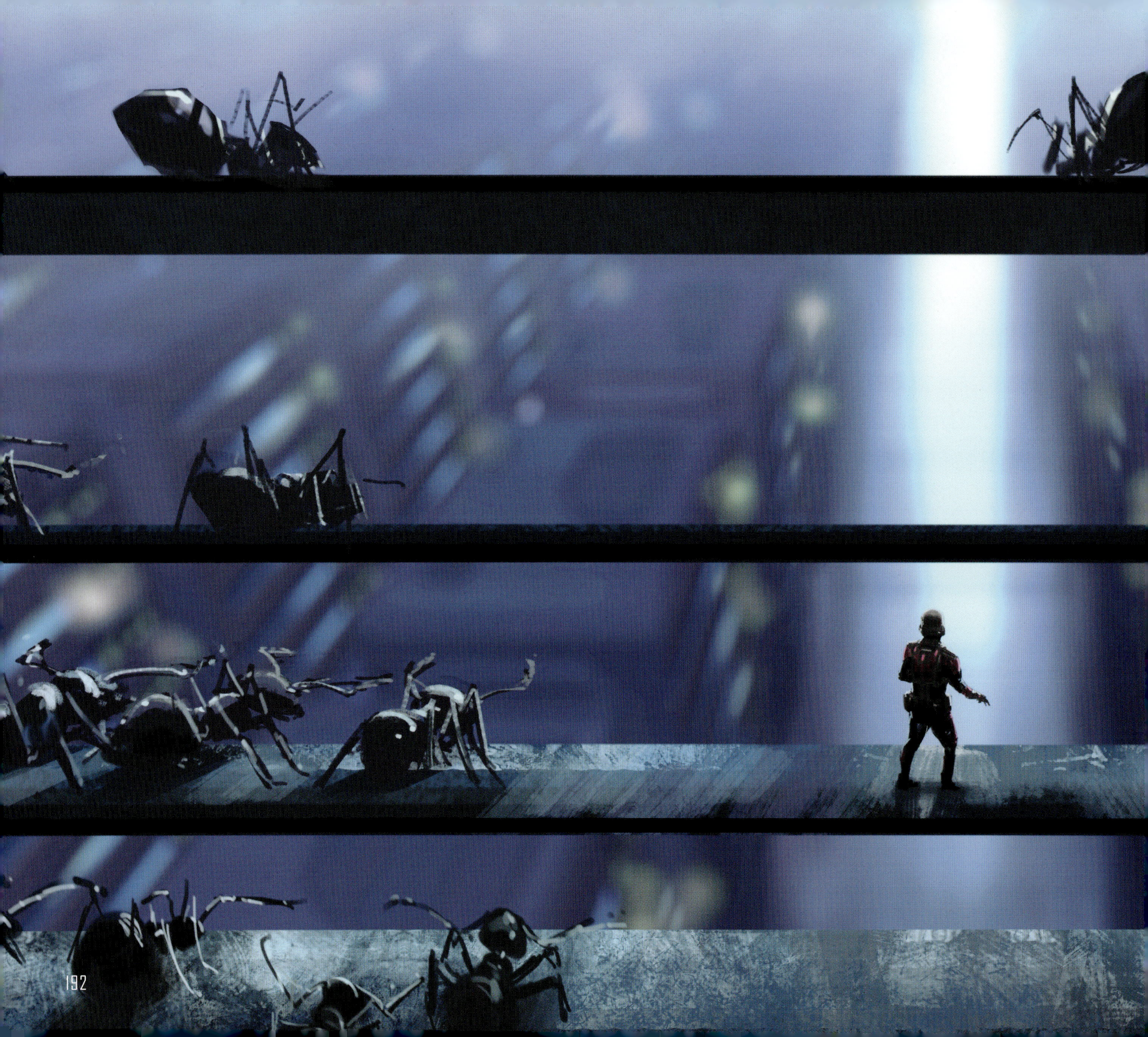

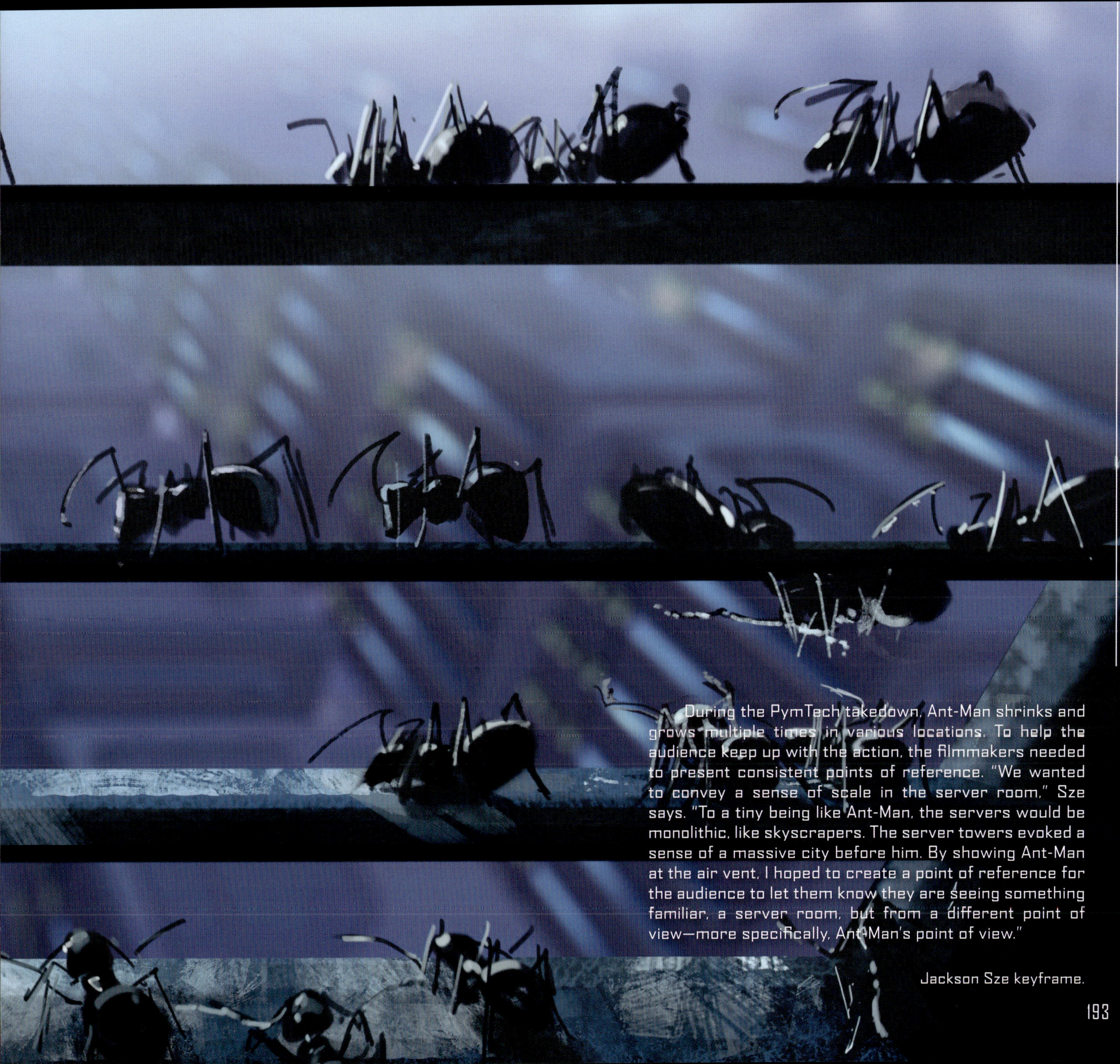

During the PymTech takedown, Ant-Man shrinks and grows multiple times in various locations. To help the audience keep up with the action, the filmmakers needed to present consistent points of reference. "We wanted to convey a sense of scale in the server room," Sze says. "To a tiny being like Ant-Man, the servers would be monolithic, like skyscrapers. The server towers evoked a sense of a massive city before him. By showing Ant-Man at the air vent, I hoped to create a point of reference for the audience to let them know they are seeing something familiar, a server room, but from a different point of view—more specifically, Ant-Man's point of view."

Jackson Sze keyframe.

"There was a documentary about ants that showcased the fascinating natural rafts that ants can build to stay buoyant," Sze explains. "When nature hands you something this good, you don't have to do much to make it interesting. With this image, I wanted to put Ant-Man on an exciting ride—much like whitewater rafting."

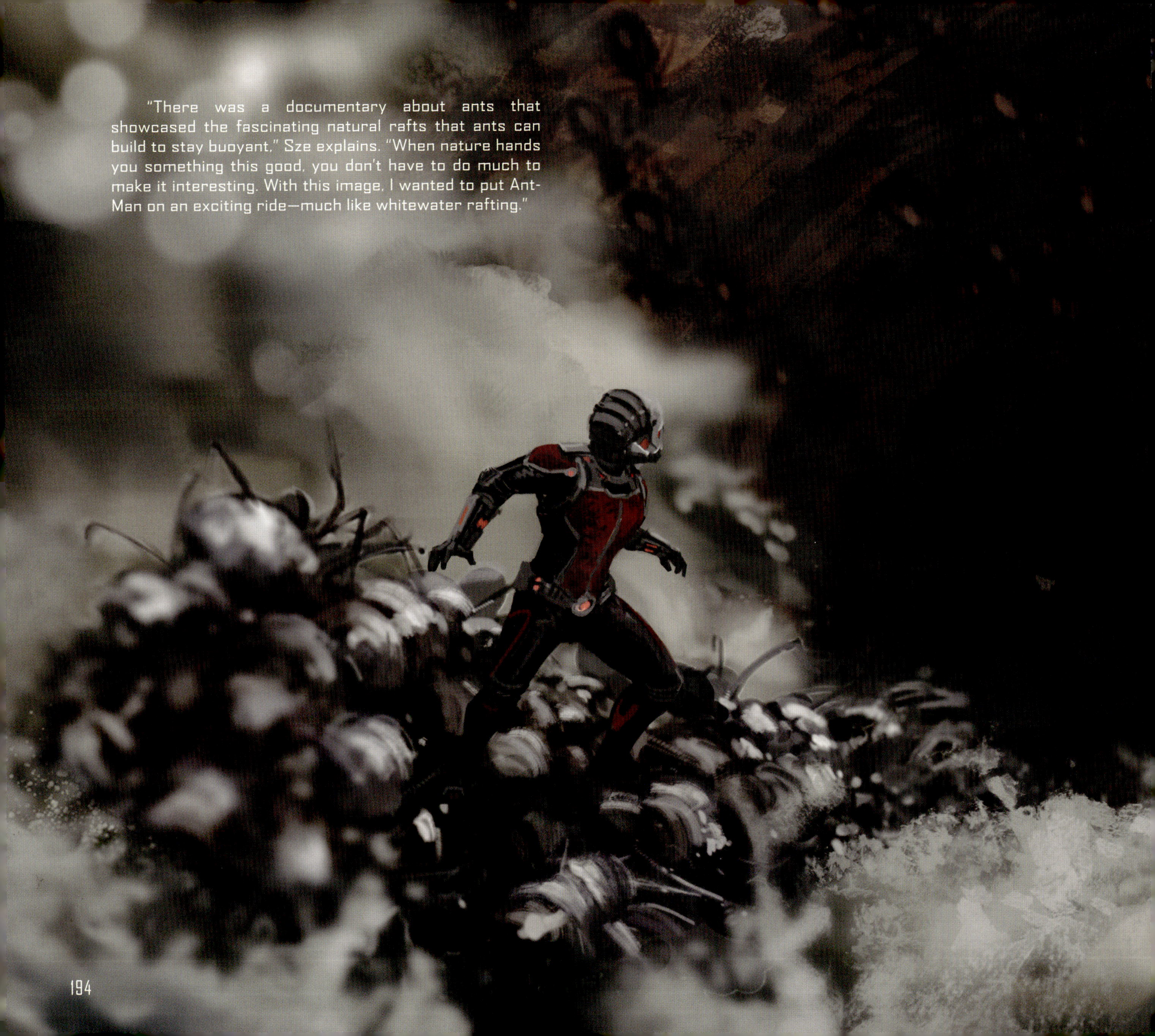

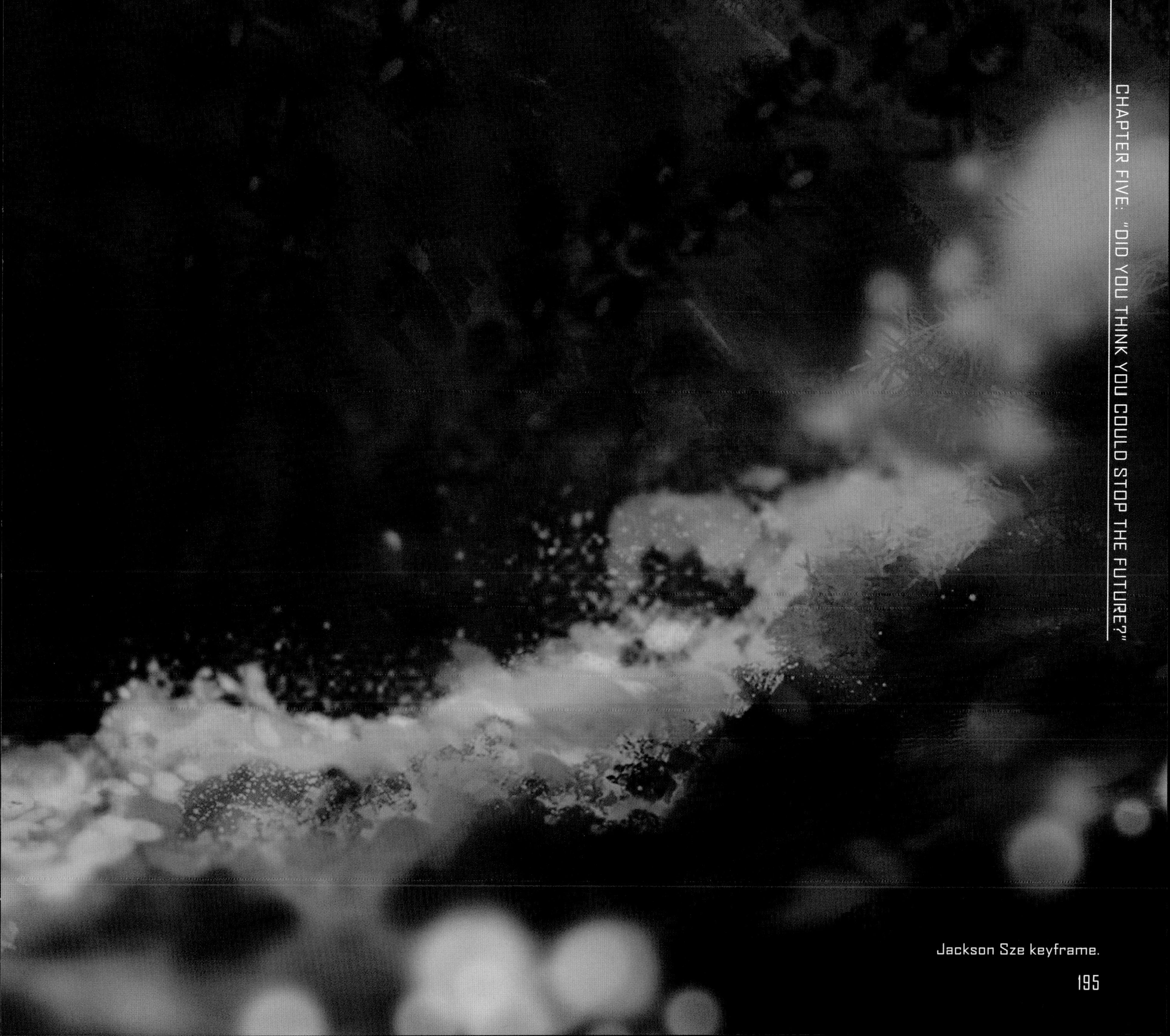

Jackson Sze keyframe.

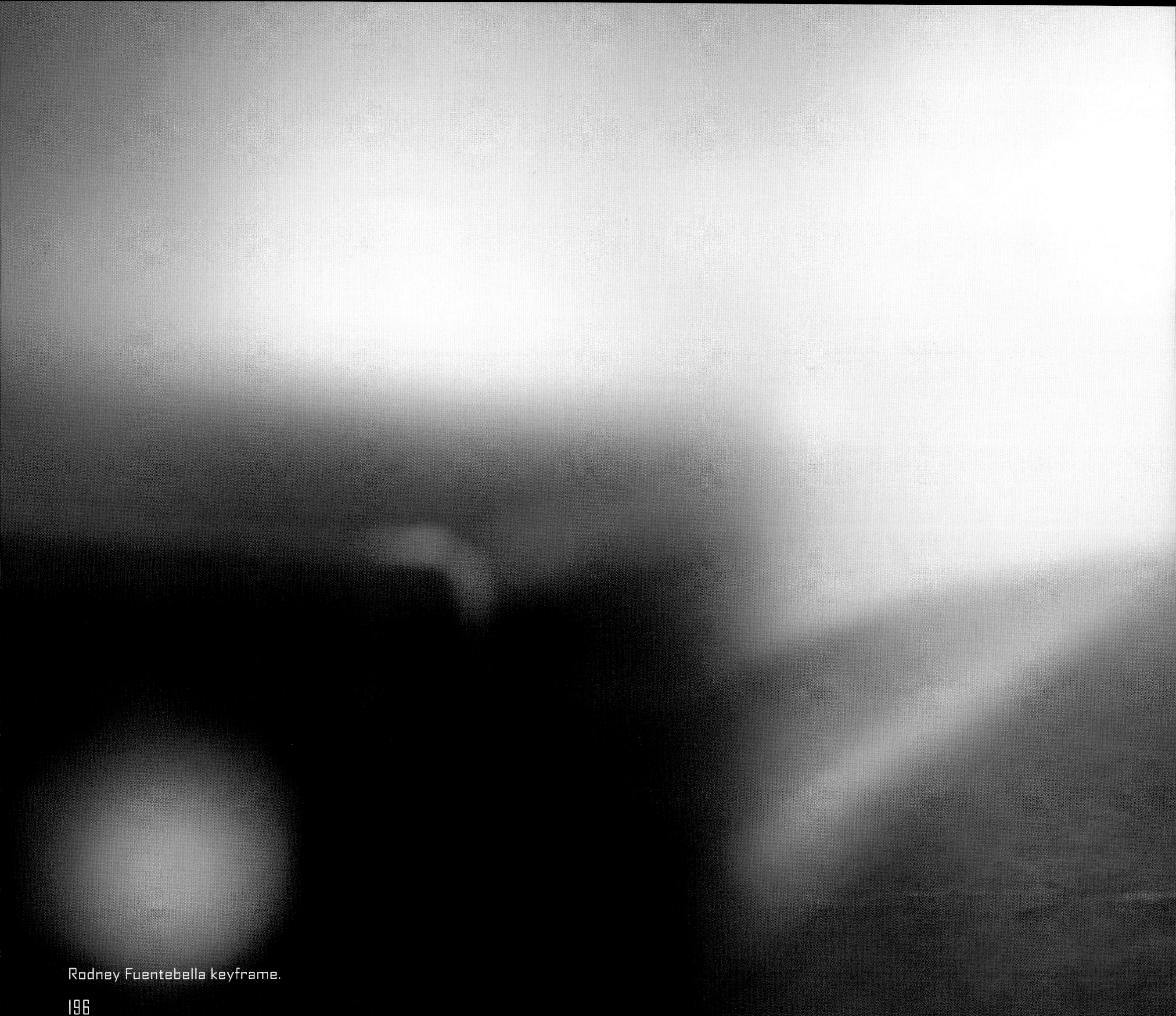

Rodney Fuentebella keyframe.

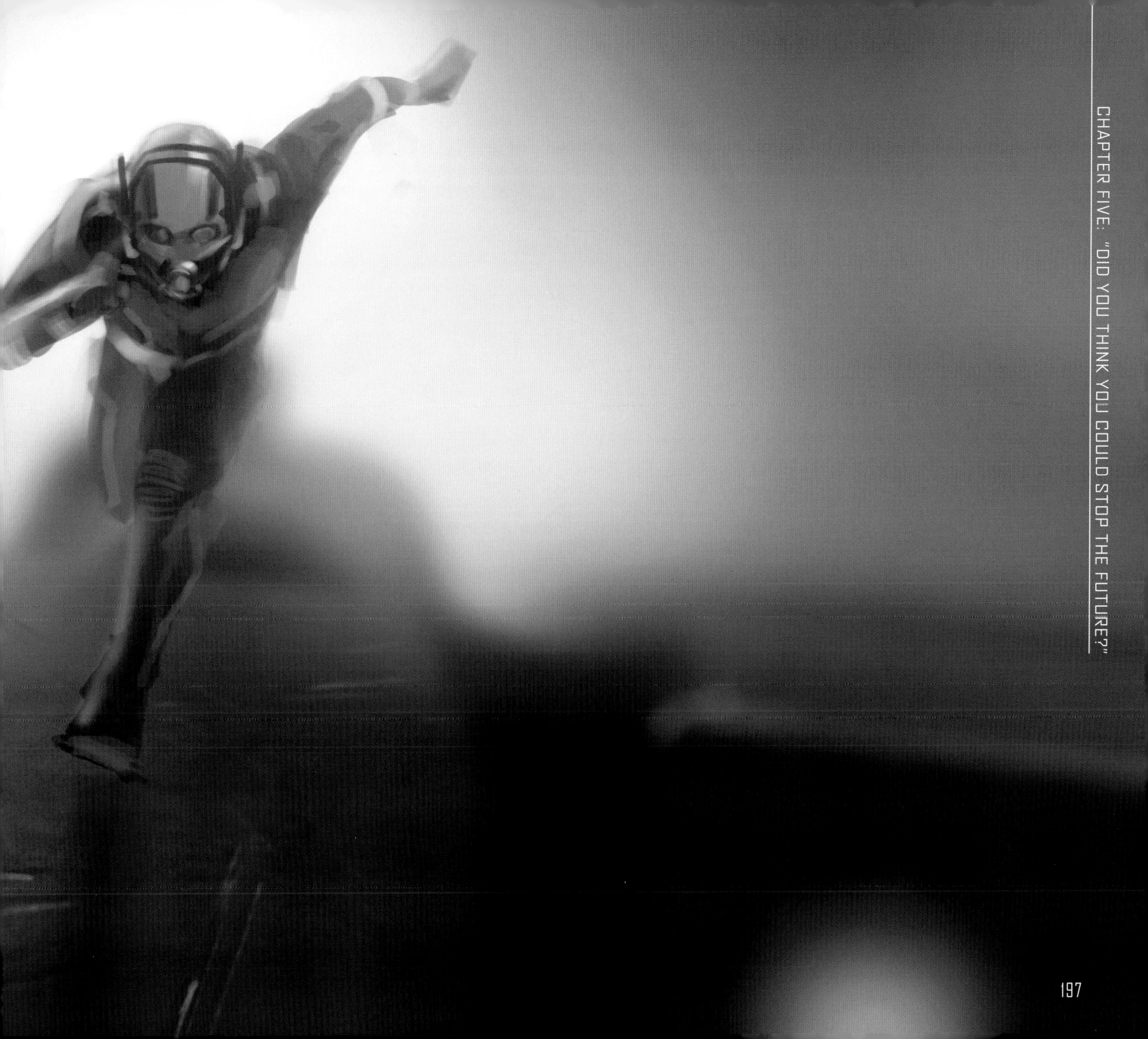

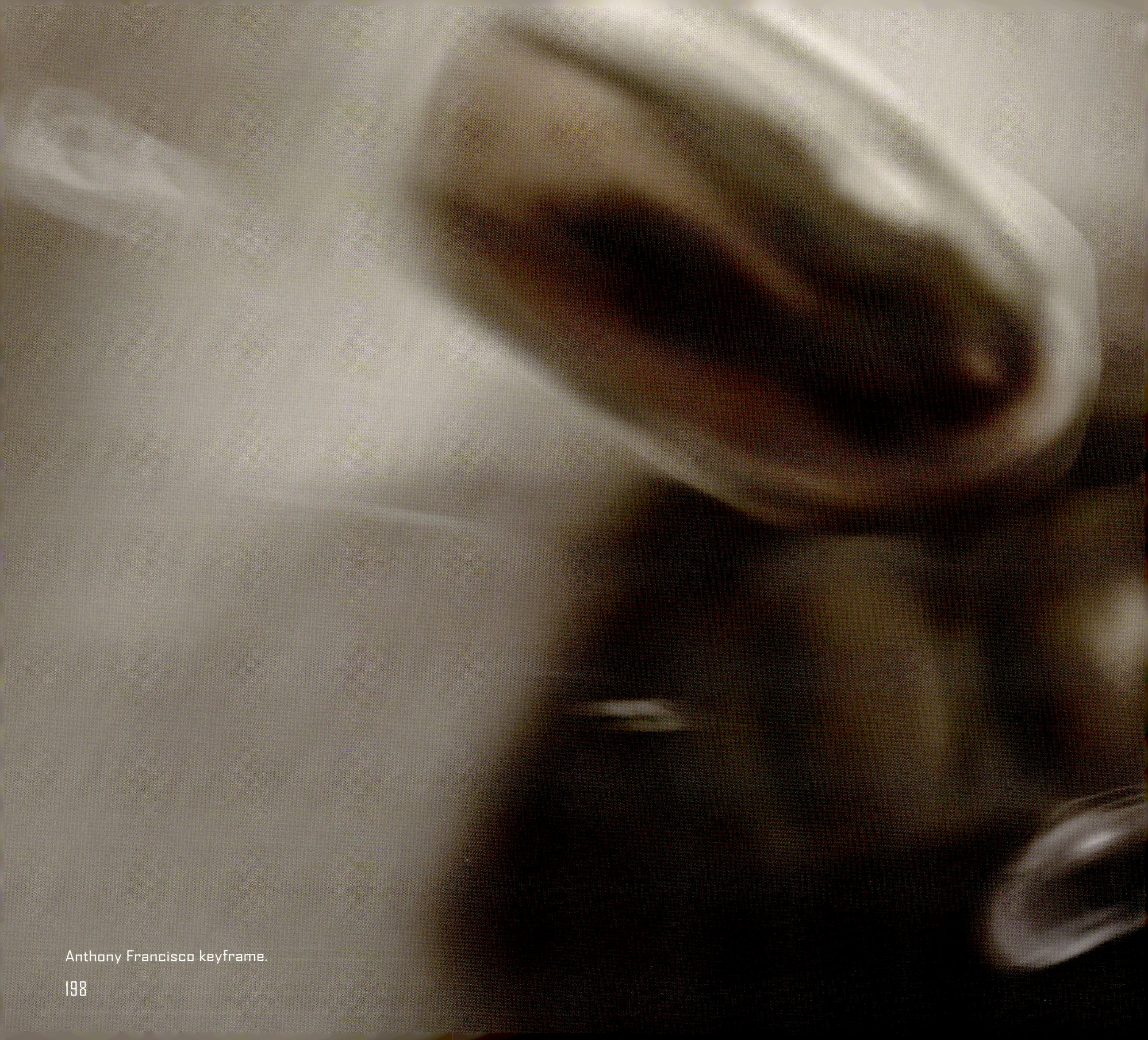

Anthony Francisco keyframe.

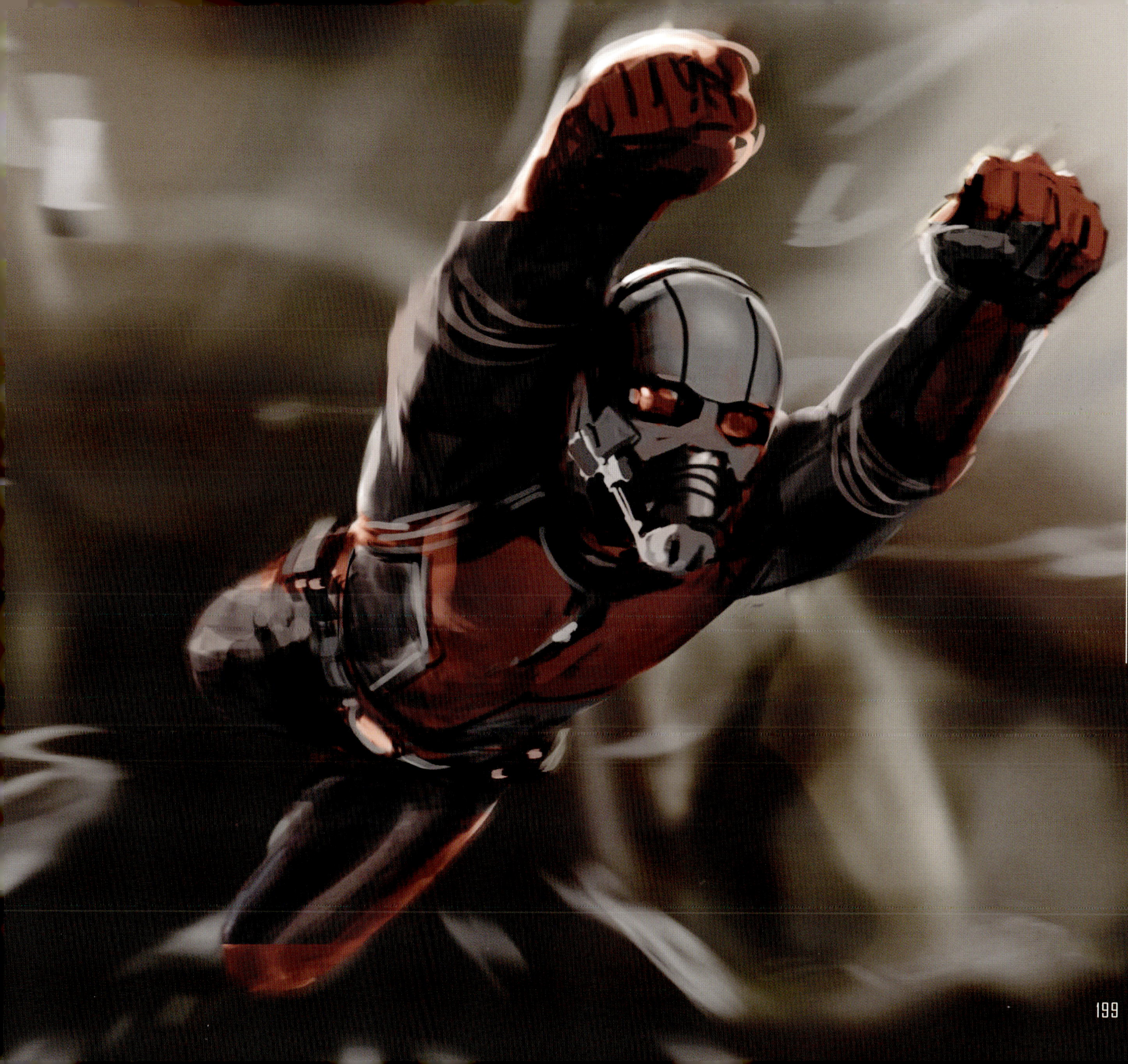

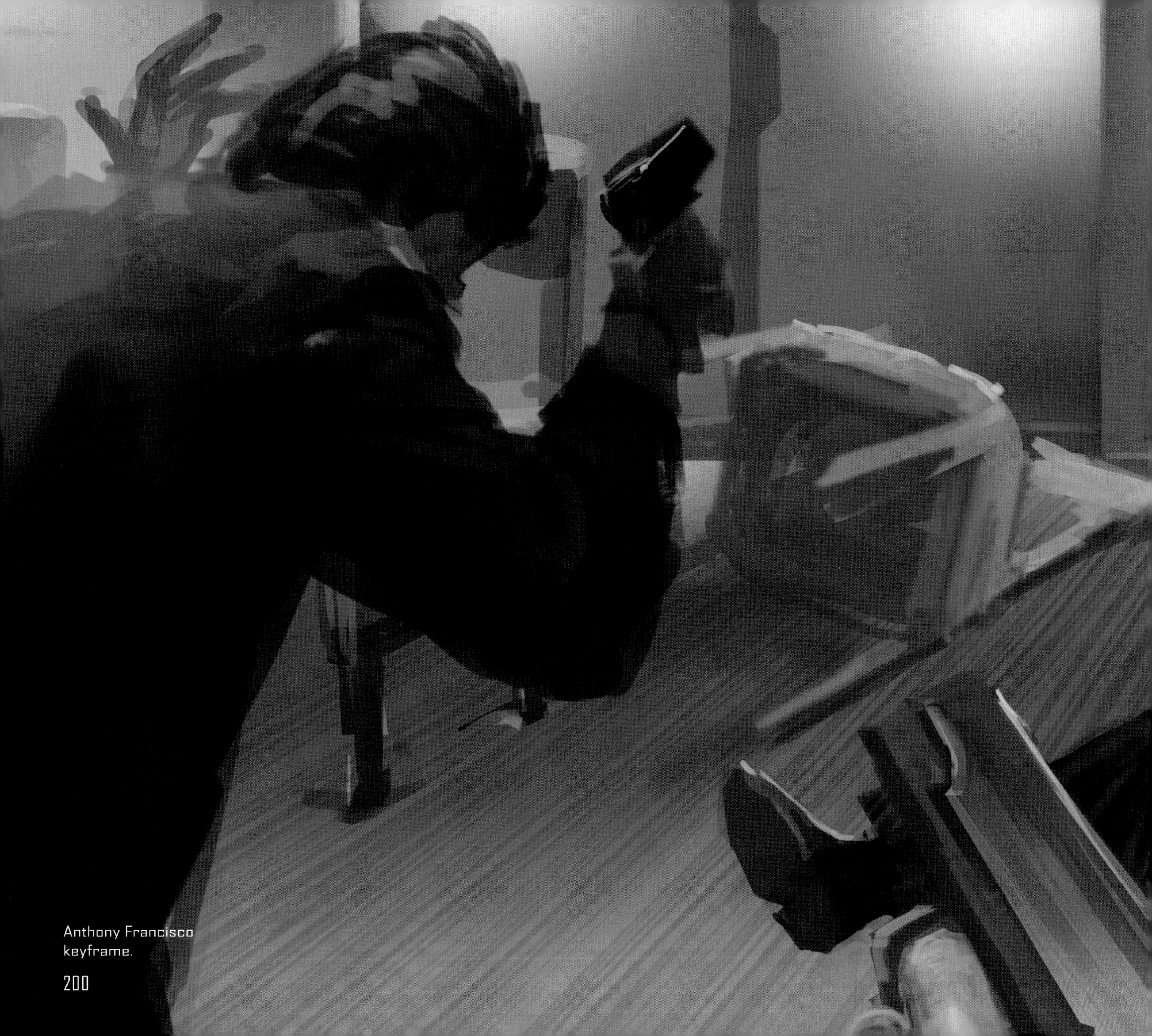

Anthony Francisco keyframe.

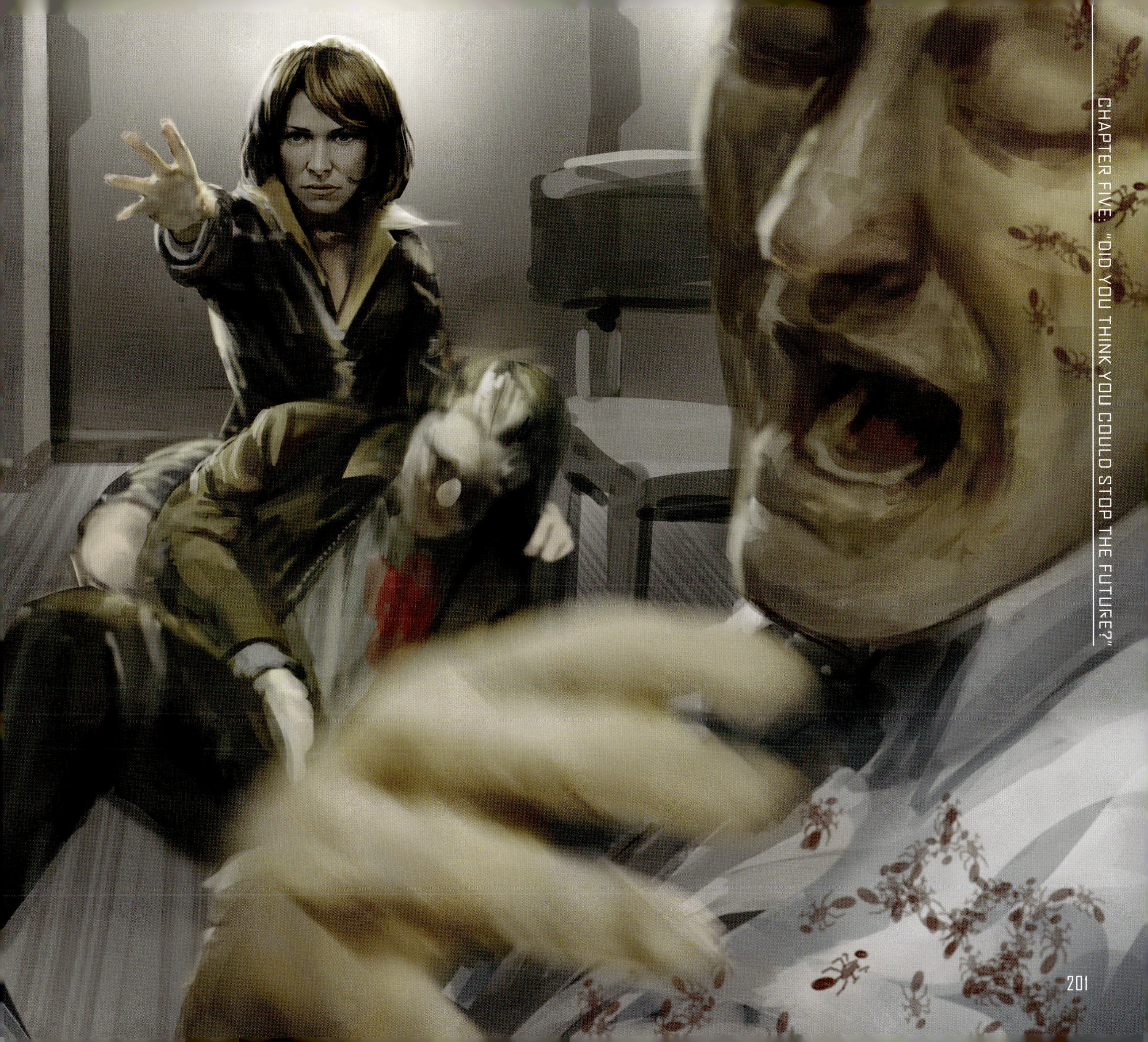

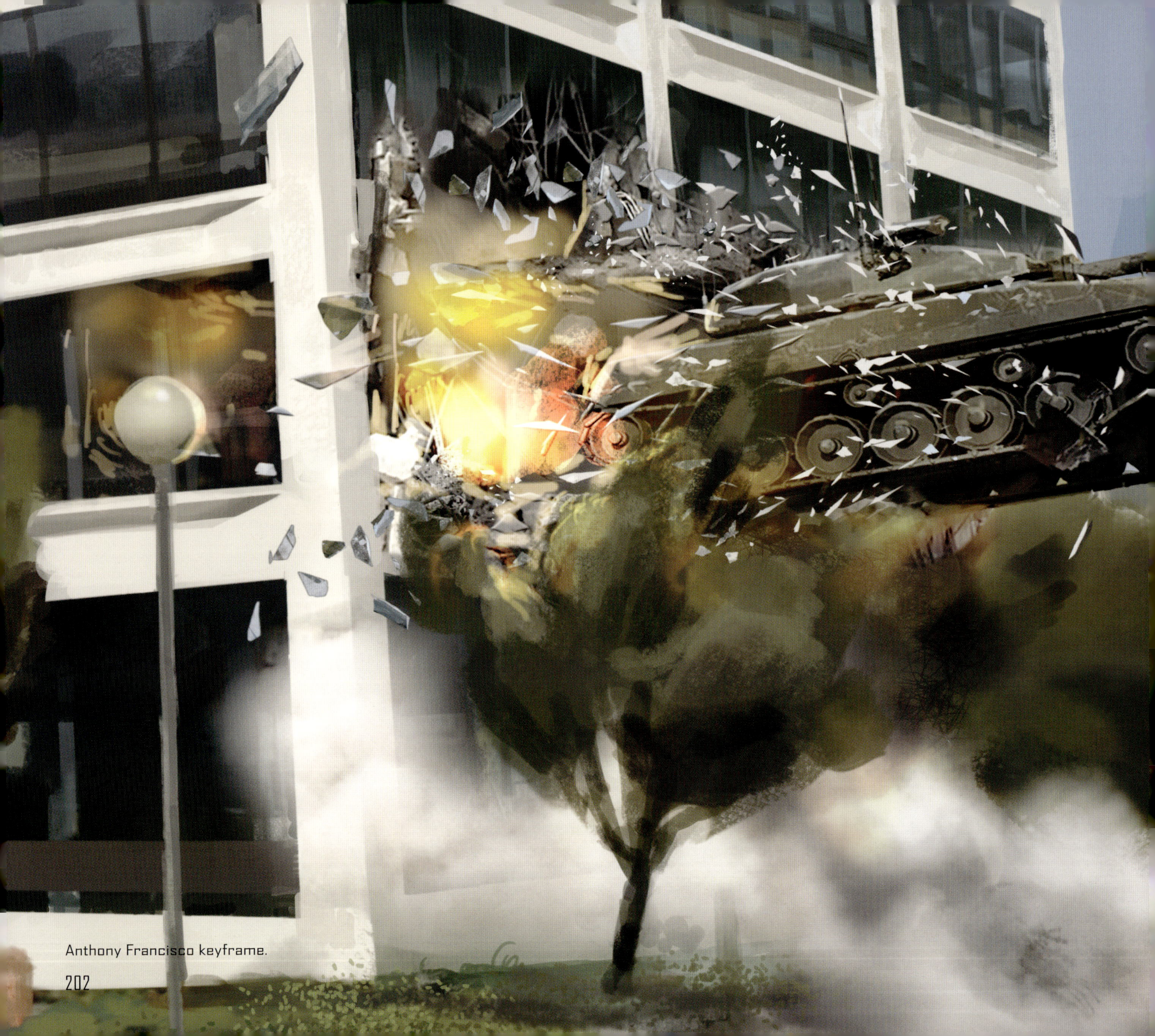

Anthony Francisco keyframe.

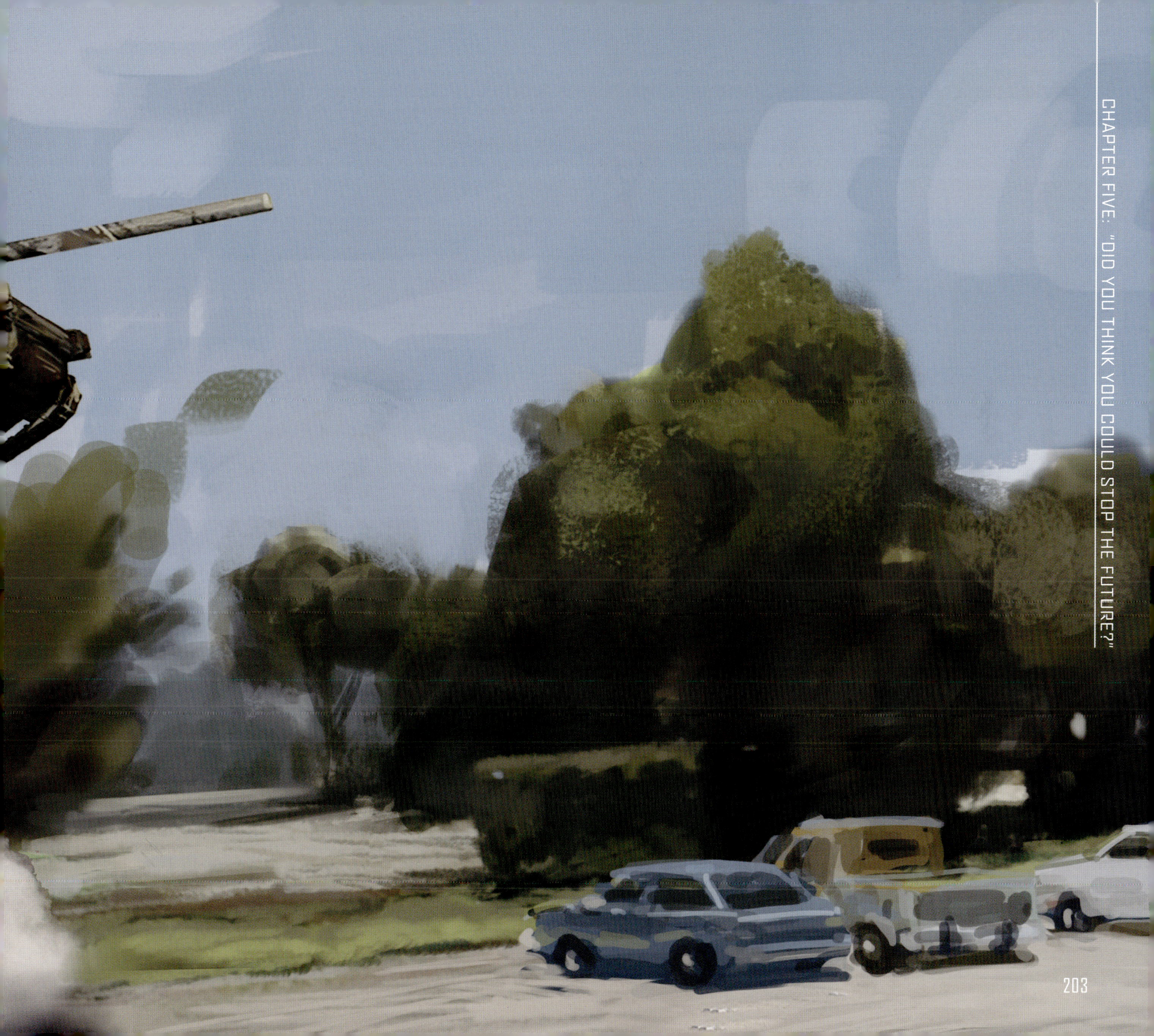

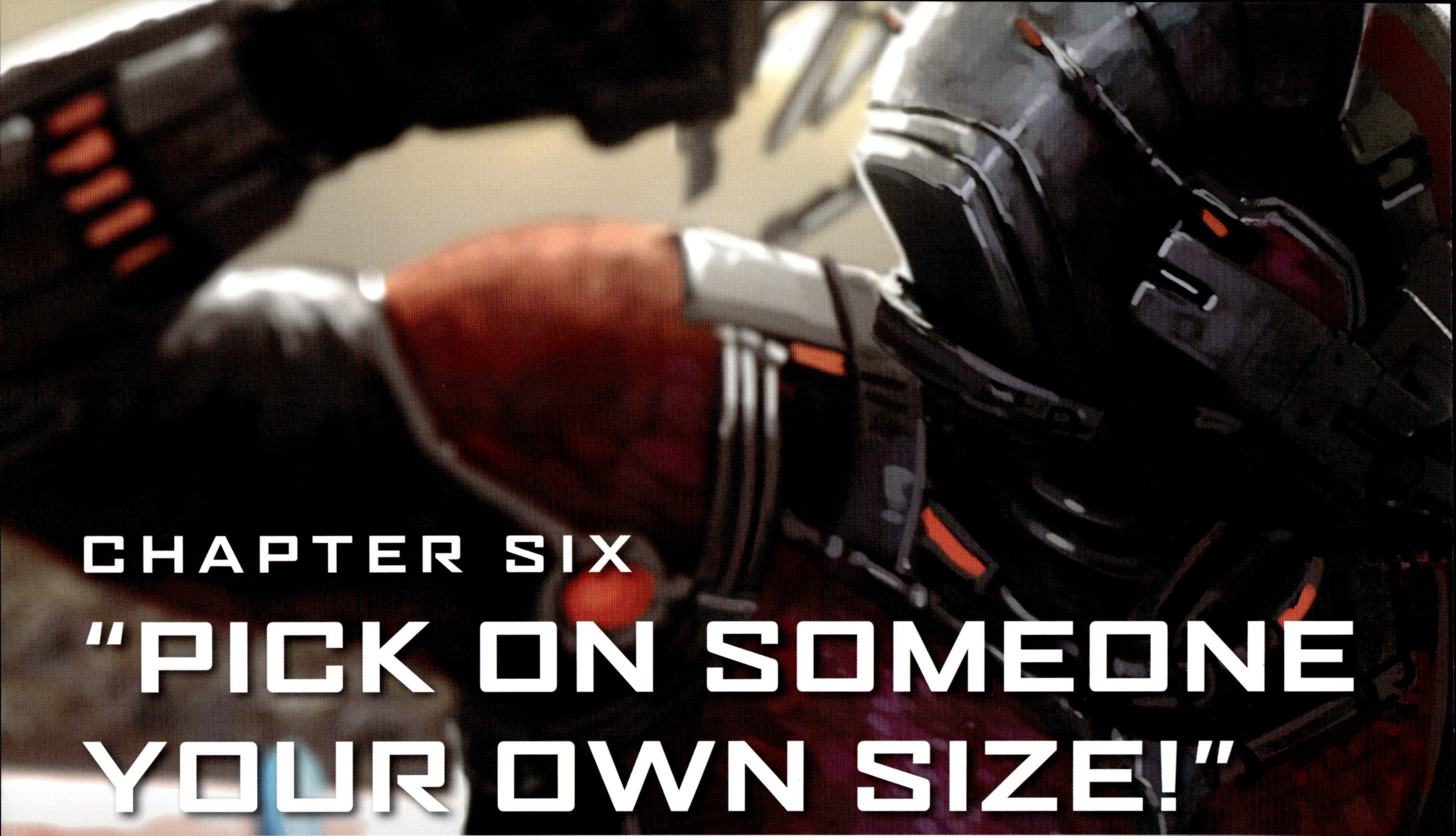

CHAPTER SIX

"PICK ON SOMEONE YOUR OWN SIZE!"

After losing PymTech, an unstable Darren Cross sets his sights on the most important thing in Scott Lang's life: his daughter. For the final showdown, Lang faces Cross in a down-and-dirty slugfest set against a most unexpected backdrop: a nine-year-old girl's bedroom. Staging this grand climax in small-scale environments—such as a toy train set and shelves cluttered with plush, stuffed animals—adds a new dimension to the Marvel Cinematic Universe. "There are limitations to all of the technology the characters use in the Marvel Universe. Ant-Man's no different, and that can add to very, very fun moments in a particular scene," says Executive Producer and President of Marvel Studios Kevin Feige. "For instance, he's fighting a character, they're both small, they're fighting on a little girl's shelf with toys being flung back and forth. Suddenly one of them grows, but the toy next to them has grown as well, and you have a plastic toy smashing out of a house and landing on top of another car and other characters sort of seeing that. Finding those ways to take a conceit and do more and more and more with it is always the fun challenge."

For Director Peyton Reed, that challenge was the pull for the entire film. "What I really loved about *Ant-Man* from the beginning, even when I read earlier drafts of the script, was that it all led to a third-act battle between the good guy and the bad guy," Reed explains. "And in most of these movies, it would be these giant global stakes—buildings blowing up and such—and here it was taking place in a little girl's bedroom. To me, when you hear that concept, it inherently makes you smile because it's such a great twist."

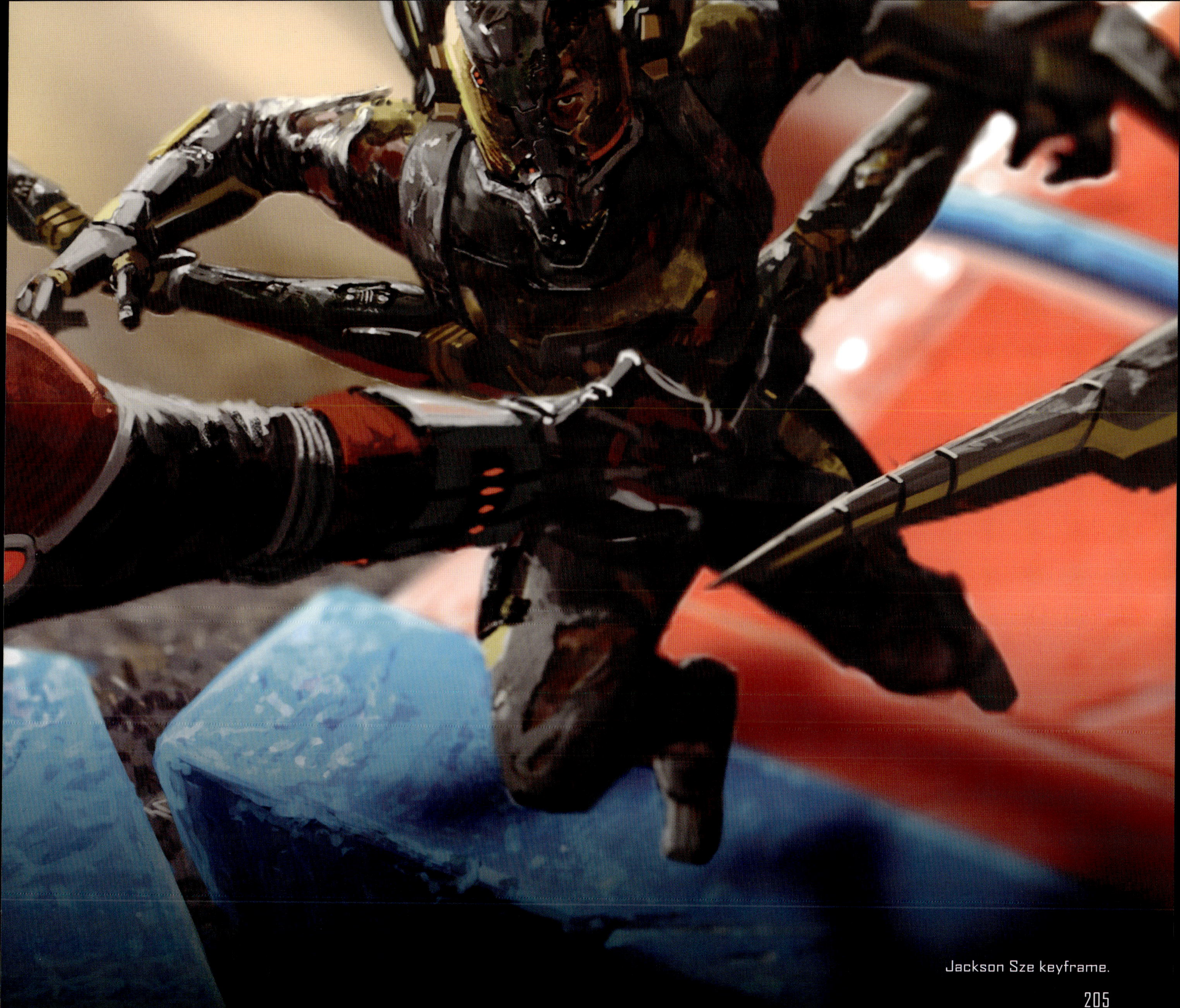

Jackson Sze keyframe.

CROSS'S ESCAPE

As PymTech goes down in flames, Darren Cross takes to the skies—the Yellowjacket suit stowed safely away in a high-tech briefcase. Ant-Man is hot on his heels, resolute that the technology must be reclaimed. Concept Artist Anthony Francisco was tasked with visualizing Darren Cross's reveal inside the suit—a beat that needed to feel iconic and powerful, even within the confines of the small aircraft. "This was the first keyframe I completed on the film," Francisco says. "I wanted to show Yellowjacket in an intimidating stance that also showcased the suit. His head and arms, both sets, envelop the space inside the vehicle—thus giving him the illusion of being even larger and more dangerous."

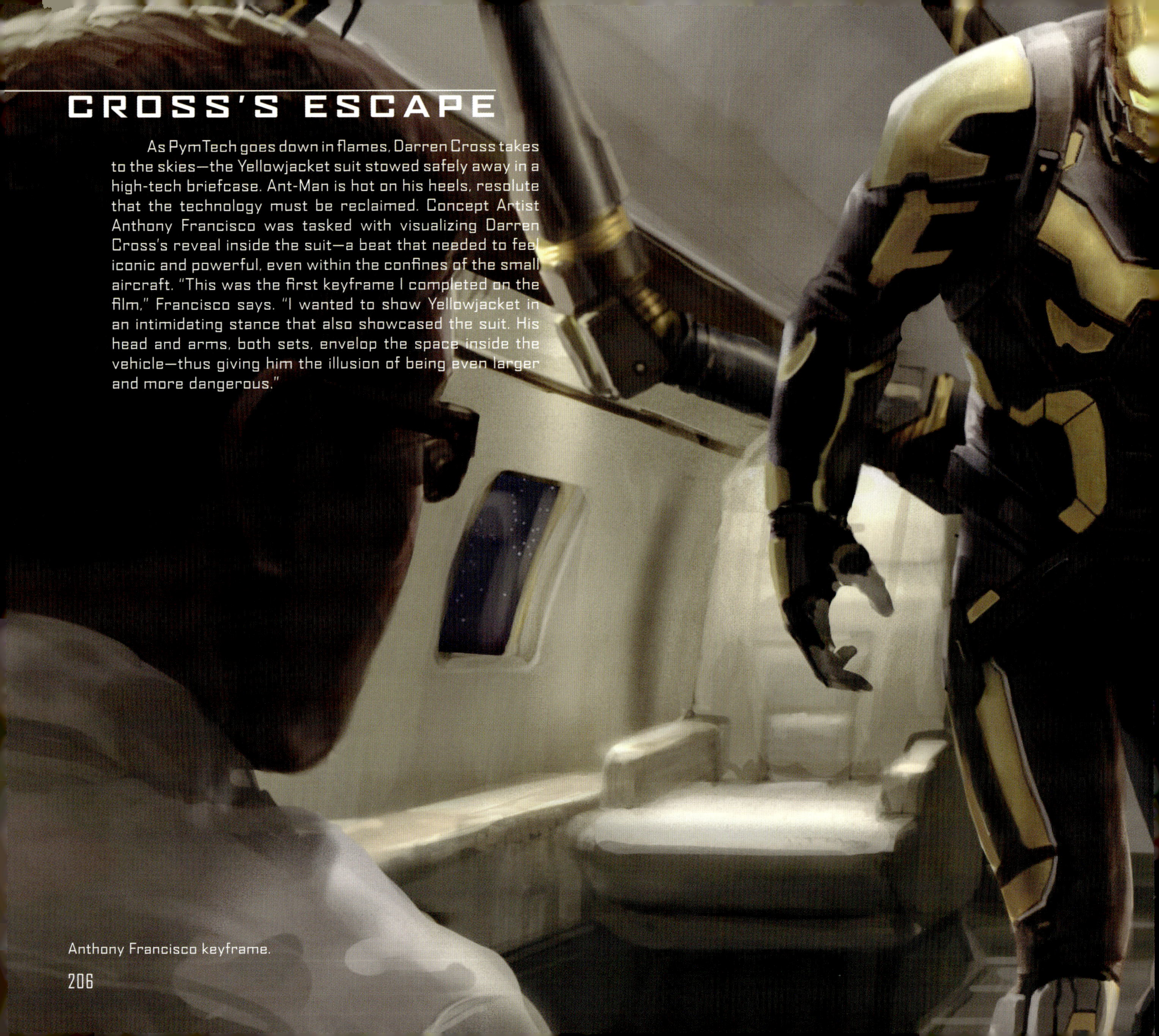

Anthony Francisco keyframe.

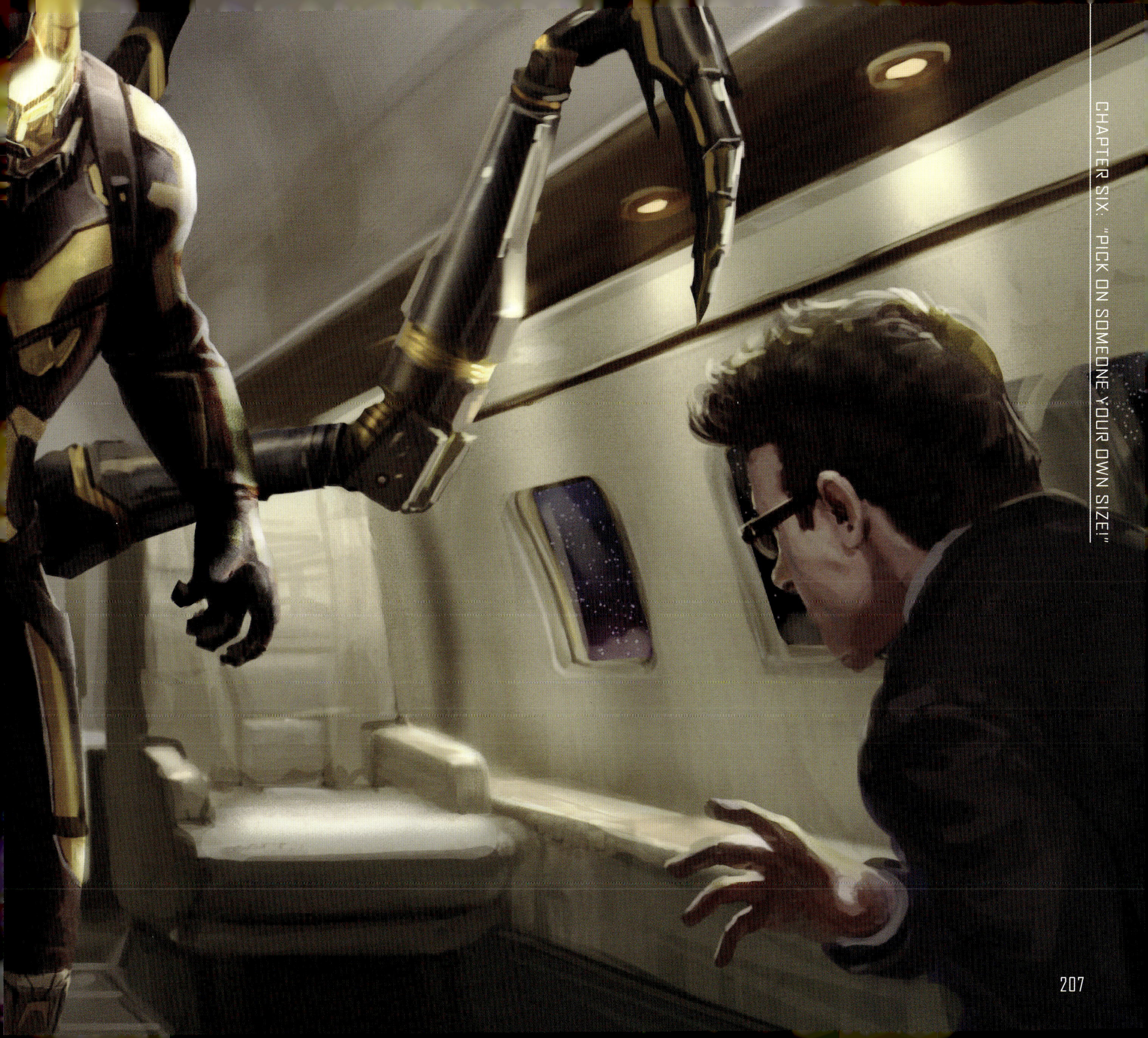

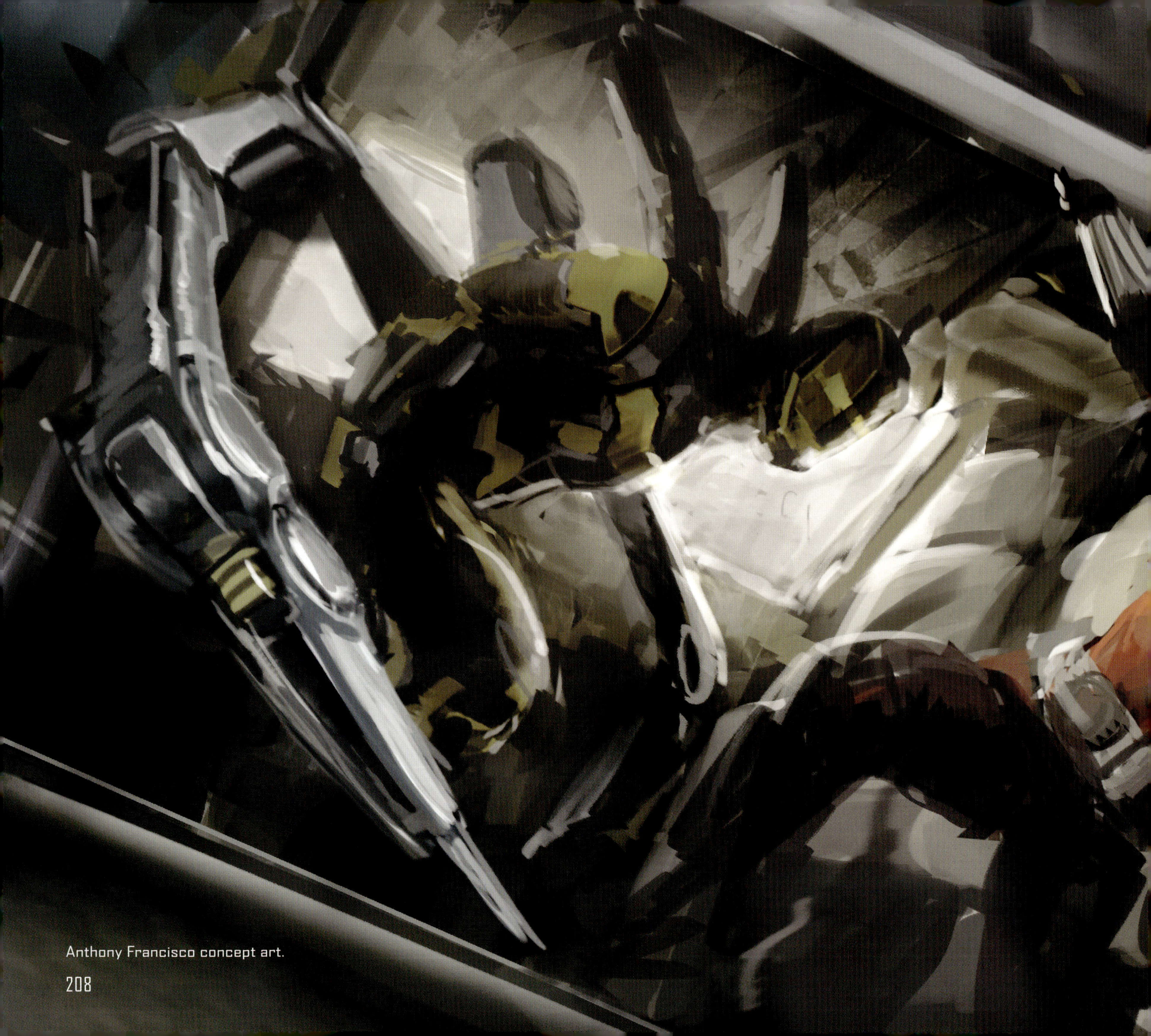

Anthony Francisco concept art.

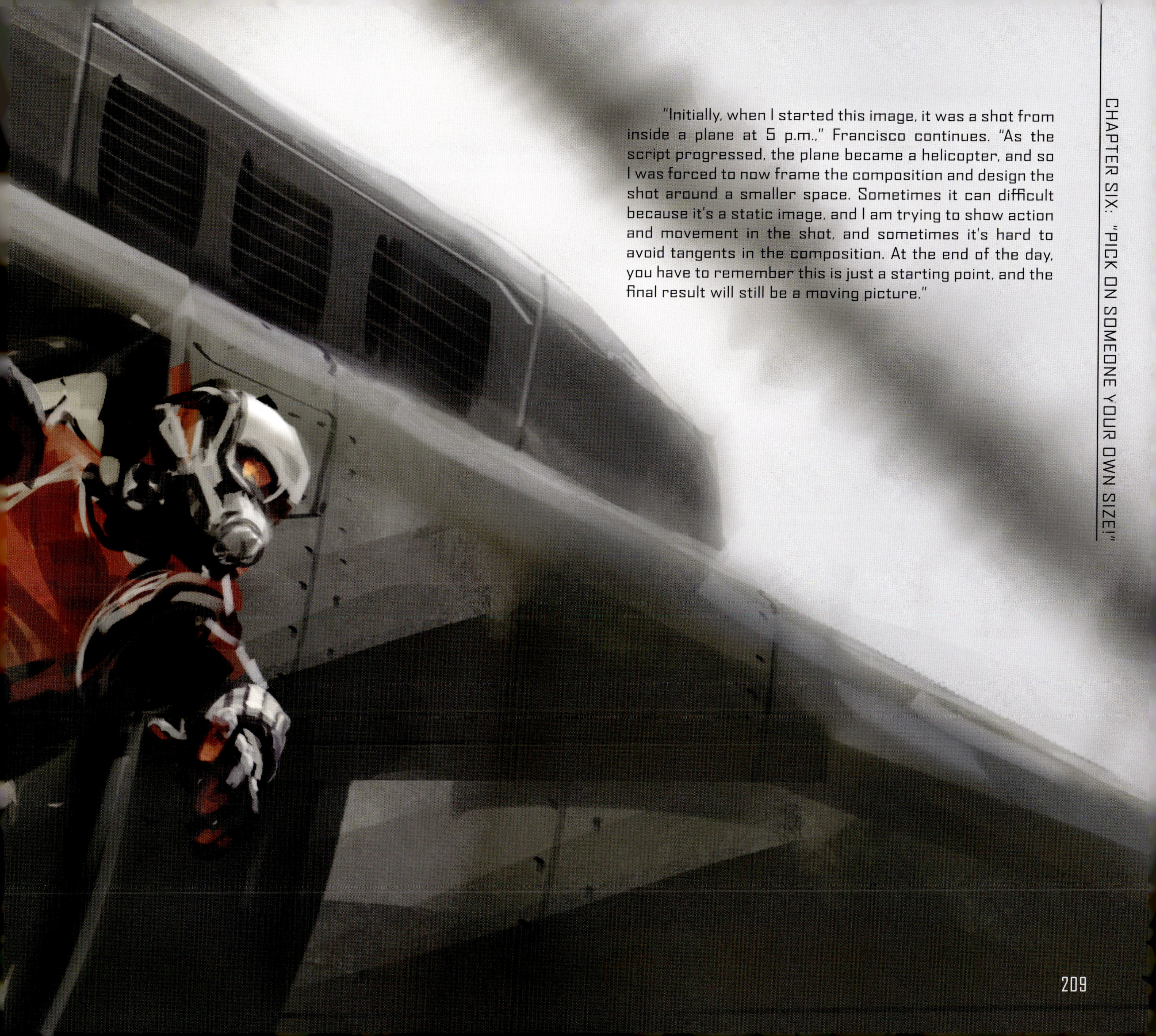

"Initially, when I started this image, it was a shot from inside a plane at 5 p.m.," Francisco continues. "As the script progressed, the plane became a helicopter, and so I was forced to now frame the composition and design the shot around a smaller space. Sometimes it can difficult because it's a static image, and I am trying to show action and movement in the shot, and sometimes it's hard to avoid tangents in the composition. At the end of the day, you have to remember this is just a starting point, and the final result will still be a moving picture."

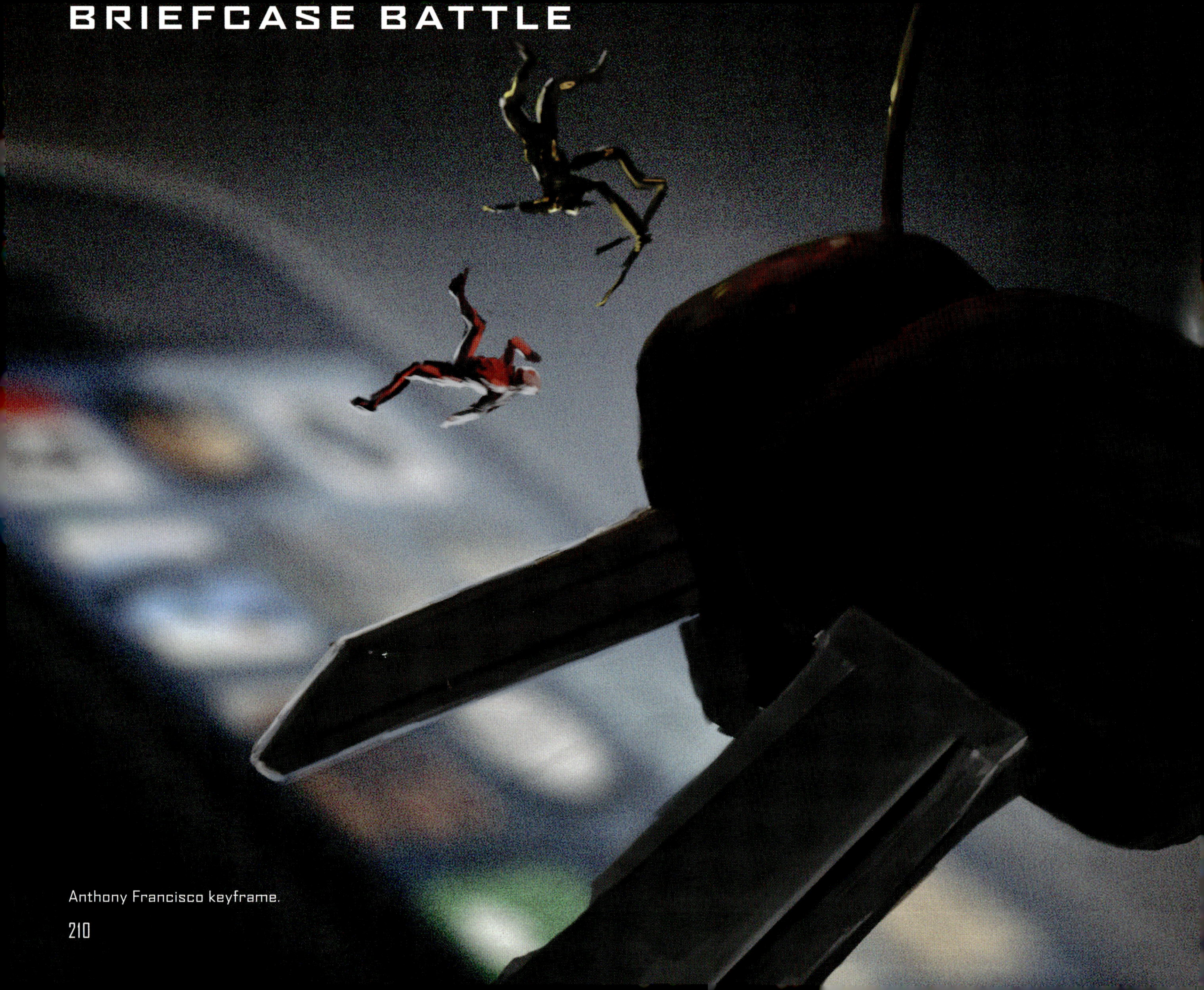

Anthony Francisco keyframe.

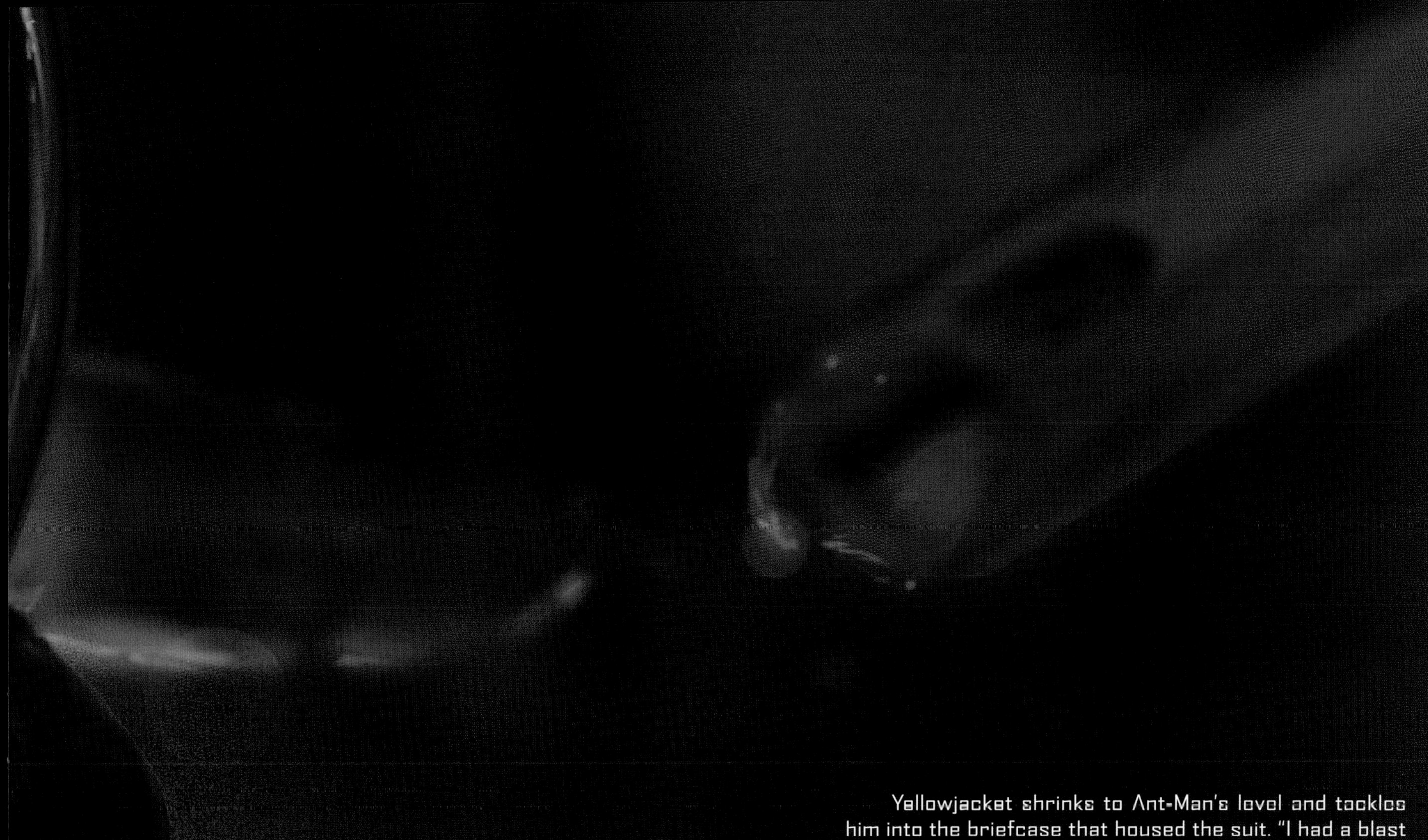

Yellowjacket shrinks to Ant-Man's level and tackles him into the briefcase that housed the suit. "I had a blast working on these keyframes," Anthony Francisco says. "These were done early on in the production, so I had nothing to really base the visuals from—all I knew was they were fighting inside a briefcase. The key thing here was to utilize the contents to help sell the scale of the characters and be creative in the placement of the light sources so that you can still believe the action is taking place inside the briefcase. Then, later, I was told that the case would be falling. So I had to design the shot around utilizing rules of freefall and how it would affect both the characters and the contents inside. Along with the light coming from the sources within the briefcase, the characters also have their own glow, which made the fight even more iconic and unique."

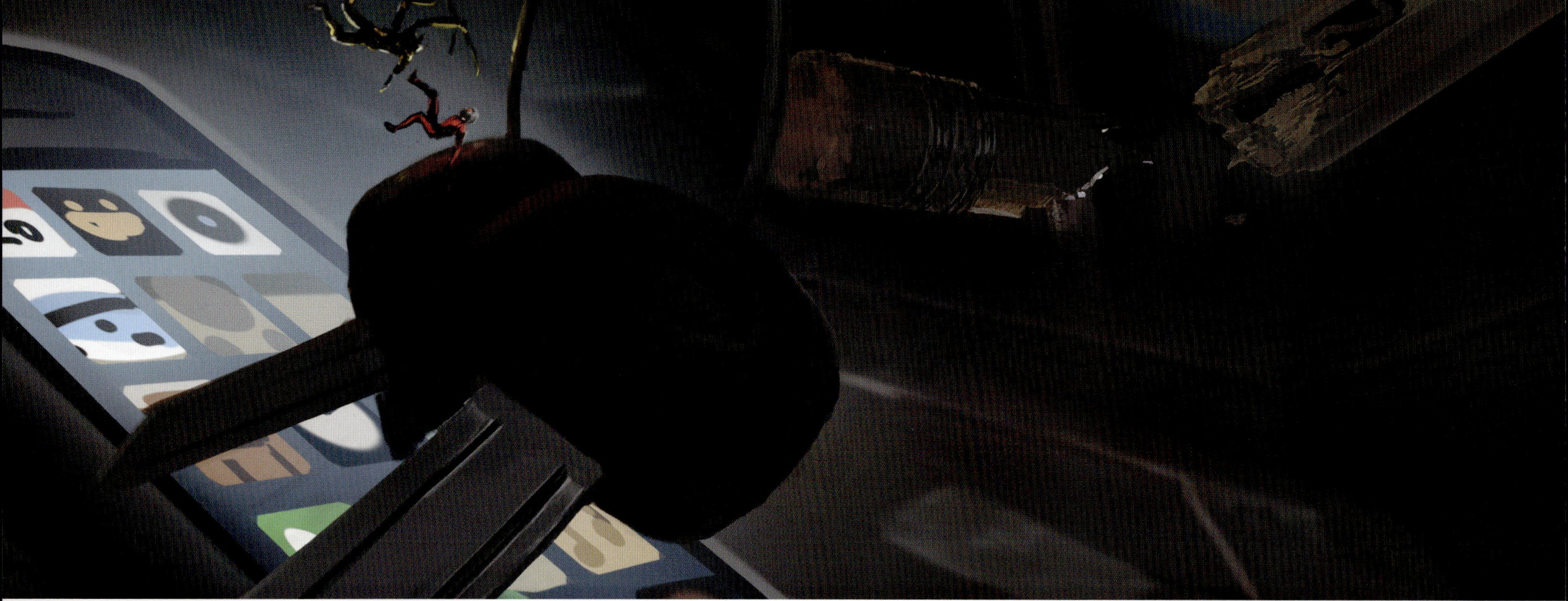

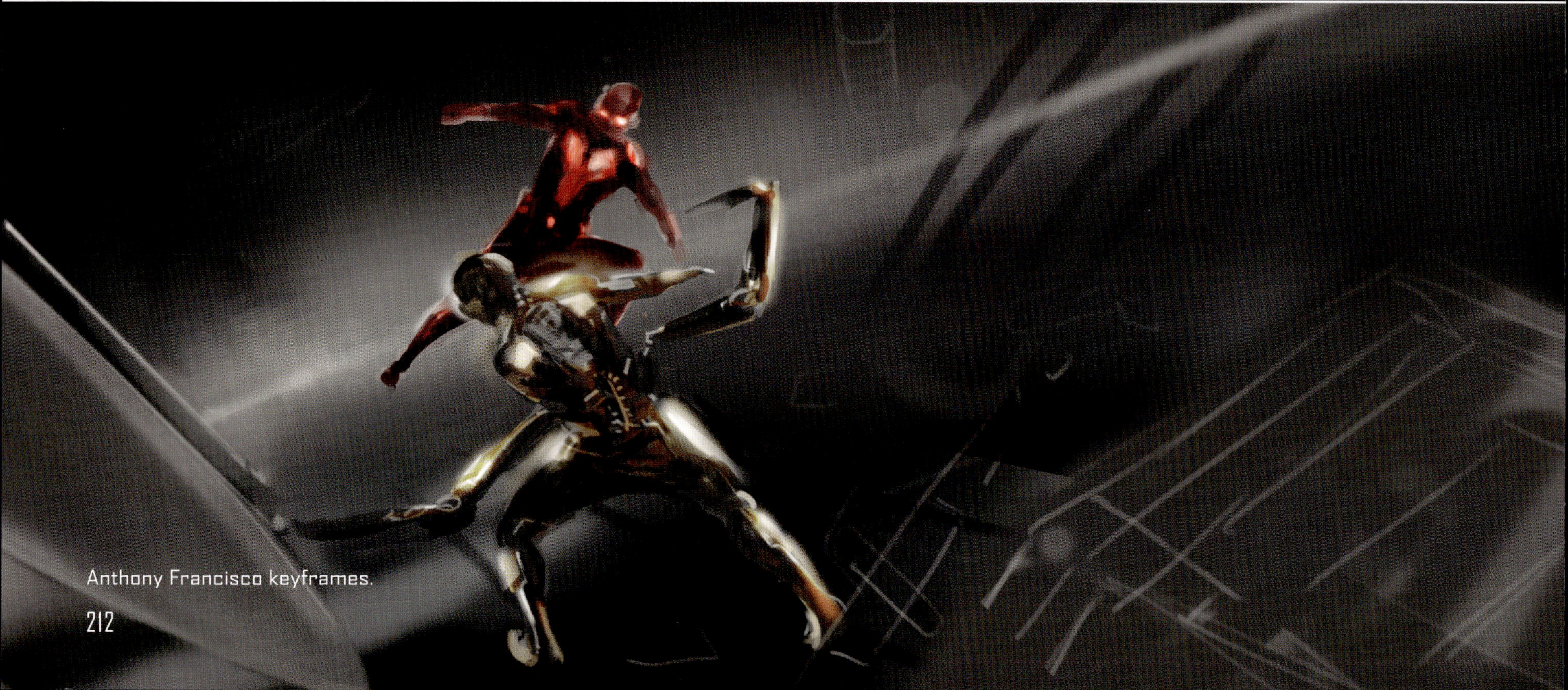

Anthony Francisco keyframes.

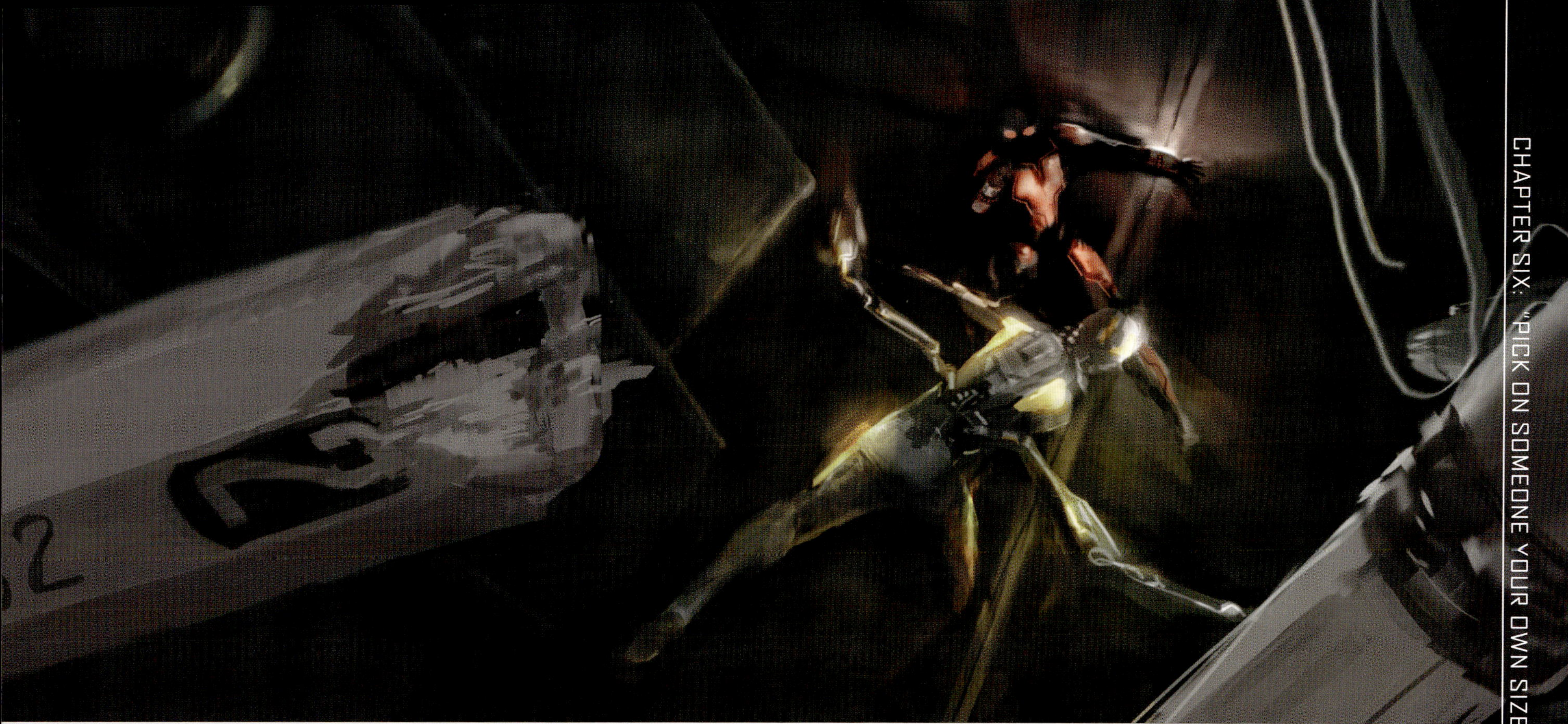

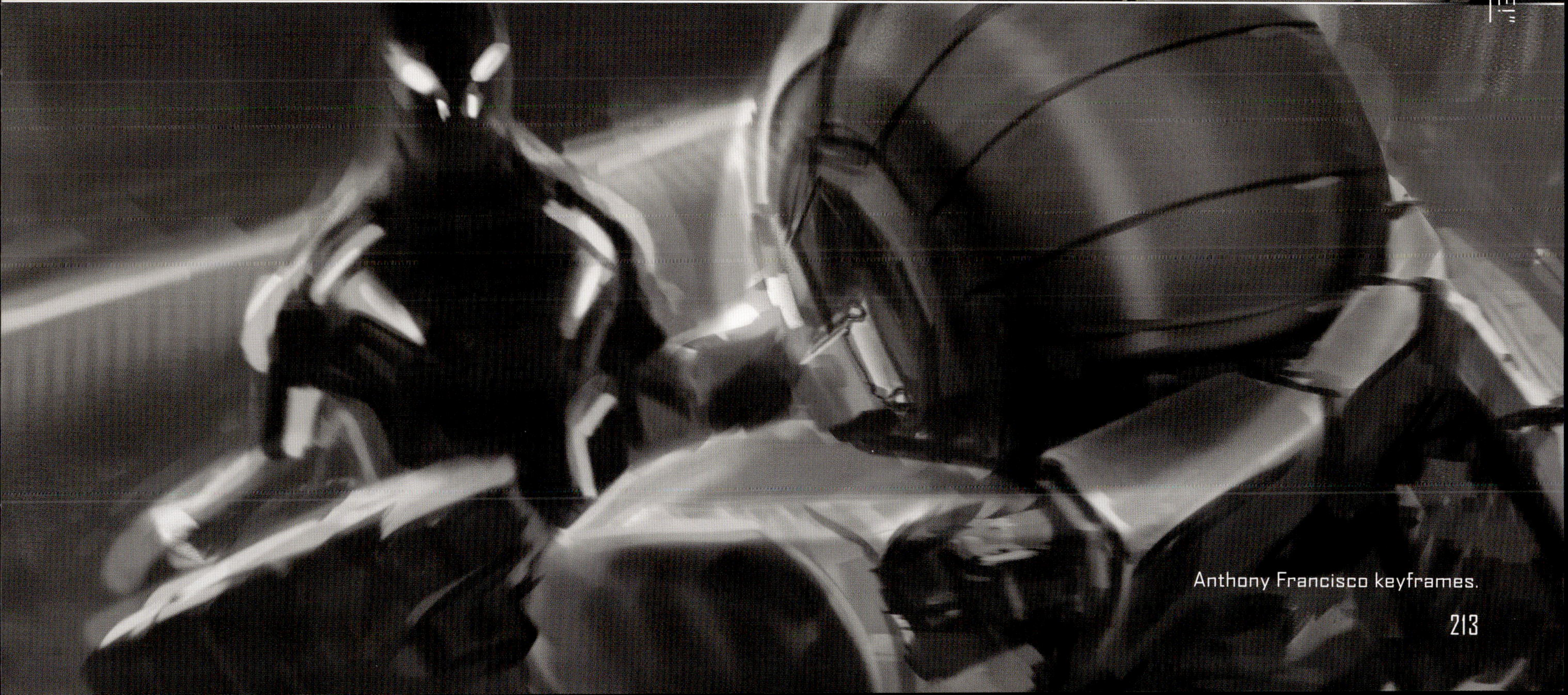

Anthony Francisco keyframes.

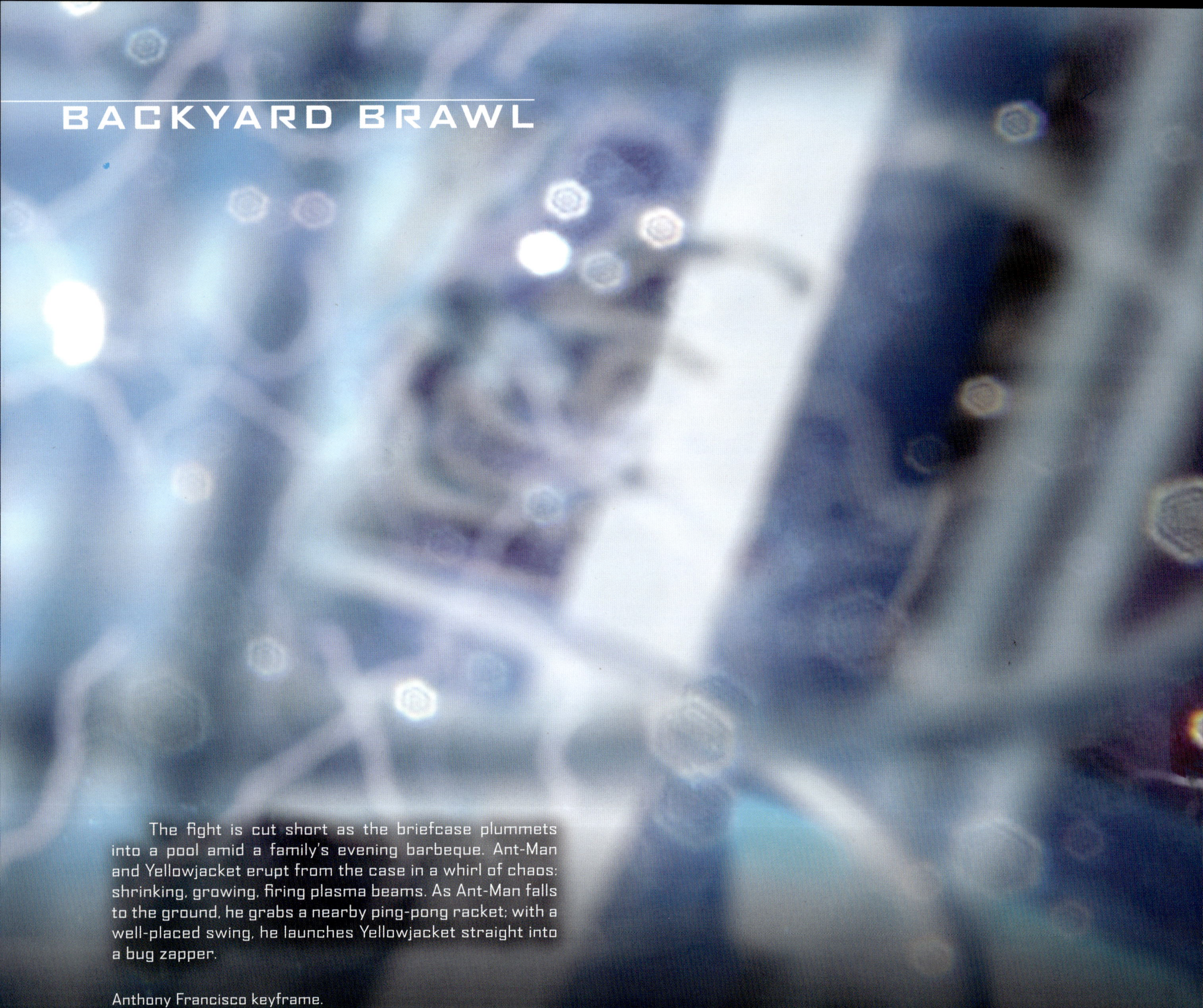

BACKYARD BRAWL

The fight is cut short as the briefcase plummets into a pool amid a family's evening barbeque. Ant-Man and Yellowjacket erupt from the case in a whirl of chaos: shrinking, growing, firing plasma beams. As Ant-Man falls to the ground, he grabs a nearby ping-pong racket; with a well-placed swing, he launches Yellowjacket straight into a bug zapper.

Anthony Francisco keyframe.

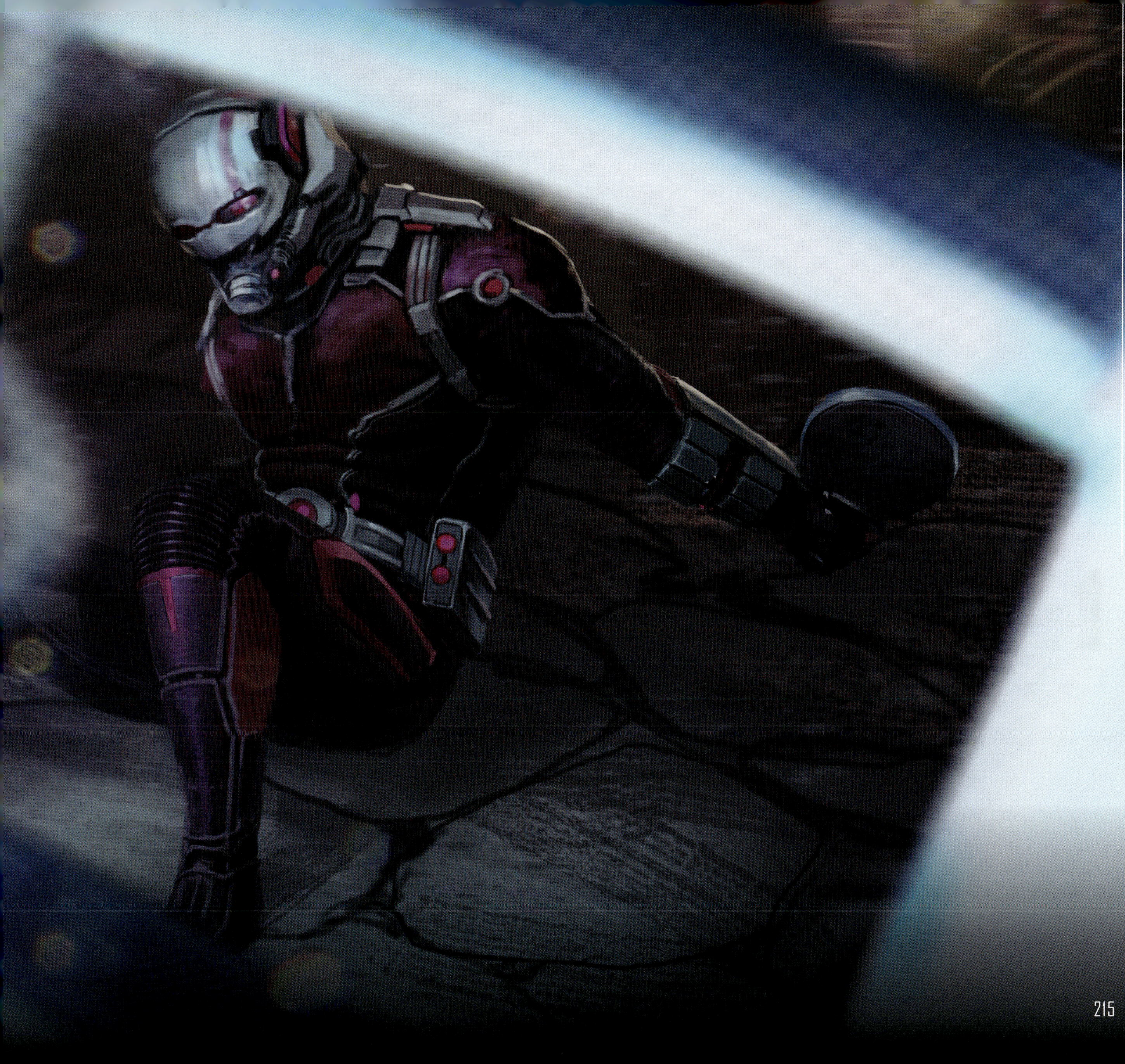

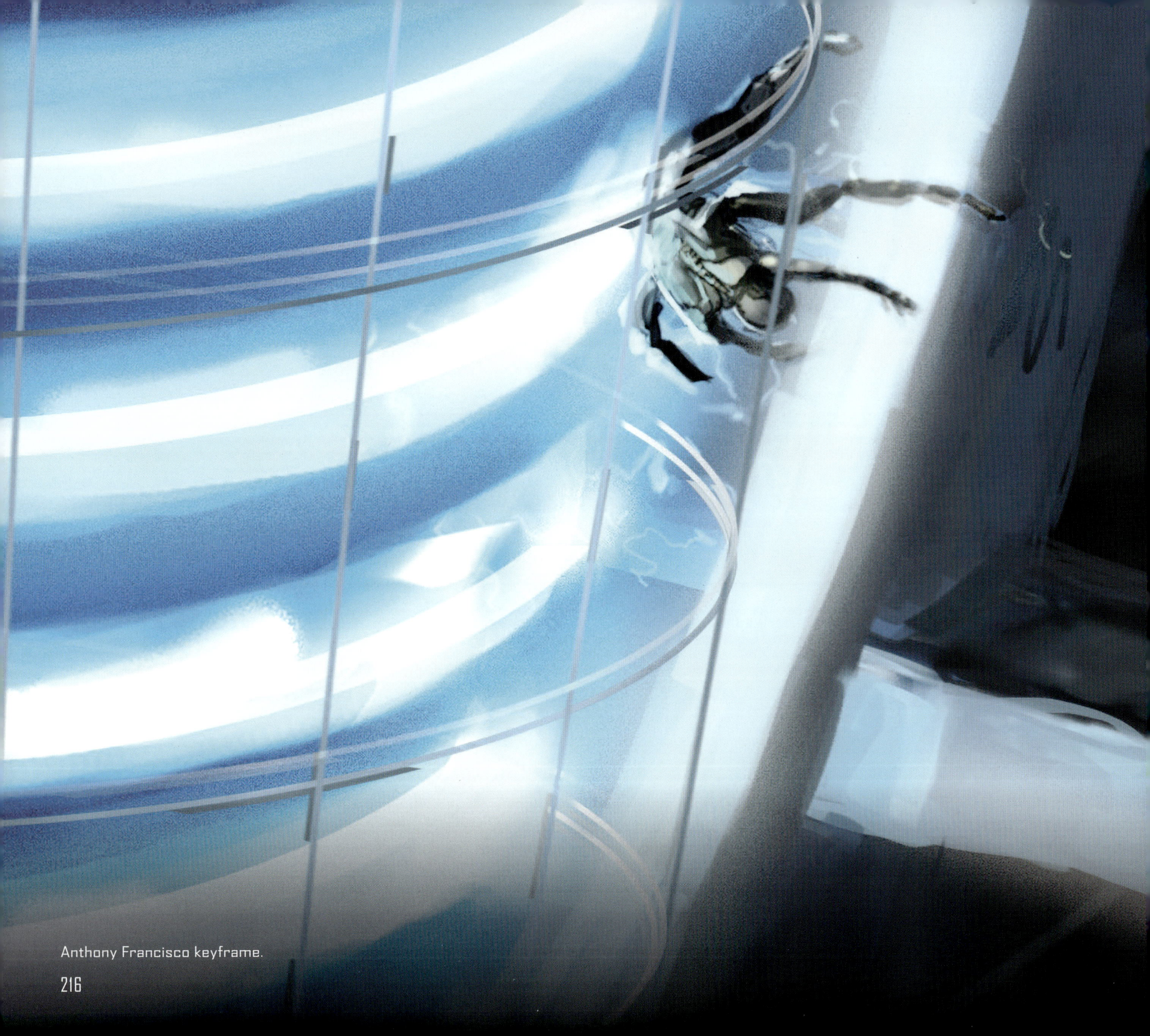

Anthony Francisco keyframe.

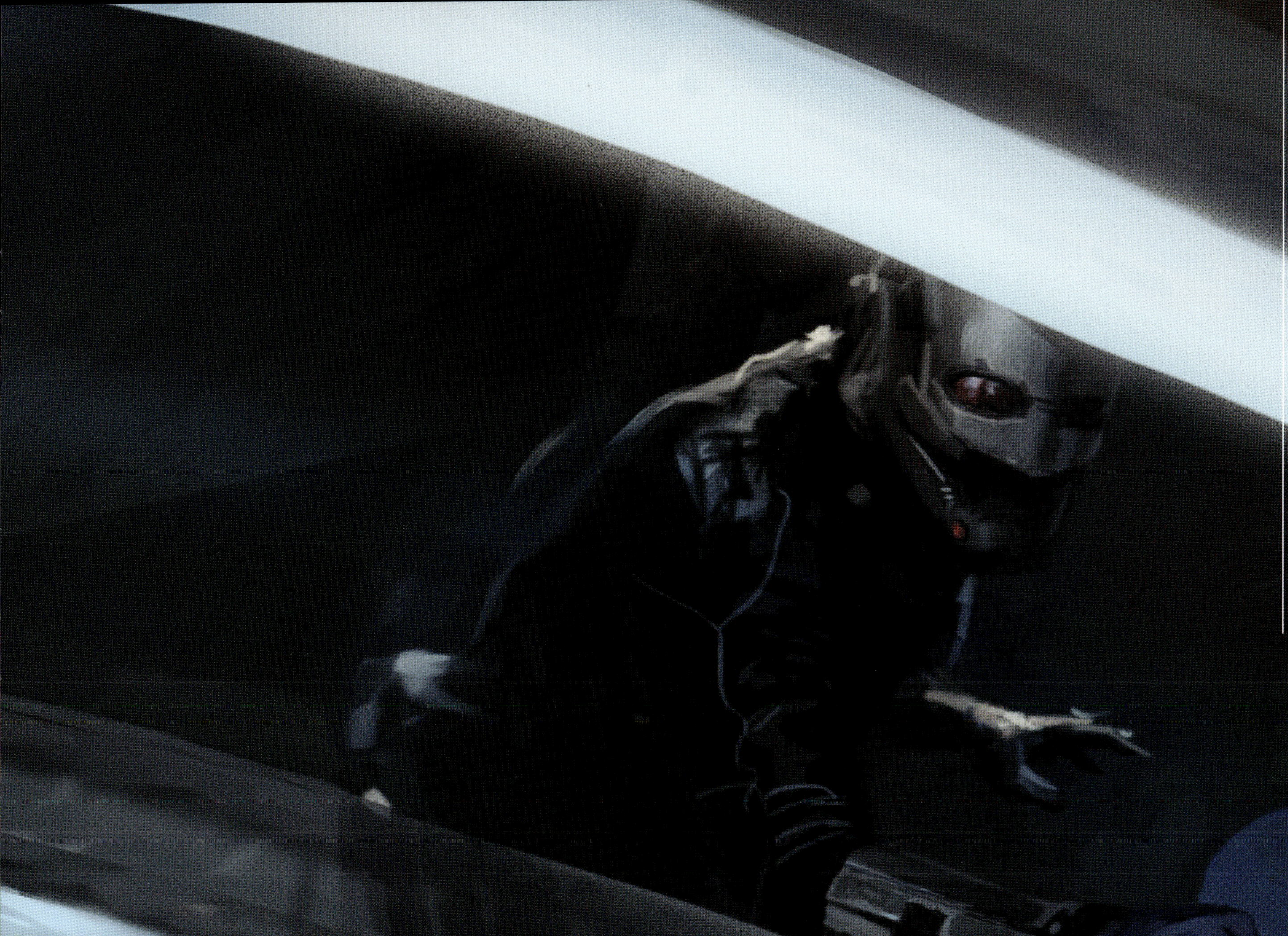

Anthony Francisco continued the fight's visual progression, culminating in the big BZZT moment. "For these zapper beats, I really wanted to explore the dynamic possibilities for various angles and depths of field," he says. "I also did a lot of research on various types of bug zappers to see which one would allow the audience to follow the action once Yellowjacket gets knocked in. The bug zapper I used was actually based off one I had at home: It had large slits on the outside, but a smaller casing inside—pretty much exactly what the script called for. It was serendipitous."

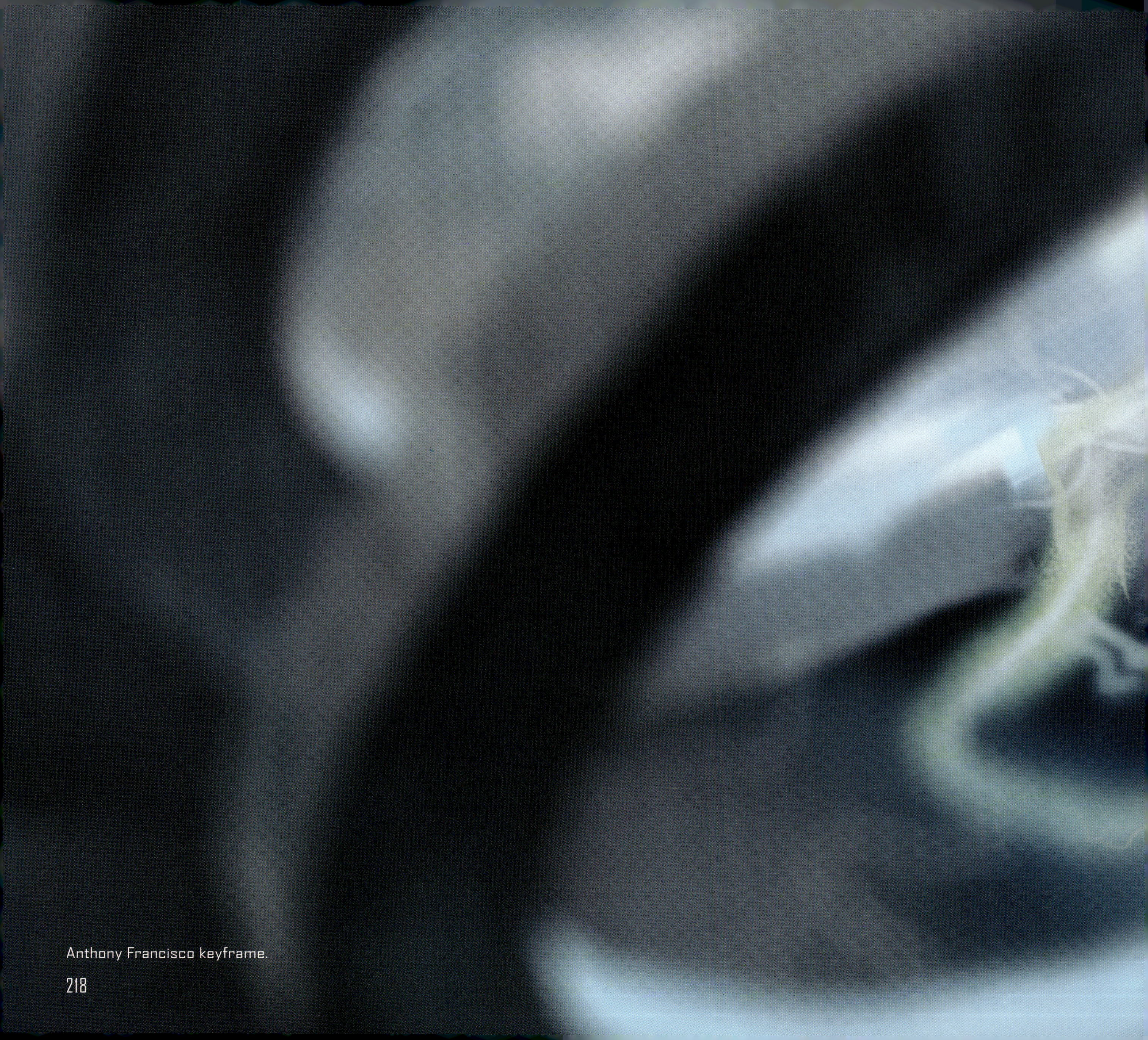

Anthony Francisco keyframe.

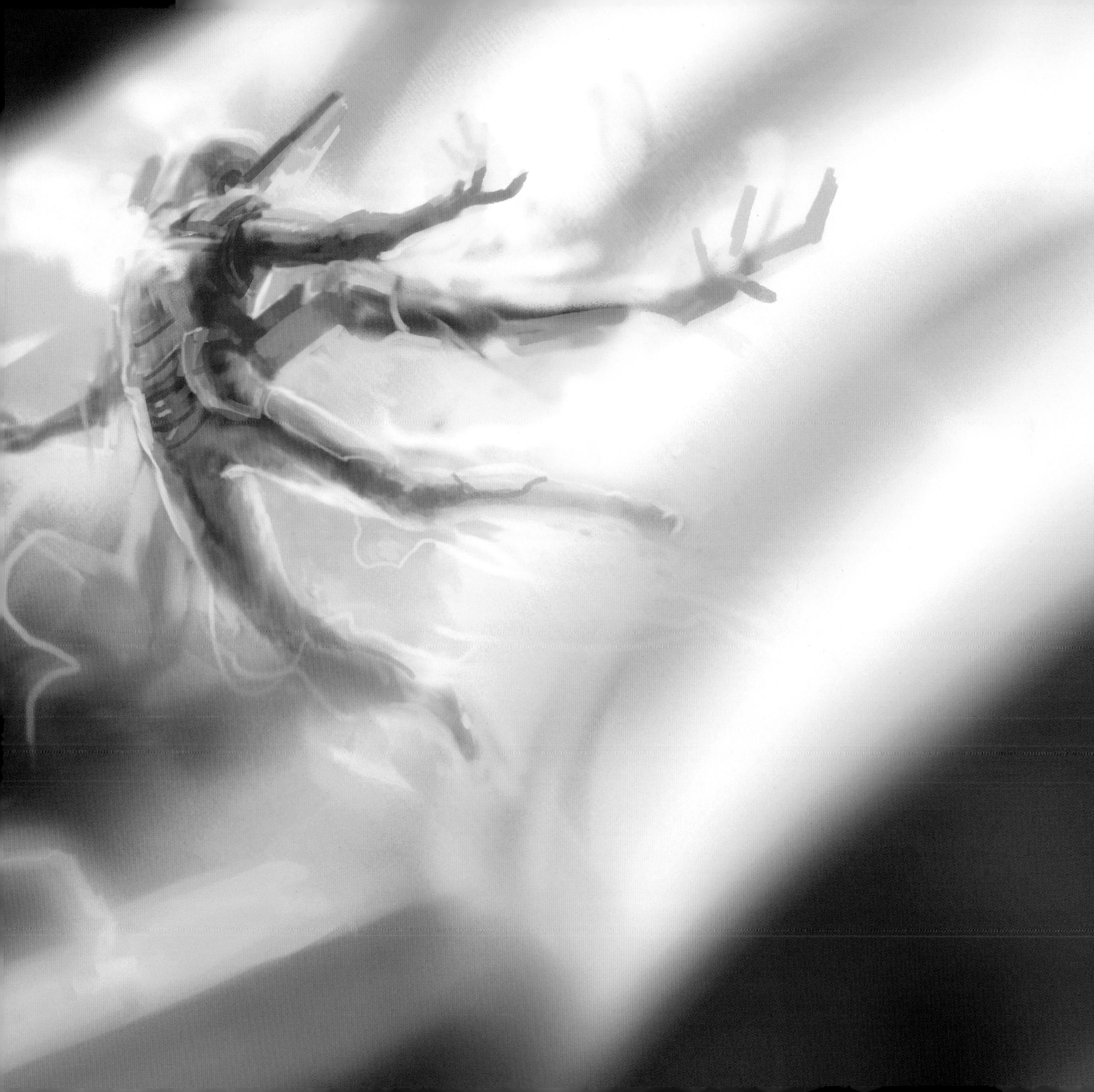

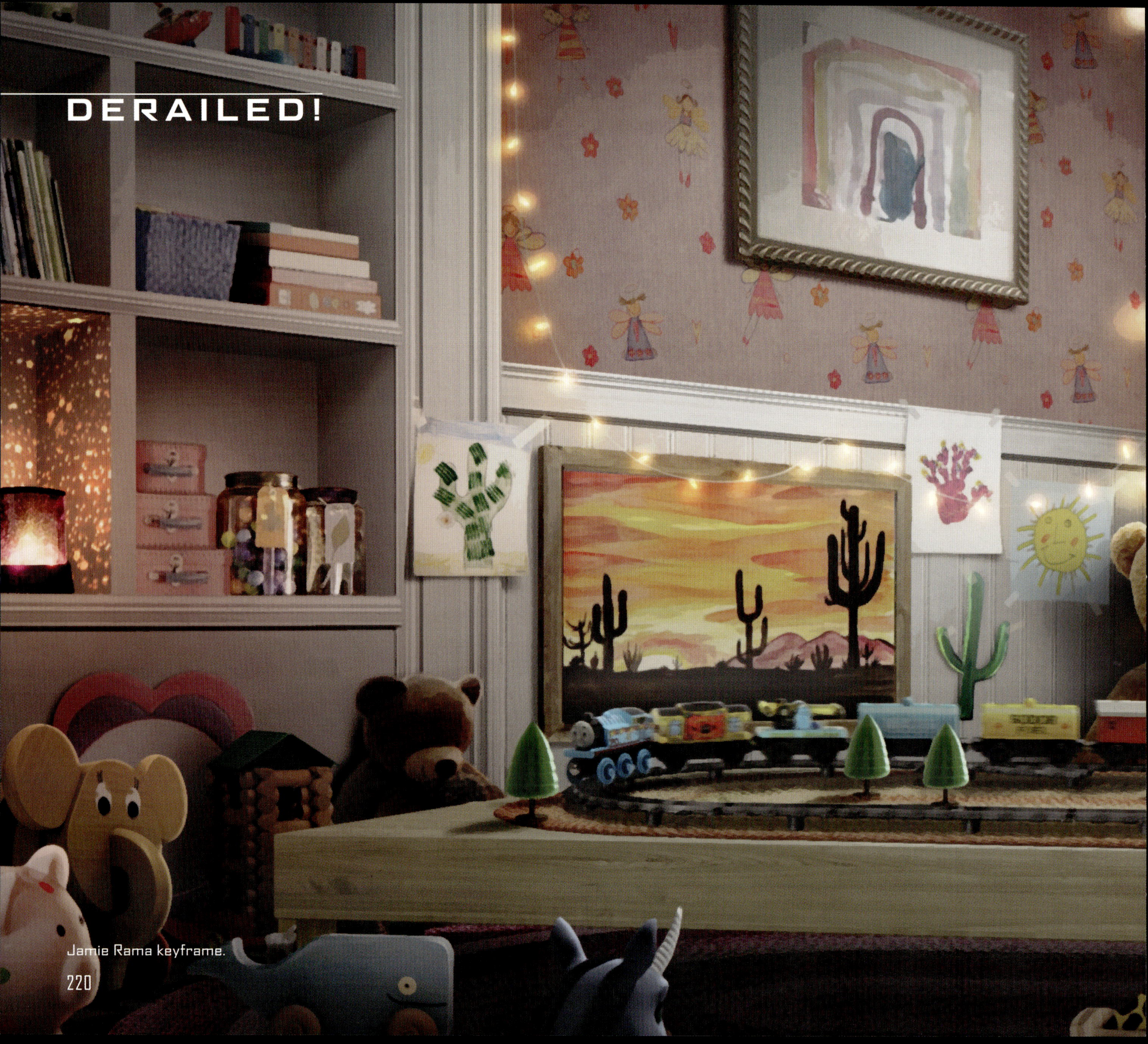

Jamie Rama keyframe.

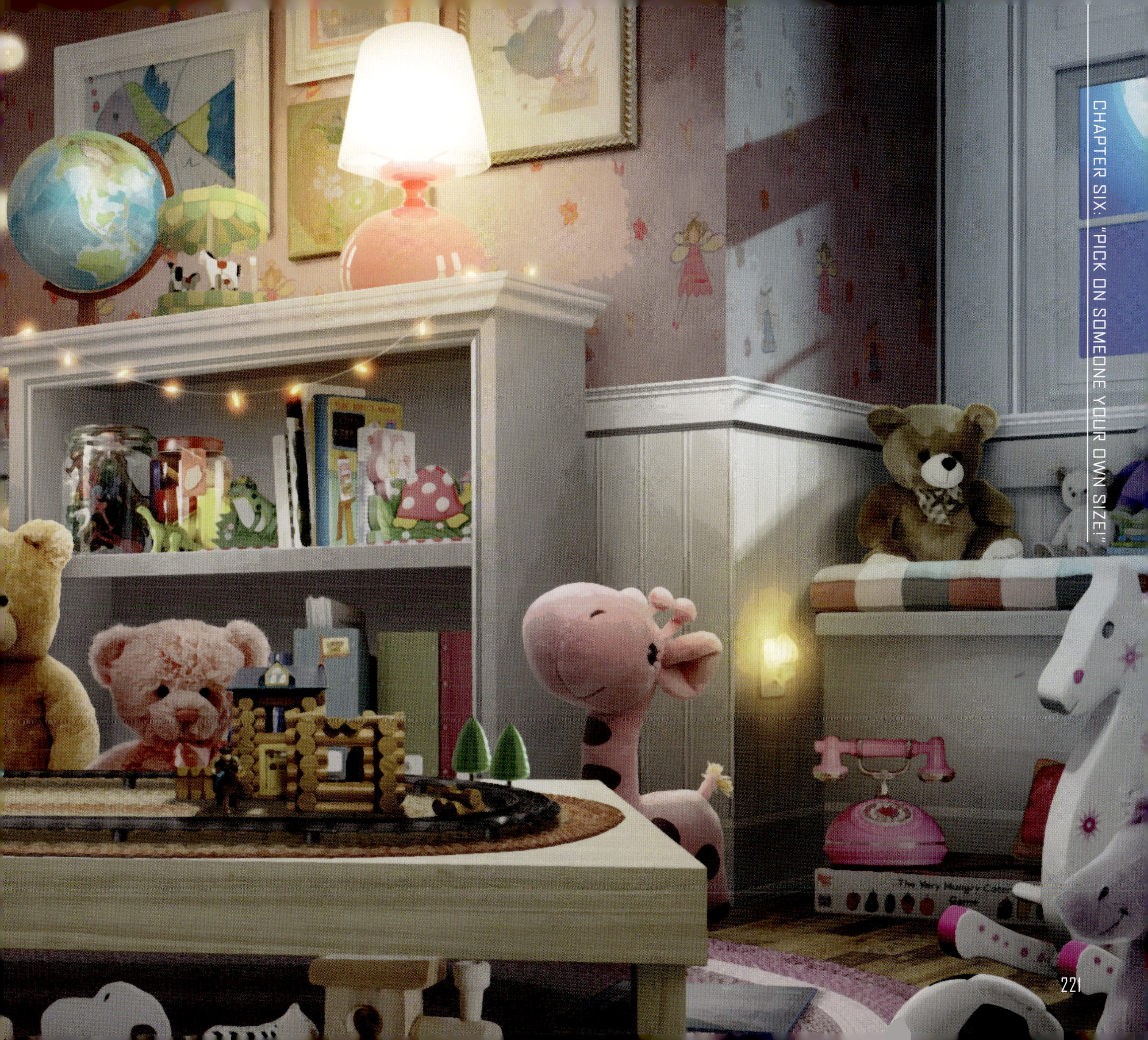

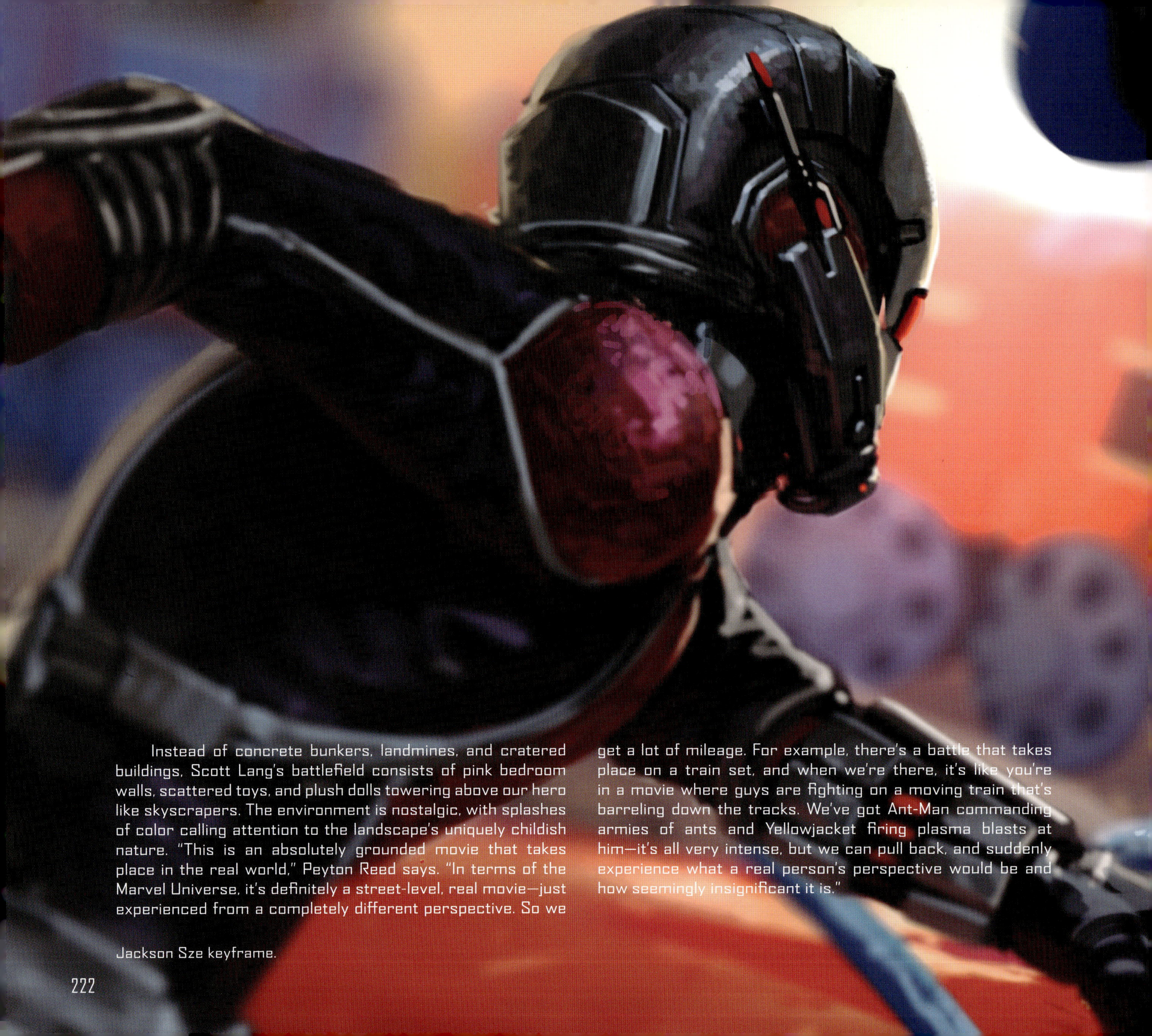

Instead of concrete bunkers, landmines, and cratered buildings, Scott Lang's battlefield consists of pink bedroom walls, scattered toys, and plush dolls towering above our hero like skyscrapers. The environment is nostalgic, with splashes of color calling attention to the landscape's uniquely childish nature. "This is an absolutely grounded movie that takes place in the real world," Peyton Reed says. "In terms of the Marvel Universe, it's definitely a street-level, real movie—just experienced from a completely different perspective. So we get a lot of mileage. For example, there's a battle that takes place on a train set, and when we're there, it's like you're in a movie where guys are fighting on a moving train that's barreling down the tracks. We've got Ant-Man commanding armies of ants and Yellowjacket firing plasma blasts at him—it's all very intense, but we can pull back, and suddenly experience what a real person's perspective would be and how seemingly insignificant it is."

Jackson Sze keyframe.

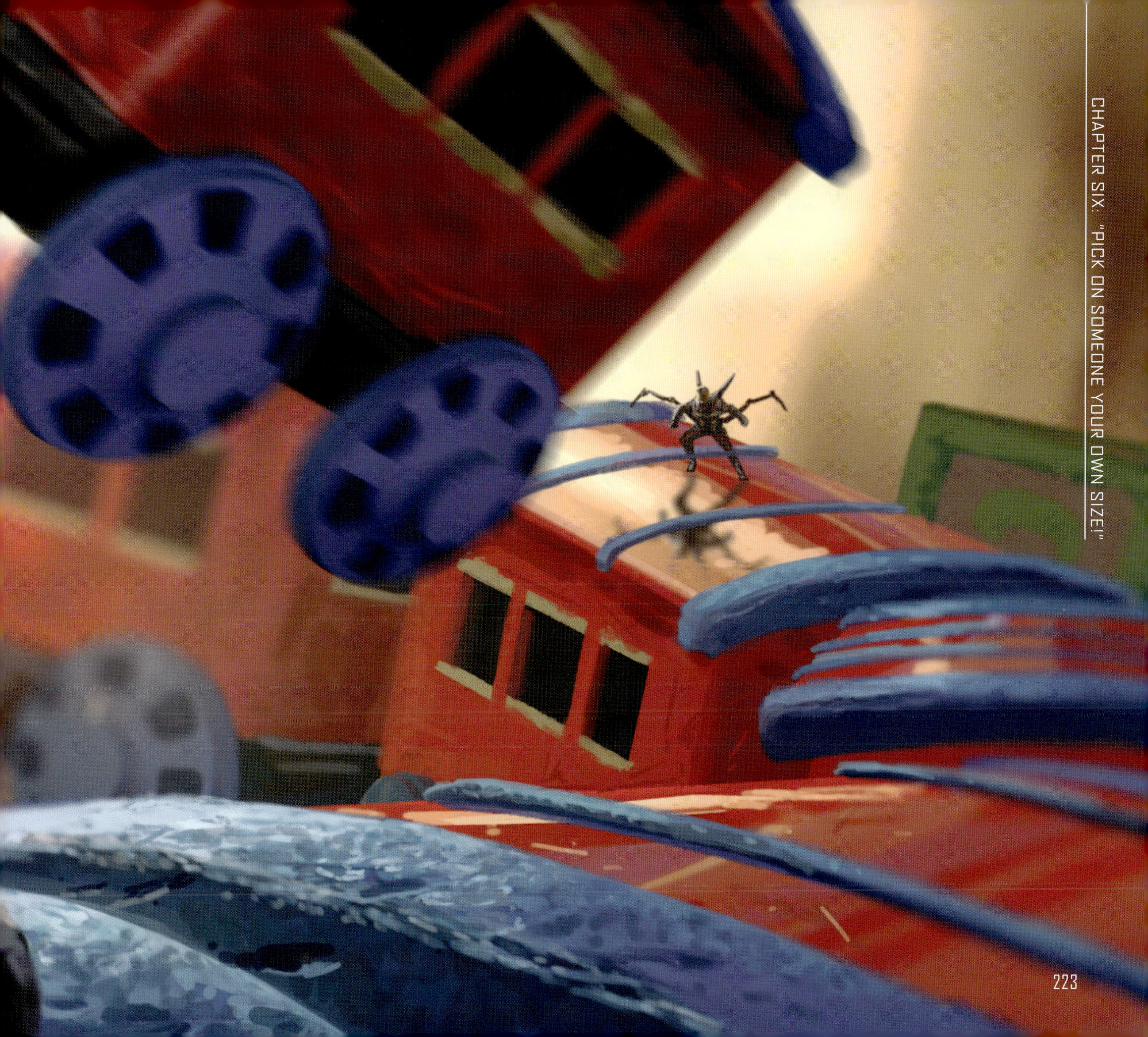

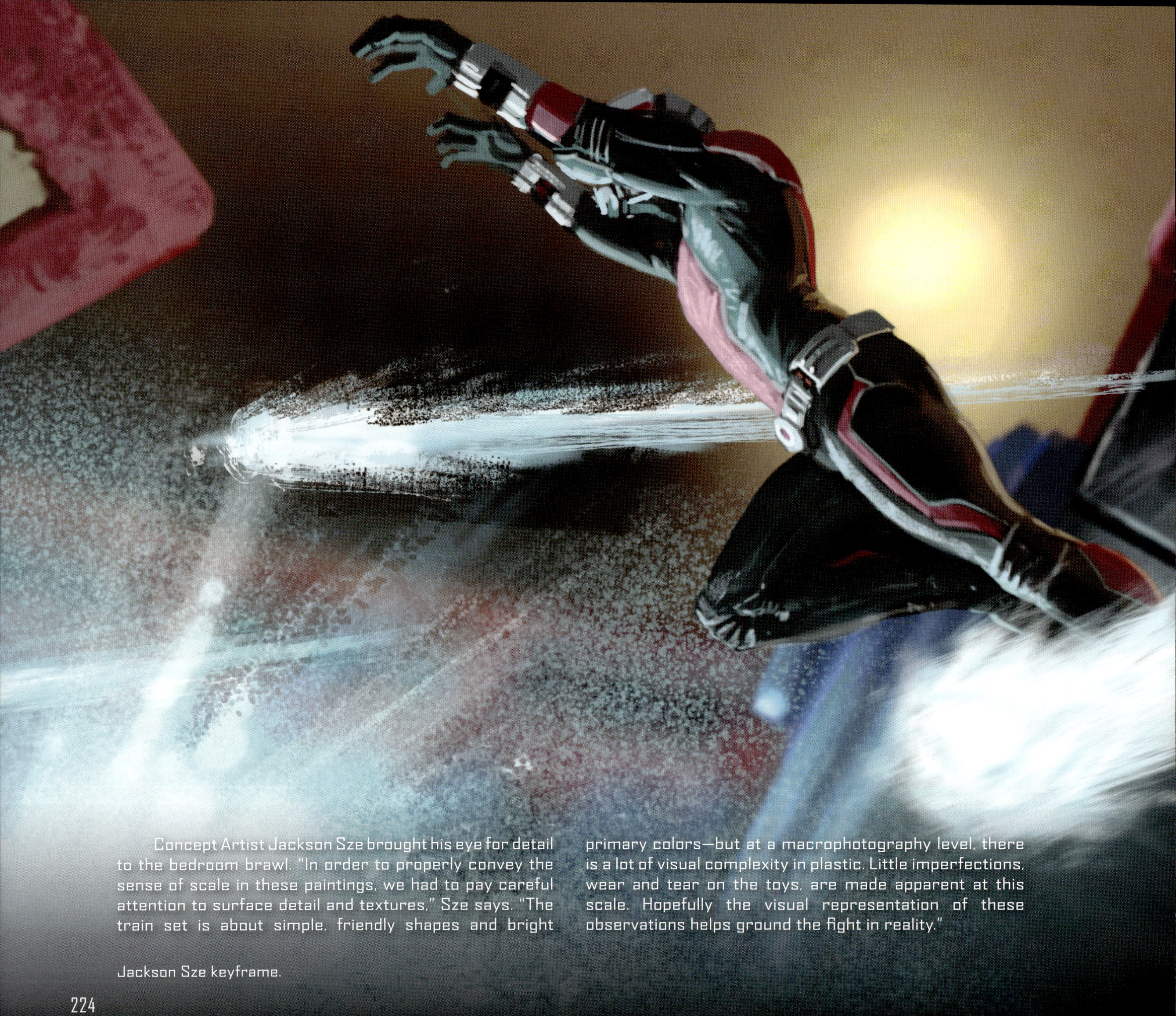

Concept Artist Jackson Sze brought his eye for detail to the bedroom brawl. "In order to properly convey the sense of scale in these paintings, we had to pay careful attention to surface detail and textures," Sze says. "The train set is about simple, friendly shapes and bright primary colors—but at a macrophotography level, there is a lot of visual complexity in plastic. Little imperfections, wear and tear on the toys, are made apparent at this scale. Hopefully the visual representation of these observations helps ground the fight in reality."

Jackson Sze keyframe.

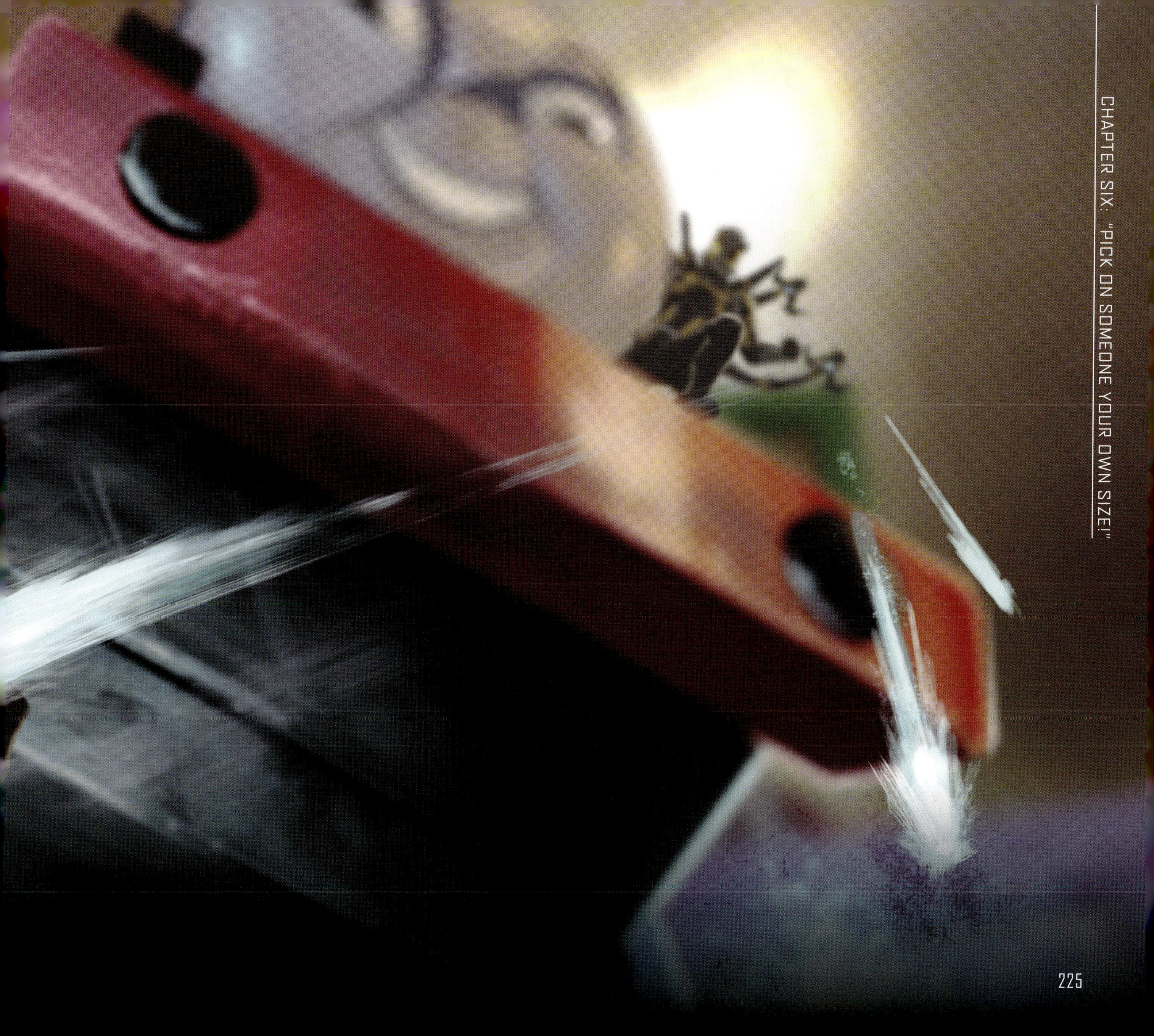

"There have been many great fight scenes filmed on trains throughout cinema," Sze continues. "It was really fun to do our take on a train fight-scene with our tiny hero and toy train set. Speaking of, being able to use Thomas the Tank Engine in the scene was a real treat. It added humor and familiarity, and reinforced the scale of the fight."

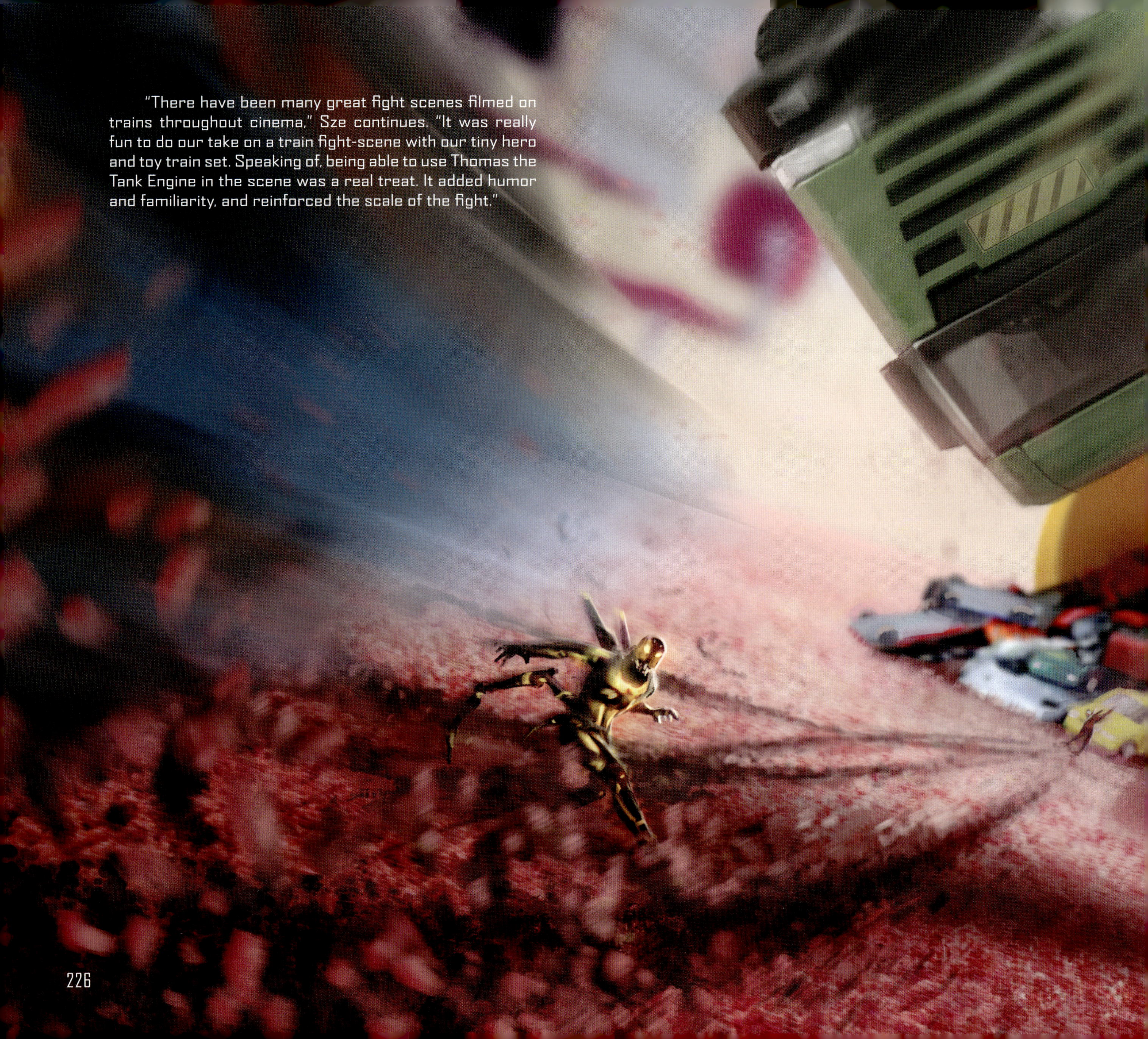

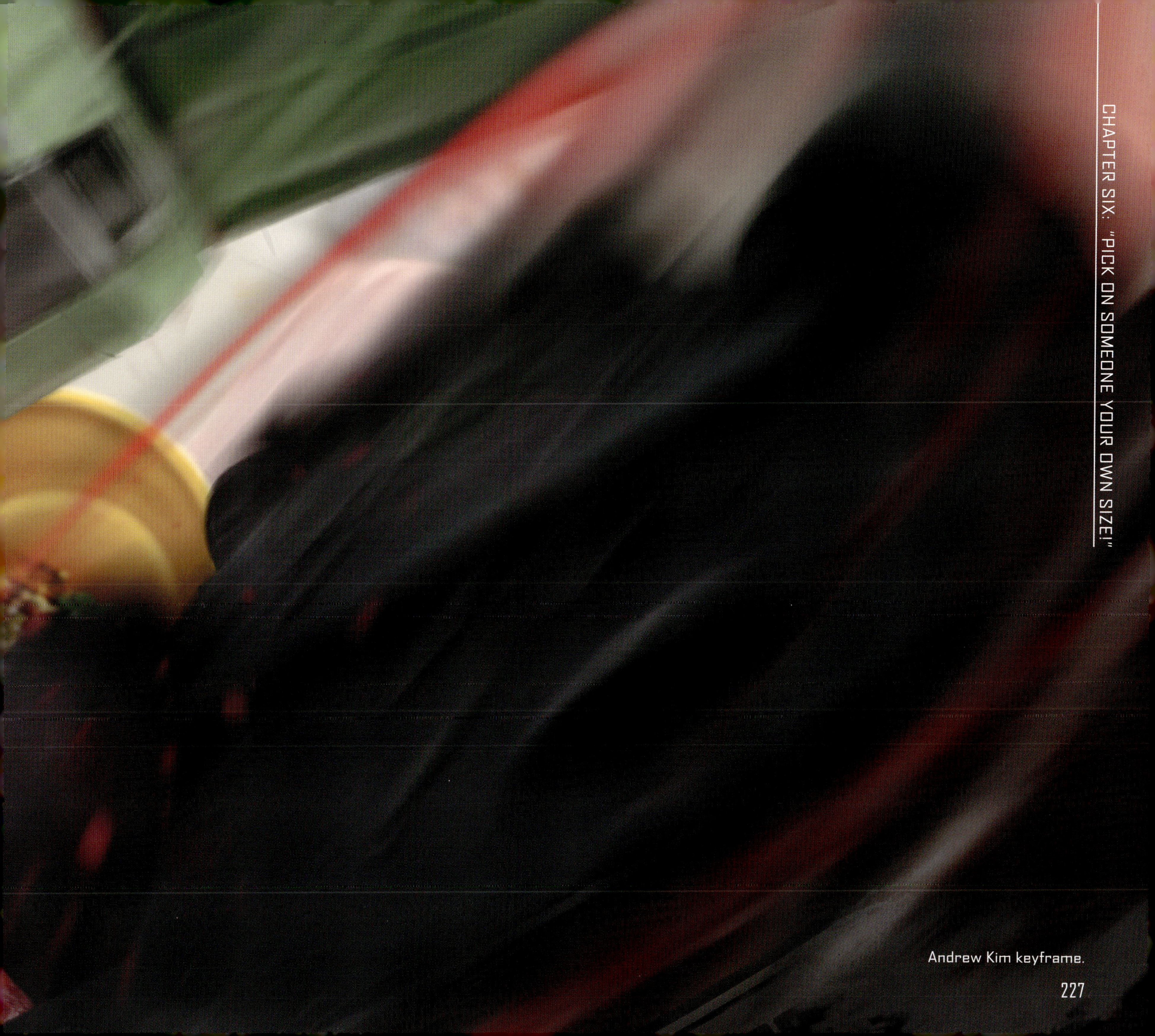

Andrew Kim keyframe.

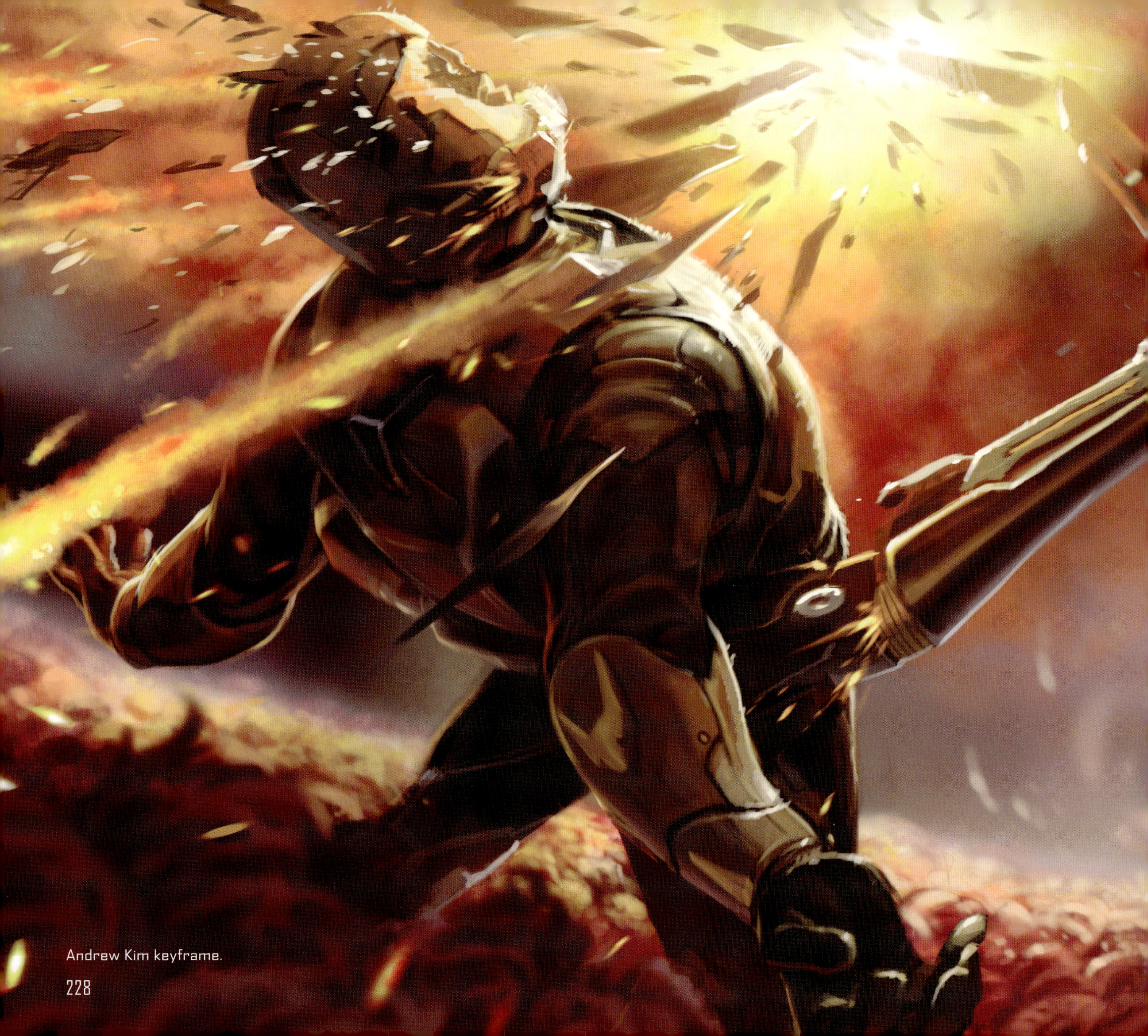

Andrew Kim keyframe.

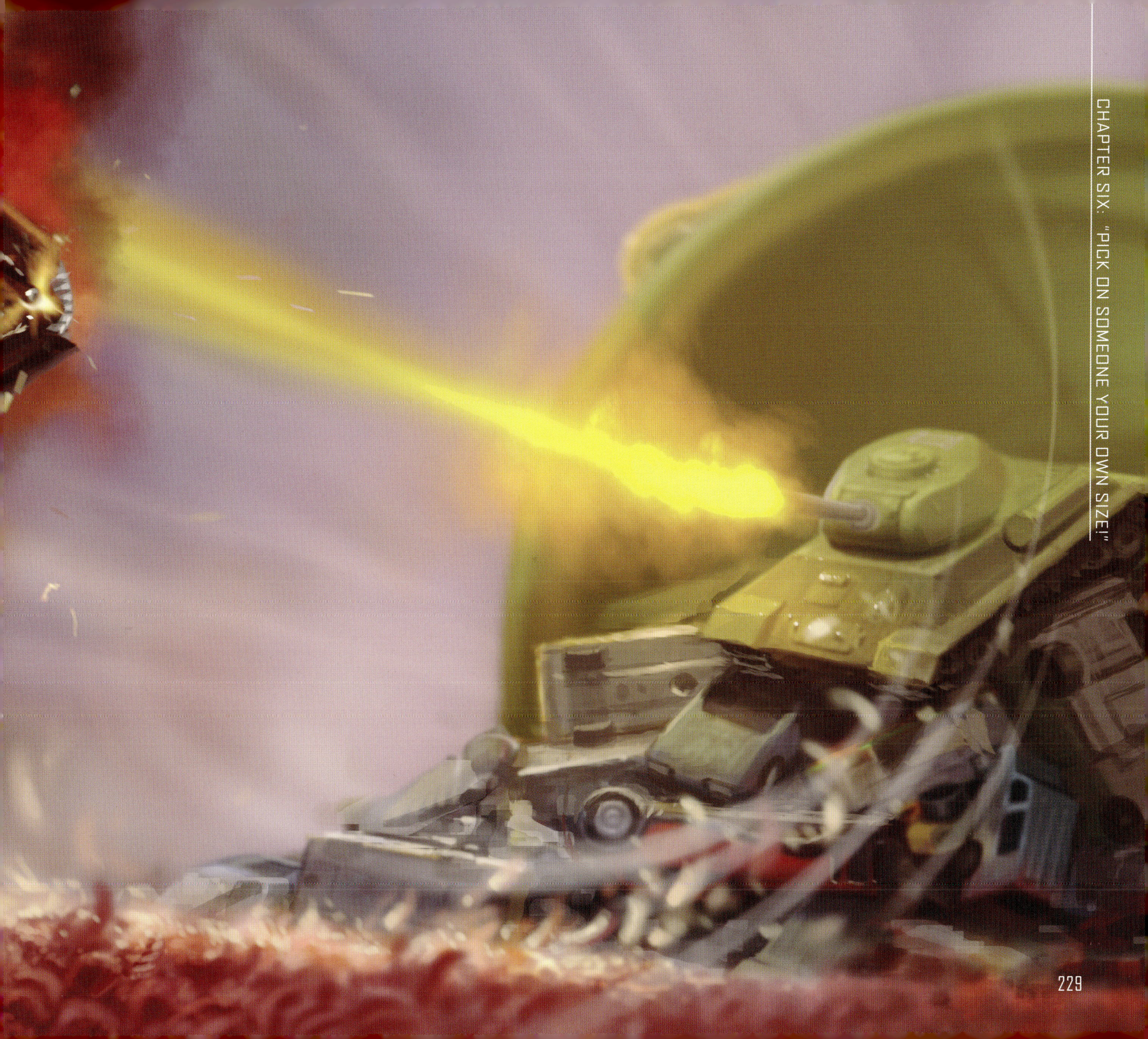

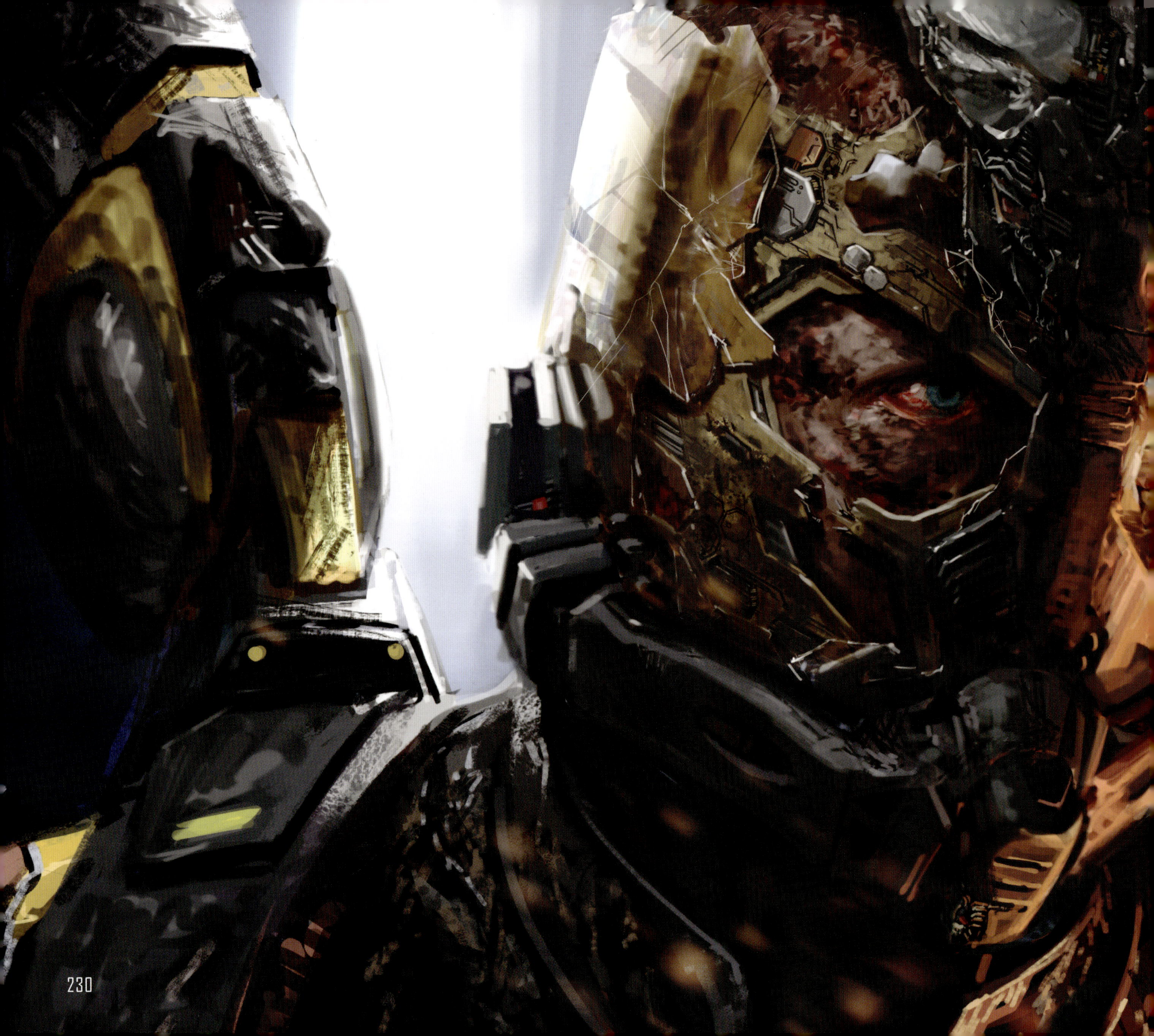

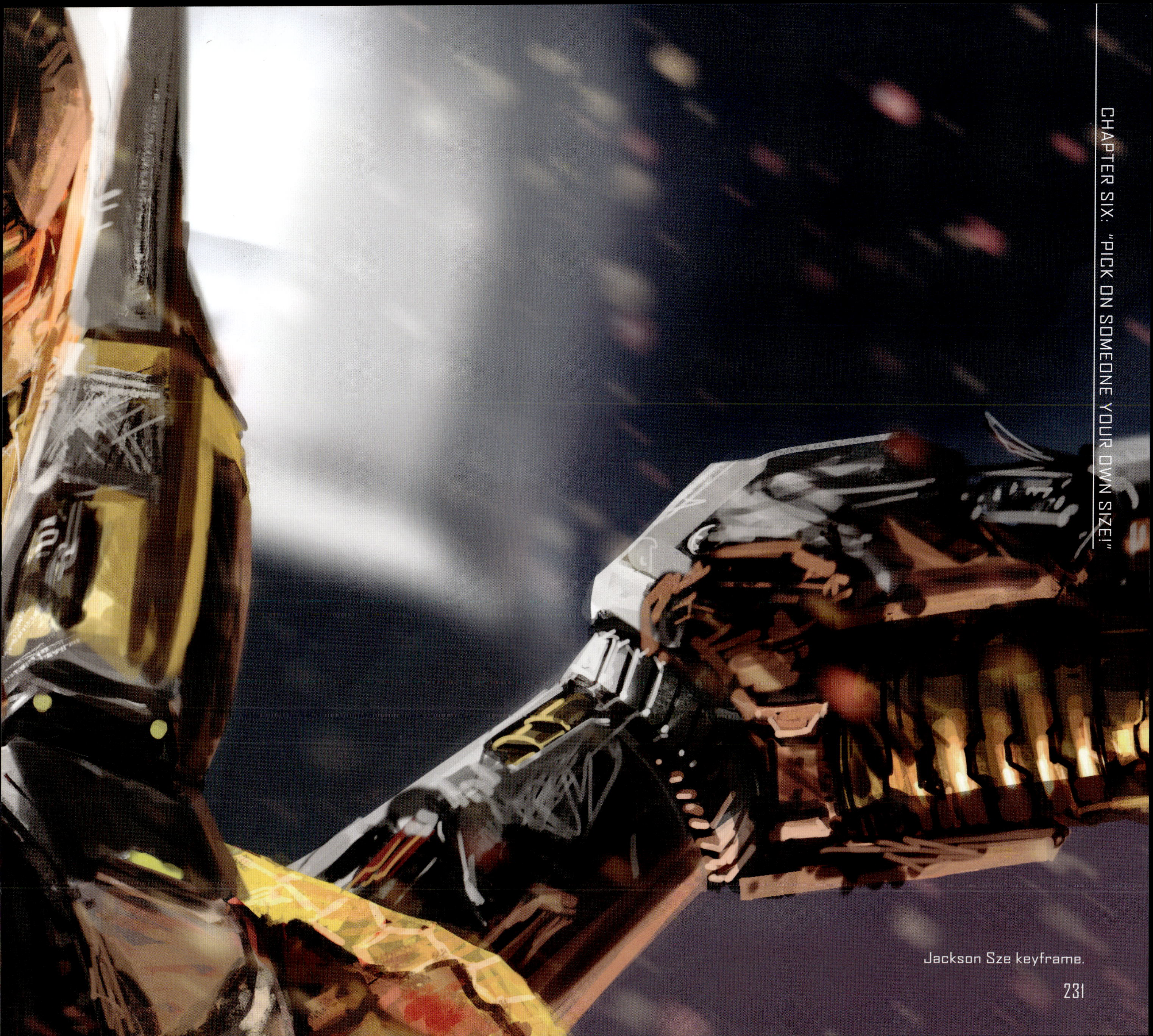

Jackson Sze keyframe.

INTO THE QUANTUM REALM

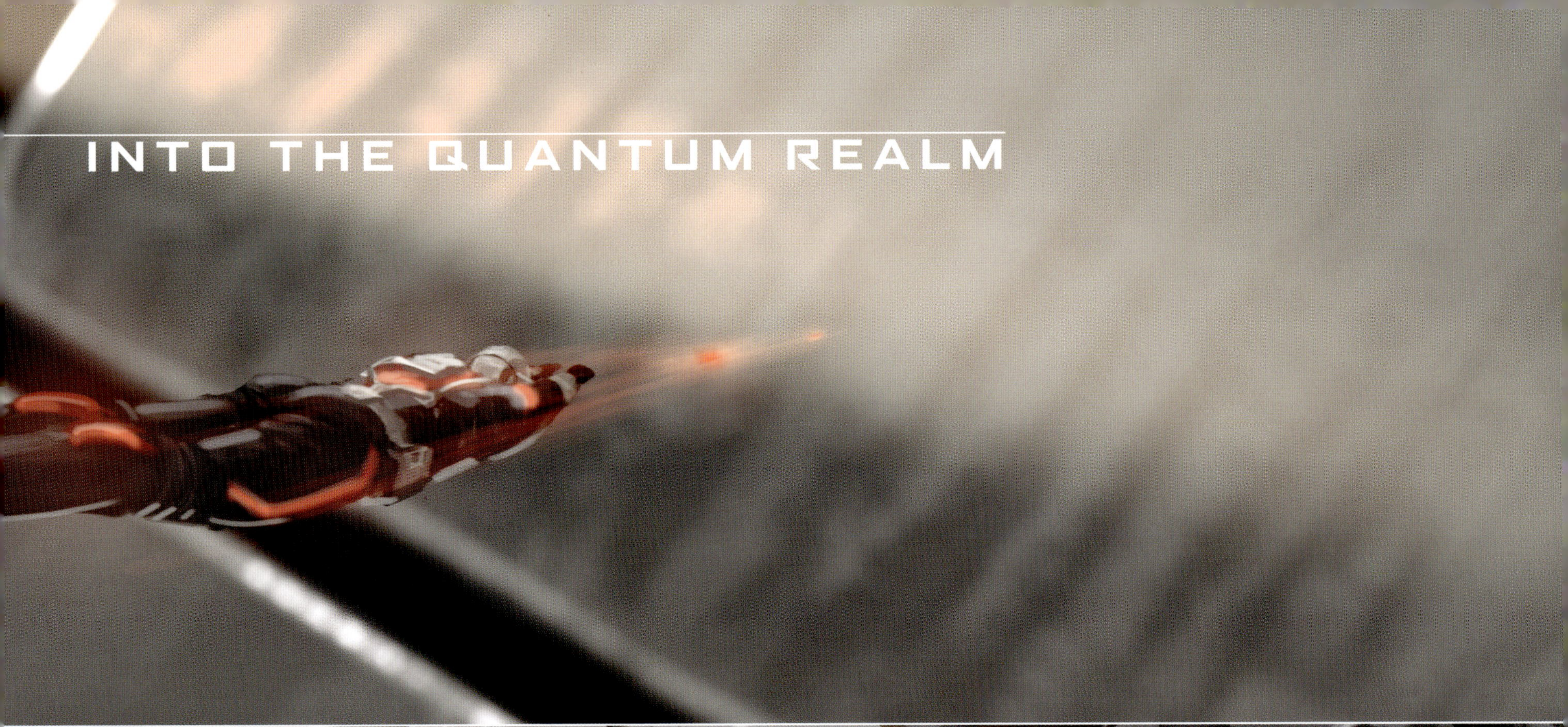

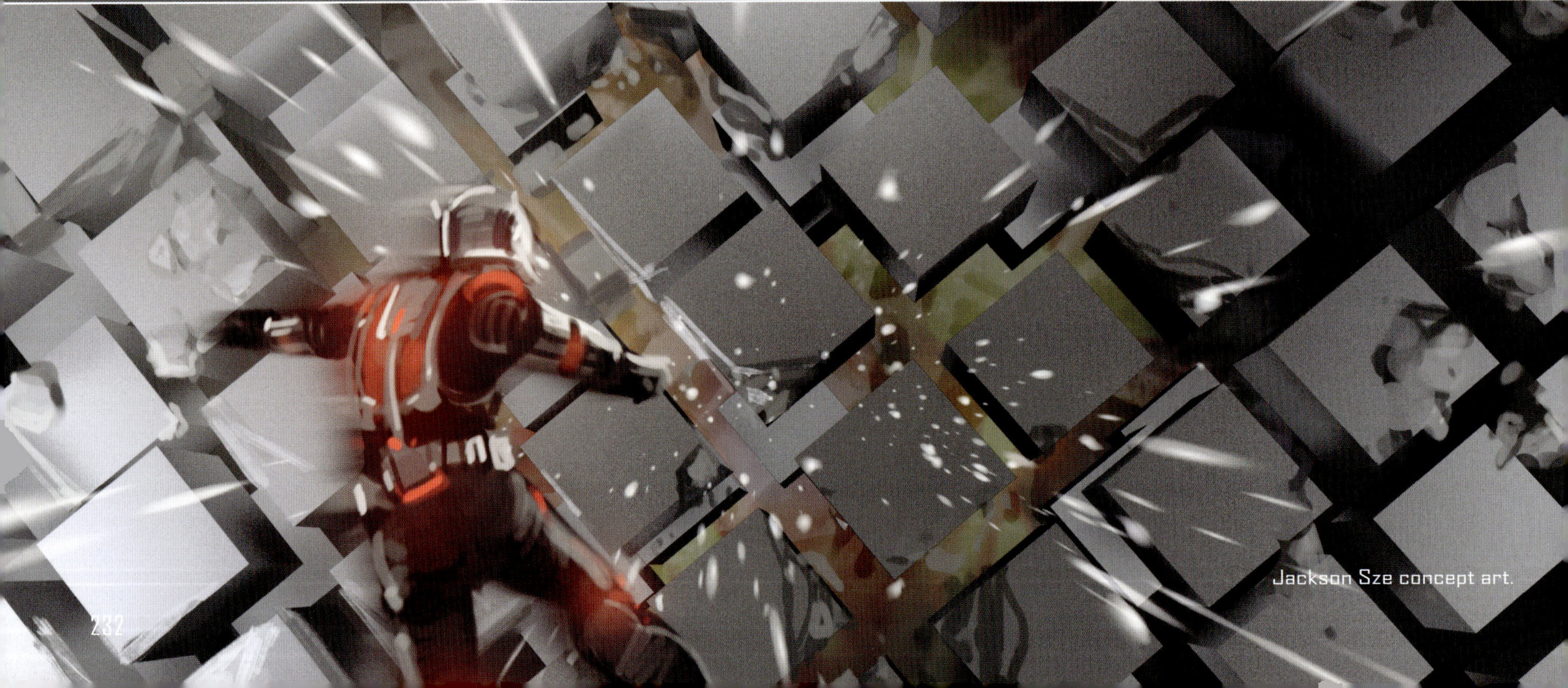

Jackson Sze concept art.

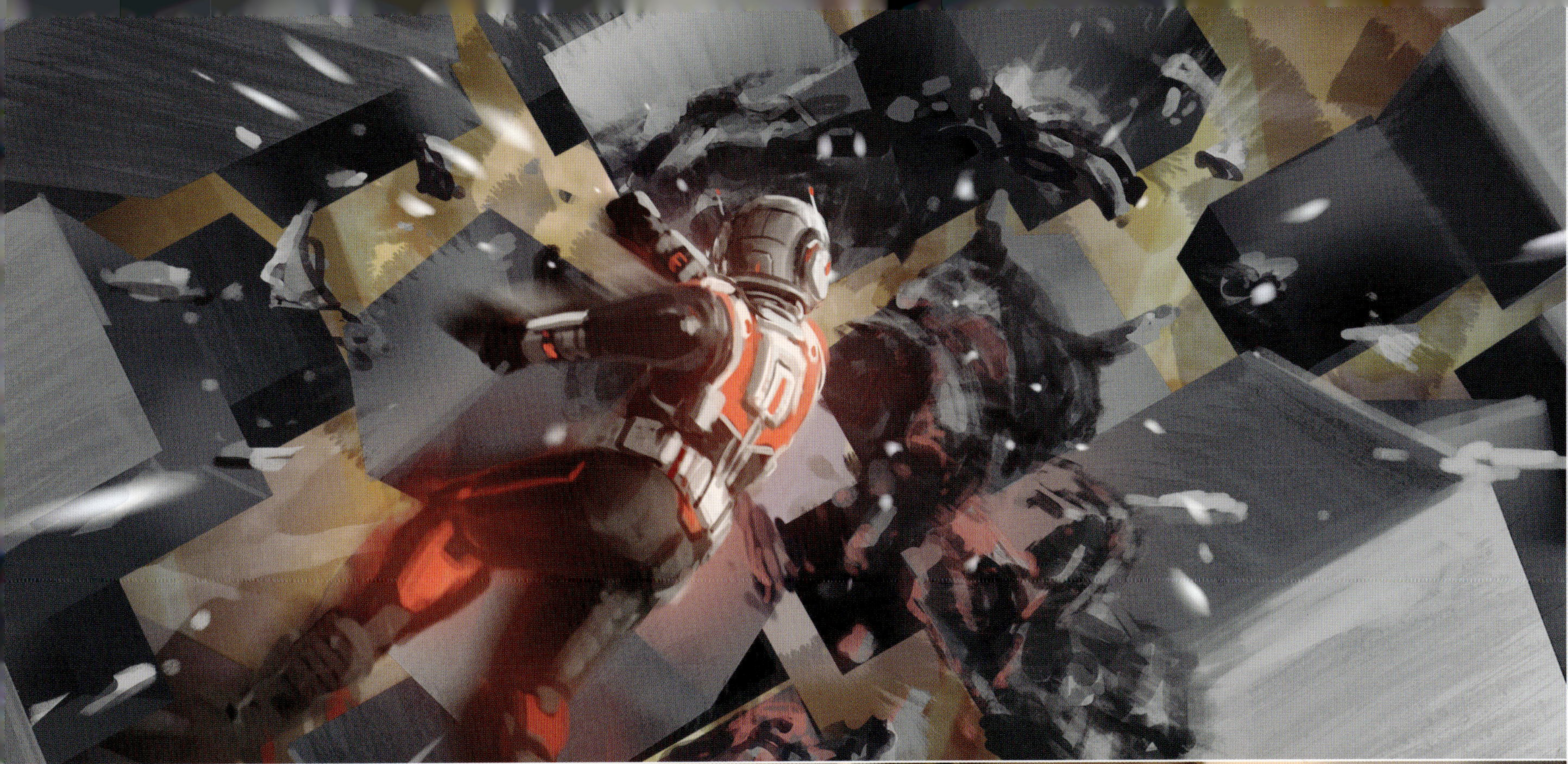

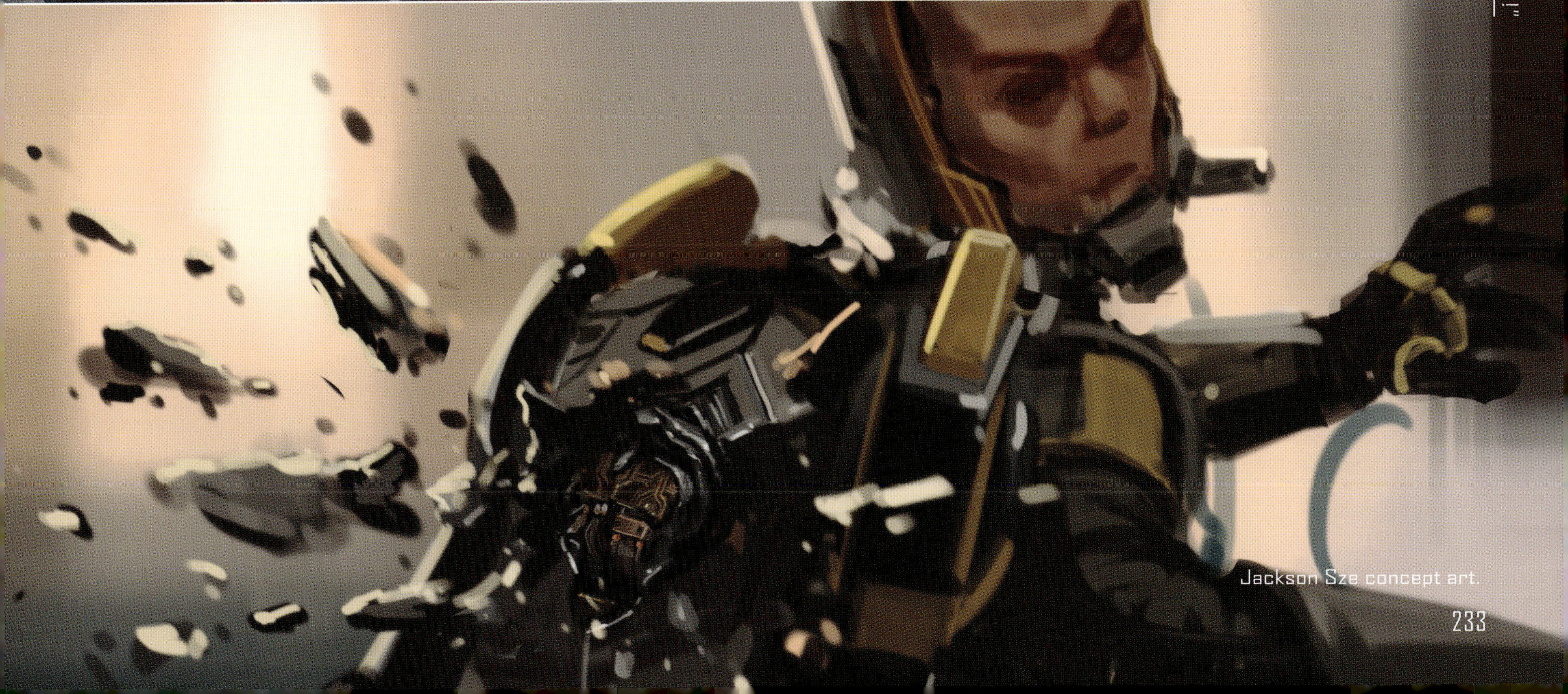

Jackson Sze concept art.

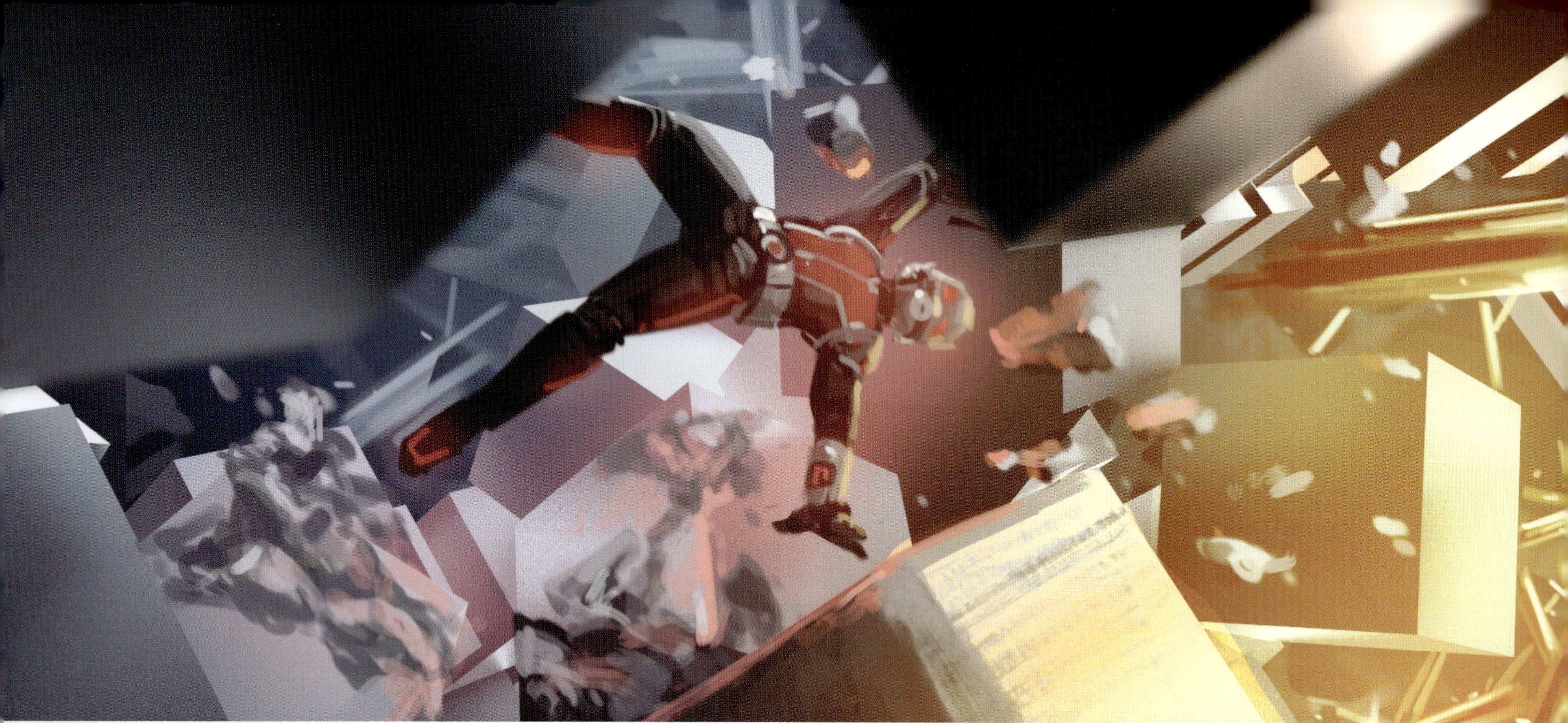

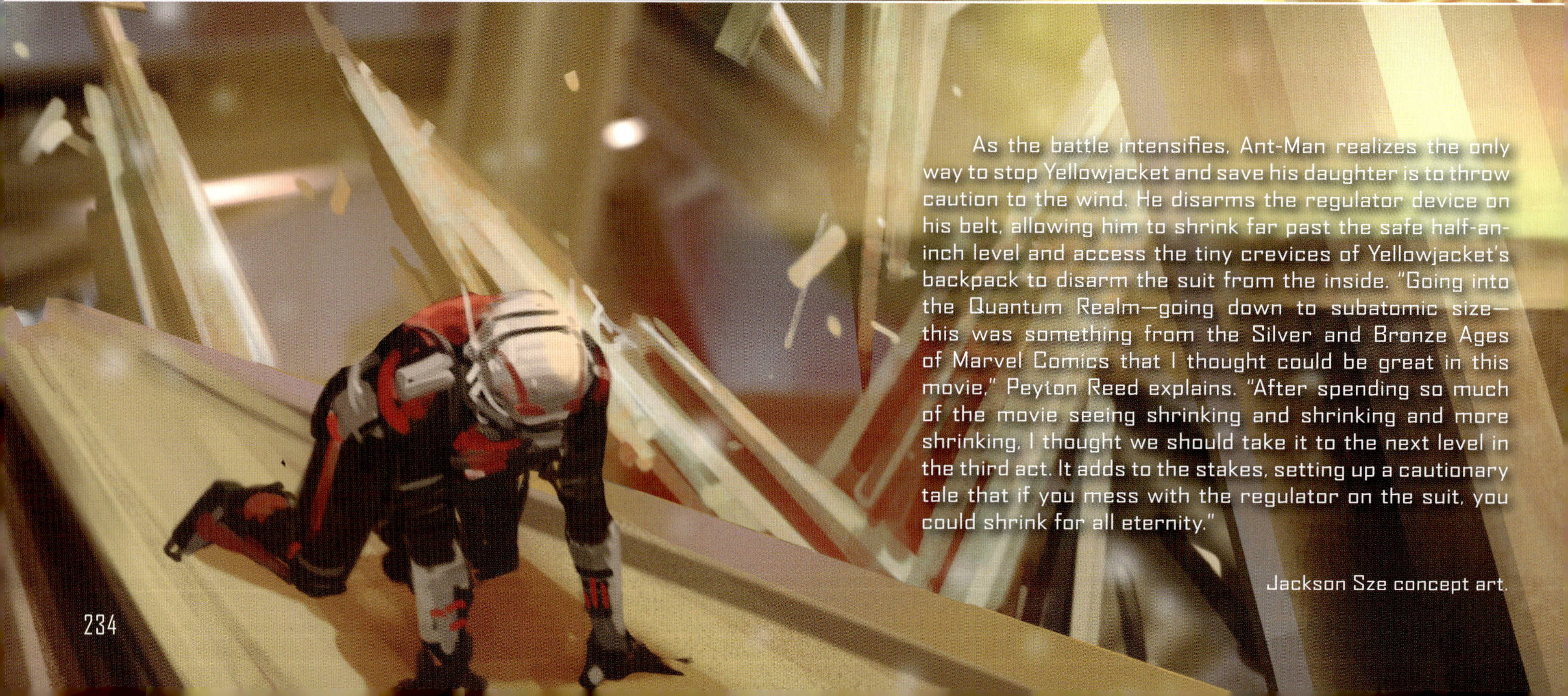

As the battle intensifies, Ant-Man realizes the only way to stop Yellowjacket and save his daughter is to throw caution to the wind. He disarms the regulator device on his belt, allowing him to shrink far past the safe half-an-inch level and access the tiny crevices of Yellowjacket's backpack to disarm the suit from the inside. "Going into the Quantum Realm—going down to subatomic size—this was something from the Silver and Bronze Ages of Marvel Comics that I thought could be great in this movie," Peyton Reed explains. "After spending so much of the movie seeing shrinking and shrinking and more shrinking, I thought we should take it to the next level in the third act. It adds to the stakes, setting up a cautionary tale that if you mess with the regulator on the suit, you could shrink for all eternity."

Jackson Sze concept art.

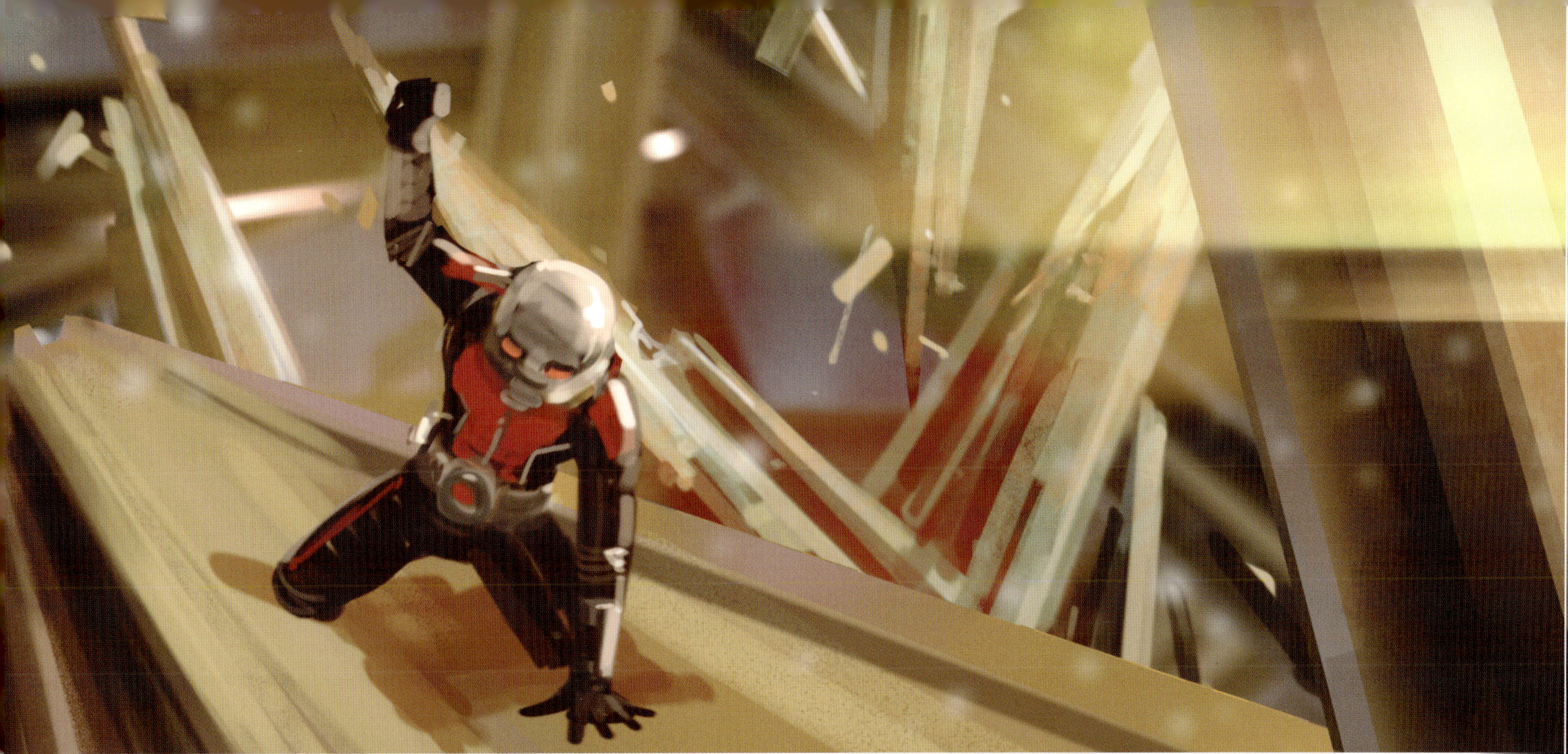

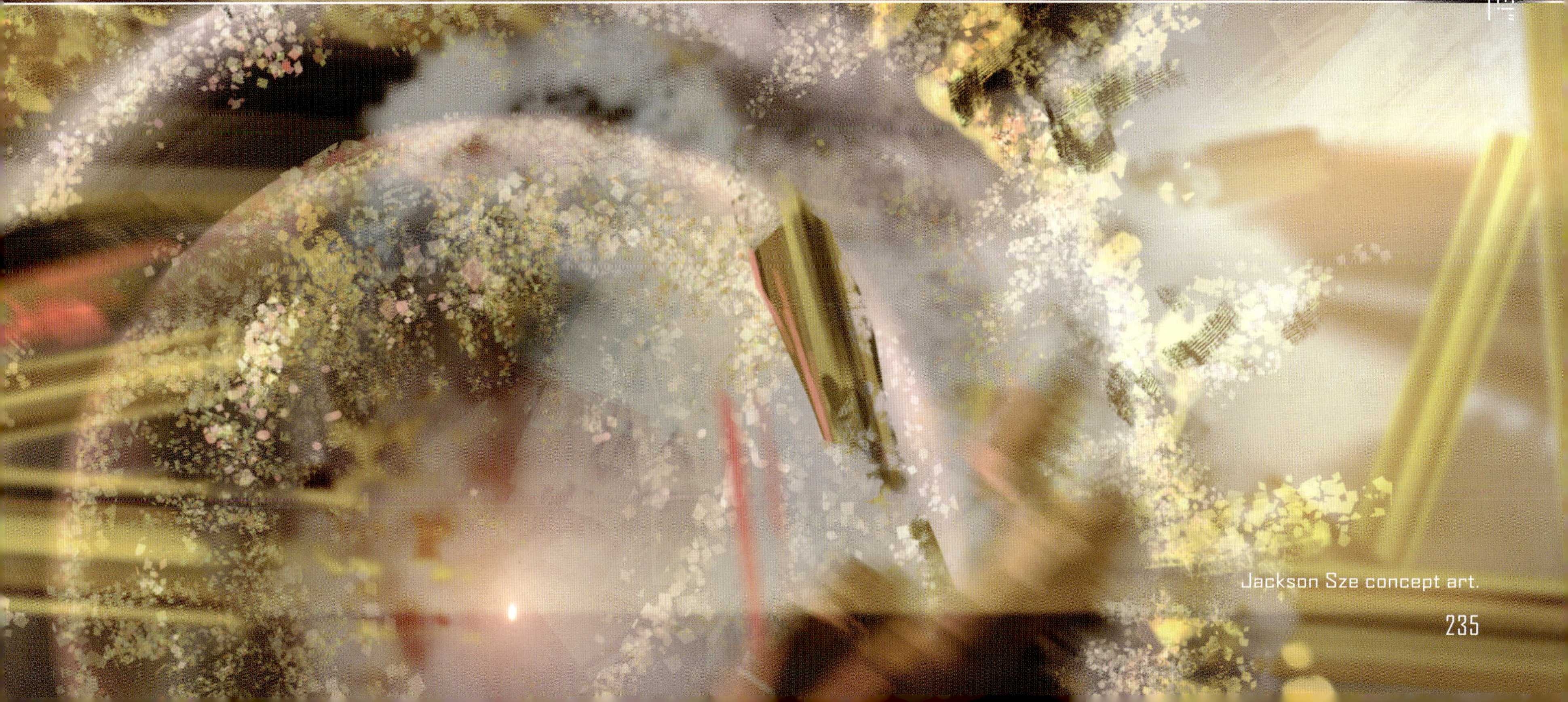

Jackson Sze concept art.

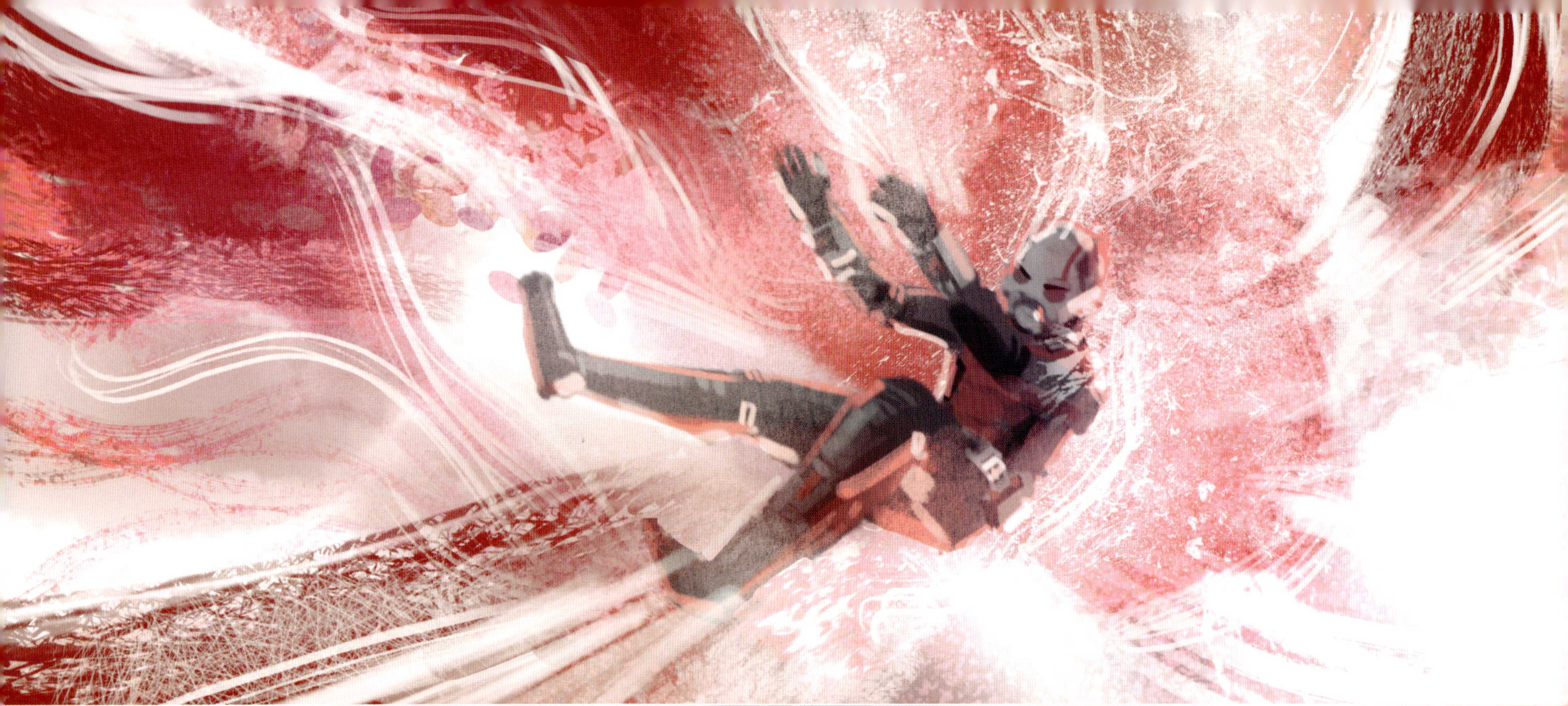

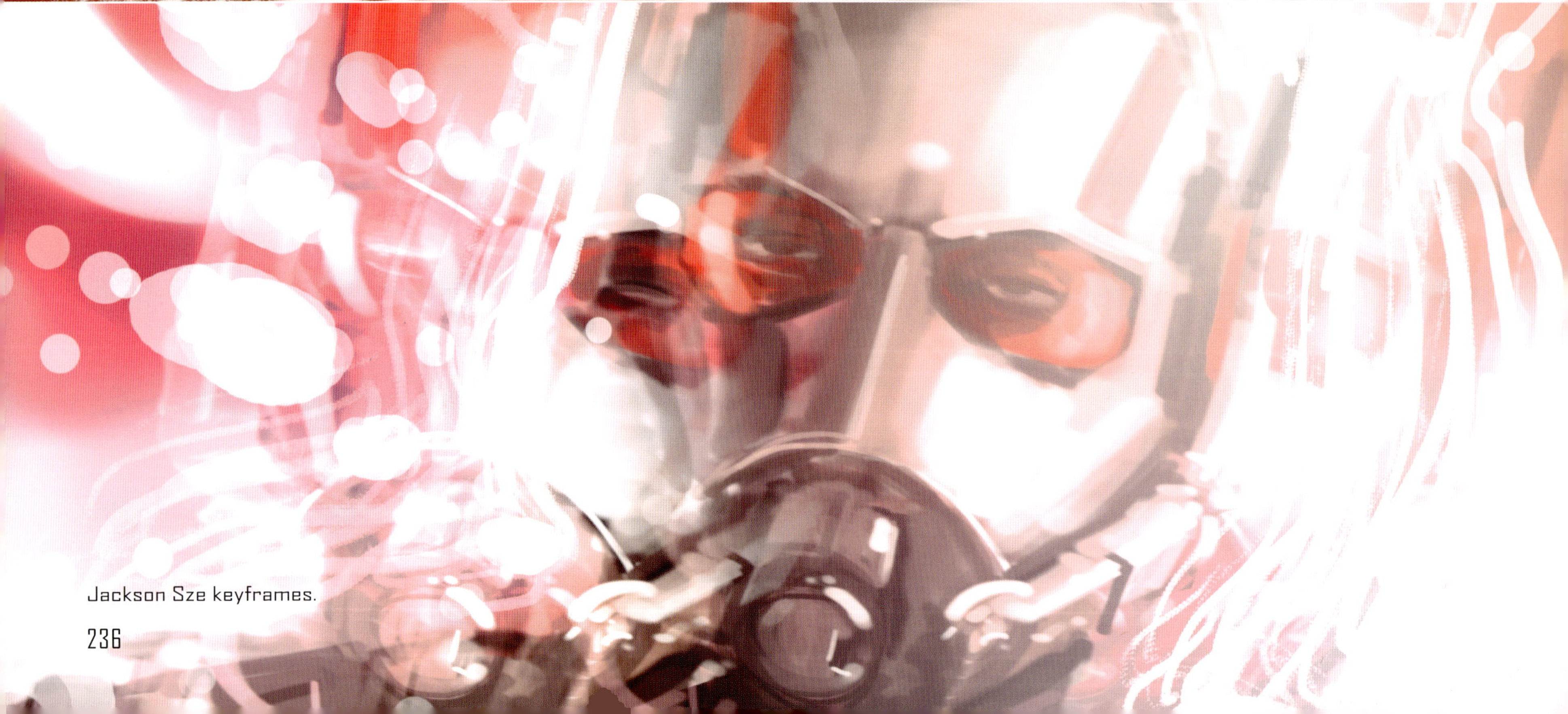

Jackson Sze keyframes.

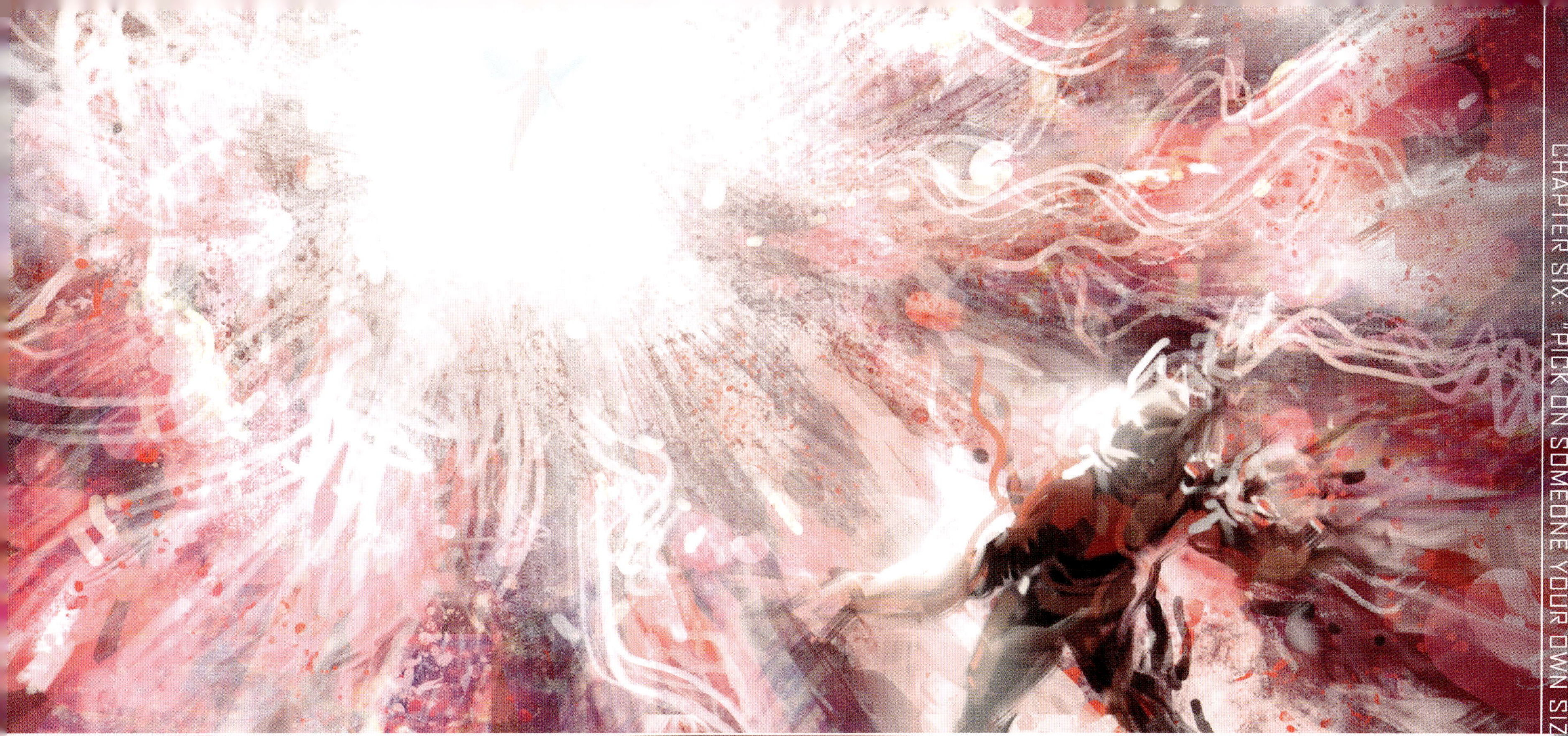

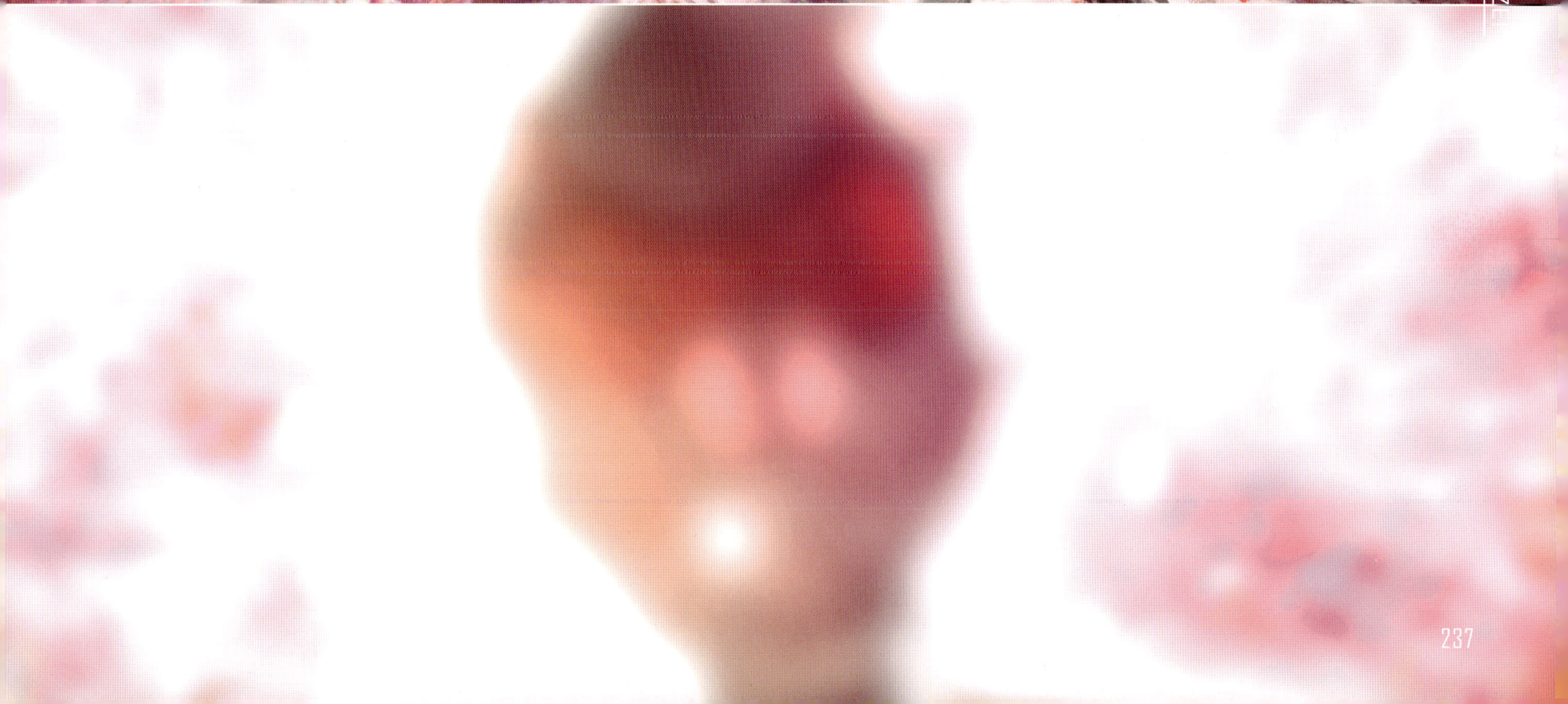

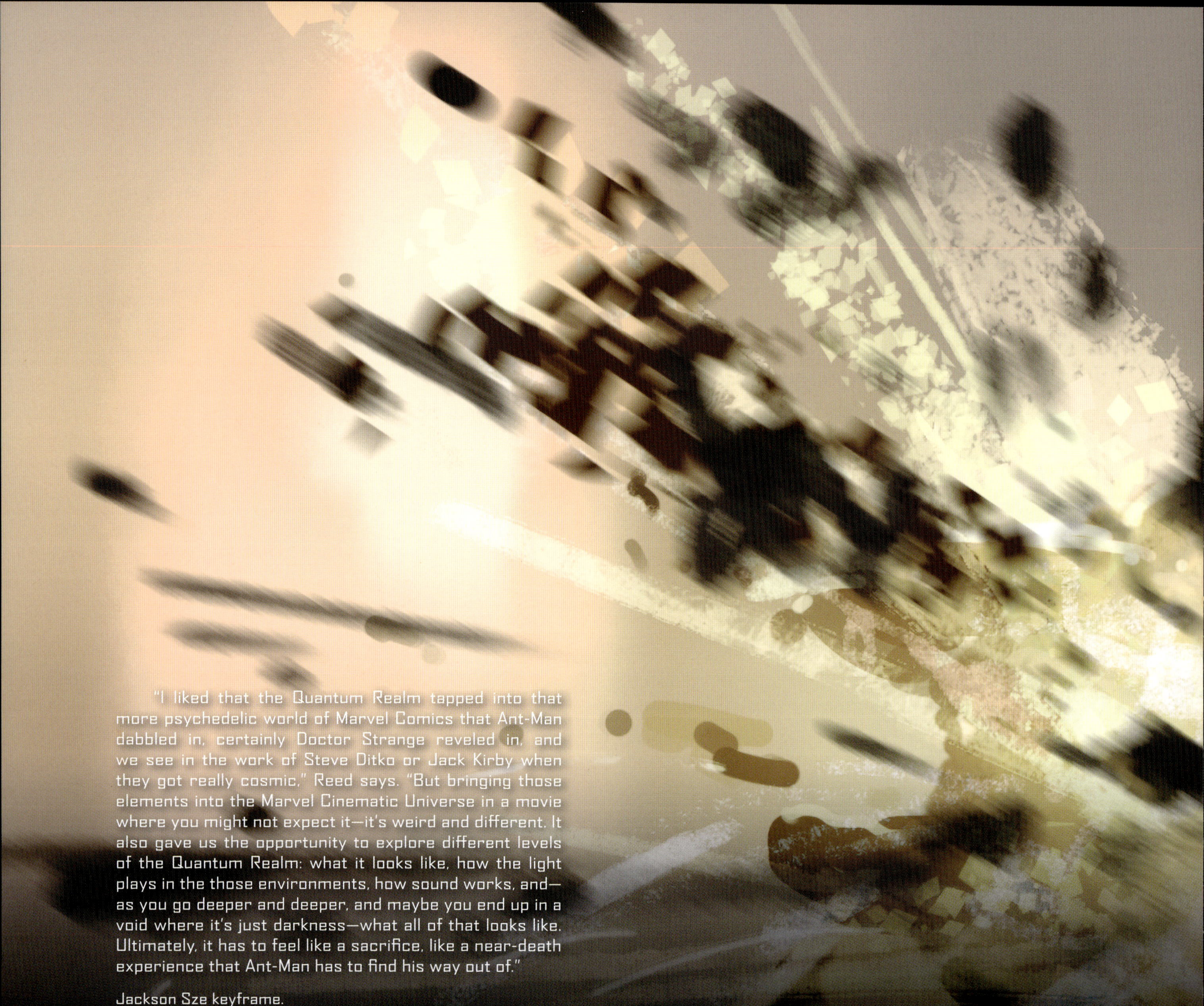

"I liked that the Quantum Realm tapped into that more psychedelic world of Marvel Comics that Ant-Man dabbled in, certainly Doctor Strange reveled in, and we see in the work of Steve Ditko or Jack Kirby when they got really cosmic," Reed says. "But bringing those elements into the Marvel Cinematic Universe in a movie where you might not expect it—it's weird and different. It also gave us the opportunity to explore different levels of the Quantum Realm: what it looks like, how the light plays in the those environments, how sound works, and—as you go deeper and deeper, and maybe you end up in a void where it's just darkness—what all of that looks like. Ultimately, it has to feel like a sacrifice, like a near-death experience that Ant-Man has to find his way out of."

Jackson Sze keyframe.

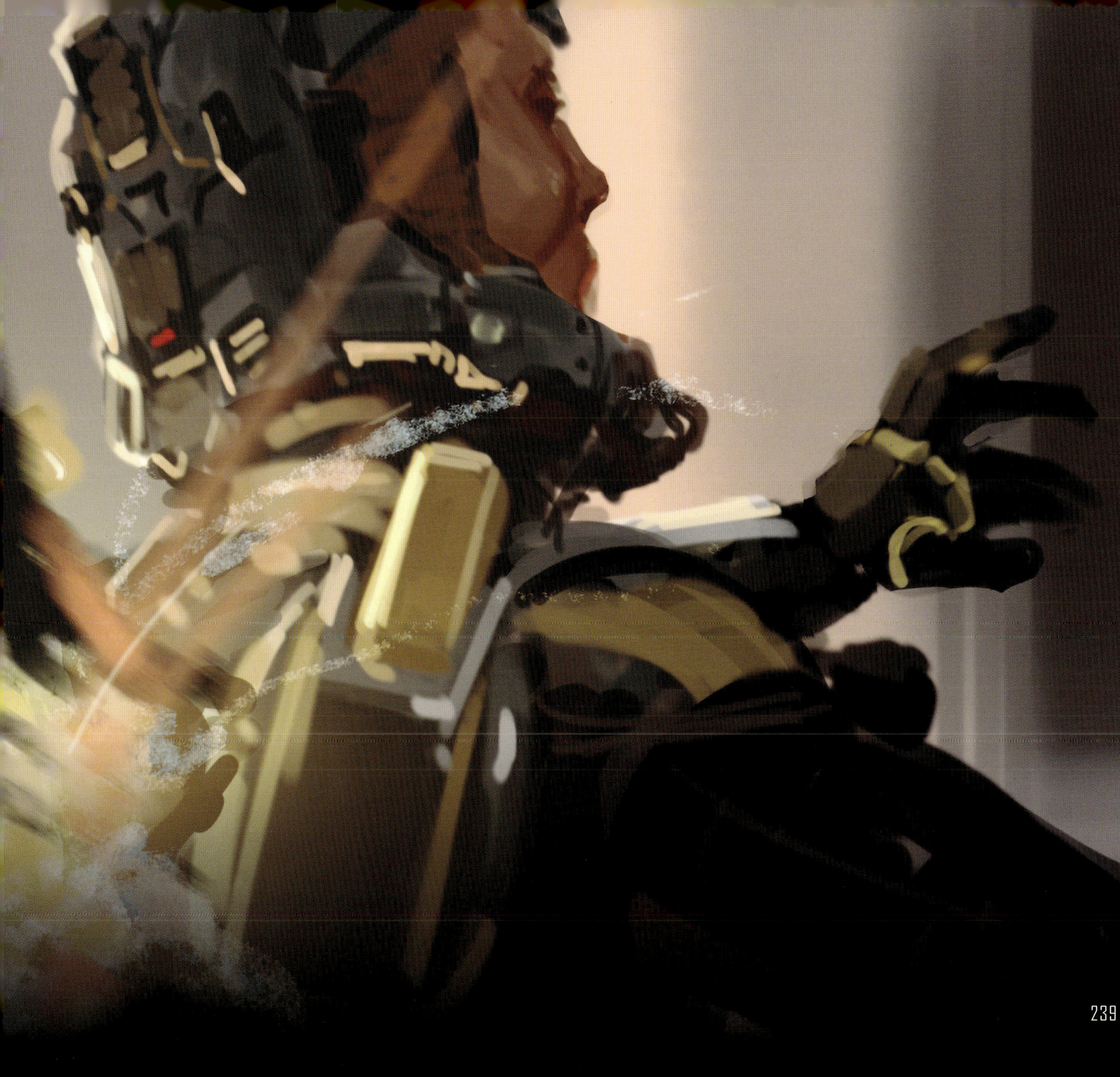

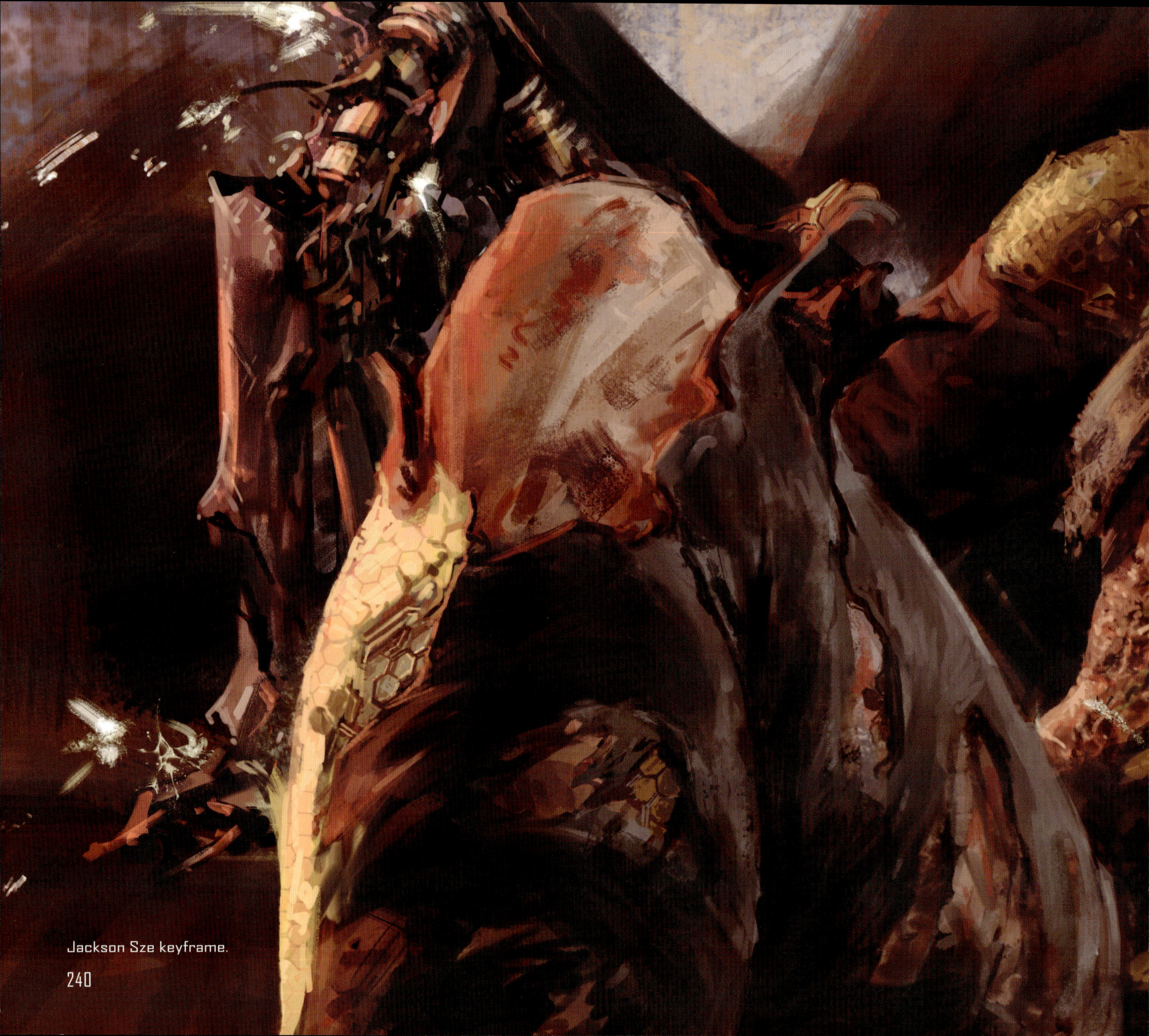

Jackson Sze keyframe.

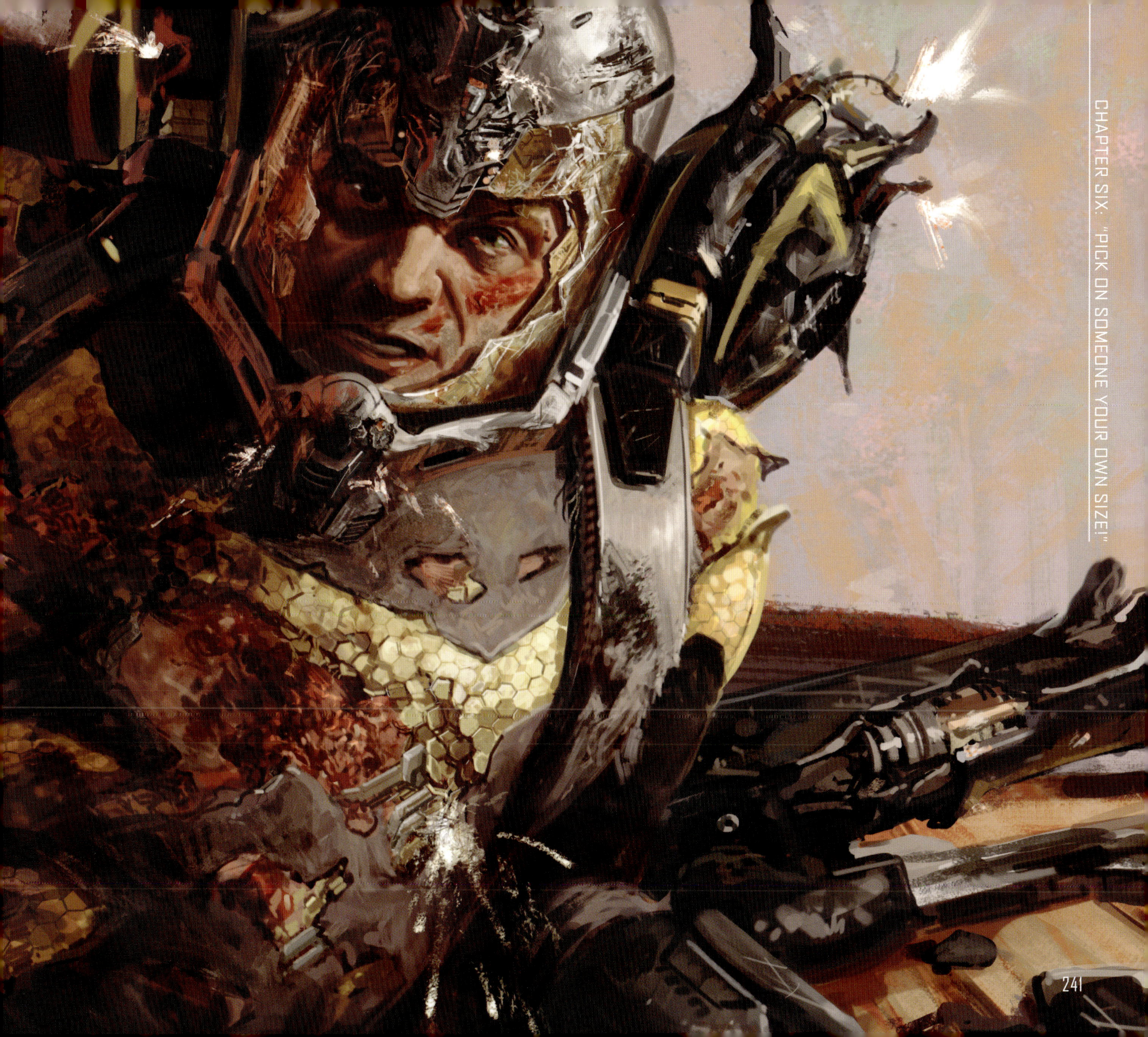

"I am not used to infusing humor into my paintings, so this was enjoyable to paint," Jackson Sze says. "Ant-Man is literally on top of the world! In his own perspective, of course. A tiny hero the world needs."

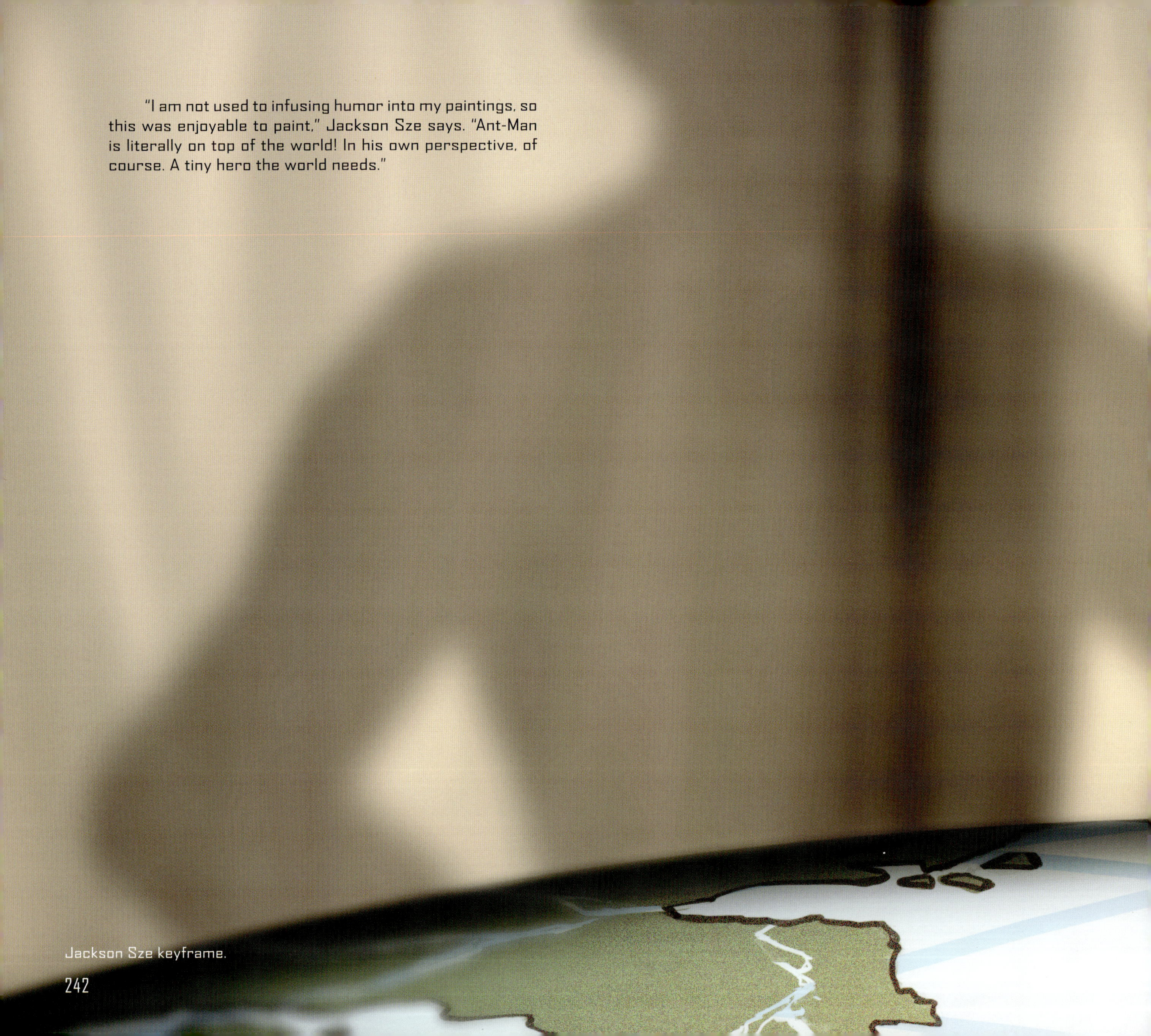

Jackson Sze keyframe.

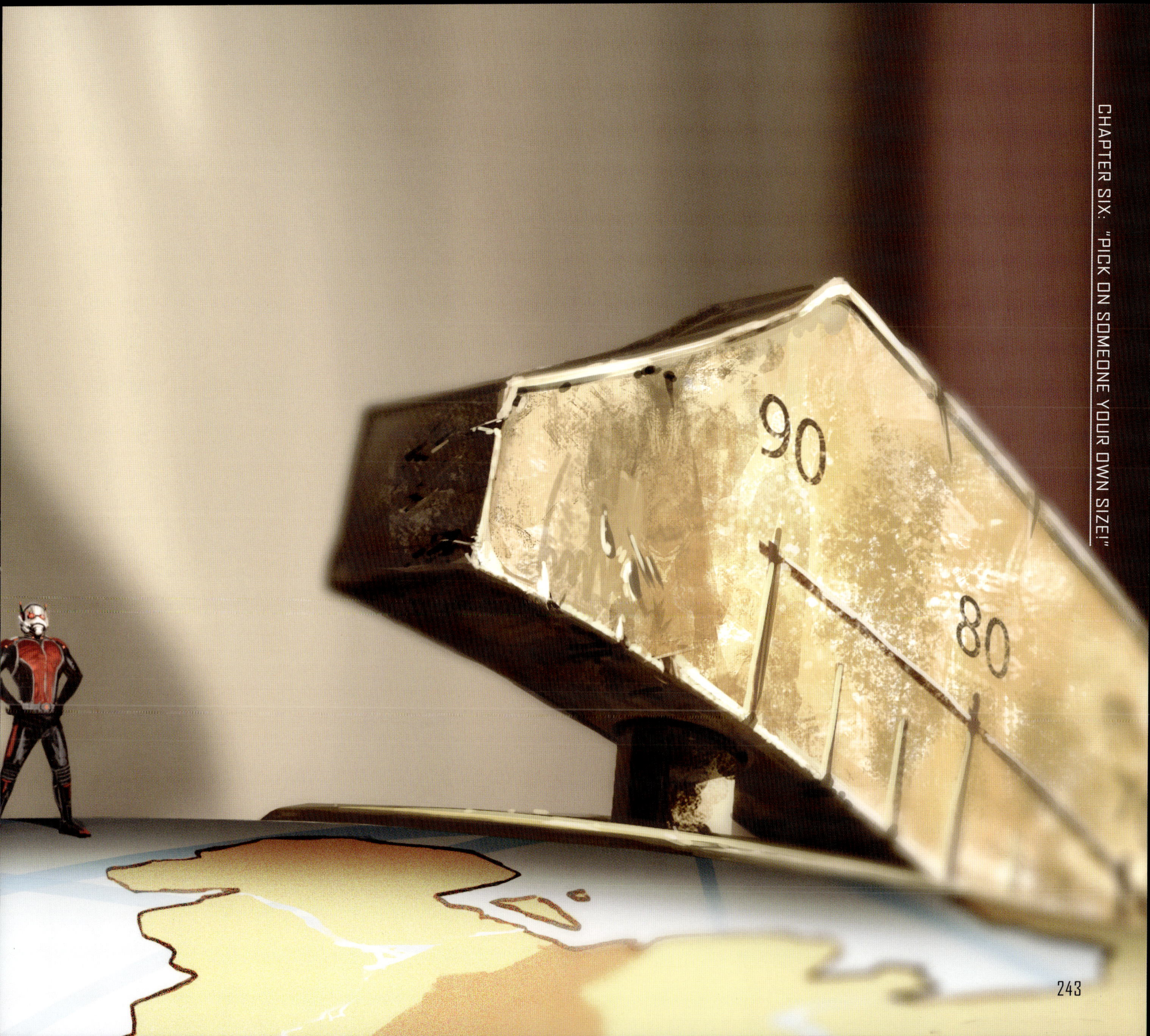
90
80

CHAPTER SEVEN

NO HAMMER. NO SHIELD. NO PROBLEM!

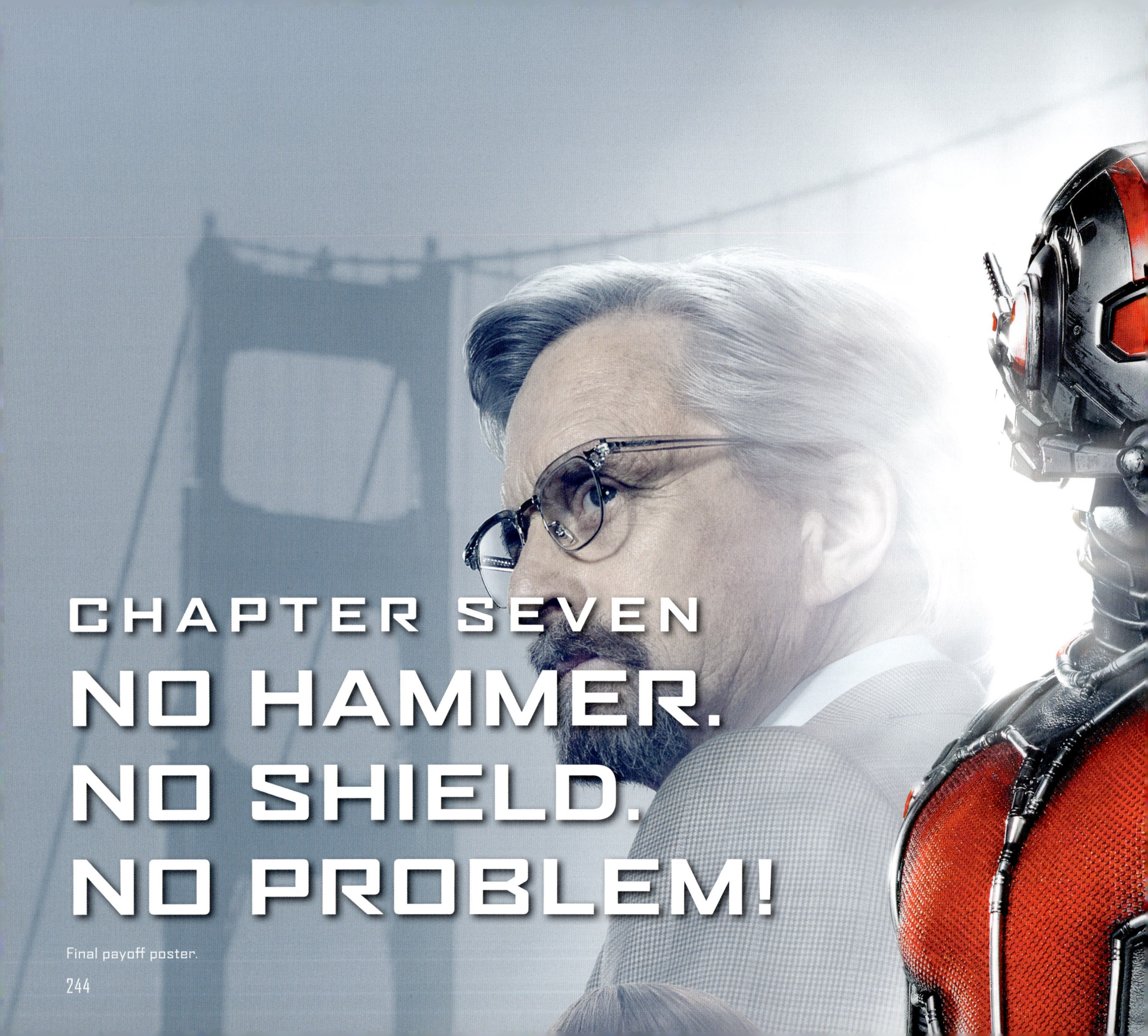

Final payoff poster.

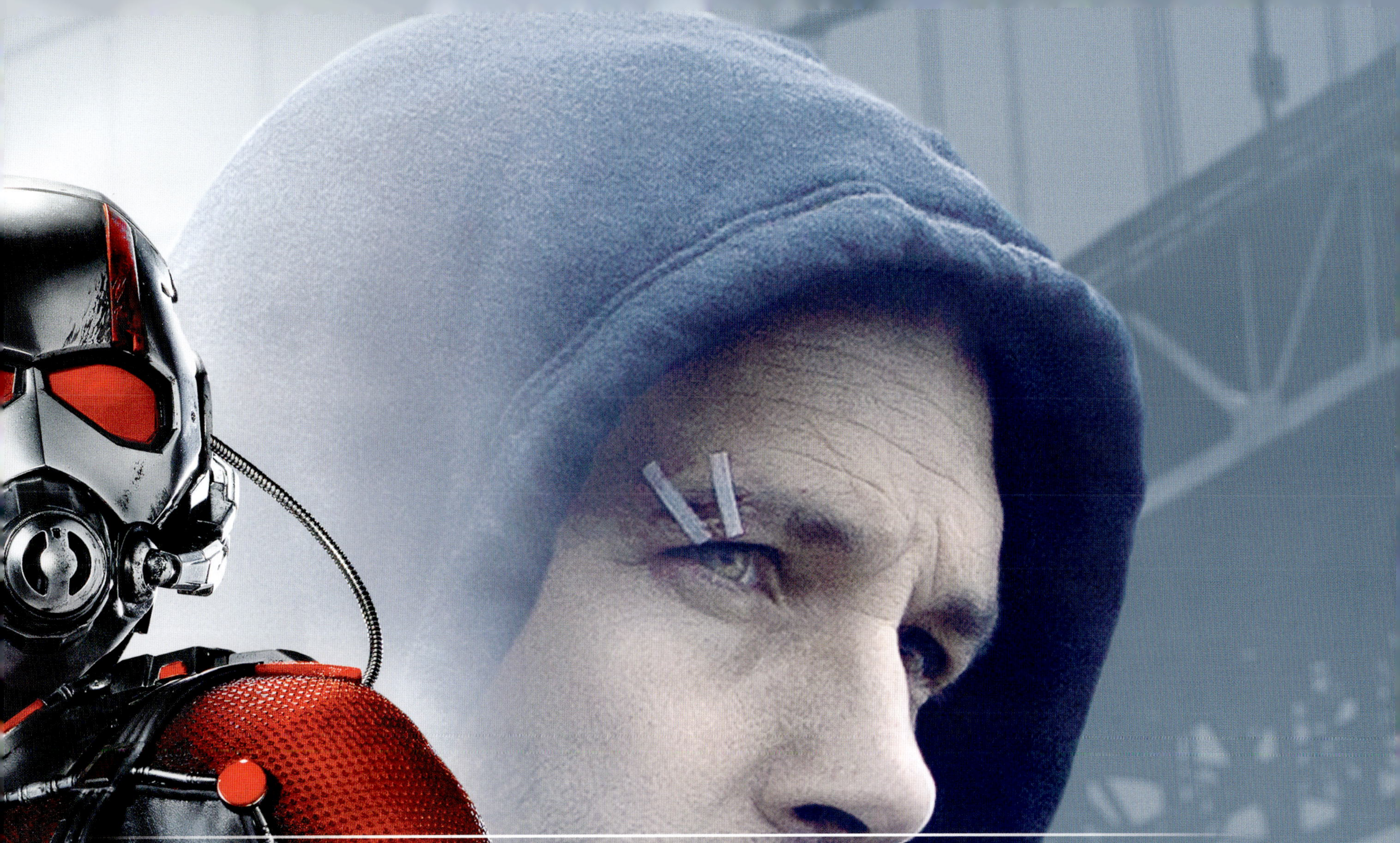

While the world had caught a glimpse of the Ant-Man costume in footage from a preliminary visual-effects test shown at the 2013 San Diego Comic-Con, the true reveal came in Andy Park's poster for the 2014 convention. Before settling on a final design, Park sketched a few rough thumbnails to capture the tone, action, and fun of Ant-Man. In the end, it was a combination of ideas from these early designs that translated into the final layout.

"I started out my career as a comic-book artist, so being able to illustrate the official San Diego Comic-Con poster for the Ant-Man film was a huge honor," Park says. "I've been lucky enough to participate alongside Ryan Meinerding and Charlie Wen on *Marvel's The Avengers* posters, as well as the latest *Avengers: Age of Ultron* posters. The approach we take with these illustrations is to essentially make them look like an amalgamation of a classic comic-book cover with an iconic movie poster. With this poster, I knew I wanted to demonstrate his growing/shrinking ability, as well as showcase Paul Rudd and Michael Douglas. Getting to include Ant-Man riding on a flying ant was a bonus. I wasn't sure if they wanted to reveal that he was going to do that, but I did include it in my thumbnail roughs. Thankfully they were totally on board with it. The Comic-Con posters are especially gratifying because they are often the first reveal of the characters in full costume. And I was happy that it was all well received by the fans."

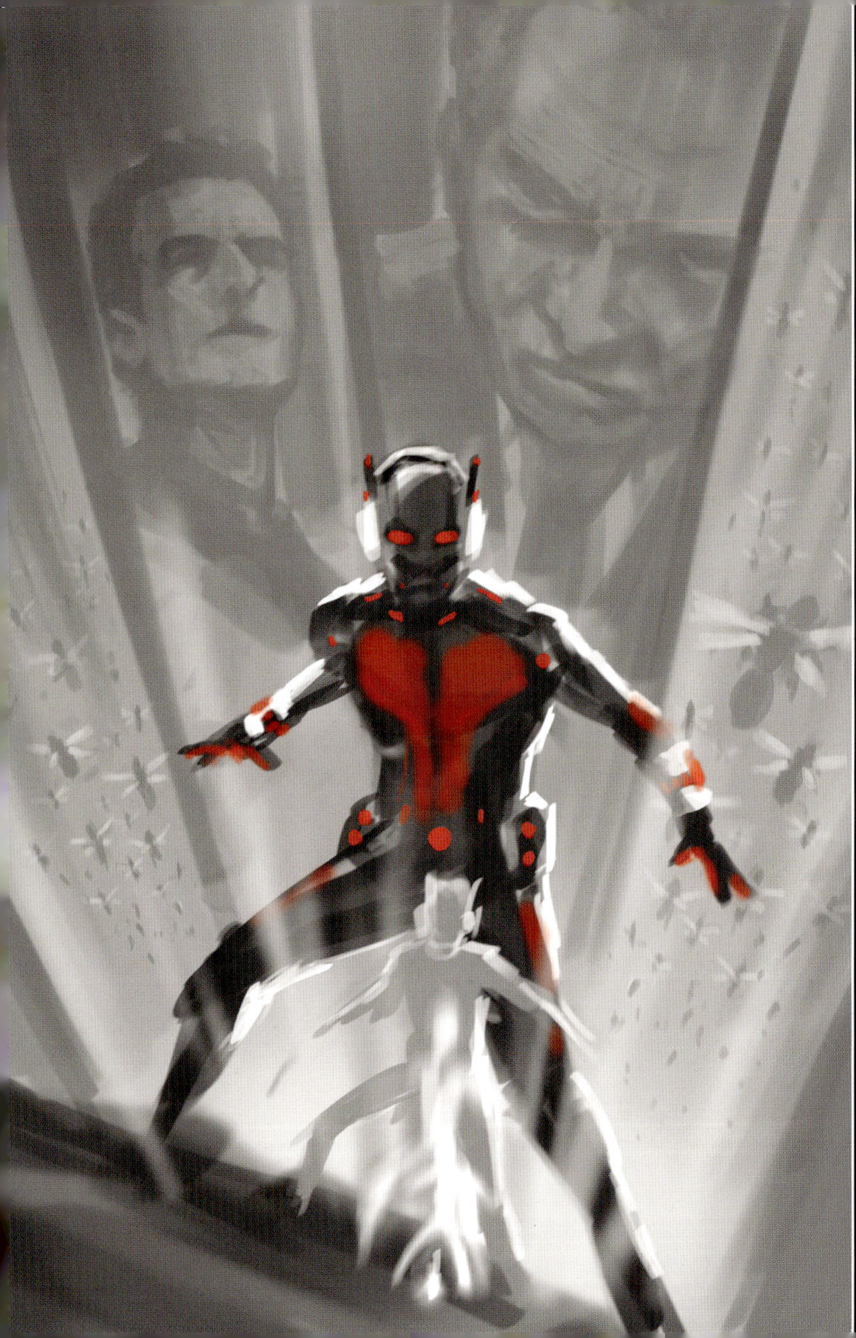
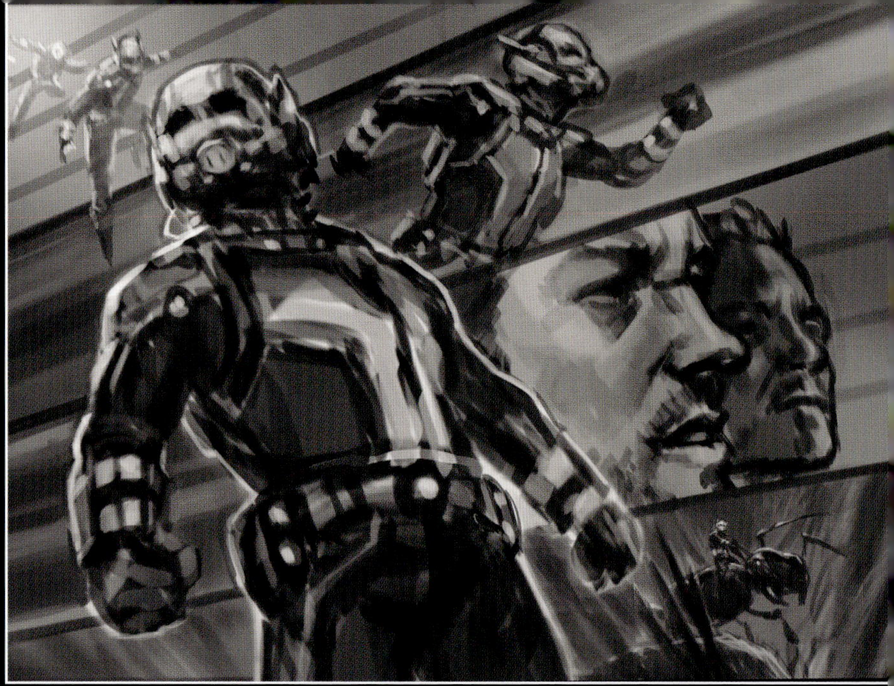
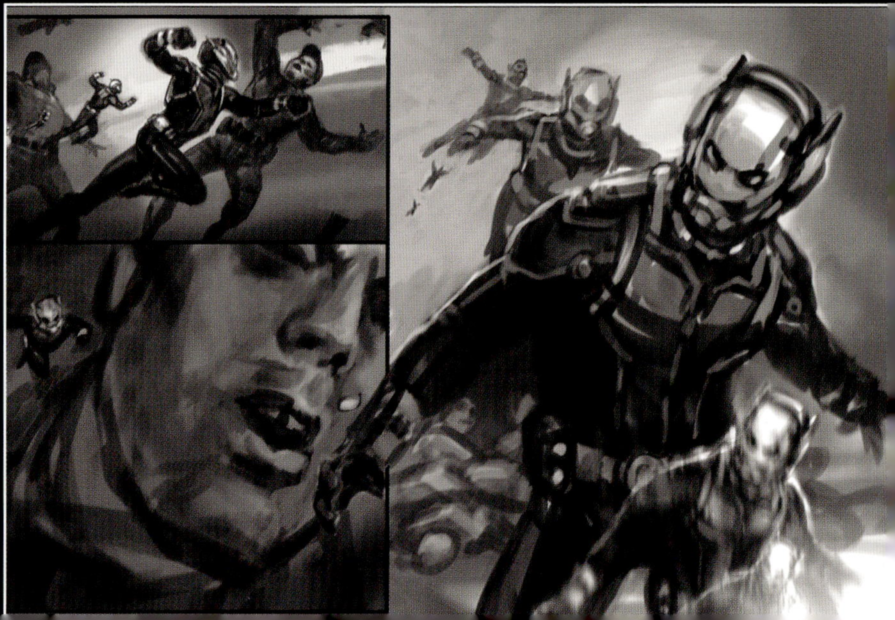

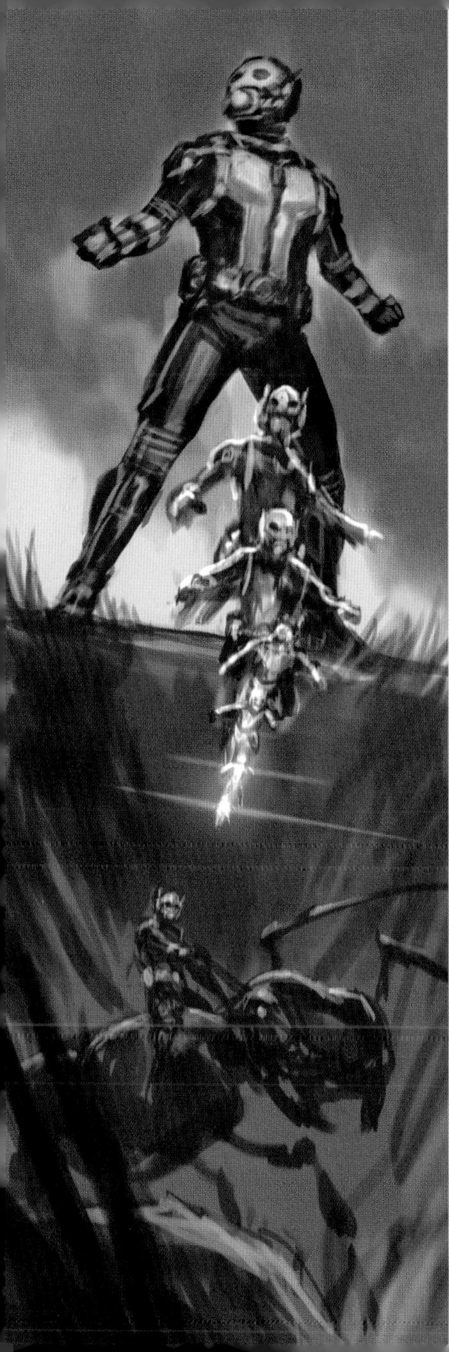

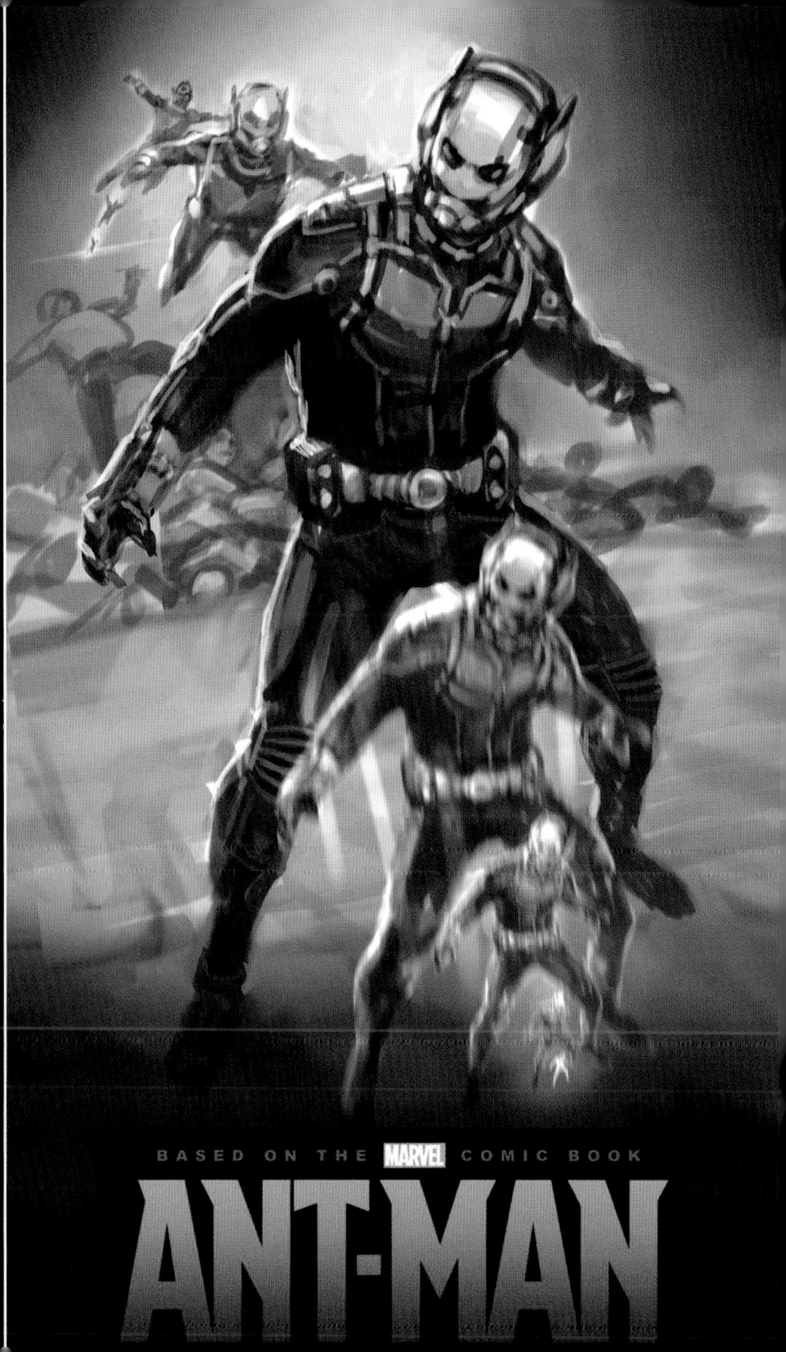
BASED ON THE MARVEL COMIC BOOK
ANT-MAN

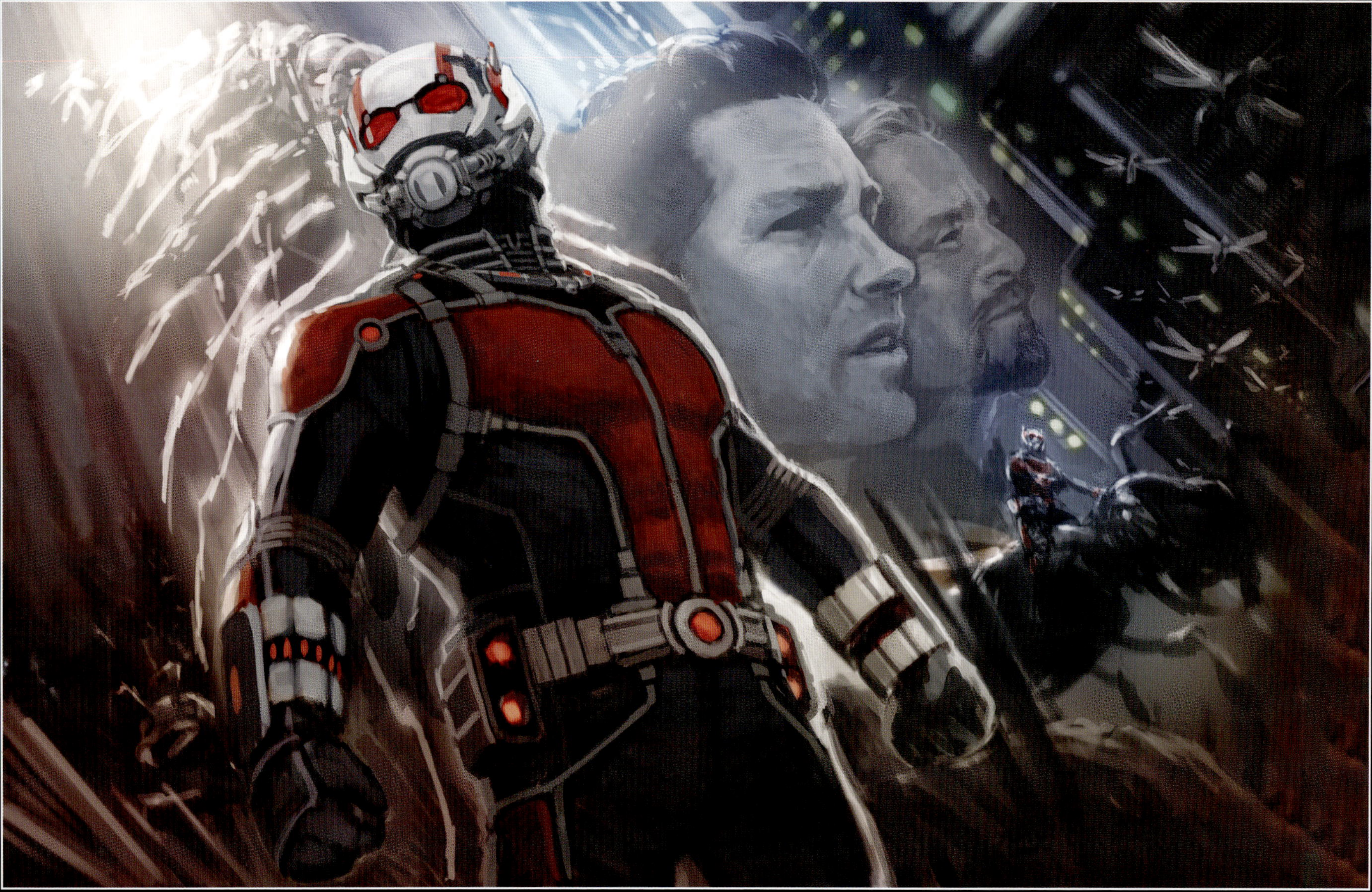

Rough for the San Diego Comic-Con collectible poster by Andy Park.

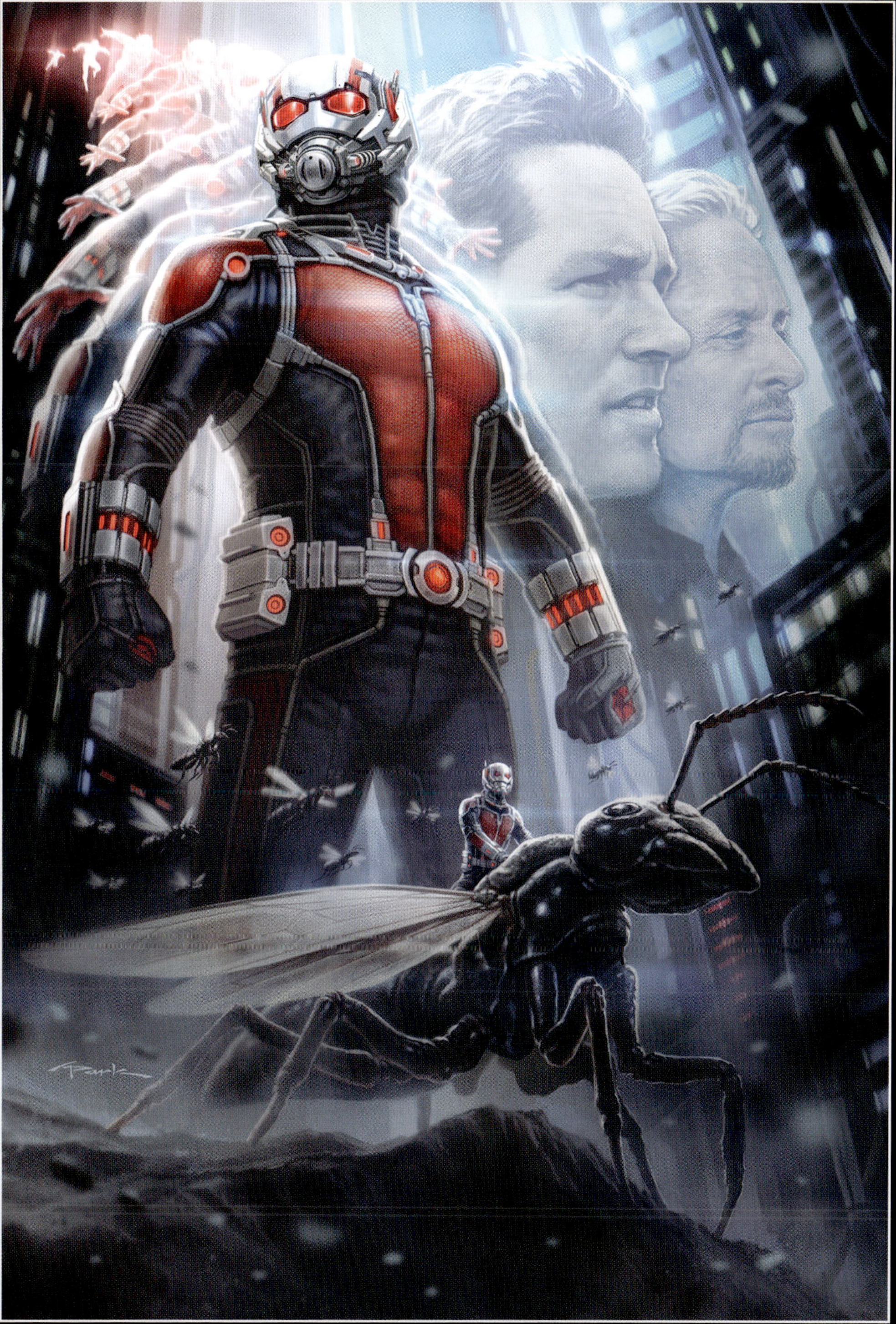

Final Comic-Con poster ar
by Andy Park.

CONTRIBUTOR BIOS 2015

Director ***Peyton Reed*** gained national attention with his feature debut *Bring It On*. The film won critical raves and opened at #1 with a $17.4 million weekend. It stayed in the top 10 for seven consecutive weeks, becoming the sleeper hit of summer 2000. It went on to sell over five million copies on DVD, spawning both a successful franchise for Universal and, most recently, a Broadway musical. Reed followed it up with 2003's *Down with Love*, a visually stunning homage to the Rock Hudson/Doris Day sex comedies of the early sixties. The film was critically acclaimed and has become a cult favorite. In 2006, Reed helmed the smash hit *The Break-Up*. The comedy/drama debuted at #1 with a $39 million opening weekend and went on to gross over $200 million worldwide. It was Universal's highest-grossing film of 2006. 2008 saw Reed direct *Yes Man*, which opened at #1 domestically and became a worldwide hit, grossing over $225 million globally. Originally from Raleigh, and a graduate of the University of North Carolina, Reed began shooting Super 8 film at the age of 13. He started his career as a documentary editor at ZM Productions. After writing and directing the award-winning short *Almost Beat* in 1989, he directed a series of high-profile, behind-the-scenes documentaries, including *The Secrets of the Back to the Future Trilogy*, *Through the Eyes of Forrest Gump*, and *The Honeymooners Anniversary Special*. Reed went on to bring his wry wit and keen sense of visual invention to an incredibly diverse range of projects, from critically-hailed comedic television (CBS's *The Weird Al Show*, HBO's *Mr. Show with Bob and David*, Comedy Central's *Upright Citizens Brigade*, Fox's *New Girl*) to music videos (She & Him, Superchunk, The Connells) to numerous commercials (Gap with Sarah Jessica Parker, Target with Isaac Mizrahi and Cisco with Ellen Page). *Ant-Man* marks his first time working with insects.

Over the past decade, Producer and Marvel Studios President **Kevin Feige** has played an instrumental role in a string of blockbuster feature films adapted from the pages of Marvel comic books. In his current role, Feige oversees all creative aspects of the company's feature film and home entertainment activities. In addition to producing Marvel's *Avengers: Age of Ultron*, he is currently producing *Ant-Man*. His previous producing credits for Marvel include *Iron Man 3*, which became the second-largest box office debut in Hollywood history behind the critically acclaimed *Marvel's The Avengers*, which Kevin also produced along with *Guardians of the Galaxy*, *Captain America: The Winter Soldier*, *Thor: The Dark World*, *Thor*, *Captain America: The First Avenger*, *Iron Man 2*, and *Iron Man*.

Executive Producer and Marvel Studios Co-President **Louis D'Esposito** served as executive producer on the blockbuster hits *Iron Man*, *Iron Man 2*, *Thor*, *Captain America: The First Avenger*, *Marvel's The Avengers*, *Iron Man 3*, *Thor: The Dark World*, *Captain America: The Winter Soldier*, and most recently *Avengers: Age of Ultron*. He is currently working on *Ant-Man*, as well as collaborating with Marvel Studios President Kevin Feige to build the future Marvel slate. As co-president of the studio and executive producer on all Marvel films, D'Esposito balances running the studio to overseeing each film from its development stage to distribution. Beyond his role as co-president, D'Esposito also directs unique filmed projects for the studio, including his Marvel One-Shot titled *Agent Carter* starring Hayley Atwell, and the short film titled *Item 47*. The project was released as an added feature on *Marvel's The Avengers* Blu-ray Disc. D'Esposito began his tenure at Marvel Studios in 2006. Prior to Marvel, D'Esposito's executive producing credits include the 2006 hit film *The Pursuit of Happyness* starring Will Smith, *Zathura: A Space Adventure*, and the 2003 hit *S.W.A.T.* starring Samuel L. Jackson and Colin Farrell.

Executive Producer **Victoria Alonso** was executive producer for writer/director Joss Whedon's *Avengers: Age of Ultron* for Marvel Studios, where she serves as executive vice president of Visual Effects and Post Production. She executive-produced James Gunn's *Guardians of the Galaxy*, Joe and Anthony Russo's *Captain America: The Winter Soldier*, Alan Taylor's *Thor: The Dark World*, Shane Black's *Iron Man 3*, as well as *Marvel's The Avengers* for Joss Whedon. She also co-produced Marvel's *Iron Man* and *Iron Man 2* with Director Jon Favreau, Kenneth Branagh's *Thor* and Joe Johnston's *Captain America: The First Avenger*. Alonso's career began at the nascency of the visual effects industry, when she served as a commercial VFX producer. From there, she VFX-produced numerous feature films, working with such directors as Ridley Scott (*Kingdom of Heaven*), Tim Burton (*Big Fish*), and Andrew Adamson (*Shrek*), to name a few.

Executive Producer **Michael Grillo** started his career in production as a DGA trainee on *Young Frankenstein* and *The Towering Inferno*. He became the second assistant director on *Fun with Dick and Jane*, *New York, New York* with Martin Scorsese, and *The Deer Hunter*, which won the Oscar for Best Picture that year. He moved up to first assistant director on numerous productions, then started his long collaboration with director Lawrence Kasdan as his first assistant director on *Body Heat* and *The Big Chill*. With Kasdan and Charles Okun, he executive produced *Silverado*, *I Love You to Death*, and *Wyatt Earp*, was co-producer on *Cross My Heart*, and produced *Grand Canyon* and *The Accidental Tourist*, for which he received an Academy Award nomination for Best Picture. Later, he produced *Defending Your Life* and *The Trigger Effect*. He was executive producer on DreamWorks' first feature film, *The Peacemaker*, and served as DreamWorks' head of feature film production management from 1996 through 2005. During that period, he oversaw such productions as *Gladiator*, *American Beauty*, and *Saving Private Ryan*. He then executive produced *The Green Hornet*, *The Amazing Spider-Man*, and *Captain America: The Winter Soldier* for Marvel. Grillo has received two DGA Awards for Best Picture as assistant director and is a member of the Academy of Motion Pictures Arts and Sciences and the Directors Guild of America.

Co-Producer **David J. Grant** joined Marvel Studios in 2008 as vice president of physical production. As Associate Producer, David oversaw production on *Iron Man 2*, *Thor*, *Marvel's The Avengers*, and *Thor: The Dark World*; as Co-Producer, he oversaw *Guardians of the Galaxy*. Current projects include *Dr. Strange* and *Guardians of the Galaxy 2*. Prior to joining Marvel Studios, David was a freelance production supervisor, having most recently supervised *Fast and Furious*, *Iron Man*, *Spider-Man 3*, *Guess Who*, and *Spider-Man 2*. He worked for 20 years with industry veteran Executive Producer Joseph Caracciolo Sr., first as his personal assistant, and later as production assistant.

Co-Producer **Brad Winderbaum** began his career at Marvel Studios in 2006 as the assistant to Louis D'Esposito on *Iron Man*. Winderbaum went on to win an Emmy Award and Webby Award in 2007 for his independently produced webseries *Satacracy 88*, then returned to Marvel to create interactive marketing campaigns for *Iron Man 2*, *Thor*, *Captain America: The First Avenger*, and *The Avengers*. Winderbaum went on to oversee the Marvel One-Shot program, and served as an executive producer on *Item 47*, *Agent Carter*, and *All Hail the King*. *Ant-Man* is the first feature film he has overseen for the studio.

Production Designer **Shepherd Frankel** was born and raised in New York City. He attended the LaGuardia School of the Arts before relocating to the West Coast and earning a master's in Architecture from the School of Architecture and Urban Planning at UCLA. Quick on his feet, upon graduating from UCLA, Frankel and his creativity were recruited to working on commercials as an asst. art director for a variety of commercial shops, including RSA for Tony Scott and Ridley Scott. His success in the commercial world led him to features, where he continued his development as an asst. art director, art director and supervising art director on various films including Rob Minkoff's *Stuart Little 1 & 2*, Andy Tennant's *Sweet Home Alabama*, Paul Thomas Anderson's *Magnolia*, Jonathan Mostow's *Terminator 3*, Raja Gosnell's *Scooby Doo 2: Monsters Unleashed*, Pitof's *Catwoman*, Tim Story's *Fantastic Four*, and Todd Phillip's *Due Date*. Frankel was a perfect fit for Marvel's fast paced *Ant-Man*, as he has previously collaborated with Marvel Studios as production designer on several Marvel One-Shots: *Item 47*, *Agent Carter*, both directed by Louis D'Esposito and *All Hail the King*, directed by Drew Pearce. His work on the additional photography of *Thor: The Dark World*, *Guardians of the Galaxy*, and *Avengers: Age of Ultron* primed him to jump in on *Ant-Man*. Prior to his Marvel experience, Frankel has had an extensive history in delivering large-scale films as well as great comedies as production designer. Some of his other previous work includes: Jason Bateman's *Bad Words*, *Couples Retreat*, directed by Peter Billingsley, and *Horrible Bosses*, *Identity Thief*, and *Four Christmases*, directed by Seth Gordon. Among his other features as production designer are Anne Fletcher's hits *Step Up* and *27 Dresses*, Richard LaGravenese's *P.S. I Love You*, and Zak Penn's *The Grand*. Between feature assignments, Frankel works with studios, directorsm and producers to develop concept presentations and design strategies for films. In addition, he has set the look for several successful television pilots and popular commercials.

Costume Designer **Sammy Sheldon Differ** graduated from The Wimbledon School of Art and began her career designing for pop promos before becoming an assistant designer on films including Ridley Scott's *Gladiator* and Jake Scott's *Plunkett & Macleane*. She went on to design costumes for Ridley Scott's *Black Hawk Down* and the mockumentary *Calcium Kid* starring Orlando Bloom. Differ has received BAFTA Film nominations for her work on *The Imitation Game*, starring Benedict Cumberbatch and Keira Knightley, and for *The Merchant of Venice*, starring Al Pacino and Jeremy Irons; and a BAFTA TV nomination for the BBC's modern adaptation of *The Canterbury Tales* and Costume Designers Guild Award nominations for Excellence in Period Film for *The Imitation Game*, and Excellence in Fantasy Film for *X-Men: First Class* and *V for Vendetta*. Other film credits include *Kick-Ass 2*, *Gulliver's Travels*, *Kick-Ass*, *The Green Zone*, *Hellboy 2: The Golden Army*, *Stardust*, *Kinky Boots*, *A Hitchhiker's Guide to the Galaxy*, and, most recently, *Ex Machina*. Sammy was born in Manchester and lives in London.

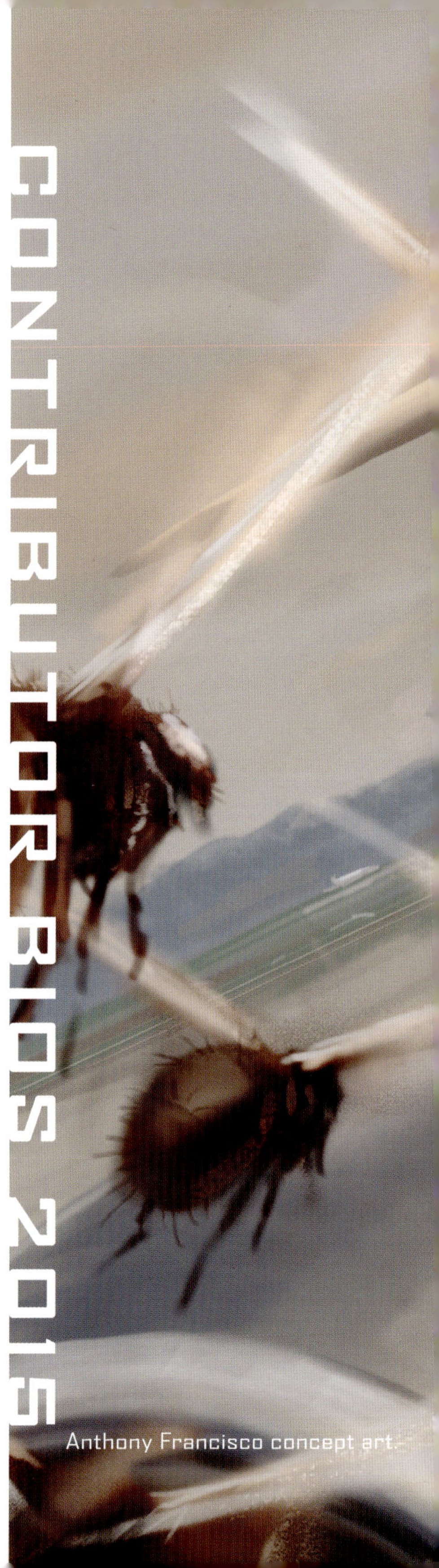

Anthony Francisco concept art.

CONTRIBUTOR BIOS 2015

Director of Photography **Russell Carpenter**, A.S.C., won an Academy Award for Best Cinematography for his beautiful imagery on *Titanic*, the enormously successful romantic drama directed by James Cameron. His two other collaborations with the director include *True Lies* and *T2-3D*. He started his career in public broadcasting in San Diego, but was soon enamored by the lure of Hollywood storytelling. He moved to and spent years toiling on non-union films before working his way onto much larger motion pictures. Carpenter teamed three times with director Joseph McGinty "McG" Nichol for two Charlie's Angels films and the Reese Witherspoon, Tom Hardy, Chris Pine film *This Means War*. His credits include two films starring Kevin Spacey: *The Negotiator* and the Las Vegas drama *21*. Some of his other credits include *The Indian in the Cupboard, Shallow Hal, Monster in Law, Awake*, and *The Ugly Truth*. Carpenter is a member of the American Society of Cinematographers.

Head of Visual Development **Charlie Wen** has held a variety of positions in the entertainment industry, ranging from concept designer to art director, on everything from feature films to video games and animation. Wen's client list reads as a virtual who's who of the industry, including Disney, Digital Domain, DreamWorks, Legendary Pictures, Marvel Studios, Darkhorse, Rhythm and Hues, Imagi Studios, Wizards of the Coast, and Sony Computer Entertainment of America. In 2005, he created Kratos and helped establish *God of War* as a monolithic action-adventure title for Sony PlayStation. Outside the production environment, Wen has given lectures on figure drawing and character design at many distinguished studios and universities. After helping establish the main character designs in *Thor*, he holds the title of head of visual development at Marvel Studios, working on *Captain America: The First Avenger, Marvel's The Avengers, Iron Man 3, Thor: The Dark World, Guardians of the Galaxy, Captain America: The Winter Soldier, Avengers: Age of Ultron*, and *Ant-Man*.

Property Master **Russell Bobbitt**'s resume includes all three of Marvel's Iron Man films, *Thor*, and *Captain America: The Winter Soldier*, and *Ant-Man*, as well as *Oz: The Great and Powerful, The Hangover, The Hangover Part II*, and J.J. Abrams' *Star Trek*. Tasked with the design, manufacturing, and acquisition of film props, as well as the establishment of prop continuity from scene to scene, Bobbitt has been developing the physical reality of iconic movies for 30 years. He has twice won Hamilton's prestigious "Behind the Camera" Award for Best Property Master. He has also won two Telly Awards for directing. He resides in Los Angeles with his wife, Tracy, and daughter Jordan.

Visual Effects Supervisor **Jake Morrison** has been blending photography and computer graphics for over 20 years. Pursuing an early interest in creating real-time visuals to be performed alongside live music, Morrison taught himself a programming language and learned video sampling techniques. This led to a career that encompassed commercials, television, and—for the last 10 years—film. Working on the VFX Vendor side, Morrison was VFX / CG supervisor and lead compositor on many projects, including Peter Jackson's *The Lord of the Rings: The Two Towers*, the Wachowskis' *The Matrix Reloaded* and *The Matrix Revolutions* before crossing over to the production side with digital effects supervisor credits on Warner Bros' *300* for Zack Snyder and the Wachowskis' *Speed Racer*. Most recently Morrison has been working with Marvel Studios and was the main VFX supervisor on *Thor: The Dark World*, Second Unit VFX supervisor on *Marvel's The Avengers*, and also provided additional VFX supervision on Kenneth Branagh's *Thor*.

Visual Effects Producer **Diana Giorgiutti**'s experience in film and television spans 35 years and includes some of Hollywood's most respected films. She is currently the visual effects producer on Marvel's *Ant-Man*, previously having taken the same role for *Thor* and *Thor: The Dark World*. Other recent projects have included work as stereo producer on Marvel's *Captain America: The First Avenger*, and the Visual Effects Producer on Baz Luhrmann's *Australia*, for which she won a Golden Satellite Award for Best Visual Effects. Giorgiutti also produced the conceptual "green light" phase on the Wachowskis' *Speed Racer*, and budget and concept development on a remake of *Logan's Run*. Prior to *Ant-Man*, Giorgiutti worked as Digital Effects Producer on the highly acclaimed *Matrix* films with the Wachowskis and Joel Silver, the first *Matrix* film winning an Oscar for Best Visual Effects. Other films include *Lords of Dogtown, Sky Captain and the World of Tomorrow, Romeo Must Die*, and *Babe: The Gallant Pig*.

Concept Artist **Andy Park** began his career illustrating comic books on titles such as *Tomb Raider, Excalibur*, and *Uncanny X-Men* for companies like Marvel, DC, and Image Comics. After about a decade in the comic-book world, he began working as a concept artist in video games and television. He was one of the leading artists creating the worlds and characters of the award-winning *God of War* franchise for Sony Computer Entertainment of America. In 2010, Park joined and has become an integral part of the team at Marvel Studios as a visual development illustrator, designing characters and keyframes for *Marvel's The Avengers, Captain America: The First Avenger, Iron Man 3, Captain America: The Winter Soldier, Thor: The Dark World, Avengers: Age of Ultron*, and the upcoming *Captain America: Civil War*.

Concept Artist **Rodney Fuentebella** has degrees in design from UCLA and Product Design from the Art Center College of Design. Born in the Philippines and raised in San Francisco, he has worked on various projects for Electronic Arts, Atari, Rhythm and Hues, DreamWorks Animation, and WIRED magazine, as well as various other entertainment and commercial projects. In film, he worked as a concept artist at Rhythm and Hues before joining the Visual Development team at Marvel Studios. Fuentebella has created key-art illustrations and character designs for *Captain America: The First Avenger, Marvel's The Avengers, Iron Man 3, Captain America: Winter Soldier, Guardians of the Galaxy, Avengers: Age of Ultron*, and the upcoming *Captain America: Civil War*.

Concept Artist **Andrew Kim** started his career in video games and has worked for studios such as Sony Santa Monica and Naughty Dog, creating characters and environments for highly claimed titles such as *Bio Shock, God of War 3*, and *Uncharted 2* and *3*. He has since joined Marvel Studios as a concept illustrator and worked on projects such as *Thor: The Dark World, Captain America: The Winter Soldier, Guardians of the Galaxy*, and *Ant-Man*.

Concept Artist **Jackson Sze** has worked in advertising, video games, television, and film for studios such as Lucasfilm Animation and Sony Computer Entertainment of America. He is a founding member of the BATTLE MiLK series of art books and is a senior concept illustrator at Marvel Studios. His projects include *Marvel's The Avengers, Thor: The Dark World*, and *Avengers: Age of Ultron*. He is currently working on the upcoming *Dr. Strange* and *Guardians of the Galaxy 2*.

Concept Artist **Anthony Francisco** worked on film and game projects before moving into movie concept art for various effects houses such as Stan Winston Studios, Rick Baker, ADI, Harlow FX, and Illusion Industries. Francisco produced art for *Superman Returns, A.I. Artificial Intelligence, Men in Black 2, Spider-Man, The Passion of the Christ, G.I Joe: Retaliation*, and *The Chronicles of Riddick*, among others. From 2004-2006, he worked as a concept artist at NCsoft Santa Monica on the *Guild Wars* and *Tabula Rasa* MMO game titles. Francisco then joined the team at Offset Software as lead concept artist to work on a fantasy-based FPS game. In 2010, he worked at Rhythm and Hues on *Hunger Games, R.I.P.D.*, and *Seventh Son*. Francisco also does illustration work for *Magic: The Gathering* and has been an instructor at Gnomon School for Visual Effects, Art Center College of Design in Pasadena, Concept Design Academy, and CGMW online. He is based in Burbank where he works on upcoming Marvel titles as part of the Visual Development team at Marvel Studios.

Storyboard Artist **David Krentz** was born in Winnipeg, Canada, and graduated from the Character Animation program at California Institute of the Arts in 1993. He was immediately hired into Walt Disney Feature Animation as a layout artist. He migrated into a lead character designer position for a four-year long stint on *Disney's Dinosaur*. His love for dinosaurs, anatomy, and character proved a valuable asset to that benchmark CG film. After leaving Disney he went on to pursue a freelance career, where he stretched his creative wings doing many different kinds of jobs on many different projects including sculpting (digital and clay), storyboarding, creature/character design, and concept illustration. He contributed to such movies as *Fantasia 2000, Dinosaur, Treasure Planet, Spider-Man 2, Valiant, The Ant Bully, Outlander, The Spiderwick Chronicles*, the *Walking with Dinosaurs* 3-D feature, *John Carter*, and *Ant-Man*. He took on the role of director for the Discovery Channel series *Dinosaur Revolution* as well as the CG animated feature film *Dinotasia* with Werner Herzog. He maintains ties to the scientific community, where he often lectures on developing performance-centric creatures for film and recreates new dinosaur finds from the bones up. He also stars in a "how to draw dinosaurs" series of DVDs and has become one of the most respected figures in the world of dinosaur art.

Storyboard Artist **Jim Magdaleno** started out as a page at Paramount Pictures. He landed a job as a production assistant in the art department on *Star Trek: The Next Generation* and worked his way up to Graphic Artist. His first job as an illustrator was on *Star Trek: Voyager*. After two seasons, he left television to do storyboards in motion pictures. His first job was on *Men in Black*. He has storyboarded over 50 films. His many credits include such films as *X-Men, Training Day, Italian Job, Iron Man 3, Dawn of the Planet of the Apes, The Equalizer, Ant-Man, Southpaw*, and three of the *Fast and Furious* films. He is currently working on a remake of *The Magnificent Seven*, starring Denzel Washington and directed by Antoine Fuqua.

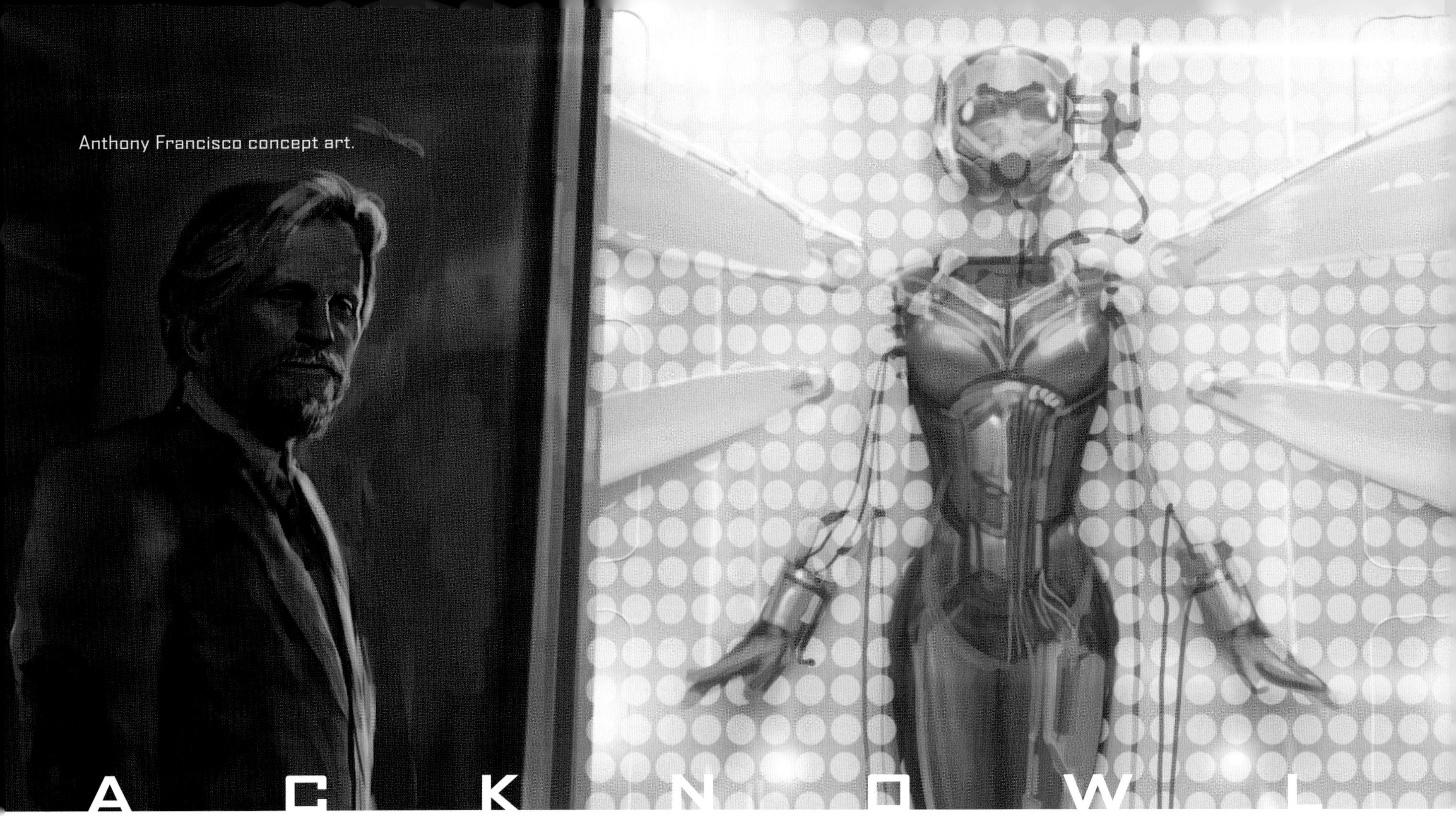

Anthony Francisco concept art.

Victoria Alonso
Dick Ayers
Jordan Boyd
John Buscema
John Byrne
Jim Carson
Dave Cockrum
Louis D'Esposito
Double Negative
Michael Douglas
John Eaves
Kevin Feige
Anthony Francisco
Shepherd Frankel
Rodney Fuentebella
Diana Giorgiutti
Austin Gorg
Michael Grillo
Andrew Kim
Jack Kirby
George Klein
Calla Klessig
Alexei Krassovsky
David Krentz
Andy Park
Bob Layton
Stan Lee

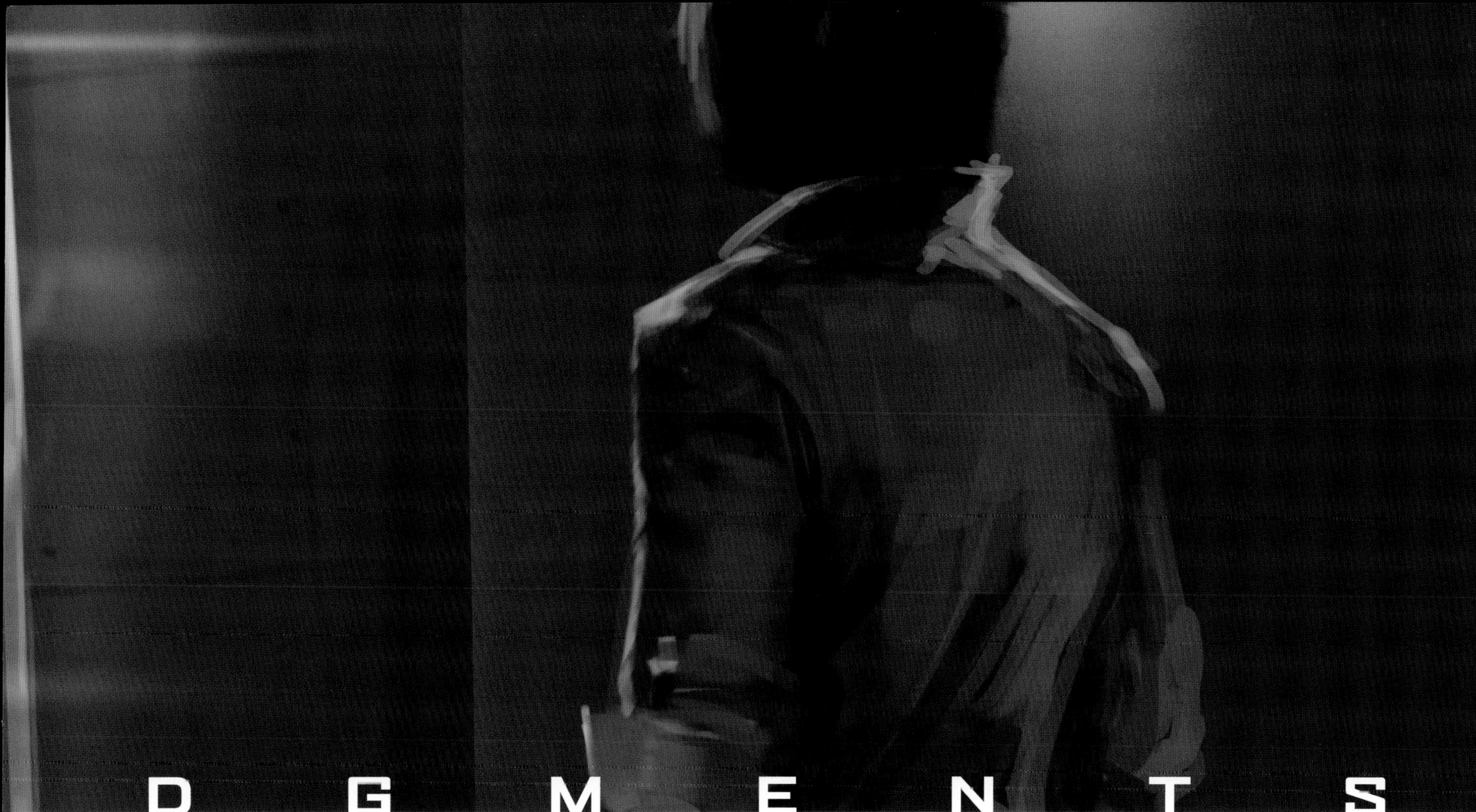

D G M E N T S

Larry Lieber
Evangeline Lilly
Jim Magdaleno
Michael McFarlane
Bob McLeod
Ryan Meinerding
David Michelinie
Jake Morrison
Tony Murphy

Josh Nizzi
Ming Pan
Manuel Plank-Jorge
Jacque Porte
Jamie Rama
Peyton Reed
Ramon Rosanas
Paul Rudd
Sammy Sheldon Differ

Nick Spencer
Corey Stoll
Jackson Sze
Third Floor
Charlie Wen
Brad Winderbaum
Dean Wolcott
Oscar Wright

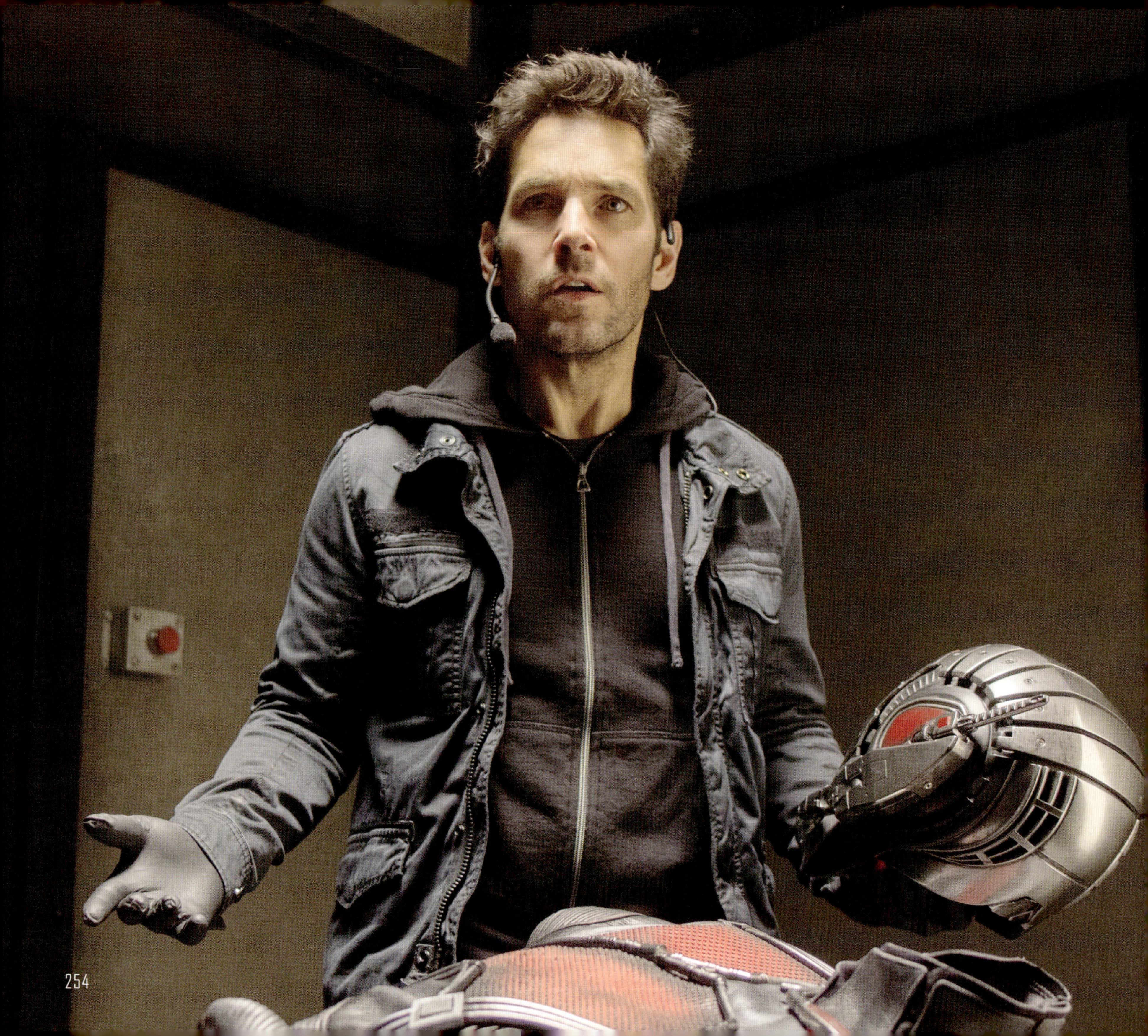

ARTISTS CREDITS

Jackson Sze
2-3, 6-7, 30-31, 36-37, 64-65, 74-79, 86-87, 94-95, 106-122, 132-135, 166-167, 170-171, 177, 190-195, 204-205, 222-225, 230-243

Jack Kirby
10-11, 14

Dick Ayers
10-11, 14

Bob Layton
12

George Klein
13

Ramon Rosanas
14

Jordan Boyd
14

Andrew Kim
16-17, 64 55, 58 58, 80-83, 131, 226-229, 246-249

Andy Park
18-25, 126-130, 172-173, 175, Cover

Rodney Fuentebella
26, 40-41, 60-63, 68-73, 164-165, 174, 196-197

Charlie Wen
27-29

Ryan Meinerding
27, 29, 173

Sammy Sheldon Differ
32-33

Jim Carson
34-35, 38-39, 43, 47-48, 97

Tim Flattery
42

Jamie Rama
44-45, 96, 98-103, 220-221

Josh Nizzi
46, 160-163

Manual Plank-Jorge
49-51, 104-105

Anthony Francisco
52-53, 56-57, 66-67, 123-125, 136-151, 155-159, 175-176, 178-179, 184-185, 198-203, 206-219, 250-253

Jim Magdaleno
80-85, 88-89, 180-183, 186-189

Dean Wolcott
105

Austin Gorg
105

Calla Klessig
105

Double Negative
110-111

Ming Pan
136-139

John Eaves
152

David Krentz
180-183, 186-189

The Third Floor
180-183, 186-189

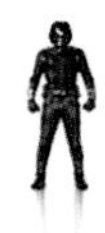